GOVERNMENT
INFORMATION ON THE
INTERNET

GOVERNMENT
INFORMATION ON THE
INTERNET

Greg R. Notess
• • •

BERNAN PRESS
LANHAM, MARYLAND

Copyright © 1997 by Bernan Press

Published 1997 by Bernan Press, an imprint of Bernan Associates,
a division of
The Kraus Organization Limited
Printed in the United States of America

99 98 97   4 3 2 1

TM

Bernan Press
4611-F Assembly Drive
Lanham, MD 20706-4391
(800) 274-4447
e-mail: info@bernan.com

ISBN: 0-89059-041-9 (Paperback)
ISBN: 0-89059-081-8 (Hardback)

TABLE OF CONTENTS

INTRODUCTION

The federal government has long strived to provide government information to the public. The Federal Depository Library Program, with libraries in every state, was established as a way for the public to access government documents. However, as the Paperwork Reduction Act and other recent federal legislative and regulatory efforts have demonstrated, Congress has expressed a growing concern over the bulk of print publications and the expense of producing them. As a solution, the Government Printing Office (GPO) and the Superintendent of Documents are exploring options for transforming government publications into electronically disseminated documents.

While the concern over the excess of paper publications has been on the rise, computer and networking technologies have evolved to a point that electronic dissemination is faster, more convenient, and can reach a larger audience. The GPO began distributing floppy disks and CD-ROMs in the 1980s. However, both kinds of disks share the same production problem that print sources face. Multiple copies of each publication still need to be created for distribution to depository libraries, government agencies, and interested private citizens.

Electronic bulletin board systems (BBS) present an alternate dissemination model. Data can be produced just once in electronic format and then uploaded to the BBS. Users can then use a computer and modem to dial into the BBS to retrieve the data. Since the 1980s government BBS, have been established for this purpose. Unfortunately, most BBS interfaces are not easy to use, and retrieving the data can be quite complex for users not familiar with BBS software. For users who live outside of the Washington, D.C. area, access to most federal BBS is a long distance phone call. In addition, users need to know if and when a specific government agency has a BBS, what kind of data is available from it, and how to connect to it.

The evolution of the Internet provided a new and efficient publication mechanism. The Internet essentially solves the access problem. The recent rise in popularity of the Internet with both the commercial and consumer sectors has made the Internet an even more attractive medium for the dissemination of government information. There is no long distance charge (beyond any associated with the Internet connection itself). Additionally, the popularity of the World Wide Web (hereafter referred to simply as the Web) provides a common and easily understood interface to information resources.

The Internet and the Web have proven to be an effective means of publishing, sharing, and disseminating a wide variety of information products. With the hypertext and graphical capabilities of the Web popularized by widely available browser software such as Netscape Navigator and Microsoft Internet Explorer, the Internet has become the significant player in the online universe.

For the U.S. federal government, the Internet and the Web are a very attractive medium for the publication and dissemination of government information. Since U.S. federal government information is free of copyrights, the Internet is a way to save money on publishing as well as a means of reaching the general public. The government has become one of the major content providers on the Web.

The abundance of government information on the Internet brings with it the need for a print directory—a source that categorizes government information available on the Web. But why bother with a directory like *Government Information on the Internet* when the Internet changes so quickly? URLs die and are reborn, and yesterday's government resources end up lost in a server crash. An online directory of these resources would be ideal, since an online directory can be updated daily. Unfortunately, any directory compiled by human effort suffers the same problem of upkeep. One thing I discovered in researching this work is that all of the online directories are incomplete and contain errors. This print directory is also vulnerable to those problems—but it has some unique advantages.

This is a snapshot in time of the history of government resources on the Internet. While many of these sites have changed significantly in a year's time, others have remained almost the same for several years. This directory will help show the development of government resources on the Internet by documenting what is available as of early 1997. In addition, a resource such as this can prove invaluable in tracking a certain site or a specific document. Even if the site is no longer at a specified URL, knowing that resources were once available means that they likely still exist on the Internet and just require a bit of work to find them. The directory has special features for librarians and savvy library users. These include an emphasis on publications available at sites and the inclusion of Superintendent of Documents (SuDoc) numbers for many publications and resources. Finally, you can browse this book while waiting for an online search engine or Web page to load.

Scope and Defining a Web Site

The intent of *Government Information on the Internet* is to enable users to access a significant portion of the government's new online world by providing subject and agency access to more than 1,200 governmental Internet resources. These include publicly accessible Internet sites provided by any part of the U.S. government and nongovernmental sites containing data that originated from the government. The primary focus is on the U.S. federal government, but there is also a chapter for state government resources, with major sites for each state, and an international chapter with selected international, intergovernmental organization, and foreign country sites. The directory is not limited to resources that are hosted on government-owned computers; rather, the decision to include a resource is based on whether the information content of a site originated in the government.

What distinguishes a single Internet resource? A book or a CD-ROM is easy to identify as single, unique, published items, although parts of a series may get a bit more complex. On the Internet, identifying a unique resource is much more difficult, if not impossible. Sometimes, a governmental agency may provide the same information through multiple access options. For example, data can be accessible from a Web page, a Gopher server, and a FedWorld BBS. Yet in each case, the document may be the same. At other times, multiple organizations may post the same data, perhaps in different formats and in different network locations.

Another difficulty in indexing Internet resources is differentiating between one resource and many. A book is generally complete in one volume, although there are the more complex cases of monographic series, multivolume works, and books with separately authored chapters. A Gopher server or Web site can contain a much more diverse collection of materials. One Web page can contain links to sites on other servers, a link to an electronic journal, and links to press releases, multi- megabyte data sets, pictures of staff, and a virtual video tour of a location. Those sites with a hierarchical structure are more easily defined as a single site at the top level page, but they often have featured pages or sections of pages that could be considered as a site in their own right.

I have tried to address this problem with two different approaches. In the first case, where multiple sites include the exact or very similar information, one record is used, and the alternative access points are included. If the information content is significantly different, separate records are used. The second approach deals with identifying a site rather than individual documents. While it is an amorphous task to try to define limits to a site in the wide open realm of hypertext, there is often a sense of order, especially on government sites, that designates a certain collection of pages as a single site.

With well over one million Web pages in the .gov domain and a few hundred thousand in the .mil domain, there is no practical way to catalog every single page. And then there are ftp archives, telnet sites, e-mail lists, newsgroups, and Gopher servers. Instead, this work concentrates on identifying distinct resources and sites. Typically, all Web pages or Gopher menu items on one single server will be included in just one entry unless there are multiple distinct groupings. For example, one server could host the Web site for two or more distinct agencies. In that case, each agency's site is listed separately.

Uniform Resource Locators

One problem that was evident in the early days of tracking information resources on the Internet was the citation difficulty. How could one person cite or even describe the exact access method for getting to a specific resource? With the advent of the Web, the Uniform Resource Locator (URL) offers a solution to uniquely identifying specific resources and providing sufficient information in a citation so that another Internet user can find it. A URL designates the Internet protocol to be used for access, the address of the host computer, the path name or login name to be used, and the file name of a specific document.

The standard example of a URL for a Web site is now quite common, thanks to advertising from the commercial sector. In its simplest form the http://www.agency.gov/ syntax refers to a hypertext transport protocol (http) connection to the computer at the address www.agency.gov. A more complex URL might be http://www.agency.gov/office/pub.html, which gives the directory path of office and a specific file name of pub.html.

Http is the common Web protocol, but other Internet protocols can be designated with URLs as well. Gopher, ftp, and telnet resources all start with their names as the protocol name. Gopher and ftp URLs can be handled quite well by most Web browsers, including the popular Netscape Navigator and Microsoft Internet Explorer. Telnet and tn3270 connections are more complex. To use URLs starting with either telnet:// or tn3270:// a user needs to have appropriate telnet and tn3270 software loaded, and the Web browser must be configured to find them.

E-mail and news URLs can usually be handled well by the popular Web browsers. Many of the mailto: URLs point to e-mail discussion groups. The subscription process for these varies and usually requires more information than is contained in a URL. For these, the URL is followed by instructions for what message or messages to insert into the body or subject of the e-mail message.

While URLs are the best way of identifying a specific Internet resource, they change all too frequently. The alternate URLs provided should help in finding at least one functioning site. In most cases, a well-run government Web site will leave a forwarding address behind at the old URL.

Detailed Explanation of Fields

Entry Number: Each record starts with an entry number. These run sequentially from the first finding aid records in the introduction to the last records in the final chapter. The entry numbers are used in all of the indexes rather than page numbers.

Title: Directly following the entry number is the title of the resource. Unfortunately, determining the title of an Internet source is not as easy as finding the title of a book. For Web sites, the title could be the title designated on the top page by the HTML <title> tags, the first major header designated by the HTML <H1> tag, and/or the title included in an initial top banner graphic. While the HTML <title> designation is the preferred choice for Web resources, it is often not used or is poorly designed. For the purposes of this directory, the listed title generally is based on the HTML title element, as long as it is at least somewhat descriptive. In some cases the title is manufactured from the <H1> element or descriptive text within the initial top banner graphic, when that represents more clearly how the site is commonly referenced. To avoid redundancy, the phrase "home page" has been left off of most titles, unless it is clearly required for the clarity of the rest of the title.

E-mail lists and USENET newsgroups usually have one distinct name, and that name will be used as their title. Telnet, ftp, and Gopher resources often do not have a distinct title. For those resources, a descriptive title has been created for the resources based on names or words used by the source to refer to itself.

As can be seen by looking at this problem, titles of Internet resources often do not uniquely identify a site. Unlike in the print world, titles of sites change frequently, as the Web site designers modify and update their sites. Consequently, a title is not the most reliable reference to a site. Only a URL can uniquely identify a resource.

Sponsoring Agency: The agency that hosts the site(s) and/or produces the information on a site is listed in this field. This generally consists of a government agency, but commercial, educational, and non-profit organizations will be listed here as well when they host or sponsor a specific resource. Most of the government agencies listed are United States federal agencies, so "United States" is left off of the front of almost all agencies. (However, entries like United States Attorney are more clearly identified with the use of "United States.") The complete organizational hierarchy is rarely shown. Rather than "United States. Department of Commerce. Bureau of the Census. Foreign Trade Division," the lowest distinct hierarchical name is used. Thus, the Census is listed as Bureau of the Census. Its division with a nondistinctive and possibly duplicative name is listed as Bureau of the Census. Foreign Trade Division.

Primary Access: URLs are used to denote the primary location of resources and the principal entryway to a site's contents. Since most agencies are moving toward maintaining a Web site as the primary access point to their Internet information resources, Web sites are generally considered to be the principal location. URLs can be written in multiple ways and still refer to the same site. The shortest possible version of a URL is the one preferred for this directory.

Alternative Access Method: Many agencies offer multiple Internet sites. Web page(s), Gopher servers, anonymous ftp sites, e-mail lists, and telnet sites that represent essentially similar resources are listed in one record. In addition, if the ftp archives or other alternative site contains only a portion of the Web resources, it will still be listed under the same record rather than as a separate entry. Different versions of Web sites are also listed here. The most common, a text version of a home page, can be very helpful to use, since it will usually load significantly quicker than a graphics-intensive page. Some older and defunct URLs are included here if they have been cited or are well known. This helps users to find the new URL by accessing the old one in the URL index.

Resource Summary: This is where the site is described briefly. The description includes the organization, principal features, menu items, and significant links. For agencies that may be unfamiliar to some, a brief description of the agency's mission can also help to predict the kind of resources available on the site. The most succinct descriptions of the site are sometimes available on the site itself. Such extracts are frequently included, but quotation marks are not used since the descriptions often change on the sites themselves. The Resource Summary will mention significant publications available on the site in electronic form. For sites offering similar resources, they are compared with the other sites. The utility of the site, its ease of use, and the potential audience may be evaluated as well.

Subject Headings: These are the index terms used to describe the primary focus of the resource. The subject headings can relate to both the subject of the agency as well as the major sections of available information. All subject headings are included in the index to provide more detailed subject access than the broad chapter topics offer.

SuDoc Numbers: This field includes Superintendent of Documents (SuDoc) numbers and titles for featured publications that are or were available through the Government Printing Office and are available on the site in online versions. The emphasis of this section is on series and serials rather than monographs and pamphlets. Assuming growth of available publications, the root SuDoc number is used rather than full SuDocs for each individual item. These SuDoc numbers are widely used in depository libraries to classify their federal government documents and can be an easy way to find an online counterpart of a print publication.

Principal Finding Aids and Starting Points

The online finding aids, pathfinders, and Internet resource guides that enable easier access to other Internet resources are some of the most highly used Internet sites. General Internet finding aids such as Yahoo!, Excite, and Infoseek are high profile and attract a large number of visitors. While they are not as well known, there are numerous finding aids that focus strictly on government information sources. Unfortunately, they vary in quality, currency, and accuracy. Some may only list a few dozen resources while others boast hundreds of entries. Well-run sites see daily updates while others do not get updated for months or even years. Government finding aids that are well organized are important tools for locating specific information sources on government Internet sites. These finding aids come in many shapes and sizes.

In the past few years, government Web sites have evolved in a many directions. For many agencies, the first versions of Web pages contained little more than a mission statement and some press releases. As additional information has been added, the organization of the sites has changed and the method of presentation has matured. One recent move on the federal level has been to create multi-agency, subject-oriented sites. Such centralized subject finding aids, sometimes called one-stop shopping sites, can be an excellent starting point in the quest for relevant government information. Many of these subject-specific finding aids are the featured sites in their respective chapters. Examples include the U.S. Business Advisor, entry 59; healthfinder, entry 367; Fedstats, entry 158; and Commonly Requested Federal Services, entry 931.

Finding aids for government information come in other formats as well. One example is the online directory that specializes in access by agency. Others take a subject approach with a specific government agency. Another more formalized movement involves the use of Government Information Locator Service (GILS) records, which offer structured directory information on specific government information products. Look under Government Information Locator Services in the subject index for some of the sites that are using GILS. The GILS records vary in quality, and many point to non-Internet-accessible resources. Thus, the promise of GILS as an efficient tool for locating government information on the Internet has not yet been realized. The other finding aids and subject directories are far more effective for locating specific resources. The subject index lists these under the Finding Aid heading and its subdivisions.

The following four entries are a few of the best general finding aids and search engines for government Internet resources. The remainder of the entries in the introduction are some of the other top general finding aids for government information.

[1] The Federal Web Locator

Sponsoring Agency: Villanova Center for Information Law and Policy

Primary Access: http://www.law.vill.edu/Fed-Agency/fedwebloc.html

Alternative Access Method: gopher://ming.law.vill.edu/11/.fedgov/

Resource Summary: The Federal Web Locator is a service provided by the Villanova Center for Information Law and Policy and is intended to be a one-stop shopping point for federal government information on the Web. It is one of the most often used general finding aids for U.S. federal government agency Web sites. It is arranged by agency hierarchy. The categories roughly mirror the arrangement of the *U.S. Government Manual* and include Federal Legislative Branch; Federal Judicial Branch; Federal Executive Branch; Federal Executive Agencies; Departments; Federal Independent Establishments and Government Corporations; Federal Government Consortium and Quasi-Official Agencies; Federal Boards, Commissions, and Committees; and Nongovernment Federally Related Sites. A rough keyword search capability is available.

Though this is one of the best finding aids for government information on the Internet, it does have some problems. Despite being an online resource that is frequently updated, some of the links are still out of date and are missing a piece of the host name. It is useful only for those who know which government agency they need to search. No subject index to the content of the Web site is available. The scope of this site is limited to the Web site and consists primarily of the official Web site of government agencies. Within these constraints, this is one of the easiest ways to find a specific agency's Web address.

Subject Heading: Finding Aid

[2] FedWorld

Sponsoring Agency: National Technical Information Service (NTIS)

Primary Access: http://www.fedworld.gov/

Alternative Access Methods: telnet://fedworld.gov
ftp://ftp.fedworld.gov/pub

Resource Summary: FedWorld is a huge site that provides access to a large quantity of government resources from many different agencies. Despite its size, the site continually increases the amount of material that it offers. Much of this material was originally available on the telnet or ftp versions of FedWorld and has been transferred to the Web. The Web site, ftp archive, and telnet version all offer slightly different information. The Web site offers site search options by keyword or by specific FedWorld Web section. For NTIS publications, FedWorld provides access to the past 30 days' worth of technical reports from the NTIS bibliographic database. This service, called NTIS OrderNow, also offers ordering information. Beyond NTIS information, the FedWorld Web site features a number of other government databases and hosts some Web sites for other agencies.

The telnet version, where FedWorld was originally available, offers access to detailed information from over 50 agencies and includes access to online ordering services, federal job opportunities, and about 100 government BBS. The ftp FedWorld features access to the FedWorld file libraries, which include more than 14,000 files including information on business, health and safety, and the environment, as well as satellite images.

FedWorld is an important and useful Web site. Although the amount of NTIS bibliographic and full-text data available is disappointingly small, the collection of resources available from other agencies makes this a substantial information resource and finding aid. The difficulty with FedWorld is knowing what data and resources it offers. With so many diverse files, data sets, and agency information, the only way to know for sure is by spending some time browsing the offerings or searching for specific keywords.

Subject Headings: Electronic Publications; Employment; Finding Aid

[3] GovBot Database of Government Web Sites

Sponsoring Agencies: Center for Intelligent Information Retrieval; National Performance Review (NPR)

Primary Access: http://ciir.cs.umass.edu/ciirdemo/Govbot

Alternative Access Methods: http://www.business.gov/Search_Online.html
http://www.business.gov/Search_Online2.html [text version]

Resource Summary: The GovBot keyword index of government Web sites uses the INQUERY software developed at the Center for Intelligent Information Retrieval. It limits its database to sites with a .gov or .mil top level domain. Within that limitation, the database contains over 300,000 Web pages, all of which are keyword searchable with GovBot. Documentation is sparse for the data gathering techniques, but search documentation is more extensive. Boolean searching is not directly available, and multiple terms are combined with an OR operator. However, look at the advanced help screen for detailed information on how to force a Boolean query (such as using #band for AND).

The primary site at the Center for Intelligent Information Retrieval gives more search options, such as title and URL limits than the U.S. Business Advisor site, although both search against the same database. The limitation by domain name will not gather all federal government sites but will include some other governmental sites such as some state governments. For that reason, the Pathway Indexer available from the Government Printing Office site can be more accurate. Note that both GovBot and the Pathway Indexer (featured in entry number 9 of this chapter) are keyword search engines and that neither provides subject access to federal Web sites. For even more comprehensive keyword searching, general Web search engines like HotBot (http://www.hotbot.com/) and Alta Vista (http://www.altavista.digital.com) should also be searched. Both of these can also be limited to searching the .gov and .mil domains.

Subject Heading: Finding Aid

[4] Government InfoMine

Sponsoring Agency: University of California, Riverside. Library

Primary Access: http://lib-www.ucr.edu/govsearch.html

Alternative Access Method: http://lib-www.ucr.edu/govpub/

Resource Summary: A service of the University of California (UC) Riverside Library, InfoMine aims to provide collections of scholarly Internet resources. This InfoMine page focuses on government information. Access to the directory is by keyword search or by browsing. The keyword search option can search by title and/or subject, and it supports Boolean searching and truncation. Alternatively, users can browse by title, subject, or both. It even supports a keyword browse.

The subject headings used are fairly detailed, allowing for more precise retrieval. The resources listed are often specific online publications, data sets, and offices rather than discrete Web sites. The detailed subject indexing, combined with the records pointing directly to specific resources, makes InfoMine's government section particularly valuable for finding resources by subject.

Because this is a campus-specific site, some of the resources point to non-Internet-accessible sites available at the UC Riverside Library. Despite those entries, this is one of the best aids for finding specific Internet-accessible government resources by subject.

Subject Heading: Finding Aid

[5] Federal Depository Library Program

Sponsoring Agency: Government Printing Office (GPO)

Primary Access: http://www.access.gpo.gov/su_docs/dpos/adpos001.html

Resource Summary: This page carries the subtitle Locating Government Information Products. It offers access to a suite of tools being developed by the Federal Depository Library Program, which directs librarians and the public to federal government information on the Internet. These tools include the GPO's online version of the *Monthly Catalog of Government Publications* and links for locating government resources on the Internet. The Browse Government Internet Sites by Topic page uses subjects based on those used in the *Subject Bibliography Index*. While not all subject headings currently have links, this offers one way of finding government information by topic.

The page titled Browse Electronic Government Information Products by Title is very useful as it provides a list of government publications by agency (including SuDoc numbers) that are accessible on the Internet. (These titles are directly linked to the Internet source.) While this page has useful navigation features, the publications list is so extensive that it takes a long time to load.

The Search for Government Information on Selected Internet Sites page links to the Search Pathway Indexer (described later in this section). For GILS records, this site features a Search the Government Information Locator Service page. This site also links to a directory of depository libraries under the heading Locate Federal Depository Libraries.

With all of these resources for locating government information, this site is an important and useful finding aid for a variety of government information. The tools are designed for use by government documents librarians, and the availability of SuDoc number information is especially valuable.

Subject Headings: Finding Aid; Government Information Locator Service (GILS); Government Publications—Bibliographies

SuDoc Number: GP 3.8: *Monthly Catalog of Government Publications*

The following finding aids, numbered 5-16, make excellent supplements to those just featured. The following entries were selected as the best from a pool of numerous finding aids that locate government resources on the Internet. See also the subject index under "Finding Aid" for other general finding aids and more specific finding aids.

[6] Finding Government Documents

Sponsoring Agency: Yale University. Library

Primary Access: http://www.library.yale.edu/govdocs/govdoc2.html

Resource Summary: This site, from the government documents department at Yale University, features access to sites by both subject and agency. It functions as a finding aid for federal, state, local, and international government sites. Subject access to federal sites is available via a list of subject headings. This site assists the user by providing textual descriptions of some of the links rather than just offering a straight list of connections.

Subject Headings: Finding Aid; Finding Aid—International; Finding Aid—States

[7] Government Information

Sponsoring Agency: Vanderbilt University. Library

Primary Access: http://www.library.vanderbilt.edu/central/govt.html

Resource Summary: This government finding aid takes a more selective approach to its listings. The page is arranged by broad topics and begins with top sites for economic, social, political, international, and consumer topics.

Subject Heading: Finding Aid

[8] Government Information Xchange

Sponsoring Agency: General Services Administration (GSA)

Primary Access: http://www.info.gov/

Alternative Access Method: http://www.info.gov/txt_index.html [text version]

Resource Summary: The GSA's listing of government sites includes federal, state, local, international, and foreign Internet resources. The Government Information Xchange was established to facilitate sharing and dissemination of information resources among federal, state, and local governments. This page combines access by topic with access by agency. Some of the many available sections include Federal Directory, State and Local Government, International Organizations, Federal Yellow Pages, Intergovernmental Collaboration, Electronic Shopping Networks, and Foreign Government. A separate collection of links is available in a scroll box.

Subject Heading: Finding Aid

[9] Search Pathway Indexer

Sponsoring Agency: Government Printing Office (GPO)

Primary Access: http://gather.access.gpo.gov/Harvest/brokers/Pathway/query.html

Resource Summary: The Pathway Indexer is a keyword search engine for federal government Web sites. While it is smaller than GovBot, with slightly over 100,000 Web pages, it targets specific federal government servers rather than simply basing its database building strategy on sites with a top level .gov or .mil domain. Users can search using Boolean operators and double quotes to index phrases. Unfortunately, the record display needs improvement—it does not display the page title, only the URL, host, and path.

Subject Heading: Finding Aid

[10] U.S. Federal Government Agencies

Sponsoring Agency: Louisiana State University. Library

Primary Access: http://www.lib.lsu.edu/gov/fedgov.html

Resource Summary: This finding aid consists of a list of federal agencies in hierarchical order—designated by indentation. While the vast majority of agencies listed are linked to their corresponding Web sites, some agencies have links to divisions and subdivisions. The structure of the index is based on the *United States Government Manual*.

This site can easily compete with the Federal Web Locator as the best place to look for a specific government agency's Web site. For those agencies that provide their own index to subsidiary divisions, such as the Department of Education, only the top level agency is included on this page.

Subject Heading: Finding Aid

[11] U.S. Government Gophers

Sponsoring Agency: University of California, Irvine

Primary Access: gopher://peg.cwis.uci.edu:7000/11/gopher.welcome/peg/GOPHERS/gov

Resource Summary: Although Gophers were at one time the major mechanism for distributing government information on the Internet, they are now a dying breed. Hundreds are still available, but many are being dismantled as the information is being moved to Web sites. However, there are still substantive resources available on government Gophers, and this is the best finding aid for locating them. The server presents an alphabetical listing of Gophers by agency name, which then connects directly to the respective Gophers.

Subject Heading: Finding Aid—Gophers

[12] U.S. Government Information

Sponsoring Agency: Cleveland State University. Bartunek Law Library

Primary Access: http://govtdoc.law.csuohio.edu/usgov.html

Resource Summary: This site provides another hierarchical index to government agencies on the Internet. The main page provides access to secondary pages for the executive, legislative, and judicial branches. It also has links to reference resources, other government agencies, and other government finding aids.

Subject Heading: Finding Aid

[13] U.S. Government Sites

Primary Access: http://www.obscure.org/~jaws/government.html

Resource Summary: This collection of government Web sites is arranged hierarchically by branch of government and by agency. Its use of frames presents an alternative to the Federal Web Locator. Unfortunately, it does not seem to be updated regularly. Many of the links still point to Gopher servers even when the respective agencies have Web sites available.

Subject Heading: Finding Aid

[14] Welcome to WINGS

Sponsoring Agency: Postal Service (USPS)

Primary Access: http://www.wings.usps.gov/

Alternative Access Method: http://www.wings.usps.gov/index_tx.html [text version]

Resource Summary: This site describes the Web Interactive Network of Government Services (WINGS), which has a goal of providing easy-to-use, integrated, electronic government customer services. The original Postal Service project planned to put WINGS information kiosks in post offices, libraries, grocery stores, and shopping malls. These kiosks could then be used to access government information. The current version provides access to federal, state, and local government customer service and information resources by agency and topic. Featured subject areas include Recreation, Jobs, Moving, Health, Retirement, and Education. The heading, Top 10, includes links to the most frequently requested services. A search feature is also available.

WINGS presents an interesting approach and some compelling design, but the content is limited. While some topics such as Moving and Jobs offer access to useful services—primarily links to USPS or White House Web pages—much of the other content is not yet available.

Subject Headings: Finding Aid; Kiosks

[15] World Wide Web Virtual Library: U.S. Government Information Sources

Sponsoring Agency: National Technology Transfer Center (NTTC)

Primary Access: http://iridium.nttc.edu/gov_res.html

Resource Summary: This index of federal government Web sites is part of the World Wide Web Virtual Library project. It provides access to agencies via headings including Executive Branches, Executive Departments, Independent Agencies, and Other Government. Rather than providing an indented list to designate hierarchy, this site puts lower-level hierarchies on separate pages. The site contains about 1,000 links.

Subject Heading: Finding Aid

[16] Yahoo! Government

Sponsoring Agency: Yahoo! Inc.

Primary Access: http://www.yahoo.com/Government/

Resource Summary: Yahoo! is one of the best known and most frequently used general Internet finding aids. Its subject classification approach which features sites rather than individual pages, makes it an obvious starting point for many searches. The government section is substantial, frequently updated, and broad in scope. It includes sections at the federal, state, local, and international levels. It also includes official and unofficial sites. The Indices section near the top of the page provides a listing of many more general government finding aids.

Though it functions far better when finding specific government agencies than when finding broad subjects, it is an excellent starting point for any government search.

Subject Heading: Finding Aid

CHAPTER 1: AGRICULTURE

Governmental agricultural information is available on a variety of topics including crop statistics, rural economic development advice, lists of inspectors, and agricultural genome research. Information on all of these and related topics can be found on the Internet. Since the majority of this agricultural information comes from the U.S. Department of Agriculture, this is the best starting point, and it is also this chapter's featured resource.

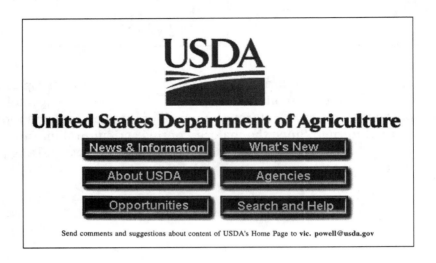

[17] U.S. Department of Agriculture

Sponsoring Agency: Department of Agriculture (USDA)

Primary Access: http://www.usda.gov/

Resource Summary: The main USDA page features sections titled News and Information, About USDA, Agencies, What's New, and Opportunities. The site includes a hierarchical guide to agricultural programs, the USDA's segment of the Government Information Locator Service (GILS), a history of the USDA in images and text, and information on the 1996 Farm Bill. Current news is available including press releases, fact sheets, backgrounders, and speeches.

The Agencies page is designed as an organizational diagram with links to departmental and agency Web sites. In addition, the site points to USDA support programs and affiliates. It provides a basic, yet easy to navigate, structure for finding component agencies within the Department of Agriculture.

This is a well-organized site with easy access to more detailed agricultural information. It is an excellent starting point for those who are not sure which agency site to investigate.

Subject Headings: Agriculture; Finding Aid—Agriculture

SuDoc Number: A 21.34: *Broadcasters Letter*

Agriculture: General Agricultural Information

[18] Agriculture Fact Book

Sponsoring Agency: Department of Agriculture (USDA)

Primary Access: http://www.usda.gov/news/pubs/factbook/contents.htm

Alternative Access Method: http://www.usda.gov/factbook/contents.html

Resource Summary: The full text of this publication is available in Adobe PDF format. The cover page PDF file was not available for verification, but it appears that this is the continuation of the annual *Fact Book of Agriculture*.

The Agriculture resources are divided into four sections. The first section covers General Agricultural Information resources as well as those sites that do not fit under the other categories. This section runs from entry numbers 18 to 31. Business Sources for agriculture, the second subchapter, features resources for rural economic development and covers entries 32-41. The third section, Extension Service, contains resources related to and originating from the Cooperative State Research, Education, and Extension Service and includes entries 42-46. The related category of Research, entries 47-58, has agricultural research and scientific sources.

This is an excellent source for overview and statistical information on U.S. agriculture.

Subject Headings: Agriculture—Full Text; Farms and Farming—Full Text

SuDoc Number: A 1.38/2: *Fact Book of Agriculture*

[19] Animal and Plant Health Inspection Service

Sponsoring Agency: Animal and Plant Health Inspection Service (APHIS)

Primary Access: http://www.aphis.usda.gov/

Alternative Access Method: gopher://gopher.aphis.usda.gov/11/AI.d

Resource Summary: The APHIS site includes a guided tour of its informational offerings, including such items as the USDA's Beagle Brigade and its Screwworm Eradication Program. Other areas on the site include publications, fact sheets, proposed regulations, information for travelers, an import-export directory, and an agency directory. In all of these areas, the focus is on information related to enforcing regulations governing the import and export of plants, animals, and certain agricultural products. Various access points to information at the site include a keyword search feature and an alphabetical subject index.

The site features a good mix of information for business professionals and the general public. It is useful for anyone with questions about transporting plant and animal products into and out of the country.

Subject Headings: Importing and Exporting; Inspectors; Travel; Veterinary Medicine

[20] The Biotechnology Information Center

Sponsoring Agency: Biotechnology Information Center (BIC)

Primary Access: http://www.nal.usda.gov/bic

Resource Summary: The BIC provides access to a variety of information services and publications covering many aspects of agricultural biotechnology. In addition to information about the BIC, the site includes many links to other agricultural biotechnology-related Internet sites. Original information on this site includes bibliographies on biotechnology topics and lists of relevant newsletters, videos, databases, and other resources. Full-text, biotechnology-related patents are available from 1994 in ASCII text.

The patents, bibliographies, and lists are some of the most valuable resources on this site. The links to other related information servers are also useful and well organized. It would be helpful if the ASCII files were converted into HTML or PDF.

Subject Headings: Biotechnology; Patents

[21] Federal Funding Sources for Rural Areas

Sponsoring Agency: National Agricultural Library (NAL)

Primary Access: gopher://gopher.nal.usda.gov/11/nalpub/ffsra95

Resource Summary: Information on this site was obtained from the online system known as Federal Funding APRS (Federal Assistance Programs Retrieval System) and the print version of this database, known as the *Catalog of Federal Domestic Assistance*. Only items related to rural topics are included. This site consists of a direct search via the WAIS database option, a list of funding sources by department, and a subject list. The descriptions of the funding sources are arranged by department.

Those with a graphical Web browser may find it easier to search the full *Catalog of Federal Domestic Assistance* (see entry number 809).

Subject Headings: Grants; Rural Development

SuDoc Number: PrEx 2.20: *Catalog of Federal Domestic Assistance*

[22] Foreign Agricultural Service

Sponsoring Agency: Foreign Agricultural Service (FAS)

Primary Access: http://ffas.usda.gov/

Resource Summary: FAS Online features information about the Service including an organizational chart, a personnel directory, and information on agricultural exporting. For exporters the page offers links titled Export Programs, U.S. Exporter Assistance, and U.S. Export Directory. For statistics and data, the site has sections including Trade Data and Analysis, Foreign Market Research, and Trade Policy. The Publications link includes a catalog of publications, press releases, commodity circulars, *AgExporter Magazine*, and fact sheets.

This site is useful for those involved in the international trade of agricultural products.

Subject Headings: Agriculture—International; Importing and Exporting

SuDoc Numbers: A 67.7/3: *AgExporter*
A 67.40: *U.S. Export Sales*

[23] Forest Service

Sponsoring Agency: Forest Service (USFS)

Primary Access: http://www.fs.fed.us/

Alternative Access Method: http://www.fs.fed.us/textonly.htm [text version]

Resource Summary: The USFS resources are extensive. Areas on the site include Introduction to the Forest Service (speeches, mission, vision and guiding principles, and directory information); The Public Forum (place for public comment on land management practices, Forest Service proposals, suggestions, complaints, and news of Forest Service activities); Enjoy the Outdoors (recreation opportunities, environmental education, wildlife, wilderness, and tourism); and Caring for the Land (ecosystem management, cooperative forestry, and fire management). Other areas include Research in the Forest Service (research papers, news, and events in the Forest Service research community); State and Private Forestry; Global Conservation; Publications and Bibliographies; Forest Service Databases, Graphics, and Software; and Outreach and Employment Opportunities.

The site provides a few publications in full text, along with various Forest Service publications catalogs. Under the Research heading, viewers can find lists of recently published reports. Users can access information on the forests in the National Forest system by forest name and by state. A search option provides keyword searching of the entire site.

The site is well organized with a substantial amount of information about the agency, its component forests, and position papers.

Subject Heading: Forestry

SuDoc Numbers: A 13.27/7: *Forest Products Laboratory: List of Publications*
A 13.141: *Gypsy Moth News*

[24] gears: Global Entomology Agriculture Research Server

Sponsoring Agencies: Agricultural Research Service (ARS); Carl Hayden Bee Research Center

Primary Access: http://gears.tucson.ars.ag.gov/

Resource Summary: This site is graphics intensive, and it contains a broad collection of information. Areas on this site include Nature Explorer, Internet Classroom Research Focus, Africanized Honey Bee (AHB) Infopage, Multimedia, and U.S. Department of Agriculture Software.

Most of the material deals with bees, and there are a number of documents available, research-oriented and educational, in HTML.

Subject Headings: Bees; Entomology

[25] Joint Agricultural Weather Facility

Sponsoring Agencies: National Oceanic and Atmospheric Administration (NOAA); World Agricultural Outlook Board

Primary Access: http://www.usda.gov/oce/waob/jawf/

Resource Summary: This site for international agricultural weather comprises crop calendars for summer and winter crops. It also contains special articles and a few publications, including access to the *Weekly Weather and Crop Bulletin.*

Subject Headings: Agriculture—International; Crops; Weather

SuDoc Number: C 55.209: *Weekly Weather and Crop Bulletin*

[26] National Integrated Pest Management Network

Sponsoring Agency: Cooperative State Research, Education, and Extension Service

Primary Access: http://www.reeusda.gov/ipm/ipm-home.htm

Resource Summary: The Integrated Pest Management (IPM) Network links to regional information servers and to other servers that describe and contain information on the program. In addition, the central server has connections to EPA Worker Protection Standards for Agricultural Workers and to USDA/Agricultural Marketing Service (AMS) Federal Pesticide Recordkeeping Requirements.

Most of the substantive information is on the peripheral servers, but this site provides a central link.

Subject Headings: Entomology; Insects; Pesticides

[27] Natural Resources Conservation Service

Sponsoring Agencies: Natural Resources Conservation Service; National Spatial Data Infrastructure (NSDI)

Primary Access: http://www.ncg.nrcs.usda.gov/

Alternative Access Method: http://www.ncg.nrcs.usda.gov/Welcome2.html [text version]

Resource Summary: This site features information including data on the Service, its offices, and technical references. The Natural Resources Conservation Service Data Clearinghouse links to information from the National Spatial Data Infrastructure (NSDI). The NSDI has links to a substantial collection of data sets and descriptions of data sets. The Workforce Organization category includes information on the agency's headquarters, centers, institutes, and regional and state offices. The Technical References category includes a number of publications in PDF format such as the *Conservation Practice Standards* and *National Engineering Handbook 20 Standards*.

The standards under the Technical References category and some of the detailed plant and soils information from the NSDI will likely be the most useful resources at this site. Many of the links are to information stored on other servers.

Subject Headings: Conservation; Soils; Standards

[28] PLANTS Database

Sponsoring Agency: National Plant Data Center

Primary Access: http://trident.ftc.nrcs.usda.gov/plants/

Alternative Access Method: ftp://trident.ftc.nrcs.usda.gov/dist/plants/

Resource Summary: The PLANTS Database provides a single source of standardized information about plants. PLANTS provides standardized plant names, symbols, and other plant attribute information. In addition, the database can generate lists of endangered and threatened plants, wetlands reports, and phylogenetic plants. Searches can be limited by state and keyword. The ftp site contains information on the distribution of plants by state.

For verifying plant names and other information, this database is an excellent choice. The search options are generally straightforward, although they can be a bit confusing for first-time users.

Subject Headings: Endangered Species; Plants

[29] Rural Information Center

Sponsoring Agency: National Agricultural Library (NAL)

Primary Access: http://www.nal.usda.gov/ric/agnic/agnic-ric.html

Alternative Access Method: gopher://gopher.nalusda.gov/11/infocntr/ric_richs

Resource Summary: This site has information on several areas including Information about the Rural Information Center and its Programs, the Rural Information Center Health Service Files, and Rural Information Center Publications. Most of the publications are NAL Quick Bibliographies on rural issues. The Health Service section includes information on federal legislation, grants, and newsletters.

This site can be used as a good starting point for finding more information on a variety of rural issues.

Subject Heading: Rural Education

[30] USDA, NRCS National Plant Data Center

Sponsoring Agencies: National Plant Data Center (NPDC); Natural Resources Conservation Service (NRCS)

Primary Access: http://trident.ftc.nrcs.usda.gov/npdc/

Resource Summary: This site features information about the Center, the cooperating agencies, and the NPDC activities. It also links to the PLANTS Database home page.

Subject Heading: Plants

[31] USDA Research, Education, and Economics

Sponsoring Agency: Department of Agriculture (USDA)

Primary Access: http://www.reeusda.gov/ree/

Resource Summary: This site consists of a few links to Research, Education, and Extension (REE) agencies such as the Agricultural Research Service; the Cooperative State Research, Education, and Extension Service; the Economic Research Service; and the National Agricultural Statistics Service. It also includes links to a REE Directory; REE Program Results Teams; the REE Strategic Plan; and REE Legislative Affairs.

Subject Headings: Agricultural Education; Agriculture—Research

Agriculture: Business Sources

[32] Farm Service Agency

Sponsoring Agency: Farm Service Agency (FSA)

Primary Access: http://www.fsa.usda.gov/

Resource Summary: The FSA site includes sections titled News and Information, About FSA, Programs, What's New, Opportunities, and Search/Help. The News and Information page includes press releases, FSA reports, and FSA background information and fact sheets. The Programs page provides access to some of the FSA publications along with information on crop insurance, emergency loans, and the latest farm bill.

Subject Headings: Conservation Reserve Program; Farms and Farming

[33] Grain Inspection, Packers, and Stockyards Administration

Sponsoring Agency: Department of Agriculture (USDA); Grain Inspection, Packers, and Stockyards Administration (GIPSA)

Primary Access: http://www.usda.gov/gipsa/

Resource Summary: The mission of GIPSA is to facilitate the marketing of grains, livestock, poultry, and meat for the overall benefit of consumers and American agriculture. This site includes information on the agency, a GIPSA directory, information from the Federal Grain Inspection Service, and information about selected GIPSA publications.

This page is useful for information about the agency, its regulations, and its inspectors and/or weighing services for the Federal Grain Inspection Service.

Subject Heading: Farms and Farming

[34] National Rural Development Council

Sponsoring Agency: National Rural Development Council (NRDC)

Primary Access: http://www.rurdev.usda.gov/nrdp/nrdp4.html

Resource Summary: This site lists agencies (with links to appropriate Web sites) that are partners in the NRDC and contains information on the NRDC steering committee. There is little original information on this site.

Subject Heading: Rural Development

[35] National Rural Development Partnership

Sponsoring Agency: National Rural Development Partnership (NRDP)

Primary Access: http://www.rurdev.usda.gov/nrdp/

Resource Summary: This site features information about the Partnership and its accomplishments. It also has links to state partners, information on the Rural Development Net, and other rural development sites. To see what activities the NRDP has been involved with, look under the heading NRDP Accomplishments: The Electronic Archive. This is a catalog of the National Rural Development Partnership successes, indexed by state and issue area.

Some areas of this site are still under construction, but it does provide basic information on the NRDP and its activities.

Subject Heading: Rural Development

[36] Rural Development, USDA

Sponsoring Agency: Department of Agriculture (USDA)

Primary Access: http://www.rurdev.usda.gov/

Alternative Access Method: gopher://199.128.87.48/

Resource Summary: This site provides access to the informational resources of the USDA's Rural Development agencies. This site features full-text documents of case studies for the Development Ideas that Work program, along with links to online discussion groups, rural development regulations, and the Rural Development Programs and Assistance section.

This is another useful site for those in rural communities and those interested in promoting rural economic development.

Subject Heading: Rural Development

[37] Rural Housing Service

Sponsoring Agency: Rural Housing Service

Primary Access: http://www.rurdev.usda.gov/agency/rhs/rhs.html

Resource Summary: This page primarily describes the agency and provides links to some of its program areas. These include Single Family Housing Programs, Multi-Family Housing Programs, and Community Programs.

Subject Heading: Rural Development

[38] Rural Utilities Service

Sponsoring Agency: Rural Utilities Service (RUS)

Primary Access: http://www.usda.gov/rus/

Resource Summary: The Rural Utilities Service Web site provides information on its programs and services. RUS features links entitled Telecommunications Program; Electric Program; Distance Learning and Telemedicine, Water and Waste Program, Water 2000, and RUS Regulations. Another section links to the RUS Success Stories page with specific tales of RUS programs that have helped to bring about a fundamental and sometimes dramatic improvement to the lives of rural citizens.

Subject Headings: Rural Development; Utilities

[39] State Rural Development Councils

Sponsoring Agency: National Rural Development Partnership (NRDP)

Primary Access: http://www.rurdev.usda.gov/nrdp/nrdpsrdc.html

Resource Summary: This page lists contact information for each of the 37 state rural development centers that are part of the National Rural Development Partnership.

There is limited information beyond the basic function of this site.

Subject Headings: Rural Development; States

[40] U.S. Agricultural Marketing Service

Sponsoring Agency: Agricultural Marketing Service (AMS)

Primary Access: http://www.usda.gov/ams/

Resource Summary: The Agricultural Marketing Service Web site provides information on the agency as well as current market news. The Program Areas page links to information about the various AMS programs and divisions. The News and Information link connects to press releases and food purchase reports. The AMS Market News Reports area provides up-to-the-minute information on commodity prices, demand, movement, volume, and quality. Other categories on the site include Services, Job Opportunities, and USDA Quality Standards.

This is an important site for anyone interested in current agricultural market statistics.

Subject Heading: Agriculture—Marketing

[41] USDA Rural Business-Cooperative Service

Sponsoring Agency: Rural Business-Cooperative Service

Primary Access: http://www.rurdev.usda.gov/agency/rbcds/html/rbcdhome.html

Resource Summary: This page describes the Rural Business-Cooperative Service. The site offers links to additional information on the Service under headings such as Rural Development, Regulations, Special Initiatives, Business Programs, Success Stories, and Employment.

This site provides an excellent starting point for finding information on the Service and its programs. It will be of most interest to businesses and rural community leaders.

Subject Heading: Rural Development

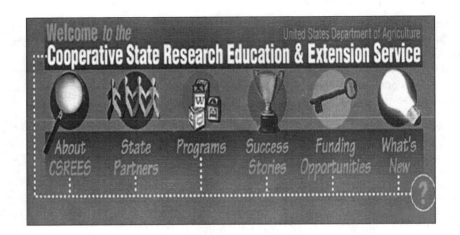

[42] Cooperative State Research Education & Extension Service

Sponsoring Agency: Cooperative State Research Education & Extension Service (CSREES)

Primary Access: http://www.esusda.gov/

Alternative Access Methods: http://www.reeusda.gov/
gopher://esusda.gov/

Resource Summary: The site features information about the mission, partners, and programs of the Cooperative State Research Education & Extension Service. Agency information includes a table of organization, a personnel directory, and the CSREES budget and funding authorization. The Funding Opportunities link provides access to information on CSREES grants. It also has a Success Stories page, which highlights successful Extension Service programs.

This is a basic, functional site that makes it easy to find information on the Extension Service and its programs.

Subject Headings: Agricultural Education; Grants—Education

[43] *Journal of Extension*

Sponsoring Agency: Cooperative State Research Education & Extension Service (CSREES)

Primary Access: http://joe.org/joe/

Alternative Access Methods: gopher://gopher.ext.vt.edu/11/joe
gopher://joe.uwex.edu/11/joe
mailto:almanac@joe.uwex.edu with "send help joe" in body
mailto:almanac@joe.org with "send help joe" in body

Resource Summary: The electronic version of the *Journal of Extension* (*JOE*) is the only version of the *Journal* currently being published—the print version ceased publication in 1994. The online version goes back to the fall of 1987. Articles are in ASCII and are accessible by date and via a keyword search engine. While the articles are stored on Gopher servers and have access from the Web page, the different Gopher servers and the almanac automated e-mail system all provide the same text.

As the only format for current issues of the *JOE*, access to the Internet and knowledge of how to retrieve articles is essential for extension personnel and librarians serving them. This refereed publication uses sophisticated, yet easy-to-use, interfaces to the electronic publication. Others seeking a model for producing an electronic periodical would be well advised to look closely at how the *JOE* is handled. Unfortunately, not all of the alternate access sites are keeping up with the current issues.

Subject Heading: Electronic Periodicals

[44] PENPages

Sponsoring Agencies: Cooperative State Research Education & Extension Service (CSREES); Department of Agriculture (USDA); Pennsylvania State University

Primary Access: gopher://penpages.psu.edu/

Alternative Access Methods: telnet://penpages.psu.edu/
http://www.cas.psu.edu/docs/CASSERVERS/Penpages.html
http://www.penpages.psu.edu/

Resource Summary: PENPages is a broad-based agricultural and nutrition resource that includes some government information along with information from other agencies and organizations. This is a large collection of information—over 12,000 documents are available. The principal federal government resources on this site include USDA press releases and market reports, MAPP (the national Cooperative Extension family database), the Cooperative Extension Service's Diversity and Pluralism Database, and various Pennsylvania-oriented resources from the Pennsylvania Department of Agriculture.

The combination of federal government documents and publications from other organizations works well. This is an important source for extension agents, and it would be even more widely used if it were converted to a Web interface and the documents were converted from ASCII to HTML format. The two Web URLs listed provide information about PENPages and a keyword search option but not about the direct access available from the Gopher.

Subject Headings: Agriculture—Full Text; Agriculture—International; Nutrition; Pennsylvania

[45] State Partners of the Cooperative State Research, Education, and Extension Service

Sponsoring Agency: Cooperative State Research Education & Extension Service (CSREES)

Primary Access: http://www.reeusda.gov/new/statepartners/usa.htm

Resource Summary: This site offers a directory of land-grant universities that are state partners of the Cooperative State Research, Education, and Extension Service. Links are provided to the Web sites of schools of forestry, higher education, home economics, veterinary science, and state extension services and experiment stations.

Subject Heading: Agricultural Education

[46] USDA Almanac

Sponsoring Agency: Cooperative State Research Education & Extension Service (CSREES)

Primary Access: mailto:almanac@esusda.gov with "send guide" in body

Alternative Access Methods: mailto:almanac@ces.ncsu.edu with "send guide" in body
mailto:almanac@oes.orst.edu with "send guide" in body
mailto:almanac@ecn.purdue.edu with "send guide" in body
mailto:almanac@empire.cce.cornell.edu with "send guide" in body
mailto:almanac@acenet.auburn.edu with "send guide" in body
mailto:almanac@wisplan.uwex.edu with "send guide" in body
mailto:almanac@ext.missouri.edu with "send guide" in body

Resource Summary: E-mailing the message "send guide" will result in a response that includes the almanac users guide. Each site contains different files available from the almanac server. For an e-mail listing of available documents, send the message "send catalog" to each address. There are many files available, including Economic Research Service report summaries, fact sheets, North American Free Trade Agreement documents, Extension Family Resource Management documents, and National Agricultural Statistics Service (NASS) reports, to name just a few of the major series available from the central server. Categories on other servers include EXTOXNET - Pesticide Information Notebook and the Home Buyers Guide at Cornell, the Aquaculture Network Information Center at Purdue, the Certified Organic Growers' Manual and Sustainable Agriculture Research and Education Projects at North Carolina State University, Sustainable Finance for Development in Africa at Missouri, and the Great Lakes Haylist from the University of Wisconsin (uwex).

There are plenty of potentially useful documents on these almanac servers. The e-mail request and deliver mechanism is effective, and it was an especially valuable resource distribution channel in the pre-Gopher and pre-Web days of the Internet. These documents would be retrieved more frequently if the almanac documents were available in HTML and directly accessible by Web clients.

Subject Heading: Agriculture—Full Text

Agricultural
Genome
Information
System

An integrated system
for agricultural genome analysis.

This is the **graphical** version of the AGIS web site. The text-only v
also available.

Databases

Conferences

Publications

Courses

Tools

Related Links

INSIDE AGIS
What AGIS is all about
What's New
Curators and Collaborators
Server Information

ANNOUNCEMENTS
AGIS Listserv

NAL RESOURCES
Plant Genome Data & Information Center
NAL Home Page
Calendar of Events

[47] Agricultural Genome Information Server

Sponsoring Agencies: Agricultural Research Service (ARS); National Agricultural Library (NAL)

Primary Access: http://probe.nalusda.gov/

Alternative Access Methods: gopher://probe.nalusda.gov:7000/
ftp://probe.nalusda.gov/pub/

Resource Summary: The Agricultural Genome Information Server (AGIS) features many highly technical genome databases along with other biological databases housed at the National Agricultural Library. The genome databases include ones for plants (cotton, soybeans, trees, sorghum, rice, maize, alfalfa, and grains); livestock (poultry, swine, sheep, and bovine), and other (including human chromosomes 21 and X, and mycobacteria). The other biological databases include those for plant chemicals, Native American food and medicinal plants, and worldwide ethnobotany.

Other links on this page include Conferences , Publications, Courses, and tools

The site contains a wealth of genome information for the researcher, but the general public may also find the other biological databases of interest.

Subject Headings: Agriculture—Statistics; Genetics; Genomes; Plants

[48] *Agricultural Outlook*

Sponsoring Agencies: Cornell University. Mann Library; Economic Research Service

Primary Access: http://usda.mannlib.cornell.edu/reports/erssor/economics/ao-bb

Alternative Access Method: gopher://mann77.mannlib.cornell.edu/11/reports/erssor/economics/ao-bb

Resource Summary: Both the summary and the full issue of this publication are available. The electronic version only contains the text of the print version; tables and graphics are not included. The earliest full issue available is from February 24, 1995. The summary issues are available two to three days before the full issue.

This is an ASCII version of the print periodical. It would be easier to browse if an HTML or PDF version were available. There is no table of contents or other mechanism to browse the ASCII version. In addition, the dates differ from the printed version. For example, the August 1995 print issue is listed as the July 26, 1995, issue online. There are also textual discrepancies between the print and the online ASCII version.

Subject Heading: Agriculture—Statistics

SuDoc Number: A 93.10/2: *Agricultural Outlook*

[49] Agricultural Research Service

Sponsoring Agency: Agricultural Research Service (ARS)

Primary Access: http://www.ars.usda.gov/

Alternative Access Method: http://www.ars-grin.gov/ars/

Resource Summary: This site is organized with the following information: About ARS, News and Information, Research, Information Resources of the National Agricultural Library, Management Team, and Job Opportunities with ARS. Most of the information in these categories describes the ARS or some of its activities. The Job Opportunities section includes vacancies in service and postdoctoral research positions. News and Information includes press releases, the *ARS Magazine*, a visitor center, and various newsletters.

The detailed descriptive information about ARS and the availability of some of its publications make this a useful site for background on the agency and as a starting point for agricultural research information.

Subject Headings: Agriculture—Statistics; Employment

SuDoc Number: A 77.517: *Methyl Bromide Alternatives*

[50] Beltsville Agricultural Research Center

Sponsoring Agencies: Agricultural Research Service (ARS); Beltsville Agricultural Research Center (BARC)

Primary Access: http://www.barc.usda.gov/

Resource Summary: This page consists primarily of a hypertext list of institutes, centers, divisions, and laboratories at BARC. Some major divisions of BARC are the Beltsville Human Nutrition Research Center, the Facilities Management and Operations Division, the Livestock and Poultry Science Institute, the Natural Resources Institute, and the Plant Sciences Institute.

Another link on this page is to a research index. This list of agricultural specialists is divided by broad topic, and then by narrower specialty. The list includes only the contact person's name, specialty, and e-mail address.

The research index would be more useful if it included addresses and phone numbers in addition to the names and e-mail addresses of the specific contact people.

Subject Headings: Agriculture—Research; Research Laboratories

[51] Economic Research Service

Sponsoring Agency: Economic Research Service (ERS)

Primary Access: http://www.econ.ag.gov/

Resource Summary: The ERS site provides economic and other social science information and analysis for public and private decisions on agriculture, food, natural resources, and rural America. The ERS produces information as a service to the general public and to help the executive and legislative branches develop, administer, and evaluate agricultural and rural policies and programs.
Their Web site divides the offerings into the following categories: About ERS, New Analysis, Products and Services, and Briefing Rooms. There are a number of online publications under Products and Services, some in HTML and others in PDF. That section also includes pointers to the collection of ERS publications at Cornell's Mann Library site.

The site features a basic and easy-to-navigate layout. The electronic publications and data sets make this a useful site for the agricultural researcher.

Subject Heading: Agriculture—Statistics

SuDoc Number: A 1.75: *Issues in Agricultural and Rural Finance*

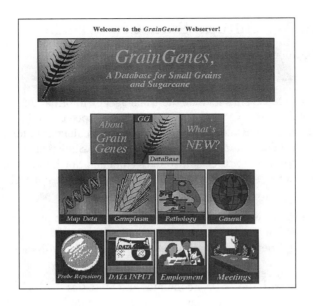

Welcome to the *GrainGenes* Webserver!

[52] GrainGenes

Sponsoring Agencies: National Agricultural Library (NAL); Plant Genome Research Program

Primary Access: http://wheat.pw.usda.gov/graingenes.html

Alternative Access Methods: gopher://probe.nalusda.gov:7002/1
gopher://greengenes.cit.cornell.edu/
mailto:waismail@probe.nalusda.gov with "help" in body
http://wheat.pw.usda.gov/ggpages/xggindex.html

Resource Summary: GrainGenes is a compilation of molecular and phenotypic information on wheat, barley, oats, rye, and sugarcane. The top level pages have links for different types of access to the database including Web, Gopher, and ACEDB (an X Window interface). There are also special connections geared toward agronomists, mappers, and pathologists. Images with descriptions from the GrainGenes database are only available via the Web connection.

Access to the actual data is available by an alphabetical browse by category and name and also by a variety of keyword searches. For researchers, another option is available for adding new data to the database.

The database contains both a substantial amount of genetic information and many links to other genome databases. The interactive and collaborative capabilities of the Internet are used to good advantage, allowing researchers to submit data for entry into the database as well as browse through data that is already included.

Subject Headings: Genetics; Genomes; Plants

[53] National Agricultural Statistics Service

Sponsoring Agency: National Agricultural Statistics Service (NASS)

Primary Access: http://www.usda.gov/nass/

Resource Summary: The NASS sites include the usual agency information, such as a mission statement and a directory of the NASS commodity and price specialists. In addition, the Agency Information section provides a catalog of published reports, a calendar of forthcoming reports, and an electronic products catalog. Under the heading NASS State Statistical Offices is an address list of all the state offices with links to three state offices (Indiana, North Carolina, and Texas) that have home pages. Another top level category, the U.S. Crop Acreage and Yield Maps, are color map images showing a range of acres harvested and yields for selected crops, by county.

The NASS Publications and Historic Data Products categories link to publications and data sets, many of which are located on the USDA Economics and Statistics System at the Cornell University Library's Web server. They also provide access to *Agricultural Statistics* available in PDF format.

This site, in combination with the USDA Economics and Statistics System, provides a substantial number of useful agricultural and crop-related resources. As stated on the top of this page, the NASS aims to provide meaningful, accurate, and objective statistical information and services for the United States, its agriculture, and its rural communities. These two sites effectively demonstrate how the Internet can be used as a dissemination mechanism for those services.

Subject Headings: Agriculture—Statistics; Crops

SuDoc Number: A 1.47: *Agricultural Statistics*

[54] National Genetic Resources Program

Sponsoring Agency: Agricultural Research Service (ARS)

Primary Access: http://www.ars-grin.gov/

Alternative Access Method: gopher://gopher.ars-grin.gov/

Resource Summary: The Germplasm Resources Information Network Web server provides germplasm information about plants, animals, microbes, and invertebrates within the National Genetic Resources Program of the U.S. Department of Agriculture's Agricultural Research Service. Each of the four germplasm databases varies in terms of scope and access points. The microbe database is not yet available, and that link only retrieves a short text file. The invertebrates databases also are not yet available, except for the one titled Releases of Beneficial Organisms in the United States and Territories. The plant and animal database links connect to substantial information resources for germplasm information, yet they are arranged quite differently. Under the National Animal Germplasm link, there is also a listing of livestock breeds.

This site will be primarily of interest to researchers, but it does include some information of more general interest such as the listings of livestock breeds.

Subject Headings: Genetics; Germplasms; Livestock

[55] *Probe*

Sponsoring Agency: Plant Genome Research Program

Primary Access: http://www.nal.usda.gov/pgdic/probe.html

Alternative Access Method: gopher://gopher.nal.usda.gov/11/infocntr/pltgen/ probe_newsl/

Resource Summary: *Probe*, the newsletter for the USDA Plant Genome Research Program, is available back to its first issue from 1991. Articles are in ASCII text on the Gopher server. The newsletter is also available in HTML starting with Volume 4, Issue 3/4 of August 1994.

Both the Gopher and Web versions are easy to browse. No full-text search option is available; however, there may not be as much demand for a search feature in a newsletter as there is in a professional journal such as the *Journal of Extension*. Unfortunately, the latest issue available is from April-June 1995.

Subject Headings: Electronic Periodicals; Genetics; Genomes; Plants—Full Text

[56] USDA Economics and Statistics System

Sponsoring Agencies: Cornell University. Mann Library; Economic Research Service (ERS); National Agricultural Statistics Service (NASS)

Primary Access: http://usda.mannlib.cornell.edu/usda/usda.html

Alternative Access Methods: http://www.mannlib.cornell.edu/usda/usda.html
gopher://usda.mannlib.cornell.edu/11/
ftp://usda.mannlib.cornell.edu/usda/
telnet://usda@usda.mannlib.cornell.edu
mailto:usda-reports@usda.mannlib.cornell.edu with "subscribe <report code>" in body

Resource Summary: This site features current and historical data on national food and agricultural developments. It forecasts the effects of changing conditions and policies on domestic and international agriculture. It contains information on production, supply, demand, utilization, prices, agricultural inputs, commodities, labor and chemical usage, international agricultural trade, and land/water conservation. These materials cover both U.S. and international agriculture topics.

Access is by title, agency, subject, or keyword search. Most reports are text files that contain time-sensitive information. Most data sets are in spreadsheet format (Lotus 1-2-3 or .wk1). These include time series data that are updated yearly.

Under the Reports heading, three groups of reports can be found: *ERS Situation and Outlook Reports*, *NASS Reports*, and *World Agricultural Outlook Board Reports*. Most of these are available back to the beginning of 1995.

The reports are also available via e-mail to the URL listed under other access points. Go to gopher://mann77.mannlib.cornell.edu/00/reports/REPORTS_EMAIL_DISTRIBUTION for a list of the report codes and further instructions.

This can be an especially valuable resource for depository libraries, as at least some of the *Situation and Outlook* reports and yearbooks ceased being distributed to depository libraries at the end of 1994.

Subject Headings: Agriculture—Full Text; Agriculture—Statistics; Crops

SuDoc Numbers: A 1.34:770: *Agriculture Statistics of the European Community*
A 1.34:863 *Agricultural Statistics of the Former USSR Republics and the Baltic States*
A 92. *NASS Reports*
A 93. *ERS Situation and Outlook Report*
A 92.9/3: *Poultry: Production and Value*
A 92.9/4: *Egg Products*
A 92.9/5: *Poultry Slaughter*
A 92.9/6: *Hatchery Production Annual—Supplement*
A 92.9/13: *Layers and Egg Production*

A 92.9/16: *Chicken and Eggs*
A 92.9/17-2: *Turkey Hatchery*
A 92.10: *Milk Production*
A 92.10/2: *Milk Production, Disposition, and Income—Supplement*
A 92.10/5: *Dairy Products—Annual Summary—Supplement*
A 92.10/7: *Dairy Products*
A 92.11: *Vegetables*
A 92.11/2-2: *Noncitrus Fruits and Nuts*
A 92.11/2-4: *Walnut Production*
A 92.11/2-5: *Almond Production*
A 92.11/3: *Cherry Production*
A 92.11/6: *Cranberries*
A 92.11/8: *Citrus Fruits*
A 92.11/10-2: *Vegetables—Annual Summary*
A 92.11/10-5: *Mushrooms*
A 92.11/11: *Potato Stocks*
A 92.12: *Farm Labor*
A 92.14: *Peanut Stocks and Processing*
A 92.14/3: *Hazelnut Production*
A 92.15: *Grain Stocks*
A 92.16: *Agricultural Prices* (monthly)
A 92.16/2: *Agricultural Prices* (annual)
A 92.17: *Meat Animals: Production, Disposition, Income*
A 92.18: *Livestock Slaughter* (annual)
A 92.18/3: *Livestock Slaughter* (monthly)
A 92.18/6: *Cattle on Feed*
A 92.18/6-2: *Cattle*
A 92.18/7: *Hogs and Pigs*
A 92.18/9: *Sheep*
A 92.18/11: *Mink*
A 92.21: *Cold Storage*
A 92.21/2: *Cold Storage Annual Summary*
A 92.24: *Crop Production*
A 92.24/2: *Crop Production - Prospective Plantings*
A 92.24/3: *Crop Values*
A 92.24/4: *Crop Production—Annual Summary*
A 92.24/5: *Farms and Land in Farms*
A 92.28/2: *Honey*
A 92.29/2-7: *International Agriculture and Trade*
A 92.29/5: *Wool and Mohair*
A 92.32: *Floriculture Crops*
A 92.40: *Farm Production Expenditures*
A 92.43: *Rice Stocks*

A 92.44: *Catfish Processing*
A 92.44/2-2: *Catfish Production*
A 92.44/3: *Trout Production*
A 92.46: *Broiler Hatchery*
A 92.47: *Cotton Ginnings*
A 92.50: *Agricultural Chemical Usage*
A 93.9/8: *Agricultural Income and Finance*
A 93.10/2: *Agricultural Outlook*
A 93.11: *Wheat Outlook*
A 93.11/2: *Feed Outlook*
A 93.11/2-3: *Wheat Yearbook*
A 93.16/3: *Food Review*
A 93.17/5-5: *U.S. Agricultural Trade Update*
A 93.23/2: *Oil Crops Outlook*
A 93.24/2: *Cotton and Wool Outlook*
A 93.25: *Tobacco*
A 93.31/3: *Sugar and Sweeteners*
A 93.43: *Outlook for U.S. Agricultural Exports*
A 93.46/3: *Livestock, Dairy, and Poultry Monthly*
A 93.46/3-2: *Poultry Outlook*
A 93.46/3-3: *Dairy Outlook*
A 93.46/3-4: *Hog Outlook*
A 93.46/3-5: *Cattle and Sheep Outlook*
A 93.46/3-6: *Aquaculture Outlook*
A 93.52: *Food Spending in American Households, 1980-1988*

[57] The USDA Research Database

Sponsoring Agencies: Community of Science; Department of Agriculture (USDA)

Primary Access: http://cos.gdb.org/best/fedfund/usda/usda-intro.html

Resource Summary: The USDA Research Database contains the information on ongoing and recently completed projects sponsored or conducted primarily within the USDA and the state university research system. Some 30,000 project summaries, including latest progress reports and lists of recent publications coming from the research, are maintained in the file on an ongoing basis.

These pages provide access to the Current Research Information System (CRIS) database from the USDA. It also includes the Human Nutrition and Information Management System subfile on nutrition research. Access points include research site, state (or foreign country), and broad topical headings. Available search fields include project number, start and end dates, institution, state, research title, and keyword.

The number of access points and search fields make this an easy database to search. This is a useful database for researchers in the agricultural and human nutrition fields.

Subject Headings: Agriculture—Research; CRIS; Nutrition

[58] World Agricultural Supply and Demand Estimates

Sponsoring Agency: Cornell University. Mann Library; Department of Agriculture (USDA)

Primary Access: http://usda.mannlib.cornell.edu/reports/waobr/wasde-bb

Alternative Access Method: gopher://mann77.mannlib.cornell.edu/11/reports/waobr

Resource Summary: This site consists of a monthly statistical report and commentary on world-wide and U.S. supply and use of standard agricultural commodities. A separate report for cotton is available each month. Issues of the report are available from January 12, 1995 (March 9, 1995, for cotton).

Reports are in ASCII, which could make importing into a spreadsheet program difficult. Otherwise, this is an excellent resource.

Subject Heading: Agriculture—Statistics

SuDoc Number: A 93.29/3: *World Agricultural Supply and Demand Estimates*

CHAPTER 2: BUSINESS AND ECONOMICS

The Internet offers some unique opportunities for disseminating government information about financial, economic, and other business related resources to the general public, business people, and government contractors. This chapter features sites that offer resources such as full-text income tax forms, patents, import restrictions, banking statistics, labor statistics, and procurement listings from the *Commerce Business Daily*.

Business information can be so varied in its origin, as well as in its utility, that no one agency has yet produced a single best source for finding other government business and economic information. The sites that do provide connections to useful resources often link to nongovernmental sites for their most substantial resources. Given these cautions, the following two featured sites can be used to find a significant portion of business and economic government resources on the Internet. The U.S. Department of Commerce provides access to other Department of Commerce resources. The U.S. Business Advisor takes a different organizational approach and offers even more links.

[59] U.S. Business Advisor

Sponsoring Agencies: National Performance Review (NPR); Small Business Administration (SBA)

Primary Access: http://www.business.gov/

Alternative Access Method: http://www.business.gov/index2.html [text version]

Resource Summary: The U.S. Business Advisor exists to provide businesses with one-stop access to federal government information, services, and transactions. While it is not yet a comprehensive starting point for business, it does contain many relevant links. It has an easy-to-navigate layout including the following categories: Common Questions, How To..., Search, Browse, and News. The first category includes basic answers to common questions. The How To section links to other government resources including expert tools, step-by-step guides, and transactions. The Search section includes a link to the GovBot search engine; GPO Access; the health, safety, and environ-ment portion of the *Code of Federal Regulations*; a FinanceNet search; and regulations under development. To their credit, the creators of the Business Advisor realize that even these search tools may not find all answers, so they provide browsing capabilities in six general business areas. The News section includes selected, business-related press releases from government agencies.

There is not a great deal of original material on this site, but the organization of links to other sites sets it apart from many others. Altogether, this is an excellent starting point for anyone looking for business information from the government.

Subject Heading: Finding Aid—Business

[60] U.S. Department of Commerce

Sponsoring Agency: Department of Commerce (DOC)

Primary Access: http://www.doc.gov/

Resource Summary: With its major focus on the business world, the Department of Commerce also has responsibility for gathering statistics and weather information. Their Web site serves as a primary information point for the Department. The General Information heading includes announcements, e-mail and telephone staff directories, and a featured DOC site of the week. The Commerce on the Web heading provides a list of DOC Web sites arranged by bureau and topical links such as Business and Trade, Economy and Statistics, Science and Technology, and Informa-tion and Business Services.

This site provides easy access to the many other Department of Commerce Internet information sources, both by agency and by topic.

Subject Headings: Business Information; Finding Aid—Business

Business and Economics: General Business Information Resources

[61] 1040 and Other Tax Information

Sponsoring Agencies: Drake Software, Inc.; Internal Revenue Service (IRS)

Primary Access: http://www.1040.com/

Resource Summary: This unofficial site mirrors official IRS forms and publications on FedWorld. It also has some federal tax forms dating back to the 1992 tax year. All forms are available in PDF format. There is also a page titled State Revenue Addresses and another page titled State Tax Forms. The State Tax Forms page includes copies of state income tax forms, also in PDF, from about 30 states. This site is a nice backup to the IRS site, and it is a useful finding aid for Internet-accessible state tax forms.

Subject Headings: Tax Forms—Federal; Tax Forms—State

SuDoc Number: T 22.2/12: *Tax Forms*

[62] Bureau of Engraving and Printing

Sponsoring Agency: Bureau of Engraving and Printing

Primary Access: http://www.bep.treas.gov

Resource Summary: The Bureau of Engraving and Printing Web site features information on the Bureau, its headquarters, and its Western Currency Facility in Ft. Worth, Texas. Available sections include Tours, Map, Stamp Forum, Public Sales, Stamps, and Play the Money Game. The game consists of matching the correct presidential picture to the correct currency.

Subject Heading: Currency

The Business and Economics resources in this chapter are subdivided broadly into four sections. The first section includes sites that contain General Business Information Resources as well as those sites that do not fit under the other three categories. This section runs from entry number 61 to 94. The Finance section includes a variety of sites related to finance, either offering financial statistics or providing financial advice. It covers entries 95-111. The third section, Government Business, includes sites from government procurement offices, which offer advice to businesses interested in getting involved with the government market, and sites from internal governmental business organizations. These are entries 112-139. Since so many government agencies will be involved in some kind of procurement activities, see also "Procurement" in the subject index or go directly to a specific agency's Web site. The last subchapter, International Commerce, Exporting, and Importing, lists a variety of sites and resources that are designed for companies interested in exporting, importing, and international commerce in general. These are entries 140-156.

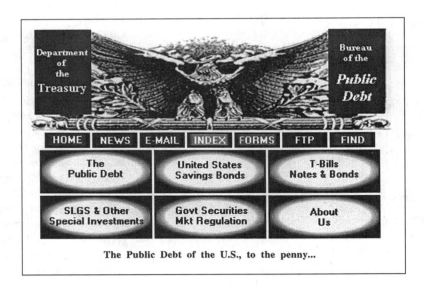

The Public Debt of the U.S., to the penny...

[63] Bureau of the Public Debt

Sponsoring Agency: Bureau of the Public Debt

Primary Access: http://www.publicdebt.treas.gov/

Alternative Access Method: ftp://ftp.publicdebt.treas.gov/

Resource Summary: The Bureau of the Public Debt site features information on the debt as well as on investments in government bonds. Some of the available categories include News; The Public Debt; United States Savings Bonds; T- Bills, Notes, and Bonds; and other special investments. The Public Debt page includes a daily debt figure, a monthly statement on the debt, historical debt figures, and a frequently-asked-questions file.

Subject Headings: Debt; Savings Bonds

SuDoc Numbers: T 63.209/5: *Tables of Redemption Values for $25 Series Bonds*
T 63.209/5-2: *Tables of Redemption Values for $50 Series EE and Series E Savings Bonds*
T 63.209/6: *Tables of Redemption Values for U.S. Savings Bonds, Series E*
T 63.209/7: *Tables of Redemption Values for U.S. Savings Bonds, Series EE*
T 63.210: *Tables of Redemption Values for U.S. Savings Notes*
T 63.215: *Monthly Statement of the Public Debt of the United States*

[64] The Digital Daily: Income Tax Forms, Instructions, Publications

Sponsoring Agency: Internal Revenue Service (IRS)

Primary Access: http://www.irs.ustreas.gov/cover.html

Alternative Access Methods: http://www.irs.ustreas.gov/plain/ [text version]
ftp://ftp.fedworld.gov/pub/irs-pdf/
ftp://ftp.fedworld.gov/pub/irs-pcl/
ftp://ftp.fedworld.gov/pub/irs-ps/
ftp://ftp.fedworld.gov/pub/irs-sgml/
ftp://ftp.fedworld.gov/pub/irs-utl/

Resource Summary: The image-intensive design of this site can take time to load, but it is an extremely well-designed site. The graphic Digital Daily, features all sorts of tax links including Tax Stats, Tax Info for You, Tax Info for Business, Electronic Services, Taxpayer Help, Tax Regs in English, IRS Newsstand, Forms and Pubs, What's Hot, Meet the Commissioner, Comments and Help, and a Site Tree.

The major resource on the IRS site is the full-text tax forms, publications, and instructions. There is also the usual brief agency description, a biography of the commissioner, a list of where to file (arranged by state), and information about where to find tax help.

The federal tax forms, instructions, and publications are available in Adobe Acrobat PDF format. The forms on this server are replicas of the official IRS forms. Most can be printed, filled out, and filed with the IRS. However, the Adobe Acrobat Reader must be installed on your computer before these forms can be viewed or printed. Some forms are available from 1991 to the present. Other formats available are compressed PCL, PostScript, and SGML (Standardized General MarkUp Language).

Access is either via a list of forms available from the FedWorld ftp site or via a keyword title search engine. The FedWorld lists are divided by file format: PCL, PDF, PS, and SGML. The UTL directory contains other documents, mostly in ASCII text or PDF format, such as the General Tax Calendar, Tip Sheets, and other help documents.

For anyone not willing to wait for tax forms in the mail, this is a commendable resource. The search engine does not always retrieve keywords from titles. Searches on form numbers work better, but a search on "Schedule C" does not bring up the records for Schedule C. At other times, the search engine does not function. For convenience, maybe someday there will be HTML forms that could be submitted (with reliable encryption) online.

Subject Headings: Tax Forms—Federal; Taxes

SuDoc Numbers: T 22.2/12: *Tax Forms*
T 22.23: *Internal Revenue Bulletin*
T 22.25: *Internal Revenue Cumulative Bulletin*
T 22.44/2: *IRS Publications*

[65] Economic Development Administration

Sponsoring Agency: Economic Development Administration (EDA)

Primary Access: http://cher.eda.doc.gov/agencies/eda/index.html

Resource Summary: This site contains descriptive information on the EDA and links to EDA services. For information on the EDA, this site features an e-mail directory, links to EDA programs and offices, and a fact sheet. Other links point to the Office of Economic Conversion Information and Other Economic Development Contacts and Resources.

Subject Heading: Economic Development

[66] Economics and Statistics Administration

Sponsoring Agency: Economics and Statistics Administration (ESA)

Primary Access: http://cher.eda.doc.gov/agencies/esa/index.html

Alternative Access Method: http://www.doc.gov/agencies/esa/index.html

Resource Summary: This site describes the Economics and Statistics Administration, which collects much of the statistical, economic, and demographic information that is made available to the public. The page links to the major ESA departments and workgroups including the Bureau of Economic Analysis, STAT-USA, and the Census Bureau. The site also has links to the ESA Reports and the Working Papers.

Users could use this site to link to the information-rich sites of its major offices, but most people are likely to go directly to those sites.

Subject Headings: Business Information; Statistics

[67] Employment and Training Administration

Sponsoring Agency: Department of Labor (DOL); Employment and Training Administration (ETA)

Primary Access: http://www.doleta.gov/

Resource Summary: The ETA site contains agency information such as a mission statement, an organizational chart, press releases, speeches, and testimony. This site also offers descriptions of ETA programs and activities links including Adult Training Programs, Dislocated Worker Programs, Employment Services, Special Population Programs, Unemployment Benefits, Unemployment Insurance Information, and Youth Training Programs. Also, the site offers information on the laws ETA administers.

The Programs and Activities category includes numerous documents useful for both those looking for work and those interested in governmental career and employment programs.

Subject Headings: Employment; Labor

[68] Employment Standards Administration

Sponsoring Agency: Department of Labor (DOL); Employment Standards Administration (ESA)

Primary Access: http://www.dol.gov/dol/esa/

Resource Summary: In addition to agency information, such as a mission statement, organizational chart, personnel directory, press releases, and information about the assistant secretary, the ESA makes relevant statutory and regulatory information available. It also has links to some ESA Programs and some online posters, and a directory for state departments of labor. The site also provides access to hot topic links near the top of the page.

Subject Headings: Employment; Labor

[69] Federal Deposit Insurance Corporation

Sponsoring Agency: Federal Deposit Insurance Corporation (FDIC)

Primary Access: http://www.fdic.gov/

Aternative Access Methods: gopher://gopher.fdic.gov/
ftp://ftp.fdic.gov/
mailto:listserv@nic.sura.net with "subscribe bulksale" in body
mailto:listserv@nic.sura.net with "subscribe FDIC-announce" in body

Resource Summary: Featuring a large collection of banking information and publications, the FDIC site offers sections such as Banking News, Public Information, Consumer News, Asset Sales Information, and a Databank. Most of the statistical publications are available on the Databank page directly or under the Statistical Publications subheading. For example, the *Quarterly Banking Profile* contains detailed statistics about FDIC-insured banks and savings institutions. The reports do not mention specific banks, but they do address the industry as a whole and by region. Some of the data is in HTML and some is in ASCII text files. Tables are available in both ASCII and Lotus 1-2-3 (.wk1), and a number of GIF files of charts are available as well.

Brief information on individual FDIC-insured institutions can be found under the Consumer heading and the FDIC Institutions subheading. These ASCII text files, one for each state, provide addresses, certification, deposits, and asset information for each institution. Other resources include year-end financial results, consumer information, and more statistics from the Division of Research and Statistics.

The FDIC appeals to both the professional and the consumer with its offerings. For the professional, the detailed statistics and various full-text reports create many opportunities for research into banking trends and specific institutions. For the consumer it offers advice, referrals to rating services, and statistics on individual institutions.

Subject Heading: Banking

SuDoc Numbers: Y 3.F 31/8:1-2:/ *Statistics on Banking*
Y 3.F 31/8:27/ *FDIC Banking Review*
Y 3.F 31/8:24/ *FDIC Consumer News*
Y 3.F 31/8:26/ *FDIC Historical Statistics on Banking*
Y 3.F 31/8:28/ *Survey of Real Estate Trends*
Y 3.F 31/8:29/ *Quarterly Banking Profile*

[70] Federal EDI Secretariat

Sponsoring Agency: National Institute of Standards and Technology (NIST)

Primary Access: http://snad.ncsl.nist.gov/dartg/edi/fededi.html
Alternative Access Method: http://snad.ncsl.nist.gov/dartg/edi/fededi-info.html [text version]

Resource Summary: This central site for federal Electronic Data Interchange (EDI) information includes a section for vendor registration, architecture documents, Implementation Conventions (ICs) open for comment, a point of contact, and both the 3040 ICs and the 3050 ICs.

Subject Heading: Electronic Data Interchange

[71] Federal Trade Commission

Sponsoring Agency: Federal Trade Commission (FTC)

Primary Access: http://www.ftc.gov/

Alternative Access Methods: gopher://gopher.ftc.gov/
ftp://ftp.ftc.gov/pub/

Resource Summary: The FTC Web site includes a variety of consumer publications and FTC rulings. Under Commission Actions, the FTC publishes complaints, decisions and orders, and final orders, in both WordPerfect 5.1 and Adobe Acrobat PDF formats. These date back to March 1996, but older documents may be added in the future. Beginning in September 1996, the FTC began adding HTML versions.

The site also describes the FTC and how it brings actions. Also provided are the FTC's organizational structure, a list of its offices, and a list of contacts for additional information. Other links connect to headings titled: News Releases; Speeches and Articles; FTC ConsumerLine (described more fully in the Ready Reference chapter); and Conferences, Hearings, and Workshops. The ftp and Gopher servers do not have all the links and documents found on the Web server.

The FTC uses a basic presentation style with just a few links, but these links connect to substantial and important resources for information from the FTC for both consumers and the business world.

Subject Headings: Cases—Full Text; Commerce; Consumer Information

SuDoc Number: FT 1.11: *Federal Trade Commission Decisions*

[72] FedWorld Davis-Bacon Act Search

Sponsoring Agencies: Department of Labor (DOL); National Technical Information Service (NTIS)

Primary Access: http://kirk.fedworld.gov/dbhome.htm

Resource Summary: The Davis-Bacon Wage Determination Database contains wage determinations made by the Department of Labor under the mandate of the Davis-Bacon Act and related legislation. The Department determines prevailing wage rates for construction-related occupations in most counties in the United States. All federal government construction contracts and most contracts for federally assisted construction over $2,000 must contain Davis-Bacon wage determinations. This FedWorld database has weekly updates, but it is only available by subscription. An out-of-date database that demonstrates how the system works is available for visitors.

Subject Headings: Construction; Davis-Bacon Act; Pay Scales

SuDoc Number: L 36.211: *General Wage Determinations Issued Under the Davis-Bacon and Related Acts*

[73] IBM Patent Server

Sponsoring Agencies: International Business Machines, Inc. (IBM); Patent and Trademark Office (PTO)

Primary Access: http://patent.womplex.ibm.com/

Resource Summary: One of the newer entries into the patent database market, this IBM site includes bibliographic data on U.S. patents for 1974 to the present. It also includes some patents issued from 1971 to 1973. Full patents are even available in GIF format for patents issued from 1980. Available search options include Patent Number Search, Boolean Text Search, and Advanced Text Search. Field searching is also available.

The server may be slow at times, especially in the retrieval of the large GIF images of the full patents. However, the inclusion of these images makes this site the most comprehensive of the free sources for patent information.

Subject Headings: Bibliographic Databases; Patents

[74] Maxwell's Taxing Times

Sponsoring Agencies: Internal Revenue Service (IRS); Maxwell Laboratories, Inc.

Primary Access: http://www.maxwell.com/tax/

Alternative Access Method: http://www.scubed.com/tax/tax.html

Resource Summary: Tax forms are available in a variety of formats for U.S. federal income tax, selected state tax forms, and Canadian federal forms. State forms are available for over half of the states. The U.S. federal tax forms are available in PDF format. There is also a link that points to the official IRS page and its forms, while another link connects to the Canadian tax agency. Other links include a list of phone numbers for requesting state tax forms and tax assistance, information on commercial tax packages, and links to other Web sites with tax information.

The S-Cubed Division of Maxwell Laboratories offers a welcome supplement to the income tax information offered by the IRS and other government organizations.

Subject Headings: Tax Forms—Canadian; Tax Forms—Federal; Tax Forms—State

SuDoc Number: T22.2/12: *Tax Forms*

[75] MicroPatent Web Services

Sponsoring Agencies: MicroPatent; Patent and Trademark Office (PTO)

Primary Access: http://www.micropat.com/

Resource Summary: This is a commercial service that provides a free display of the past four weeks of patents by classification and of the past two weeks by keywords. Prior to the past four weeks, first-page images are available only by patent number. For very recent patents, the full text of the patent is available in HTML. Online images of patents are available back to 1976, patent number 3930791.

With custom viewing software, the first page of all patents can be viewed for free. However, even free searching and viewing requires registration (which is also free). The patent side of the Web site also offers free searching of the *Official Gazette*. The trademark side of the Web site is also a commercial search service for trademarks. There is a demonstration database available for free.

The search options are rather limited since they can only be used for very recent patents. For users who already know patent numbers, MicroPatent is a good place to look. Full patents are available for immediate download, or by e-mail, fax, or standard mail for competitive prices. To view images and the patents themselves, users must download and install their patent viewing software, which is currently only available for Microsoft Windows.

Subject Headings: Patents; Trademarks

SuDoc Number: C 21.5: *Official Gazette*

[76] Mine Safety and Health Administration

Sponsoring Agency: Mine Safety and Health Administration (MSHA)

Primary Access: http://www.msha.gov/

Alternative Access Methods: gopher://gopher.msha.gov/
telnet://bbs@bbs.msha.gov/

Resource Summary: This site features agency information including a mission statement and enabling legislation. Other categories include press releases, speeches, special reports, congressional testimony, statutory and regulatory information, MSHA Regulations, MSHA Policies and Information Bulletins, Safety and Health Hazard Alerts, Information Bulletins, Fatal Mining Accident Reports, Mining Accident and Injury Statistics, Proposed and Final Regulations, and Public Hearings.

Many of the links point to documents in ASCII text on the Gopher server, but some, such as the press releases, are available in HTML. There is a substantial number of documents available on these servers.

Subject Headings: Labor; Mining

SuDoc Number: L 38.17/2: *MSHA Program Information Bulletin*

[77] Minority Business Development Agency

Sponsoring Agency: Minority Business Development Agency (MBDA)

Primary Access: http://cher.eda.doc.gov/agencies/mbda/index.html

Resource Summary: The MBDA site provides information about the Agency and contact information. A description of the Agency includes sections on key responsibilities, activities and services, and departments or workgroups.

It provides basic information about the agency, but the site features no special databases or electronic publications.

Subject Headings: Business Information; Minorities

[78] Office of the Comptroller of the Currency

Sponsoring Agency: Department of the Treasury. Office of the Comptroller of the Currency (OCC)

Primary Access: http://www.occ.treas.gov/

Resource Summary: The Office of the Comptroller of the Currency is an independent bureau of the Treasury Department that oversees the nation's federally chartered banks and the financial regulations that pertain to those banks. The Web site topics are arranged around Who, What, How, When, and Where. Who covers OCC personnel and What features information on the national banks, including the Community Reinvestment Act public evaluations in WordPerfect format and the *Quarterly Derivatives Fact Sheet*. How includes banking regulations, press releases, enforcement activities, and the *Weekly Bulletin* of applications. When and Where cover the history of OCC and office locations.

For those in the banking industry, this site contains a great deal of information. The site is well organized, despite the unusual structure, and it includes a site search option as well.

Subject Headings: Banking; Law Enforcement; Regulations; Regulations—Compliance

SuDoc Number: T 12.3/2: *Weekly Bulletin*

[79] Office of Thrift Supervision

Sponsoring Agency: Department of the Treasury. Office of Thrift Supervision

Primary Access: http://www.access.gpo.gov/ots/

Resource Summary: This site presents descriptive information on the Office of Thrift Supervision, including a brief mission statement and biographical information on the director. It also has press releases, employment opportunities, and a quarterly thrift update.

Subject Heading: Banking

SuDoc Number: T 71.7: *Office of Thrift Supervision News*

[80] SBA: Small Business Administration

Primary Access: http://www.sba.gov/

Alternative Access Methods: http://www.sbaonline.sba.gov/
http://www.sba.gov/textonly/ [text version]
gopher://www.sbaonline.sba.gov/
ftp://www.sbaonline.sba.gov/
telnet://sbaonline.sba.gov/

Resource Summary: The Small Business Administration site provides a variety of resources for small businesses. Agency information is available under the headings of Learn about SBA, SBA Offices and Partners, and Your Local SBA Resources. Choosing the Local SBA Resources link leads the user through some image maps for choosing their state. Under each state, information is presented in the following categories: Local SBA Offices; Calendar of Events; Service Corps of Retired Executives; Small Business Development Centers; Preferred/Certified Lenders; Small Business Investment Companies; Approved Microloan Participants; Business Information Centers; Disaster Area Offices; and Small Business Innovation Research Awards.

Three SBA programs that offer assistance to small businesses are listed under the heading Starting Your Business. The Financing Your Business link leads to information on a variety of SBA loan programs. Another category, Expanding Your Business, describes an export assistance program; ways of getting involved with federal procurement, and the Small Business Innovation Research Program. The Library of SBA Files page provides access to many brief text files of advice for small business.

There are plenty of useful and interesting resources on this site for those involved with small businesses. For business users in need of timely assistance, the most useful section is probably the local contacts for each state.

Subject Heading: Small Businesses

[81] Shadow Patent Office

Sponsoring Agencies: Patent and Trademark Office (PTO); Electronic Data Systems

Primary Access: http://www.spo.eds.com/patent.html

Resource Summary: This is a commercial service for searching the full text of patents back to January 1972. The database is updated weekly. The full text of the patents and full search services are available to customers, for a fee. There is also a free service option that provides browsing the past year's worth of patent titles and numbers by week and major classifications. The free service also gives access to the *Manual of Classification*, which is updated every three months.

For those who want to keep up to date with the most recent patents, the free access to recent patent titles could be used in conjunction with MicroPatent's free first-page images and limited full-text HTML versions. The free search service is not as useful as that available from QPAT-US or the USPTO/CNIDR U.S. Patent Bibliographic Database Search site. However, the *Manual* is very useful, and it is more current than that which is available from STO's Internet Patent Search System.

Subject Heading: Patents

SuDoc Number: C 21.12: *Manual of Classification*

[82] Small Business Advancement National Center

Sponsoring Agencies: Small Business Advancement National Center (SBANC); Small Business Administration (SBA)

Primary Access: http://www.sbaer.uca.edu/

Alternative Access Methods: gopher://www.sbaer.uca.edu/
ftp://www.sbaer.uca.edu/
mailto:listserv@www.sbaer.uca.edu with "sub sbaer-l" in body

Resource Summary: Funded by the Small Business Administration, the SBANC and its home page attempt to provide small businesses, entrepreneurs, educators, economic development officers, and small business counselors with the necessary resources to further their business and economic goals. They have collected a broad variety of information related to small businesses. There is a Small Business Tip of the Week heading, a list of upcoming events, SBANC newsletters in HTML, and links to small business resources from a variety of nongovernmental organizations.

This is a useful information resource for small businesses; however, most of the information and links are nongovernmental in origin.

Subject Heading: Small Businesses

[83] Small Business Development Centers

Sponsoring Agency: Small Business Administration (SBA)

Primary Access: http://www.smallbiz.sunycentral.edu/sites.htm#SBDC

Resource Summary: Two lists are available on this site. The first is a directory of all Small Business Development Centers (SBDCs) which includes a complete state-by-state roster of all SBDCs. The second is a list of SBDCs on the Internet (for connections to SBDCs with Gopher or Web sites). These lists give quick and easy access for identifying local Small Business Development Centers.

Subject Headings: Economic Development; Small Businesses

[84] Small Business Innovation Research Awards

Sponsoring Agencies: Community of Science; Small Business Administration (SBA)

Primary Access: http://cos.gdb.org/best/fedfund/sbir/sbir-intro.html

Resource Summary: Small Business Innovation Research (SBIR) Awards are granted to small U.S. companies in an effort to promote their growth and development. The SBA compiles a database of these SBIR awards, while the Community of Science provides a searchable interface with options to search all awards since 1983, to search by agency, and to search in specific states. Like other Community of Science federal databases, they do an excellent job of providing a powerful search interface to the database.

Subject Headings: Grants; Small Businesses

[85] STO's Internet Patent Search System

Sponsoring Agencies: Patent and Trademark Office (PTO); Source Translation and Optimization (STO)

Primary Access: http://sunsite.unc.edu/patents/intropat.html

Resource Summary: This patent site offers access to the *Manual of Classification*, to the *Index to the U.S. Patent Classification*, and to some patent titles and abstracts. The patent title data go from patent number 3500000 to December 1993. Abstracts are only available for 1981-1989.

Other patent-related resources available from this site are: phone numbers for various PTO offices; PTO examining goups—key personnel and contact points; special PTO P.O. boxes for sending materials to the PTO; and the Crystal City Public Patent Searching Room. Also included are PTO depository libraries across the country; U.S. patent filing fees; preparation of patent drawings—PTO guide; current Patent Cooperation Treaty (PCT) countries and future expansion; and information on the Paris Convention for intellectual property protection. The *Manual of Classification* and the *Index to the U.S. Patent Classification* are available in ASCII text and can be browsed alphabetically or by broad categories.

The *Manual of Classification* and the *Index to the U.S. Patent Classification* are only current as of December 1993. In fact, the whole site does not seem to have been updated very recently. This site is best for browsing the *Manual* or the *Index*.

Subject Heading: Patents

SuDoc Numbers: C 21.12: *Manual of Classification*
C 21.12/2: *Index to the U.S. Patent Classification*

[86] Total Quality Management in DOE

Sponsoring Agency: Department of Energy (DOE). Office of Quality Management

Primary Access: http://www.doe.gov/html/quality/tqmhome.html

Resource Summary: This site contains a brief introductory statement and three links. One link is to an HTML publication, *Total Quality Management Implementation Guidelines*. Another connects to the DOE Defense Programs page, and the third gives access to the Total Quality Management (TQM) Training database. This database includes numerous TQM training courses with course title, description, location, cost, and course number.

There is not a great deal of information on TQM on this site, but it does give an idea of how one government agency is trying to implement TQM ideas.

Subject Heading: Total Quality Management

[87] U.S. Customs Service

Sponsoring Agency: Customs Service

Primary Access: http://www.customs.ustreas.gov/

Resource Summary: The main Customs Service features sections titled Importing Exporting, Traveler Information, Enforcement Activities, and About U.S. Customs. Another section is labeled Report Smuggling.

The Importing Exporting section gives relevant rules and regulations and additional information on such topics as intellectual property, marking country of origin, and importing a car. Traveler Information gives advice for properly going through customs when traveling internationally.

This site provides a good overview of the agency and basic information about Customs for travelers and the business community.

Subject Headings: Customs; Immigration; Importing and Exporting; Travel

[88] U.S. Department of Labor

Sponsoring Agency: Department of Labor (DOL)

Primary Access: http://www.dol.gov/

Resource Summary: The main Department of Labor site presents the HTML format that most of the component departments and agencies use. It has information about the administrator, the agency, press releases, speeches, testimony, regulatory information, grants and contracts information, and a description of the agency's programs and activities. In addition, this top-level site has links to subsidiary DOL agencies and their Web sites. The site has some topical access with subject links such as minimum wage, teen safety, pension search, and welfare to federal work.

If you understand the organization of this page, it is easier to find information here than on other DOL Web sites. This site is also useful for locating DOL by topic.

Subject Headings: Labor; Regulations

[89] U.S. Patent and Trademark Office

Sponsoring Agency: Patent and Trademark Office (PTO)

Primary Access: http://www.uspto.gov/

Resource Summary: This site provides substantial information from the Patent and Trademark Office. The top level page contains the link Public Information, and it also includes recent news. For information on patents, the PTO site offers categories such as Search Patents, Weekly Data, Download Forms, and Order Patent Copies.

The About the Patent and Trademark Office page features basic information about the agency and on how to apply for patents and trademarks. The latter is available in HTML versions of the standard introductory publications: *General Information Concerning Patents*, *Basic Facts about Patents*, and *Basic Facts about Registering a Trademark*. These publications are also available in a variety of word processor formats, as are the applications that are available in Adobe PDF format. The *PTO Annual Report* can be found along with speeches and press releases on the same page. A listing of patent and trademark libraries and information about the Patent and Trademark Depository Library (PTDL) program are available from the PTDLs link.

Other resources available include an employee locator, a list of patent attorneys registered with the PTO, and current announcements and public hearings. Under the Public Information heading, the PTO now offers an option for searching the patent classification system, *Official Gazette* notices, and the Trademark Acceptable Identification of Goods and Services Manual.

This is an excellent collection of resources for anyone interested in the patent or trademark process, with one major exception—the PTO pages do not include the *Official Gazette* or the full text of any patents or trademarks. The Internet Town Hall offered an experimental Internet publication of patent information from 1994. This experiment ended October 1, 1995, and on September 26, 1995, the PTO announced that they would provide free-to-the-public patent information on their home page. This free version takes the form of the CNIDR U.S. Patents Projects (http://patents.cnidr.org/), which is linked to this page.

Subject Headings: Patents; Trademarks

SuDoc Numbers: C 21.1/2: *Commissioner of Patents and Trademarks Annual Report*
C 21.2: P 27/18 *Basic Facts about Patents*
C 21.2: R 26/ *Basic Facts about Registering a Trademark*
C 21.5: *Official Gazette*
C 21.26/2: *General Information Concerning Patents*

[90] United States Mint

Sponsoring Agency: Mint

Primary Access: http://www.ustreas.gov/treasury/bureaus/mint/

Alternative Access Method: http://www.usmint.gov/

Resource Summary: Other than a brief description of the agency, the U.S. Mint page has only a few other links. One links to information on the director, and another links to information on a gift collection.

The page could be improved by describing, with images, more of the commemorative and special coins that the Mint issues. As the site is developed, expect the alternate URL to become the primary one.

Subject Heading: Currency

[91] USPTO/CNIDR Patent Project

Sponsoring Agencies: Center for Networked Information Discovery and Retrieval (CNIDR); Patent and Trademark Office (PTO)

Primary Access: http://patents.cnidr.org/

Resource Summary: This project has brought the full bibliographic patent database and a full-text database of AIDS patents to the Internet public for free. The bibliographic database is kept current and dates back to 1976. It includes patent number, date, inventors, assignee, application number, date files, patent classes, references cited, and abstracts. In addition, the entries include a mention of how many claims have been filed. The full-text versions of patents are not available on this site, but there is information about how to order patents from the U.S. Patent and Trademark Office.

There are three types of search options: simple, two-term Boolean, and advanced. In the advanced search, field searching is available. In all three search options, the searcher can either search a single year at a time, or in predefined groups including the entire database. Results can be requested sorted in reverse chronological order or ranked by relevance. For those wanting to search by patent classification, there is a browsable database of the U.S. patent classification system. It can be browsed by class and then by subclass, but it is not currently searchable.

The free availability of the bibliographic patent database is a significant addition to Internet information resources. While some will still want free online access to the actual patents, this is still a major step forward in providing patent information to the public. One problem with the service is that long or complex searches can time out due to the load on the server. Thus, it is not as dependable as a commercial patents database such as QPAT-US.

Subject Headings: AIDS (disease)—Full Text; Bibliographic Databases; Patents

[92] Welcome to QPAT-US

Sponsoring Agencies: Patent and Trademark Office (PTO); Questel-Orbit

Primary Access: http://www.qpat.com/

Resource Summary: Questel-Orbit's QPAT-US service offers a bibliographic patent database of the front page information for all U.S. patents issued since 1974. It requires registration, but searching is free. For those willing to pay, QPAT-US also offers a full-text database of U.S. patents issued since 1974. For both services, the search interface is one of the most sophisticated available via a Web form, with Boolean operators, field searching, date limits, and search tracking. In the display, there are hypertext links to other patent abstracts available from the system. There is also a convenient Order button for those wanting to purchase a paper copy.

QPAT-US is one of the best database implementations on the Web. After registering, it is far easier to use than the official USPTO/CNIDR U.S. Patent Bibliographic Database Search site listed earlier in this chapter.

Subject Headings: Bibliographic Databases; Patents

[93] Welcome to the United States National Labor Relations Board

Sponsoring Agency: National Labor Relations Board (NLRB)

Primary Access: http://www.nlrb.gov/

Alternate Access Method: http://netsite.esa.doc.gov/nlrb/

Resource Summary: After a description of the NLRB, there is a link to a list of Government Information Locator Service records for NLRB products under the Information Locator section. There is also a list of regional NLRB offices with addresses and phone numbers, but no e-mail addresses or Web pages. Under the heading Board Opinions there is a section featuring National Labor Relations Board Decisions in PDF format. These are slip opinions that are actually housed on the STAT-USA Web server. Only the most current 60 days' worth of opinions are available.

While there is not a great deal of information available on this site, the NLRB Decisions will be of interest to those following labor law.

Subject Headings: Cases—Full Text; Collective Bargaining; Government Information Locator Service (GILS); Labor Unions

[94] Women's Business Ownership

Sponsoring Agency: Small Business Administration (SBA). Office of Women's Business Ownership

Primary Access: http://www.sbaonline.sba.gov/womeninbusiness/

Alternative Access Method: http://www.sbaonline.sba.gov/textonly/womeninbusiness/ [text version]

Resource Summary: This site contains links to other sites related to women in business and to some conference announcements. Also included are numerous programs and resources including: the Demonstration Training Program, Women's Network for Entrepreneurial Training Mentoring. Interagency Committee on Women's Business Enterprise, Women's Prequalification Pilot Loan Program, Federal Procurement Pilot Program for Women-Owned Businesses, SBA Women's Business Ownership Representatives, and Statistics on Women-Owned Businesses. While the statistics section is brief, there is also a link to a more detailed Census Bureau report. One valuable resource at this site is the FAQ, listed as Most Commonly Asked Questions.

Much of the information at this site refers to financial assistance and grant programs available to women in business. This is a good place to begin searching for such information.

Subject Headings: Small Businesses; Women

Business and Economics: Finance

[95] Army Financial Management

Sponsoring Agency: Assistant Secretary of the Army for Financial Management and Comptroller

Primary Access: http://www.asafm.army.mil/

Resource Summary: With a variety of information on army accounting and financial management practices, this site features sections titled Budget, Business Practices, Finance, Interactive Services, Pentagon, Publications, Proponency, and Resource Analysis. There are numerous publications—arranged alphabetically—in the Publications section and also scattered elsewhere on the site. These include the *Green Book* (which contains the army budget), the army's *Annual Financial Report*, and the companion guide *Serving the Nation*, among many others.

Subject Headings: Accounting; Financial Management

[96] Board of Governors of the Federal Reserve

Sponsoring Agency: Federal Reserve Board

Primary Access: http://www.bog.frb.fed.us/

Resource Summary: This main site of the Federal Reserve Board includes information about the Federal Reserve System and its publications. Available sections about the Board include Press Releases, Welcome to the Federal Reserve Board, Testimony and Speeches, and Regulation and Supervision. The Federal Open Market Committee section includes access to the *Summary of Commentary on Current Economic Conditions*, commonly known as the *Beige Book*, which includes anecdotal information on current economic conditions. The Reports to Congress section includes a PDF version of their *Annual Report*. The Publications section features access to PDF versions of selected *Federal Reserve Bulletin* articles. This site also provides links to Federal Reserve banks and other units of the Federal Reserve System.

This site offers a substantial body of information from the Board, although it would be helpful to have the full text of the *Federal Reserve Bulletin* available.

Subject Heading: Banking

SuDoc Numbers: FR 1.1: *Annual Report*
FR 1.3: *Federal Reserve Bulletin*

[97] Commodity Futures Trading Commission

Sponsoring Agency: Commodity Futures Trading Commission (CFTC)

Primary Access: http://www.cftc.gov/

Resource Summary: The CFTC Web site features a variety of information on commodities trading. Categories include Commission Information, Commitments of Traders, Press Releases, Enforcement, Speeches, Publications, Weekly Advisory, Opinions and Orders, and Reparations. The Commitments of Traders area includes *Commitments of Traders in Futures* reports in a compressed, comma-delimited format for loading into a spreadsheet. Both the long form and short form data reports are available. Some of the reports are available back to 1986.

With the Press Releases, Weekly Advisories, and the *Commitments of Traders in Futures* reports, this site should be of interest to anyone following the commodity futures market.

Subject Headings: Commodities; Futures

SuDoc Number: Y 3.C 73/5:9-3/ *Commitments of Traders in Futures*

[98] Department of the Treasury

Sponsoring Agency: Department of the Treasury

Primary Access: http://www.ustreas.gov/

Alternative Access Method: http://www.ustreas.gov/txtonly.htm [text version]

Resource Summary: The Department of the Treasury Web site features access to the Department's bureaus as well as information on the Department. The What's New section contains press releases, speeches, and the Treasury's Electronic Library. The category, Treasury Offices, gives Internet links to the component Treasury bureaus.

A Tours and Treasures page provides general interest information on the building. The Browse section provides subject access to material from the Department and its bureaus. Other available agency information includes a directory of top agency officials and a mission statement.

The majority of substantial information resources are located within the bureaus' own pages.

Subject Heading: Economics

[99] ED/OIG

Sponsoring Agency: Department of Education (ED). Office of Inspector General (OIG)

Primary Access: http://www.ed.gov/offices/OIG/edoig.html

Resource Summary: This page briefly describes the Office and has links to two regional offices. The site has links to other resources both inside and outside of the department, but it has very little original material.

Subject Heading: Auditing

[100] ED/OIG Philadelphia

Sponsoring Agency: Department of Education (ED). Office of Inspector General (OIG). Philadelphia Office

Primary Access: http://www.netaxs.com/~edoig/home.html

Resource Summary: There is very little original information at this site. There are, however, links to other resources. The most useful of the external links is gathered on the Government Auditor's Resource Page, which is compiled by one of the staff members.

Subject Heading: Auditing

[101] EDGAR Database

Sponsoring Agency: Securities and Exchange Commission (SEC)

Primary Access: http://www.sec.gov/edgarhp.htm

Alternative Access Methods: ftp://ftp.sec.gov/edgar/
gopher://gopher.sec.gov/
http://www.town.hall.org/edgar/edgar.html [former site, no longer active]

Resource Summary: As stated by the SEC, the Electronic Data Gathering, Analysis, and Retrieval (EDGAR) database performs automated collection, validation, indexing, acceptance, and forwarding of submissions by companies and others who are required by law to file forms with the U.S. Securities and Exchange Commission. The SEC's primary purpose is to increase the efficiency and fairness of the securities market for the benefit of investors, corporations, and the economy by accelerating the receipt, acceptance, dissemination, and analysis of time-sensitive corporate information filed with the agency. Documents available through EDGAR include several different forms, the best known of which are probably the 10-K, 10-Q, and proxy statements. The documents available on EDGAR are all in raw ASCII format.

Searching uses a WAIS index of the header information in each document, and options include Boolean searching. Under Custom Filing Retrieval Tools, there are a number of forms interfaces, which enable more advanced searching.

There are limits to what data is available on EDGAR. This site allows you to retrieve any 1994 and 1995 filings to the Securities and Exchange Commission that are available to the public. Non-electronic filings, and filings made prior to 1994, will not be available here. As of May 1996 all public domestic companies are required to make their filings on EDGAR, except for cases of hardship and documents that are not permitted to be filed electronically. Other documents may be filed on EDGAR voluntarily thus, they may or may not be available on EDGAR.

The SEC made the EDGAR system available for free on the Internet after an NSF funded a demonstration project (located at http://www.town.hall.org/edgar/edgar.html) with New York University and the nonprofit Internet Multicasting Service (IMS). At the end of the grant funding, IMS announced that it would shut down the popular experiment, and the SEC finally brought up its own version. The raw EDGAR data provided here is a valuable resource for anyone interested in corporate financial information.

The EDGAR database is also still available via New York University (http://edgar.stern.nyu.edu/), and that is an excellent backup for the SEC site. See the description of the NYU EDGAR Development Site in this chapter (entry number 109).

Subject Headings: Corporations—Finance; EDGAR

[102] Federal Reserve Bank of Chicago

Sponsoring Agency: Federal Reserve Bank of Chicago

Primary Access: http://www.frbchi.org/

Resource Summary: The Federal Reserve Bank of Chicago features a wide range of banking information. The Federal Reserve heading includes employment opportunities, a calendar of events, the location of Federal Reserve Banks, and glossaries of various financial terms. The Economic Information page provides regional economic highlights, monetary policy, economic indicators, and financial data sections. Opening rates and treasury offerings are available under the Government Securities link. The Publications and Speeches page includes papers by Reserve economists, online annual reports, and several newsletters. This site also offers separate sections for bankers, educators, and the media.

There is a substantial amount of financial information at this site, both statistics and text.

Subject Headings: Banking; Economics—Statistics

[103] Federal Reserve Bank of Philadelphia

Sponsoring Agency: Federal Reserve Bank of Philadelphia

Primary Access: http://www.phil.frb.org/

Resource Summary: The Federal Reserve Bank of Philadelphia provides a variety of information both on the Bank and on regional statistics. Available sections include Our Organization; News and Views; Economics; Publications and Presentations; and Banks, Thrifts, and Credit Unions.

More regional in focus than the other Federal Reserve Bank sites, this site provides useful information for those interested in this particular region—the Third Reserve District, which comprises two-thirds of Pennsylvania, the southern half of New Jersey, and all of Delaware.

Subject Headings: Banking; Financial Statistics

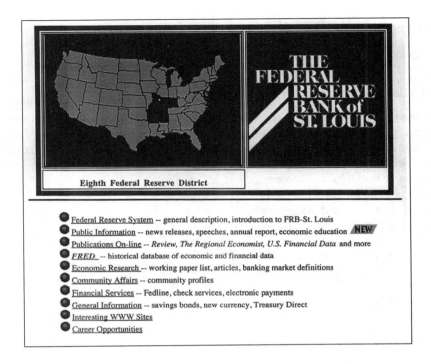

Eighth Federal Reserve District

- Federal Reserve System -- general description, introduction to FRB-St. Louis
- Public Information -- news releases, speeches, annual report, economic education **NEW**
- Publications On-line -- *Review, The Regional Economist, U.S. Financial Data* and more
- *FRED* -- historical database of economic and financial data
- Economic Research -- working paper list, articles, banking market definitions
- Community Affairs -- community profiles
- Financial Services -- Fedline, check services, electronic payments
- General Information -- savings bonds, new currency, Treasury Direct
- Interesting WWW Sites
- Career Opportunities

[104] Federal Reserve Bank of St. Louis

Sponsoring Agency: Federal Reserve Bank of St. Louis

Primary Access: http://www.stls.frb.org/

Resource Summary: This site includes general descriptions of the Federal Reserve Bank of St. Louis and the Federal Reserve System. Other sections include job postings, community profiles, and Federal Reserve Economic Data (FRED). FRED provides historical U.S. economic and financial data, including daily U.S. interest rates, monetary and business indicators, exchange rates, and regional economic data for the Eighth Federal Reserve District covering Arkansas, Illinois, Indiana, Kentucky, Mississippi, Missouri, and Tennessee.

This is one of the easiest Federal Reserve sites to use. Much of the statistical data are composed of national figures, so this site can be used by those interested in the nation as a whole and not just for the states covered in this district.

Subject Headings: Economics—Statistics; Financial Statistics

[105] FinanceNet E-mail Lists and Newsgroups

Sponsoring Agency: Office of the Vice President

Primary Access: mailto:listproc@financenet.gov with "subscribe <list>" in body
news:gov.topic.admin.finance.* using news.financenet.gov as news server

Resource Summary: The following lists can be subscribed to by e-mail or read as newsgroups. For e-mail delivery, send an e-mail message to listproc@financenet.gov with "subscribe <list>" in the body of the message. Replace <list> with the appropriate list name. For news access, set the news server to news.nsf.gov. The following groups can be found in the fnet. hierarchy. In other words, the newsgroup name would be fnet.accounting or fnet.fin-jobs.

accounting - Accounting Issues

aga - Association of Government Accountants

asset-liab-mgt - Asset and Liability Management

budget-net - Budget Net

calendar - Financial Management Events Calendar

daily-sales - Daily Sales Notice from *Commerce Business Daily*

fin-audits - Financial Audits

fin-jobs - Finance Related Job Opportunities

fin-policy - Financial Policy

fin-reporting - Financial Reporting

fin-systems - Financial Systems

fin-training - Financial Training

general - General List

gfoa - Government Financial Officers

govsales - Government Asset Sales

int-controls - Internal Controls

muninet - International Institute of Municipal Clerks

news - Financial News and Announcements

payroll - Payroll Issues

perf-measures - Performance Measures

procurement - Procurement Issues

state-county - State County Issues

travel - Travel Issues

There are two newsgroups without an e-mail list counterpart: fnet.sectornet and fnet.fnet. Two of the mailing lists recorded above do not have newsgroup counterparts: calendar and daily-sales. While e-mail and news can be effective information-sharing mechanisms, most of these are not high-volume lists.

Subject Headings: Accounting; E-mail Lists; National Performance Review

[106] Financial Management Service

Sponsoring Agency: Department of the Treasury. Financial Management Service (FMS)

Primary Access: http://www.fms.treas.gov/

Resource Summary: The Financial Management Service site features a broad range of resources related to financial management and government bonds. The full text of the *Treasury Bulletin* is available in PDF format back to 1996. It also provides access to information on consolidated financial statements, savings bonds, and procurement opportunities. Some featured sections of the site include Accounting Resources, Activities and Contacts, Condition of the Federal Government, Products and Services, Publications, and Regulations and Guidance. The Publications page provides access to the PDF versions of many FMS titles.

Subject Headings: Financial Management; Government Bonds

SuDoc Numbers: T 63.103/2: *Treasury Bulletin*
T 63.113/2: *Monthly Treasury Statement of Receipts and Outlays of the United States Government*
T 63.113/3: *Consolidated Financial Statements of the United States Government*
T 63.121: *Treasury Reporting Rates of Exchange*
T 63.128: *Financial Connection*

[107] Home Mortgage Disclosure Act

Sponsoring Agencies: Federal Reserve Board; Right-to-Know Network

Primary Access: http://rtk.net/www/data/hmda_gen.html

Resource Summary: Hosted by a non-governmental organization, this site provides a variety of access points to the *Home Mortgage Disclosure Act Data*. Users can search by area, bank, and market. The file covers all banks, savings and loans, savings banks, and credit unions with assets over $10 million and at least one branch in a metropolitan area. Records provide information on the lender's mortgage loan applications including the type of loan; the location of the property; the race, gender, and income of the applicant; and whether the application was approved. The site also offers summarized national statistics on the HMDA database.

Subject Headings: Home Mortgage Disclosure Act (HMDA); Mortgages

SuDoc Number: FR 1.63 *Home Mortgage Disclosure Act Data*

[108] National Credit Union Administration

Sponsoring Agency: National Credit Union Administration (NCUA)

Primary Access: http://www.ncua.gov/

Alternative Access Methods: http://www.ncua.gov/text.html [text version]
http://www.ncua.gov/frameindex.html [frames version]
http://www.ncua.gov/lobby.html [Java version]

Resource Summary: The National Credit Union Administration is an independent federal agency that supervises and insures credit unions. Their Web site offers statistics and publications from the NCUA. Some of the available sections include Organization, About Credit Unions, News, Credit Union Data, Reference Information, and Download Files and Software. Most of the online publications can be found under the Reference Information section.

Subject Headings: Banking; Credit Unions

SuDoc Numbers: NCU 1.8:B 99/ *Federal Credit Union Bylaws*
NCU 1.19: *NCUA Letters to Credit Unions*
NCU 1.20: *NCUA News*

[109] NYU EDGAR Development Site

Sponsoring Agencies: New York University (NYU). Stern School of Business; Securities and Exchange Commission (SEC)

Primary Access: http://edgar.stern.nyu.edu/

Resource Summary: This site provides access to the same SEC filings described in the entry for the SEC EDGAR Database (entry number 101). Sponsored by the New York University Stern School of Business, the opening page has a very different design when compared to the SEC site. Most of the other links answer questions or describe projects of the school, but the main EDGAR database is accessible under the link titled Get Corporate SEC Filings.

This is a much more efficient starting point for finding EDGAR data than is on the SEC site, primarily because this site permits searching of the database on either server. Thus, if one is down or malfunctioning, the other is readily accessible. In addition, thanks to the sponsorship of several companies, the NYU site has also added features, such as a search by Zacks Industry Code, that are not available on the SEC server.

Subject Headings: Corporations—Finance; EDGAR

[110] U.S. Securities and Exchange Commission

Sponsoring Agency: Securities and Exchange Commission (SEC)

Primary Access: http://www.sec.gov/

Alternative Access Methods: http://www.sec.gov/textindx.htm [text version]
ftp://ftp.sec.gov/

Resource Summary: The SEC site's major offering is its EDGAR database, described earlier in this chapter. In addition to the link to the EDGAR database, the site features sections titled About the SEC; Investor Assistance and Complaints, SEC Digests and Statements, Small Business Information, Current SEC Rulemaking, and Enforcement Actions. The *SEC Annual Report* and *The SEC News Digest* are available under the SEC Digests and Statements section.

Subject Headings: Corporations—Finance; EDGAR; Investments; Stock Exchanges

SuDoc Numbers: SE 1.1: *SEC Annual Report*
SE 1.25/12: *The SEC News Digest*

[111] Woodrow: Federal Reserve Bank of Minneapolis Information Service

Sponsoring Agency: Federal Reserve Bank of Minneapolis

Primary Access: http://woodrow.mpls.frb.fed.us/

Resource Summary: This site features a variety of resources. Under The Federal Reserve heading, there is a tour of the bank in Minneapolis, background information on the bank and the Federal Reserve System, press releases, and a description and pictures of the new 1996 currency, including the new $100 bill. The Research and Data area includes the complete and current *Beige Book*, including information for all the regions and a map to show region boundaries. It also includes a section for the Ninth District Economy with topical subdivisions and interest and exchange rate charts. The Publications heading features selections from the *fedgazette*, the *Region*, and the *Annual Report*, along with some reports from the bank's research division.

Well organized and easy to navigate, this site is a rich resource for nationwide banking information and for region-specific information.

Subject Headings: Banking; Currency; Economics—Statistics

Business and Economics: Government Business ────────────

[112] Acquisition Reform Net

Sponsoring Agencies: National Performance Review (NPR); Office of Federal Procurement Policy

Primary Access: http://www-far.npr.gov/

Alternative Access Method: http://www-far.npr.gov/NTindex.html [non-table version]

Resource Summary: With the goal of fostering measurable breakthroughs in the way that the federal government obtains goods and services, this site features the following categories: Reference Corner, Acquisition Opportunities, Acquisition Best Practices, and Training On Demand.

This is a good site for advice and links to actual procurement opportunities, and it points to regulations available on other sites.

Subject Headings: Acquisitions; Procurement

SuDoc Number: GS 1.6/10: *Federal Acquisition Regulations*

[113] Army Acquisition Corps

Sponsoring Agency: Department of the Army. Acquisition Corps (AAC)

Primary Access: http://www.sarda.army.mil/dacm/

Resource Summary: The AAC home page is designed to assist the AAC staff and the acquisition workforce in obtaining professional development information. The site includes career opportunities, career development guidelines, career management updates, professional publications, and education and training opportunities.

This site includes material related to both military and civilian issues, so it is useful to anyone interested in training and job opportunities in government acquisitions.

Subject Headings: Acquisitions; Military Training; Professional Development

[114] *Commerce Business Daily* [Community of Science]

Sponsoring Agency: Department of Commerce (DOC). Office of Field Services

Primary Access: http://cos.gdb.org/repos/cbd/cbd-intro.html

Resource Summary: This is a commercial service targeted at organizations. The *Commerce Business Daily* can be browsed by category, and search options are available by agency, by classification, and by keyword in the synopsis.

The service is easy to use, with all the necessary search options. It compares favorably with the Government Contractor Resource Center at http://www.govcon.com/ except that the Government Contractor site is free

Subject Headings: Electronic Periodicals; Procurement

SuDoc Number: C 1.76: *Commerce Business Daily*

[115] *Commerce Business Daily* [Loren Data Corp.]

Sponsoring Agency: Department of Commerce (DOC). Office of Field Services

Primary Access: http://www.ld.com/

Alternative Access Method: http://www.rahul.net/nps/ [former site, still works]

Resource Summary: This is a commercial service, but it does offer free access to the most recent edition of the *Commerce Business Daily (CBD)* in HTML. The commercial subscription service delivers portions of the *CBD* via e-mail, based on specific criteria when the account is established.

For those who would prefer to receive only relevant portions of the *CBD* and receive it via e-mail, this may be a good alternative to having to search each day on a free service such as the Government Contractor Resource Center.

Subject Headings: Electronic Periodicals; Procurement

SuDoc Number: C 1.76: *Commerce Business Daily*

[116] *Commerce Business Daily* Internet Smart System

Sponsoring Agencies: Department of Commerce (DOC). Office of Field Services; United States Information Corporation

Primary Access: telnet://guest@cbd.savvy.com

Resource Summary: This is a commercial service, although there is a free two-week trial account. The ASCII full text of the *Commerce Business Daily* for the previous few months is accessible, but only one issue at a time. Search options include a category or a keyword search. Alternatively, you can set up a personal profile for searching. Results are available on screen, or they can be sent via e-mail or ftp.

The absence of a multi-issue search is a significant drawback to this system. The presence of more advanced search options would be nice as well. The free service at the Government Contractor Resource Center (http://www.govcon.com/) is much more sophisticated.

Subject Headings: Electronic Periodicals; Procurement

SuDoc Number: C 1.76: *Commerce Business Daily*

[117] Defense Logistics Services Center

Sponsoring Agency: Defense Logistics Services Center (DLSC)

Primary Access: http://www.dlsc.dla.mil/

Resource Summary: On the top level page, this site offers two headings: Customer Service, and Products and Services. The DLSC site also features access to the Commercial and Government Entity (CAGE) file. The CAGE Code is a five-position code that identifies contractors doing business with the federal government, NATO member nations, and other foreign governments. The CAGE code is used to support a variety of mechanized systems throughout the government. New CAGE codes can be requested online, and existing codes are available in searchable databases.

Although it is a military site, this can be very useful for contractors working with any segment of the federal government. It is especially valuable for accessing CAGE information.

Subject Headings: CAGE Codes; Contractors; Military Logistics; Procurement

SuDoc Numbers: D 7.43: *loglines*
D 7.34: *Sealed Bid/Invitation to Bid*

[118] Defense Supply Center, Columbus

Sponsoring Agencies: Defense Supply Center, Columbus (DSCC); Department of Defense (DoD)

Primary Access: http://www.dscc.dla.mil/

Alternative Access Method: telnet://131.74.160.39

Resource Summary: The DSCC, a DoD procurement and supply center, offers information on its Web site under headings such as Customer Advocacy, Information, Internal Support, Legal Office, Material Management, New Stuff, Office, Procurement Support, Reference, Technical Support, and Tenant Activities. It also offers information and a telnet link to the DSCC bulletin board.

This site is primarily of interest to those in the DoD procurement business. It does not, however, offer easy access to an inventory listing.

Subject Heading: Procurement

[119] DOE Office of Procurement and Assistance Management

Sponsoring Agency: Department of Energy (DOE). Office of Procurement and Assistance Management

Primary Access: http://www.pr.doe.gov/

Resource Summary: This page contains information related to internal DOE procurement. It provides announcements, contact personnel, an organizational structure, and some general information about procurement.

This site is most useful to those in procurement in the DOE. Changes are made often on this page so check back.

Subject Heading: Procurement

[120] Doing Business with the Department of Energy

Sponsoring Agency: Department of Energy (DOE). Office of Procurement and Assistance Management

Primary Access: http://www.pr.doe.gov/prbus.html

Resource Summary: This page is designed to assist companies and the public, including small disadvantaged businesses, educational institutions, governmental entities, and individuals, on how to do business with the DOE. It features basic information on how to do business with the DOE, contact personnel, information for small businesses, and business opportunities with the DOE.

This is a useful resource for those wanting government contracts with the DOE. While there are not many original resources, it provides valuable information about procedures and contacts.

Subject Heading: Procurement

[121] Electronic Mail Task Force Report

Sponsoring Agencies: Department of Health and Human Services (HHS). Assistant Secretary for Management and Budget; National Performance Review (NPR)

Primary Access: gopher://gopher.os.dhhs.gov:70/1/dhhs/os/asmb

Resource Summary: This site consists of the report, *Governmentwide Electronic Mail for the Federal Government,* which consists of a single ASCII text file. The report addresses the use of e-mail within government organizations and assesses its ability to increase government efficiency. The report is dated April 1, 1994.

Subject Heading: E-mail

[122] Federal Acquisition Institute Training Materials

Sponsoring Agencies: Federal Acquisition Institute (FAI); General Services Administration (GSA)

Primary Access: http://www.gsa.gov/staff/v/training.htm

Resource Summary: This is the Federal Acquisition Institute's Web site for procurement training. Categories of information include FAI News, FAI Procurement Curriculum, FAI Certification Workbooks, Training Organizations, an FAI Publication of the Month, Procurement Hot Spots, and Future Plans in the FAI. According to the last category, their goal is to move to an online university, which would use the Web and other electronic delivery mechanisms to offer training.

This site specifically targets its materials at training federal employees in the acquisitions and procurement realms. The site contains useful information for non-federal personnel with interests in those areas as well.

Subject Headings: Acquisitions; Higher Education; Procurement

[123] Federal Acquisition Jumpstation

Sponsoring Agencies: Federal Aviation Administration (FAA); Marshall Space Flight Center; Office of Federal Procurement Policy

Primary Access: http://procure.msfc.nasa.gov/fedproc/home.html

Resource Summary: This page provides a hierarchical listing of procurement and acquisitions Web sites, arranged by agency.

This is an effective page, created for the purpose of listing links to procurement and acquisitions sites. Its basic layout and broad coverage make it a successful site.

Subject Headings: Acquisitions; Finding Aid—Business; Procurement

[124] FinanceNet

Sponsoring Agencies: National Science Foundation (NSF); Office of the Vice President

Primary Access: http://www.financenet.gov/

Alternative Access Methods: telnet://pula.financenet.gov/
gopher://gopher.financenet.gov/
ftp://ftp.financenet.gov/
mailto:info@financenet.gov

Resource Summary: Established by Vice President Gore's National Performance Review, FinanceNet covers topics in public financial management. The site is operated by the National Science Foundation. FinanceNet aims to link government financial management administrators, educators, and taxpayers to catalyze continuous improvements in the productivity of government personnel and in the stewardship of and accountability for taxpayer resources. The site has many sections, but featured ones include What is FinanceNet?; FinanceNet What's New Page; Government Asset Sales; U.S. Federal Financial Management; State and Local Financial Management; International Public Financial Management; FinanceNet Topics; and Employment, Education, and Training.

For those involved in the National Performance Review and for government financial managers, this site contains a considerable collection of useful information.

Subject Headings: Financial Management; National Performance Review

[125] General Services Administration *Federal Acquisition Regulations*

Sponsoring Agency: General Services Administration (GSA)

Primary Access: http://www.gsa.gov/far/

Alternative Access Method: http://www.gsa.gov/far/pdf_home.html [for PDF format]

Resource Summary: This version of the *Federal Acquisition Regulations (FAR)* provides access to HTML and PDF versions of the regulations. The only access point for both formats is a table of contents listing. No search option is available. For searching the regulations, try either the version of the *FAR* at the Government Contractor Resource Center (http://www.govcon.com/), which allows keyword searching, including Boolean operators, or try the Harvest search engine available on the Acquisition Reform Net (http://www-far.npr.gov:80/Harvest/brokers/ARNFARs/query.html).

Subject Heading: Regulations—Full Text

SuDoc Number: GS 1.6/10: *Federal Acquisition Regulations*

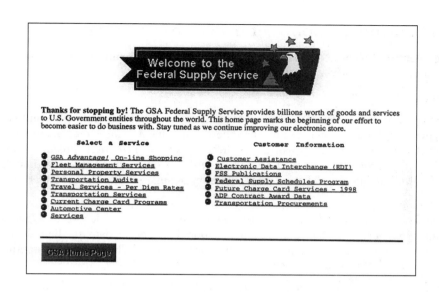

[126] General Services Administration Federal Supply Service

Sponsoring Agency: General Services Administration (GSA). Federal Supply Service (FSS)

Primary Access: http://www.fss.gsa.gov/

Resource Summary: This is a central location for information on procuring items from the FSS. The page includes the following categories: GSA Advantage Online Shopping, Personal Property Services, Travel Services, Fleet Management Services, Aircraft Management Services, Transportation Services, Electronic Data Interchange, Future Charge Card Services, and Customer Assistance.

The Advantage Online Shopping section is set up to provide supply catalogs with up-to-date pricing information, and it is the most useful part of this resource. While it will be most useful to those in government purchasing, it could be used by the general public to obtain pricing data. There is a brief description of the service, but there is not much substantive information beyond brief listings.

Subject Headings: Procurement; Property Management

SuDoc Number: GS 2.17: *MarkeTips*

[127] Government Contractor Resource Center

Sponsoring Agencies: Defense Logistics Agency; Department of Commerce (DOC). Office of Field Services; General Services Administration (GSA)

Primary Access: http://www.govcon.com/

Resource Summary: This is a free site, supported by advertising, but registration is required. A number of government publications can be found here, including the *Commerce Business Daily (CBD)* under the Current Business Opportunities heading, and the *Federal Acquisition Regulations*, the *Federal Information Resources Management Regulations*, the *Standard Industrial Classification Manual*, and the *Defense Logistics Agency Acquisition Regulation* under the Information Center heading.

For the *Commerce Business Daily*, a form entry can be used to search for keywords. Options include limits by agency, supply category, and publication date. For the date, the limit defaults to the current issue but can be changed to the past one to eight weeks. The issues, back to August 15, 1995, are also available by direct browsing.

Of all the free and commercial Internet sites that offer the *CBD*, this one has the most features and search options. In addition, it has the advantage of being coupled with the full text of various acquisitions regulations and other government and non-government contractor resources. The ads that support the service are not very intrusive, and since they are targeted at contractors, they can be informative and helpful as well.

Subject Headings: Electronic Periodicals; Procurement; Regulations—Full Text

SuDoc Numbers: C 1.76: *Commerce Business Daily*
D 7.6/5: *Defense Logistics Agency Acquisition Regulation*
GS 1.6/10: *Federal Acquisition Regulations*
GS 12.15/2: *Federal Information Resources Management Regulations/Federal Acquisition Regulations*
PrEx 2.6/2: In 27/987 *Standard Industrial Classification Manual*

[128] GSA Mid-Atlantic Region

Sponsoring Agency: General Services Administration (GSA). Mid-Atlantic Region

Primary Access: http://tsd.r3.gsa.gov/

Resource Summary: This site provides basic information about the services offered by this regional GSA office, including government vehicle auctions, technical services, and federal supply services.

This is a useful site for people wanting to contact the GSA in this region.

Subject Headings: Auctions; Procurement

[129] Kennedy Space Center Office of Procurement

Sponsoring Agency: Kennedy Space Center (KSC)

Primary Access: http://www.ksc.nasa.gov/procurement/

Resource Summary: The purpose of this site is to provide easy access to KSC procurement information. It accomplishes this goal through categories such as Business Opportunities; Abstract of Offers; Contract Awards; Search National Aeronautics and Space Administration (NASA) Synopses; Procurement Reference Documents; Kennedy Space Center Construction Clauses; NASA's Acquisition Forecast (FY 1995); MidRange Procurement Pilot Test Program; and How to Do Business with Kennedy Space Center.

This site is useful for those wanting government contracts with the Kennedy Space Center or NASA in general.

Subject Headings: Acquisitions; Procurement

[130] Logistics Policy Staff

Sponsoring Agency: Department of Health and Human Services (HHS). Office of Grants and Acquisition Management

Primary Access: http://www.os.dhhs.gov/progorg/sais/sais.html

Alternative Access Method: gopher://gopher.os.dhhs.gov/1/Topics/Lognet/

Resource Summary: The Web site describes the Logistics Policy Staff's functions, which focus on the logistics of property management. The Gopher site and the Policies section of the Web site are called LogNet, and they include a calendar of events, training opportunities, and an agency directory and organizational chart. The more substantial resources include a number of publications available in HTML and ASCII including *Logistics Management Manual*, *Contractor's Guide for Management of Government Property*, and *Property Custodian's Guide*.

For government property managers, there are a number of useful full-text documents at these sites.

Subject Headings: Acquisitions; Property Management

[131] Marshall Space Flight Center Procurement

Sponsoring Agency: Marshall Space Flight Center

Primary Access: http://procure.msfc.nasa.gov/

Resource Summary: This site provides information on procurement and acquisitions opportunities at the Center. Significant categories of information include Business Opportunities, Synopses of Contract Awards, Procurement Reference Documents, and How to Do Business with Marshall Space Flight Center.

This site is useful for those wanting government contracts with the Marshall Space Flight Center.

Subject Headings: Acquisitions; Procurement

[132] NASA Acquisition Internet Service

Sponsoring Agency: National Aeronautics and Space Administration (NASA)

Primary Access: http://procurement.nasa.gov/

Resource Summary: The NASA Acquisition Internet Service (NAIS) site provides a central point of Internet contact for businesses interested in NASA acquisitions and procurement opportunities.

Subject Headings: Acquisitions; Procurement

[133] NASA Ames Acquisitions

Sponsoring Agency: Ames Research Center (ARC)

Primary Access: http://procurement.nasa.gov/EPS/ARC/class.html

Alternative Access Method: http://procure.arc.nasa.gov/Acq/Acq.html

Resource Summary: The NASA Ames Acquisitions site features the sections entitled Business Opportunities, Awards, Search Just Ames Acquisition Documents, and How to Do Business with Ames Research Center.

This site is useful for those interested in gaining government contracts with the Center. Check both URLs, since the address is currently changing.

Subject Headings: Acquisitions; Procurement

[134] National Electronic Commerce Resource Center Program

Sponsoring Agency: Electronic Commerce Resource Center (ECRC)

Primary Access: http://www.ecrc.ctc.com/

Resource Summary: This site and the program aim to promote awareness and implementation of electronic commerce and related technologies into the civil-military industrial base. The program consists of the ECRC Technology Development Testbed, ECRC Team Integrators, and Regional ECRCs. The site also features sections called The Possibilities with Electronic Commerce and Course Calendar.

This could be a useful site for those exploring the options of electronic commerce with the U.S. military, but there is a lack of depth to the site.

Subject Headings: Acquisitions; Electronic Data Interchange (EDI); Military

[135] Office of Inspector General

Sponsoring Agency: Department of the Interior (DOI). Office of Inspector General (OIG)

Primary Access: http://www.access.gpo.gov/doi/

Alternative Access Method: http://info.er.usgs.gov/doi/office-of-inspector-general.html

Resource Summary: While the alternate URL simply describes the office and gives addresses and phone numbers for regional offices, the main site includes access to an OIG Reports database of publicly released audit reports. It also gives hotline information for reporting fraud, waste, and abuse in the Department of the Interior.

Subject Headings: Auditing; Reports—Full Text

[136] Panama Canal Commission

Sponsoring Agency: Panama Canal Commission

Primary Access: http://www.pananet.com/pancanal/

Resource Summary: Featuring operational information on the Panama Canal, this site offers a General Information section and one for Procurement Information and Acquisition. The General Information section includes headings such as Press Releases, Panama Canal Commission Organization, Panama Canal Operations, Panama Canal History, Other Information, and Panama Canal Photographs. The other section covers information on doing business with the Panama Canal Commission.

This site provides general information on the Canal, current toll charges for users of the Canal, and an opportunity for businesses to bid on procurement contracts. For anyone interested in any of these areas, this is a useful site.

Subject Headings: Acquisitions; Panama Canal; Shipping

[137] Policy, Management, and Budget

Sponsoring Agency: Department of the Interior (DOI). Policy, Management, and Budget

Primary Access: http://www.doi.gov/policy-management-budget.html

Resource Summary: This page describes the Policy, Management, and Budget office and links to other descriptive documents for its component offices and systems including: Acquisition and Grant Management, Human Resources, Office of Aircraft Services, Office of Financial Management, Office of Information Resources Management, Office of Environmental Policy and Compliance, and Departmental Administrative Systems.

Subject Headings: Acquisitions; Planning

[138] Small Business Innovation Research and Small Business Technology Transfer Programs

Sponsoring Agencies: Defense Technical Information Center (DTIC); Small Business Innovation Research Program (SBIR); Small Business Technology Transfer (STTR)

Primary Access: http://www.dtic.mil/dtic/sbir

Resource Summary: This site hosts information on the Small Business Innovation Research (SBIR) and the related Small Business Technology Transfer (STTR) programs. It includes the full text from 97.1 DoD SBIR Solicitation and the DoD STTR Solicitation. The link to SBIR/STTR services contains information on technical information support for SBIR.

The information is very specific to these two programs and primarily of interest to participants or applicants.

Subject Headings: Small Businesses; Technology Transfer

[139] Surplus U.S. Government Sales

Sponsoring Agency: Defense Reutilization and Marketing Service

Primary Access: http://www.drms.dla.mil/

Alternative Access Method: http://www.drms.dla.mil/oldhome.html

Resource Summary: This site features a publicly accessible, searchable database of items available at public auctions and sales. Other significant sections include a List of Catalogs, Regional Zone Sales, Support Numbers, and a Recycling Control Point. It has recently added online bidding. It also features the Reutilization, Transfer, and Donations database.

Anyone interested in buying from the government or just investigating what is available should check out this site.

Subject Headings: Auctions; Marketing

Business and Economics: International Commerce, Exporting, and Importing

[140] Asia-Pacific Technology Program

Sponsoring Agencies: Asia-Pacific Technology Program; Department of Commerce (DOC). Office of International Technology Policy and Programs

Primary Access: http://www.ta.doc.gov/aptp/aptp.htm

Alternative Access Method: http://www.gwjapan.org/html/xjtlb.html

Resource Summary: This page describes the program and its major activities. The site assists U.S. researchers in accessing and utilizing Japanese, Chinese, and Korean sources of science and technology. It links to pages with information on scientific and technical information from each of the three countries. The Japan section includes a detailed Scientific and Technical Information page, including descriptions of what other federal agencies are doing to monitor Japanese technology. To link to the *Japanese Technical Literature Bulletin* try the alternate URL, which has ASCII versions from March 1993 to July 1995.

Most of the information on this site relates to Japan. More information regarding programs involving the other Asia-Pacific countries would be helpful. This can be a useful resource, especially for information about Japanese technology.

Subject Headings: Asia; Importing and Exporting; Japan—Trade; Scientific and Technical Information

SuDoc Number: C 1.90: *Japanese Technical Literature Bulletin*

[141] Big Emerging Markets

Sponsoring Agency: International Trade Administration (ITA)

Primary Access: http://www.stat-usa.gov/itabems.html

Resource Summary: This site describes the Big Emerging Markets (BEMs) program, which targets exports to countries such as Poland, Indonesia, South Africa, and India. Brief HTML files offer advice on exporting to the countries listed as BEMs. Specific information can be found on each of the countries.

This is useful for anyone looking for economic information on the BEMs.

Subject Heading: Importing and Exporting

[142] BISNIS Online

Sponsoring Agencies: Business Information Service for the Newly Independent States (BISNIS); International Trade Administration (ITA)

Primary Access: http://www.itaiep.doc.gov/bisnis/bisnis.html

Alternative Access Method: http://www.iep.doc.gov/bisnis/bisnis.html

Resource Summary: BISNIS offers a four-line description and the following links for assisting U.S. businesses in trade with Russia: Latest U.S. Embassy Cables; Daily Ruble/U.S. Dollar Exchange Rates; BISNIS Market Information and Business Leads; BISNIS Reports and Publications; and Sources of Finance for Trade and Investment in the NIS.

BISNIS is a useful resource for businesses or individuals wanting to learn more about trade with Russia and business opportunities in that region.

Subject Headings: Importing and Exporting; Russia

SuDoc Number: C 61.42: *The BISNIS Bulletin*

[143] Bureau of Export Administration

Sponsoring Agency: Department of Commerce (DOC). Bureau of Export Administration (BXA)

Primary Access: http://www.bxa.doc.gov/

Resource Summary: The Bureau of Export Administration offers descriptive resources on its Web site. There is the usual descriptive information on the agency under headings such as BXA Programs, Press Releases, BXA Mission, Call Us, and Locations. The Encryption page features information on commercial encryption export controls and regulations and criteria related to encryption technologies. Other sections include Export Administration Regulations Marketplace, Fact Sheets, Violations, Regulations, and Resources.

This is a useful site for businesses investigating export regulations and for all those on the Internet following the controversy on export controls on encryption technologies.

Subject Headings: Encryption; Importing and Exporting

[144] Bureau of International Labor Affairs

Sponsoring Agency: Department of Labor (DOL). Bureau of International Labor Affairs (ILAB)

Primary Access: http://www.dol.gov/dol/ilab/

Resource Summary: ILAB includes information about the agency including a mission statement, a partial directory, descriptions of component departments, a short biography of the under secretary, and some full-text press releases from 1995. Under the Media Releases section is an online report on child labor.

Subject Headings: International Trade; Labor

[145] CEEBICNet

Sponsoring Agencies: International Trade Administration (ITA). International Economic Policy Group; Central and Eastern Europe Business Information Center (CEEBIC)

Primary Access: http://www.itaiep.doc.gov/eebic/ceebic.html

Resource Summary: CEEBICNet offers information on marketing and export to Central and Eastern Europe including CEEBIC Market Information and Trade Leads, Latest U.S. Embassy Cables, Subscribe to CEEBIC Publications, Small Business Corner, Back Issues of the Central and Eastern Europe Commercial Update, and Connect Directly to Central and East European Countries.

The site contains useful information for those interested in the markets in Central and Eastern Europe.

Subject Headings: Eastern Europe; Importing and Exporting; Marketing; Small Businesses

[146] The Commercial Service of the U.S. Department of Commerce

Sponsoring Agency: International Trade Administration (ITA)

Primary Access: http://www.ita.doc.gov/uscs/

Alternative Access Method: http://www.ita.doc.gov/ita_home/itauscs.html

Resource Summary: This page describes the Commercial Service, which aims to assist U.S. companies in exporting. The site provides directories of its Export Assistance Centers for locations in each of the states and in about 70 foreign offices. Another page describes the Commercial Service's programs, which are designed to help small and medium-sized U.S. businesses start or expand their export efforts. The site also has brief educational guides to finding exporting information.

This is an excellent site for businesses or individuals that are beginning to explore the possibilities for exporting products.

Subject Headings: Importing and Exporting; International Trade

[147] Export Import Bank

Sponsoring Agency: Export-Import (Ex-Im) Bank of the United States

Primary Access: http://www.exim.gov/

Alternative Access Method: http://www.exim.gov/textonly.html [text version]

Resource Summary: This official home page of the Export-Import Bank has information on the Bank's services and programs. It provides press releases, a history, fact sheets, and a contacts directory. The Programs page features sections such as Program Overview, Medium and Long Term Guarantees, Insurance Programs, Working Capital Guarantee Program, Project Finance Programs, Ex-Im Bank Fees, Small Business Programs, Environmental Programs, and Aircraft Finance Programs. The Publications section features press releases, publications lists, and some online reports.

Subject Headings: Banking; Importing and Exporting

[148] GEMS - Global Export Market Information System

Sponsoring Agency: International Trade Administration (ITA). International Economic Policy Group

Primary Access: http://www.itaiep.doc.gov/

Resource Summary: The Global Export Market Information System (GEMS) is designed to provide country and region information for American exporters. It consists of links to its major programs, including the Central and Eastern Europe Business Information Center Online; BISNIS Online; NAFTA Online; Special American Business Internship Training (SABIT); and Big Emerging Markets. The site also boasts a WAIS search feature, which can search across documents from the different programs.

This site is mostly useful as a link to the individual programs and for its search feature.

Subject Heading: Importing and Exporting

[149] Import Administration

Sponsoring Agencies: Import Administration (IA); International Trade Administration (ITA)

Primary Access: http://www.ita.doc.gov/import_admin/records/

Resource Summary: As the agency that enforces laws and agreements to prevent unfairly traded imports and to safeguard jobs and the competitive strength of American industry, the IA home page begins with a description of the agency's mission. The site also offers access to documents about IA topics such as foreign trade zones and statutory imports. There is a glossary, annual report, and *Federal Register* decisions regarding antidumping and countervailing duty cases.

This site provides a useful agency overview and information on antidumping, countervailing duty cases, and the GATT Uruguay Round.

Subject Heading: Importing and Exporting

U.S. Department of Commerce
International Trade Administration

"... dedicated to helping U.S. businesses
compete in the global marketplace..."

[150] International Trade Administration—Trade Information

Sponsoring Agency: International Trade Administration (ITA)

Primary Access: http://www.ita.doc.gov/

Resource Summary: The ITA Web site includes some agency information under the heading About the ITA. The Press Room link provides access to press releases and speeches. Two other major headings include Information Directory and Assistance Centers. The Information Directory has topical links to Regions and Countries, Industries, Cross Cutting Programs, and Trade Statistics. The Assistance Centers section includes the Trade Information Center, Export Assistance Centers, and Import Administration. The Trade Statistics page provides access to a number of well-known publications. These include selected tables from the *U.S. Industrial Outlook* and the full text of its successor, the *U.S. Global Trade Outlook*. Some of the online publications have only selected portions of the print version available on the Internet.

The numerous links to substantial information repositories make this site a good first choice for export-related information.

Subject Heading: Importing and Exporting

SuDoc Numbers: C 61.28/2: *U.S. Foreign Trade Highlights*
C 61.34: *U.S. Industrial Outlook*
C 61.34/2: *U.S. Global Trade Outlook*
C 61.35/2: *LA/C Business Bulletin*
C 61.2:M 56/4 *Metropolitan Area Exports*

[151] International Trade Commission

Sponsoring Agency: International Trade Commission (ITC)

Primary Access: http://www.usitc.gov/

Alternative Access Method: ftp://ftp.usitc.gov/pub/

Resource Summary: The International Trade Commission's site includes a basic description of the Commission along with some press releases. It also features ITC publications and reports, employment opportunities, a bibliography of trade-related law journal articles, and a list of ITC trade analysts by commodity or service assignments.

The Reports and Publications section features a number of serials. The quarterly *Industry, Trade, and Technology Review* is available in a self-extracting WordPerfect format for the past few issues. The monthly *International Economic Review* is available for the past few months in PDF format. Another significant ITC publication, available under the Tariffs subcategory, is the *Harmonized Tariff Schedule of the United States*. It is available in several self-extracting WordPerfect files.

The page is somewhat hard to understamd in presentation, but the availability of the tariff schedules and the two serials in full-text formats make this an important resource for international trade information.

Subject Headings: Electronic Periodicals; Employment; Importing and Exporting; International Trade

SuDoc Numbers: ITC 1.10: *Harmonized Tariff Schedule of the United States*
ITC 1.29: *International Economic Review*
ITC 1.33/2: *Industry, Trade, and Technology Review*

[152] NAFTA Online

Sponsoring Agency: International Trade Administration (ITA). International Economic Policy Group

Primary Access: http://www.itaiep.doc.gov/nafta/nafta.html

Resource Summary: This site contains the full text of the North American Free Trade Agreement (NAFTA) in ASCII text, a searchable NAFTA market research database, and a NAFTA border page featuring information on the border areas.

The site could be improved with the addition of an HTML version of NAFTA. The market research database is misleading in the label; it actually links to the full Global Export Market Information System database, which includes countries outside of the scope of NAFTA.

Subject Headings: Canada; Importing and Exporting; Mexico

[153] Special American Business Internship Training Program

Sponsoring Agencies: International Trade Administration (ITA); Special American Business Internship Training Program (SABIT)

Primary Access: http://www.itaiep.doc.gov/sabit/sabit.html

Resource Summary: The Special American Business Internship Training Program (SABIT) assists U.S. companies and organizations working in the New Independent States (NIS) by funding training programs for managers and scientists from the former Soviet Union. Applications for companies and NIS trainees are available for the SABIT Program, the SABIT Standards Program, and the SABIT Defense Conversion Program. Other files describe the various programs, SABIT successes, and AMBIT, the American Management and Business Internship Training Program.

The combination of both descriptions and applications can help users decide whether SABIT fits their needs.

Subject Headings: Importing and Exporting; Russia

[154] Trade Development Unit

Sponsoring Agency: International Trade Administration (ITA). Trade Development Unit

Primary Access: http://www.ita.doc.gov/ita_home/itatdhom.html

Resource Summary: This page consists primarily of a description of the Unit and its functions. It also has links to other ITA programs and information on various industry groups.

Subject Headings: Importing and Exporting; International Trade

[155] U.S. Ex-Im Bank

Sponsoring Agency: Export-Import (Ex-Im) Bank of the United States

Primary Access: http://www.tradecompass.com/us_exim/

Resource Summary: While this site is an unofficial one, their goal is to provide accurate and useful information electronically to commercial bankers, exporters, export consultants, brokers, government entities, and others interested in Ex-Im Bank. This page features HTML press releases, ASCII committee meeting minutes, an ASCII internal policy handbook, ASCII fact sheets on exports to particular countries, a list of Ex-Im Bank seminars, and other miscellaneous publications.

This site includes an impressive array of information. The general scope of the available information will be of most interest to those actively involved in the export and import business.

Subject Headings: Banking; Importing and Exporting

Welcome to the

United States Trade Representative's Homepage

[156] United States Trade Representative

Sponsoring Agency: Trade Representative (USTR)

Primary Access: http://www.ustr.gov/

Resource Summary: Beyond the seal of the USTR, this page provides a variety of sections and publications, including the categories Mission, History, People, Reports, Speeches, Testimony, and Agreements. Agreements includes information on NAFTA and the Summit of the Americas Trade Ministerial. The Reports area includes a number of full-text reports including the *National Trade Estimate Report on Foreign Trade Barriers* and the *Trade Policy Agenda and Annual Report of the President of the United States on the Trade Agreements Program* in HTML.

The availability of the reports in HTML provides an important source of information on trade deficits and trade barriers. For anyone researching trade policies with a specific country, this is an excellent source of information.

Subject Headings: International Trade; Negotiations; North American Free Trade Agreement (NAFTA)

SuDoc Numbers: PrEx 9.10: *National Trade Estimate Report on Foreign Trade Barriers*
PrEx 9.11: *Trade Policy Agenda and Annual Report of the President of the United States on the Trade Agreements Program*

CHAPTER 3: CENSUS AND OTHER STATISTICS

The government, especially the Census Bureau, produces a great quantity of statistical reports. These statistics can appear in press releases, report series, monographic publications, and distinct databases. The Internet provides an excellent medium for broad dissemination of these statistics, and many agencies, including the Census Bureau, have begun to make use of it for just this purpose. Statistics are available on many sites in many forms. Entries listed in this chapter include sites whose major content is statistical as well as agencies that focus on the production of statistics. However, many sites listed in other chapters also include statistics and statistical reports. Search in the index for a particular subject area or go directly to a specific agency's site.

Of all the statistical sites, two Census Bureau resources are the featured sites for this chapter. The 1990 U.S. Census LOOKUP sites provide a huge amount of data from the 1990 Census of Population and Housing. For anyone just looking for statistics from the 1990 Census, the LOOKUP sites can provide one-stop browsing of an incredible wealth of data. As the major statistical agency for the government, the U.S. Census Bureau site is another excellent starting point for finding various census information beyond the scope of the 1990 Census.

[157] 1990 U.S. Census LOOKUP

Sponsoring Agencies: Bureau of the Census; Lawrence Berkeley National Laboratory (LBL)

Primary Access: http://cedr.lbl.gov/cdrom/doc/lookup_doc.html

Alternative Access Methods: http://bigsur.lbl.gov/cdrom/lookup
http://parep2.lbl.gov/cdrom/lookup
http://www.census.gov/cdrom/lookup
http://library.monterey.edu/cdrom/lookup
http://indian.monterey.edu/cdrom/lookup

Resource Summary: These sites provide access to data from the 1990 Census of Population and Housing. LOOKUP is an experimental Web server used for retrieving data from the following 1990 U.S. Census Summary Tape Files (a Web client with forms capability is required):
STF1A (State, County, Tract, Place, MSA, MCD, and parts)
STF3A (State, County, Tract, Place, Urban, Area, MSA, MCD, and parts)
STF1C and STF3C (Nation, State, County, MSA)
STF1D and STF3D (Congressional Districts): (103rd at LBL, 104th at Census Bureau)
STF3B (ZIP codes)

This site is an extraordinary resource. CD-ROMs are useful for distribution of large databases, but their public accessibility is much more difficult to enable on a large scale. This experiment has successfully bridged the gap and provides the Internet community with a significant portion of the 1990 Census statistics. It is still experimental, and they have detailed bug reports that describe some of the problems. The browser-dependent bugs list is quite useful, and a feature that more Web sites using complex forms should include.

Unfortunately, the future of this resource may be in jeopardy. In August 1995, Department of Energy funding for the CD-ROM activities was discontinued. The Bureau of the Census has provided limited funding to temporarily maintain the existing system. The Census Bureau funding allows for no development and only limited user support. Although the site states that additional funding is needed to maintain the system beyond October 1, 1996, it is still functioning in 1997. Even without further development, this is a very useful resource.

Subject Headings: Demographics; Statistics

SuDoc Numbers: C 3.282: *1990 Census of Population and Housing STF 1*
C 3.282/2: *1990 Census of Population and Housing STF 3*

[158] Fedstats: One Stop Shopping Federal Statistics

Sponsoring Agency: Federal Interagency Council on Statistical Policy

Primary Access: http://www.fedstats.gov/

Resource Summary: The Fedstats site was established with the goal of providing easy access to a broad range of statistics that are offered by more than 70 federal agencies. Primary access methods include the links Agencies, Programs, Regional Statistics, and Press Releases. For finding specific statistics, Fedstats offers an A to Z subject index and direct keyword searching. Note that the keyword search is only searching pages from some of the agencies, but not all. The Fast Facts section links to a few sources for commonly requested statistics such as the PDF version of the *Statistical Abstract*. The Policy page has links to information on statistical policy and electronic dissemination plans, while the Contacts page links directly to personnel directories pages from some of the constituent agencies.

This site is an excellent demonstration of a new direction in federal government Web sites, that of a central subject approach. However, due to the great quantity of government statistics, it is quite difficult to produce a site that quickly points to exactly the statistic an individual is seeking. This site is most useful to people who already have a good idea of which agency produces certain statistics and the exact name of a specific statistical measure. For those with more general information needs, this site can be difficult to navigate.

Subject Heading: Finding Aid—Statistics

[159] U.S. Census Bureau

Sponsoring Agency: Bureau of the Census

Primary Access: http://www.census.gov/

Alternative Access Methods: http://www.census.gov/index.txtonly.html [text version]
ftp://ftp.census.gov/pub/
telnet://cenbbs.census.gov/
gopher://gopher.census.gov/ [no longer supported]

Resource Summary: The Census site provides access to a wide range of census materials and data. While all of the census reports and statistical series published by the Bureau are not available online, a great deal of recent statistical releases can be found on this site. Press releases show up under the News heading. The Subjects A-Z page features an alphabetical list of topics and publications.

Information about the agency is available under the heading About the Census Bureau. This includes a number of employee directories that can help refer people to an appropriate Census official. The Access Tools link features a variety of ways to search and view available statistics, including access by maps, links to 1990 Census CD-ROMs, the Tiger Map Server, and other software data extraction tools.

The Search button presents a variety of search options, including searches by keyword, place name, map point, and one for Census staff. The keyword options feature a master HTML index search, with support for Boolean operators. Other keyword indexes are categorized as major indexes, in which the full content of documents are indexed, and minor indexes where only the titles are indexed.

On the commercial side, the Census offers CenStats and CenStore. CenStats, a commercial service, provides access to Census Bureau databases including some of their CD-ROMs and all Census Bureau publications released since January 1, 1996. Depository libraries can receive a free password, but other users must pay a subscription fee. CenStore provides information on Census publications and data products that are for sale.

Overall, the Census offers a significant amount of readily accessible statistical data and recent statistical press releases. This should be one of the first sites to check for demographic and economic statistics. There are so many different resources that it can be difficult to find specific statistics, but the sophisticated search options available from the top page make the process easier. The CenStats service makes publications available in PDF format. While it is convenient to have access to all of the data online, browsing for specific statistics in a PDF file can be difficult. Both the free and commercial side of the site need further development in making statistical tables easily accessible for the general public.

Subject Headings: Demographics; Statistics

SuDoc Numbers: C 3.6/2: F 76 *Guide to Foreign Trade Statistics*
C 3.6/2: F 49/6/ *Governments Finance and Employment Classification Manual*

C 3.24 *Census of Manufactures*
C 3.24/9 *Annual Survey of Manufactures*
C 3.31 *1992 Census of Agriculture*
C 3.134: *Statistical Abstract of the United States*
C 3.134/2: C 83/2/ *County and City Data Book*
C 3.145/6: *Quarterly Tax Survey*
C 3.158: *Current Industrial Reports*
C 3.163/3: *Census Catalog and Guide*
C 3.163/7: *Monthly Product Announcement*
C 3.186: P 25/EL *State Population Estimates*
C 3.186: P-25/P 94 *State Population Projections: 1995 to 2025*
C 3.204/3: *County Business Patterns*
C 3.216 *Census of Mineral Industries*
C 3.233/5: TC 92 *1992 Census of Transportation: Truck Inventory and Use Survey*
C 3.238: *Census and You*
C 3.242: *Quarterly Public Employee Retirement*
C 3.245 *1992 Census of Construction Industries*
C 3.255 *1992 Census of Retail Trade*
C 3.256 *1992 Census of Wholesale Trade*
C 3.257 *1992 Census of Service Industries*
C 3.266: *Consolidated Federal Funds Report*
C 3.266: *Federal Expenditure by State*
C 3.267: *Quarterly Financial Report for Manufacturing, Mining and Trade Corporations*
C 3.291: FC 92 *1992 Census of Financial, Insurance, and Real Estate Industries*
C 3.292: UC 92 *1992 Census of Transportation, Communications, and Utilities*

The Census and Other Statistics resources in this chapter are subdivided broadly into three sections. The first subchapter covers sites that include general statistical resources as well as sites that do not fit under the other subcategories. This section runs from entry numbers 160 to 169. Demographics, the second section, includes the majority of the Census sites along with other pages offering demographic statistics and covers entries 170-183. The third section, Economic Statistics, includes sites whose statistical publications cover economic issues, and includes entries 184-191.

Census and Other Statistics: General

[160] Bureau of Justice Statistics

Sponsoring Agencies: Bureau of Justice Statistics (BJS); National Criminal Justice Reference Service (NCJRS)

Primary Access: http://www.ojp.usdoj.gov/bjs/

Alternative Access Methods: ftp://www.ojp.usdoj.gov/pub/bjs/
telnet://ncjrs@ncjrsbbs.aspensys.com/

Resource Summary: This site describes the BJS and its various data series. It also has links to the full text of recent reports and press releases, with some dating back to 1988. They are primarily available in ASCII text, although the newest ones are also available in PDF. The reports and press releases are also available on the NCJRS BBS, available at the alternate URL of (telnet://ncjrs@ncjrsbbs.aspensys.com/).

This is a rich site for recent criminal justice statistics.

Subject Heading: Criminal Justice—Statistics

SuDoc Numbers: J 29.2:C 26 *Federal Criminal Case Processing*
J 29.9/6: *Sourcebook of Criminal Justice Statistics*
J 29.11/3: *Capital Punishment*
J 29.11/6: *Probation and Parole*
J 29.11/7: *PrisonersJ*
29.11/10: *Criminal Victimization*
J 29.11/11: *Felony Sentences in State Courts*
J 29.11/11-2: *Felony Sentences in the United States*
J 29.11/15: *Prosecutors in State Courts*
J 29.17: *Correctional Populations in the United States*
J 29.20: *Compendium of Federal Justice Statistics*

[161] Bureau of Transportation Statistics

Sponsoring Agency: Bureau of Transportation Statistics (BTS)

Primary Access: http://www.bts.gov/

Alternative Access Methods: gopher://gopher.bts.gov/
http://www.bts.gov/toolbar/contents/ [text version]
ftp://ftp.bts.gov/

Resource Summary: In addition to information about the agency and a BTS publications and data products list, this site includes some substantial collections of data. The National Transportation Library includes many full-text documents and reports from the BTS and other sources. To access the documents use either the keyword index search or one of the top-level subject categories.

The Briefing Room has press releases, announcements, and the latest statistics. It also has a link to the latest *National Transportation Statistics* and *Highway Statistics* volumes, which are available in PDF with some tables in Excel, Lotus 1-2-3, and even HTML formats. Earlier issues of the *National Transportation Statistics* are available on the Gopher and ftp sites. The Products and Services page provides access to press releases, information on BTS services, and a listing of BTS products. Other available categories on the main page include Geographic Information Services, BTS Programs, and Databases. The Databases page provides access to data from the Commodity Flow Surveys, On-Time Airline Statistics, *Highway Statistics*, the *FAA Statistical Handbook of Aviation*, and the *Fatal Accident Reporting System*.

There is a substantial amount of transportation data available at this site, but the publications are not always easy to find. Some are under Databases, while others are under Products or Briefing Room. Having one page with access to all of them would be a helpful improvement. Even so, this site has extensive resources and should be of interest to anyone seeking transportation statistics.

Subject Headings: Aeronautics; Geographic Information Systems; Transportation—Statistics

SuDoc Numbers: TD 2.23: *Highway Statistics*
TD 4.20: *FAA Statistical Handbook of Aviation*
TD 8.27: *Fatal Accident Reporting System*
TD 10.9: *National Transportation Statistics*

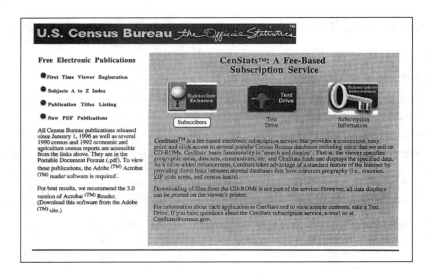

[162] CenStats: An Electronic Subscription Service

Sponsoring Agency: Bureau of the Census

Primary Access: http://www.census.gov/apsd/www/censtats.html

Resource Summary: This new, fee-based service from the Census Bureau provides online access to many Census reports not available on the free sites. Subscription plans are available for single publications, series of publications, or for the entire collection. All Federal Depository Libraries, official data centers, and other organizations with formal affiliations with the Census Bureau will have free access to CenStats. Almost all of the publications are only available in PDF format. The reports can be browsed by subject and by title, although the title listing is also arranged by different subject categories, not just by an alphabetical list of titles.

Many of the large publications are only available in a single PDF file while others, such as the *Statistical Abstract,* are divided into sections. In either scenario, an entire document or section needs to be downloaded to see just one table, and for those who do not know the publications very well, it can be difficult to determine which section may have an appropriate table. Adding a brief notice with the size of the PDF files would enable users to realize how long it might take to download a specific file. Even better, there ought to be some HTML versions of the documents available with a master index or a keyword search of table titles available.

Subject Headings: Demographics; Economics—Statistics

[163] Census Mailing Lists

Sponsoring Agency: Bureau of the Census

Primary Access: mailto:majordomo@census.gov with "subscribe <list>" in body

Resource Summary: The following e-mail lists are available on the census.gov server. Send an e-mail message to majordomo@census.gov with "subscribe <list>" in the body of the message. Replace <list> with the appropriate list name listed below. Send the messages "help lists" and "lists," on separate lines, to the same address for additional instructions. The following descriptions are from the response to the "lists" command:

agfs - Respond to users' questions about agriculture
ces - Center for Economic Studies
compendia - Answer users' questions about *U.S. Statistical Abstracts*
econweb - User feedback from the econ pages
febnet - Federal Executive Board Network
ftd - Respond to users' questions about foreign trade
genealogy - helping genealogists
geoweb - GeoWEB Project Support List
govs - Respond to feedback from users
gweos - Government Wide Electronic Online Service
mcd - Respond to users' questions
metadata - Census Metadata Discussion Group
press-release - Census Press Releases
product-announce - Census Product Announcements
pub-contract - Lawyers discuss Federal Public Contract Law
svsd - Respond to users' questions
themapit - let users draw maps with data

Subject Headings: E-mail Lists; Statistics

[164] Census Publication Titles

Sponsoring Agency: Bureau of the Census

Primary Access: http://www.census.gov/mp/www/pub/

Resource Summary: This is a subject listing of Census Bureau publications. It features information on ordering the documents from the Government Printing Office (GPO), and it provides a link to the GPO home page to check which depository libraries receive specific Census documents. In addition, the actual data from the *Current Industrial Reports* is available in ASCII full-text format.

This site is useful for checking details, including availability and price, about Census publications. The availability of full-text *Current Industrial Reports* leads to the hope that more of the other publications will also become available from this page.

Subject Heading: Publication Catalogs

SuDoc Number: C 3.158 *Current Industrial Reports*

[165] Census State Data Centers

Sponsoring Agency: Bureau of the Census

Primary Access: http://www.census.gov/sdc/www/

Alternative Access Method: http://www.census.gov/ftp/pub/sdc/www/

Resource Summary: Via a clickable image map or an alphabetical list, basic contact information for each state's Census Data Centers can be found, along with a graphical designation of services available at each. In addition, there is a hypertext list of those Census State Data Centers that have their own home pages.

This site has good basic directory information, including Internet contact addresses, for the state data centers.

Subject Heading: States—Statistics

U.S. Census Bureau *the Official Statistics*

TIGER Mapping Service
The "Coast to Coast" Digital Map Database.

Welcome to the home page for the TIGER Map Service, a project sponsored by the U.S. Bureau of the Census. The goal of this service is to provide a public resource for generating high-quality, detailed maps of anywhere in the United States, using public geographic data.

Try out TMS Version 2.5, now with additional layers! (requires table support)

If your browser doesn't support tables, you can still use TMS Version 1.3.1, which draws good maps as well.

For more information...

- Background and General Information about the TMS project
- Technical Details & Credits
- Frequently Asked Questions (FAQ)
- The TIGER home page
- Applications and Links from Other Sites that use TMS
- Current Features and Future Plans for the TMS
- How to Request TMS maps directly from your own HTML web pages or CGI script.
- Cyber Awards for TMS has more information about the Tiger data and products.
- Ordering and Product Information.
- GIS Gateway page.

Please email general comments and suggestions to: TMS@Census.GOV

[166] Census TIGER Map Service

Sponsoring Agency: Bureau of the Census

Primary Access: http://tiger.census.gov/

Resource Summary: The TIGER Map Service (TMS) is a project sponsored by the U.S. Bureau of the Census. The goal is to provide a public resource for generating high-quality, detailed maps of any place in the United States, using public geographic data. Using TMS version 2.5 for browsers that support tables or TMS version 1.3.1 for those that do not, this site can produce maps from the TIGER data. With a connection to the U.S. Gazetteer, maps can be found by entering a city and/or ZIP code. Or, enter a specific latitude and longitude along with a size in degrees designation to retrieve census maps for a specific location. Layers of data can be "forced on" or "forced off" and map census level and themes can be specified.

This is a great site for those interested in Geographic Information Systems (GIS) or maps in general. Be warned that maps may take a while to be created—this is a prototype, so do not be discouraged if it seems slow. The site responds slowly, but considering the behind-the-scenes processing going on, it is an amazing feat to be able to produce these maps at all.

The site is also important for Web page developers who want to include one of the maps as an inline image on other pages. There is a open interface to images allowing any user to request maps directly to inline in other documents.

Subject Headings: Geographic Information Systems; TIGER Census Mapping Data

[167] Government Information Sharing Project

Sponsoring Agency: Bureau of the Census

Primary Access: http://govinfo.kerr.orst.edu/

Alternative Access Method: http://govinfo.kerr.orst.edu/index.text.html [text version]

Resource Summary: The Government Information Sharing Project is a project that makes government CD-ROMs available on the Internet. In some cases, the search interface on the Internet is easier to use than the one that comes on the CD-ROM. The site divides its offerings into Demography, Economics, and Education. The Demography section provides access to *USA Counties on CD-ROM*; *Census of Population and Housing, 1990* including Summary Tape Files 1 and 3; Population Estimates by Age, Sex, and Race; and the *Equal Employment Opportunity File*. The Economics heading provides access to the *Consolidated Federal Funds Report*; the *Census of Agriculture* for 1982, 1987, and 1992; the *Economic Census* for 1992; the *Regional Economic Information System*; and *U.S. Imports/Exports History*. The Education section features the *School District Databook Profiles*.

The interface, which utilizes clickable image maps and forms functions to make the data request, is fairly straightforward. Response time is quick. Overall, it is an incredibly well-implemented interface to significant data sets available on these CD-ROMs.

Subject Headings: Agriculture—Statistics; Demographics; Economics—Statistics

SuDoc Numbers: C 3.134/6: *USA Counties*
C 3.266/2: *Consolidated Federal Funds Report, 1985-95*
C 3.277:CD-AG 92-1 B *Census of Agriculture, 1992: Geographic Area Series 1B*
C 3.277:CD-EC 92-1 I *Economic Census, 1992: Report Series 1I*
C 3.278/2: *U.S. Imports History*
C 3.278/3: *U.S. Exports History*
C 3.282: *1990 Census of Population and Housing STF 1*
C 3.282/2: *1990 Census of Population and Housing STF 3*
C 3.283:CD 90-EEO-1 *1990 Census of Population and Housing, Equal Employment Opportunity File*
C 59.24: *REIS: Regional Economic Information System*
ED 1.308: SCH 6/6 *School District Data Book*

[168] The TIGER Page

Sponsoring Agency: Bureau of the Census

Primary Access: http://www.census.gov/geo/www/tiger/

Resource Summary: The Topographically Integrated Geographic Encoding and Referencing (TIGER) pages give an overview of the TIGER system from the Census Bureau. Technical documentation, introductions, user notes, sample file sets for the TIGER/Line '92, TIGER/Line '95, and the Census Tract Street Index files are available in HTML format. It also has a section on related products and information.

This is a good site for information on TIGER products. However, maps produced from the actual TIGER data sets are not available on this site. For those, see the Census Tiger Mapping Service (TMS) Home Page at http://tiger.census.gov/

Subject Headings: Geographic Information Systems; TIGER Census Mapping Data

[169] University of Virginia Library Social Sciences Data Center

Sponsoring Agency: University of Virginia. Library

Primary Access: http://www.lib.virginia.edu/socsci/

Resource Summary: This site offers a substantial set of government statistics resources. While not all of its resources are from the federal government, many of its popular resources are. The Interactive Data Resources page is the primary section for access to major government CD-ROM resources such as the *County and City Data Book*, *National Income and Product Accounts*, *REIS: Regional Economic Information System*, *State Personal Income*, *Uniform Crime Reports*, and the *Standard Industrial Classification Manual*. It also provides access to the *Public Use Microdata Samples* (PUMS) from the 1990 Census.

Like the Government Information Sharing Project from the University of Oregon, this is an important site. The University of Virginia should be commended for making so many popular government CD-ROMs available on the Internet.

Subject Headings: Social Science Research; Statistics

SuDoc Numbers: C 3.134/2:C 83/2/ *County and City Data Book*
C 3.285: *Public Use Microdata Samples* (PUMS)
C 59.11/5: *National Income and Product Accounts*
C 59.24: *REIS: Regional Economic Information System*
C 59.25: *State Personal Income*
J 1.14/7: *Uniform Crime Reports for the United States*
PrEx 2.6/2:In 27/987 *Standard Industrial Classification Manual*

Census and Other Statistics: Demographics

[170] *County and City Data Book*

Sponsoring Agency: Bureau of the Census

Primary Access: http://www.census.gov/stat_abstract/ccdb.html

Alternative Access Method: ftp://ftp.census.gov/pub/statab/ccdb/

Resource Summary: This site includes 17 tables from the *County and City Data Book*. Tables are in ASCII text format, and a compressed Lotus 1-2-3 (.wk1) format is available. This is only a small portion of what is available in the full print publication.

Subject Heading: Demographics

SuDoc Number: C 3.134/2:C 83/2/ *County and City Data Book*

[171] Data Extraction System

Sponsoring Agency: Bureau of the Census

Primary Access: http://www.census.gov/DES/www/welcome.html

Alternative Access Methods: http://www.census.gov/ftp/pub/DES/www/welcome.html
telnet://desuser@www.census.gov/

Resource Summary: This site enables users to request a custom-made table from the statistics in the following data set: Survey of Income and Program Participation, Current Population Survey, American Housing Survey, and Consumer Expenditure Survey. A series of prompts allows users to specify exactly what the generated data set will look like. After the request has been sent, users are notified by automatic e-mail when the file is ready. Users then need to retrieve the file, via FTP or the Data Extraction System (DES) Web site, before it expires on the server.

DES is designed for advanced users of Census data. Some knowledge of database structure and the specific data elements in each of the files makes it much easier to maneuver through the prompts. Regardless, this is an important and useful source for obtaining customized statistical reports.

Subject Headings: Data Products; Demographics

[172] EASI Quick Reports and Analysis

Sponsoring Agencies: Bureau of the Census; Easy Analytic Software, Inc. (EASI)

Primary Access: http://www.easidemographics.com/free_reports.html

Resource Summary: This commercial site uses data from the Census Bureau to provide free access to a large quantity of demographic reports. These free reports can be requested by using one of several geographic variables and reports. The reports are quite detailed and provide EASI's own rankings of the specified geographic area.

Although the free reports are designed as an advertising tool for their commercial software, the available data can be quite useful to others as well. Unfortunately, the date and specific source of the data are not clearly identified.

Subject Heading: Data Products

[173] Field Division

Sponsoring Agency: Bureau of the Census. Field Division

Primary Access: http://www.census.gov/field/www/

Alternative Access Methods: http://www.census.gov/field/www/index.txt.html [text version] http://www.census.gov/ftp/pub/field/www/

Resource Summary: This site uses a clickable image map, or an alternative text page, for access to the home pages of the 12 regional offices of the field division. In addition, there is a list of telephone numbers, job openings, and abstracts of the surveys that the division carries out.

Subject Heading: Demographics

[174] Historical Demographic, Economic, and Social Data of the U.S.

Sponsoring Agencies: Bureau of the Census; Harvard University; Inter-university Consortium for Political and Social Research (ICPSR)

Primary Access: http://icg.harvard.edu/census/

Resource Summary: The data made available on this site at Harvard University, in conjunction with ICPSR, are available for each of the decennial census reports between 1790 and 1860. Coverage is available for all counties in most states during this time period. Subject coverage includes population and a variety of other factors, depending on which date is chosen.

This is one of the few sites that provides historical U.S. census data. The forms-based interface is easy to use and the generated HTML output is easy to browse, as long as too many variables are not requested.

Subject Heading: Demographics—Historical

[175] Housing and Household Economic Statistics

Sponsoring Agency: Bureau of the Census. Housing and Household Economic Statistics Division

Primary Access: http://www.census.gov/hhes/www/

Alternative Access Method: http://www.census.gov/ftp/pub/hhes/www/

Resource Summary: In addition to information on the division and its products and publications, this site contains detailed housing economic statistics. Household economic statistics are available in the following categories: health insurance, income and poverty, labor force, poverty dynamics, program participation dynamics, small area income and poverty estimates, and wealth.

This is a useful supplement to housing statistics found in the various sites with data from the 1990 Census of Population and Housing.

Subject Heading: Housing—Statistics

[176] Integrated Public Use Microdata Series

Sponsoring Agency: Bureau of the Census

Primary Access: http://www.hist.umn.edu/~ipums/

Alternative Access Method: ftp://ftp.hist.umn.edu/

Resource Summary: Integrated Public Use Microdata Series (IPUMS) is a database consisting of 23 samples of the U.S. Census from 1850 to 1990. The IPUMS assigns the consistent codes to the different samples and integrates their documentation. The main page provides access to the data and to the documentation under links titled Download Entire IPUMS Samples, Create Extracts of IPUMS Files, Download Other Census Data Files, and Download the IPUMS Documentation. This site is primarily of use to researchers running detailed statistical studies using Census sample data.

Subject Headings: Data Products; Demographics—Historical

[177] International Programs Center

Sponsoring Agency: Bureau of the Census. International Programs Center (IPC)

Primary Access: http://www.census.gov/ipc/www/

Alternative Access Method: http://www.census.gov/ftp/pub/ipc/www/

Resource Summary: This site describes the Center and its work. It also includes a list of its publications and data products, information on world population, and a training program schedule. Selected databases, such as the International Database and the HIV/AIDS Surveillance Database, can be downloaded and run on a local PC. A Publications and Reports page lists publications from the IPC, some of which are available online in PDF format.

This is a useful site for those interested in demographics beyond the U.S.

Subject Headings: AIDS (disease); Demographics—International

[178] Map Stats

Sponsoring Agency: Bureau of the Census

Primary Access: http://www.census.gov/datamap/www/

Resource Summary: This is one of the links from the *Statistical Abstract* page and a link from the main Census Bureau page. It includes a list of Federal Information Processing Standards (FIPS) codes for counties and for Metropolitan Statistical Areas (MSAs). Access is via a clickable image map of the U.S. or via an alphabetical list of states. After selecting the state, information is available for the whole state, congressional district, or county. For each area, the display gives population, links to Census maps of the area, detailed demographics from the 1990 Census CD-ROMs via LOOKUP, a general profile from *USA Counties*, and an economic profile from *County Business Patterns*. For state records, there are also population estimates, profiles from the *Statistical Abstract*, and a summary of state government finances.

Comparable in scope to the U.S. Gazetteer at http://tiger.census.gov/cgi-bin/gazetteer, this is a very user-friendly approach to providing statistics on states and counties from multiple sources.

Subject Heading: FIPS Codes

SuDoc Numbers: C 3.134: *Statistical Abstract of the United States*
C 3.134/6: *USA Counties*
C 3.204/3 *County Business Patterns*

[179] Pop Clocks

Sponsoring Agency: Bureau of the Census

Primary Access: http://www.census.gov/main/www/popclock.html

Resource Summary: Two population clocks, or pop clocks, give up-to-the-minute estimates of the population. The United States Pop Clock estimates the resident population of the U.S. at the current minute and gives a brief explanation of how the estimate is derived. The World Pop Clock estimates the current minute's world population, lists monthly estimates for the next year, includes a World Vital Events Per Time Unit Table, gives estimates of the world population from 1950 to 2050, and provides notes on the estimates.

This is useful both as a population estimate resource and as a demonstration of the advantages of an online system that can change its data every minute.

Subject Headings: Demographics—Forecasts; Demographics—International

[180] Population Topics

Sponsoring Agency: Bureau of the Census. Population Division

Primary Access: http://www.census.gov/population/www/

Alternative Access Method: http://www.census.gov/ftp/pub/population/www/

Resource Summary: This site links to a variety of population statistics. Some of the sections include Population Estimates, Population Projections, Social and Demographic Characteristics Data, 1995 Test Results, 1990 Census Data, and Historical Census Data. Each of these sections can lead to a substantial collection of demographic statistics. Formats for the statistical and text publications available on this site vary between ASCII text, HTML, and PDF.

This is an important site for anyone searching for current, historical, or future population statistics.

Subject Headings: Demographics; Demographics—Forecasts; Demographics—Historical

[181] U.S. Census Data at Lawrence Berkeley National Laboratory

Sponsoring Agencies: Bureau of the Census; Lawrence Berkeley National Laboratory (LBL)

Primary Access: http://cedr.lbl.gov/mdocs/LBL_census.html

Alternative Access Method: telnet://seedis.lbl.gov/

Resource Summary: Nationwide data from the 1970, 1980, and 1990 U.S. Censuses are available at Lawrence Berkeley National Laboratory. This is the upper level page for the Census LOOKUP program, which provides detailed 1990 Census data via its interface to the 1990 Census CD-ROMs. In addition, it has information on access to the SEEDIS (Socio-Economic Environmental Demographic Information System) database with information from the 1980 Census and other older data. SEEDIS is available at the telnet URL listed, although support is not available and only two sessions can occur at once. The Small-Area Census Data section links to information on other older data sets.

As they say themselves, the LBL data archive is believed to be the most complete collection of U.S. Census data on the Internet. The combination of the CD-ROM LOOKUP connection and information on other collections makes this one of the first stops for both old and new Census data.

Subject Heading: Demographics—Historical

[182] U.S. Demography

Sponsoring Agencies: Bureau of the Census; Consortium for International Earth Science Information Network (CIESIN)

Primary Access: http://www.ciesin.org/datasets/us-demog/us-demog-home.html

Alternative Access Method: ftp://ftpserver.ciesin.org/pub/census/

Resource Summary: The Demography home page is part of an initiative to identify, document, and provide simple access to demographic information. First on this page is a detailed descriptive listing of several key demographic data sets. The major data holdings can be found under the Archive of Census Related Products category, which currently contains 17,000+ files spanning 4,000+ MB in compressed ASCII files.

At a glance, this page appears to offer easy access to standard statistical compilations. After realizing that most of these links are only to descriptions of these standard data sets, users must navigate through a series of ftp directories to get to actual data sets. Only the advanced users may want to take the time to find the necessary data. For the advanced users, there is also an option to try the CIESIN Data Exploration Software for access to the Public Use Microdata Samples (PUMS) data sets.

Subject Headings: Data Products; Demographics

[183] U.S. Gazetteer

Sponsoring Agency: Bureau of the Census

Primary Access: http://tiger.census.gov/cgi-bin/gazetteer

Resource Summary: This Gazetteer is used to identify places to view the Tiger Map Server and the 1990 Census LOOKUP. Search statements can include simply a city or place name, a place name and two-letter state abbreviation (this requires a comma between the two), or a five-digit ZIP code. The Census STF-1A files used to create the database can be downloaded from this site as well. Search results contain 1990 population, latitude and longitude, ZIP code(s), and links to Census maps (from the TIGER files) of the area and to the Census CD-ROM LOOKUP programs for detailed demographics on the location.

The link construction makes this one of the easiest methods for finding detailed demographics and maps for specific U.S. locations. The Census Data Maps at http://www.census.gov/stat_abstract/ profile.html provide similar information for states and counties but also link to county information from other sources.

Subject Headings: Gazetteers; Geography; Place Names

Census and Other Statistics: Economic Statistics —————

[184] BEA

Sponsoring Agency: Bureau of Economic Analysis (BEA)

Primary Access: http://www.bea.doc.gov/

Resource Summary: Many BEA publications are only available electronically on the subscription service STAT-USA. The BEA Web site does provide some information about the agency including employment opportunities, a customer service statement, and a telephone contact list. The data that is available for free on this site includes selected BEA press releases, selected data series from the *Survey of Current Business*, and the *User's Guide to BEA Information*, available in both ASCII and PDF format. The *Guide* describes the different BEA publications and their release schedule. Most of the other substantive links merely describe BEA publications and give STAT-USA subscription information.

With so many government agencies going to great lengths to make their publications available for free on the Internet, it is a bit frustrating that the BEA, with its important statistical series online, only provides their information through a subscription service. For STAT-USA subscribers, it is easier to find the relevant statistic directly on STAT-USA rather than by going through the BEA site.

Subject Heading: Economics—Statistics

SuDoc Numbers: C 59.11: *Survey of Current Business*
C 59.8:B 89/ *User's Guide to BEA Information*

[185] Bureau of Labor Statistics

Sponsoring Agency: Bureau of Labor Statistics (BLS)

Primary Access: http://stats.bls.gov/

Alternative Access Methods: gopher://stats.bls.gov/
ftp://stats.bls.gov/

Resource Summary: The Bureau of Labor Statistics site is an important source with a significant collection of economic statistics. Under the BLS Information heading is the BLS mission statement, a list of senior management officials without addresses or phone numbers, information on the Senior Research Fellow Program, and international training descriptions. Press releases from the agency, in ASCII text format, are located under the Publications heading.

The Economy at a Glance link makes good use of the HTML tables feature by presenting current statistics on the labor market, hours and earnings, the Consumer Price Index (CPI), and Producer Price Index (PPI). The Publications link contains very little data and few full-text publications beyond the press releases.

The majority of actual data from BLS publications can be reached from either the Data or Surveys and Programs categories. Data can be accessed by category and uses HTML forms. The user marks specific statistics, output format, display header, delimiter, and time period. Some of the time series data go back to 1913.

This is a major statistical site with advanced capabilities. The use of forms to get custom-made tables of labor and economic data, in either space delimited or comma delimited formats, is very useful for anyone wanting specific statistics. Statistics can be browsed on screen or downloaded for analysis in spreadsheets. The BLS should be commended both for advanced uses of HTML as shown in the Economy at a Glance table, and for remembering other users by providing an ASCII version of the same table.

Subject Headings: Economics—Statistics; Labor—Statistics

SuDoc Numbers: L 2.3/4: *Occupational Outlook Handbook*
L 2.3/18: *Consumer Expenditure Survey*
L 2.38/3 to L 2.38/10: *Consumer Price Index* data
L 2.46/6: to L 2.46/9: *Employee Benefit Survey* data
L 2.61 *Producer Price Indexes* data
L 2.117: *Employment Cost Index*
L 2.121 to L 2.122 *Occupational Compensation Survey* data

[186] Business Cycle Indicators

Sponsoring Agencies: Bureau of Economic Analysis; Global Exposure Interactive

Primary Access: http://www.globalexposure.com/

Alternative Access Method: http://www.globalexposure.com/bcinoframes/bci.html [no frames version]

Resource Summary: This commercial site features time series of the BEA's business cycle indicators from 1948 to 1995. However, it presents the data only in charts and in some sample spreadsheet formats. The site advertises a software product, which has many features for manipulating this economic data. The charts and sample spreadsheet information are provided for free to entice potential customers.

Given the limits of this site in providing only charts and sample spreadsheet data, anyone looking for a specific numeric figure cannot easily retrieve it from this site. However, the site would be useful for someone wanting a quick graphical display of a business cycle indicator time series.

Subject Heading: Economics—Statistics

[187] Electronic Bulletin Board

Sponsoring Agency: Department of Commerce (DOC)

Primary Access: telnet://ebb.stat-usa.gov/

Alternative Access Method: http://www.stat-usa.gov/BEN/databases.html

Resource Summary: Full use of the telnet version of the BBS requires a registration plus per minute charges—guest users can log on with limited access to files. The Web page is part of STAT-USA and is not divided into sections. Available files include Federal Reserve Board reports, Gross Domestic Product (GDP) data, National Income and Product Accounts (NIPA) data, economic indicators, Bureau of Labor Statistics (BLS) employment statistics, Consumer Price Index (CPI) and Producer Price Index (PPI), import trade data, exports by commodity, the *U.S. Industrial Outlook*, and much more. Download options include X/Y/ZModem, Kermit, screen capture, and ASCII.

There are a great number of useful statistical data sets and press releases on this BBS. However, the BBS interface and the cost severely limit the appeal. The absence of e-mail or ftp delivery options make it difficult to download data over the Internet. Even so, for those who learn the system and need one single source for a vast amount of government economic statistics, this is a great resource. The Web version on STAT-USA is much easier to use, but it is also requires a fee to use.

Subject Headings: Economics—Statistics; Importing and Exporting

[188] NAICS—North American Industry Classification System

Sponsoring Agency: Bureau of the Census

Primary Access: http://www.census.gov/pub/epcd/www/naics.html

Resource Summary: The NAICS codes will replace the Standard Industrial Classification (SIC) codes that have been used for so many years to designate industries in government statistical reports. The new NAICS is planned to become effective in the U.S. on January 1, 1997. All federal agencies that collect establishment-based data are expected to utilize the new system. This site includes many published documents related to NAICS including the complete hierarchy and coding system for the NAICS structure. Another table matches the 1997 NAICS to the 1987 SIC. The documents are all available in PDF and ASCII formats.

As reports are published using the new NAICS codes, this site will become indispensable for finding appropriate NAICS codes and for comparing older reports with SIC codes to the new reports with NAICS codes.

Subject Headings: North American Industry Classification System (NAICS);SIC Codes

[189] The New England Electronic Economic Data Center

Sponsoring Agencies: Federal Reserve Bank of Boston; Bureau of Economic Analysis (BEA)

Primary Access: gopher://neeedc.umesbs.maine.edu/

Alternative Access Method: ftp://neeedc.umesbs.maine.edu/

Resource Summary: This site contains historical data published in the Federal Reserve Bank of Boston's New England Economic Indicators (about 90 variables from 1969 for all states and some metropolitan areas) and gross state product data for New England from the Bureau of Economic Analysis. Most files are ASCII, comma delimited spreadsheet files.

No finding aid or index is available. Few explanatory text files help in navigating these files. Thus, it is difficult to find specific information. This site will be of most interest to researchers.

Subject Headings: Economics—Statistics; Financial Statistics

[190] STAT-USA

Sponsoring Agency: Economics and Statistics Administration

Primary Access: http://www.stat-usa.gov/

Alternative Access Methods: http://www.stat-usa.gov/stat-usa.textonly.html [text version]
gopher://gopher.stat-usa.gov/ [no longer maintained]
ftp://ftp.stat-usa.gov/ [no longer maintained]

Resource Summary: STAT-USA is a fee-based service, although free passwords are available for depository libraries. Its principal offerings are The National Trade Data Bank; The National Economic, Social, and Environmental Data Bank; The Economic Bulletin Board Lite Edition; The Global Business Procurement Opportunities; and The Bureau of Economic Analysis (BEA). A reorganization of the site that occurred in early 1996 lists all of these sources under STAT-USA Databases.

Alternative access is available through other top level menu choices including information by subject, frequently requested statistics, publications of interest, and daily economic news. Within each of the database categories, the data sets are listed and may be searchable with the INQUERY search engine. The *Commerce Business Daily* is included in the Global Business category. The BEA section includes the full text of the *Survey of Current Business* back to January 1995, and it is available by date and broad topic although not by INQUERY searching.

STAT-USA is not always easy to use. The reorganization of the site in early 1996 created problems for some browsers and graphics drivers. The text would scroll off the white section and into the much more difficult to read colored section of the page. Some documents are in PDF format, while others are in plain ASCII. The new ability to browse by subject and the other top level options help in navigation, but it is still not the most intuitive organization. The search engine still needs significant improvements. While there is a great deal of economic and statistical information at this site, it would be more popular if it were free to all users.

Subject Headings: Business Information; Economics—Statistics

SuDoc Numbers: C 1.76: *Commerce Business Daily*
C 1.88: *National Trade Data Bank*
C 1.88/2: *National Economic, Social, and Environmental Data Bank*
C 1.91/2: *STAT-USA Newsletter*
C 59.11: *Survey of Current Business*

[191] U.S. International Trade Statistics

Sponsoring Agency: Bureau of the Census. Foreign Trade Division

Primary Access: http://www.census.gov/foreign-trade/www/

Alternative Access Method: http://www.census.gov/ftp/pub/foreign-trade/www/

Resource Summary: This site features news and data on trade statistics. Some of the available sections are International Trade Reports (including press rleases); Schedule B Commodity Lookup and Other Classification Schedules; Correct Way to Fill Out the Shipper's Export Declarations; *Guide to Foreign Trade Statistics*; Other Services and Ordering Information; and Who's Who in Foreign Trade.

Subject Headings: Economics—Statistics; Importing and Exporting; International Trade

CHAPTER 4: CONGRESS

In the past few years, the United States Congress has made substantial efforts to contribute information to the Internet and to disseminate information online. This chapter lists resources about Congress, its activities, and its members. While some of these sites offer legal information, see Chapter 9—Legal Information for resources that focus specifically on the law.

The featured site in this chapter is the U.S. House of Representatives. The House Web site is one of the best finding aids for congressional information from both chambers. It serves as an excellent starting point for information on legislation, legislative activity, and members of Congress.

[192] U.S. House of Representatives

Sponsoring Agency: House of Representatives

Primary Access: http://www.house.gov/

Alternative Access Methods: http://www.house.gov/welcomex.html [text version]
gopher://gopher.house.gov/

Resource Summary: The U.S. House of Representatives' Web service provides public access to legislative information and to other U.S. government information services. It presents details on the members, committees, and organizations of the House.

This site includes sections such as The Legislative Process, Annual Schedule, Write Your Representative, Internet Law Library, Visitor Information, and Educational Links. Details are also provided on bills and resolutions currently under consideration in Congress, as well as the voting results of each member on various measures. Visitor maps, the text of the Constitution, and the Declaration of Independence are also included. The Legislative Process page presents information on current legislation in both the House and the Senate. The full text of bills and some reports are available, but hearings are not.

The site is very well organized, has a substantial amount of original material, and is one of the best resources for finding congressional information. It will become even more useful when the full-text versions of hearings become available.

Subject Headings: Constitution; Declaration of Independence; Legislation—Full Text; Members of Congress—Directories

Congress: General

[193] Commission on Security and Cooperation in Europe

Sponsoring Agency: Commission on Security and Cooperation in Europe (CSCE)

Primary Access: http://www.house.gov/csce/

Resource Summary: The Commission on Security and Cooperation in Europe, better known as the Helsinki Commission, is an independent government agency created by Congress and includes members of Congress. Their Web site has few links, which include Hot Topics, Press Releases, List of Commission Publications, and the *Digest*—the Commission's monthly newsletter. The List of Commission Publications includes access to a number of hearings housed on the House of Representatives' Gopher.

Subject Headings: Europe; Human Rights; National Security

SuDoc Number: Y 4.SE 2/11: *CSCE Digest*

The congressional resources in this chapter are subdivided broadly into three sections. The first section covers general congressional resources as well as sites that do not fit under the other two headings. This section runs from entry number 193 to 209. Directories, the second subchapter with entries 210-214, contains resources that provide access to information on the members of both chambers of Congress. See also the directory listings available on both the House and Senate Web sites. The third section, Voting, includes sites that report or rate the voting records of each individual member of Congress. This section includes entries 215-220.

[194] Congressional Budget Office

Sponsoring Agency: Congressional Budget Office (CBO)

Primary Access: gopher://gopher.cbo.gov:7100/1

Alternative Access Method: http://gopher.cbo.gov:7100/0/reports/online

Resource Summary: The CBO still makes most of its full-text reports available via a Gopher server. The alternate URL provides easier Web access to the reports that are available online.

Subject Heading: Budget

SuDoc Numbers: Y 10.2:EL 2/3 *Emerging Methods for Making Electronic Payments*
Y 10.2:G 28/2 *Who Pays and When? An Assessment of Generational Accounting*
Y 10.2:H 53/3 *High-Tech Highways*
Y 10.2:W 29/5 *The Safe Drinking Water Act: Case Study of an Unfunded Mandate*
Y 10.13: *Reducing the Deficit: Spending and Revenue Options*
Y 10.17: *The Economic and Budget Outlook*
Y 10.19: *An Analysis of the President's Budgetary Proposals*

[195] Congressional Research Service Reports

Sponsoring Agencies: Congressional Research Service (CRS); National Library for the Environment

Primary Access: http://www.cnie.org/nle/crs_toc.shtml

Resource Summary: Made available by the National Library for the Environment, a project of the non-governmental Committee for the National Institute for the Environment, this site offers access to over 100 short *Congressional Research Service Reports* on environmental issues. The *Reports* are classified in broad subject listings. There is no alphabetical title list, but there is a keyword search option.

The National Library for the Environment should be commended for making some of the *Congressional Research Service Reports* available since they are not available through the depository library system.

Subject Headings: Congressional Research; Environmental Issues; Reports—Full Text

[196] FECInfo

Sponsoring Agency: Federal Election Commission (FEC)

Primary Access: http://www.tray.com/fecinfo/

Resource Summary: This is an unofficial site that uses FEC data and presents it in an easy-to-use format. Founded by a former manager of the official FEC site, this site aims to be a non-partisan source for learning who contributed to a specific candidate's campaign. Under the FECInfo Database Queries section, the page maps a variety of ways to retrieve contribution information. These include ways of looking up contributors by occupation, name, and ZIP code; public action committee information; and contribution information for specific candidates. The databases include information dating back to the 1993-1994 election cycle.

This is a well-designed site that makes it easy to find information on campaign contributions at the congressional and presidential levels. While much of the same data is available on the official FEC site, the packaging of FECInfo makes it even easier to find.

Subject Headings: Campaign Contributions; Elections; President

[197] Federal Election Commission

Sponsoring Agency: Federal Election Commission (FEC)

Primary Access: http://www.fec.gov/

Alternative Access Methods: http://www.fec.gov/1996/txindex.html [text version]
ftp://ftp.fec.gov/

Resource Summary: By using a simple design approach and few links from the home page, the FEC Web site presents a substantial amount of useful information for voters. It contains sections including The Citizen's Guide to Contributions and the Law, which links to various HTML and PDF publications from the FEC. It also contains the sections Financial Information About Candidates, Parties, and PACs, including information on presidential, House, and Senate candidates. Access is by state or by name. The same information is available from a few previous elections on the ftp server.

This site also provides access to recent press releases and electronic versions of the National Mail Voter Registration form, along with information about which states accept it.

Subject Headings: Campaign Contributions; Elections; Public Action Committees; Voting

SuDoc Numbers: Y 3.El 2/3: 15/ *FEC Reports on Financial Activity*
Y 3.El 2/3: 2 EX 7/ *Independent Expenditures*
Y 3.El 2/3: 11/ *The Record*
Y 3.El 2/3: *Guide to Supporting Federal Candidates*

[198] GAO Daybook [e-mail list]

Sponsoring Agency: General Accounting Office (GAO)

Primary Access: mailto:majordomo@www.gao.gov with "subscribe daybook" in body

Alternative Access Method: news:alt.politics.org.misc

Resource Summary: This e-mail list sends out announcements of new GAO reports. The GAO Daybook is the daily listing of released GAO reports and testimony. Those reports that are available electronically are available through GPO Access. The daily listing is also posted to the newsgroup, and is thus available by mail or news.

This site is useful for those users who need up-to-date information on new GAO reports but don't want to check GPO Access or the GAO Web site on a daily basis.

Subject Heading: Reports—Bibliography

[199] General Accounting Office

Sponsoring Agency: General Accounting Office (GAO)

Primary Access: http://www.gao.gov/

Alternative Access Method: mailto:info@www.gao.gov

Resource Summary: The GAO has been using the Internet (e-mail) for dissemination of its reports for years. However, it took longer than many other agencies to come to the Web. Its current Web offerings include GAO Reports and Testimony, Comptroller General Decisions and Opinions, GAO Policy and Guidance Materials, Special Publications and Software, and What's New About GAO. Most of the GAO Reports are accessible via GPO Access, but this site also has links which provide access to the most frequently requested reports and to the most recent reports. The reports listed in these categories are directly accessible in PDF format.

The Comptroller General Decisions are also accessible on GPO Access (since January 1996), and the most recent 60 days of decisions are also on this Web server. The GAO publishes many reports and decisions, and this Web site is one of the best ways to gain access to these documents.

Subject Headings: Cases—Full Text; Reports—Full Text

SuDoc Numbers: GA 1.1: *Comptroller General's Annual Report*
GA 1.5: *GAO Comptroller General Decisions*
GA 1.13: *GAO Reports and Testimony*

[200] Govline Congressional Committee Transcripts Feed

Sponsoring Agencies: Congress; Software Tool and Die, Inc.

Primary Access: http://world.std.com/govline/

Alternative Access Method: mailto:govline@world.std.com

Resource Summary: The Govline Congressional Committee Transcript Service is a commercial wire service that delivers complete electronic texts of all testimonies submitted to U.S. congressional committees. It also provides all special, joint, select, and subcommittee sessions as well as witness lists and other pertinent materials. Delivery is via a Usenet news feed. Full-text testimonies are typically delivered within 24 hours of the close of the committee or subcommittee session. Texts are delivered as available throughout the day. Volume is dependent upon congressional activity, but when Congress is in full session volume runs at about 50-100 texts per day (i.e., about 1-2MB of text per day).

Subject Heading: Congressional Testimony—Transcripts

[201] Institute for Better Education Through Resource Technology

Sponsoring Agency: Institute for Better Education Through Resource Technology (IBERT)

Primary Access: http://ibert.org/

Resource Summary: This non-governmental, non-profit institute offers access to federal budget information. Its Civix Database offers a compilation of all agency budget requests submitted to Congress, thus providing one of the most detailed listings of federal budget line items found anywhere. Access to detailed information requires stepping through a hierarchy of agencies and programs. The Deficit History section features a table of the history of the deficit, receipts, and outlays of the federal government dating back to 1901.

This is an excellent resource for anyone searching for specific line item budget information.

Subject Heading: Budget

[202] John C. Stennis Center for Public Service

Sponsoring Agency: John C. Stennis Center for Public Service

Primary Access: http://www.stennis.gov/

Resource Summary: The John C. Stennis Center for Public Service was created by Congress in 1988 to promote and strengthen public service in America at all levels of government. The Web site consists primarily of information on the Center such as its mission statement, the board of trustees, the director's welcome, and a guest register. The primary substantive offerings are available under the Stennis Center Programs link. Each of the programs listed has a brief description of the program, usually two or three screens' worth, and sometimes further descriptive links.

This site is designed well, but there is not a great deal of original information.

Subject Heading: Public Service

[203] Office of Technology Assessment

Sponsoring Agency: Office of Technology Assessment (OTA)

Primary Access: http://www.ota.nap.edu/

Alternative Access Methods: http://www.wws.princeton.edu/~ota/
http://www.access.gpo.gov/ota/
http://bilbo.isu.edu/ota/ota.html
http://www.ota.gov/ [defunct]
ftp://otabbs.ota.gov/pub/ [defunct]
telnet://public@otabbs.ota.gov [defunct]

Resource Summary: Shortly after the disbandment of OTA at the end of 1995, the official OTA sites became unavailable. However, a number of other sites volunteered to host the information. The OTA Web site included directory information for both OTA programs and staff, the OTA publications catalog, OTA report briefs, selected full-text OTA reports in ASCII (and some in PDF), and a listing of work in progress. The work in progress section included contact information for the project director and an estimated publication date.

While the report briefs are helpful, press releases are not included on the server, and they would have been a useful addition. The work in progress section was not kept up-to-date. Many of the listed projects had estimated publication dates that were long past even before the OTA closed down. The full text reports are the most substantial portion of this site.

Subject Headings: Congress; Reports—Full Text

SuDoc Number: Y 3.T 22/2:7/ *OTA Reports*

[204] Penny Hill Press

Sponsoring Agency: Congressional Research Service (CRS)

Primary Access: http://www.clark.net/pub/pennyhill/pennyhill.html

Resource Summary: This commercial press offers delivery of Congressional Research Service publications. This site includes a classified listing of available reports with abstracts.
The information offering could be improved by adding access to the abstracts by author and by date.

Subject Headings: Bibliographic Databases; Congressional Research

[205] U.S. Commission on Immigration Reform

Sponsoring Agency: Commission on Immigration Reform

Primary Access: http://www.utexas.edu/lbj/uscir/

Resource Summary: This site features sections including the Commission's Mandate, People, and Activities. The Activities section includes subsections titled Reports to Congress, Research Papers, Site Visits, Research Activities, and Congressional Testimony. The site also has a section describing internship opportunities with the Commission.

This is a useful site for those researching immigration reform policies and legislation.

Subject Heading: Immigration

[206] U.S. Senate Bibliographies

Sponsoring Agencies: North Carolina State University (NCSU); Senate

Primary Access: http://www.lib.ncsu.edu/stacks/senatebibs/

Alternative Access Method: ftp://ftp.ncsu.edu/pub/ncsu/senate/

Resource Summary: NCSU produces monthly bibliographies of Senate hearings, prints, and publications from title page proofs received weekly from the Senate Library. The bibliographies go back to the 98th Congress.

These bibliographies are primarily of interest to the depository library community, but they could also be useful for researchers.

Subject Headings: Depository Libraries; Legislation—Bibliographies

[207] The United States Capitol

Sponsoring Agency: Architect of the Capitol

Primary Access: http://www.aoc.gov/

Resource Summary: The Congress' home gets its own Web page with this site. Information available here includes the Capitol's construction history, its museum rooms and major spaces, its architects, the Capitol grounds, works of art at the Capitol, current projects at the Capitol, a brief bibliography, and answers to frequently asked questions.

For basic information about the building, this is a useful and informative site. It could be improved with the addition of more images of the exterior and interior of the building.

Subject Heading: Capitol Building

[208] United States Congress

Sponsoring Agencies: Congress; Government Printing Office (GPO)

Primary Access: http://www.gpo.gov/congress/

Resource Summary: This GPO page on Congress includes links to a variety of congressional publications made available by GPO. These include the *Congressional Pictorial Directory*, the *Official Congressional Directory*, *Economic Indicators*, calendars of the House and Senate, and reports and documents from the House and Senate. Access to congressional reports and documents is via a WAIS search.

Most of the documents on this page will be readily accessible from other major congressional and legislative sites such as the House Web server, THOMAS, and GPO Access. The page does provide a useful overview of what is available, but it does not clearly identify how far back in time the different publications are available.

Subject Headings: Legislation; Members of Congress—Directories

SuDoc Numbers: X *Congressional Record*
Y 1.2/2: *House Calendars*
Y 1.3/2: *Senate Calendars*
Y 4.Ec 7: *Economic Indicators*
Y 4.P 93/1:1/ *Official Congressional Directory*
Y 4.P 93/1:1 P/ *Congressional Pictorial Directory*

[209] The United States Senate

Sponsoring Agency: Senate

Primary Access: http://www.senate.gov/

Alternative Access Method: gopher://gopher.senate.gov/

Resource Summary: The Senate site provides information on contacting senators and a mechanism for senators and senate committees to disseminate electronic documents. Various press releases, senate reports, and testimony are accessible by senator and by committee. Other sections give information about Senate committees, the history of the Senate, a virtual tour of the Senate, and a Senate art and photo gallery.

Not nearly as ambitious as the House of Representatives' Web Page, the Senate site does provide useful information about senators and the Senate itself. While it includes information on legislative action, it is not a site for full-text legislative information.

Subject Headings: Members of Congress—Directories; Reports—Full Text

Congress: Directories

[210] CapWeb: The Internet Guide to the U.S. Congress

Sponsoring Agencies: Congress; Net.Capital, Inc.

Primary Access: http://www.capweb.net/directory.html

Resource Summary: This commercial site offers more than just directories to Congress, but the directories that are available here are easy-to-use. Information on each member includes Washington address, phone number, fax number, e-mail address, URL, party affiliation, picture, and committee assignments. Access is available by name, state, party, and committee.

This site makes an excellent directory for basic information on members of Congress.

Subject Headings: Members of Congress—Directories

[211] Congress.Org

Sponsoring Agencies: Capital Advantage; Issue Dynamics, Inc.

Primary Access: http://www.congress.org/

Resource Summary: Congress.Org provides a variety of congressional directories. It includes links to secondary pages including Congressional Directory, Finding Your Member, House Committees, and Senate Committees. The Congressional Directory page provides access alphabetically, by state, and by committee. The Find Your Member page uses ZIP codes to find specific members. The records for each member provide detailed information including term number, room number, home town, previous occupation, education, birthplace, religion, spouse, and more. It even provides some information on the member's staffers. It includes House and Senate committee assignments and room numbers for the current session.

This is one of the best and most comprehensive Internet-accessible directories for Congress.

Subject Heading: Members of Congress—Directories

[212] Congressional Directories

Sponsoring Agencies: Congress; University of Michigan. Documents Center

Primary Access: http://www.lib.umich.edu/libhome/Documents.center/congdir.html

Alternative Access Method: gopher://una.hh.lib.umich.edu/11/socsci/poliscilaw/uslegi/ [defunct]

Resource Summary: Dating back to the 103rd Congress, the directory entries include party designation, state, name, Washington office address, phone number, and fax number. There are separate lists for both the House and the Senate as well as for e-mail addresses and Web sites. The listings by chamber are in ASCII file, so e-mail addresses and Web sites are not hyperlinked from those lists.

This site is useful for its archives of previous Congressional sessions as well as the current one.

Subject Heading: Members of Congress—Directories

[213] Congressional E-mail directory

Primary Access: http://www.webslingerz.com/jhoffman/congress-email.html

Resource Summary: This directory of e-mail addresses is made available by WebslingerZ and Jeffrey Hoffman. This site only provides an e-mail address for members of Congress with no additional directory information or party affiliation. Access is by state or via keyword search. The e-mail addresses and names of the individuals that have e-mail addresses are linked to a mailto: URL for sending e-mail straight from the directory. Members of Congress without e-mail addresses are also listed, although the site encourages the public to demand that they get an e-mail address.

Subject Heading: Members of Congress—Directories

[214] The Zipper

Sponsoring Agency: Stardot Consulting, Ltd.

Primary Access: http://www.voxpop.org/zipper/

Resource Summary: Submit a five-digit ZIP code to this unofficial site and get the district number, name, address, phone number, party affiliation, and e-mail address for the representative and senator in that area. There is also a built-in correction mechanism to help correct any possible errors. Because it uses a ZIP code database, the Zipper only claims an accuracy of about 85 percent. While the built-in correction mechanism option helps, be sure to verify the information returned by this database in an official source.

Subject Headings: Congressional Districts; ZIP Codes

Congress: Voting

[215] American Voter on the Job

Sponsoring Agencies: Congress; Congressional Quarterly, Inc. (CQ)

Primary Access: http://voter.cq.com/cq_job.htm

Resource Summary: This site from CQ provides information on specific members of Congress. This includes general profiles, recent floor speeches, bills introduced, and committee votes. Search access is by last name, ZIP code, or state.

This makes an excellent supplement to the floor vote information available on the Congressional Quarterly's VoteWatch site, since that site does not include voting records from committees. The profiles and floor speeches also make this a site worth visiting for anyone interested in the voting records and activities of particular members of Congress.

Subject Headings: Members of Congress; Voting Records

[216] C-SPAN Roll Call Vote Search

Sponsoring Agency: C-SPAN

Primary Access: http://congress.nw.dc.us/c-span/subjvote.html

Resource Summary: This page presents a single search box for roll call votes. A user can enter a keyword and choose the chamber and which session to search. It does not offer a search by member or bill number. The results provide a list of names in a scroll box for yeas, nays, and those not voting.

Subject Heading: Voting Records

[217] Congressional Observer Publications: U.S. Congressional Votes

Sponsoring Agency: Congressional Observer Publications, Inc.

Primary Access: http://www.proaxis.com/~cop/congvts.htm

Resource Summary: This commercial service provides all votes from the current congressional session and older ones back to 1993. Nonsubscribers have access to the current day's votes and featured votes. The free version gives only the numbers of votes, the subscriber version includes voting records for each member of Congress on each vote.

Subject Heading: Voting Records

[218] Congressional Quarterly's VoteWatch

Sponsoring Agencies: Congress; Congressional Quarterly, Inc. (CQ)

Primary Access: http://pathfinder.com/CQ/

Resource Summary: This commercial site uses a forms interface to request voting records for "key votes." Available search options include name, state, ZIP code, and/or voting district of a particular member of Congress; time period of voting (up to 18 months); popular bill name or keyword; and broad subject areas. The results give the yea or nay votes by phrases that describe the bill, rather than by a bill number. These phrases are hypertext linked to descriptions of the vote written by *Congressional Quarterly* (CQ) staff writers.

This can be an extremely useful resource for the public. It should state more clearly that it does not include all voting records but only those that CQ defines as "key votes."

Subject Heading: Voting Records

[219] Find Out How Congress Voted

Sponsoring Agencies: Congress; Congressional Quarterly, Inc. (CQ)

Primary Access: http://pathfinder.com/cgi-bin/congress-votes

Resource Summary: This is another access point to CQ's voting records. Enter a ZIP code on this site to view the voting records for members of Congress from that area. Note that these are only the key votes, and not all of the votes that occurred.

Subject Heading: Voting Records

[220] Voter Information Services

Sponsoring Agency: Voter Information Services, Inc.

Primary Access: http://www.vis.org/

Resource Summary: This site provides ratings of the voting record for each member of Congress. The ratings come from a range of organizations, both conservative and liberal. More specific voting records are available for a fee.

Note that the site is only updated four times a year. The commercial products may be of interest to the political consultant, but other Internet sources can provide the same kind of information for the casual user.

Subject Heading: Voting Records

CHAPTER 5: EDUCATION

Given that a great deal of the research and development of the Internet occurred in the educational realm, finding significant government sources on education should come as no surprise. Many sites target teachers and students in grades kindergarten through 12 (commonly referred to as K-12) with lesson plans, interactive learning programs, and materials written specifically for children. Many government agencies have also seen the public relations wisdom of providing basic material for educational users. This chapter includes sites with resources for a wide range of educational endeavors. The sites and agencies in this chapter focus primarily on education. Many of the sites listed elsewhere in this directory offer lesser links for educators and/or students, but those offerings are relatively minor compared to the rest of the site's resources.

The featured sites in this chapter are AskERIC and Online Educational Resources from the Ames Research Center. The AskERIC site provides access to much of the ERIC Clearinghouses' educational material. The Online Educational Resources page links to numerous educational sites with a focus on science education.

[221] AskERIC

Sponsoring Agency: Educational Resources Information Center (ERIC)

Primary Access: http://ericir.syr.edu/

Alternative Access Methods: gopher://ericir.syr.edu/
ftp://ericir.syr.edu/

Resource Summary: AskERIC is the Internet-based education information service of the ERIC System. Major sections of the AskERIC system are the AskERIC Question and Answer service, ERIC lesson plans, the ERIC database, and links to the ERIC clearinghouses. Users of the Question and Answer service can submit questions on educational topics to AskERIC and receive responses by e-mail. A collection of lesson plans is available in the Virtual Library section. This area also features AskERIC InfoGuides, an ERIC Conference Schedule, Television Series Companion Materials, and other educational resources.

Access to the ERIC database, from 1989 forward, is via HTML forms using the PLS, Inc., search engine. This does permit simple Boolean searches and field searching. Full-text offerings at this site include the AskERIC InfoGuides and the ERIC Digests. Archives of messages posted on education listservs are also available.

With the Question and Answer service, the ERIC database, and the lesson plans this site is an important starting point for educators' introduction to the Internet. The ERIC database access could be expanded to include older information, and it could use more advanced search options such as setting limits and increasing the maximum retrieval set size. More lesson plans could be added and more could be converted to HTML. Still, these are minor criticisms of an excellent and important educational resource.

Subject Headings: Educational Resources; Lesson Plans

[222] Online Educational Resources

Sponsoring Agency: Ames Research Center (ARC)

Primary Access: http://quest.arc.nasa.gov/OER/

Resource Summary: Although this is a government-sponsored site, it lists much more than just government resources for education. Links to educational resources are organized in the following categories: Educational Organizations and Programs; University and College Resources; Resource Lists and Subject Trees on Education; Museums and Expositions Online; Online Libraries; Collaborative Technology Resources, Projects, and Datasets; and Search Pages and Resource Discovery Engines.

This is an excellent finding aid for general educational resources, especially for science education.

Subject Heading: Finding Aid—Education

Education: General

[223] Directorate for Education and Human Resources

Sponsoring Agency: National Science Foundation (NSF). Directorate for Education and Human Resources (EHR)

Primary Access: http://red.www.nsf.gov/

Resource Summary: The EHR page includes links to the various EHR divisions including Graduate Education; Undergraduate Education, Experimental Program to Stimulate Competitive Research (EPSCoR); and Elementary, Secondary, and Informal Education. Other links connect to Technology in Education, Science at Home, Teacher Links, Programs, and Publications. Many of these links connect to non-governmental sites. However, the publications category includes selected full-text documents, and the Programs link lists numerous EHR-sponsored programs descriptions.

With its many links to external resources, this site is a good starting point for science education materials.

Subject Headings: Science Education; Technology Education

The education resources in this chapter are subdivided broadly into three sections. The first section covers sites that are considered general educational resources as well as sites that do not fit under the other categories. This section runs from entry numbers 223 to 236. Higher Education, the second section, features resources related to college, university, and other adult educational institutions and covers entries 237-260. The third section, K-12, contains resources targeted at the K-12 community and includes entries 261-288.

[224] ERIC Clearinghouse on Assessment and Evaluation

Sponsoring Agencies: Educational Resources Information Center (ERIC); Clearinghouse on Assessment and Evaluation

Primary Access: http://ericae2.educ.cua.edu/

Alternative Access Method: http://ericae2.educ.cua.edu/intbod.stm [non-frames version]

Resource Summary: In addition to information on the ERIC system, the Clearinghouse itself, and the ERIC bibliographic database, this site offers much more. Substantial resources can be found under the headings Test Locator, Full Text Documents, Assessment FAQ, and K-12 Educational Resources. The Test Locator connects to searchable bibliographic databases of tests from Buros, Pro-Ed, and the Educational Testing Service.

Numerous documents are listed in a side frame under the heading Assessment and Evaluation. These include alternative assessment, goals and standards, personnel evaluation, test construction, and test reviews. Other headings include News and Test Schedules; Essays, Bibliographies, and Resources; and Information About Other Testing Projects. Under the K-12 Educational Resources section, there is a link to a list of educational resources from Canada, standards and benchmarks, and information on a K-12 assessment e-mail list.

There is a substantial body of test and assessment information on this site. Anyone interested in educational assessment and learning measurement should explore the documents here.

Subject Headings: Educational Assessment; Testing

[225] ERIC Clearinghouse on Counseling and Student Services

Sponsoring Agencies: Educational Resources Information Center (ERIC); Clearinghouse on Counseling and Student Services (CASS)

Primary Access: http://www.uncg.edu/~ericcas2/

Alternative Access Method: gopher://ericir.syr.edu/11/Clearinghouses/16houses/CASS

Resource Summary: The ERIC CASS site includes a description of the Clearinghouse, a text and audio greeting, information about ordering CASS publications, and upcoming CASS conferences. As is the case at most ERIC clearinghouses, digests from CASS are available in the supervisory collection, the assessment collection, and other single digests. The Gopher site consists of a single text file describing the Clearinghouse.

At this point, the ERIC/CASS *Digests* are the major resource at this site. They are also developing a Counselor and Therapist Support System (CATS 2), which may contain useful resources when it is completed.

Subject Headings: Counseling; Student Services

[226] ERIC Clearinghouse on Education Management

Sponsoring Agencies: Educational Resources Information Center (ERIC); Clearinghouse on Education Management (CEM)

Primary Access: http://darkwing.uoregon.edu/~ericcem/

Alternative Access Method: gopher://ericir.syr.edu/11/Clearinghouses/16houses/CEM

Resource Summary: In addition to some descriptive information about this ERIC Clearinghouse, there are the usual links to information about CEM publications and to full-text ERIC digests from ERIC/CEM. The Gopher site consists of a single text file describing the Clearinghouse.

At this point, there is not as much material on this site as there is on some of the other ERIC Clearinghouse sites.

Subject Heading: Educational Management

[227] ERIC Clearinghouse on Information and Technology

Sponsoring Agencies: Educational Resources Information Center (ERIC); Clearinghouse on Information and Technology (ERIC/IT)

Primary Access: http://ericir.syr.edu/ithome/

Alternative Access Method: gopher://ericir.syr.edu/11/Clearinghouses/16houses/CIT

Resource Summary: The ERIC Information and Technology site features ERIC/IT *Digests* and various other documents from the Clearinghouse. The News and Information category only includes one undated press release. The New section offers information on new ERIC/IT monographs. The Publications page provides links to monographs, *Digests*, minibibliographies, and an ERIC/IT newsletter.

Subject Headings: Educational Technology; Library Science

[228] ERIC Clearinghouse on Languages and Linguistics

Sponsoring Agencies: Educational Resources Information Center (ERIC); Clearinghouse on Languages and Linguistics (CLL)

Primary Access: http://www.cal.org/ericcll/

Alternative Access Method: gopher://ericir.syr.edu/11/Clearinghouses/16houses/CLL/ERIC_LL

Resource Summary: This site features ERIC *Digests* and *Minibibs* from the ERIC CLL. The About ERIC/CLL link retrieves a document describing the Clearinghouse and its services. Other links include ERIC/CLL Publications, ERIC/CLL Newsletter, and the Center for Applied Linguistics.

Subject Heading: Language Arts Education

[229] ERIC Clearinghouse on Teaching and Teacher Education

Sponsoring Agencies: Educational Resources Information Center (ERIC); Clearinghouse on Teaching and Teacher Education

Primary Access: http://www.ericsp.org/

Alternative Access Method: gopher://ericir.syr.edu/11/Clearinghouses/16houses/ERIC_SP

Resource Summary: The ERIC Clearinghouse on Teaching and Teacher Education Web site features information on the Clearinghouse and Internet resources for teachers. Under the Becoming a Teacher heading, the site links to a number of full-text *InfoCards*. The Internet Resources for Teachers section links to pages on lesson plans and placement services. The Clearinghouse Publications heading features links to *Digests* from the Clearinghouse and a publications list.

Subject Headings: Lesson Plans; Teaching

[230] The ERIC Database

Sponsoring Agency: Educational Resources Information Center (ERIC)

Primary Access: http://ericir.syr.edu/Eric/

Alternative Access Method: http://www.cua.edu/www/eric_ae/search.html

Resource Summary: The Web version of the ERIC database uses the Web forms feature to search and supports Boolean operators and field searching. The database only covers information back to 1989. The initial form only includes room for three search words, but the form can be expanded as needed. Search results are displayed in a very basic HTML format. The alternate site lists numerous other sites that offer partial or whole access to ERIC, sometimes through telnet or tn3270 connections.

Providing free access to the most popular index for education makes these ERIC access points a very significant resource for the education community.

Subject Heading: Bibliographic Databases

SuDoc Numbers: ED 1.310: *Resources in Education*
ED 1.310/4: *Current Index to Journals in Education*

[231] ERICPages

Sponsoring Agencies: Educational Resources Information Center (ERIC); National Library of Education

Primary Access: http://www.aspensys.com/eric/

Alternative Access Method: gopher://aspensys3.aspensys.com:70/11/education/eric

Resource Summary: Although hosted on a contractor's server rather than on a government computer, this site has a well-organized overview of the ERIC system and its component clearinghouses. Featured links include AskERIC, the National Parent Information Network, the National Library of Education, and other information on the ERIC system. *ERIC Review* is available on the Gopher.

This is a useful alternative entry point to the ERIC system of resources if AskERIC is unavailable. It is also useful for verifying addresses or other contact information.

Subject Heading: Educational Resources

SuDoc Number: ED 1.331: *ERIC Review*

[232] The Learning Web at the U.S. Geological Survey

Sponsoring Agency: Geological Survey (USGS)

Primary Access: http://www.usgs.gov/education/

Resource Summary: The Learning Web is dedicated to K-12 education, exploration, and life-long learning. The site contains links to educational resources offered by the USGS along with a section for teaching earth sciences information, a link to volcano information, and a Living in the Learning Web page that investigates topics that affect people every day. One of the most intriguing is the Ask a Geologist service, where K-12 students can send questions via e-mail to the program and a USGS geologist will reply.

This is useful for teachers interested in finding geologic educational resources and for students looking for basic earth science information.

Subject Headings: Geology; Science Education; Volcanoes

[233] NASA Langley Office of Education

Sponsoring Agency: Langley Research Center (LaRC)

Primary Access: http://edu-www.larc.nasa.gov/edu/OED.html

Resource Summary: The Langley Research Center Office of Education was created to effectively promote and facilitate services, resources, and programs between the Center and the larger education community. The Office of Education provides an education program from kindergarten through the postdoctoral level for students, teachers, and university faculty. Unfortunately, all the information on this site is merely descriptive. Other than descriptions of various programs and facilities of the Office of Education, the only links are to higher level servers, the page creator, and one of its institutes.

The audience for this site would benefit from actual online publications, lesson plans, program applications, and a higher information content in general.

Subject Heading: Science Education

[234] National Center for Education Statistics

Sponsoring Agency: National Center for Education Statistics (NCES)

Primary Access: http://www.ed.gov/NCES/

Alternative Access Methods: gopher://gopher.ed.gov:10000/
ftp://ftp.ed.gov/ncesgopher/

Resource Summary: Providing a wealth of educational statistics, the NCES Web site provides numerous areas for visitors to browse. The site starts with information on the NCES with a link to information on NCES and a What's New section, which features recently released publications and datasets as well as new features of the site. The body of online publications can be found under the headings Publications, Data and Surveys, Education At-A-Glance, and Frequently Asked Education Questions. Within the Publications section, frequently referenced statistical reports are available in HTML format. Other reports are available in PDF format, while some of the older reports are on the Gopher server in zipped WordPerfect 5.1 or Word 2.0a formats.

Other top level categories include Projects with Partners, which describes collaborative efforts between NCES and other organizations; Locate an Expert at NCES, which helps find an NCES expert; and a Search NCES option with keyword search capability for the HTML portion of their Web site. Note that the Search NCES option will not search within the text of PDF reports or documents on the Gopher server.

For anyone searching for statistics related to any form of education, this site should be the first place to visit. Although statistical reports are only available from the past few years, some of the reports include time series data. In addition, the major reports are in HTML, which permits easy browsing and keyword searching.

Subject Headings: Educational Statistics; Statistics

SuDoc Numbers: ED 1.109: *Condition of Education*
ED 1.120: *Projections of Education Statistics*
ED 1.302:P 94 *Projections of Education Statistics to 2006*
ED 1.326: *Digest of Education Statistics*
ED 1.327: *Youth Indicators*
ED 1.329: *Dropout Rates in the United States*

[235] U.S. Department of Education

Sponsoring Agency: Department of Education (ED)

Primary Access: http://www.ed.gov/

Alternative Access Method: gopher://gopher.ed.gov/

Resource Summary: This site contains the usual mission statements, staff directory, electronic publications, press releases, and more. The basic presentation is available within the following categories: Welcome, News, Guides, Money Matters, Secretary's Initiatives, People and Offices, Programs and Services, Publications, Other Sites, Search, and Picks of the Month. The Gopher and the Web pages are not exactly the same—some links from the Web pages point to resources on the Gopher server.

As one of the most obvious starting points for information on and about education, this site packs a great deal of information into its various categories. While much of the information was first made available on the Gopher server, most is now available in the Web pages.

Subject Heading: Educational Resources

SuDoc Numbers: ED 1.8:ST 9/5/ *The Student Guide: Financial Aid from the Department of Education*
ED 1.8:T 22/3/ *A Teacher's Guide to the U.S. Department of Education*
ED 1.41: *Progress of Education in the United States of America*
ED 1.303/2: *OERI Bulletin*

[236] Urban Education Web

Sponsoring Agencies: Educational Resources Information Center (ERIC); Clearinghouse on Urban Education

Primary Access: http://eric-web.tc.columbia.edu/

Alternative Access Method: gopher://ericir.syr.edu/11/Clearinghouses/16houses/CUE

Resource Summary: The Web portion is known as UEWeb (Urban Education) and is dedicated to urban students, their families, and the educators who serve them. The site describes the Clearinghouse on Urban Education and has a link to information on urban/minority families that is housed on the National Parent Information Network. The Publications category lists publications of the Clearinghouse with links to those available full-text online. Many of the online publications are also accessible under the Major Subject Areas category, with sections on equity and cultural diversity, urban teachers, curriculum and instruction, compensatory education, and administration and finance. Another link connects to resources of interest to Historically Black Colleges and Universities (HBCUs).

This site features numerous full-text publications of interest to those involved with urban education at the primary, secondary, and higher education levels.

Subject Headings: Higher Education; Minorities; Urban Education

Education: Higher Education

[237] Air Force Institute of Technology

Sponsoring Agency: Air Force Institute of Technology (AFIT)

Primary Access: http://www.afit.af.mil/

Resource Summary: The AFIT site covers some of the major AFIT educational directions including graduate education and professional continuing education. The site also features an online course catalog and class schedule.

This site provides an excellent overview to AFIT and its programs.

Subject Headings: Air Force; Higher Education—Military

[238] Air University

Sponsoring Agency: Air University

Primary Access: http://www.au.af.mil/

Resource Summary: This site includes the University's course catalog, faculty and staff directories, an Air University Press publications catalog, and a database of ongoing research at the University. Special projects include SPACECAST 2020 and 2025—a Chief of Staff of the Air Force study to explore and share ideas on air and space capabilities for the future.

The site provides a well-organized and informative page about the University and is useful for students and those interested in research at Air University.

Subject Headings: Air Force; Higher Education—Military

[239] Army Logistics Management College

Sponsoring Agency: Army Logistics Management College (ALMC)

Primary Access: http://www.almc.army.mil/

Resource Summary: The Army Logistics Management College site features information on the College and its schools. It offers an online course catalog and an online version of *Army Logistician*.

Subject Headings: Higher Education—Military; Military Logistics

SuDoc Number: D 101.69: *Army Logistician*

[240] Command and General Staff College

Sponsoring Agency: Command and General Staff College

Primary Access: http://www-cgsc.army.mil/

Resource Summary: This site offers information on the College, its training programs, and its organizations. It features online versions of *Military Review* and *Prairie Warrior*.

Subject Heading: Higher Education—Military

SuDoc Number: D 110.7: *Military Review*

[241] Computational Science Education Project

Sponsoring Agency: Oak Ridge National Laboratory (ORNL)

Primary Access: http://csep1.phy.ornl.gov/csep.html

Alternative Access Method: http://csep2.phy.ornl.gov/csep.html [mirror]

Resource Summary: The Computational Science Education Project (CSEP) page provides an introduction to high performance computing issues as a preparation for research and studies in computational science and computational engineering. The intended audience is students in science and engineering at the advanced undergraduate level and higher. This site includes a constantly changing textbook in HTML and sample lectures in HTML. The project is mirrored at about a dozen other sites, which are also listed on this page.

The textbooks, known as e-books, can be navigated with an image map or a table of contents. The image maps have had problems on occasion. This site features useful material for undergraduates in computer science and/or electrical engineering.

Subject Headings: Computer Science—Education; Electronic Books

[242] Defense Language Institute Foreign Language Center

Sponsoring Agency: Defense Language Institute (DLI)

Primary Access: http://www.dli.army.mil/

Alternative Access Method: telnet://lingnet.army.mil

Resource Summary: This DLI site is set up to complement the DLI's mission to train, sustain, and evaluate foreign language skills in the DoD and other government agencies. Thus, the site offers information about DLI programs in the main categories of Train, Sustain, Evaluate, and About DLI. In addition, it has a small section titled Support Activities. The telnet URL connects to LingNet, the Defense Language Institute's bulletin board system.
The site is primarily of interest to those eligible for and interested in DLI language training.

Subject Heading: Higher Education—Military

[243] Division of Graduate Education

Sponsoring Agency: National Science Foundation (NSF). Division of Graduate Education

Primary Access: http://red.www.nsf.gov/EHR/GERD/index.html

Resource Summary: This resource describes a number of the Division's programs and initiatives that offer assistance to graduate students in the sciences. Some of the programs are specifically aimed at minorities and/or women.

This site is well organized and features basic information about the programs.

Subject Headings: Grants—Education; Higher Education; Minorities; Women

[244] Division of Undergraduate Education

Sponsoring Agency: National Science Foundation (NSF). Division of Undergraduate Education (DUE)

Primary Access: http://www.ehr.nsf.gov/EHR/DUE/start.htm

Resource Summary: The DUE focuses on improving undergraduate education in sciences, mathematics, and engineering. These Web documents describe the agency and its programs as well as staff listings, award announcements, and press releases. Other DUE publications available on this Web site include the DUE newsletter and program and proposal guides.

This is a useful resource for anyone interested in DUE or any of its programs.

Subject Headings: Higher Education—Undergraduate; Science Education

[245] ERIC Clearinghouse for Community Colleges

Sponsoring Agencies: Educational Resources Information Center (ERIC); Clearinghouse for Community Colleges

Primary Access: http://www.gseis.ucla.edu/ERIC/eric.html

Alternative Access Method: gopher://ericir.syr.edu/11/Clearinghouses/16houses/CCC

Resource Summary: The Web site features an audio file of a speech by President Clinton, a description of the ERIC system, some ERIC digests and bibliographies, community college links, and information on contacting the Clearinghouse. The Gopher consists of a single text file describing the Clearinghouse and some bibliographies produced by the Clearinghouse.

While this site is not as rich in resources as some of the other ERIC Clearinghouses, it is a good starting point for information on community colleges.

Subject Headings: Community Colleges; Higher Education

[246] ERIC Clearinghouse on Adult, Career, and Vocational Education

Sponsoring Agencies: Educational Resources Information Center (ERIC); Clearinghouse on Adult, Career, and Vocational Education (ACVE)

Primary Access: http://coe.ohio-state.edu/cete/ericacve

Alternative Access Method: gopher://ericir.syr.edu/11/Clearinghouses/16houses/CACVE

Resource Summary: The ERIC Clearinghouse on Adult, Career, and Vocational Education contains a substantial number of publications online. These include ERIC *Digests* from ACVE and other publications under the headings Myths and Realities, Trends and Issues Alerts, and Practice Application Briefs. These publications are in HTML format on the Web server and ASCII format on the Gopher server. The site also has general background information on ACVE, a staff directory, and links to related sites.

Subject Headings: Adult Education; Vocational Education

[247] ERIC Clearinghouse on Higher Education

Sponsoring Agencies: Educational Resources Information Center (ERIC); Clearinghouse on Higher Education (HE)

Primary Access: http://www.gwu.edu/~eriche/

Alternative Access Method: gopher://ericir.syr.edu/11/Clearinghouses/16houses/CHE

Resource Summary: This ERIC Clearinghouse offers descriptive information on its activities and publications. Information is available under the headings HE Clearinghouse, New and Noteworthy, and FAQ. Publications are found under the Library heading and include ERIC *Digests* from HE and Critical Issues Bibliography Sheets. The ERIC Reports section offers access to a catalog of reports.

Subject Heading: Higher Education

[248] Graduate School, USDA

Sponsoring Agency: Department of Agriculture (USDA). Graduate School

Primary Access: http://grad.usda.gov/

Alternative Access Methods: gopher://grad.usda.gov/
telnet://bbs.grad.usda.gov:23/

Resource Summary: This site contains information about the School, including its course catalog, frequently asked questions, and online registration.

Subject Headings: Agricultural Education; Higher Education—Agriculture

[249] Marine Corps University

Sponsoring Agency: Marine Corps University

Primary Access: http://www-mcu.mqg.usmc.mil/

Resource Summary: This is a newer site with many links still under construction. Major categories include Marine Corps University Headquarters, Marine Corps Research Center, Doctrine, Resident Courses, Non Resident Courses, Professional Military Education (PME), and PME Courses. The site includes descriptive information on different aspects of the University and its programs. It does not yet have detailed course information, but it does include a database of faculty expertise.

This site needs further development, but it still offers a sense of what the Marine Corps University is involved in.

Subject Headings: Higher Education—Military; Marines

[250] Minority University Space Interdisciplinary Network

Sponsoring Agency: Goddard Space Flight Center (GSFC)

Primary Access: http://muspin.gsfc.nasa.gov/

Alternative Access Method: gopher://muspin.gsfc.nasa.gov/

Resource Summary: Minority University Space Interdisciplinary Network (MU-SPIN) is designed for Historically Black Colleges and Universities (HBCUs), and Other Minority Universities (OMUs). The focus of the program is on the transfer of advanced computer networking technologies to HBCUs and OMUs and their use for supporting multidisciplinary research. Many of the substantive resources are located in the MU-SPIN Resource Center, which is on the Gopher server. Other links from the Web server point to other related Web sites, and the usual agency information.

MU-SPIN offers services such as hands-on training of faculty and students in accessing resources available over the Internet; hands-on training of technical staff in local area and campus network installation, management, and user support; technical sessions at annual conferences; and technical video lectures on network-related issues.

For minority colleges and universities, this is an important resource for high-tech and computer networking information and training.

Subject Headings: Computer Networking; Higher Education; Minorities

[251] NASA Academy

Sponsoring Agencies: Ames Research Center (ARC); Dryden Flight Research Center; Goddard Space Flight Center (GSFC); Marshall Space Flight Center; National Aeronautics and Space Administration (NASA)

Primary Access: http://university.gsfc.nasa.gov/SA/academy.html

Resource Summary: This is the central page for various NASA Academy summer programs for college students in science, math, engineering, or computer science. NASA Academy programs are available from both the Goddard and Marshall Space Flight Centers. The listings from Goddard are more extensive, with descriptions of the Academies from 1993 through the present. Goddard's links also include a copy of the application for the next summer's Academy.

The information on these pages will be of interest to college students interested in careers or further study with NASA and also to their counselors.

Subject Heading: Higher Education

[252] National Defense University

Sponsoring Agency: National Defense University (NDU)

Primary Access: http://www.ndu.edu/

Resource Summary: This military institute of higher education has a Web site with an online course catalog. Other categories include links to the university's component colleges, which include Armed Forces Staff College, Industrial College of the Armed Forces, Institute for National Strategic Studies, Information Resources Management College, and the National War College. Each of the links contains descriptive information about the colleges.

This Web site presents a well-organized and informative overview of the NDU. The NDU catalog and the descriptions of the colleges provide a substantial body of information.

Subject Heading: Higher Education—Military

SuDoc Number: D 5.416: *McNair Papers* (series)

[253] Naval Postgraduate School

Sponsoring Agency: Naval Postgraduate School (NPS)

Primary Access: http://www.nps.navy.mil/

Alternative Access Method: gopher://peacock.nps.navy.mil/

Resource Summary: Like many university home pages, the Naval Postgraduate School provides information on the NPS, its departments, NPS policies, and a course catalog and schedule (from Peacock, the Gopher server).

This site is useful for students and staff at NPS as well as for outsiders interested in public information from and/or about the school.

Subject Heading: Higher Education—Military

[254] Office of Postsecondary Education

Sponsoring Agency: Department of Education (ED). Office of Postsecondary Education (OPE)

Primary Access: http://www.ed.gov/offices/OPE/

Resource Summary: In addition to announcements, the OPE directories, and an overview of OPE divisions, this site features one section with information for students and another with information for schools. The student section contains the full text of *The Student Guide: Financial Aid from the U.S. Department of Education* in HTML and ASCII format, and other information on financial aid, including the Direct Loan Program, the Free Application for Federal Student Aid (FAFSA), FAFSA Express (downloadable software), State Guaranty Agencies, and State Higher Education Agencies. Under the Schools category, there are a number of links to information about higher education programs and the Fund for the Improvement of Postsecondary Education.

This is a very useful site with a substantial body of information sources of interest to both students and financial aid offices.

Subject Headings: Financial Aid; Student Services

SuDoc Numbers: ED 1.8:ST 9/5/ *The Student Guide: Financial Aid from the Department of Education*
ED 1.40/5: *Direct Loan Newsletter*

[255] Office of University Programs at NASA Goddard Space Flight Center

Sponsoring Agency: Goddard Space Flight Center (GSFC). Office of University Programs (OUP)

Primary Access: http://university.gsfc.nasa.gov/

Resource Summary: The OUP site describes the mission of the office and links to pages with descriptions of its programs for institutions and individuals. It also has links to the NASA Academy, the Graduate Student Researchers Program, and the NASA/University of Maryland Baltimore County (UMBC) Research Fellowship "Kiosk" program. Other OUP programs with links include the Resident Researchers Associateship Program, the Director's Discretionary Fund, and the Research and Technology Report in full text, HTML format.

This is a useful page for students, faculty, or administrators at universities that want to increase connections with NASA.

Subject Headings: Higher Education; Space—Research

[256] Project EASI: Easy Access for Students and Institutions

Sponsoring Agency: Department of Education (ED)

Primary Access: http://easi.ed.gov/

Resource Summary: The site describes Project EASI (Easy Access for Students and Institutions) and gives the current status of this project. Project EASI is a collaborative effort among a diverse group of government, business, and education leaders initiated by the U.S. Department of Education to reengineer the country's postsecondary education financial aid delivery system. The site features sections titled Planning For Your Education, Applying to School, Receiving Financial Aid, and Repaying Your Loan. Another option allows public feedback on the project.

Subject Headings: Financial Aid; Project EASI

[257] The Uniformed Services University of the Health Sciences

Sponsoring Agency: Uniformed Services University of the Health Sciences (USUHS)

Primary Access: http://www.usuhs.mil/

Resource Summary: This site provides basic information about the University in the following categories: What's New at USUHS! USUHS Mission; Message from the Dean; USUHS Location and Directions; Admission Requirements; Graduate Programs; and Graduate School of Nursing. Pages for USUHS departments, a personnel directory, and the *Fourth Year Course Catalog* are accessible.

This is a well-organized site with basic descriptive information about the institution. A link to a description of the research programs at the University would be helpful.

Subject Headings: Higher Education—Medical; Higher Education—Military

[258] United States Air Force Academy

Sponsoring Agency: Air Force Academy

Primary Access: http://www.usafa.af.mil/

Alternative Access Method: ftp://ftp.usafa.af.mil/

Resource Summary: Main top level categories include Admissions, Athletics, Staff Chaplain, and Dean of Faculty. There seems to be more information in the Admissions and Athletics categories than the other two. Other options include searchable e-mail address directories, one for cadets and another for faculty and staff.

Subject Headings: Air Force; Higher Education—Military

[259] United States Military Academy

Sponsoring Agency: Military Academy (USMA)

Primary Access: http://www.usma.edu/

Resource Summary: This West Point Web site features the following categories: USMA Admissions Information; USMA Agencies and Departments; USMA Supported Mailing Lists; Other Places to Look; Search for E-mail Addresses; Online Utilities, References, and Journals; USMA Internet Policies and Guidelines; and USMA Web Weekly Usage Statistics. The admissions information is fairly detailed, but under the Agencies and Departments heading, only a few departments and support agencies are included along with *Mathematica Militaris*, an online journal. Most of the online utilities are Web related.

Subject Headings: Electronic Periodicals; Higher Education—Military; *Mathematica Militaris*; West Point

[260] The United States Naval Academy

Sponsoring Agency: Naval Academy (USNA)

Primary Access: http://www.nadn.navy.mil/

Resource Summary: This site contains information typical of college and university Web pages. The top level listing links to information on the Naval Academy Superintendent, General Information About the Academy, Departments and Divisions, Information Resources, and an index to all the USNA Web pages. It does not contain a course catalog, but that might be available on the USNA Gopher (which is only available to USNA personnel).

This is a well-designed and informative site for USNA staff and students as well as others interested in the Naval Academy.

Subject Headings: Higher Education—Military; Navy

[261] Ames Teacher Resource Center

Sponsoring Agency: Ames Research Center (ARC)

Primary Access: http://quest.arc.nasa.gov/trc/trc2/trchome.html

Resource Summary: The page is almost exclusively descriptive of the Center, which is located at the National Aeronautics and Space Administration Ames Research Center, Moffett Field, California. It serves educators in the western states (Alaska, Arizona, California, Hawaii, Idaho, Montana, Nevada, Oregon, Utah, Washington, Wyoming) and trust territories of the Pacific Islands. This page provides contact information, hours, and a listing of the types of educational materials available.

This site is most useful for those who want to visit or contact the Center. It would be even more useful if the lesson plans, curriculum materials, or publications were available online.

Subject Heading: Science Education

[262] ArtsEdge

Sponsoring Agency: John F. Kennedy Center for the Performing Arts

Primary Access: http://artsedge.kennedy-center.org/

Alternative Access Method: http://artsedge.kennedy-center.org/aetext.html [text version]

Resource Summary: ArtsEdge is a major resource for educators and students in the arts. A lengthy bibliographic list of curricula can be browsed and searched by keyword or topic. There is a long list of arts organizations, news and calendars from the Kennedy Center, a jobs listing, links to related Web sites, and more. Included in the For Students section are pages titled Young Artist Showcase and Student Research Pages, and links to Web sites both by and for students.

Well designed, this site should be a primary stopping point for anyone involved in arts education.

Subject Heading: Art—Study and Teaching

[263] CEC ERIC Clearinghouse on Disabilities and Gifted Education

Sponsoring Agencies: Council for Exceptional Children (CEC); Educational Resources Information Center (ERIC); Clearinghouse on Disabilities and Gifted Education

Primary Access: http://www.cec.sped.org/ericec.htm

Alternative Access Method: gopher://ericir.syr.edu/11/Clearinghouses/16houses/ERIC_EC

Resource Summary: This site includes text files describing ERIC and the Clearinghouse. It has numerous full-text ERIC *Digests* in categories including Cultural Diversity, Early Childhood, Gifted, Instruction and Management, Other Disabilities, Policies and Procedures, and Learning Disabilities. It also provides some online fact sheets and minibibliographies.

Subject Headings: Disabilities; Gifted and Talented Education

[264] Census Bureau Educational Materials

Sponsoring Agency: Bureau of the Census

Primary Access: http://www.census.gov/ftp/pub/edu/www/

Resource Summary: This site includes selected HTML documents describing how Census data can be used in K-12 education as well as selected curricula and teaching resources for specific topics such as diversity.

It would be even more useful to educators if additional teaching resources using Census materials were added to the site. Unfortunately, due to budget constraints, the education curriculum program at the Census Bureau has been suspended. No updates or revisions to these materials is forthcoming.

Subject Headings: Curricula; Demographics—Educational Resources

[265] Division of Elementary, Secondary, and Informal Education

Sponsoring Agency: National Science Foundation (NSF). Division of Elementary, Secondary, and Informal Education (ESIE)

Primary Access: http://red.www.nsf.gov/EHR/ESIE/index.html

Resource Summary: The Division of Elementary, Secondary, and Informal Education page includes a description of ESIE and has information on the director. The two major categories are Programs and Initiatives, and Publications. Under Programs and Initiatives, information on eligibility, deadlines, and a description is available for the following programs: Teacher Enhancement Program, Instructional Materials Development Program, Informal Science Education Program, Presidential Awards for Excellence in Science and Mathematics Teaching, and Young Scholars Program. The three publications consist of two program guidelines and a list of summer opportunities for teachers.

This site is most useful for those interested in the specific programs of ESIE.

Subject Headings: Mathematics Education; Science Education

[266] ECENET-L [e-mail list]

Sponsoring Agencies: Educational Resources Information Center (ERIC); Clearinghouse on Elementary and Early Childhood Education (EECE)

Primary Access: mailto:listserv@vmd.cso.uiuc.edu "subscribe ecenet-l" in body

Alternative Access Method: http://ericps.ed.uiuc.edu/eece/listserv/ecenet-l.html

Resource Summary: ECENET-L is a listserv discussion list for people interested in early childhood education. The list invites participation from representatives of professional associations and government agencies, faculty and researchers, students and teachers, parents, and librarians. The intent is to make this a list for people to come together to share ideas, resources, problems, and solutions related to early childhood education.
The address for this list may change. Check at the Web site for up-to-date information.

Subject Headings: E-mail Lists; Elementary Education

[267] ECPOLICY-L [e-mail list]

Sponsoring Agencies: Educational Resources Information Center (ERIC); Clearinghouse on Elementary and Early Childhood Education (EECE)

Primary Access: mailto:listserv@postoffice.cso.uiuc.edu "subscribe ecpolicy"

Alternative Access Method: http://ericps.ed.uiuc.edu/eece/listserv/ecpol-l.html

Resource Summary: ECPOLICY-L provides a forum for discussion of policy issues related to young children. Suggested topics include providing information about the development, care, and education of young children for state, federal, and local policymakers; raising the awareness of policymakers, educators, the media, and parents about the issues important to the future of young children; and encouraging responsiveness of the early childhood community to public issues affecting children.

Subject Headings: Child Care; E-mail Lists; Elementary Education

[268] Eisenhower National Clearinghouse

Sponsoring Agencies: Department of Education (ED). Office of Educational Research and Improvement (OERI); Department of the Interior (DOI); Eisenhower National Clearinghouse for Mathematics and Science Education

Primary Access: http://www.enc.org/

Alternative Access Methods: telnet://enc.org/
gopher://gopher.enc.org/

Resource Summary: Funded by OERI, the Eisenhower National Clearinghouse (ENC) offers many links to governmental and non-governmental resources. The Resource Finder provides access to a bibliographic database of electronic and print curriculum resources. It also features categories titled Digital Dozen (a monthly top 12 online resources list), Online Documents (including HTML versions of journal articles), and Other ENC Online Publications. Two categories link to external resources: Lessons and Activities, and Educational Resources.

This site provides many documents with high quality content in the broad fields of mathematics and science education. The access points to the bibliographic database and the many full-text online sources are easy to navigate.

Subject Headings: Bibliographic Databases; Educational Resources; Lesson Plans; Mathematics Education; Science Education

The ERIC Clearinghouse for Science, Mathematics, and Environmental Education (ERIC/CSMEE) is one of 16 clearinghouses in the ERIC system. The Clearinghouse collects and processes all the science, mathematics, and environmental education materials included in the ERIC database, and also offers an array of products and services of special interest to educators. Though the Clearinghouse strives to meet the needs of all learners, special attention is given to the needs of minorities, females, and those who are differently abled.

Science Education Resources

Mathematics Education Resources

Environmental Education Resources

[269] ERIC Clearinghouse for Science, Mathematics, and Environmental Education

Sponsoring Agencies: Educational Resources Information Center (ERIC); Clearinghouse for Science, Mathematics, and Environmental Education (CSMEE)

Primary Access: http://www.ericse.org/

Alternative Access Methods: http://www.ericse.ohio-state.edu/
gopher://gopher.ericse.ohio-state.edu/

Resource Summary: The Web server for the ERIC Clearinghouse for Science, Mathematics, and Environmental Education (ERIC/CSMEE) features bulletins and digests from the Clearinghouse. There is also information about CSMEE, links to other educational resources, an option for sending comments to the Clearinghouse, and a link to the Gopher.

The Gopher also includes the bulletins and digests, as well as some categories not readily accessible from the Web page. These include a Publications List, ERIC/CSMEE Journal Coverage, ERIC/CSMEE Partners, and ERIC/CSMEE Information Central. The Information Central area includes lesson plans and information guides.

For those in science, math, and/or environmental education, this site offers numerous resources. The availability of documents in full-text format combined with links to other resources make this a useful information resource.

Subject Headings: Environmental Education; Mathematics Education; Science Education

[270] ERIC Clearinghouse on Elementary and Early Childhood Education

Sponsoring Agencies: Educational Resources Information Center (ERIC); Clearinghouse on Elementary and Early Childhood Education (EECE)

Primary Access: http://ericps.crc.uiuc.edu/

Alternative Access Methods: http://ericps.ed.uiuc.edu/
gopher://ericps.ed.uiuc.edu/

Resource Summary: The ERIC Clearinghouse on Elementary and Early Childhood Education offers descriptive information on the Clearinghouse, links to external education resources, connections to other components in the ERIC system, and lists of its available publications. These include ready searches, newsletters, excerpts from books, and ERIC *Digests* from EECE, some of which are available in Spanish. This site also lists electronic discussion groups sponsored by ERIC/EECE.

This is a useful collection of materials on elementary education, early childhood education, and parenting.

Subject Headings: Elementary Education; Parents and Parenting

[271] ERIC Clearinghouse on Reading, English, and Communications

Sponsoring Agencies: Educational Resources Information Center (ERIC); Clearinghouse on Reading, English, and Communications (REC)

Primary Access: http://www.indiana.edu/~eric_rec/

Alternative Access Method: gopher://gopher.indiana.edu:1067/11/eric_rec/gopher

Resource Summary: Like other ERIC Clearinghouses, this one features information on ERIC and on the REC. It also lists its available publications and ERIC *Digests*. The presentation is quite different, with headings such as ERIC Who, The Book Store, and Interactive ERIC Online. The Family Learning category features parent involvement materials, read-along stories, helpful tips for parents, and information on a senior partners pen pal program. A number of conferences and workshops are listed under Professional Development Resources, and available videos are under Videos.

The page design features many graphics and some large video files. However, the organization could be condensed and made easier to navigate with the presence of a button bar and/or more distinct, descriptively titled categories.

Subject Headings: Communications; Language Arts Education; Reading

[272] ERIC Clearinghouse on Rural Education and Small Schools Program Description

Sponsoring Agencies: Educational Resources Information Center (ERIC); Clearinghouse on Rural Education and Small Schools (CRESS)

Primary Access: http://www.ael.org/erichp.htm

Alternative Access Method: gopher://ericir.syr.edu:70/11/Clearinghouses/16houses/CRESS

Resource Summary: The Clearinghouse on Rural Education and Small Schools offers a brief description of the CRESS, a list of staff, and a section called Hot Items. A topical section features ERIC *Digests*, prepacked searches, and directories on subject categories such as American Indians and Alaska Natives, Mexican Americans, Migrant Education, Outdoor Education, Rural Education, and Small Schools.

Different from the other Clearinghouses in organization, this site manages to present substantial resources in its topical specialties.

Subject Headings: American Indians; Minorities; Rural Education

[273] ERIC Clearinghouse on Social Studies/Social Science Education

Sponsoring Agencies: Educational Resources Information Center (ERIC); Clearinghouse on Social Studies/Social Science Education (ChESS)

Primary Access: http://www.indiana.edu/~ssdc/eric-chess.html

Alternative Access Method: gopher://ericir.syr.edu/11/Clearinghouses/16houses/CHESS

Resource Summary: The ERIC/ChESS home page features the usual description of ERIC and of ChESS, a publications list, and a list of ERIC/ChESS digests. Other top level links connect to other ERIC sites and other social studies resources.

Unlike many of the other ERIC sites, not even the *Digests* are available in full text from the ChESS site. As of early 1997, this page had not been updated since 1995.

Subject Heading: Social Studies Education

[274] GLOBE Program

Sponsoring Agencies: Environmental Protection Agency (EPA); National Aeronautics and Space Administration (NASA); National Oceanic and Atmospheric Administration (NOAA); National Science Foundation (NSF)

Primary Access: http://www.globe.gov/

Alternative Access Method: http://globe.fsl.noaa.gov/

Resource Summary: Global Learning and Observations to Benefit the Environment (GLOBE) is a worldwide network of students, teachers, and scientists working together to study and understand the global environment. This site offers information on the program and is used by participants in the program. The program involves students in taking environmental measurements. Over 3,000 schools have already submitted over hundreds of thousands of data reports based on observations by GLOBE student scientists. The data is accessible to anyone, and there is information on how new schools can register to be included in the program.

With participating schools from all over the world, this kind of collaborative project demonstrates how the Internet can be used in a K-12 environment. In addition, the Web site is well designed and makes navigation easy even for those not familiar with GLOBE.

Subject Headings: Environmental Education; Global Change; Science Education

[275] IITA K-12 Project

Sponsoring Agency: Lewis Research Center (LeRC)

Primary Access: http://www.lerc.nasa.gov/Other_Groups/K-12/

Resource Summary: The Information Infrastructure Technology and Applications (IITA) K-12 Program is part of a governmentwide high-performance computing program. It is an educational program designed to increase the computer literacy of K-12 students. This site includes K-12 project descriptions, a list of accomplishments, teacher training programs, and classroom projects. It also provides links to other external governmental and non-governmental resources.

Subject Headings: Computer Science—Education; High Performance Computing

[276] Learning Page of the Library of Congress

Sponsoring Agency: Library of Congress (LC)

Primary Access: http://lcweb2.loc.gov/ammem/ndlpedu/

Resource Summary: This page is designed specifically for educators and is intended to assist educators (and students) in finding materials within the National Digital Library collection on the Web.

The page is well designed and well organized. The access points meet many information needs.

Subject Headings: Lesson Plans; Libraries; National Digital Library Program

[277] MIDDLE-L [e-mail list]

Sponsoring Agencies: Educational Resources Information Center (ERIC); Clearinghouse on Elementary and Early Childhood Education (EECE)

Primary Access: mailto:listserv@vmd.cso.uiuc.edu "subscribe middle-l" in body

Alternative Access Method: http://ericps.ed.uiuc.edu/eece/listserv/middle-l.html

Resource Summary: MIDDLE-L provides a place for sharing ideas, resource information, and problems and their solutions related to middle level education. It is intended for middle level educators, teacher educators, and others interested in education at the middle level.

The address for this list may change. Check at the Web site for up-to-date information.

Subject Headings: E-mail Lists; Middle School Education

[278] NASA Classroom of the Future

Sponsoring Agencies: National Aeronautics and Space Administration (NASA); Wheeling Jesuit College

Primary Access: http://www.cotf.edu/

Resource Summary: The NASA Classroom of the Future program at Wheeling Jesuit College sponsors this page. It features descriptive information about the program, including a virtual tour of the Center for Educational Technologies at Wheeling. The three main projects of the Classroom of the Future program are Astronomy Village, BioBLAST, and Exploring the Environment. All three are computer-based instructional modules, but not necessarily Web based. This site provides information on the projects and their current stage of development.

This site is useful for those interested in computer-based instruction and science education.

Subject Headings: Educational Technology; Science Education

[279] NASA K-12 Internet: Live from the Hubble Space Telescope

Sponsoring Agencies: Ames Research Center (ARC); National Aeronautics and Space Administration (NASA)

Primary Access: http://quest.arc.nasa.gov/livefrom/hst.html

Alternative Access Method: mailto:listmanager@quest.arc.nasa.gov with "subscribe updates-hst" in body

Resource Summary: In the spring of 1996, for the first time, students in grades K-12 had a chance to use the Hubble Space Telescope (HST). The Space Telescope Science Institute (which operates Hubble) contributed three HST orbits to the Passport to Knowledge educational project for this purpose. The planets Neptune and Pluto have been selected as targets for original observations by students who will serve as Hubble Space Telescope "Co-Investigators," working alongside some of America's foremost astronomers.

This site provides news, featured events, a video broadcast schedule, and background information on the project. The mailing list is designed to provide the latest announcements on the project. Other mailing lists are available for discussion of the project.

This is another excellent example of how the Internet can aid in collaborative projects with students and teachers in K-12.

Subject Headings: Hubble Telescope; Space

[280] National Child Care Information Center

Sponsoring Agencies: Administration for Children and Families; Educational Resources Information Center (ERIC); National Child Care Information Center (NCCIC)

Primary Access: http://ericps.crc.uiuc.edu/nccic/

Alternative Access Method: http://ericps.ed.uiuc.edu/nccic/

Resource Summary: NCCIC is an Adjunct ERIC Clearinghouse for Child Care cosponsored by the Child Care Bureau of the Administration for Children and Families and the ERIC Clearinghouse on Elementary and Early Childhood Education. The site provides information on the Center and its sponsors, a list of child care organizations, a Tribal Child Care Resource Directory, and the full text of NCCIC's *Child Care Bulletin*.

The collection of child care resources available here makes this a useful site for anyone searching the Internet for information on child care issues.

Subject Heading: Child Care

[281] National Clearinghouse for U.S.-Japan Studies

Sponsoring Agencies: Clearinghouse on Social Studies/Social Science Education (ChESS); Educational Resources Information Center (ERIC); Indiana University East Asian Studies Center

Primary Access: http://www.indiana.edu/~japan/

Resource Summary: This Web site features many links to material related to Japan. The primary focus is on educational material, and almost all of it is in English. Two major databases are the Clearinghouse's bibliographic index available at the Database Search link and its database of K-12 lesson plans on Japan under the heading Teaching Resources. Other top level categories include Publications, Japan Links, and Our Affiliates.

This is an excellent site for those interested in teaching children about Japan.

Subject Headings: Japan; Lesson Plans

[282] The National Education Goals Panel

Sponsoring Agency: National Education Goals Panel

Primary Access: http://www.negp.gov/

Resource Summary: The National Education Goals Panel is a bipartisan and intergovernmental body of federal and state officials created to monitor, assess, and report annually on state and national progress toward achieving the National Education Goals, commonly known as Goals 2000. The Web site offers a description of the panel and of National Education Goals. It also features sections titled Commonly Asked Questions, Popular Publications, Progress Toward the Goals, Publication Request Form, and Data Search.

Subject Headings: Educational Assessment; Goals 2000

[283] National Parent Information Network

Sponsoring Agencies: Educational Resources Information Center (ERIC); Clearinghouse on Elementary and Early Childhood Education (EECE)

Primary Access: http://ericps.crc.uiuc.edu/npin/

Alternative Access Methods: http://ericps.ed.uiuc.edu/npin/
gopher://ericps.ed.uiuc.edu/11/npin

Resource Summary: The National Parent Information Network (NPIN) provides information and communications capabilities to parents and those who work with parents. Full-text materials have been reviewed by persons outside the ERIC system for reliability and usefulness. Publications, brochures, and other materials that are merely listed here have not been reviewed and are included for informational purposes only.

Major categories on this site include Parent News, Parents AskERIC, Resources for Parents, Resources for Those Who Work With Parents, ERIC Information and Materials, and Internet Resources for Parents and Those Who Work With Parents. The Resources for Parents page features full-text publications including ERIC *Digests* and other brochures, pamphlets, and newsletters.

While many of the resources available through NPIN are available directly from the ERIC Clearinghouses or other sources, pulling them together in a clear organization makes the materials more readily accessible.

Subject Heading: Parents and Parenting

[284] PARENTING-L [e-mail list]

Sponsoring Agencies: Educational Resources Information Center (ERIC); Clearinghouse on Elementary and Early Childhood Education (EECE)

Primary Access: mailto:listserv@postoffice.cso.uiuc.edu with "subscribe" in body

Alternative Access Method: http://ericps.ed.uiuc.edu/eece/listserv/parent-l.html

Resource Summary: PARENTING-L is an Internet discussion group on topics related to parenting children (including child development, education, and child care) from birth through adolescence. Discussion ranges from family leave and parental rights issues, to parents as partners in their children's education, to the changes in children as they leave high school and begin college or get their first job.

Subject Headings: E-mail Lists; Parents and Parenting

[285] Question: NASA K-12 Internet Initiative

Sponsoring Agencies: Ames Research Center (ARC); National Aeronautics and Space Administration (NASA)

Primary Access: http://quest.arc.nasa.gov/

Resource Summary: The K-12 Internet Initiative, also known as Quest, aims to provide support and services for schools, teachers, and students to fully utilize the Internet, and its underlying information technologies, as a basic tool for learning. One major approach to this is to sponsor collaborative projects with students, teachers, and NASA scientists. This site includes reports and other documents from the projects and announcements of upcoming ones.

Another major section lists sources of financial support from a variety of governmental and non-governmental grant agencies. This site also features categories including Using the Net in School, Which Schools Are Online, and NASA Online Resources. In most of these categories, the pages contain text with hypertext links throughout.

The organization of material requires a bit more reading than other sites and it makes finding items within these documents more time consuming. However, this is a good starting point for teachers who are new to the Net.

Subject Headings: Educational Resources; Grants—Education

[286] REGGIO-L [e-mail list]

Sponsoring Agencies: Educational Resources Information Center (ERIC); Clearinghouse on Elementary and Early Childhood Education (EECE)

Primary Access: mailto:listserv@postoffice.cso.uiuc.edu with "subscribe reggio-l" in body

Alternative Access Methods: gopher://ericir.syr.edu/11/Listservs/REGGIO-L
http://ericps.ed.uiuc.edu/eece/listserv/reggio-l.html

Resource Summary: REGGIO-L is a listserv discussion list co-owned by the Merrill-Palmer Institute at Wayne State University and ERIC Clearinghouse on Elementary and Early Childhood Education at the University of Illinois. REGGIO-L is a place where early childhood educators, researchers, students, parents, and others who have an ongoing interest in the Reggio Emilia approach to early childhood education can discuss the educational philosophy behind the program, teaching approaches and essential elements of the program, its adaptation in the United States, and other related topics.

The Gopher site contains an archive of postings to this list. The address may change, but check the Web site for a current e-mail address for the listserv.

Subject Headings: E-mail Lists; Elementary Education

[287] SAC-L [e-mail list]

Sponsoring Agencies: Educational Resources Information Center (ERIC); Clearinghouse on Elementary and Early Childhood Education (EECE)

Primary Access: mailto:listserv@postoffice.cso.uiuc.edu "subscribe sac-l" in body

Alternative Access Method: http://ericps.ed.uiuc.edu/eece/listserv/sac-l.html

Resource Summary: SAC-L is a discussion list for people interested in school-age care, planning, resources, activities, funding, staff development, and related subjects.

Subject Headings: Child Care; E-mail Lists

[288] TEACHART - Art Curriculum Teachers [e-mail list]

Sponsoring Agency: Smithsonian Institution

Primary Access: mailto:listserv@sivm.si.edu with "sub teachart name" in body

Resource Summary: This is an e-mail discussion list. It is sponsored and hosted by the Smithsonian for the National Museum of African Art (NMAA) Art Curriculum Teacher Conference.

Subject Headings: Art—Study and Teaching; E-mail Lists

CHAPTER 6: ENVIRONMENT

Government agencies have made a variety of environmental resources available on the Internet. This chapter includes environmental, biological, weather, climatological, public lands, oceanography, and pollution resources. Some of the information is aimed at research scientists, while other sites offer resources for the general public. See also the Earth Sciences section in Chapter 13 and the Science and the Energy subchapter in Chapter 16—Technology and Engineering.

No single finding aid encompasses all the topics that these sites offer. The two featured sites for this chapter—the Environmental Protection Agency and the new NOAA Web sites—offer access to some of the best environmental information available, especially when both are used.

[289] Environmental Protection Agency

Sponsoring Agency: Environmental Protection Agency (EPA)

Primary Access: http://www.epa.gov/

Alternative Access Methods: gopher://gopher.epa.gov/
ftp://ftp.epa.gov/

Resource Summary: This is the central, top level site for information from the EPA. Major divisions include You and Your Environment, featuring public information, and Collection of Resources, with more detailed information on the EPA and its divisions and programs. The Collection of Resources offers links to EPA offices, regions, laboratories, programs, initiatives, press releases, and an events calendar. Numerous EPA documents are available in HTML and/or PDF formats under the Publications link. The You and Your Environment section features access by kind of user, including the categories Kids; Students and Teachers; Concerned Citizens; Researchers and Scientists; Business and Industry; and State, Local; and Tribal Governments.

This is an excellent entry point into a vast quantity of EPA documents and data. By combining it with a search of the main NOAA site, you should easily find many of the Internet-accessible environmental resources.

Subject Headings: Consumer Information; Environmental Issues; Hazardous Waste

SuDoc Numbers: EP 1.21: *Catalog of Publications: Office of Science and Technology*
EP 1.111: *Monthly Hotline Reports*
EP 5.1:P 43/ *Office of Pesticides Programs Annual Report*

[290] NOAA

Sponsoring Agency: National Oceanic and Atmospheric Administration (NOAA)

Primary Access: http://www.noaa.gov/

Alternative Access Method: http://www.noaa.gov/noaa-image-home.html [imagemap version]

Resource Summary: This site is designed well and it includes a variety of information on the agency, including the categories NOAA in the News, NOAA's Proposed Budget, Frequently Asked Questions, Job Vacancy Announcements, Line and Program Offices, and more. Beyond agency information, most of the content links are to sources on various Web sites from the NOAA's component divisions and offices.

The major informational sections of this site are under the following topics: Rebuild Fisheries, Seasonal and Interannual Forecasts, Protected Species, Coastal Ecosystems Health, Long Term Global Change, Warnings and Forecasts, Navigation and Positioning, Satellites, Fleet, Environmental Information Services, and High Performance Computing and Communications.

Given the broad scope of environmental topics that NOAA agencies cover, this site can be used as a finding aid for environmental information that might fall under NOAA's domain. Used in conjunction with the EPA home page, it should help in finding the major government sources for environmental information.

Subject Headings: Atmospheric Studies; Global Change; Oceanography; Satellites

SuDoc Number: C 55.53 *NOAA Reports*

The Environment resources in this chapter are subdivided into five sections. The first section includes general resources as well as sites that do not fit under the other categories. This section runs from entry number 291-302. Biology, the second subchapter, features resources in the biological sciences and covers entries 303-318. The third section, Climate and Weather, covers climatology and weather resources in entries 319-335. Oceans, covering entry numbers 336-354, includes oceanographic resources and sites related to coastal science. The last subchapter, Pollution, features environmental sites that focus on pollution-related topics. This section covers entry numbers 355-365.

Environment: General

[291] *Access EPA*

Sponsoring Agency: Environmental Protection Agency (EPA)

Primary Access: http://www.epa.gov/Access

Alternative Access Methods: http://www.epa.gov/Contacts/Access/
gopher://gopher.epa.gov/11/Contacts/Access
telnet://epaibm.rtpnc.epa.gov/ [under Public Access, OLS, A]

Resource Summary: This is the full text of the third edition of *Access EPA*, the directory of environmental information resources. The 1993 version was available in HTML format with links to chapters and to sections. The 1995/96 edition is supposed to be available via an ftp server, but was not yet available in early 1997. The 1993 edition is still available on the Gopher server and at the alternate Web URL. It was, however, removed from the original Web site. The page makes a note that the 1995/96 version will not be available in HTML, but the latest version is available via the telnet URL.

This is one of the most useful directories for locating specific environmental information. It is unfortunate that the Web version has been removed, but at least the old version is still available on the Gopher and a current version is available via telnet.

Subject Heading: Environmental Issues—Directories

SuDoc Number: EP 1.8/13: Ac 2/ *Access EPA*

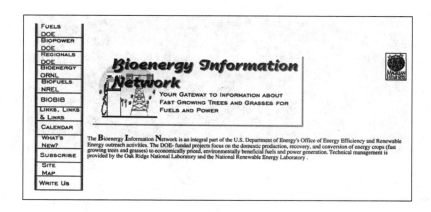

The Bioenergy Information Network is an integral part of the U.S. Department of Energy's Office of Energy Efficiency and Renewable Energy outreach activities. The DOE- funded projects focus on the domestic production, recovery, and conversion of energy crops (fast growing trees and grasses) to economically priced, environmentally beneficial fuels and power generation. Technical management is provided by the Oak Ridge National Laboratory and the National Renewable Energy Laboratory .

[292] Biofuels Information Network

Sponsoring Agencies: Oak Ridge National Laboratory (ORNL); National Renewable Energy Laboratory (NREL)

Primary Access: http://www.esd.ornl.gov/bfdp

Resource Summary: This page provides links to various research programs investigating liquid and gaseous fuels produced from dedicated energy crops such as grasses and fast-growing short-rotation trees. The projects focus on the domestic production, recovery, and conversion of these feedstocks to economically priced, environmentally beneficial fuels such as ethanol, methanol, and biodiesel. The major categories on the site are Fuels, Biopower, Bioenergy, Biofuels, and Regionals. Each category features numerous full-text reports, white papers, and program descriptions.

Included in these pages is the BioBib—a small bibliographic database of articles, conference proceedings, other reports of research in the biofuels area, and NREL's BioFuels Database. These databases, though small, provide over 1,000 citations to the BioFuels literature.

For anyone interested in what is happening with renewable energy and biofuels, this is an information-rich resource.

Subject Headings: Bibliographic Databases; Biofuels; Crops; Renewable Energy

[293] Bureau of Land Management National Home Page

Sponsoring Agency: Bureau of Land Management (BLM)

Primary Access: http://www.blm.gov/

Alternative Access Methods: http://www.blm.gov/nhp/text_nhp.html [text version]
ftp://ftp.blm.gov/pub/
http://www.gpo.gov/blm/

Resource Summary: The main categories on the BLM site are Message from the Director, Breaking News, What is the BLM?, State by State Information, BLM Points of Interest, Calendar of Events, and Public Contact Directory. The Breaking News section includes press releases, speeches, legislative actions, and regulatory actions. BLM Points of Interest lists BLM-managed lands organized by state. For each unit, it gives a brief description, location, contact person, phone number, and e-mail address if available. The State by State Information section provides links to Internet sites for state and regional BLM offices. Not all states are included in the BLM Points of Interest and State by State Information pages since the BLM primarily manages lands in several western states.

For anyone interested in the BLM, its management, BLM lands, recreational philosophy, and other aspects of the BLM, this is a site worth checking.

Subject Heading: Public Lands

SuDoc Numbers: I 53.1: *Bureau of Land Management Annual Report*
I 53.1/2: *Public Land Statistics*

[294] Chemicals in the Environment OPPT Chemical Fact Sheets

Sponsoring Agency: Environmental Protection Agency (EPA). Office of Pollution Prevention and Toxics (OPPT)

Primary Access: http://www.epa.gov/opptintr/chemfact/

Alternative Access Method: gopher://gopher.epa.gov/11/Offices/PestPreventToxic/Toxic/chemfact/chemical

Resource Summary: These fact sheets provide a brief summary of information on selected chemicals. Each fact sheet covers a particular chemical's identity, production and use, environmental fate, and health and environmental effects. The sheets also include a list of laws under which the chemical is regulated, phone numbers, and the names of EPA offices and other agencies one can call or contact for more information. Each fact sheet is also accompanied by a chemical summary—a technical support document that provides detailed technical information on the chemical named in the fact sheet. The files are formatted in ASCII.

Although these sheets are currently only available for selected chemicals, they provide a quick summary of useful information about each one.

Subject Heading: Chemical Information—Full Text

[295] Council on Environmental Quality

Sponsoring Agencies: Council on Environmental Quality (CEQ); Executive Office of the President

Primary Access: http://www.whitehouse.gov/CEQ/

Alternative Access Method: http://www.whitehouse.gov/CEQ/index-plain.html [text version]

Resource Summary: The CEQ site includes a keyword search engine and four main categories including More About CEQ, The Clinton Administration, NEPANet, and What's New. NEPANet gathers a wide variety of NEPA-related information including the text of the law, related regulations, and other similar links. The More About CEQ section includes a basic description and some recent *Annual Reports*.

There is little original content on the site; most of it consists of links to other related sites. The full text of the *Annual Reports* is one of the most useful features of the site.

Subject Headings: Environmental Issues; National Environmental Policy Act (NEPA)

SuDoc Number: PrEx 14.1: *Annual Report of the Council on Environmental Quality*

[296] Department of Energy NEPA Web

Sponsoring Agency: Department of Energy (DOE)

Primary Access: http://www.eh.doe.gov/nepa/

Resource Summary: This site summarizes some of the DOE's activities related to NEPA. The DOE NEPA Analyses page provides access to databases of information on DOE environmental impact statements (EIS), mitigation action plans, and environmental assessments. This includes access to the full text of some EISs. Other sections of this site include DOE NEPA Announcements, NEPA Links, DOE NEPA Tools, and DOE NEPA Process Information.

Subject Headings: Environmental Impact Statements; National Environmental Policy Act (NEPA)

[297] Environmental Management Web Information Services

Sponsoring Agency: Department of Energy (DOE). Office of Environmental Management (EM)

Primary Access: http://www.em.doe.gov/

Alternative Access Method: http://www.em.doe.gov/menu/?tindex.html [text version]

Resource Summary: This office's Web site covers a number of different topics, with links such as EM Public Information Resources; Regulatory Information, Waste Management, Environmental Restoration, Science and Technology, and Cross Cutting Programs. Reports, speeches, newsletters, and other documents are available in HTML format. There is a full-text search engine available for most pages that uses a Boolean-enabled WAIS search engine.

Subject Headings: Environmental and Occupational Health; Nuclear Energy; Pollution; Waste Management

[298] Environmental Research Laboratories

Sponsoring Agencies: Environmental Research Laboratories; National Oceanic and Atmospheric Administration (NOAA)

Primary Access: http://www.erl.noaa.gov/

Resource Summary: This page provides links to NOAA's Environmental Research Laboratories, which carry out fundamental research, technology development, and services to improve understanding of the Earth, its oceans and inland waters, the lower and upper atmosphere, and space. This page is useful primarily for connecting to the Web sites of the specific labs.

Subject Heading: Research Laboratories

[299] Mining Health and Safety Research, DOE

Sponsoring Agencies: Bureau of Mines; Department of Energy (DOE). Mining Health and Safety Research Program

Primary Access: http://www.usbm.gov/

Resource Summary: Formerly the site of the now-defunct Bureau of Mines, this is the current site for the DOE's Mining Health and Safety Research Program, one of the surviving pieces of the Bureau of Mines. This site provides information from that program, as well as a number of other links to former Bureau of Mines sites. For the information on the program, the site features categories titled Health and Safety Research Overview, Worker Health, Worker Safety, and Disaster Prevention.

With the Bureau of Mines being closed, the host part of the URL may change in the future.

Subject Headings: Environmental and Occupational Health; Mining

[300] ParkNet: The National Park Service Place

Sponsoring Agency: National Park Service (NPS)

Primary Access: http://www.nps.gov/

Alternative Access Method: http://www.nps.gov/index_txt.htm [text version]

Resource Summary: ParkNet is the NPS' official Web site and the primary source for information on America's National Parks. One featured category, Visit Your National Parks, provides access to brief information on each of the individual NPS units. Access is by name, state, region, or theme. There is also a featured park of the month. Other main sections include Links to the Past, for information on historical units; Park Smart, for education and interpretation links; Info Zone, for job opportunities, partnerships, planning, and legislation; and Nature Net, covering natural resources data and publications of the NPS.

For those interested in the NPS, specific parks, or park research, there is a great deal of information on this site. Information on each park unit should be expanded—some parks have detailed entries, but not all do. More links to related sites, such as unofficial pages or related pages, would also be helpful.

Subject Headings: National Parks; Public Lands

SuDoc Numbers: I 29.3/4 *Park Science*
I 29.114 *NPS Statistical Abstract*

[301] U.S. Department of the Interior

Sponsoring Agency: Department of the Interior (DOI)

Primary Access: http://www.doi.gov/

Resource Summary: Primarily an entry point to other DOI sites, Interior on the Web provides a number of access points to the DOI and its component agencies. The most substantive information is available under the main classifications, which are Index to Topics; What We Do, which includes links, arranged by subject, to DOI, and external sites; News and Press Releases from the DOI which is in HTML format and has links to press releases from component bureaus and services; Bureaus, Offices, and Committees, which has links to the many organizations under the DOI; and Customer Satisfaction Reports, which includes Agency Customer Satisfaction Reports for the year. Other classifications include Education and Outreach, which links to the DOI Eisenhower databases of educational programs and to other educational links; Training links to DOI training centers; Employment and Volunteer Opportunities; and Locator (People, Function, and Organization), which has links to various DOI agency directories. Other links connect to help files, a DOI Web search option, a Web tutor, and a disclaimer.

The site is well organized, and its multiple access points to various DOI resources make it easy to use. Some of the internal links lead to dead ends, but overall the site is well maintained.

Subject Heading: Conservation

SuDoc Number: I 1.116: *People Land and Water*

[302] Water Resources of the United States

Sponsoring Agency: Geological Survey (USGS)

Primary Access: http://water.usgs.gov/

Alternative Access Method: http://h2o.usgs.gov/

Resource Summary: As one of the major subject-oriented USGS Web sites, this one covers USGS materials related to water resources. *National Water Conditions* is featured prominently along with headings for Water Data, Publications and Products, Programs, and Your State. In a move to save money and provide a wider distribution for the *National Water Conditions*, it is no longer available in paper but only on the Internet. The electronic version contains tables, charts, and maps, in addition to explanatory text. Back issues are available back to October 1993. The *Selected Water Resources Abstracts* is a bibliographic database with citations back to 1939.

The *Selected Water Resources Abstracts* is available through a WAIS gateway and does not always work properly. However, most of the other data and information resources on this site are easily accessible and provide a significant amount of useful information on water resources.

Subject Headings: Bibliographic Databases; Streamflow Data; Water Supply

SuDoc Numbers: I 19.13/3: *National Water Summary*
I 19.42: *National Water Conditions*
I 1.94/2: *Selected Water Resources Abstracts*

Environment: Biology

[303] Biological Resources Division

Sponsoring Agency: Geological Survey (USGS). Biological Resources Division (BRD)

Primary Access: http://www.nbs.gov/

Alternative Access Method: http://www.nbs.gov/indextxt.html [text version]

Resource Summary: The National Biological Service was moved under the authority of the USGS and renamed the Biological Resources Division in September 1996. Thus, despite the host name, the NBS site is now the BRD site. Rich with graphic images of birds, plants, and insects, the site features information on a broad range of biological topics. The primary sections include National Biological Information Infrastructure, About the BRD, Science, News and Information, Partnerships, and Features. The Science page includes National Programs, Current Projects, Publications, and Science by State. The Publications page provides links to subsidiary organizations' publications pages as well as to *Biological Science Reports* and *Information and Technology Reports.* The News and Information section features press releases, fact sheets, and information bulletins.

With information for children, the general public, and researchers, this site offers one of the best government starting points for general biological information. The domain name may change on this site sometime in the future. If so, check under the main USGS site for the new location.

Subject Heading: Biology—Research

[304] CONSLINK - The Conservation Network [e-mail list]

Sponsoring Agency: Smithsonian Institution

Primary Access: mailto:listserv@sivm.si.edu with "sub conslink name" in body

Resource Summary: This e-mail discussion list, sponsored and hosted by the Smithsonian, covers conservation topics. The following electronic newsletters are distributed through CONSLINK: *Biodiversity Conservation Strategy Update*; *Boletin Humedales de Mexico*; *Conservation Digest - The Journal of Biopolitics*; *Environment Information Systems in Sub-Saharan Africa*; *Heron Conservation News*; *Captive Breeding Specialist Group News*; *Deer Specialist Group News*; *Society for Conservation Biology Newsletter*; *Tragopan - Pheasant Specialist Group Newsletter*; *Tropinet*; *USAID Environment and Natural Resources News*; and the *Biological Conservation Newsletter*.

Subject Headings: Conservation; E-mail Lists

[305] CRUST-L Crustacean Systematics, Distribution, Ecology [e-mail list]

Sponsoring Agency: Smithsonian Institution

Primary Access: mailto:listserv@sivm.si.edu with "sub crust-l name" in body

Resource Summary: This is an e-mail discussion list sponsored and hosted by the Smithsonian. Topics include crustacean systematics, distribution, and ecology.

Subject Headings: Conservation; Crustaceans; E-mail Lists

[306] Environmental Management Technical Center

Sponsoring Agency: Environmental Management Technical Center (EMTC)

Primary Access: http://www.emtc.nbs.gov/

Resource Summary: The EMTC is a river-related inventory, monitoring, research, spatial analysis, and information-sharing program. Their Web site offers a wide variety of biological, physical, spatial, graphic, and written information relating to the Upper Mississippi River System and adjoining geographic areas. It provides access to specific information on fish, vegetation, invertebrates, water quality, water levels, aerial photography, satellite imagery, scientific publications, and geographic information systems maps, coverages, and applications. The Other Services and Related Web Sites section provides training manuals and answers to frequently asked questions as well as points to other sites. Under Publications and Reports, a few Project Status Reports and the EMTC's newsletter, *River Almanac*, are available in PDF format.

This site offers a substantial amount of information for researchers interested in river ecology along the upper Mississippi.

Subject Headings: Ecology—Research; Fisheries Management; Mississippi River; Rivers; Water Supply

SuDoc Number: I 73.16: *River Almanac*

[307] Fish and Wildlife Service

Sponsoring Agency: Fish and Wildlife Service (FWS)

Primary Access: http://www.fws.gov/

Resource Summary: The Fish and Wildlife Service Web site provides information on the agency including recent announcements, employment opportunities, and press releases. Under the What We Do page, other FWS pages are available by office and subject. The subject listing is called keywords and includes pages titled Ecosystems, Habitat Conservation, Directives, Endangered Species, Ducks, Fire, Fish, Migratory Birds and Waterfowl, Refuges, Wetlands, Laws, and Wilderness.

Some of the categories have more substantial information than others, but overall, the FWS pages include a great deal of information. The variety of information will appeal to many different audiences.

Subject Headings: Endangered Species; Fish and Fishing; Wildlife

SuDoc Numbers: I 49.77: *Endangered Species Bulletin*
I 49.98 *National Survey of Fishing, Hunting, and Wildlife-Associated Recreation*
I 49.100/3: *Waterfowl Population Status*
I 49.100/4: *Waterfowl 2000: The Plan's Newsletter*
I 49.106/5: *Mourning Dove Breeding Population Status*
I 49.106/6: *American Woodcock Harvest and Breeding Population Status*
I 49.111:INTERNET *MAT Update*

[308] Forest Ecosystem Dynamics

Sponsoring Agency: Goddard Space Flight Center (GSFC)

Primary Access: http://forest.gsfc.nasa.gov/

Resource Summary: The Forest Ecosystem Dynamics (FED) Project is concerned with modeling and monitoring ecosystem processes and patterns in response to natural and anthropogenic effects. The FED Web site serves to disseminate project information, archive spatial and scientific data sets, and demonstrate the linking of ecosystem and remote sensing models. The site features some descriptive information on the project, along with a Fed Imagery Archive, a FED Spatial Data Archive, and an Ecosystem Modeling Interface. Most of the images are of a couple of areas in Maine, but the FED Spatial Data Archive includes unrestricted geographic information system data.

While most of this site will only be of interest to ecological researchers in the remote sensing and geographic information systems areas, some of the image archive may be useful for the general public.

Subject Headings: Ecology—Research; Forestry; Geographic Information Systems; Remote Sensing

[309] Great Lakes Information Network

Sponsoring Agencies: Environmental Protection Agency (EPA). Great Lakes National Program Office; Great Lakes Environmental Research Laboratory; National Telecommunications and Information Administration

Primary Access: http://www.great-lakes.net/

Alternative Access Methods: gopher://gopher.great-lakes.net:2200/
ftp://ftp.great-lakes.net/pub/great-lakes/
mailto:majordomo@great-lakes.net with "lists" in body
Resource Summary: The Great Lakes Information Network (GLIN) is a cooperative project that provides a place for people to find information relating to the Great Lakes region. Topics covered include the economy, the environment, human health, tourism, news, events, and weather. Many discussion lists on Great Lakes topics are hosted on the e-mail list server.

Subject Heading: Great Lakes

[310] Gulf States Marine Fisheries Commission

Sponsoring Agency: Gulf States Marine Fisheries Commission (GSMFC)

Primary Access: http://www.southwind.com/gsmfc/

Resource Summary: The Gulf States Marine Fisheries Commission (GSMFC) was authorized by Congress as an organization of the five states (Texas, Louisiana, Mississippi, Alabama, and Florida) whose coastal waters are part of the Gulf of Mexico. Their Web site describes their activities with categories such as Overview of the GSMFC; GSMFC Programs; Publications; Employment Opportunities; Upcoming Meetings; and Listing of Marine Toxic Blooms, Fish Kills, and Other Events in the Gulf of Mexico.

For those involved with interstate fisheries management issues in the Gulf of Mexico region, the information on the GSMFC projects should be very useful.

Subject Headings: Fisheries Management; Gulf of Mexico

[311] LLNL Biology and Biotechnology Research Program

Sponsoring Agency: Lawrence Livermore National Laboratory (LLNL). Biology and Biotechnology Research Program

Primary Access: http://www-bio.llnl.gov/

Resource Summary: Offering basic descriptive information on the Program and its research areas, this site features the following categories: Quick Program Overview, Research in Progress, Research Highlights, Publications, Program Organization and Funding Sources, Laboratory Facilites and Staff, and Educational Opportunities. The Publications section includes a list of publications authored by members of the Program.

With its brief descriptions of research conducted by the Program, past and present, this site will be primarily of interest to other researchers in biotechnology.

Subject Headings: Biology; Biotechnology

[312] MAMMAL-L Mammalian Biology [e-mail list]

Sponsoring Agency: Smithsonian Institution

Primary Access: mailto:listserv@sivm.si.edu with "sub mammal-l name" in body

Resource Summary: This is an e-mail discussion list on the biology of mammals. It is sponsored and hosted by the Smithsonian.

Subject Headings: E-mail Lists; Mammals

[313] National Marine Fisheries Service

Sponsoring Agency: National Marine Fisheries Service (NMFS)

Primary Access: http://kingfish.ssp.nmfs.gov/

Resource Summary: The detailed agency page includes recent press releases, a directory of data resources, information on grants for research and development, connections to the agency's various offices, and more. Full-text version of two reports, *Our Living Oceans* and *Fisheries of the United States*, are available by chapter. Graphics, such as images of southeastern U.S. marine fish and global sea surface temperature maps, provide a multimedia presence, as do the assorted whale songs and links to salmon Web pages. A publications list gives bibliographic information for ordering technical reports from the agency.

The NMFS offers a complementary variety of information resources, from the general interest whale songs to the research grant information. Anyone interested in marine fisheries should take a look at this page.

Subject Headings: Fish and Fishing; Statistics

SuDoc Numbers: C 55.1/2: *Our Living Oceans*
C 55.309/2-2: *Fisheries of the United States*

[314] Northwest Fisheries Science Center

Sponsoring Agencies: Northwest Fisheries Science Center; National Marine Fisheries Service (NMFS)

Primary Access: http://listeria.nwfsc.noaa.gov/

Resource Summary: This site describes the Center, its mission, and its programs. The Information Center page includes basic descriptive information on the Center. The Research Program's links include Coastal Zone and Estuarine Studies, Environmental Conservation, Fisheries Analysis and Monitoring, and Utilization Research. The Publications area offers bibliographic lists and a few full-text reports in the NOAA *Technical Memorandum* series.

This site should be useful to fisheries researchers and to those interested in fisheries management in the Northwest. One area of general interest is the live Web cam located in their Aqualab.

Subject Headings: Fish and Fishing; Fisheries Management

[315] Office of Inventory and Monitoring

Sponsoring Agencies: Geological Survey (USGS). Biological Resources Division (BRD). Office of Inventory and Monitoring

Primary Access: http://www.im.nbs.gov/

Resource Summary: Formerly the NBS Office of Inventory and Monitoring, it is now under the USGS BRD. This site aims to provide reliable information on the status and trends of the nation's plant and animal life. It also strives to identify populations, species, and ecosystems at risk before they become threatened or endangered; to determine the factors causing the observed trends; and to provide tools for forecasting future trends based on alternative policy and management decisions. The site offers categories for Software, Designing a Monitoring Program, Amphibians, Butterflies, Birds, and Other Species.

This site will be useful for anyone involved with an inventory and monitoring program as well as for those interested in these species for which monitoring programs are available.

Subject Headings: Amphibians; Birds; Butterflies; Endangered Species

[316] Office of Protected Resources

Sponsoring Agency: National Marine Fisheries Service (NMFS). Office of Protected Resources

Primary Access: http://kingfish.ssp.nmfs.gov/tmcintyr/prot_res.html

Resource Summary: The Office of Protected Resources coordinates marine species protection, conservation, and restoration. This Web site provides basic information documents about the Marine Mammals Protection Act and the Endangered Species Act and a listing of endangered and threatened species and recovery efforts. This list of protected or endangered marine mammals has a hyperlink from each species that provides information on the Office's program for that species.

Subject Headings: Endangered Species; Fish and Fishing; Mammals

[317] Pacific States Marine Fisheries Commission

Sponsoring Agency: Pacific States Marine Fisheries Commission (PSMFC)

Primary Access: http://www.psmfc.org/

Resource Summary: The Pacific States Marine Fisheries Commission, authorized by Congress in 1947, is one of three interstate commissions dedicated to resolving fishery issues. It serves as a forum for discussion, working for coastwide consensus of state and federal authorities. Their Web site offers information in categories named About PSMFC, PSMFC Projects, PSMFC Personnel, and PSMFC Publications. All of these sections offer more descriptive information about the PSMFC and its activities.

This site will be of interest to anyone in fisheries management in the area served by the PSMFC.

Subject Heading: Fisheries Management

[318] South Atlantic Fishery Management Council

Sponsoring Agency: South Atlantic Fishery Management Council

Primary Access: http://www.safmc.nmfs.gov/

Resource Summary: The South Atlantic Fishery Management Council is responsible for the conservation and management of fish stocks within the 200-mile limit of the Atlantic off the coasts of North Carolina, South Carolina, Georgia, and east Florida to Key West. Their site features information about the Council, including members, staff, committees, and advisory panels. It also includes the following categories: Council Press Page, with press releases and newsletters; the Council Publications Page; and the Council Searchable Databases. This last section does not yet have any link or searchable database available, but its presence on the page intimates that one or more will soon be available.

Subject Heading: Fisheries Management

Environment: Climate and Weather

[319] Arkansas-Red Basin River Forecast Center

Sponsoring Agencies: Arkansas-Red Basin River Forecast Center; National Weather Service (NWS)

Primary Access: http://info.abrfc.noaa.gov/

Alternative Access Method: gopher://info.abrfc.noaa.gov/
Resource Summary: This site includes forecast and precipitation data for this river basin, along with pictures of the rivers. Another link allows the public to submit precipitation and river stage reports.

Subject Headings: Rivers; Water Supply

[320] The Climate Diagnostics Center

Sponsoring Agency: Climate Diagnostics Center

Primary Access: http://www.cdc.noaa.gov/

Resource Summary: This site offers access to a variety of climatic data sets and software. Abstracts of some publications and Neural Network Predictions of El Niño are also available.

Given the highly technical nature of most of the material at this site, it is primarily of interest to researchers in climatology.

Subject Headings: Climatology; El Niño

[321] Climate Monitoring and Diagnostics Laboratory

Sponsoring Agency: Climate Monitoring and Diagnostics Laboratory

Primary Access: http://www.cmdl.noaa.gov/

Alternative Access Method: ftp://ftp.cmdl.noaa.gov/

Resource Summary: This site describes the lab and its research projects. It provides links to information on ongoing research at the lab including aerosols, carbon cycle, atmospheric ozone, and solar radiation. It also includes a staff directory, research data on the ftp server, and citations with abstracts to results published by lab scientists.

This well-organized site has substantial research-level information. It would be even more helpful to have the full text of articles published by lab scientists instead of simply abstracts.

Subject Headings: Atmospheric Studies; Climatology

[322] Climate Prediction Center

Sponsoring Agencies: Climate Prediction Center; National Centers for Environmental Prediction

Primary Access: http://nic.fb4.noaa.gov/

Alternative Access Methods: http://nic.fb4.noaa.gov/altindex.html [text version]
ftp://nic.fb4.noaa.gov/pub/nws/nmc/cac/htdocs/

Resource Summary: The Climate Prediction Center provides a wide variety of climatological data including long-term predictions, historical times series, analysis, assessment, and applications. Information on winds, stratospheric conditions, El Niño, temperature and precipitation long-term predictions, and special climatic condition summaries are available under the products and data headings on this page.

The site is useful for the weather and climate researcher, although some of the data will be of interest to the general public.

Subject Headings: Climatology; El Niño; Weather

SuDoc Numbers: C 55.129/2: *Climate Bulletin*
C 55.194: *Climate Diagnostics Bulletin*

[323] Decoded Offshore Weather Data

Sponsoring Agency: National Data Buoy Center (NDBC)

Primary Access: http://www.ems.psu.edu/cgi-bin/wx/offshore.cgi

Resource Summary: This site gives access to decoded offshore weather observations from numerous regions around the world. These observations are primarily from moored buoys and ships crossing the oceans and are provided as raw data.

The data comes from the National Data Buoy Center, and is much easier to browse and read on the Interactive Marine Observations site at http://www.nws. fsu.edu/buoy/.

Subject Headings: Oceanography; Weather

[324] Forecast Systems Laboratory

Sponsoring Agency: Forecast Systems Laboratory

Primary Access: http://www.fsl.noaa.gov/

Resource Summary: This site describes the lab and its research mission. Data products include a variety of Colorado weather data, analyses, and predictions. More specific information comes from the divisions, each of which has its own page: Aviation Division, Demonstration Division, Facility Division, Forecast Research, Modernization Division, and Systems Development Division.

Although it can be frustrating in that some of the data products are restricted to internal use only, this site offers useful data for the meteorologic researcher.

Subject Heading: Weather

[325] Geophysical Fluid Dynamics Laboratory

Sponsoring Agency: Geophysical Fluid Dynamics Laboratory (GFDL)

Primary Access: http://www.gfdl.gov/

Resource Summary: Beginning with a choice between explanatory introductory material or a full-color tour, this site presents categories including Research Projects, Computational Support, and Administration. The Research Projects include the subcategories Climate Dynamics, Radiation and Clouds, Middle Atmosphere Dynamics and Chemistry, Experimental Prediction, Oceanic Circulation, Observational Studies, Hurricane Dynamics, and Mesoscale Dynamics. The Research Projects area also has some online GFDL bibliographies. The Computational Support page provides links to data sets, software, and user guides.

This site provides a good overview of the lab and its projects. The more detailed information will be of most interest to researchers.

Subject Headings: Climatology; Oceanography

[326] Global Hydrology and Climate Center

Sponsoring Agency: Marshall Space Flight Center

Primary Access: http://wwwghcc.msfc.nasa.gov/

Resource Summary: Most links on this site are to external sources. There is a brief description of the Center, a mission statement, links to cooperative partners, a phone list, and information on visiting the Center. The three primary sources available, listed as "Items of Interest," are Employment Opportunities, Optical Transient Detector (Space-Borne Lightning Sensor), and Current Precipitation Products and Movies. Of these, the last link appears to be available only for registered users since it requires a username and password.

There is not a great deal of original material at this site.

Subject Headings: Climatology; Hydrology

[327] Mission to Planet Earth

Sponsoring Agency: National Aeronautics and Space Administration (NASA)

Primary Access: http://www.hq.nasa.gov/office/mtpe/

Alternative Access Method: http://www.hq.nasa.gov/office/mtpe/MTPE_text.htm [text version]

Resource Summary: Mission to Planet Earth (MTPE) is a NASA research program that is striving to discover patterns in climate that will help in long-term prediction of environmental events such as floods and severe winters. The Web site features the following sections: MTPE Missions, Science of the Earth System, Access to Data, and Publications and Education Programs. The Science of the Earth System section explains some of the basics of climatology while the Access to Data area provides a list of links to many other climatological sites. The MTPE Missions section describes ways in which NASA is acquiring climatological information, including remote sensing. The Publications and Education Programs section offers MTPE Education Reports and links to many educational programs related to MTPE.

This site is geared more toward the education community than to research scientists. Students and teachers can find a broad collection of useful climatological material on this site.

Subject Headings: Climatology; Remote Sensing

SuDoc Number: NAS 1.53/3: *Research Announcements*

[328] National Center for Atmospheric Research

Sponsoring Agency: National Center for Atmospheric Research (NCAR)

Primary Access: http://www.ncar.ucar.edu/

Alternative Access Methods: http://www.ncar.ucar.edu/althome.html [non frames version] telnet://weather@weather.rap.ucar.edu/

Resource Summary: The National Center for Atmospheric Research site features information on the Center and its research areas. Agency information is available from the NCAR mission statement and their most recent *Annual Scientific Report*. Other links include NCAR Divisions and Programs (presenting detailed information on each, sometimes including personnel directories and publications); Resources, Facilities, and Services (including information on NCAR supercomputers, library, and project support); Research Data Archives (links and descriptions of major data archive holdings and availability); Weather and Related Information (mostly links to external resources); News, Updates, and Deadlines (press releases, job opportunities, and seminars).

NCAR offers a substantial body of online information. Their resources are of use to both NCAR researchers and to the general public interested in meteorology and the atmospheric sciences.

Subject Heading: Atmospheric Studies

[329] National Centers for Environmental Prediction

Sponsoring Agency: National Centers for Environmental Prediction (NCEP)

Primary Access: http://www.ncep.noaa.gov/

Alternative Access Method: http://www.ncep.noaa.gov/altindex.shtml [text version]

Resource Summary: This site links to the Web sites for the component NCEP centers, which include the Aviation Weather Center, the Climate Prediction Center, the Environmental Modeling Center, the Hydrometeorological Prediction Center, the Marine Prediction Center, the Space Environment Center, the Storm Prediction Center, and the Tropical Prediction Center.

Subject Headings: Climatology; Storms

[330] National Climatic Data Center

Sponsoring Agency: National Climatic Data Center

Primary Access: http://www.ncdc.noaa.gov/

Resource Summary: This major repository site for climatological data features the following categories: What's New; What's Hot; Products, Publications and Services; Online Data Access; Interactive Visualization of Climate Data; Climate Research Programs; and World Data Center for Meteorology. Of these, the Online Data Access contains numerous data sets and series, including monthly precipitation, daily surface summaries, temperature and pressure figures, and even a Nineteenth Century U.S. Climate Data Set. The Publications category includes some special reports on recent major weather events such as the Blizzard of '96.

This should be one of the first sites to visit when looking for recent or time series climatological data.

Subject Headings: Climatology; Weather

[331] National Severe Storms Laboratory

Sponsoring Agency: National Severe Storms Laboratory

Primary Access: http://www.nssl.uoknor.edu/

Resource Summary: The National Severe Storms Laboratory offers information on its research program, which is involved with all aspects of severe weather. The Web site features sections including General Information, The Weather Room, and Scientific Research. The Publications section, under Scientific Research, contains some full-text articles and preprints by lab personnel.

Subject Heading: Storms

[332] National Weather Service

Sponsoring Agency: National Weather Service (NWS)

Primary Access: http://www.nws.noaa.gov/

Resource Summary: This well-organized site begins with a series of links to weather information: Forecasts and Warnings, Facsimile Charts, Climate, and Snow Cover. The forecasts are not as easily accessible here as through more traditional Internet sources such as the Weather Underground, but the forecasts are available. The charts are available in TIF format, which may require users to configure and/or download a viewer. This site also has links to the regional NWS offices, information on NWS headquarters, a set of Frequently Asked Questions, a site search option, and information on modernization.

This site contains a large quantity of current weather information. Anyone interested in weather should browse this site.

Subject Heading: Weather

SuDoc Number: C 55.127 *Aware*

[333] NESDIS

Sponsoring Agency: National Environmental Satellite, Data, and Information Service (NESDIS)

Primary Access: http://ns.noaa.gov/NESDIS/NESDIS_Home.html

Resource Summary: The NESDIS page consists primarily of links to component NESDIS agencies such as the National Climatic Data Center. In addition, it features recent images of hurricanes, press releases, as well as an organizational chart.

Subject Headings: Climatology; Hurricanes; Weather

[334] Pacific Marine Environmental Laboratory

Sponsoring Agency: Pacific Marine Environmental Laboratory

Primary Access: http://www.pmel.noaa.gov/pmelhome.html

Resource Summary: This site describes the lab, its mission, programs, and available data sets. The personnel directory is supplemented by some personal home pages. The Publications link includes a search form for National Technical Information Service (NTIS) reports from the lab and other published papers. Abstracts only are available for published articles by lab personnel. A few full-text papers are available under the Outstanding Scientific Papers category. Data access includes Interactive Access to Tropical Atmosphere-Ocean (TAO) Buoy Data (Realtime and Historical), Live Access to Climate Databases via the FERRET Program, and Data from the CoAxial Segment of the Juan de Fuca Ridge. Software is available for access to the data. The site also includes detailed information on El Niño on the El Niño Theme Page.

The site is well organized and has good bibliographies, full-text publications, and data sets of interest to the research scientist.

Subject Headings: El Niño; Oceanography

[335] Tropical Prediction Center

Sponsoring Agencies: National Hurricane Center (NHC); National Centers for Environmental Prediction; Tropical Prediction Center (TPC)

Primary Access: http://www.nhc.noaa.gov/

Alternative Access Method: ftp://ftp.nhc.noaa.gov/pub/forecasts

Resource Summary: This site features graphs of tropical cyclones, information on past hurricanes, and Tropical Prediction Center/National Hurricane Center (TPC/NHC) products. The products section includes information on tropical cyclones in the Atlantic and the eastern Pacific. The alternate ftp site includes an archive of all storm advisories.

This server can be slow, but it is an excellent source of information on current and past hurricanes and cyclones.

Subject Headings: Cyclones; Hurricanes

[336] Coastal Ecosystems Program

Sponsoring Agency: Fish and Wildlife Service (FWS)

Primary Access: http://www.fws.gov/~cep/cepcode.html

Resource Summary: This site describes the Coastal Ecosystems Program and its mission. It lists a number of existing programs, some of which have pages describing them in more detail.

This page could use further development, including detailed descriptions of all the programs and a staff directory.

Subject Heading: Coastal Ecology

[337] Coastal Engineering Research Center

Sponsoring Agency: Coastal Engineering Research Center (CERC)

Primary Access: http://bigfoot.cerc.wes.army.mil/

Alternative Access Method: ftp://bigfoot.cerc.wes.army.mil/pub/

Resource Summary: The research activities of CERC are the major focus of this page. Some of the links describe CERC and include access to a directory, the organizational structure, a virtual tour of the field research facility, and a coastal activities calendar. One featured research area is Tsunami, with links to experiments, contact people, and the International Workshop on Long Wave Runup Models. The other featured area for research data is the Coastal Engineering Data Retrieval System (CEDRS) available under the Wind, Wave, and Water Level Data link. CEDRS is a database of wind, wave, and water level data for the coastline of the United States used to assist the coastal engineer. Data are organized as files in directories linked to locations. The hierarchy is by water body, region, and station. A variety of publications are available including some technical notes and research from the Dredging Research Program. The HTML version of the *CERCular* is available, but only one issue was listed (December 1995). The site also features a link with a listing of positions available.

Subject Headings: Army; Oceanography; Tsunami

SuDoc Number: D 103.42/11: *CERCular*

[338] Coastal Programs Division

Sponsoring Agency: National Ocean Service. Coastal Programs Division (CPD)

Primary Access: http://www.nos.noaa.gov/ocrm/cpd/

Resource Summary: This site consists primarily of information about the Division and its administration of the National Coastal Zone Management Program. It features links to its mission statement, an organizational chart, staff information, and participating states. The links to participating states are available via an image map, an alphabetical list, and by regions.

Subject Headings: Coastal Ecology; Oceanography

[339] Environmental Technology Laboratory

Sponsoring Agency: Environmental Technology Laboratory

Primary Access: http://www.etl.noaa.gov/

Resource Summary: This site describes the lab and provides links to publications and research data. The Environmental Technology Laboratory features oceanic and atmospheric research and the development of new remote-sensing systems. The publications include the *25th Anniversary Brochure* and the *1993 Annual Brochure*. The lab information section includes an ASCII staff directory, an organizational chart, and a map of Boulder, Colorado.

Subject Headings: Atmospheric Studies; Oceanography—Research; Radar; Remote Sensing

[340] Fleet Numerical Meteorology and Oceanography Center

Sponsoring Agency: Fleet Numerical Meteorology and Oceanography Center (METOC)

Primary Access: http://www.fnoc.navy.mil/

Resource Summary: This site, emblazoned with METOC in its opening graphic, includes data on oceanographic models, satellite images of the U.S. (infrared and visual), access to the Navy Oceanographic Data Distribution System (NODDS) at different levels for authorized military use vs. civilian use, and the usual mission statement. The METOC Data section is currently restricted to authorized, government users only.

Due to restrictions, this site will mainly be of interest to military personnel with authorization to access the data sets.

Subject Headings: Oceanography; Weather

[341] Interactive Marine Observations

Sponsoring Agencies: National Data Buoy Center (NDBC); National Weather Service-Tallahassee

Primary Access: http://www.nws.fsu.edu/buoy/

Resource Summary: The Interactive Marine Observations site provides near-real-time access to decoded marine weather observations as reported by buoys and Coastal Marine Automated Network stations that are maintained by the NDBC. Generally, the data for the current hour for any station becomes available about 15 minutes after the hour. Access is by image map, station ID, or region.

This site should prove useful for researchers and boating enthusiasts.

Subject Headings: Oceanography; Weather

[342] JPL PO.DAAC

Sponsoring Agencies: Jet Propulsion Laboratory; Physical Oceanography Distributed Active Archive Center (PO.DAAC)

Primary Access: http://podaac-www.jpl.nasa.gov/

Alternative Access Method: ftp://podaac.jpl.nasa.gov/pub/

Resource Summary: The Physical Oceanography Distributed Active Archive Center (PO.DAAC) archives and distributes data relevant to the physical state of the oceans. The main offerings from this site can be found in their Data Catalog. The site includes a number of help links including information on how to order and retrieve data from PO.DAAC. Three featured categories of data include Advanced Very High Resolution Radiometers Pathfinder Data and Subsetting Routines, Subsets of Multi-Channel Sea Surface Temperature Data, and Topex/Poseidon Images and Animations.

The data available from PO.DAAC appears to be of interest to researchers. Some data sets in the Data Catalog are available by ftp, but they do not have direct links to the ftp URL. However, not all items in the Data Catalog are available on the Internet.

Subject Heading: Oceanography

[343] National Data Buoy Center

Sponsoring Agency: National Data Buoy Center (NDBC)

Primary Access: http://seaboard.ndbc.noaa.gov/

Alternative Access Method: ftp://seaboard.ndbc.noaa.gov/

Resource Summary: The National Data Buoy Center (NDBC) site provides buoy-measured environmental data and an overview of the NDBC. Real-time data is available, although this page links to other sources for this data. Archival data is available on this page, at the ftp site, and at a few external sites as well. A couple of graphs show data from recent hurricanes.

Primary uses include learning about the agency and finding links to Internet-accessible sites that have NDBC data.

Subject Headings: Data Products; Hurricanes; Oceanography

[344] National Oceanographic Data Center

Sponsoring Agency: National Oceanographic Data Center (NODC)

Primary Access: http://www.nodc.noaa.gov/

Alternative Access Methods: gopher://gopher.nodc.noaa.gov/
mailto:listproc@gopher.nodc.noaa.gov with "subscribe ocean_list name" in body

Resource Summary: The National Oceanographic Data Center provides ocean data management and ocean data services. Links on the page include sections titled NODC Overview, NODC Headquarters Offices, NODC Liaison Offices, How to Obtain NODC Products and Services, How to Submit Data to NODC, and NODC Contact Points. The Products and Services section features access to an online data catalog; databases of physical, chemical, and biological oceanographic data; and a publications list. Most of the available information is designed for researchers.

The contents on the Gopher server are very similar to those on the Web page. The NODC Bulletin Board Service is available on the Gopher server and/or via the e-mail list. Messages are posted on the Gopher, and an archive of old messages can be found there as well.

The available data sets and the listing of other data products (available off of the Internet) can be useful for researchers.

Subject Heading: Oceanography—Research

[345] NOAA/AOML Physical Oceanography Division

Sponsoring Agency: Atlantic Oceanographic and Meteorological Laboratory (AOML). Physical Oceanography Division (PHOD)

Primary Access: http://www.aoml.noaa.gov/phod/

Resource Summary: The AOML/PHOD page includes links to information from the Drifting Buoy Data Assembly Center, the Pan American Climate Studies, Upper Ocean Thermal Center, Indian Ocean Repeat Hydrography, Atlantic Climate Change Program, and Florida Current Acoustic Doppler Current Profiler (ADCP) data.

This site is a well-organized collection of research information and oceanographic data from PHOD. It will be most useful for oceanographic researchers.

Subject Headings: Oceanography; Weather

[346] NOAA/Atlantic Oceanographic and Meteorological Laboratory

Sponsoring Agency: Atlantic Oceanographic and Meteorological Laboratory (AOML)

Primary Access: http://www.aoml.noaa.gov/

Resource Summary: The AOML page provides a brief description of the lab, a searchable staff directory, and a list of ongoing projects. The Products and Services section includes the following categories: Monthly Color Acoustic Doppler Current Profiler Plots, Equatorial Pacific Trajectories and Analysis, Global Drifter Population Maps, Monthly Drifter Maps, and some *ACCP Notes*—the newsletter of the Atlantic Climate Change Program.

This site provides a good overview of the lab and its research mission. The Products and Services category contains the major substantive resources on the site.

Subject Headings: Oceanography; Preprints; Weather

[347] NOAA Coastal and Estuarine Oceanography Branch

Sponsoring Agency: Coastal and Estuarine Oceanography Branch (CEOB)

Primary Access: http://www-ceob.nos.noaa.gov/

Resource Summary: The Coastal and Estuarine Oceanography Branch is responsible for traditional products such as the U.S. Tide and Tidal Current Tables. Over the decades, it has also developed a monitoring and numerical modeling capability in support of safe navigation and coastal research. The Web site does not include the tide tables, but it does offer a four-day tide and tidal current prediction. Under the heading Real-Time/Forecast Information, the site features sections titled Physical Oceanographic Real-Time Systems; Coastal Forecast System Simulations; Chesapeake Area Forecasting Experiment; and Tampa Bay Forecasting Project. Under the Coastal Ecosystem Health Projects heading, there are links to Maui Algal Bloom Project, Long Island Sound Model Run Animation, and Monitoring and Modeling of Ocean Dumpsites and Sewage Outfalls. Each link has information on the project or links to actual data.

While it does not make the complete tide table available, this can be a useful site for someone just looking for current estimates. However, the estimates are limited to only selected stations.

Subject Headings: Oceanography; Tides

[348] NOAA Environmental Information Services

Sponsoring Agencies: Environmental Information Services (EIS); National Oceanic and Atmospheric Administration (NOAA)

Primary Access: http://www.esdim.noaa.gov/

Alternative Access Methods: gopher://gopher.esdim.noaa.gov/
telnet://noaadir@esdim1.esdim.noaa.gov:23/

Resource Summary: A broad range of the NOAA data sets and other data products are available from these sites. The top Web page is arranged in a question and answer format with questions such as What data products are available from the NOAA? What can you do with data from the NOAA? and How can I find data available from the NOAA? Sections of the site include NOAA National Data Centers, NOAA Participation in National and International Organizations and Joint Offices, and Other Services Provided by the NOAA Environmental Information Services.

The NOAA Data Set Catalog, the NOAA Environmental Services Data Directory (NOAADIR), and the NOAA National Environmental Data Referral Service (NEDRES) are available on the Gopher site. With the telnet URL access for the Master Directory, they all provide different ways for finding NOAA data products.

Subject Headings: Data Products; Oceanography; Satellite Imagery; Weather

[349] NOAA National Ocean Service

Sponsoring Agency: National Ocean Service (NOS)

Primary Access: http://www.nos.noaa.gov/

Resource Summary: The NOS is the primary civil agency within the federal government that is responsible for the health and safety of our nation's coastal and oceanic environment. Their Web site features a virtual guided tour and links that include Features, Products and Services, Index of Contents, Servers Upstream, Servers Downstream, Links to Ocean and Coastal Resources, and About This Server. Many of the links are either to external sources or to other NOS agency Web sites.

Subject Heading: Oceanography

[350] Office of Coast Survey

Sponsoring Agency: Office of Coast Survey

Alternative Access Method: http://chartmaker.ncd.noaa.gov/alternate.html [non-table version]

Primary Access: http://chartmaker.ncd.noaa.gov/

Resource Summary: The Coast Survey is the official chart-making agency. It manages nautical chart data collections and information programs. This site describes the Survey and its activities. It offers information on nautical charting, hydrography, and distances between ports. The site also offers lists of the Coast Survey's publications and charts and provides ordering information.

Subject Headings: Coastlines; Maps and Mapping

[351] Office of Ocean and Coastal Resource Management

Sponsoring Agency: Office of Ocean and Coastal Resource Management (OCRM)

Primary Access: http://www.nos.noaa.gov/ocrm/

Resource Summary: According to the Web site, "OCRM combines the expertise of managers and planners, scientists, and environmental advocates to balance the preservation of valuable ocean and coastal resources with the need for compatible economic development of the coastal zone." Most of their site has links to other National Ocean Service sites or to other external sources related to coastal information.

Subject Headings: Coastal Ecology; Oceanography

[352] OLLD

Sponsoring Agency: Ocean and Lake Levels Division (OLLD)

Primary Access: http://www.olld.nos.noaa.gov/

Alternative Access Method: telnet://guest@wlnet2.nos.noaa.gov/

Resource Summary: The OLLD Web site features a wealth of data including Great Lakes data and tidal information. The pages include a list of reporting stations, data reports of storm events, benchmark information, and relative sea level trends tables. Featured sections of the Web site include Publications, Data Resources, Tide and Tidal Current Predictions, and Physical Oceanographic Real-Time Systems. The telnet address provides access to data from stations and includes the following categories: Six-Minute Data for Tidal Locations, Six-Minute Data for Great Lakes Locations, Hourly Height Data for Tidal Locations, Monthly Mean Data for Tidal Locations, and Accepted 19-Year Station Datums (1960-1978).

Subject Headings: Data Products; Great Lakes; Oceanography; Tides

[353] ORCA Information Service

Sponsoring Agency: Office of Ocean Resources Conservation and Assessment (ORCA)

Primary Access: http://seaserver.nos.noaa.gov/

Resource Summary: This site provides access to a variety of information about ORCA including the mission and organization of ORCA, its data products, publications, and updates on ORCA projects. Under the What Information is Available heading, there is access to the ORCA corporate database, which includes hundreds of data product offerings. Two major access routes are available: Thematic Information Stories or Spatial-topical Information Selection. The former allows direct access to stories on given topics, while the latter allows the use of spatial and temporal criteria.

Subject Headings: Coastlines; Oceanography

[354] Sanctuaries and Reserves Division

Sponsoring Agency: National Ocean Service. Sanctuaries and Reserves Division

Primary Access: http://www.nos.noaa.gov/ocrm/srd/

Resource Summary: Marine Sanctuaries and Estuarine Research Reserves along the coasts of the U.S. are listed on this site by name, state, and region. The site also features press releases, a publications list, and a statement on biodiversity.

Subject Headings: Coastlines; Sanctuaries

Environment: Pollution

[355] Air and Radiation Division, Region 5, USEPA

Sponsoring Agency: Environmental Protection Agency (EPA). Air and Radiation Division

Primary Access: http://www.epa.gov/ARD-R5/

Resource Summary: This server comes from EPA region 5 which serves the Midwest. Despite being a regional server, it boasts a great number of documents. Most are listed under their Products and Services heading and include Acid Rain, Air Quality, Air Toxics, CFC's, Refrigerants, Air Conditioning and the Ozone Layer; Environmental Justice; Facilities, Emissions, Enforcement, and Compliance; Great Lakes/Great Waters; Permitting; and Radon, Indoor Air Quality, Radiation, Electric, and Magnetic Fields.

A Local News and Events link has weekly activity reports and press releases. It also has numerous links to other sources of information on air pollution, the Clean Air Act, and other EPA offices.

An information-rich site, the division has done an admirable job in both content and organization.

Subject Headings: Acid Rain; Air Pollution

[356] Air Resources Laboratory

Sponsoring Agency: Air Resources Laboratory

Primary Access: http://www.erl.noaa.gov/arl/arl.html

Resource Summary: This page describes the lab and its research projects and divisions with no further links to data or publications.

Subject Headings: Climatology; Air Pollution—Research

[357] Chemicals in the Environment Public Access Information

Sponsoring Agency: Environmental Protection Agency (EPA). Office of Pollution Prevention and Toxics

Primary Access: http://www.epa.gov/cie/

Alternative Access Method: gopher://gopher.epa.gov/11/Offices/ PestPreventToxic/Toxic/cie/

Resource Summary: This newsletter is designed to help people find out about the EPA's information products that are related to chemicals. Issues of the newsletter are available in a mixture of formats—some are in WordPerfect 6.1 for Windows format, others are in ASCII, and yet others are in PDF or HTML.

Subject Headings: Chemical Information—Full Text; Electronic Periodicals; Hazardous Waste—Full Text

[358] DoD Environmental Security

Sponsoring Agency: Department of Defense (DoD). Office of the Under Secretary of Defense for Environmental Safety

Primary Access: http://www.acq.osd.mil/ens/

Resource Summary: This site consists primarily of information about the organization which aims to invest in pollution prevention to reduce the cost of cleanup and compliance, to promote technology innovations to obtain better and cheaper environmental performance, and to support community revitalization with fast-track cleanup of closed or realigned facilities.

Unfortunately, the site includes very little information beyond the description of the agency. The few additional documents include DoD directives and instructions, information on the Environmental Security Technology Certification Program (ESTCP), and information on Environmental Scholarships and Fellowships from the DoD.

Subject Headings: Environmental and Occupational Health; Pollution

[359] Enviroene - Assisting Pollution Prevention Implementation

Sponsoring Agencies: Environmental Protection Agency (EPA); Idaho National Engineering Laboratory

Primary Access: http://es.inel.gov/

Resource Summary: Enviroene combines a number of resources on pollution prevention projects and research. Several of the main links on this document connect to pollution prevention (known on this site as P2) documents and to programs from other Internet sites. The Pollution Prevention Programs in the United States section contains a great deal of information on local programs. The Solvent Substitution Data System section lists a number of governmental and nongovernmental data resources on substitutes for various solvents.

The *EPA Sector Notebooks* are publications, available in PDF and various WordPerfect formats, that contain a comprehensive environmental profile, industrial process information, pollution prevention techniques, pollutant release data, regulatory requirements, compliance/enforcement history, innovative programs, and contact names.

This site combines locally produced resources with links to external resources and establishes a good starting point for finding information on pollution prevention.

Subject Headings: Pollution; Solvents

SuDoc Number: EP 1.2:P 94/ *EPA Sector Notebooks*

[360] Great Lakes National Program Office

Sponsoring Agency: Environmental Protection Agency (EPA). Great Lakes National Program Office (GLNPO)

Primary Access: http://www.epa.gov/glnpo/

Resource Summary: In addition to providing information about the Program, the Great Lakes National Program Office aims to restore and maintain the physical, chemical, and biological integrity of the Great Lakes Basin ecosystem. This site features information on their projects including pollution prevention, monitoring, and human health. Other sections include Visualizing the Lakes, with an online *Great Lakes Atlas,* and Ecopage which includes information on green landscaping, mining ideas, and a state of the ecosystem report.

Subject Headings: Great Lakes; Pollution

[361] Hazardous Waste Remedial Actions

Sponsoring Agencies: Department of Energy (DOE); Hazardous Waste Remedial Actions Program (HAZWRAP)

Primary Access: http://www.ornl.gov/HAZWRAP/

Resource Summary: HAZWRAP, the Hazardous Waste Remedial Actions Program, works with federal, state, and local agencies in the United States and abroad to develop effective and affordable solutions to environmental problems. This Web site describes their areas of expertise under the Services/Capabilities heading. These areas include Clean Air Act Compliance, Decontamination and Decommissioning, Demilitarization, Environmental Biotechnology, Hydrogeology, Pollution Prevention, and Waste Management, among many other related fields. The other main headings, the HAZWRAP Team, the HAZWRAP Difference, and Partnering with HAZWRAP, provide more information about the organization.
Organizations that might need HAZWRAP's services should be aware of this Web site.

Subject Headings: Hazardous Waste; Pollution

[362] NOAA Great Lakes Environmental Research Laboratory

Sponsoring Agency: Great Lakes Environmental Research Laboratory

Primary Access: http://www.glerl.noaa.gov/

Alternative Access Methods: gopher://gopher.glerl.noaa.gov/
ftp://ftp.glerl.noaa.gov/

Resource Summary: This site describes the Lab, its mission, and its programs. Other links connect to recent news from the lab, current activities, and a historical overview. The lab produces many data sets, but only a few are available on the server. Data sets are available in their Great Lakes Coast Watch series, Great Lakes Ice Data series, and Lake Erie Forecasting System. The Publications section includes yearly reports, publications lists, publications abstracts, and a few technical memoranda.

Subject Headings: Great Lakes; Limnology; Water Pollution

[363] Oil Spill Public Information Center

Sponsoring Agency: Oil Spill Public Information Center (OSPIC)

Primary Access: http://www.alaska.net/~ospic/

Resource Summary: The OSPIC seeks to provide information about the Exxon Valdez oil spill. This site serves as part of the virtual library of information on the oil spill. It includes a description of the events, a map of the spill area, the current status of the area, images from the event, and samples of free documents.

This can be a very useful source for both the general public and researchers interested in the Exxon Valdez oil spill.

Subject Heading: Exxon Valdez Oil Spill

[364] Technology Transfer Network 2000

Sponsoring Agency: Environmental Protection Agency (EPA). Office of Air Quality Planning

Primary Access: http://ttnwww.rtpnc.epa.gov/

Alternative Access Methods: telnet://ttnbbs.rtpnc.epa.gov:23/
ftp://ttnwww.rtpnc.epa.gov/

Resource Summary: Originally a BBS accessible only by telnet, Technology Transfer Network 2000 is now available on the Web and by ftp. It consists of a collection of information from 14 other EPA systems, including the Aerometric Information Retrieval System, the Air Pollution Training Institute, the Clean Air Act Amendments, the Clearinghouse for Inventories and Emission Factors, and the Office of Radiation and Indoor Air.

Subject Headings: Air Pollution; Technology Transfer

[365] U.S. EPA Office of Air and Radiation

Sponsoring Agency: Environmental Protection Agency (EPA). Office of Air and Radiation

Primary Access: http://www.epa.gov/oar/

Alternative Access Methods: http://www.epa.gov/oar/oarhomet.html [text version]
gopher://www.epa.gov/11/Offices/Air/

Resource Summary: This site includes a lot of information about air pollution and air radiation. The top level image map packs many links into one image. Some of the major sections include Basic Facts, Publications, Resources, Organization, and Regulations.

Featured topics include Ozone Layer, Acid Rain, Automobiles, Indoor Air, Urban Air, Air Toxics, Radiation, and Pollution Prevention. Some of the publications available include Acid Rain Program Publications, UV Index Documents, Radon Publications, Consumer Information, *Measuring Air Quality—The Pollutant Standards Index*, *The Plain English Guide to the Clean Air Act*, and *The Health Effects Notebook for Hazardous Air Pollutants*. Available databases include Aerometric Information Retrieval System (AIRS) and the Energy Star Product Database.

Many of the topics covered on this site are of broad interest to researchers and to the general public. It is well worth a visit from anyone interested in acid rain, air pollution, or radon.

Subject Headings: Acid Rain; Air Pollution; Consumer Information; Radiation; Radon

CHAPTER 7: HEALTH SCIENCES

Medical information on the Internet in general ranges from fad diets to highly technical research databases. The government medical information resources provide a degree of authority not always available from other purported health science Internet sites. Within the many government sites offering health sciences resources are full-text, online periodicals, genetic research databases, public health information, and AIDS resources.

The following three featured health sciences sites are useful as entryways to the wealth of government medical information on the Internet. Those interested in information on a specific disease may want to start with the Centers for Disease Control and Prevention sites. The National Institutes of Health site contains many resources of interest to researchers and to the general public. For more consumer-oriented resources, the U.S. Department of Health and Human Services site is a good starting point.

[366] Centers for Disease Control and Prevention

Sponsoring Agency: Centers for Disease Control and Prevention (CDC)

Primary Access: http://www.cdc.gov/

Alternative Access Methods: http://www.cdc.gov/cdctext.htm [text version]
ftp://ftp.cdc.gov/

Resource Summary: This starting point for the substantial holdings on CDC Web sites features the usual information about the agency including links to the CDC's component centers, institutes, and offices. Other featured categories include Health Information, Travelers' Health, Publications and Products, Data and Statistics, Training and Employment, and Funding. The Travelers' Health section includes a link to the full text of *Health Information for International Travel*. Although the text of that document is housed on the CDC Wonder server, it is easier found on this site.

The researcher or the general public interested in finding information on various diseases would be well advised to take a look at this site. The information is well organized and the pages are easy to navigate. They even have a search feature for the CDC Web pages. The combination of the search feature and the information accessible from this page make it a useful finding aid for government health information on diseases.

Subject Headings: Diseases; Epidemiology; Preventive Medicine; Travel

SuDoc Numbers: HE 20.7315: *Health Information for International Travel*
HE 20.7511: *Summary of Sanitation Inspections of International Cruise Ships*

[367] healthfinder⁽ᵀᴹ⁾ - A Gateway Consumer Health Information Web Site

Sponsoring Agency: Department of Health and Human Services (HHS)

Primary Access: http://www.healthfinder.gov/

Resource Summary: Launched April 15, 1997, healthfinder is a gateway consumer health information Web site. This site is designed to assist consumers in finding government health information on the Internet. It links to selected online publications, databases, Web sites, support and self-help groups, and government health agencies. The selected links are intended to offer reliable health information sources for the public. The Pubs page provides a search option by keyword and age group. The Tour page has broad topical access to resources. To enable communication, the Talk page lists toll-free numbers, Web sites for support and self-help groups, and collections of online discussion groups.

This site is an excellent starting point for finding health information on the consumer level, rather than from other sources, which provide technical information geared toward medical practitioners and researchers. Its search options work well, but a larger collection of subjects to browse would be helpful.

Subject Headings: Consumer Information; Finding Aid—Health

[368] National Institutes of Health

Sponsoring Agency: National Institutes of Health (NIH)

Primary Access: http://www.nih.gov/

Alternative Access Method: gopher://gopher.nih.gov/

Resource Summary: The NIH site is one of the principal starting points for finding health sciences information from the government. The Web site features the following links: Welcome to NIH, News and Events, Health Information, Grants and Contracts, Scientific Resources, and Institutes and Offices. The Welcome to NIH link provides an introduction to the NIH, which includes an employee directory and maps of the NIH campus in Bethesda, Maryland. The News and Events link features an events calendar, special reports, and employment information. The Health Information link includes a selection of prominent NIH health resources such as CancerNet, AIDS information, Clinical Alerts, the Women's Health Initiative, and the NIH Information Index (a subject-word guide to diseases and conditions under investigation at NIH).

The Grants and Contracts link features NIH funding opportunities and application kits, grant policy, and award data. Among other databases, the Grants page provides access to award data including the Computer Retrieval of Information on Scientific Projects (CRISP) system—a biomedical database that contains basic information on current research ventures supported by the Public Health Service. CRISP is housed on the Gopher server, and it contains records dating back to 1972. There is also a link to the CRISP thesaurus.

The Scientific Resources category is broad and covers NIH research news, research training information, a list of NIH research labs on the Web, and computer and network support for NIH scientists. The Institutes and Offices section lists the many component NIH organizations, most of which are listed separately in this directory.

The NIH works in a significant portion of the health sciences field. The NIH Internet sites contain significant holdings of information about the NIH and its component organizations. But more importantly, they contain an important body of sources in the health sciences for the general public, health science researchers, and health science professionals.

Subject Headings: Diseases; Health; Health Sciences

SuDoc Number: HE 20.3013 *CRISP Biomedical Research Information*

[369] U.S. Department of Health and Human Services

Sponsoring Agency: Department of Health and Human Services (HHS)

Primary Access: http://www.os.dhhs.gov/

Alternative Access Methods: http://www.os.dhhs.gov/hpagetxt.html [text version]
gopher://gopher.os.dhhs.gov/

Resource Summary: The HHS page uses the following topics for access to more detailed information: About HHS; News and Public Affairs; Search; Consumer Information; What's New; HHS Research, Policy, and Administration; and Employee Information. The HHS selection provides access to the operating divisions, institutes, centers, and offices of HHS.

Under the Consumer Information link, selected offerings of component HHS agencies are available via an alphabetical subject list and by frequently requested subjects. To make it easier to find information on frequently requested subjects across multiple HHS sites, this section, along with the Search section, features a searchable database of selected HHS Internet resources. The database contains brief descriptions and links that lead directly to information on the constituent HHS sites.

The site also contains press releases, speeches, congressional testimony, and a searchable database of HHS phone numbers. The HHS Web pages provide access to a large amount of health sciences material from component agencies. The searchable database and multiple access points make this site one of the primary sources of federal government health information.

Subject Headings: Finding Aid—Health; Health

The Health Sciences resources are divided into three sections. The first section consists of sites that are general health science information resources and sites that do not fit under the other categories. This section runs from entry numbers 370 to 416. Diseases, the second subchapter, contains resources related to specific diseases or groups of diseases and covers entries 417-434. The third section, Research, with entries 435-458, includes sites dealing with health sciences research efforts.

Health Sciences: General

[370] Administration on Aging

Sponsoring Agency: Administration on Aging (AoA)

Primary Access: http://www.aoa.dhhs.gov/

Alternative Access Method: gopher://gopher.os.dhhs.gov:70/11/dhhs/aoa/

Resource Summary: The AoA Web site features resources for the elderly, their families, and professionals working with the aged. The site includes a description complete with a phone number of the Eldercare Locator—a nationwide directory assistance service designed to help older persons and caregivers locate local support resources for aging Americans. A Web version of the Locator is under construction. The site also includes a welcome from the administrator, press releases, and a What's New section.

There are two major links, which are titled Information and the National Aging Information Center (NAIC). The Information link includes statistical publications, ElderAction HTML pamphlets, and the publication *Age Pages*. The NAIC link provides access to additional electronic publications, data sets, and forums. It also features access to searchable databases.

Four links are not yet available, including the Eldercare Locator, Image Database, Variable Reference System, and Directory of Aging Organizations. The bibliographic database is supposed to be functional but often results in error messages. Once the problems are fixed, the database will describe materials produced by Administration on Aging grantees funded under Title IV of the Older Americans Act of 1965 (Public Law 89-73). Title IV of the Act supports demonstrations, research, training projects, and a number of institutes and centers such as the National Resource Centers on Native American Elders, Long-Term Care, Long-Term Care Ombudsman, and Elder Abuse, as well as the National Eldercare Institutes.

Some of the publications available on this site include the *Resource Directory for Older People* and the *Age Pages*. The Gopher site includes some documents not yet available on the Web site, such as the executive summary of the 1994 *Annual Report*.

This site includes a great deal of useful information on aging, the elderly, and health care for the elderly. Once the incomplete portions of this site are finished, it should be even more useful.

Subject Headings: Bibliographic Databases; Elderly

SuDoc Numbers: HE 1.201: *Administration on Aging Annual Report*
HE 20.3861: *Age Pages*
HE 20.3868: *Resource Directory for Older People*

[371] Archives of *FDA Consumer* Magazines

Sponsoring Agency: Food and Drug Administration (FDA)

Primary Access: http://www.fda.gov/fdac/fdacindex.html

Resource Summary: This site links to issues of the *FDA Consumer* dating back to April 1989. The older issues are available through a gateway to the FDA BBS in ASCII format. Many, but not all, of these older issues are available in their entirety. Since the July/August 1995 issue, the full text of *FDA Consumer* is available in HTML. Selected graphics are included as well.

This is a frequently referenced title, and having an electronic version available and accessible is an important public service on the part of the FDA. They should be commended for putting this publication online.

Subject Headings: Consumer Information—Full Text; Electronic Periodicals

SuDoc Number: HE 20.4010: *FDA Consumer*

[372] Armed Forces Institute of Pathology

Sponsoring Agency: Armed Forces Institute of Pathology (AFIP)

Primary Access: http://www.afip.mil/

Resource Summary: The Armed Forces Institute of Pathology is involved with education, consulting, and research in pathology. Their Web site features information on their research and consultation services. Available publications include an annual report and *The AFIP Letter*.

Subject Headings: Higher Education—Medical; Pathology

SuDoc Number: D 101.117: *The AFIP Letter*

[373] ATSDR

Sponsoring Agency: Agency for Toxic Substances and Disease Registry (ATSDR)

Primary Access: http://atsdr1.atsdr.cdc.gov:8080/

Resource Summary: Like so many other government pages, ATSDR's home page begins with information about the agency including job announcements, goals, and organizational structure. However, the ATSDR offerings go well beyond that. The site offers a wide variety of information sources on toxic substances, public health assessment, and public education on hazardous substances. The ToxFAQs and Public Health Summaries sections summarize information about hazardous substances taken from the ATSDR Toxicological Profiles. *The Environmental Data Needed for Public Health Assessments* is a guidance manual published by ATSDR that describes the general purpose and focus of a public health assessment.

The primary link on the ATSDR site is the Hazardous Substance Release/Health Effects Database (HazDat). HazDat contains information on the release of hazardous substances from Superfund sites or from emergency events. It also gives information on the effects of these hazardous substances on the health of human populations. The following information is included in HazDat: site characteristics, activities and events, contaminants found, contaminant media and maximum concentration levels, impact on population, and community health concerns. Additional information can be found regarding ATSDR public health threat categorization, ATSDR recommendations, environmental fate of hazardous substances, exposure routes, and physical hazards on this site.

In addition, HazDat contains substance-specific information such as the ATSDR Priority List of Hazardous Substances, health effects by route and duration of exposure, metabolites, interactions of substances, susceptible populations, and biomarkers of exposure and effects.

This is an excellent site for finding toxicological data and information on hazardous substances.

Subject Headings: Environmental and Occupational Health; Health Assessment; Superfund Sites; Toxic Substances; Toxicology

[374] CDC National Center for Environmental Health

Sponsoring Agency: National Center for Environmental Health (NCEH)

Primary Access: http://www.cdc.gov/nceh/oncehhom.htm

Resource Summary: The NCEH site features the category NCEH Programs and Activities, which includes the headings Health Effects of Environmental Hazards, Emergency Response, Public Health Surveillance, Laboratory Standardization Programs, Infants and Children, Women's Health, and Disabilities Prevention.

Other top level categories include About NCEH, What's New, Calendar of Events, Training and Employment, and Publications and Products. The Publications and Products section includes a list of publications by NCEH authors, full-text fact sheets and brochures, books, and *Morbidity and Mortality Weekly Report* articles by NCEH authors. Under the Books link, full-text versions of *Preventing Lead Poisoning in Young Children* and *Basic Housing Inspection* can be found.

An array of environmental health topics are covered by the NCEH site. For people interested in environmental health topics, this site is worth a look.

Subject Headings: Environmental and Occupational Health; Lead

SuDoc Numbers: HE 20.7302:L 46/2/991 *Preventing Lead Poisoning in Young Children*
HE 20.7002:H 81/2 *Basic Housing Inspection*

[375] CDC Wonder on the Web

Sponsoring Agency: Centers for Disease Control and Prevention (CDC)

Primary Access: http://wonder.cdc.gov/

Resource Summary: CDC Wonder provides a single point of access to a variety of CDC reports, guidelines, and even numeric public health data. The numeric databases can provide the numbers and rates of many diseases including sexually transmitted diseases, cancer cases, and deaths in the United States. Users can request data for any disease and demographic group by submitting special queries against available datasets. CDC Wonder also provides free-text search facilities and document retrieval for several important text datasets including the *Morbidity and Mortality Weekly Report* from 1982 to the present and the CDC Prevention Guidelines.
To submit a query, CDC Wonder requires a user ID and password. There is no charge for registration, and there is an anonymous registration option. Non-anonymous registration allows access to "sensitive databases" which are only available to members of "secure groups."

Subject Headings: Health Statistics; Public Health

SuDoc Number: HE 20.7009: *Morbidity and Mortality Weekly Report*

[376] Clinical Center

Sponsoring Agencies: National Institutes of Health (NIH); Warren Grant Magnuson Clinical Center

Primary Access: http://www.cc.nih.gov/

Resource Summary: The Clinical Center, the research hospital at the NIH, is involved in a variety of clinical studies. Their Web site features an About the Clinical Center section with organizational information, Center news, and patient resources. It also includes a Health Information section with lists of published reports, books, and videos, as well as a Medical and Scientific Education section with staff research papers.

This site aims at a primarily internal audience, but there is information of value here for anyone interested in research at the Clinical Center.

Subject Headings: Clinical Medicine; Medical Research

[377] Comprehensive Epidemiologic Data Resource

Sponsoring Agency: Department of Energy (DOE)

Primary Access: http://cedr.lbl.gov/

Alternative Access Method: gopher://cedr.lbl.gov/

Resource Summary: The Department of Energy developed the Comprehensive Epidemiologic Data Resource (CEDR) Program to provide public access to health and radiation exposure data concerning DOE installations. Most of the data derive from DOE epidemiologic studies. For a starting point, use the Access link to connect to the CEDR Catalog to obtain information on the CEDR Program and on the types of data available through CEDR. The Browsing CEDR Data and Documentation section offers public access to CEDR data and another access point for registered CEDR users. The site also features a few white papers on topics related to CEDR data.

For anyone concerned with exposure to radiation at any DOE-operated facility, this is an important site.

Subject Headings: Epidemiology; Radiation

SuDoc Number: E 1.20/3:0339 *CEDR, Comprehensive Epidemiologic Data Resource*

[378] DoD Telemedicine Test Bed

Sponsoring Agency: Department of Defense (DoD)

Primary Access: http://www.matmo.army.mil/

Resource Summary: This telemedicine site includes a wide range of documents, images, and other information on telemedicine. It includes a weekly electronic newsletter, *TeleMed*, which contains recent news on telemedicine topics. Other sections on this site include Telemedicine in Bosnia, DoD Clinical Cases, the Telemedicine Bibliography, the Telemedicine Project Directory, and the Telemedicine Photo Album.

For health professionals interested in current uses of telemedicine, this site features useful information and discussions of actual uses. For anyone interested in learning more about telemedicine, this site is a good resource even though it is aimed more at the practitioner than the general public.

Subject Headings: Bosnian Conflict; Telemedicine

[379] DOE Office of Human Radiation Experiments

Sponsoring Agency: Department of Energy (DOE). Office of Human Radiation Experiments

Primary Access: http://www.ohre.doe.gov/

Alternative Access Method: http://raleigh.dis.anl.gov/

Resource Summary: This is a U.S. Department of Energy project designed to provide public access to human radiation experiment records and related information. This is an innovative project used to identify and make public federal government records from the Cold War era that are of interest to researchers as well as to the general public. This work includes document declassification as well as a systematic effort to gain intellectual control over the DOE's records.

For access to this database of declassified documents, the Human Radiation Experiments Information Management System (HREX) offers two search modes, standard and experts. Other documents that can be searched include overview documents, record series descriptions, historical photos, and a link to the most recently declassified documents.

This is an impressive resource for those interested in radiation experiments on humans. The search interface is functional and it links to scanned images of the original documents. This site presents a treasure trove of primary material for researchers.

Subject Headings: Medical Research; Radiation

[380] Environment, Safety, and Health Technical Information Services

Sponsoring Agency: Department of Energy (DOE). Office of Environment, Safety, and Health

Primary Access: http://tis.eh.doe.gov/

Resource Summary: The DOE's Environment, Safety, and Health Technical Information Services (TIS) is a collection of information services designed for safety and health professionals. The top level page provides both a graphical and a text interface along with access to the TIS mission statement and organization. The Documents and Publications page includes bulletins, newsletters, regulatory information, and congressional testimony.

Subject Headings: Environmental and Occupational Health; Safety

[381] Environmental Health Clearinghouse

Sponsoring Agencies: Information Ventures, Inc.; National Institute of Environmental Health Sciences (NIEHS)

Primary Access: http://infoventures.com/e-hlth/

Alternative Access Method: mailto:envirohealth@niehs.nih.gov

Resource Summary: The main function of the Environmental Health Clearinghouse is to answer questions on environmental health issues. The Web site features factsheets on specific health issues or specific chemicals, provides answers to selected questions, and offers various methods of sending questions to the Clearinghouse. It is staffed by junior and senior scientists trained in environmental health issues.

Subject Heading: Environmental and Occupational Health

[382] FDA Approved Animal Drug Data Base

Sponsoring Agency: Food and Drug Administration (FDA). Center for Veterinary Medicine (CVM)

Primary Access: http://scholar.lib.vt.edu/ejournals/vetfda.html

Alternative Access Method: gopher://borg.lib.vt.edu/11/vetFDA

Resource Summary: This searchable database includes records for all animal drug products approved by the FDA for safety and effectiveness. The search engine uses a single line entry in both the Gopher and the Web version, but Boolean operators can be used. Updated quarterly, records in the database include fields such as tradename, sponsor, ingredients, species, route of administration, drug forms, and *Code of Federal Regulations* information.

The database records are clearly formatted, even though they are primarily in ASCII text. This is a useful database for veterinarians and anyone interested in official FDA information on specific animal drugs.

Subject Headings: Drugs; Veterinary Medicine

[383] FDA Center for Food Safety and Applied Nutrition

Sponsoring Agencies: Center for Food Safety and Applied Nutrition (CFSAN); Food and Drug Administration (FDA)

Primary Access: http://vm.cfsan.fda.gov/

Resource Summary: This page consists almost entirely of links to other resources. The link to CFSAN Food and Consumer Information is the one that actually links to information from CFSAN itself. That page includes topics on food safety including Plant Toxin Information, Consumer Advice and Material for Educators, Cosmetics, Food Additives, Foodborne Illness, and Food Labeling. Other topics include Nutrition and Dietary Supplement Information, Pesticides and Chemical Contaminants, Press Releases, Congressional Testimony, Seafood Information, and Women's Health.

This site contains some informative documents on food safety and nutrition. Unfortunately, some documents are mixed in with numerous links to external sites and can be difficult to find.

Subject Headings: Food Safety; Nutrition

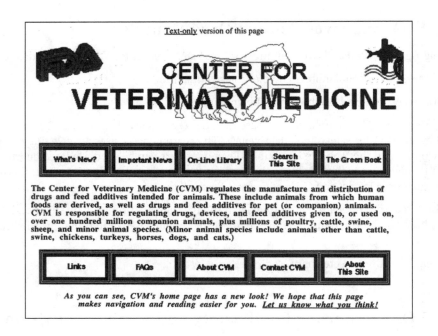

CENTER FOR VETERINARY MEDICINE

| What's New? | Important News | On-Line Library | Search This Site | The Green Book |

The Center for Veterinary Medicine (CVM) regulates the manufacture and distribution of drugs and feed additives intended for animals. These include animals from which human foods are derived, as well as drugs and feed additives for pet (or companion) animals. CVM is responsible for regulating drugs, devices, and feed additives given to, or used on, over one hundred million companion animals, plus millions of poultry, cattle, swine, sheep, and minor animal species. (Minor animal species include animals other than cattle, swine, chickens, turkeys, horses, dogs, and cats.)

| Links | FAQs | About CVM | Contact CVM | About This Site |

As you can see, CVM's home page has a new look! We hope that this page makes navigation and reading easier for you. Let us know what you think!

[384] FDA Center for Veterinary Medicine

Sponsoring Agency: Food and Drug Administration (FDA). Center for Veterinary Medicine (CVM)

Primary Access: http://www.cvm.fda.gov/

Resource Summary: The FDA CVM Web site includes a great deal of information about the CVM and its component parts including phone directories and organizational charts. The site also features recent news from the CVM and an Information and Resources Library. This Library acts as a central location for public CVM documents of interest to animal drug developers and manufacturers, veterinarians, consumers, and pet owners.

The Information and Resources Library offers a few issues of *FDA Veterinarian* magazine, the booklet *FDA and the Veterinarian*, Adverse Drug Experience Reporting summaries, and Information for Consumers pamphlets, all in HTML.

The site provides a disclaimer which states that the information on the Web server is only intended to be a general summary of information for the public and consumers. It does not take the place of the actual regulations. Regardless, it can be useful to those in the animal drug business and consumers.

Subject Heading: Veterinary Medicine

SuDoc Numbers: HE 20.4410: *FDA Veterinarian*
HE 20.4402:F 73/ *FDA and the Veterinarian*

[385] Food and Drug Administration

Sponsoring Agency: Food and Drug Administration (FDA)

Primary Access: http://www.fda.gov/

Alternative Access Methods: http://www.fda.gov/hometext.html [text version]
telnet://bbs@fdabbs.fda.gov

Resource Summary: The FDA BBS has been an important source of FDA information and publications for years. Many of those documents are now available on the FDA home page and its component agency pages. The main categories include FDA News, Biologics, Cosmetics, Foreign Language, Foods, Medical Devices/Radiological Health, Field Operations/Imports, Human Drugs, Animal Drugs, and Toxicology. Additional choices link to information on the FDA, product approvals, and orphan products. Another section includes information for special audiences including Teens, Industry, Media, and Health Professionals. The site also includes a search capability for the entire site.

The home page can be confusing when searching for specific items and subsidiary agencies under the given categories. It would be helpful if there were a publications category that gathered links to all of the available publications.

Subject Heading: Drugs

SuDoc Numbers: HE 20.4039: *FDA Enforcement Report*
HE 20.4003/3: *FDA Medical Bulletin*
HE 20.4619: *Mammography Matters*

[386] Food and Drug Administration Center for Drug Evaluation and Research

Sponsoring Agencies: Center for Drug Evaluation and Research (CDER); Food and Drug Administration (FDA)

Primary Access: http://www.fda.gov/cder/

Alternative Access Method: gopher://gopher.cder.fda.gov/

Resource Summary: The Center for Drug Evaluation and Research Web site features descriptive information about the Center under the heading, About CDER. The Drug Information section includes a variety of links to resources on drugs, including the full text of the 1995 *National Drug Code Directory* which is located on the Gopher. Other sections on the top level page include Regulatory Guidance and What's New.

Subject Heading: Drugs

SuDoc Number: HE 20.4012: *National Drug Code Directory*

[387] Food and Nutrition Information Center

Sponsoring Agencies: Food and Nutrition Information Center (FNIC); National Agricultural Library (NAL)

Primary Access: http://www.nal.usda.gov/fnic/

Alternative Access Method: gopher://gopher.nalusda.gov/11/infocntr/fnic

Resource Summary: The FNIC sites focus on providing information to the consumer on the topics of food, nutrition, food labels, and school meals. The site includes the full text of the 1995 edition of *Nutrition and Your Health: Dietary Guidelines for Americans* in both HTML and PDF versions and the 1990 edition in HTML. Other categories include the Healthy Eating Index, Food Service Management, Food Labeling Education, Foodborne Illness Education Information Center, Healthy School Meals Resource System, and ARS/USDA Nutrition Information.

This site contains a substantial number of documents on food and nutrition. While the professional nutritionist may want to look elsewhere for more advanced information, the resources on this site should prove quite useful for the general public.

Subject Headings: Nutrition; School Meals
SuDoc Number: A 1.77:232 *Nutrition and Your Health: Dietary Guidelines for Americans*

[388] Food Safety and Inspection Service

Sponsoring Agency: Food Safety and Inspection Service (FSIS)

Primary Access: http://www.usda.gov/agency/fsis/

Resource Summary: FSIS is the public health agency in the Department of Agriculture responsible for ensuring that meat, poultry, and egg products are safe, wholesome, and accurately labeled. The FSIS Web site offers information concerning the agency, its activities, and food safety issues. Main categories include Mission and Activities, News and Information, Publications, Consumer Education and Information, and Organization/Program Areas. These sections contain a number of online factsheets, newsletters, and lists of recalls.

For consumers concerned with food safety, this site offers a variety of useful resources.

Subject Headings: Consumer Information; Food Safety; Inspectors

SuDoc Number: A 110.19: *The Food Safety Educator*

[389] Hazardous and Medical Waste Program

Sponsoring Agencies: Army Center for Health Promotion and Preventive Medicine; Directorate of Environmental Health Engineering; Hazardous and Medical Waste Program

Primary Access: http://chppm-meis.apgea.army.mil/

Resource Summary: This site features sections on Compliance, Military Item Disposal Instructions, Pollution Prevention, Special Studies and Technologies, Training, and Program Management. Hazardous and Medical Waste Program Information Papers are available on a number of subjects, including waste disposal. The ProAct Fact Sheets provide information so that members of the military can respond to hazardous waste proactively and dispose of it properly.

Subject Headings: Army; Hazardous Waste; Medical Waste

[390] Health Resources and Services Administration

Sponsoring Agency: Health Resources and Services Administration (HRSA)

Primary Access: http://www.hrsa.dhhs.gov/

Resource Summary: This site includes information through sections titled Overview and Programs, News and Public Affairs, Grants and Contracts, Staff Directory, Job Opportunities, and Upcoming Events. Most of the information available from the site describes the agency and its component bureaus. Other than press releases, no publications are directly available from the HRSA site. However, the section titled Overview and Programs lists the individual bureaus and offices which provide some fact sheets and other publications. The component bureaus of the HRSA are the Office of the Administrator, Bureau of Primary Health Care, Bureau of Health Professions, Bureau of Health Resources Development, Maternal and Child Health Bureau, Office of Rural Health Policy, and Center for Managed Care.

A centralized list of available publications would be a nice addition to this site. While it contains some useful information on public health, it is not yet a major source.

Subject Headings: Grants—Health Sciences; Public Health

[391] Health Services/Technology Assessment Text

Sponsoring Agencies: Agency for Health Care Policy and Research (AHCPR); National Library of Medicine (NLM); Preventive Services Task Force

Primary Access: http://text.nlm.nih.gov/

Alternative Access Methods: http://text.nlm.nih.gov/ftrs/gateway
gopher://gopher.nlm.nih.gov/11/hstat/
ftp://nlmpubs.nlm.nih.gov/hstat/
telnet://hstat@text.nlm.nih.gov/

Resource Summary: Health Services/Technology Assessment Text (HSTAT) provides access to full-text documents in the area of health care decision making. HSTAT includes AHCPR *Clinical Practice Guidelines* and *Quick Reference Guides for Clinicians*; AHCPR consumer brochures; *Health Technology Assessment Reports*; and National Institutes of Health (NIH) consensus development conference and technology assessment reports. HSTAT also provides Warren G. Magnuson Clinical Center research protocols; HIV/AIDS Treatment Information Service (ATIS) resource documents; Substance Abuse and Mental Health Services Administration (SAMHSA) treatment improvement protocols; and the *Guide to Clinical Preventive Services*.

Each of the categories is accessible either by a table of contents, which lists each of the component reports, or via a search mechanism, which searches for diagnosis, sign, symptom, or other phrase or key words. HSTAT provides a significant body of full-text documents within its limited subject area.

Subject Headings: Health Care Management; Reports—Full Text

SuDoc Numbers: HE 1.6/3:C 61/3 *Guide to Clinical Preventive Services*
HE 20.6512/7: *Health Technology Assessment Reports*
HE 20.6520: *Clinical Practice Guidelines*
HE 20.6520/2: *Quick Reference Guides for Clinicians*

[392] HIV/AIDS Surveillance Report

Sponsoring Agency: Centers for Disease Control and Prevention (CDC)

Primary Access: http://www.cdc.gov/nchstp/hiv_aids/stats/hasrlink.htm

Alternative Access Methods: gopher://gopher.niaid.nih.gov:70/11/aids/csr
gopher://cdcnac.aspensys.com:72/11/4

Resource Summary: These semiannual reports contain detailed statistics on the incidence of HIV and AIDS in the United States. The electronic versions start in 1993 and are available in PDF and ASCII format.

These reports have been available in print for a number of years at varying frequencies. The online versions are easy to use and browse.

Subject Heading: AIDS (disease)—Full Text

SuDoc Number: HE 20.7011/38 *HIV/AIDS Surveillance Report*

[393] Indian Health Services

Sponsoring Agency: Indian Health Services (IHS)

Primary Access: http://www.ihs.gov/

Alternative Access Method: http://www.tucson.ihs.gov/

Resource Summary: The IHS site includes the section Recruitment Pages which contains a job vacancies area, facilities information, and an IHS Tour. This site also includes the section, IHS Employees InfoNet, which offers information for IHS health care professionals and other employees; the IHS Communications Page which includes a list of publications and entries in the *Congressional Record*; and a monthly feature article. Available IHS publications include the *IHS Primary Care Provider* in HTML format from December 1994 to July 1995 and in PDF format since August 1995. Additionally, there is an index to the *IHS Primary Care Provider* for 1981-1994.

An expansion of the site is planned which will continue to target four main groups: IHS employees, congressional liaisons, tribal liaisons, and the public. While this site offers something for each of these groups, the new plan should make the IHS site even more effective at delivering additional information and content to all of these groups.

Subject Headings: American Indians; Minorities

SuDoc Number: HE 20.9423: *IHS Primary Care Provider*

[394] International Health Program Office

Sponsoring Agency: International Health Program Office (IHPO)

Primary Access: http://www.cdc.gov/ihpo/homepage.htm

Resource Summary: The IHPO pages contain information related to the IHPO mission of collaborating with other nations and international organizations to promote healthy lifestyles and to prevent excess disease, disability, and death. The top level page presents sections titled About IHPO, International Health Information for Travelers, Publications, and Centers for Disease Control's (CDC) Global Health Programs and Activities. Another major section is the Major Program Areas, which includes the subsections International Emergency and Refugee Health; Community and Facility Development and Evaluation; Populations in Transition; Global Health Policy; Global Information Resources, Support, and Training; and CDC Global Health Services. Rather than pointing to separate pages for each category, the IHPO page includes the secondary links on the top level page.

Although there are not a substantial number of resources on this site, breaking the categories into separate pages would make it easier to navigate.

Subject Headings: Health Promotion—International; Travel

[395] Lab of Neurosciences

Sponsoring Agency: National Institute on Aging (NIA). Laboratory of Neurosciences (LNS)

Primary Access: http://adobe.nia.nih.gov/

Resource Summary: This site features information on the LNS Memory and Aging Program. It includes some neuroimaging pictures, an online application for participation in an LNS study, and an e-mail directory for the lab.

It seems that little has been updated on this server since mid-1995. More recent information from LNS would be a useful addition.

Subject Headings: Elderly; Memory; Neurology

[396] Lister Hill National Center for Biomedical Communications

Sponsoring Agencies: Lister Hill National Center for Biomedical Communications; National Library of Medicine (NLM)

Primary Access: http://www.nlm.nih.gov/about_nlm/organization/lister_hill/ lhncbc.html

Resource Summary: This page primarily describes the activities of the Center, its divisions, and its director. One of the few links available connects to a fact sheet on the Unified Medical Language System (UMLS).

Subject Headings: Biomedical Information; Unified Medical Language System (UMLS)

[397] *Morbidity and Mortality Weekly Report*

Sponsoring Agency: Centers for Disease Control and Prevention (CDC)

Primary Access: http://www.cdc.gov/epo/mmwr/mmwr.html

Alternative Access Methods: ftp://ftp.cdc.gov/pub/Publications/mmwr/
mailto:lists@list.cdc.gov with "subscribe mmwr-toc" in body

Resource Summary: The *Morbidity and Mortality Weekly Report* (MMWR), along with its other associated reports, has been a standard source for detailed statistics. The online version presents the full text of each issue of the *MMWR* in Adobe PDF format dating back to January 1993, Volume 42, Issue 1. Each issue for 1995 forward also has an HTML preview, which includes the titles and first paragraphs from each article. A searchable index of the *MMWR,* along with other publications such as the *Surveillance Summaries* and the *Recommendations and Reports,* goes back to 1993.

The CDC has done a commendable job of converting this publication to an online format. It is well organized, and it is relatively easy to find articles by date as well as by keyword using the searchable index. Although this site does not offer issues prior to January 1993, earlier issues of *MMWR* are available on the CDC Wonder site.

Subject Headings: Electronic Periodicals; Health Statistics

SuDoc Numbers: HE 20.7009: *Morbidity and Mortality Weekly Report*
HE 20.7009: *MMWR Summary of Notifiable Diseases*
HE 20.7009/2: *MMWR CDC Surveillance Summaries*
HE 20.7009/2-2: *MMWR Recommendations and Reports*

National Center for Health Statistics

How to...	News Releases and Fact Sheets
About NCHS	Frequently Asked Questions
What's New	FEDSTATS and Other Sites
Coming Events	Customer Satisfaction Survey
Products	Search
Data Warehouse	E-mail

[398] National Center for Health Statistics

Sponsoring Agency: National Center for Health Statistics (NCHS)

Primary Access: http://www.cdc.gov/nchswww/nchshome.htm

Resource Summary: The NCHS site is especially rich in PDF versions of many of their reports. The What's New section announces recently released reports and press releases. Other press releases can be found under the News Releases and Fact Sheets section. The press releases are divided by year and then by topic. Reports are found under the Publications category, a subsection of the NCHS Products section. Among the available reports are *Vital and Health Statistics, Advance Data from the Vital and Health Statistics, National Health Interview Series, Monthly Vital Statistics Report, Health United States*, and the *NCHS Catalog of University Presentations*. Information on how to order print publications and where to write for vital records is also available in the same area.

Not all of the reports in a given series are available on the NCHS site, and those that are available go back to 1994 at the earliest. Even so, this site contains a substantial number of major sources of health statistics. One major publication that is lacking at this point is an online version of the *Vital Statistics of the United States.*

Subject Heading: Health Statistics

SuDoc Numbers: HE 20.6209 *Vital and Health Statistics*
HE 20.6209/3 *Advance Data from the Vital and Health Statistics*
HE 20.6209/4 *National Health Interview Series*
HE 20.6217: *Monthly Vital Statistics Report*
HE 20.7042/: *Health United States*
HE 20.6225: *NCHS Catalog of University Presentations*

[399] National Center for Injury Prevention and Control

Sponsoring Agency: National Center for Injury Prevention and Control (NCIPC)

Primary Access: http://www.cdc.gov/ncipc/ncipchm.htm

Resource Summary: NCIPC seeks to reduce morbidity, disability, mortality, and costs associated with injuries outside the workplace. Their Web site features top level links to the Center's divisions which include: Acute Care, Rehabilitation, and Disabilities; Unintentional Injury Prevention; and Violence Prevention. Other top level categories include About the NCIPC; What's New; Research Grants and Funding Opportunities; Scientific Data, Surveillance, and Injury Statistics; and Publications and Resources. This last category includes a number of bibliographies of NCIPC publications, ordering information, and a few publications in various formats.

Detailed injury mortality statistics and the few available full-text publications are the major features of this site.

Subject Headings: Injuries; Preventive Medicine; Violence—Prevention

[400] National Health Information Center

Sponsoring Agencies: National Health Information Center (NHIC); Office of Disease Prevention and Health Promotion (ODPHP)

Primary Access: http://nhic-nt.health.org/

Resource Summary: The NHIC Web site features health information for the consumer. The Health Information Resource Database includes 1,100 organizations and government offices that provide health information upon request. Entries include contact information, brief descriptive abstracts, and information about the publications and services that the organizations provide. This section also includes a list of toll-free numbers for health information. The Publications page offers a publications list, information on Healthy People 2000, and a list of national health observances such as Diabetic Eye Disease Awareness Month.

Subject Heading: Consumer Information

[401] National Immunization Program

Sponsoring Agency: National Immunization Program (NIP)

Primary Access: http://www.cdc.gov/nip/home.htm

Alternative Access Method: http://www.cdc.gov/nip/shock.htm [Shockwave version]

Resource Summary: The NIP site includes sections titled What's New; Frequently Asked Questions; About NIP; and Publications, Products, and Services. The Products part features downloadable software called Clinical Assessment Software Applications (CASA). The Publications page is empty, and the Services page lists some toll-free help line numbers.

Beautifully designed, this site is quite graphics intensive, which can make for slow loading over a modem connection—the alternate Shockwave site takes even longer. The site is well organized; however, when compared to other CDC, sites it is still lacking in content.

Subject Heading: Immunization

[402] National Institute of Child Health and Human Development

Sponsoring Agency: National Institute of Child Health and Human Development (NICHD)

Primary Access: http://www.nih.gov/nichd/

Resource Summary: The NICHD site has an employment opportunity section, an organizational chart, a couple of reports, and a few *NICHD News Notes*.

This site offers very little information beyond the *News Notes,* which are basically press releases.

Subject Heading: Human Development

SuDoc Number: HE 20.3364/3: *NICHD News Notes*

[403] National Institute of Environmental Health Sciences

Sponsoring Agency: National Institute of Environmental Health Sciences (NIEHS)

Primary Access: http://www.niehs.nih.gov/

Resource Summary: The NIEHS site links to a wide variety of information in the environmental health area. One major resource is an electronic version of *Environmental Health Perspectives* and its supplements. Unfortunately, it only includes abstracts and the table of contents. The abstracts database is searchable and contains information dating back to 1974. Other major links, listed separately, include the National Toxicology Program and the Environmental Health Clearinghouse. Agency information includes some background on NIEHS, an events calendar, employment opportunities, research funding, and contact information.

While this site links to a substantial body of environmental health documents, the addition of the full text for *Environmental Health Perspectives* would be welcome.

Subject Headings: Environmental and Occupational Health; Grants—Health Sciences

SuDoc Number: HE 20.3559: *Environmental Health Perspectives*

[404] National Institute on Aging

Sponsoring Agencies: Alzheimer's Disease Education and Referral Center (ADEAR); National Institute on Aging (NIA)

Primary Access: http://www.nih.gov/nia/

Alternative Access Method: http://www.cais.com/adear/

Resource Summary: The NIA Web site features a range of information on aging from NIA announcements to grant information to fact sheets for the public. The What's New section features appointments, upcoming events, employment opportunities, press releases, and media advisories of significant findings from NIA-supported research. The NIA Research section lists extramural aging research at other institutions throughout the country and intramural research on the NIH campus and at the Gerontology Research Center. The Funding and Training section covers available NIA grants, the application process, and research training related to aging. The Health Information section offers publications on health and aging topics for both health professionals and the public. One link under Publications leads to the NIA's Alzheimer's Disease Education and Referral Center (ADEAR). ADEAR contains a referral service, publications on Alzheimer's, and news on current NIA research about the disease.

The NIA provides a good mix of information on this site for researchers, health professionals, and the public. While not all of the publications listed are available online, an increasing number are accessible in HTML format. The Alzheimer's disease material may be especially useful to the general public.

Subject Headings: Aging; Alzheimer's Disease; Elderly; Grants—Health Sciences

[405] National Institute on Alcohol Abuse and Alcoholism

Sponsoring Agency: National Institute on Alcohol Abuse and Alcoholism (NIAAA)

Primary Access: http://www.niaaa.nih.gov/

Resource Summary: The NIAAA site features many of the same categories as other National Institutes of Health sites: Welcome, Publications and Databases, News and Events, and Grants/Contracts Information. The Publications section includes the full text of the *Alcohol Alerts* along with table of contents and summaries from many other NIAAA publications.

The site is useful to the general public for introductory information on alcoholism. It is also beneficial to the researcher looking for grant opportunities and to the individual looking for a list of NIAAA publications.

Subject Headings: Alcoholism; Grants—Health Sciences

SuDoc Number: HE 20.8322: *Alcohol Alert*

[406] NIOSH

Sponsoring Agency: National Institute of Occupational Safety and Health (NIOSH)

Primary Access: http://www.cdc.gov/niosh/homepage.html

Resource Summary: This NIOSH site provides information about NIOSH and related activities. Featured sections include the National Occupational Research Agenda; Meetings, Conferences and Symposia; NIOSH Respirator Information; NIOSH Activities in the 50 States; NIOSH Publications; and NIOSH Database Information.

Under NIOSH Publications, a number of publications and publication lists can be found. This includes lists of *Criteria for a Recommended Standard* . . . series, *NIOSH Alerts*, and *NIOSH Current Intelligence Bulletins (CIBs)*. The full text of some of the publications is available. The 1994 *NIOSH Manual of Analytical Methods* and a few of the Health Hazard Evaluation Program summaries are also available, although the *Manual* is only available in WordPerfect 5.1 format. Agency information on the NIOSH Web includes a small NIOSH directory, employment opportunities, research fellowships, and NIOSH activities in the 50 states.

The NIOSH site does not make the best use of Web design and layout, but with a little digging in some of the categories, a substantial number of full-text documents can be found.

Subject Heading: Environmental and Occupational Health

SuDoc Numbers: HE 20.7108:994/ *NIOSH Manual of Analytical Methods*
HE 20.7110: *Criteria for a Recommended Standard* . . .
HE 20.7123: *NIOSH Alerts*
HE 20.7115: *NIOSH Current Intelligence Bulletins (CIBs)*
HE 20.7125: *Health Hazard Evaluation Summaries*

[407] OASD Health Affairs

Sponsoring Agency: Department of Defense (DoD). Office of the Assistant Secretary of Defense (Health Affairs) (OASD)

Primary Access: http://www.ha.osd.mil/

Resource Summary: This DoD site features a number of health topics related to the military. The Web page includes sections on the Computer/Electronic Accommodations Program (CAP), Medical Readiness, Persian Gulf Illness, Clinical Issues, PharmacoEconomic Center, Health Affairs Acquisitions, and Legislative Material. The Persian Gulf Illness site includes some full-text reports on the Gulf War Veterans' Disease (listed on the site as Persian Gulf Illness).

The Persian Gulf Illness section of this site is likely to be the portion most widely used by the general public. Other sections should be of interest to those in the military with health concerns.

Subject Headings: Gulf War Veterans' Disease; Medicine—Military Support

[408] Occupational Safety and Health Administration

Sponsoring Agency: Occupational Safety and Health Administration (OSHA)

Primary Access: http://www.osha.gov/

Alternative Access Methods: http://www.osha-slc.gov/
gopher://gabby.osha-slc.gov/

Resource Summary: The OSHA Web site contains a substantial number of pages and documents both on the agency and on its regulations and publications. Major categories include Media Releases, Publications, Programs and Services, Compliance Assistance, Statistics and Data, Standards, and Other OSHA Documents. While some OSHA publications such as their *Fact Sheets* are under the Publications category, others can be found under different sections. For example, the *Standard Industrial Classification Manual* is available under Statistics and Data.

Also under the Statistics and Data section, frequently cited OSHA Standards can be searched by Standard Industrial Classification number. Use the search feature to get to the full text of the standards and regulations along with interpretations. Agency information available on the site includes directories, press releases, a mission statement, and an OSHA planning document.

While there is a substantial collection of documents available on this site, and the top level page is fairly well organized, it can still be difficult to find specific OSHA information. The site would be much improved if the full-text versions of OSHA regulations were directly linked from all mentions of them.

Subject Heading: Environmental and Occupational Health

SuDoc Numbers: L 35.24: *Fact Sheets*
PrEx 2.6/2:In 27/987 *Standard Industrial Classification Manual*

[409] Office of the Assistant Secretary for Planning and Evaluation

Sponsoring Agency: Department of Health and Human Services (HHS). Assistant Secretary for Planning and Evaluation (ASPE)

Primary Access: http://aspe.os.dhhs.gov/

Alternative Access Method: gopher://gopher.os.dhhs.gov/11/dhhs/os/aspe

Resource Summary: The Office of the Assistant Secretary for Planning and Evaluation is responsible for policy analysis and advice, policy development, strategic and implementation planning, and coordination and conduct of evaluation and policy research for the Department of Health and Human Services. The ASPE home page offers a sampling of work in selected policy areas including Comparisons of the Major Immigration and Welfare Reform Proposals; Children and Youth Policy Issues and Programs; Economic Support for Families; Disability, Aging, and Long-Term Care; Teen Pregnancy; and the HHS Fatherhood Initiative.

Other features of the page include a list of grant winners for research on poverty, the Policy Information Center with its searchable database of program evaluation abstracts, HHS Poverty Guidelines, and an HHS issues forum. The site also features a PDF version of *Trends in the Well-Being of America's Children and Youth*. The Gopher site only includes a searchable version of the Program Information Center evaluation abstracts.

The ASPE home page is a good starting point for information on public health policy and issues.

Subject Headings: Planning; Public Health

SuDoc Number: HE 1.63: *Trends in the Well-Being of America's Children and Youth*

[410] Prevent Chronic Diseases - NCCDPHP

Sponsoring Agency: National Center for Chronic Disease Prevention and Health Promotion (NCCDPHP)

Primary Access: http://www.cdc.gov/nccdphp/nccdhome.htm

Resource Summary: The NCCDPHP home page features background information on chronic diseases, infant mortality, the cost-effectiveness of prevention, priorities, and state participation in NCCDPHP grant programs. Additionally, the site has information on NCCDPHP major program areas including surveillance, disease prevention and control, modification of risk factors, comprehensive approaches, and maternal and infant health.

Also on this page is a PDF version of *Physical Activity and Health: A Report of the Surgeon General.* This site also includes the *Executive Summary,* press releases, at-a-glance summaries, and ordering information for the full 1996 Report.

Although there are few in-depth documents available on this page, it does provide good background information on agency programs and on chronic diseases and their prevention.

Subject Headings: Diseases; Preventive Medicine

SuDoc Number: HE 20.7602:P56 *Physical Activity and Health: A Report of the Surgeon General. Executive Summary*

[411] Reducing the Burden of Diabetes

Sponsoring Agencies: Centers for Disease Control and Prevention (CDC); National Center for Chronic Disease Prevention and Health Promotion

Primary Access: http://www.cdc.gov/nccdphp/ddt/ddthome.htm

Resource Summary: Sponsored by the Division of Diabetes Translation, this site is concerned with translating scientific research findings into health promotion, disease prevention, and treatment strategies. The documents available on this site aim to reduce the burden of diabetes and to provide research-based information to the public. Major categories include What's New, Vision/ Mission Statement, Diabetes At-a-Glance, National Diabetes Fact Sheet, State-Based Diabetes Control Programs, Information for Health Care Practitioners, and Diabetes Articles from CDC. Other sections are under construction but should be available soon.

Even though a number of sections of the site are still being built, this site provides general information on diabetes along with more in-depth sections focusing on research. It is a useful site to visit for those interested in diabetes.

Subject Headings: Consumer Information—Full Text; Diabetes

[412] Substance Abuse and Mental Health Services Administration

Sponsoring Agency: Substance Abuse and Mental Health Services Administration (SAMHSA)

Primary Access: http://www.samhsa.gov/

Alternative Access Method: ftp://ftp.samhsa.gov/

Resource Summary: This site features information in sections such as SAMHSA's Programs and Service, Weekly Report, Statistical Information on Drug Abuse and Mental Health, Strategic Plan, Managed Care Initiatives, 1996 Funding Opportunities, and Events and Conferences. The Weekly Report page gives an update on the agency's activities including grant announcements, new publications, conference events, and much more. The Statistical section gives a description of both the *Substance Abuse and Mental Health Statistics Sourcebook* and the *National Household Survey on Drug Abuse*, which are actually available on the FTP server in Envoy format.

For statistical information on drug abuse, research grant funding opportunities, and general information on SAMSHA, this site proves to be useful.

Subject Headings: Drug Abuse; Grants—Health Sciences; Mental Health; Statistics

SuDoc Numbers: HE 20.402:SO 8 *Substance Abuse and Mental Health Statistics Sourcebook* HE 20.402:D 84/ *National Household Survey on Drug Abuse*

[413] Surgeon General's Advanced Desktop

Sponsoring Agencies: Brooks Air Force Base; Department of the Air Force. Surgeon General

Primary Access: http://usafsg.brooks.af.mil/

Alternative Access Method: http://usafsg.brooks.af.mil/frame3.html [frames version]

Resource Summary: This site includes a fair amount of information about the Surgeon General and the Air Force Medical Service including mission, values, goals, vision, and strategies. On the other hand, beyond external links, there is little on the site that goes beyond describing the agency and what it is doing. It would be of interest to those seeking information on military health strategies.

Subject Heading: Medicine—Military Support

[414] U.S. Army Center For Health Promotion and Preventive Medicine

Sponsoring Agency: Center For Health Promotion and Preventive Medicine (CHPPM)

Primary Access: http://chppm-www.apgea.army.mil/

Resource Summary: The top of this page begins with information about CHPPM, its mission, commander, fax number, organizational chart, and more. The remainder of the page displays a substantial body of links to many subsidiary pages. Some of the categories include Army Industrial Hygiene, Directorate of Health Promotion and Wellness, Entomological Sciences Program, Ground Water and Solid Waste Program, Water Supply Management Program, Environmental Noise Program, Hazardous and Medical Waste Program, Health Hazard Assessment Program, Laser and Optical Radiation Hazards Program, Medical Safety and Health Program, and Occupational Health Management Information System. Each of these categories, along with the others, gives a description of the program or office. Many of them provide additional documents on their topic or subject area.

The top level page is not easy to navigate but the site does have a substantial amount of information on health promotion. Though targeted at a military audience, there is also useful information for the general public.

Subject Headings: Army; Environmental and Occupational Health; Preventive Medicine

[415] Unique Physician Identifier Numbers

Sponsoring Agencies: Health Care Financing Administration (HCFA); Medical College of Wisconsin

Primary Access: http://www.fps.mcw.edu/www/upin.html

Alternative Access Method: gopher://gopher.cpg.mcw.edu/11gopher_root_upin%3A%5B000000%5D

Resource Summary: The Medical College of Wisconsin has purchased the original Unique Physician Identifier Numbers (UPIN) database from the federal government, reformatted the data elements, and indexed the files. Due to the massive size of the database, they have divided the file by states. Like its print counterpart, the *Medicare Unique Physician Identification Number Directory*, the database contains information on physicians in both solo and group practice who provide services for which claims are submitted to a Medicare carrier and for which payment is made under Medicare. Physicians practicing solely within health care maintenance organizations or other prepaid capitation systems are not included.

After choosing a specific state, the search interface is a simple entry box that will accept Boolean queries. The database includes physician name, specialty, credentials, Medicare Provider Identification Number (PIN), and ZIP code of the practice setting.

This database is primarily of interest to health care workers looking for a UPIN or Medicare PIN while filling out Medicare forms. The database can be used by the public to search by ZIP code and specialty to find a physician in a specific geographic area.

Subject Headings: Medicare and Medicaid; Physicians

SuDoc Number: HE 22.414: *Medicare Unique Physician Identification Number Directory*

[416] Welcome to MEDSITE

Sponsoring Agencies: Brooks Air Force Base; Medical Systems Implementation and Training Division

Primary Access: http://www.medsite.brooks.af.mil/

Alternative Access Method: telnet://newuser@medsva.brooks.af.mil

Resource Summary: MEDSITE, which takes its name from Medical Systems Implementation and Training Element, divides its offerings into MEDSITE Team Pages, Deployment Schedules, Deployable Composite Health Care System (CHCS), and CHCS Functionality Training.

The offerings from MEDSITE may be of interest to those researching the military medical response and support capabilities.

Subject Heading: Medicine—Military Support

[417] AIDS Bibliography

Sponsoring Agency: National Library of Medicine

Primary Access: gopher://gopher.nlm.nih.gov/11/bibs/aids

Alternative Access Method: ftp://nlmpubs.nlm.nih.gov/bibs/aids

Resource Summary: These bibliographies are straight ASCII files of references to journal articles, monographs, and audiovisuals. These are large text files, arranged alphabetically by subject. Only citations are included and there are no abstracts. The online version starts with October 1995.

While these are monthly publications, updates are infrequent and can be as much as six months behind.

Subject Headings: AIDS (disease); Bibliographic Databases

SuDoc Number: HE 20.3615/3: *AIDS Bibliography*

[418] CDC National AIDS Clearinghouse Web Server

Sponsoring Agency: Centers for Disease Control and Prevention (CDC)

Primary Access: http://www.cdcnac.org/

Alternative Access Methods: ftp://cdcnac.org/pub/cdcnac/
gopher://cdcnac.org:72/
mailto:listserv@cdcnac.aspensys.com with "sub aidsnews name" in body

Resource Summary: The National Aids Clearinghouse (NAC) includes reference and referral services, culturally specific educational materials, publications, clinical trials information, treatment information, and the AIDS Daily Summary which, according to the site, is a "news clipping service to help keep up with AIDS-related news."

This well designed Web site links to the other Internet services of the NAC and provides clear contact information for other types of communication with the Clearinghouse. This is a good starting point for government information on AIDS and HIV.

Subject Heading: AIDS (disease)

[419] Gulf War Veterans' Illnesses

Sponsoring Agency: Presidential Advisory Committee on Gulf War Veterans' Illnesses

Primary Access: http://www.gwvi.gov/

Resource Summary: This site comes from the President's Advisory Committee and includes information on the Committee's activities. Major links include Committee Purpose, Committee Members, Meetings Schedule, Meeting Transcripts, Interim Report, and Updates. The *Interim Report* is actually the meeting transcripts and is in HTML. The transcripts are also available in one downloadable zip file.

This is a good source for information about the Committee's activities and for information on the Gulf War Veterans' Disease. See also the GulfLINK site.

Subject Headings: Gulf War Veterans' Disease; Persian Gulf War 1991; Veterans—Health Care

SuDoc Number: Pr 42.8:AD 9/INT.REPT *Interim Report, Presidential Advisory Committee on Gulf War Veterans' Illnesses*

[420] GulfLINK

Sponsoring Agencies: Defense Technical Information Center (DTIC); Persian Gulf War Veterans' Illnesses Senior Level Oversight Panel

Primary Access: http://www.dtic.mil/gulflink/

Resource Summary: This site contains documents related to the possible causes of the illnesses being reported by veterans of the Persian Gulf War of 1991. GulfLINK includes a substantial collection of documents including reports, congressional testimony, and declassified documents. The declassified documents are in ASCII and are searchable by keyword and browsable by release date.

Other documents on the site include press releases, fact sheets, bibliographies, and speeches. Altogether, these create a sizable database of resources on the Gulf War Veterans' Disease. This collection is of use to veterans, health care workers, and researchers.

Subject Headings: Gulf War Veterans' Disease; Persian Gulf War 1991; Veterans—Health Care

[421] The Missing GulfLINK Files

Sponsoring Agency: Insignia Publishing Company, Inc.

Primary Access: http://www.insigniausa.com/gulflink.htm

Alternative Access Methods: http://insigniausa.com/gulflink.exe [entire collection in self-extracting format]
http://www.ozbod.demon.co.uk/gulflink/
http://www.rpi.edu/~bellw/billz_home/grunts/gulflink.html

Resource Summary: These 308 controversial files comprise a variety of official documents related to the Gulf War Veterans' disease. Originally posted on GulfLINK, they were removed for security reasons on February 8, 1996. The DoD returned 82 of these files to the Web site on August 30, 1996 and all 308 files are now available from this site and its mirrors. These are the copies of the files, as originally posted on GulfLINK.

These sites show that once documents are posted on the Internet, it can be difficult to remove them. The documents were removed from GulfLINK so they could be reviewed again for any classified information. They may all become available again on GulfLINK, but for now, these sites provide an excellent service for anyone interested in the Gulf War Veterans' disease.

Subject Heading: Gulf War Veterans' Disease

[422] National Cancer Institute

Sponsoring Agency: National Cancer Institute (NCI)

Primary Access: http://www.nci.nih.gov/

Alternative Access Method: gopher://www.nci.nih.gov/

Resource Summary: While the first categories listed are Intramural Research, Extramural Research, Technology Transfer, Administrative, Public Information, and International Cancer Information Center, the main body of the site can be found under Cancer Information Service. That page connects to CancerNet (described earlier in this chapter). The Research section links to the Web pages of NCI laboratories and its divisions. An HTML version of the *NCI Fact Book* is available under the Public Information offerings category. The International Cancer Information Center link goes straight to CancerNet.

Most users interested in information on cancer will be better served by going directly to CancerNet. This site is most useful for information specifically about the National Cancer Center.

Subject Heading: Cancer

SuDoc Number: HE 20.3174: *NCI Fact Book*

[423] National Center for HIV, STD, and TB Prevention

Sponsoring Agency: National Center for HIV, STD, and TB Prevention (NCHSTP)

Primary Access: http://www.cdc.gov/nchstp/od/nchstp.html

Alternative Access Method: http://www.cdc.gov/nchstp/od/Text/nchstp.html [text version]

Resource Summary: As the name of the agency implies, the NCHSTP Web site features three main sections that correspond to the agency's three main divisions: HIV/AIDS Prevention, STD Prevention, and TB Elimination. Each of the division pages contains links to relevant *Morbidity and Mortality Weekly Reports* along with a few other publications. The HIV/AIDS Prevention page contains the largest number of information sources including statistics, trials, treatment, funding, and conferences.

For information on any of the three areas covered by NCHSTP, this site is worth a visit. It offers sources for both researchers, patients, and the public.

Subject Headings: AIDS (disease); Sexually Transmitted Diseases (STD); Tuberculosis (TB)

[424] National Center for Infectious Diseases

Sponsoring Agency: National Center for Infectious Diseases (NCID)

Primary Access: http://www.cdc.gov/ncidod/ncid.htm

Alternative Access Methods: ftp://ftp.cdc.gov/pub/EID/
mailto:lists@list.cdc.gov with "subscribe EID-TOC" in body

Resource Summary: One major resource on this site is the electronic version of the journal *Emerging Infectious Diseases* (*EID*). The goals of *EID* and the NCID Web site are to promote the recognition of new and reemerging infectious diseases and to improve the understanding of factors involved in disease emergence, prevention, and elimination. *EID* has an international scope and is intended for professionals in infectious diseases and related sciences. The Web site contains the table of contents from the current and previous issues, instructions to authors, and information about the *EID*. The articles are available in HTML, PDF, ASCII, and PostScript formats.

Other sections of the NCID site include Selected Prevention and Control Areas; Publications (other than *EID*); and New, Reemerging, and Drug Resistant Infections. The alternate URLs only provide access to *EID*.

Especially within the online pages of *EID*, this site contains a great deal of information on the prevention and control of traditional, new, and reemerging infectious diseases both in the United States and around the world.

Subject Headings: Electronic Periodicals; Infectious Diseases

SuDoc Number: HE 20.7009/7: *Emerging Infectious Diseases*

[425] National Heart, Lung, and Blood Institute

Sponsoring Agency: National Heart, Lung, and Blood Institute (NHLBI)

Primary Access: http://www.nhlbi.nih.gov/nhlbi/nhlbi.html

Alternative Access Method: gopher://gopher.nhlbi.nih.gov/

Resource Summary: Most of the content of the site still remains on the Gopher server, but the Web site is being constructed and has links to sources on the Gopher. The Web site includes a few NHLBI publications and announcements in HTML and the NHLBI *Fact Book* in PDF. The Gopher includes information about the NHLBI, its organization, and personnel. It also features directories for press releases, education programs, advisory committees, and documents.

The Web site needs to be more clearly organized, and the movement of documents from the Gopher to the Web server would make this a more useful resource.

Subject Headings: Heart Disease; Smoking

[426] National Institute of Allergy and Infectious Diseases

Sponsoring Agency: National Institute of Allergy and Infectious Diseases (NIAID)

Primary Access: http://www.niaid.nih.gov/

Alternative Access Methods: http://www.niaid.nih.gov/textonly.htm [text version]
gopher://gopher.niaid.nih.gov/
gopher://odie.niaid.nih.gov/

Resource Summary: The NIAID home page features information from the agency where scientists work to develop new and improved ways to diagnose, treat, and prevent infectious diseases and disorders of the immune system. On this site, users can explore research on AIDS, tuberculosis, and other infectious diseases, allergic and immunologic diseases, asthma, transplantation, and more. The agency information on this site includes press releases, job openings, calendars of events, publications, and clinical trials recruitment. On the research side, the site lists research activities and resources including the AIDS reagent program catalog. For those seeking grants, the NIAID Extramural Information Center is now available.

While the Web site and the Gopher server cover many types of infectious diseases and allergies, these sites are especially useful for access to information on AIDS.

Subject Headings: AIDS (disease); Allergies; Infectious Diseases

[427] National Institute of Arthritis and Musculoskeletal and Skin Diseases

Sponsoring Agency: National Institute of Arthritis and Musculoskeletal and Skin Diseases (NIAMS)

Primary Access: http://www.nih.gov/niams/

Resource Summary: The NIAMS Web site provides public information, research databases, and grant opportunities in the fields of rheumatology, orthopedics, dermatology, metabolic bone diseases, heritable disorders of bone and cartilage, inherited and inflammatory muscle diseases, and sports medicine. Featured categories include About NIAMS, News and Events, Health Information, Scientific Resources, Grants and Contracts, Clinical Studies, and Reports. While some of these sections have very little content, the Grants and Contracts category and the Clinical Studies section provide more detailed information. The Health Information section includes the full text of pamphlets on such diseases as Lyme disease, fibromyalgia, and psoriasis.

While the NIAMS Web site is not as rich in content as some of the other NIH sites, it does have some basic information of interest to both researchers and the public.

Subject Headings: Arthritis; Diseases; Grants—Health Sciences

[428] National Institute of Diabetes and Digestive and Kidney Disease

Sponsoring Agency: National Institute of Diabetes and Digestive and Kidney Disease (NIDDK)

Primary Access: http://www.niddk.nih.gov/

Resource Summary: The NIDDK site features information on disorders covered by the agency, including diabetes, digestive diseases, endocrine diseases, hematologic diseases, kidney diseases, nutrition and obesity, and urologic diseases. Three bibliographic databases: Diabetes, Digestive Diseases, and Kidney and Urologic Diseases, reference health education material. Agency information includes an NIDDK staff directory, press releases, research funding, and postdoctoral positions.

Under each disease, the information content is useful but slim. But the bibliographic databases greatly enhance the usefulness of the site for finding additional resources.

Subject Headings: Diabetes; Diseases

[429] National Institute of Mental Health

Sponsoring Agency: National Institute of Mental Health (NIMH)

Primary Access: http://www.nimh.nih.gov/

Alternative Access Method: gopher://gopher.nimh.nih.gov/

Resource Summary: The NIMH site features the categories Publications and Education Programs, Grants and Contracts, Studies Seeking Volunteers, and Information on the NIMH. Information on the agency includes press releases, descriptions of the component offices and departments, and an NIMH events calendar. This section also has some basic information on mental illnesses. Under the Publications section, several recent pamphlets and general publications are available in HTML format. Many of these are in the *Decade of the Brain* series.

The NIMH Web site offers a small but informative body of literature on mental illnesses. While some of the information will be of interest primarily to researchers in mental health, other sections such as Publications can be useful to the general public.

Subject Headings: Depression; Grants—Health Sciences; Mental Health

SuDoc Numbers: HE 20.8102:Al 7/ *You Are Not Alone: Mental Health/Mental Illness*
HE 20.8102:AN 9 *Anxiety Disorders: Decade of the Brain*
HE 20.8102:B 52/2/ *Decade of the Brain: Bipolar Disorder*
HE 20.8102:B 73/3 *Decade of the Brain: Learning Disorders*
HE 20:8102:B 73/4 *Alzheimer's Disease*
HE 20.8102:D 36/2 *Attention Deficit Hyperactivity Disorder*
HE 20.8128:D 44/ *Plain Talk About Depression*
HE 20.3002:D 44/5/ *Depression: Effective Treatments are Available*
HE 20.8102:D 44/17 *If You're Over 65 and Feeling Depressed*
HE 20.8102:D 44/18 *Helpful Facts About Depressive Illness*
HE 20.8102:D 63/9 *Eating Disorders: Decade of the Brain*
HE 20.8102:OB 7/ *Obsessive-Compulsive Disorder: Decade of the Brain*
HE 20.8102:P 19/2 *Panic Disorder*
HE 20.8102:P 19/3 *Understanding Panic Disorder*
HE 20.8102:SCH 3/6 *Schizophrenia: Questions and Answers*
HE 20.8102:T 71/2/ *Getting Treatment for Panic Disorder*

[430] National Institute of Neurological Disorders and Stroke

Sponsoring Agency: National Institute of Neurological Disorders and Stroke (NINDS)

Primary Access: http://www.nih.gov/ninds/

Resource Summary: A primary category on the NINDS Web site is titled Health Information, which features information about selected neurological disorders, clinical trials, and clinical alerts and advisories. The Funding Information section provides details on NINDS grants and contracts, research training and development programs, ongoing program announcements, and requests for applications. Agency information on the NINDS site includes employment opportunities, press releases, and its organizational structure.

Although the site lacks substantial online publications beyond the brief documents found in the Health Information section, these can be useful in providing a quick overview on many neurological disorders.

Subject Headings: Grants—Health Sciences; Neurology; Strokes

[431] National Institute on Deafness and Other Communication Disorders

Sponsoring Agency: National Institute on Deafness and Other Communication Disorders (NIDCD)

Primary Access: http://www.nih.gov/nidcd/

Alternative Access Method: http://www.aerie.com/chid/nidcd/dctest.html

Resource Summary: Like many of the other NIH institutes, the NIDCD Web site features the sections: About the NIDCD, News and Events, Current Research, Health Information, and Grants and Contracts. Along with a few full-text pamphlets, the Health Information section includes the NIDCD Information Clearinghouse and its Deafness and Communication Disorders Database. This database provides titles, abstracts, and information and educational materials on deafness and other communication disorders.

The bibliographic database offers a useful supplement to the materials that are available in full text from the Web site.

Subject Headings: Bibliographic Databases; Deafness; Grants—Health Sciences

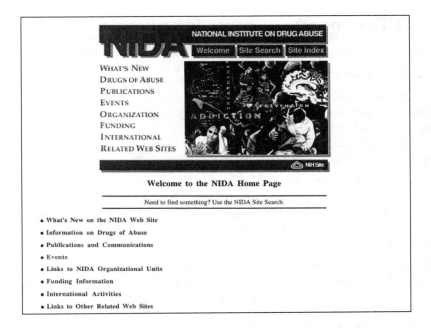

[432] National Institute on Drug Abuse

Sponsoring Agency: National Institute on Drug Abuse (NIDA)

Primary Access: http://www.nida.nih.gov/

Alternative Access Method: http://www.nida.nih.gov/NIDATOCtext.html [text version]

Resource Summary: The NIDA site includes its many categories on a long Web page. These categories include About NIDA; Events; NIDA Organizational Units; Publications and Communications; and Funding Information. The Publications and Communications section includes the full text of *NIDA Notes* dating back to 1995, and it also includes a few *NIDA Research Reports*.

The most substantial content on the NIDA site can be found in the Funding Information and Publications and Communications sections. The top level page could be redesigned to make it easier to navigate.

Subject Headings: Drug Abuse; Grants—Health Sciences

SuDoc Numbers: HE 20.8217/4: *NIDA Notes*
HE 20.8217/7: *NIDA Research Reports*

[433] NCI's CancerNet Cancer Information

Sponsoring Agencies: National Cancer Institute (NCI); National Institutes of Health (NIH)

Primary Access: http://wwwicic.nci.nih.gov/

Alternative Access Methods: gopher://gopher.nih.gov/11/clin/cancernet
mailto:cancernet@icicb.nci.nih.gov with "help" in body
http://imsdd.meb.uni-bonn.de/cancernet/cancernet.html
http://biomed.nus.sg/Cancer/welcome.html
gopher://biomed.nus.sg/11/NUS-NCI-CancerNet

Resource Summary: The CancerNet database has long been one of the most substantial and reliable information sources available on the Internet. Unlike other Internet sources, CancerNet not only comes from a reliable source for cancer information, NCI, but it states that all information located on the service has been reviewed by oncology experts and is based on the results of current research.

The main page provides access to the CancerNet database at different levels: Patients and the Public, Health Professionals, and Basic Researchers. The Patients and the Public section features General Information on Cancer, Treatment Information, Detection, Prevention and Genetics, Supportive Care Information, and Clinical Trial Information. From a number of these categories, CancerNet provides access to detailed HTML documents on different types of cancer from the Physician Data Query (PDQ) system.

The categories of data under the Health Professionals heading are similar to those for patients. Many of the links connect to PDQ documents; however, the documents are written for a more advanced level of medical understanding. There is also a link to topic searches from CancerLit on over 70 predefined cancer topics.

The Basic Researcher page links to the *Journal of the National Cancer Institute* (containing news and article abstracts only, not full text), the NCI Cooperative Breast Cancer Tissue Research Database, the AIDS Malignancy Bank Database, and the Cooperative Human Tissue Network.

The alternate sites mirror the data from the main CancerNet site, although the organization of the data may differ. In addition, the mirror sites may not always have the most up-to-date version of the database.

CancerNet is an incredible resource providing detailed and reliable information on many cancer topics. This is definitely a must-see site for information on cancer.

Subject Headings: Cancer; Consumer Information—Full Text; Medical Research

SuDoc Number: HE 20.3161: *Journal of the National Cancer Institute*

[434] Office of Disease Prevention and Health Promotion

Sponsoring Agency: Office of Disease Prevention and Health Promotion (ODPHP)

Primary Access: http://odphp.osophs.dhhs.gov/

Alternative Access Method: gopher://odphp.osophs.dhhs.gov/

Resource Summary: The ODPHP Web page consists primarily of announcements and links to ODPHP-sponsored sites such as the National Health Information Center. Some publications are not available in both ASCII and PDF formats—most of the ASCII documents are on the Gopher server.

Despite a basic design and a small range of content, the number of full-text publications make it a useful site for general health information. The addition of a full text keyword search option would make the documents more accessible.

Subject Headings: Health Promotion; Preventive Medicine

Health Sciences: Research

[435] Biology of the Mammary Gland

Sponsoring Agency: National Institutes of Health (NIH). Section of Developmental Biology

Primary Access: http://alice.dcrt.nih.gov/~mammary/

Resource Summary: This Web site serves as a forum to integrate various aspects of mammary gland biology and to promote collaborations and exchange of ideas, knowledge, and resources on that subject. It features a searchable Animal Models database, the New Tools and Technologies category, and user-submitted mini reviews on timely topics related to the biology of the mammary gland. Other sections include a BBS for messages, meeting announcements, information on the whey acidic protein, and some literature listings. This site is aimed primarily at researchers.

Subject Headings: Biology—Research; Genetics

[436] Edison

Sponsoring Agency: National Institutes of Health (NIH). Office of Policy for Extramural Research Administration

Primary Access: http://era.info.nih.gov/

Resource Summary: NIH grantees are required by law to report on activities involving the disposition of certain intellectual property rights that result from federally funded research. In order to facilitate compliance for cases involving inventions, patents, and licenses that have resulted from NIH funding agreements, the Office of Policy for Extramural Research Administration developed this online Extramural Invention Information Management System (code-named Edison). Edison has been designed to streamline grantees' administrative tasks in complying with the law.

This site is designed specifically for NIH grantees. It is of use only to those who fall under the provisions of the law and who have chosen to use this mechanism as an alternative to completing paper documentation.

Subject Headings: Intellectual Property; Regulations—Compliance

[437] FAA Civil Aeromedical Institute

Sponsoring Agencies: Civil Aeromedical Institute (CAMI); Federal Aviation Administration (FAA)

Primary Access: http://www.cami.jccbi.gov/

Resource Summary: The Civil Aeromedical Institute handles medical certification, research, and education in aviation safety. Their Web site offers resources related to CAMI research areas including Pilot Aeromedical Certification Records and Standards; Aviation Medical Examiner, Physiology and Survival; Human Behavior and Aviation Environment; Toxicology and Aircraft Accident, Protection, and Survival; and Preventive Medicine, Education, and Research. The Publications page provides access to technical report citations, the *Federal Air Surgeon's Medical Bulletin*, brochures, and the *Aviation Medical Examiners Directory*.

This is an excellent resource for researchers in aviation medicine and aviation safety.

Subject Heading: Aeronautics—Medical Aspects

SuDoc Number: TD 4.211: *Aviation Medical Examiners Directory*

[438] Frederick Cancer Research and Development Center

Sponsoring Agencies: Frederick Cancer Research and Development Center (FCRDC); National Cancer Institute (NCI)

Primary Access: http://www.ncifcrf.gov:1994/

Resource Summary: This site from the FCRDC appears to be primarily aimed at FCRDC personnel. It features the sections General Information; Administrative Offices; Computing Resources; Scientific/Research Programs; Research Support Services; and Campus Services/Facilities.

The FCRDC home page is of use to FCRDC staff and to those interested in learning more about the FCRDC.

Subject Headings: Cancer; Medical Research; Research Laboratories

[439] GenoBase Database Gateway

Sponsoring Agency: National Institutes of Health (NIH). BioInformatics and Molecular Analysis Section

Primary Access: http://specter.dcrt.nih.gov:8004/

Resource Summary: This experimental GenoBase server uses tables and various query capabilities to provide access to an NIH copy of GenoBase, which is a Prolog-based, object-oriented molecular biology database. This includes European Molecular Biology Laboratory and Swiss-Prot. The Web version includes a substantial subset of the data in GenoBase, but not all. The page also has a long list of other links to important molecular biology resources.

The detailed research-level information available from this site makes it of most interest to the research scientist.

Subject Headings: Genetics; Molecular Biology

[440] GrantsNet

Sponsoring Agencies: Department of Health and Human Services (HHS); National Performance Review (NPR)

Primary Access: http://www.os.dhhs.gov/progorg/grantsnet/

Alternative Access Methods: gopher://gopher.os.dhhs.gov/1/Topics/grantsnet/
mailto:listserv@list.nih.gov with "subscribe gnet-l name" in body

Resource Summary: GrantsNet is a tool for finding and exchanging information about HHS and selected other federal grant programs. It aims to provide government resources to the general public in a more accessible and meaningful manner. It contains information on how to search for funding opportunities and how to administer awards.

This can be a useful site for anyone pursuing grant funding from HHS or anyone interested in the process.

Subject Heading: Grants—Health Sciences

[441] Internet Grateful Med

Sponsoring Agency: National Library of Medicine (NLM)

Primary Access: http://igm.nlm.nih.gov/

Resource Summary: Internet Grateful Med is a fee-based gateway system that interacts with the user and then connects to the Medlars databases on the user's behalf. The Web version of the Grateful Med software makes for easier connections to Medline and other MEDLARS databases over the Internet. The Web version has many of the features of the regular Grateful Med software, including the addition of an online connection to the Unified Medical Language System Metathesaurus. The service can be used by anyone with a Grateful Med or Medlars account.

While this Web version can be a little slow, it is a major improvement over the older version of Grateful Med, which connected over the phone lines. The connection to the Metathesaurus with the Find Related button and the Analyze Search feature make searching Medline easier for the novice searcher.

Subject Headings: Bibliographic Databases; Medical Research; Medline; Unified Medical Language System (UMLS)

[442] John E. Fogarty International Center

Sponsoring Agency: John E. Fogarty International Center (FIC)

Primary Access: http://www.nih.gov/fic/

Resource Summary: The FIC aims to improve people's health through the promotion of international cooperation and advanced study in the biomedical sciences. The FIC fosters research partnerships between American scientists and foreign counterparts through grants, fellowships, exchange awards and international agreements. The FIC Web site serves as one means for sharing such information. The main categories include About the Fogarty International Center; Publications (which contains directories of grants); Regional Information; Research and Training Opportunities; Scholars-in-Residence; and News and Vacancy Announcements.

For health sciences researchers interested in international study, this is an important site.

Subject Heading: Health Promotion—International

[443] Laboratory of Structural Biology

Sponsoring Agency: Laboratory of Structural Biology

Primary Access: http://www.mgsl.dcrt.nih.gov/docs/start.html

Alternative Access Method: http://aqueous.labs.brocku.ca/osfile.html

Resource Summary: This site features information on the osmotic stress method and the measurements of macromolecular forces. It offers preprints on macromolecular forces and the osmotic stress method in general. The alternate site only mirrors the archive of osmotic pressure data of various osmotic agents measured at different external conditions.

Subject Headings: Osmotic Stress; Research Laboratories; Thermodynamics

[444] Lawrence Berkeley National Laboratory Human Genome Center

Sponsoring Agencies: Human Genome Center; Lawrence Berkeley National Laboratory (LBL)

Primary Access: http://www-hgc.lbl.gov/GenomeHome.html

Alternative Access Method: ftp://genome.lbl.gov/pub/seq/

Resource Summary: The LBL Genome Sequencing Center is a large-scale sequencing operation. Sequences available here include 1.9 megabases of human sequence (mostly 5q31) and 3.5 megabases of Drosophila Melanogaster sequence (in collaboration with the Berkeley Drosophila Genome Project). The sequences are available on the ftp site. Human Genome Center groups linked on the site include Automation, Biology, Informatics, and Sequencing. This Web site also includes information on the Human Genome Center, its personnel, and its organization.

This site features substantial data sets for genome researchers.

Subject Headings: Genetics; Genomes

[445] MEDLARS Information Retrieval

Sponsoring Agency: National Library of Medicine (NLM)

Primary Access: telnet://medlars.nlm.nih.gov/

Resource Summary: The Medical Literature Analysis and Retrieval System (MEDLARS) databases, including Medline, are available for a fee to anyone that signs up for an account. Telnet access to the databases simply provides an alternate mode of access to the MEDLARS system compared to the more traditional direct phone lines or public data network access.

For a Web interface to the MEDLARS databases, try Internet Grateful Med (described separately), which still requires a MEDLARS account.

Subject Headings: Bibliographic Databases; Medline

SuDoc Number: HE 20.3612 *Index Medicus*

[446]   The National Center for Biotechnology Information

Sponsoring Agencies: National Center for Biotechnology Information (NCBI); National Library of Medicine (NLM)

Primary Access: http://www.ncbi.nlm.nih.gov/

Alternative Access Methods: gopher://ncbi.nlm.nih.gov/
ftp://ncbi.nlm.nih.gov/Home.html
mailto:retrieve@ncbi.nlm.nih.gov with "help" in body
mailto:blast@ncbi.nlm.nih.gov with "help" in body

Resource Summary: This NCBI site includes huge databases of genetic information including GenBank, the DNA Sequence Database; the Online Mendelian Inheritance in Man (OMIM), a catalog of human genes and genetic disorders; Entrez, which includes a subset of Medline, the NCBI protein database, and the NCBI nucleotide database; and Basic Local Alignment Search Tool (BLAST) for searching for sequences. The site includes information on submitting new sequences using BankIt, along with detailed explanations of how to use the e-mail interfaces to BLAST and GenBank.

This is an important site for genome and genetic sequence researchers. The site provides access to multiple databases with detailed help files for use in searching the databases. NCBI gives multiple means of accessing the data.

Subject Headings: Biotechnology; BLAST; GenBank; Genetics; Genomes; Molecular Biology; OMIM

SuDoc Numbers: HE 20.3624: *Entrez*
HE 20.3624/2: *NCBI Newsletter*

[447] National Center for Human Genome Research

Sponsoring Agency: National Center for Human Genome Research (NCHGR)

Primary Access: http://www.nchgr.nih.gov/

Resource Summary: Numerous links to genome databases and resources can be found on this NCHGR site. The main categories include The Human Genome Project, Genome and Genetic Data, Intramural Research, Grant Information, Policy and Public Affairs, and About NCHGR. Links to the databases such as GenBank are in the Genome and Genetic Data section; however, they are all external databases. In the Grant Information section there is a searchable database of NCHGR grants, which gives a list of grants in different sort orders.

Beyond the links to external resources, of which there are many, this site primarily consists of agency information.

Subject Headings: Genetics; Genomes

[448] National Center for Research Resources

Sponsoring Agencies: National Center for Research Resources (NCRR); National Institutes of Health (NIH)

Primary Access: http://www.ncrr.nih.gov/

Resource Summary: The NCRR site features a variety of resources for biomedical researchers. The link About NCRR includes general information including a mission statement, an organizational chart, a strategic plan, employment opportunities, and staff directory. The NCRR Extramural Activities and NCRR Intramural Activities sections include descriptions of, and information about, NCRR extramural and intramural funding opportunities. The Grants Information section has information about both NIH and NCRR grants opportunities. Access to Research Resources includes directories of NCRR-supported research resources and information on how to access them. The News, Publications, and Program Highlights section features current events, press releases, publications, program highlights, and information about the National Advisory Research Resources Council.

A useful site for the health sciences researcher seeking grant funding, the NCRR site is also useful for finding information about current research studies.

Subject Headings: Genetics; Grants—Health Sciences; Medical Research

SuDoc Number: HE 20.3013/6: *Research Resources Reporter*

[449] National Center for Toxicological Research

Sponsoring Agency: National Center for Toxicological Research (NCTR)

Primary Access: gopher://gopher.nctr.fda.gov/

Alternative Access Method: http://www.fda.gov/opacom/hptoxic.html

Resource Summary: While the alternate Web page provides a brief description of the agency, the only link is to the NCTR Gopher site. Even the Gopher site is fairly sparse, with a couple of text files that describe NCTR, its Gopher, and the Third International Conference on Phytoestrogens (from 1995). The site also has a folder on phytoestrogens with a text file describing phytoestrogens and containing a large phytoestrogens bibliography.

NCTR conducts peer-reviewed scientific research in anticipation of the Food and Drug Administration's regulatory needs. However, their Internet sites provide information on only a very small portion of the activities in which they are involved.

Subject Headings: Phytoestrogens; Toxicology

[450] National Eye Institute

Sponsoring Agency: National Eye Institute (NEI)

Primary Access: http://www.nei.nih.gov/

Resource Summary: The National Eye Institute Web site features the categories NEI Vision Exhibit at the Franklin Institute, NEI Funding Information, Publications, NEI Sponsored Clinical Studies, and NEI Intramural Research. Under the Publications link there are a few resources for the general public and the education community, but most of the other resources will be primarily of interest to researchers.

Subject Headings: Grants—Health Sciences; Ophthalmology; Vision

[451] National Institute of Dental Research

Sponsoring Agency: National Institute of Dental Research (NIDR)

Primary Access: http://www.nidr.nih.gov/

Alternative Access Method: http://www.aerie.com/nohicweb/

Resource Summary: The NIDR site offers a substantial collection of documents and information on dental research. The main links are Welcome to NIDR (including its mission, organization, staff directories, visitor information, and employment opportunities); Research Highlights; News, Publications, and Health Information (including the National Oral Health Information Clearing-house); Oral Health Research at NIDR; NIDR Programs; and Funding Information (listing NIDR grant programs, requests for applications, and requests for proposals). The National Oral Health Information Clearinghouse features the Oral Health Database. This bibliographic database includes a variety of health-related materials and educational resources that fall outside the scope of more technical, research-based collections. It has a strong patient education focus and high-lights materials such as fact sheets, brochures, videocassettes, newsletter articles, catalogs, and other educational resources for patients and professionals.

Along with a few full-text publications and the detailed grant information, the Oral Health Data-base makes this site an important stop for practical information on dental and oral health.

Subject Headings: Bibliographic Databases; Dentistry; Grants—Health Sciences

[452] National Institute of General Medical Sciences

Sponsoring Agency: National Institute of General Medical Sciences (NIGMS)

Primary Access: http://www.nih.gov/nigms/

Alternative Access Method: http://www.gdb.org/coriell.html

Resource Summary: NIGMS supports basic biomedical research that is not targeted at specific diseases but rather lays the foundation for advances in disease diagnosis, treatment, and prevention. The NIGMS Web site contains a Funding Information category, which includes program announcements, grant award mechanisms, application dates, and a grant list. The Science Education section features some full-text publications including *Why Do Basic Research?* and *Medicines by Design*. Agency information includes press releases, a staff listing, employment opportunities, and visitor information. The alternate URL hosts the NIGMS *Catalog of Cell Cultures and DNA Samples*.

Of most interest to researchers working with NIGMS, the site does have a bit to offer the public in terms of its explanations of the importance of basic research.

Subject Heading: Medical Research

SuDoc Numbers: HE 20.3452:R 31/3 *Why Do Basic Research?*
HE 20.3464: *Catalog of Cell Cultures and DNA Samples*

[453] National Institute of Nursing Research

Sponsoring Agency: National Institute of Nursing Research (NINR)

Primary Access: http://www.nih.gov/ninr/

Resource Summary: The National Institute of Nursing Research site features the categories Documents and Publications, Extramural Research, and Intramural Research. The Documents and Publications link includes an NINR fact sheet, the National Nursing Research Agenda, and brief descriptions of current research. The Extramural Research category lists science and staff contacts, ongoing program announcements, funded NINR grantees and trainees, types of research, and funding application procedures. The Intramural Research section describes current programs, ongoing protocols, and training opportunities.

Agency information includes a welcome message from the director, press releases, mission statement, NINR organization, and a section on the National Advisory Council.

This site is well organized and provides easy access to its information on federally funded nursing research.

Subject Heading: Nursing

[454] National Institute on Disability and Rehabilitation Research

Sponsoring Agency: National Institute on Disability and Rehabilitation Research (NIDRR)

Primary Access: http://www.ed.gov/offices/OSERS/NIDRR/

Resource Summary: This site features reports on current research projects at NIDRR. The site offers the sections Information About the National Institute on Disability and Rehabilitation Research, Current NIDRR Research, NIDRR Publications, and Other Disability and Rehabilitation Resources.
This will be primarily of interest to researchers in the disabilities area.

Subject Heading: Disabilities

[455] National Toxicology Program

Sponsoring Agencies: National Center for Toxicological Research (NCTR); National Institute of Environmental Health Sciences (NIEHS); National Institute of Occupational Safety and Health (NIOSH); National Toxicology Program (NTP)

Primary Access: http://ntp-server.niehs.nih.gov/

Alternative Access Method: ftp://ntp-ftp-server.niehs.nih.gov/NTP_Reports/

Resource Summary: The National Toxicology Program conducts toxicity/carcinogenesis studies on agents suspected of posing hazards to human health. Chemical-related study information is submitted to NIEHS and is archived and maintained—more than 800 chemical studies are on file. Much of this information is available on the NTP Web server including the *Annual Plan*, the *Annual Report on Carcinogens*, NTP Abstracts and Study Results database, and information on the status of NTP studies. The Abstracts and Study Results database is searchable and includes long-term carcinogenesis studies, short-term toxicity studies, immunotoxicity studies, reproductive toxicity studies, and teratology studies. The Chemical Health and Safety Information database is searchable by chemical name and by Chemical Abstracts Service registry number.

This site contains a significant amount of toxicological data for researchers and for those interested in the scientific basis for the regulation of toxic chemicals.

Subject Headings: Chemical Information; Toxic Substances; Toxicology

SuDoc Numbers: HE 20.23/2: *Annual Plan for Fiscal Year ... / National Toxicology Program*
HE 20.23/4: *Annual Report on Carcinogens*

[456] The NIH Grants Database

Sponsoring Agencies: Community of Science; National Institutes of Health (NIH)

Primary Access: http://cos.gdb.org/best/fedfund/nih-intro.html

Resource Summary: The NIH Grants database contains information about all current NIH grants including a complete listing, for each institution, of dollar amounts for grants awarded. It is updated at least every two weeks. Although the database is housed on the non-government Community of Science server, the data is received from the NIH.

The search interface gives many different options for searching including grant amounts, years left in grant, state, ZIP code, institution, and project number. The records include keywords which can then be directly searched from the results record.

This is an impressive search interface. At the top level screen, the following search options and subset search options are provided:
 *Search All Current NIH Grants
 *Search New NIH Grants
 *Search Grants Funded by Specific Institutes in the NIH
 *Search NIH Grants Received by Selected Universities
 *Search NIH Grants in Specific States
 *NIH Sponsored Clinical Trials
 *AIDS and HIV Research Funded by the NIH
 *Transgenic Animals and Gene Targeting
 *Cancer and Oncology Research Funded by the NIH
 *Drug and Pharmacology Studies Funded by the NIH
 *Research on Alzheimer's Disease Funded by the NIH
 *Research on Aging Funded by the NIH
 *Genetic Mapping Funded by the NIH
 *Genome Project Studies Funded by the NIH
 *Toxicology Research Funded by the NIH
 *Meetings, Conferences, and Workshops Supported by the NIH

Subject Headings: Grants—Health Sciences; Medical Research

[457] Space Biomedical Research Institute

Sponsoring Agencies: Johnson Space Center; Space Biomedical Research Institute

Primary Access: http://www.jsc.nasa.gov/sa/sd/sd5.html

Resource Summary: The main page describes the Space Biomedical Research Institute and has brief sections titled History, Goals, Vision, and Personnel all on one page. Under the goal of "Identify physiologic limitations to man's capability in space flight" is a link to an unpublished document entitled *Humans in Space*. This document examines, in detail, the question of whether human beings can live and work in space. It also provides an introduction to the basic problems and theories of space biomedical research.

While the main page is fairly brief in terms of information content, the *Humans in Space* document is quite extensive and serves as an excellent introductory overview to health problems of humans in space.

Subject Headings: Biomedical Information; Space—Effects on Humans—Research

[458] Welcome to Naval Dental Research Institute

Sponsoring Agency: Naval Dental Research Institute (NDRI)

Primary Access: http://support1.med.navy.mil/NDRI/

Resource Summary: This site features information in the following sections Naval Dental Research Institute Information, Patents and Licensing Opportunities, Product Information, and Email Addresses. Current research efforts are listed under the heading, Product Information. More information on past research is available under the Naval Dental Research Institute Information section.

This site is of narrow interest, but it does offer a useful overview of current research programs.

Subject Headings: Dentistry; Medical Research

CHAPTER 8: INTERNATIONAL

The United States is by no means the only country that offers government information on the Internet. While the primary focus of this directory is United States federal government information, information from other governments and intergovernmental organizations can also be very useful. This chapter is much more selective than the other chapters of this book; it includes only primary international sites. In the Other Countries section, resource summaries are omitted partly since some of the sites do not provide an English version.

Numerous finding aids provide access to country information on the Internet. A smaller number offer links to international governmental information. Of these, none are comprehensive, but the four featured sites for this chapter provide a starting point.

Featured Sites

[459] Geneva International

Primary Access: http://geneva.intl.ch/geneva-intl/

Alternative Access Method: http://geneva.intl.ch/geneva-intl/fgi.htm [French version]

Resource Summary: Geneva International focuses on international organizations located in Geneva. The home page provides an interactive forum for information exchange, current international news analyzed from a Geneva perspective, and a presentation of cultural and social events in the city itself. The main point of interest for government information is the database which covers hundreds of international institutions, permanent missions, and companies in Geneva. Access to the database includes thematic, keyword, and geographic access along with access by type of organization (for example, United Nations organizations or agencies, intergovernmental organizations, non-governmental organizations, and permanent missions). The institutions included in the Geneva International Database cover a wide range of social, technical, and scientific themes.

This site is one of the best starting points for finding international organizations since the offices of many international organizations are located in Geneva.

Subject Headings: Finding Aid—International Organizations; Geneva

[460] International Documents Task Force

Sponsoring Agency: Government Documents Round Table (GODORT). International Documents Task Force (IDTF)

Primary Access: http://www.library.nwu.edu/govpub/idtf/welcome.html

Resource Summary: While this site is primarily designed for the IDTF and its members, its listings of Internet resources from other governments and for intergovernmental organizations is one of the best starting points for international governmental sites. Under the section entitled Links to Selected International Organizations, a well-organized list provides links to Web sites of many intergovernmental organizations. Links are also available to the press releases and publications for each organization, provided they are available. The Links to National Governments category lists central and some subsidiary government sites for other countries.
On the library side, this site provides basic information about the IDTF including sections entitled IDTF Officers, Meeting Minutes and Announcements, and the IDTF Agency Liaison Program. Another section, IGO Miscellany, is designed to cover frequently asked questions.

The IDTF Web site is sparse in terms of design, yet it excels in information content both as a finding aid for intergovernmental organization sites and for sites of other countries. While not as detailed in its foreign coverage as the Electronic Frontier Foundation site, it is more timely. It also contains substantial information for international documents librarians.

Subject Headings: Documents Librarians; Government Publications— International; Finding Aid—International Organizations

[461] Links to Government Servers and Information

Sponsoring Agency: Electronic Frontier Foundation (EFF)

Primary Access: http://www.eff.org/govt.html

Alternative Access Method: http://home.pages.de/~anzinger/govt/europa.html [European segment only]

Resource Summary: The Electronic Frontier Foundation has compiled an extensive list of international, national, regional, and local governmental and government-related servers on the Internet. Under the U.S. Federal Government Executive Branch heading alone, over 450 links are listed. This is a hierarchical index of government information sources organized by continent, country, and then by smaller divisions. Under the heading Country Listings, the links are further categorized under such headings as Federal Information, Political Parties, and Representations in Other Countries.

This is one of the most useful finding aids, although Americans would probably prefer not having to page down so far to get to the U.S. entries. Note that when a Web, Gopher, and ftp site are each available, each one is listed separately. The international coverage is especially good. Unfortunately, it is not being updated frequently enough—the document itself gives the last update as October 12, 1995. Unless it is updated soon, it will no longer be as valuable and accurate as it has been in the past. The alternate URL, which only includes the European portion of these pages, is being updated more frequently.

Subject Headings: Finding Aid—International—Foreign Governments; Finding Aid—International Organizations

[462] Yahoo! Government: Countries

Sponsoring Agency: Yahoo! Inc.

Primary Access: http://www.yahoo.com/Government/Countries/

Resource Summary: This section of the well-known Yahoo! directory of Internet resources covers government sites from almost 100 other countries. While some of the entries are pretty slim, sometimes listing an embassy contact or a list of e-mail addresses, other entries include numerous government links in the specific country.

While this listing is not too comprehensive, it is an excellent starting point for finding at least one link to government sites in the listed countries. It also has the advantage of being updated frequently.

Subject Heading: Finding Aid—International—Foreign Governments

The International resources are divided into three sections. The first includes a few general international government information sites as well as sites that do not fit under the other categories. This section runs from entry numbers 463 to 465. Intergovernmental Organization, the second section, features resources from or about selected intergovernmental agencies and organizations, and covers entries 466-478. The third section, Other Countries, starts with a few general finding aids (entries 479-482) to government information from the government of countries other than the United States. The fourth section continues with brief entries for major government sites in other countries, arranged alphabetically by the country name. These include entry numbers 483-583. This chapter is not comprehensive. Rather, it includes selected sites for international government resources.

International: General

[463] *Social Indicators of Development*

Sponsoring Agencies: Consortium for International Earth Science Information Network (CIESIN); World Bank

Primary Access: http://www.ciesin.org/IC/wbank/sid-home.html

Resource Summary: The *Social Indicators of Development* contains the World Bank's most detailed data collection for assessing human welfare in order to provide a picture of the social effects of economic development. Data are presented for over 170 economies, omitting only those for which data are inadequate. CIESIN has an experimental Web interface to this data available in two ways: using Web forms and using the CIESIN Gateway software. Using the Gateway software requires downloading, installing, and proper Web client configuration before it can be used.

Subject Headings: Developing Countries; Statistics

[464] *Trends in Developing Economies*

Sponsoring Agencies: Consortium for International Earth Science Information Network (CIESIN); World Bank

Primary Access: http://www.ciesin.org/IC/wbank/tde-home.html

Resource Summary: *Trends in Developing Economies* (TIDE) provides brief economic reports on most of the World Bank's borrowing countries. CIESIN has an experimental Web interface to the 1995 edition of this publication. The interface is available in two ways: using Web forms and using the CIESIN Gateway software. Using the Gateway software requires downloading, installing, and proper Web client configuration before it can be used.

Subject Headings: Developing Countries; Economics—Statistics

[465] The World List

Primary Access: http://www.law.osaka-u.ac.jp/legal-info/worldlist/worldlst.htm

Alternative Access Method: http://www.law.osaka-u.ac.jp/legal-info/worldlist/frame.htm [frame version]

Resource Summary: The World List covers non-U.S. law-related resources on the Internet. It includes references to over 60 countries, providing links to a broad range of legal materials. The list often includes links to university and general Web sites.

The list is updated infrequently, but it can be a good starting point for finding legal materials from other countries.

Subject Headings: Finding Aid—Laws—International; Legislation—International

International: Intergovernmental Organizations ————————

[466] Europa

Sponsoring Agency: European Union (EU)

Primary Access: http://europa.eu.int/

Resource Summary: Europa offers information on the European Union's goals and policies. Europa is a common endeavor of the EU's institutions and is run by the European Commission. Europa features categories titled About the EU, The Union's Institutions, On the Record (official EU documents), On the Political Agenda, Publications, Newsroom, and Governments Online.

The On the Record section contains the headings: Green Papers, White Papers, Treaties, and Press Releases. The papers are available in multiple languages and in multiple formats including HTML, PDF, WordPerfect, and Microsoft Word. The full-text versions of press releases are not yet available on the Web; they are only available through commercial database providers. Brief news flashes can be found in the Newsroom section.

Europa includes a good overview of the European Union, while the Governments Online section provides an excellent list of member countries' governmental Web sites. This is an excellent starting point for those searching for governmental and intergovernmental information on Europe.

Subject Headings: Europe; International Trade

[467] Inter-American Development Bank

Sponsoring Agency: Inter-American Development Bank (IDB)

Primary Access: http://www.iadb.org/

Alternative Access Methods: http://www.iadb.org/IDB/Text/words.htm [text version]
http://www.iadb.org/epp.htm [Spanish version]

Resource Summary: The Inter-American Development Bank was established to help accelerate economic and social development in Latin America and the Caribbean. Their Web site features sections entitled Development Research and Policy; News Services; Publications; What's New; Project Documents; About the IDB; Socioeconomic and Trade Data; Operational Policies; Private Sector; Independent Investigation; Business Opportunities; and the Inter-American Investment Corporation. Some of these categories contain little data including the Publications section which is a publications catalog with no online offerings. The Projects Documents section is one of the more substantial sections with details on the many IDB projects. The Socioeconomic and Trade Data section offers a few data sets including income distribution data, hemispheric trade, population, prices, and national accounts for countries in South and Central America. The News Service section includes press releases and *The IDB*, a newsletter.

This site could be greatly expanded, but as it stands, it does offer some useful statistics and press releases from the IDB.

Subject Headings: Banking; Rural Development

[468] NATO Official Home Page

Sponsoring Agency: North Atlantic Treaty Organization (NATO)

Primary Access: http://www.nato.int/

Alternative Access Methods: http://www.vm.ee/nato/ [mirror site]
gopher://gopher.nato.int/

Resource Summary: The main categories on this site include Welcome to NATO; The NATO Family (a list of agencies and commands); Latest News; and Web Archive. The Web Archive includes full-text fact sheets, press releases, the *NATO Handbook*, speeches, and the *NATO Review*. The News section features news from NATO and the Peace Implementation Forces (IFOR). Another IFOR link includes documents related to the NATO operation in Bosnia.

While only a small subset of their printed publications are available, these Internet sites do provide a significant collection of documents from and about NATO. It is an excellent source of information on the organization. One improvement would be to provide a search engine for their full site, including the online publications.

Subject Headings: Bosnian Conflict; NATO

[469] OECD Online

Sponsoring Agency: Organisation for Economic Co-operation and Development (OECD)

Primary Access: http://www.oecd.org/

Alternative Access Methods: http://www.oecd.fr/
http://www.oecd.fr/enligne.html [French version]

Resource Summary: OECD Online contains descriptive information about the OECD, its activities, and its member countries. Major categories include About OECD; Activities; Member Countries; News and Events; Publications; and Search. The Publications section includes ordering information and a list of publications, but no online versions except for the *OECD Letter*. Press releases are available under the News and Events section along with some full-text publications that are available to journalists with the use of the correct password.

The site contains useful descriptive information about the OECD, but it would benefit from more free online content such as HTML editions of their publications or selected statistics. The French version of the site is not an exact mirror of the English version and appears to be an older incarnation.

Subject Headings: Economic Development—International; Economics—International

[470] The Organization of American States

Sponsoring Agency: Organization of American States (OAS)

Primary Access: http://www.oas.org/

Alternative Access Method: http://www.oas.org/shomepag.htm [Spanish version]

Resource Summary: The Organization of American States Web site features information on the Organization and its involvements. Major sections include Public Information; Programs and Issues; Member States and Observers; and Current Issues. Under Public Information, OAS provides press releases, speeches, and selected documents. The Programs and Issues section covers current OAS involvements including trade, democracy, environment, human rights, drug abuse control, and telecommunications and information infrastructure.
This is an excellent resource for information about the OAS and its activities.

Subject Headings: Human Rights; North America; South America

[471] UNICEF

Sponsoring Agency: United Nations Children's Fund (UNICEF)

Primary Access: http://www.unicef.org/

Alternative Access Method: gopher://gopher.unicef.org/

Resource Summary: UNICEF presents a site filled with information on international children's rights, the abuse of children, and children's materials. The site features the following sections: Newsline; About UNICEF; Information; Greeting Cards; UNICEF Worldwide; Child Rights; Voices of Youth; Support UNICEF; and UNICEF Search. Some publications can be found in the Information section including *The State of the World's Children 1996*, *The Progress of Nations 1996*, and the *UNICEF Annual Report 1996*. The material and activities for children are in the Voices of Youth section. Other categories have information on the agency, its activities, its greeting card program, and how to contribute to UNICEF.

The UNICEF sites are a treasure trove of information about children and UNICEF's activities on behalf of children.

Subject Heading: Children

[472] United Nations Headquarters

Sponsoring Agency: United Nations (UN)

Primary Access: http://www.un.org/

Alternative Access Methods: http://www.un.org/textindex.html [text version]
gopher://gopher.un.org/
gopher://gopher.undp.org/

Resource Summary: The UN Headquarters site features a variety of information and documents about the UN. The UN Overview section includes the links: UN Charter, UN Organs, Secretaries-General, and Member States. Online full-text documents are available in the UN News category which includes the *UN Journal*, daily highlights, and press releases. Other information can be found under UN Documents, which includes documents from the Secretary-General, the General Assembly, the Security Council, and the Economic and Social Council. Other featured sections include Global Issues; Departments; Information Resources; Photos; Conferences; and Publications and Sales.

For basic information on the UN and its activities, this site provides an excellent starting point.

Subject Heading: United Nations

[473] United Nations Scholars' Workstation

Sponsoring Agencies: United Nations (UN); Yale University

Primary Access: http://www.library.yale.edu/un/unhome.htm

Resource Summary: The United Nations Scholars' Workstation gives access to a collection of texts, finding aids, data sets, maps, and pointers to print and electronic information. The site covers United Nations studies including disarmament, economic and social development, environment, human rights, international relations, international trade, peacekeeping, and population and demography. Some sections are subject to access restrictions in accordance with Yale University's licensing agreements.

Unlike so many Internet sites, the Scholars' Workstation refers to both print and electronic resources. The great advantage to this is that users can be directed to appropriate information resources regardless of format. Since the Workstation is aimed at serving users at Yale, there is a definite slant toward resources accessible at Yale and detailed information on the UN Studies Program at Yale. However, the other sections can be useful to others interested in the United Nations as well.

Subject Headings: Finding Aid—International; Human Rights; United Nations

[474] United Nations System

Sponsoring Agency: United Nations (UN)

Primary Access: http://www.unsystem.org/

Alternative Access Method: http://www.unsystem.org/indfx.html [French version]

Resource Summary: This site is the official Web site locator for the UN system of organizations. It includes an Alphabetic Index of all United Nations Organizations (UNOs) with their abbreviations and the city where the headquarters is located. The other option is the Official Classification of the United Nations System of Organizations with its explanation of the various categories of UNO including programs, specialized agencies, autonomous organizations, and inter-agency bodies. Under Frequently Requested Information, the site gives a listing of which UNOs have online information for frequently requested items.

For finding component UN organizations' Web sites, this should be the first site to check. The listings are easy to browse, and they denote which agencies have a presence on the Internet.

Subject Headings: Finding Aid—International Organizations; United Nations

[475] UTLink: University of Toronto G7 Information Centre

Sponsoring Agency: Group of Seven (G7)

Primary Access: http://www.g7.utoronto.ca/

Resource Summary: This site organizes and provides access to materials and sites related to the G7, its summits, and other meetings. Categories include About the G7, G7 Summit Meetings, G7 Ministerial and Other Meetings, G7-Related Documents from Member States, Scholarly Publications and Papers, and Other G7 Information Sites. Documents within the G7 Information Centre site can be retrieved by country, year, subject, and other search options.

This should be a starting point for any search of G7-related material. Coverage is excellent and the site is well organized and easy to navigate.

Subject Headings: Economic Development; International Trade

[476] The World Bank

Sponsoring Agencies: International Finance Corporation (IFC); Multilateral Investment Guarantee Organization (MIGA); World Bank

Primary Access: http://www.worldbank.org/

Resource Summary: This site concentrates on information about the World Bank, its programs, and two constituent organizations, the IFC and MIGA. The primary categories include About the World Bank, Current Events, Press Releases and Bank News, Country/Project Information, Sectoral Information, Publications, Research Studies, The Inspection Panel, Visit the IFC, Visit the MIGA, and Search. The Press Releases category is one of the most informative sections of the site featuring current news and information about the World Bank's activities. Using the Search feature can help find World Bank projects in specific countries or on specific topics.

This site contains a great deal of information about the World Bank and its many projects.

Subject Headings: Banking; International Finance

[477] World Health Organization

Sponsoring Agency: World Health Organization (WHO)

Primary Access: http://www.who.ch/

Alternative Access Method: gopher://gopher.who.org/

Resource Summary: Major resources available from the World Health Organization site include the *World Health Report, WHO Weekly Epidemiological Record*, and the WHO Statistical Information System. Between these three sources the site offers a significant collection of international health statistics. The site provides much more beyond these resources including sections on World Health Day, Public Information and Newsletters, Outbreaks and World No-Tobacco Day, International Travel and Health, and Publications. Agency information includes sections for the WHO Library, Vacancies, WHO Headquarters' Major Programmes, WHO's Regional and Other Offices, and E-mail Address Directories.

This site offers a substantial amount of international health statistical information and textual health information.

Subject Headings: Health; Health Statistics

[478] World Trade Organization

Sponsoring Agency: World Trade Organization (WTO)

Primary Access: http://www.wto.org/

Alternative Access Methods: http://www.wto.org/homefra.htm [French version]
http://www.wto.org/homespa.htm [Spanish version]
http://www.unicc.org/wto/homefra.htm [French version]
http://www.unicc.org/wto/homespa.htm [Spanish version]

Resource Summary: The World Trade Organization Web site features information about the WTO and some online publications. Major categories include About the WTO; Press Releases; Trade Policy Reviews; The WTO in Depth; The Uruguay Round; International Trade; Trade and Environment; Publications; WTO Membership; and Vacancy Notices. Under the International Trade heading, there is a full-text version of *International Trade Trends and Statistics*. The Trade Policy Reviews and the Press Releases categories are the other sections with full-text online publications.

This is an excellent site for learning more about the WTO. It also contains some useful information and statistics on international trade.

Subject Headings: International Trade

International: Other Countries

[479] Foreign Government Resources/ Comprehensive Site Listings

Sponsoring Agency: University of Michigan. Documents Center

Primary Access: http://www.lib.umich.edu/libhome/Documents.center/forcomp.html

Alternative Access Method: http://www.lib.umich.edu/libhome/Documents.center/frames/ forcomfr.html [frames version]

Resource Summary: The frames version of this Web site is easier to navigate than the no-frames version. In addition to providing pointers to many other lists of foreign government Web sites, this site has its own list. The frames version provides access via continent, country, and subject. In the country listings, there are brief annotations for the type of information available on each of the servers.

Although this is not the easiest list to navigate, it contains a substantial number of links to government sites in other countries.

Subject Heading: Finding Aid—International—Foreign Governments

[480] Inter-Parliamentary Union

Sponsoring Agency: Inter-Parliamentary Union (IPU)

Primary Access: http://www.ipu.org/

Alternative Access Method: http://www.ipu.org/french/welcome.htm [French version]

Resource Summary: The IPU is an international organization of parliaments from different countries. The IPU Web site features two databases and links to parliamentary Web sites around the world. The two databases are PARLINE and PARLIT. For all countries with a national legislature, the PARLINE database provides general information on each parliament's chambers, a description of the electoral system, the results of the most recent elections, and information on the working of the presidency of each chamber. PARLIT is a bibliographical database covering parliamentary law and legislative elections throughout the world. It covers literature back to 1992. Other main sections of the site include Structure and Functioning; Main Areas of Activity; Publications; and Press Releases.

For anyone interested in the legislative bodies of other countries, this is an information-rich site to visit, especially in the two databases available here.

Subject Headings: Bibliographic Databases; Finding Aid—International—Parliaments; Parliaments

[481] Links to Web Sites on National Parliaments

Primary Access: http://www.soc.umn.edu/~sssmith/Parliaments.html

Resource Summary: This page presents a simple list of hot links to Web sites supported by, relating to, or somehow about parliamentary bodies from different countries. The entries range from the Estonian Riigikogu to the Nicaraguan National Assembly and the Israeli Knesset. Toward the bottom of the page is a short list of International and Regional Parliamentary Institutions. This is an excellent finding aid. Though it is simple in design and lacking much descriptive text, it is useful for locating parliamentary Web pages.

Subject Headings: Finding Aid—International—Parliaments; Parliaments

[482] Services: The Source for National Governments, Banks, Financial Information, and More

Sponsoring Agency: The Internationalist, Inc.

Primary Access: http://www.internationalist.com/INTRNTNL/service.html

Resource Summary: This is part of the the Internationalist—The Center for Business Information Web site. This part is arranged alphabetically by country. While it includes more than just government links, each country listing will include a Government Links section.

This is not the most comprehensive site for finding other countries' government links; however, it can be used to supplement some of the other international government finding aids.

Subject Heading: Finding Aid—International—Foreign Governments

International: Major Government Sites in Other Countries ——————

Andorra

[483] Govern d'Andorra

Sponsoring Agency: Andorra. Government

Primary Access: http://www.andorra.ad/govern/

Subject Heading: Andorra

Angola

[484] Republic of Angola Politics

Sponsoring Agency: Angola. Government

Primary Access: http://www.angola.org/politics/index.htm

Subject Heading: Angola

Argentina

[485] Ministerio de Economía Obras y Servicios Públicos

Sponsoring Agency: Argentina. Government

Primary Access: http://www.mecon.ar/

Alternative Access Methods: http://www.mecon.ar/default.htm [English version]
http://www.mecon.ar/econom.htm [Spanish version]

Subject Heading: Argentina

Australia

[486] Australian Government

Sponsoring Agency: Australia. Government

Primary Access: http://gov.info.au/

Subject Heading: Australia

[487] Australian Parliament

Sponsoring Agency: Australia. Parliament

Primary Access: http://www.aph.gov.au/

Subject Headings: Australia; Parliaments

Austria

[488] Bundesministerium für auswärtige Angelegenheiten

Sponsoring Agency: Austria. Government

Primary Access: http://gov.austria-info.at/bmaa/dindex.html

Subject Heading: Austria

Belgium

[489] Belgian Federal Government Online

Sponsoring Agency: Belgium. Government

Primary Access: http://belgium.fgov.be/

Subject Heading: Belgium

[490] Sénat de Belgique - Belgische Senaat - Belgisches Senat - Belgian Senate

Sponsoring Agency: Belgium. Parliament

Primary Access: http://www.senate.be/

Subject Headings: Belgium; Parliaments

Brazil

[491] Senado Federal do Brasil

Sponsoring Agency: Brazil. Parliament

Primary Access: http://www.senado.gov.br/

Subject Headings: Brazil; Parliaments

[492] Web do Governo do Brasil

Sponsoring Agency: Brazil. Government

Primary Access: http://www.mare.gov.br/

Alternative Access Methods: http://www.mare.gov.br/english/homeing.htm [English version] http://www.mare.gov.br/spanish/homespa.htm [Spanish version]

Subject Heading: Brazil

Canada

[493] Canadian Government Information on the Internet

Sponsoring Agency: Mount Allison University. Library

Primary Access: http://library.uwaterloo.ca/discipline/Government/CanGuide/

Subject Headings: Canada; Finding Aid—Canada

[494] Champlain: Canadian Information Explorer

Sponsoring Agencies: Canada. Government; General Network Services, Inc.

Primary Access: http://champlain.gns.ca/

Alternative Access Method: http://champlain.gns.ca/champlainf.html [French version]

Subject Heading: Canada

[495] Government of Canada/Gouvernement du Canada

Sponsoring Agency: Canada. Government

Primary Access: http://canada.gc.ca/

Alternative Access Methods: http://canada.gc.ca/main_e.html [English version] http://canada.gc.ca/main_f.html [French version]

Subject Heading: Canada

[496] Parliamentary Internet Parlementaire

Sponsoring Agency: Canada. Parliament

Primary Access: http://www.parl.gc.ca/english/

Alternative Access Methods: http://www.parl.gc.ca/francais/ [French version]
gopher://gopher.parl.gc.ca

Subject Headings: Canada; Parliaments

Chile

[497] Congreso Nacional de Chile

Sponsoring Agency: Chile. Parliament

Primary Access: http://www.congreso.cl/

Alternative Access Method: http://www.congreso.cl/texto.html [text version]

Subject Headings: Chile; Parliaments

Colombia

[498] Gobierno Colombiano

Sponsoring Agency: Colombia. Government

Primary Access: http://www.presidencia.gov.co/gobierno/gobierno.html

Subject Heading: Colombia

Costa Rica

[499] Gobierno de Costa Rica

Sponsoring Agency: Costa Rica. Government

Primary Access: http://www.casapres.go.cr/

Subject Heading: Costa Rica

Croatia

[500] Sabor Republike Hrvatske

Sponsoring Agency: Croatia. Parliament

Primary Access: http://www.sabor.hr/

Subject Headings: Croatia; Parliaments

[501] Vlada Republike Hrvatske - The Government of the Republic of Croatia

Sponsoring Agency: Croatia. Government

Primary Access: http://www.vlada.hr/

Subject Heading: Croatia

Czech Republic

[502] Narodni Informacni Stredisko Ceske Republiky

Sponsoring Agency: Czech Republic. Government

Primary Access: http://www.nis.cz/

Subject Heading: Czech Republic

[503] Parliament of Czech Republic, Chamber of Deputies

Sponsoring Agency: Czech Republic. Parliament

Primary Access: http://www.psp.cz/

Subject Headings: Czech Republic; Parliaments

Denmark

[504] Datacentralens Center for Datakommunikation

Sponsoring Agency: Denmark. Government

Primary Access: http://www.sdn.dk/

Subject Heading: Denmark

Ecuador

[505] Ministerio de Relaciones Exteriores del Ecuador

Sponsoring Agency: Ecuador. Government

Primary Access: http://www.mmrree.gov.ec/

Alternative Access Method: http://www.mmrree.gov.ec/ingles/indexe.htm [English version]

Subject Heading: Ecuador

Estonia

[506] Estonian Ministry of Foreign Affairs

Sponsoring Agency: Estonia. Government

Primary Access: http://www.vm.ee/

Alternative Access Methods: http://www.vm.ee/home.html [English version]
http://www.vm.ee/german/ [German version]
http://www.vm.ee/francais/ [French version]
http://www.vm.ee/venekeel/ [Russian version]
http://www.vm.ee/ukr/ [Ukrainian version]

Subject Heading: Estonia

Finland

[507] Suoman Eduskunta

Sponsoring Agency: Finland. Parliament

Primary Access: http://www.eduskunta.fi/

Subject Headings: Finland; Parliaments

[508] Suomen Tasavallan Presidentti

Sponsoring Agency: Finland. Government

Primary Access: http://www.tpk.fi/

Subject Heading: Finland

France

[509] AdmiNet - The French Government

Sponsoring Agency: France. Government

Primary Access: http://www.adminet.com/gouvernement.html

Subject Heading: France

[510] Bienvenue a L'Assemblée Nationale

Sponsoring Agency: France. Parliament

Primary Access: http://www.assemblee-nat.fr/

Subject Headings: France; Parliaments

[511] Page d'accueil Sénat

Sponsoring Agency: France. Parliament

Primary Access: http://www.senat.fr/

Alternative Access Method: http://www.senat.fr/asomm.html [English version]

Subject Headings: France; Parliaments

Gambia

[512] The Republic of the Gambia

Sponsoring Agency: Gambia. Government

Primary Access: http://www.gambia.com/

Subject Heading: Gambia

Georgia

[513] Parliament of Georgia

Sponsoring Agency: Georgia (country). Parliament

Primary Access: http://www.parliament.ge/

Subject Headings: Georgia (country); Parliaments

Germany

[514] Bundesämter, Bundesministerien, und Bundeländer

Sponsoring Agency: Germany. Government

Primary Access: http://www.laum.uni-hannover.de/iln/bibliotheken/bundesamter.html

Subject Heading: Germany

[515] Deutscher Bundestag - German Parliament

Sponsoring Agency: Germany. Parliament

Primary Access: http://www.bundestag.de/

Subject Headings: Germany; Parliaments

Ghana

[516] The Republic of Ghana

Sponsoring Agency: Ghana. Government

Primary Access: http://www.ghana.com/republic/index.html

Subject Heading: Ghana

Greece

[517] Hellenic Republic Ministry of Foreign Affairs

Sponsoring Agency: Greece. Government

Primary Access: http://www.mfa.gr/

Subject Heading: Greece

Hong Kong

[518] Hong Kong Government Information Centre

Sponsoring Agency: Hong Kong. Government

Primary Access: http://www.info.gov.hk/

Subject Heading: Hong Kong

Hungary

[519] Magyar Országgyûlés Hivatal

Sponsoring Agency: Hungary. Parliament

Primary Access: http://www.mkogy.hu/

Subject Headings: Hungary; Parliaments

[520] Prime Minister's Office, Hungary

Sponsoring Agency: Hungary. Government

Primary Access: http://www.meh.hu/

Subject Heading: Hungary

Iceland

[521] Heimasíða Alþingis

Sponsoring Agency: Iceland. Parliament

Primary Access: http://www.althingi.is/

Alternative Access Methods: http://www.althingi.is/~wwwadm/upplens.html [English version] http://www.althingi.is/~wwwadm/uppldan.html [Dutch version]

Subject Headings: Iceland; Parliaments

[522] Stjórnarrá> Íslands

Sponsoring Agency: Iceland. Government

Primary Access: http://www.stjr.is/

Alternative Access Method: http://www.stjr.is/en/stjren01.htm [English version]

Subject Heading: Iceland

India

[523] The Indian Parliament

Sponsoring Agency: India. Parliament

Primary Access: http://alfa.nic.in/

Subject Headings: India; Parliaments

Indonesia

[524] Department of Foreign Affairs Republic of Indonesia (Deplu)

Sponsoring Agency: Indonesia. Government

Primary Access: http://www.dfa-deplu.go.id/

Subject Heading: Indonesia

Ireland

[525] Rialtas na hÉireann

Sponsoring Agency: Ireland. Government

Primary Access: http://www.irlgov.ie/

Subject Heading: Ireland

Israel

[526] Israel Foreign Ministry

Sponsoring Agency: Israel. Government

Primary Access: http://www.israel-mfa.gov.il/

Subject Heading: Israel

Italy

[527] Ministero delle Finanze

Sponsoring Agency: Italy. Government

Primary Access: http://www.finanze.interbusiness.it/

Subject Heading: Italy

Japan

[528] Japanese Government-Related Web Servers

Sponsoring Agency: Japan. Government

Primary Access: http://www.epa.go.jp/html/government_wwws.html

Subject Heading: Japan

[529] Ministry of Posts and Telecommunications

Sponsoring Agency: Japan. Government

Primary Access: http://www.mpt.go.jp/

Alternative Access Method: http://www.mpt.go.jp/index-e.html [English version]

Subject Heading: Japan

[530] The National Diet of Japan

Sponsoring Agency: Japan. Parliament

Primary Access: http://fuji.stanford.edu/Diet/diet1.html

Subject Headings: Japan; Parliaments

Kuwait

[531] State of Kuwait

Sponsoring Agency: Kuwait. Government

Primary Access: http://www.moc.kw/

Alternative Access Methods: http://www.moc.kw/english.html [English version]
http://www.moc.kw/arabic.html [Arabic version]

Subject Heading: Kuwait

Latvia

[532] Parliament of the Republic of Latvia

Sponsoring Agency: Latvia. Parliament

Primary Access: http://www.saeima.lanet.lv/

Alternative Access Methods: http://www.saeima.lanet.lv/latvian/ [Latvian version]
http://www.saeima.lanet.lv/english/ [English version]

Subject Headings: Latvia; Parliaments

[533] Valsts Nozîmes Datu Pârraides Tîkls

Sponsoring Agency: Latvia. Government

Primary Access: http://www.gov.lv/

Alternative Access Method: http://www.gov.lv/english/ [English version]

Subject Heading: Latvia

Lithuania

[534] Lietuvos Respublikos Seimas

Sponsoring Agency: Lithuania. Parliament

Primary Access: http://rc.lrs.lt/

Subject Headings: Lithuania; Parliaments

Luxembourg

[535] Le Grand-Duché de Luxembourg

Sponsoring Agency: Luxembourg. Government

Primary Access: http://www.restena.lu/gover/

Subject Heading: Luxembourg

Malaysia

[536] Parlimen Malaysia

Sponsoring Agency: Malaysia. Government

Primary Access: http://www.parlimen.gov.my/

Alternative Access Methods: http://www.parlimen.gov.my/bi.htm [English version] http://www.parlimen.gov.my/bm.htm [Malay version]

Subject Heading: Malaysia

[537] Prime Minister's Office

Sponsoring Agency: Malaysia. Government

Primary Access: http://smpke.jpm.my:1025/

Subject Heading: Malaysia

Malta

[538] Official Maltese Government

Sponsoring Agency: Malta. Government

Primary Access: http://www.magnet.mt/

Subject Heading: Malta

Morocco

[539] Kingdom of Morocco/Royaume du Maroc

Sponsoring Agency: Morocco. Government

Primary Access: http://www.mincom.gov.ma/

Subject Heading: Morocco

Netherlands

[540] Ministerie van Verkeer en Waterstaat

Sponsoring Agency: Netherlands. Government

Primary Access: http://www.minvenw.nl/

Alternative Access Method: http://www.minvenw.nl/engWelcome.html [English version]

Subject Heading: Netherlands

[541] Parlement

Sponsoring Agency: Netherlands. Parliament

Primary Access: http://www.dds.nl/overheid/pdc/parlement.html

Subject Headings: Netherlands; Parliaments

New Zealand

[542] New Zealand Government

Sponsoring Agency: New Zealand. Government

Primary Access: http://www.govt.nz/

Subject Heading: New Zealand

[543] New Zealand Government Online Blue Pages

Sponsoring Agency: New Zealand. Government

Primary Access: http://www.gwr.govt.nz/

Alternative Access Method: http://www.gwr.govt.nz/text/BluePages.html [text version]

Subject Heading: New Zealand—Finding Aid

[544] New Zealand Parliamentary Home Page

Sponsoring Agency: New Zealand. Parliament

Primary Access: http://www.poli.govt.nz/

Subject Headings: New Zealand; Parliaments

Nicaragua

[545] Asamblea Naçional de Nicaragua

Sponsoring Agency: Nicaragua. Parliament

Primary Access: http://www.asamblea.gob.ni/

Subject Headings: Nicaragua; Parliaments

[546] Banco Central de Nicaragua

Sponsoring Agency: Nicaragua. Government

Primary Access: http://www.bcn.gob.ni/

Subject Heading: Nicaragua

Norway

[547] ODIN-Offentlig Dokumentasjon og Informasjon i Norge

Sponsoring Agency: Norway. Government

Primary Access: http://odin.dep.no/

Subject Heading: Norway

[548] Stortingets Informasjonstjener

Sponsoring Agency: Norway. Parliament

Primary Access: http://www.stortinget.no/

Alternative Access Method: http://www.stortinget.no/eng/engpag.htm [English version]

Subject Headings: Norway; Parliaments

Pakistan

[549] Pakistan's Armed Forces

Sponsoring Agency: Pakistan. Government

Primary Access: http://ravi.lums.edu.pk/~b98008/services.html

Resource Summary: This is an unofficial Web site.

Subject Heading: Pakistan

Peru

[550] Congreso de la República

Sponsoring Agency: Peru. Parliament

Primary Access: http://161.132.29.12/

Alternative Access Method: http://ucongr01.congreso.gob.pe/ [may change]

Subject Headings: Parliaments; Peru

[551] Sector Govierno - Peru

Sponsoring Agency: Peru. Government

Primary Access: http://ekeko.rcp.net.pe/rcp/rcp-gob.html

Subject Heading: Peru

Poland

[552] Kancelaria Senatu

Sponsoring Agency: Poland. Parliament

Primary Access: http://www.senat.gov.pl/

Subject Headings: Parliaments; Poland

[553] Republic of Poland

Sponsoring Agency: Poland. Government

Primary Access: http://www.urm.gov.pl/

Subject Heading: Poland

[554] Sejm Rzeczypospolitej Polskiej

Sponsoring Agency: Poland. Parliament

Primary Access: http://www.sejm.gov.pl/

Alternative Access Method: http://www.sejm.gov.pl/sejm_eng.htm [English version]

Subject Headings: Poland; Parliaments

Portugal

[555] Entidades Governamentais

Sponsoring Agency: Portugal. Government

Primary Access: http://www.sapo.pt/culturais/governo/

Subject Heading: Portugal

Romania

[556] Parliament of Romania - Bucharest

Sponsoring Agency: Romania. Parliament

Primary Access: http://dias.vsat.ro/

Subject Headings: Parliaments; Romania

[557] Romanian Government Room

Sponsoring Agency: Romania. Government

Primary Access: http://www.guv.ro/

Alternative Access Methods: http://www.guv.ro/govroom.html [text version]
http://www.guv.ro/index.html [frames version]
http://www.kappa.ro/guv/ [mirror]

Subject Heading: Romania

Russia

[558] Infobase - Russian Legislation on the Net

Sponsoring Agency: Russia. Government

Primary Access: http://www.inforis.ru/infobase

Subject Headings: Legislation—International; Russia

Saudi Arabia

[559] Royal Embassy of Saudi Arabia

Sponsoring Agency: Saudi Arabia. Government

Primary Access: http://imedl.saudi.net/

Alternative Access Method: http://imedl.saudi.net/mainpagetxt.html [text version]

Subject Heading: Saudi Arabia

Singapore

[560] Parliament House of Singapore

Sponsoring Agency: Singapore. Parliament

Primary Access: http://www.gov.sg/parliament/

Subject Headings: Parliaments; Singapore

[561] The Singapore Government

Sponsoring Agency: Singapore. Government

Primary Access: http://www.gov.sg/

Alternative Access Method: http://www.gov.sg/indextext.html [text version]

Subject Heading: Singapore

Slovakia

[562] Slovak Information Agency

Sponsoring Agency: Slovakia. Government

Primary Access: http://www.sia.gov.sk/

Subject Heading: Slovakia

Slovenia

[563] Center Vlade za Informatiko

Sponsoring Agency: Slovenia. Government

Primary Access: http://www.sigov.si/

Subject Heading: Slovenia

[564] Republic of Slovenia National Assembly

Sponsoring Agency: Slovenia. Government

Primary Access: http://www.sigov.si/dz/edz-ds.html

Subject Heading: Slovenia

South Africa

[565] Sangonet Open Government

Sponsoring Agency: South Africa. Government

Primary Access: http://wn.apc.org/opengov/

Subject Heading: South Africa—Finding Aid

[566] South African Government of National Unity

Sponsoring Agency: South Africa. Government

Primary Access: http://www.polity.org.za/gnu/

Subject Heading: South Africa

South Korea

[567] Ministry of Information and Communication

Sponsoring Agency: South Korea. Government

Primary Access: http://www.mic.go.kr/

Subject Heading: South Korea

Spain

[568] Administración Pública

Sponsoring Agency: Spain. Government

Primary Access: http://www.map.es/

Subject Heading: Spain

Sri Lanka

[569] Sri Lanka General Information - Government

Sponsoring Agency: Sri Lanka. Government

Primary Access: http://www.cs.cf.ac.uk/Sri_Lanka/_General/gov.html

Resource Summary: This is an unofficial Web site.

Subject Heading: Sri Lanka

Sweden

[570] Information Rosenbad

Sponsoring Agency: Sweden. Government

Primary Access: http://www.sb.gov.se/

Subject Heading: Sweden

Switzerland

[571] Confoederatio Helvetica - Swiss Confederation

Sponsoring Agency: Switzerland. Government

Primary Access: http://www.admin.ch/

Subject Heading: Switzerland

[572] Palais Fédéral - Berne - Suisse

Sponsoring Agency: Switzerland. Government

Primary Access: http://www.admin.ch/PD/

Subject Headings: Parliaments; Switzerland

Taiwan

[573] Government Information Office

Sponsoring Agency: Taiwan. Government

Primary Access: http://www.gio.gov.tw/

Alternative Access Methods: http://www.gio.gov.tw/info/nation/fr/ [French version]
http://www.gio.gov.tw/info/nation/sp/ [Spanish version]
http://www.gio.gov.tw/info/nation/ge/ [German version]
http://www.gio.gov.tw/info/nation/jp/ [Japanese version]

Subject Heading: Taiwan

Thailand

[574] Office of the Prime Minister

Sponsoring Agency: Thailand. Government

Primary Access: http://www.nectec.or.th/bureaux/opm/

Subject Heading: Thailand

[575] Parliament Thailand

Sponsoring Agency: Thailand. Parliament

Primary Access: http://www.parliament.go.th/

Subject Headings: Parliaments; Thailand

Trinidad and Tobago

[576] Discover Trinidad and Tobago - Government

Sponsoring Agency: Trinidad and Tobago. Government

Primary Access: http://www.trinidad.net/trini/govern.htm

Subject Heading: Trinidad and Tobago

Turkey

[577] Ministry of Foreign Affairs

Sponsoring Agency: Turkey. Government

Primary Access: http://www.mfa.gov.tr/

Subject Heading: Turkey

Ukraine

[578] Ministry for Internal Affairs of Ukraine

Sponsoring Agency: Ukraine. Government

Primary Access: http://www.mia.gov.ua/

Subject Heading: Ukraine

[579] Verkhovna Rada of Ukraine

Sponsoring Agency: Ukraine. Government

Primary Access: http://www.rada.kiev.ua/welcome.html

Subject Headings: Parliaments; Ukraine

United Kingdom

[580] CCTA Government Information Service

Sponsoring Agencies: United Kingdom. Government; United Kingdom. Central Computer and Telecommunications Agency (CCTA)

Primary Access: http://www.open.gov.uk/

Alternative Access Method: http://www.open.gov.uk/index2.htm [text version]

Subject Heading: United Kingdom

[581] New United Kingdom Official Publications Online (NUKOP)

Sponsoring Agency: United Kingdom. Government

Primary Access: http://www.soton.ac.uk/~nukop/

Subject Headings: Documents Librarians; Finding Aid—International; United Kingdom

[582] United Kingdom Parliament

Sponsoring Agency: United Kingdom. Parliament

Primary Access: http://www.parliament.uk/

Subject Headings: United Kingdom; Parliaments

Vatican

[583] The Holy See

Sponsoring Agency: Vatican. Government

Primary Access: http://www.vatican.va/

Subject Heading: Vatican City

CHAPTER 9: LEGAL INFORMATION

Law enforcement and legal information resources have been a major online information resource for many years. Commercial services such as Westlaw and Lexis/Nexis have offered an incredible amount of legal information resources to the commercial online community. On the Internet, only a small portion of that depth of legal information is available for free, and that portion is growing. It is also more eclectic, with press releases, law enforcement documents, and regulatory information. This chapter focuses on a broad range of legal information. See also the chapter on Congress for information about Congress, members of Congress, and their voting records.

The four featured resources for this chapter provide a substantial amount of legislative and law enforcement information, with many in full text. GPO Gate is the best access point for the full-text legislative information that is made available from the many GPO Access sites. For law enforcement information, the Justice Information Center is an excellent starting point with statistics and full-text reports available from a variety of Department of Justice agencies. The Library of Congress' THOMAS site is one of the best known finding aids for recent legislation. Meanwhile, for other law sources, the U.S. House of Representatives Internet Law Library includes a number of important resources.

[584] GPO Gate at University of California [GPO Access]

Sponsoring Agencies: Government Printing Office (GPO); Congress

Primary Access: http://www.gpo.ucop.edu/

Resource Summary: GPO Gate, the GPO Access gateway for the University of California system takes a completely different approach to designing software for access to the GPO Access databases. With the evolution of front-end software which is used to connect to these GPO Access WAIS databases, GPO Gate is one of the most highly developed gateways, it is constantly being improved.

GPO Gate is designed to assist users on how to easily access the laws, regulations, reports, data and other information provided through the GPO Access system. They succeed in doing this by providing a scripted interface that shields the user from the peculiarities of WAIS searching. Remarkably, it is done without sacrificing any of the advanced search features that are available.

For example, the Quick Search option—which is prominently accessible from the first screen of the top level page—provides a basic form entry for all of the databases. The databases are listed in a scrollable list. Underneath the list is a four-box form which allows Boolean searches of up to three words or phrases which can then be further limited based on specific title words. The Quick Search also provides options for sorting alphabetically or by relevance score and for changing the default number of results displayed.

More advanced search options are available under the headings of Select Databases by Title and Select Databases by Subject. Helpful descriptive information about each of the databases can be found under Listing and Description of all Databases section.

For users of the *Federal Register*, GPO Gate provides a separate search form under the topic, Search Federal Register. This form gives a scripted access to the *Federal Register* for specific dates and in specific sections. One other scripted interface can be found by following the Today! button. This option allows easy access to the latest issues of the frequently issued publications in GPO Access, such as the *Congressional Record* and the House and Senate *Calendars*.

GPO Gate is the best way to search the GPO Access databases. The emphasis on ease of use and the demonstrated understanding of what kind of information people are seeking from these databases combine to make GPO Gate the easiest and most reliable gateway to use. Other versions of front-end software designed to reach GPO Access (including GPO's own version) are listed later in this chapter. While they should give access to the content of the same databases, none provide that information as easily as GPO Gate.

Subject Headings: Decisions—Full Text; Legislation—Full Text; Reports—Full Text; Regulations—Full Text

SuDoc Numbers: AE 2.106: *Federal Register*
AE 2.106/3: *Code of Federal Regulations*
AE 2.106/4: *Privacy Act Issuances*
AE 2.108/2: *United States Government Manual*
AE 2.110: *Public Laws*
GA 1.5: *GAO Comptroller General Decisions*
GA 1.5/A: *GAO Reports*
I 1.1/7: *Reports of the Office of the IG*
Pr 42.9: *Economic Report of the President*
PrEx 2.3: *Unified Agenda*
PrEx 2.8: *Budget of the United States Government*
X *Congressional Record*
X 1.1: *Congressional Record Index*
Y 1.1/3: *Senate Documents*
Y 1.1/5: *Senate Reports*
Y 1.1/7: *House Documents*
Y 1.1/8: *House Reports*
Y 1.2/2: *House Calendars*
Y 1.2/5: *United States Code*
Y 1.2:R 86/2/ *House Rules Manual*
Y 1.3/2: *Senate Calendars*
Y 1.4/1: *Senate Bills*
Y 1.4/6: *House Bills*
Y 1.6: *History of Bills and Resolutions*
Y 4.Ec 7: *Economic Indicators*
Y 4.H 81/3:C 15/5 *Campaign Finance Reform Legislation: The Role of Political Parties*
Y 4.P 93/1: *Congressional Directory*

[585] Justice Information Center

Sponsoring Agencies: Department of Justice (DOJ); National Criminal Justice Reference Service (NCJRS)

Primary Access: http://www.ncjrs.org/

Alternative Access Methods: http://ncjrs.aspensys.com/
gopher://ncjrs.org:71/
ftp://ncjrs.org/pub/ncjrs/
mailto:askncjrs@aspensys.com

Resource Summary: This site is sponsored by the National Criminal Justice Reference Service (NCJRS) which responds to queries from law enforcement and corrections officials, lawmakers, judges and court personnel, and researchers. The site contains an amazing number of publications on a wide range of criminal justice and law enforcement topics. The documents are primarily in ASCII format, but an increasing number are available in HTML or PDF format. The categories listed on the main page include: Corrections; Courts; Crime Prevention; Criminal Justice Statistics; Drugs and Crime; International; Juvenile Justice; Law Enforcement; Research and Evaluation; and Victims. These topic sections include both electronic publications housed on these servers and links to external Internet resources.

Access to the publications is available through the topics or via a WAIS full-text keyword search. The site also includes a catalog of NCJRS print publications, a list of federal grants available from the DOJ, and a conference calendar.

NCJRS is a collection of clearinghouses supporting all bureaus of the DOJ Office of Justice Programs including the National Institute of Justice, the Office of Juvenile Justice and Delinquency Prevention, the Bureau of Justice Statistics, the Bureau of Justice Assistance, and the Office for Victims of Crime. It also supports the Office of National Drug Control Policy.

The vast number of publications available from the Justice Information Center makes this a very useful site for criminal justice statistics and recent reports.

Subject Headings: Criminal Justice; Criminal Justice—Full Text

SuDoc Numbers: J 24.2:D 84 *Drugs of Abuse*
J 28.24:V 66/4 *Victims of Childhood Sexual Abuse: Later Criminal Consequences*

[586] THOMAS: Legislative Information on the Internet

Sponsoring Agencies: Congress; Library of Congress (LC)

Alternative Access Method: http://www.congress.gov/

Primary Access: http://thomas.loc.gov/

Resource Summary: THOMAS is Congress' attempt to make federal legislative information freely available to the Internet public. A team from the Library of Congress brought the THOMAS system online in January 1995, at the beginning of the 104th Congress. The first database made available was Bill Text, followed shortly by Congressional Record Text, Bill Summary and Status, Hot Bills, the *Congressional Record Index*, and the Constitution. More recently, Committee Reports for the 104th Congress have been added along with links to House and Senate committee home pages. The Historical Documents section features historic congressional documents such as the Federalist Papers, the Declaration of Independence, and Constitutional Convention and Continental Congress broadsides. All historic documents are searchable as a collection and are also individually searchable and browsable.

The many legislative databases on THOMAS can be browsed or searched using the INQUERY search engine. INQUERY employs a relevance-ranking algorithm for searching. Experienced searchers who wish to use Boolean searching may use native INQUERY syntax to override the relevance-ranking default.

For more details on the origin of THOMAS, see "Newt's Net: An Interview with Don Hones, Newt Gingrich's System Integrator and the Creator of the THOMAS Server" *Internet World* 6(8):44-48, August 1995.

This is one of the most widely used Internet sources for legislative information. While it does not yet access all congressional documents as quickly as some might like, it does make a significant body of legislation easily available to the public. Since THOMAS receives its files from the Government Printing Office, one of the GPO Access sites such as GPO Gate may be a more current source of information. In addition, the LEGI-SLATE commercial service offers more value-added content to its federal legislative databases than is available from THOMAS.

Subject Heading: Legislation—Full Text

SuDoc Numbers: X *Congressional Record*
X 1.1: *Congressional Record Index*
Y 1.4/1: *Senate Bills*
Y 1.4/6: *House Bills*
Y 1.1/7:101-139 *How Our Laws Are Made*

Internet Law Library

The U.S. House of Representatives Internet Law Library Welcome!

[587] U.S. House of Representatives Internet Law Library

Sponsoring Agency: House of Representatives

Primary Access: http://law.house.gov/

Alternative Access Method: http://law.house.gov/home.htm [frames version]

Resource Summary: This is one of the most comprehensive listings of Internet-accessible resources for law. Developed by House Information Resources as part of a demonstration project, the Internet Law Library provides easy access to law-related Internet resources. The directories available on this site include over 1,600 links to law resources of the Internet. While not all of the resources are produced by the U.S. government or housed on government servers, many of them are. Featured full-text law sources at the Internet Law Library include the *U.S. Code* and the *Code of Federal Regulations (CFR)*.

The main sections of the Internet Law Library are titled: About the House Internet Law Library; U.S. Federal Laws (arranged by original published source); U.S. Federal Laws (arranged by agency); U.S. State and Territorial Laws; Laws of Other Nations; Treaties and International Law; Laws of All Jurisdictions (arranged by subject); Law School Law Library Catalogues and Services; Attorney and Legal Profession Directories; and Law Book Reviews and Publishers.

The Personal Library Software search engine that is used for sources housed on this server such as the *U.S. Code* and the *CFR* is very useful for certain searches. Unfortunately, a search which entails finding a specific section of one of the codes is more complex.

Subject Headings: Finding Aid—Laws; Legislation—Full Text; Regulations—Full Text

SuDoc Numbers: AE 2.106/3: *Code of Federal Regulations*
Y 1.2/5: *United States Code*

Legal Information: General

The Legal Information resources are divided into three sections. The first section includes general legal information resources as well as sites that do not fit under the other categories. This section runs from entries 588 to 617. Courts, the second section, with entries 618-639, contains resources about court cases and about the courts themselves. The third section, Law Enforcement, features sites related to the enforcement of laws and regulations and includes entries 640-659

[588] Advertising Law Internet Site

Sponsoring Agencies: Arent Fox; Federal Trade Commission (FTC)

Primary Access: http://www.webcom.com/~lewrose/

Resource Summary: Along with a collection of non-governmental advertising law information, this site includes a variety of documents from the FTC. These include the full text of the Advertising Guidelines and Enforcement Policy Statements, which cover topics such as food advertising, environmental claims, deceptive pricing, testimonials, and more. It also includes sections entitled: FTC Trade Regulation Rules; FTC Consumer Brochures; and FTC Business Compliance Manuals.

This site is a useful adjunct to the FTC site and has online publications that are not available on the FTC site.

Subject Heading: Trade Law

SuDoc Number: FT 1.32: *Facts for Consumers*

[589] Americans with Disabilities Act

Sponsoring Agency: Department of Justice (DOJ). Civil Rights Division

Primary Access: http://www.usdoj.gov/crt/ada/adahom1.htm

Resource Summary: The Americans with Disabilities Act (ADA) site features information on enforcement of the ADA, certification, and technical assistance. Under the Enforcement heading, *Enforcing the ADA: Status Reports* are available along with press releases and information on how to file complaints. The site also offers the following categories: Toll-Free ADA Information Line, New or Proposed Regulations, and the ADA Technical Assistance Grant Program.

Surprisingly, the ADA page does not provide a link to the text of the Act itself—it can be found on the Civil Rights Division pages. This site will be most useful to those trying to comply with ADA rather than for those seeking information about ADA.

Subject Heading: Disabilities

SuDoc Number: J 1.106: *Enforcing the ADA: Status Reports*

[590] Americans with Disabilities Act Document Center

Sponsoring Agencies: Department of Justice (DOJ); Equal Employment Opportunity Commission (EEOC); National Institute on Disability and Rehabilitation Research (NIDRR)

Primary Access: http://janweb.icdi.wvu.edu/kinder/

Resource Summary: This non-governmental site contains copies of the Americans with Disabilities Act of 1990 (ADA); ADA regulations; technical assistance manuals prepared by the EEOC or the DOJ; and other technical assistance documents sponsored by NIDRR and reviewed by EEOC or DOJ. Most of these documents are in text format. The site also links to many other sites containing information on the ADA or disabilities in general.

Many of the documents that are in text format do not have .txt extensions, which can cause some Web browsers to try to interpret them as HTML files. Other than that problem, this is a useful collection of materials related to the ADA.

Subject Headings: Americans with Disabilities Act; Disabilities

[591] Bureau of Alcohol, Tobacco, and Firearms

Sponsoring Agency: Bureau of Alcohol, Tobacco, and Firearms (ATF)

Primary Access: http://atf.ustreas.gov/

Alternative Access Methods: http://www.atf.ustreas.gov/
http://www.ustreas.gov/treasury/bureaus/atf/atf.html

Resource Summary: After the mission statement, this site includes the categories: ATF Office Directory; Firearms Information; and Alcohol Information. The Firearms Information section offers a few publications as well as documents about the Brady Law which should be of interest to those on both sides of the gun control debate. In response to church burnings, the site offers a Church Threat Assessment Guide. It also features a section on customer service plans and standards and a section for seized property, with information about auctions and the sale of seized property. This section will be of interest to those who track government auctions. This site as a whole is useful for finding basic information about the ATF and its activities.

Subject Headings: Alcoholic Beverages; Auctions; Gun Control; Firearms; Law Enforcement

SuDoc Number: T 70.18: *Federal Firearms Licensee Newsletter*

[592] Civil Division

Sponsoring Agency: Department of Justice (DOJ). Civil Division

Primary Access: http://www.usdoj.gov/civil/civil.html

Resource Summary: This brief page provides two categories entitled, Overview of Civil Division and Online Brochure for the Civil Division. These sections describe the role of the Civil Division as the government's law firm which represents more than 100 federal agencies, individual employees, members of Congress, the federal judiciary, and the people of the United States.

Other than providing a basic description of the Division, this site has little to offer.

Subject Heading: Litigation

[593] Civil Rights Division

Sponsoring Agency: Department of Justice (DOJ). Civil Rights Division

Primary Access: http://www.usdoj.gov/crt/

Alternative Access Method: gopher://gopher.usdoj.gov/1/crt

Resource Summary: Beginning with an Overview of the Civil Rights Division, this site offers a variety of court documents, speeches, and statutes relating to civil rights. One of the most substantial sections is entitled Americans with Disabilities Act Information, which includes the full text of the Act.

Be sure to check the Gopher as well as the Web site, as the Gopher contains additional documents. While the site does not provide a general overview on civil rights, there are a few useful documents here.

Subject Headings: Americans with Disabilities Act; Civil Rights; Disabilities

[594] Community Relations Service

Sponsoring Agency: Department of Justice (DOJ). Community Relations Service

Primary Access: http://www.usdoj.gov/offices/crs.html

Resource Summary: This page describes the Service and lists phone numbers for its regional offices. Other than that, there is little information on this page.

Subject Headings: Civil Rights; Community Relations[595] Comptroller General Decisions

[595] Comptroller General Decisions

Sponsoring Agency: General Accounting Office (GAO). Comptroller General

Primary Access: http://www.gao.gov/decisions/decision.htm

Resource Summary: This site provides, in HTML and PDF formats, access to the full text of the decisions issued within the past 60 days. The decisions are accessible under the following categories: Appropriations; Bid Protests; Civilian Personnel Pay and Allowances; Military Personnel Pay and Allowances; Household Goods; Freight Loss and Damage; Transportation Rates; and Other Decisions. There is also a keyword and concept search feature. For older decisions, there is a link to the database on GPO Access which goes back to January 1996.

While the decisions are also available on one of the GPO Access databases, this version provides a good explanation and easy access to the most recent decisions.

Subject Heading: Decisions—Full Text

SuDoc Number: GA 1.5: *GAO Comptroller General Decisions*

[596] Counterpoint Publishing

Sponsoring Agency: Counterpoint Publishing

Primary Access: http://www.counterpoint.com/

Alternative Access Method: gopher://gopher.counterpoint.com/

Resource Summary: Counterpoint sells access to the full text of the *Code of Federal Regulations (CFR)*, *Commerce Business Daily (CBD)*, and the *Federal Register*, in addition to some other resources. The databases are available via both Gopher or Web in HTML. Counterpoint also offers delivery of its databases via telnet and newsgroups. The search options include browse and keyword search capabilities. The keyword searches can use Boolean operators, proximity operators, and phrase searching.

While Counterpoint offers one of the most sophisticated Gopher connections to the standard resources, they have been a bit slower in developing more feature-rich Web interfaces. They face some stiff competition with the free offering of the *CBD* at the Government Contractor Resource Center (http://www. govcon.com/), free access to the *Federal Register* at many depository library GPO Access gateways (such as GPO Gate at http://www.gpo.ucop.edu/), and free access to the *Code of Federal Regulations* (http://law.house.gov/cfr. htm). In some cases the free versions boast more advanced and/or easier-to-use search options. However, Counterpoint's *CFR* has been much more current than the free version. In addition, the *Federal Register* goes back July 1991 on Counterpoint, whereas the GPO Access versions only go back to 1994.

Subject Headings: Electronic Periodicals; Procurement; Regulations—Full Text

SuDoc Numbers: AE 2.106: *Federal Register*
AE 2.106/3: *Code of Federal Regulations*
C 1.76: *Commerce Business Daily*

[597] Envirotext

Sponsoring Agency: Environmental Protection Agency (EPA)

Primary Access: http://tamora.acsiom.org/info/envirotext/

Alternative Access Method: http://tamora.cs.umass.edu/info/envirotext/

Resource Summary: Envirotext contains databases covering federal, state, Indian tribal, and agency-specific laws and legislation. Envirotext includes the complete *United States Code*, environmentally related sections of the *Code of Federal Regulations,* and the *Federal Register* which is updated daily. It also includes most Indian tribal codes, a complete set of Indian tribal agreements and treaties, and a set of all international agreements and treaties. The Indian tribal dataset is unique and solely maintained by Envirotext. The search interface uses the INQUERY search engine developed by the Center for Intelligent Information Retrieval.

The home page links to explanatory material, but the main body of the above mentioned sources are found under the heading, Use Envirotext. All of the databases can be searched together or individually. The search engine uses INQUERY. If all databases are searched at once, it can be difficult to tell from which database the source originates. With so many databases, it would help to have a way of identifying the source of a specific document. Even so, the availability of the unique tribal databases and the amount of full-text legal material available through Envirotext make this an important resource.

Envirotext claims that the databases are current and that they are updated when new versions are available from the Government Printing Office. However, this is neither an official government site nor a specifically legal-oriented site, so use with caution. Despite their attempts to keep the information up-to-date, the *CFR* description gives dates of over a year ago.

Subject Headings: American Indians—Law and Legislation; Environmental Issues—Law and Legislation; Legislation—Full Text; Regulations—Full Text

SuDoc Numbers: AE 2.106: *Federal Register*
AE 2.106/3: *Code of Federal Regulations*
Y 1.2/5: *United States Code*

[598] Equal Employment Opportunity Commission

Sponsoring Agency: Equal Employment Opportunity Commission (EEOC)

Primary Access: http://www.eeoc.gov/

Resource Summary: The Equal Employment Opportunity Commission features a number of its publications and regulations on their site. The main sections include Press Releases, Laws Enforced by the EEOC, Fact Sheets and Related Information, and Other EEOC Publications. The other EEOC publications are mostly in PDF format and include relevant sections from the *Code of Federal Regulations* and other EEOC documents.

Since the bulk of the material on this site is legal information, it will be of most interest to people wanting to browse the federal laws and regulations relevant to equal opportunity.

Subject Headings: Employment; Equal Opportunity

[599] Federal Bureau of Prisons

Sponsoring Agency: Federal Bureau of Prisons

Primary Access: http://www.bop.gov/

Alternative Access Method: http://www.usdoj.gov/bureaus/bop.html

Resource Summary: The main sections on this site include Quick Facts, Inmate Management Directives, Inmate Information, Documents, and Facilities Directory. The Inmate Management Directives section includes program statements in HTML or WordPerfect format. Inmate Information offers advice on how to find information about federal inmates. The alternate URL gives a one-page description of the Bureau.

While this site offers few documents or publications, the section on finding information about federal inmates may be useful.

Subject Heading: Prisons and Prisoners

[600] Federal Energy Regulatory Commission

Sponsoring Agency: Federal Energy Regulatory Commission (FERC)

Primary Access: http://www.fedworld.gov/ferc/ferc.html

Resource Summary: These pages describe the FERC and its areas of regulatory authority. All of the material is descriptive, and there are no regulations in full-text format available on this site.

The site would be more useful if it included some full-text documents from the FERC or links to them elsewhere.

Subject Headings: Energy; Regulations

[601] Fish and Wildlife Laws, Regulations, Policies, and Congressional Information

Sponsoring Agency: Fish and Wildlife Service (FWS)

Primary Access: http://www.fws.gov/~pullenl/wildlaw/fdigest.html

Resource Summary: This site features laws, regulations, and legislation related to fish and wildlife management. It has many links to external legal sources, but it also includes some unique documents as well. The site includes excerpts from the privately published *State Wildlife Laws Handbook* and information from the forthcoming *Federal Wildlife and Related Laws Handbook*. The section, Laws Enforced by U.S. Fish and Wildlife Service, lists citations and summaries.

This site could be improved by linking the citations in the Laws Enforced by the U.S. Fish and Wildlife Service section to the actual text which is available from other Internet resources which offer the *U.S. Code* or *Code of Federal Regulations*.

Subject Headings: Fish and Fishing—Legislation; Wildlife—Legislation

[602] GPO Access [sites using SWAIS]

Sponsoring Agencies: Congress; Government Printing Office (GPO)

Primary Access: telnet://sled:sled@sled.alaska.edu

Alternative Access Methods: telnet://guest:visitor@aztec.asu.edu
telnet://csn.carl.org
telnet://library@pldvax.pueblo.lib.co.us
telnet://themis.law.ualr.edu
telnet://gpo@library.georgetown.edu
telnet://ida.lib.uidaho.edu
telnet://library:library@unicorn.morehead-st.edu
telnet://gpo@indigo.lib.lsu.edu
telnet://info@gsvms2.cc.gasou.edu
telnet://guest@telnet.coin.missouri.edu
telnet://catalog.cwru.edu
telnet://portals.pdx.edu:806
telnet://lias.psu.edu
telnet://library@lib.ursinus.edu
telnet://visitor@osfn.rhilinet.gov
telnet://new@199.249.190.57
telnet://pac@atlas.tntech.edu
telnet://library@msuvx1.memphis.edu
telnet://link@link.tsl.texas.gov
telnet://gwis:gwis@gwis.virginia.edu
telnet://library@spl.lib.wa.us

Resource Summary: These connections to the GPO Access databases use the SWAIS (Simple Wide Area Information Service) client, either directly or through a Gopher gateway. After connecting to one of the listed URLs, a number of other steps are often required to find the GPO Access option. Look under headings such as Federal Government, Government Printing Access, or Library to find the actual connection to GPO Access.

The vt100 interface of SWAIS and the multiple steps required to connect to GPO Access through these gateways make this approach less intuitive and less user friendly than the Web GPO Access gateways such as GPO Gate. Even so, for those with only a vt100 connection to the Internet, and for local users at these sites, the SWAIS gateways still connect to the same underlying databases, and they can be used to effectively retrieve information.

Subject Headings: Decisions—Full Text; Legislation—Full Text; Regulations—Full Text; Reports—Full Text

SuDoc Numbers: AE 2.106: *Federal Register*
AE 2.106/3: *Code of Federal Regulations*
AE 2.106/4: *Privacy Act Issuances*
AE 2.108/2: *United States Government Manual*
AE 2.110: *Public Laws*
GA 1.5: *GAO Comptroller General Decisions*
GA 1.5/A: *GAO Reports*
I 1.1/7: *Reports of the Office of the IG*
Pr 42.9: *Economic Report of the President*
PrEx 2.3: *Unified Agenda*
PrEx 2.8: *Budget of the United States Government*
X *Congressional Record*
X 1.1: *Congressional Record Index*
Y 1.1/3: *Senate Documents*
Y 1.1/5: *Senate Reports*
Y 1.1/7: *House Documents*
Y 1.1/8: *House Reports*
Y 1.2/2: *House Calendars*
Y 1.2/5: *United States Code*
Y 1.2:R 86/2/ *House Rules Manual*
Y 1.3/2: *Senate Calendars*
Y 1.4/1: *Senate Bills*
Y 1.4/6: *House Bills*
Y 1.6: *History of Bills and Resolutions*
Y 4.Ec 7: *Economic Indicators*
Y 4.H 81/3:C 15/5 *Campaign Finance Reform Legislation: The Role of Political Parties*
Y 4.P 93/1: *Congressional Directory*

[603] GPO Access [with Lynx]

Sponsoring Agencies: Congress; Government Printing Office (GPO)

Primary Access: telnet://library@library.unc.edu then press 2 twice

Resource Summary: This interface uses Lynx via a telnet connection to search the GPO Access databases.

For those without access to a graphical Web client, this provides an alternative to using SWAIS at the many SWAIS GPO Access gateways.

Subject Headings: Decisions—Full Text; Legislation—Full Text; Regulations—Full Text; Reports—Full Text

SuDoc Numbers: AE 2.106: *Federal Register*
AE 2.106/3: *Code of Federal Regulations*
AE 2.106/4: *Privacy Act Issuances*
AE 2.108/2: *United States Government Manual*
AE 2.110: *Public Laws*
GA 1.5: *GAO Comptroller General Decisions*
GA 1.5/A: *GAO Reports*
I 1.1/7: *Reports of the Office of the IG*
Pr 42.9: *Economic Report of the President*
PrEx 2.3: *Unified Agenda*
PrEx 2.8: *Budget of the United States Government*
X *Congressional Record*
X 1.1: *Congressional Record Index*
Y 1.1/3: *Senate Documents*
Y 1.1/5: *Senate Reports*
Y 1.1/7: *House Documents*
Y 1.1/8: *House Reports*
Y 1.2/2: *House Calendars*
Y 1.2/5: *United States Code*
Y 1.2:R 86/2/ *House Rules Manual*
Y 1.3/2: *Senate Calendars*
Y 1.4/1: *Senate Bills*
Y 1.4/6: *House Bills*
Y 1.6: *History of Bills and Resolutions*
Y 4.Ec 7: *Economic Indicators*
Y 4.H 81/3:C 15/5 *Campaign Finance Reform Legislation: The Role of Political Parties*
Y 4.P 93/1: *Congressional Directory*

[604] GPO Access Databases

Sponsoring Agencies: Congress; Government Printing Office (GPO)

Primary Access: http://www.access.gpo.gov/su_docs/aces/aaces002.html

Alternative Access Methods: http://thorplus.lib.purdue.edu/gpo/
http://www.suffolk.lib.ny.us/gpo/

Resource Summary: Many versions of GPO Access offer a WAIS connection to full-text databases. (See the list below with SuDoc numbers for a list of available databases.) The WAIS searches can be effective for general concept and keyword searches, but it is often more difficult to search by field or with a given citation.

The GPO Access databases are listed alphabetically in a scrollable box, and underneath the box is a single search box for the query. Queries must use the proper WAIS syntax, such as having Boolean operators in all uppercase letters. (These peculiarities are detailed in the Help section.) Most of the databases start in 1994, but the *Congressional Record Index* goes back to 1992.

While this is a functional interface, the search syntax is not intuitive. Ironically, most other GPO Access gateway sites use software developed originally at Purdue. It is interesting to note that Purdue now uses the GPO software interface. While this version of GPO Access is more functional than Purdue's original verion, GPO Gate provides a much more powerful search interface with many more advanced options.

Subject Headings: Decisions—Full Text; Legislation—Full Text; Reports—Full Text; Regulations—Full Text

SuDoc Numbers: AE 2.106: *Federal Register*
AE 2.106/3: *Code of Federal Regulations*
AE 2.106/4: *Privacy Act Issuances*
AE 2.108/2: *United States Government Manual*
AE 2.110: *Public Laws*
GA 1.5: *GAO Comptroller General Decisions*
GA 1.5/A: *GAO Reports*
I 1.1/7: *Reports of the Office of the IG*
Pr 42.9: *Economic Report of the President*
PrEx 2.3: *Unified Agenda*
PrEx 2.8: *Budget of the United States Government*
X *Congressional Record*
X 1.1: *Congressional Record Index*
Y 1.1/3: *Senate Documents*
Y 1.1/5: *Senate Reports*
Y 1.1/7: *House Documents*
Y 1.1/8: *House Reports*
Y 1.2/2: *House Calendars*
Y 1.2/5: *United States Code*
Y 1.2:R 86/2/ *House Rules Manual*
Y 1.3/2: *Senate Calendars*
Y 1.4/1: *Senate Bills*
Y 1.4/6: *House Bills*
Y 1.6: *History of Bills and Resolutions*
Y 4.Ec 7: *Economic Indicators*
Y 4.H 81/3:C 15/5 *Campaign Finance Reform Legislation: The Role of Political Parties*
Y 4.P 93/1: *Congressional Directory*

[605] GPO Access Gateways

Sponsoring Agencies: Congress; Government Printing Office (GPO)

Primary Access: http://bubba.ucc.okstate.edu/wais/GPOAccess/

Alternative Access Methods: http://www.amherst.edu/amherst/admin/library/amherstGPO.html
http://www.lib.auburn.edu/gpo/
http://www.lib.lsu.edu/gpo/
http://www.lib.montana.edu/GOVDOC/gpo.html
http://sailor.lib.md.us/forms/gpo.html
http://govinfo.uky.edu/
http://mel.lib.mi.us/gpo/
http://www.unm.edu/~cmclean/gpo.html
http://www.library.unt.edu/gpo/
http://www.lib.utk.edu/gpo/GPOsearch.html
http://lawlib.wuacc.edu/washlaw/doclaw/gpoacc.html
http://winslo.ohio.gov/gpo/
http://www.library.nwu.edu/gpo/

Resource Summary: The GPO Access gateways provide another means of searching the GPO Access databases. The search query form is available toward the bottom of the page and the search must be entered using the proper WAIS syntax, such as entering Boolean operators in all capital letters. Some sites provide help files and instructions while others do not. Not all of the sites have all of the GPO Access databases available.

While these sites may be useful to local patrons, they may not work as well as the GPO's own GPO Access or GPO Gate. The gateways will not work if the Internet connection is down, since they must still make the connection to the WAIS server at GPO. If the Internet connection is working, GPO Gate or GPO's GPO Access should be available. Given the greater search capabilities at GPO Gate, that site will serve most needs better than any of these gateways.

Subject Headings: Decisions—Full Text; Legislation—Full Text; Regulations—Full Text; Reports—Full Text

SuDoc Numbers: AE 2.106: *Federal Register*
AE 2.106/3: *Code of Federal Regulations*
AE 2.106/4: *Privacy Act Issuances*
AE 2.108/2: *United States Government Manual*
AE 2.110: *Public Laws*
GA 1.5: *GAO Comptroller General Decisions*
GA 1.5/A: *GAO Reports*
I 1.1/7: *Reports of the Office of the IG*
Pr 42.9: *Economic Report of the President*
PrEx 2.3: *Unified Agenda*
PrEx 2.8: *Budget of the United States Government*
X *Congressional Record*
X 1.1: *Congressional Record Index*
Y 1.1/3: *Senate Documents*
Y 1.1/5: *Senate Reports*
Y 1.1/7: *House Documents*
Y 1.1/8: *House Reports*
Y 1.2/2: *House Calendars*
Y 1.2/5: *United States Code*
Y 1.2:R 86/2/ *House Rules Manual*
Y 1.3/2: *Senate Calendars*
Y 1.4/1: *Senate Bills*
Y 1.4/6: *House Bills*
Y 1.6: *History of Bills and Resolutions*
Y 4.Ec 7: *Economic Indicators*
Y 4.H 81/3:C 15/5 *Campaign Finance Reform Legislation: The Role of Political Parties*
Y 4.P 93/1: *Congressional Directory*

[606] LEGI-SLATE

Sponsoring Agencies: Congress; LEGI-SLATE, Inc.

Primary Access: http://www.legislate.com/

Alternative Access Method: gopher://gopher.legislate.com/

Resource Summary: LEGI-SLATE is a fee-based service providing access to federal legislation and regulations. The Web offers a front end to the LEGI-SLATE Gopher Service as well as a Windows client program. From the top level page, choose the link Federal Services. This link includes information about all bills and resolutions introduced in Congress since 1993 by specific bill number, LEGI-SLATE subject term, sponsor, chamber and type of legislation, words in the official title, and words in full text. Selected portions of the information are available for free to non-subscribers. However, the full text of the bills, the Hot Bills category, and references from the *Washington Post*, *National Journal*, and *CQ Weekly Report* are only accessible to subscribers.

For regulations, the LEGI-SLATE Gopher features the full text of the *Federal Register* since January 3, 1994. No part of the regulations section is accessible to non-subscribers. The main Web page also includes links to LEGI-SLATE News, State Services, and Legislative Highlights. The State Services section describes LEGI-SLATE products which provide state information. The Legislative Highlights section features a few recently signed bills with full LEGI-SLATE information. This provides an excellent example of what the full service offers to subscribers.

The subscriber service offers more information about current bills than any of the other free Internet-accessible legislative information sources. For non-subscribers, the lack of access to the full text of the bills and other menu items becomes frustrating rather quickly. The free service could be used to verify information found on THOMAS or the House Web server, but otherwise this server is of most use to subscribers.

The server is a Gopher+ server, which uses some forms for processing information requests. Gopher+ is not always handled well by some Web browsers and will not work at all with older Gopher clients. The latest versions of Netscape Navigator and Internet Explorer seem to be able to handle the LEGI-SLATE Gopher, even though they run into problems with other Gopher+ servers.

Subject Headings: Legislation—Full Text; Regulations—Full Text

[607] NASA Office of Legislative Affairs

Sponsoring Agency: National Aeronautics and Space Administration (NASA)

Primary Access: http://www.hq.nasa.gov/office/legaff/

Resource Summary: This site is designed for tracking legislation related to NASA and its programs. Information is available in these categories: NASA Appropriations; NASA Authorization; Fiscal Year Budget; NASA Legislative Activities Report; Hearing Calendar; Month In Review; and Fiscal Year Budget Spreadsheet. The page also has links to relevant congressional reports and bills.

This should be a useful site for those interested in tracking legislation and funding for NASA programs. It also has a wonderful animated GIF image of a space shuttle flying out of the dome of the Capitol building.

Subject Heading: Space—Legislation

[608] Office for Victims of Crime

Sponsoring Agencies: Department of Justice (DOJ); National Criminal Justice Reference Service (NCJRS); Office for Victims of Crime

Primary Access: http://www.ncjrs.org/ovchome.htm

Resource Summary: As part of the National Criminal Justice Reference Service's site, this page gives a basic description of the Office and its mission. The primary links point to the parts of the Justice Information Center that contain victim-related information including domestic violence, child abuse, elderly victims, bias-related violence, victim rights, and victim compensation to practitioners, policymakers, researchers, and crime victims.

Subject Heading: Victims

[609] Policy Works

Sponsoring Agency: Regulatory Information Service Center

Primary Access: http://policyworks.gov/org/main/mi/linkit.htm

Resource Summary: The Regulatory Information Service Center undertakes projects that will facilitate development of and access to information about federal regulatory and deregulatory activities. It accomplishes this by gathering and publishing information on federal regulations and their effects on society. This site includes information on the Center such as its organization, contact information, and links to other federal sites. Some of the available categories of information include Key Issues, Virtual Library, Regulations and Policies, and Learning Center.

This is a useful site to browse for those interested in the policy issues related to regulations.

Subject Heading: Regulations

[610] Postal Rate Commission

Sponsoring Agency: Postal Rate Commission (PRC)

Primary Access: http://www.prc.gov/

Resource Summary: The Postal Rate Commission Web site features recent full-text offerings under the headings: PRC Opinions and Decisions; Docketed Cases; *Federal Register* Notices; Congressional Testimony; Papers; and Speeches. Another section describes the work of the PRC while the Employment Information section lists job notices.
While these full-text offerings do not go back very far, there are a wide variety of sources. This site useful to those tracking the activities of the PRC and anyone interested in future rate increases.

Subject Headings: Cases—Full Text; Mailing Rates; Regulations—Full Text

[611] Telecommunications Act of 1996

Sponsoring Agency: Federal Communications Commission (FCC)

Primary Access: http://www.fcc.gov/telecom.html

Resource Summary: This site includes the full text of the Act in both ASCII and HTML. In addition, the site includes materials related to the implementation of the Act such as a draft schedule of implementation from the FCC and notices from the *Federal Register*. The document also includes links to other resources about the Act.

While recent bills are available in full-text format from GPO Access, the value-added portions of this site demonstrate the potential that the Internet has for making information even more accessible. Not only does the FCC provide a link to an HTML version of the bill, but they have tried to gather other documents and their own regulations that pertain to this specific Act.

Subject Headings: Communications; Telecommunications

SuDoc Number: AE 2.110: 104-104 *Telecommunications Act of 1996*

[612] U.S. Copyright Office

Sponsoring Agencies: Library of Congress (LC); Copyright Office

Primary Access: http://lcweb.loc.gov/copyright/

Resource Summary: The Copyright Office Web site includes basic information about the Office such as hours, location, speeches, and press releases. While the listings under the General Information and Publications category are brief, they contain a substantial number of important copyright documents. The *Copyright Information Circulars*, including *Copyright Basics*, the *Catalog of Copyright Entries*, and many copyright forms can all be easily found and retrieved. The forms are in PDF format, and the page provides detailed instructions on how to properly print the forms.

Simple in design and organization, this site does an exemplary job of providing frequently requested documents and information in an easy-to-find manner.

Subject Heading: Copyright

SuDoc Numbers: LC 3.4/2: *Copyright Information Circulars*
LC 3.4/2:1 *Copyright Basics*
LC 3.6/6: *Catalog of Copyright Entries*

[613] United States Attorneys

Sponsoring Agency: United States Attorneys

Primary Access: http://www.usdoj.gov/usao/usao.html

Resource Summary: This page includes a multiple screen description of the U.S. Attorneys. It includes online press releases and links to its districts and to the Executive Office for United States Attorneys.

Beyond the press releases and description, there is not a great deal of information on this site.

Subject Heading: Litigation

[614] United States Department of Justice

Sponsoring Agency: Department of Justice (DOJ)

Primary Access: http://www.usdoj.gov/

Alternative Access Method: gopher://gopher.usdoj.gov/

Resource Summary: The Department of Justice Web site begins with a brief introduction to the Department followed by a few choices for access to more information. DOJ organizations can be browsed by organizational structure or alphabetically by organization name. There is also a Topical Index section and a Justice Department Issues, News, and Topics of Interest area. Separate links connect to the Gopher server and to press releases.

Beyond finding a specific DOJ agency or browsing press releases, the Topical Index may be the most useful section of the site. Still under construction, its subject approach can help users find relevant DOJ Internet resources. Unfortunately, there is no keyword search option yet available.

Subject Headings: Judicial System; Law Enforcement

SuDoc Number: J 1.104: *Civil Rights Forum*

[615] United States Parole Commission

Sponsoring Agency: Parole Commission

Primary Access: http://www.usdoj.gov/bureaus/parole.html

Resource Summary: This page describes the Commission and its works. There is a link to Status of the U.S. Parole Commission which gives information on recent activities and changes.

There is little information on this site beyond the descriptions.

Subject Headings: Parole; Prisons and Prisoners

[616] The United States Sentencing Commission

Sponsoring Agency: Sentencing Commission (USSC)

Primary Access: http://www.ussc.gov/

Resource Summary: This official site contains information on the Commission and the commissioners. In addition to the full text from a *Federal Register* notice which revised sentencing guidelines, the site includes a list of a number of online publications including the *Annual Report* and the *Guidelines Manual*.

The USSC has put together a worthwhile site which is well-organized and includes an important publication in HTML full text.

Subject Headings: Criminal Justice; Sentencing

SuDoc Numbers: Y 3.SE 5:1/ *Annual Report*
Y 3.SE 5:8 G 94/ *Guidelines Manual*

[617] Will T. Bill

Sponsoring Agency: House of Representatives

Primary Access: http://www.unipress.com/will-t-bill.html

Resource Summary: Will T. Bill provides a Web forms interface to the House of Representatives' WAIS database of full-text legislation from both the House and the Senate. Since this makes direct calls on the House WAIS server, it is only available when the server is up (from 6:00 A.M. to 1:00 A.M. EST).

Will T. Bill only works properly if your Web browser is configured to handle WAIS queries. A WAIS proxy server may need to be designated in the browser's settings to handle these kind of searches. This service was more useful before the Web versions of GPO Access and THOMAS became available. Both of those services are now easier to use and more reliable than Will T. Bill.

Subject Heading: Legislation—Full Text

[618] Antitrust Division

Sponsoring Agency: Department of Justice (DOJ). Antitrust Division

Primary Access: http://www.usdoj.gov/atr/atr.htm

Alternative Access Methods: gopher://gopher.usdoj.gov/11/atr/
http://gopher.usdoj.gov/atr/atr.htm

Resource Summary: The Antitrust Division uses its Internet site to provide full-text cases, information about the division and its activities, and press releases. The Antitrust Guidelines portion is meant to make businesses and consumers aware of the current guidelines that must be followed in different areas of commerce. The Antitrust Archives include the headings Civil and Criminal Antitrust Cases, Antitrust Appellate Briefs, Business Review Letters, and Bank Merger Transactions. The cases are listed alphabetically and only go back to about 1994. The Antitrust Cases section includes more than just the decisions, it also includes memoranda, complaints, orders, and declarations. These, and most of the other publications available on this site, are not items available through the depository library system. Most of the documents are available in HTML, but some are only available in PDF or WordPerfect formats.

This site offers a surprising amount of full-text information. The plain design of the top page could discourage users from spending enough time here to find the detailed records that are available.

Subject Headings: Antitrust Law; Cases—Full Text

[619] Court of Appeals for the Ninth Circuit

Sponsoring Agencies: Court of Appeals. Ninth Circuit; Villanova Center for Information Law and Policy

Primary Access: http://www.law.vill.edu/Fed-Ct/ca09.html

Resource Summary: Electronic versions of the decisions from the Ninth Circuit of the Federal Court of Appeals are available at this site from June 1995 to the present. The electronic versions are available only in ASCII format. Access to the decisions is by month, by first or second party name (not yet available), and via a keyword search. The cases are available in HTML, ASCII, and by fax to specific area codes.

This is an excellent resource for recent case decisions. The HTML versions are not fully marked up, with most of the text appearing similar to the ASCII version. However, this site delivers important documents.

Subject Heading: Cases—Full Text

[620] The Federal Court Locator

Sponsoring Agency: The Villanova Center for Information Law and Policy

Primary Access: http://www.law.vill.edu/Fed-Ct/fedcourt.html

Resource Summary: This site has links to court opinions that are available on the Internet. The Federal Court Locator is a service provided by the Villanova Center for Information Law and Policy and is intended to be the home page for the federal court system on the Internet. This page provides links to information concerning the federal judiciary, including slip opinions.

While most of the federal circuit courts have their own entry in this directory, this site is useful for locating changed addresses and/or other federal courts on the Internet.

Subject Heading: Finding Aid—Laws

[621] Federal Courts

Sponsoring Agency: Administrative Office of the United States Courts

Primary Access: http://www.uscourts.gov/

Resource Summary: The site includes some electronic documents from the agency including press releases, a hypertext document—*Understanding the Federal Courts*, and selected articles from the Agency's newsletter—*The Third Branch*. Another document, the *Directory of Electronic Public Access Systems*, lists numbers for Bulletin Board Systems (BBS) that disseminate court cases.

Understanding the Federal Courts gives a good introductory overview of the structure of the U.S. court system. The *Directory* is a useful source for finding a BBS for a specific court.

Subject Heading: Judicial System

SuDoc Numbers: JU 10.2:C83/3/ *Understanding the Federal Courts*
JU 10.3/2: *The Third Branch*

[622] The Federal Judicial Center

Sponsoring Agency: Federal Judicial Center (FJC)

Primary Access: http://www.fjc.gov/

Resource Summary: While the top level page has few links, the Federal Judicial Center site does have a substantial number of online publications. Under the heading About the FJC, the site includes the usual descriptive information along with the FJC *Annual Report*. The Publications section is the major area for finding full-text reports, some of which are listed with their SuDoc numbers below. There is also information on Breast Implant Litigation.

The FJC Web site is well worth exploring for information on the federal courts, judges, and the judiciary system.

Subject Headings: Breast Implants; Judges; Judicial System; Litigation

SuDoc Numbers: JU 13.1: *Annual Report - Federal Judicial Center*
JU 13.8/3: *Guideline Sentencing Update*
JU 13.8/4: *Habeas and Prison Litigation Case Law Update*
JU 13.13/2: *State-Federal Judicial Observer*
JU 13.13/2-3: *International Judicial Observer*
JU 13.15 *The Court Historian*

[623] Fedworld/FLITE Supreme Court Decisions

Sponsoring Agencies: Department of the Air Force; Supreme Court

Primary Access: http://www.fedworld.gov/supcourt/

Resource Summary: The Federal Legal Information Through Electronics (FLITE) database of Supreme Court opinions is now available from Fedworld. The file consists of over 7,000 Supreme Court opinions dating from 1937 through 1975, from volumes 300 through 422 of the *U.S. Reports*. Access is by party name or a keyword search on the full text.

Access to FLITE only occurred after a long battle with the air force using Freedom of Information Act requests. The air force finally agreed to release the historic Supreme Court opinions portion of FLITE "as a matter of discretion." This database is also supposed to be available through GPO Access sometime in the future. Its availability adds a significant amount of case law material to the other case law sites that are freely available on the Internet.

Subject Heading: Cases—Full Text

SuDoc Number: JU 6.8: *U.S. Reports*

[624] FindLaw: Supreme Court Opinions

Sponsoring Agencies: Findlaw, Inc.; Supreme Court

Primary Access: http://www.findlaw.com/casecode/supreme.html

Resource Summary: FindLaw, one of the premiere finding aids for Internet law sources, has made a major improvement over other free offerings of Supreme Court opinions. These full-text HTML versions of the cases go all the way back to volume 200 of the *U.S. Reports*, from 1906. Access to the cases is available by citation, year, a party name search, and a full-text search. The cases themselves have hypertext links from references to other cases available through FindLaw. In addition, at the top of each case is a link to a search for other cases in this database that cite the displayed case. The formatting includes indentation and the *U.S. Report* page breaks, but no italics or underlining.

This is an important new free source for Supreme Court opinions. In addition, it offers greater coverage than any of the other free sources.

Subject Heading: Cases—Full Text

SuDoc Number: JU 6.8: U.S. Reports

[625] Oyez Oyez Oyez: A Supreme Court Web Resource

Sponsoring Agency: Supreme Court

Primary Access: http://oyez.at.nwu.edu/

Resource Summary: This unofficial site features information on major constitutional cases heard and decided by the Supreme Court of the United States. In addition, it includes RealAudio files, which contain digitial audio recordings of the Court's oral arguments and opinion announcements from sources in the National Archives.

Subject Heading: Cases—Sound Recordings

[626] Seventh Circuit

Sponsoring Agencies: Court of Appeals. Seventh Circuit; Chicago-Kent College of Law. Center for Law and Computers

Primary Access: http://www.kentlaw.edu/7circuit/

Alternative Access Method: http://www.kentlaw.edu/7circuit/indexstd.html [non-frames version]

Resource Summary: Electronic versions of the opinions from the Seventh Circuit of the Federal Court of Appeals are available from May 1995 to the present in HTML and Rich Text Format. Access is by month of decision, first party, second party, or keyword search.

This site provides easy-to-use and straightforward access to these cases. While the time period is limited, this is an excellent resource for recent cases.

Subject Heading: Cases—Full Text

[627] Supreme Court Decisions

Sponsoring Agencies: Legal Information Institute (LII); Supreme Court

Primary Access: http://www.law.cornell.edu/supct/

Alternative Access Methods: ftp://ftp.cwru.edu/hermes/
mailto:listserv@listserv.law.cornell.edu with "subscribe liibulletin" in body

Resource Summary: The Legal Information Institute has provided an incredibly useful service by providing this front-end to recent Supreme Court cases that are disseminated through Project Hermes. Cases are available back to May 1990 and are accessible by date, first party name, or second party name. A topic index provides access to these cases by broad legal topics. There is also a keyword search option. This site provides HTML versions of the syllabus and opinions for each case. For many cases, it also provides a WordPerfect version.

On the ftp site, files retain the names they had when they were received from the Supreme Court. The extensions are .O for the opinion, .S for the syllabus, .C for concurring opinions, and .D for Dissenting opinions. The files are available in multiple formats, organized in directories by the format type. The most usable versions are ASCII files with a .filt extension. The ASCII-orig contains the raw ASCII files and the ASCII directory contains all of the filtered ASCII files. The WordPerfect directory contains files in WordPerfect 5.1 format, and the briefs directory contains selected briefs in TIFF image files. The Atex subdirectory contains the original files received from the Supreme Court in the Atex 8000 Document Processing and Typesetting system format. The xywrite directory contains the same files with the Atex codes stripped out or converted into xywrite commands. The ASCII subdirectory contains the same files as processed by a locally developed filtering program designed to remove the typesetting codes while retaining as much of the look of the document as possible.

Each opinion consists of an optional syllabus, the opinion, and optionally concurring and dissenting opinions—each is contained in a separate file. A syllabus is associated with most of the opinions and summarizes the ruling. The files are named as they are received from the Court. Filtered files have .filt appended to the end of the name.

Most of the features of the typeset document, such as bolding, italicizing, use of fonts, and other similar characteristics are lost in the translation to ASCII. The resulting filtered documents, however, are quite readable on most displays. The WordPerfect and HTML versions do retain some of the typesetting features. The LII Bulletin is an e-mail current awareness service which includes syllabi of U.S. Supreme Court decisions in bulletin format within hours after their release.

Originally the actual files that contain the Court decisions were located at the ftp site at Case Western Reserve University. However, the LII now has a direct Hermes feed. It is far easier and more efficient to obtain the cases through the Cornell Legal Information Institute Web front-end. Note that ASCII versions do not contain footnotes while the WordPerfect files do. To retrieve any of the other format types, use the ftp site.

Subject Heading: Cases—Full Text

SuDoc Number: JU 6.8/B: *Slip Opinions of the United States Supreme Court*

[628] Tarlton Law Library - U.S. Court of Appeals - Fifth Circuit

Sponsoring Agencies: Court of Appeals. Fifth Circuit; University of Texas at Austin Law Library

Primary Access: http://www.law.utexas.edu/us5th/us5th.html

Resource Summary: The Fifth Circuit site includes selected full-text documents as well as full-text cases. The publications include *Plan Under the Criminal Justice Act for Representation on Appeal*, *Rules Governing Complaints of Judicial Misconduct or Disability*, and *Federal Rules of Appellate Procedure*. Case materials are available for decisions rendered and published electronically since 1992. The cases are available in HTML and RTF formats. Users may sort cases by docket number or date of opinion. Keyword searching can be used for the appellant and appellee information or against the full text of the entire database.

Forms are used for access points though they may not always function well. Although only relatively recent cases are available, the cases on this site are older than some of the other circuit court sites. This is a valuable resource for cases and for the full-text documents.

Subject Heading: Cases—Full Text

[629] U.S. Court of Appeals, Eighth Circuit

Sponsoring Agencies: Court of Appeals. Eighth Circuit; Washington University School of Law

Primary Access: http://www.wulaw.wustl.edu/8th.cir/

Alternative Access Method: ftp://ftp.wulaw.wustl.edu/8th.cir/

Resource Summary: This site features the Eighth Circuit Court of Appeal's calendar and full-text cases from November 1995. These electronic versions are available in ASCII format. Access is by party name or by keyword in the description.

This site does have all the features of the other circuit court sites and the time period is even more limited for the availability of cases. However, they should be commended for starting to make these cases available on the Internet.

Subject Heading: Cases—Full Text

[630] U.S. Court of Appeals, Federal Circuit

Sponsoring Agencies: Court of Appeals. Federal Circuit; Georgetown University Law Center Library

Primary Access: http://www.ll.georgetown.edu/Fed-Ct/cafed.html

Resource Summary: Electronic versions of the opinions from the Federal Circuit of the Federal Court of Appeals are available from August 1995 to the present. The electronic versions are available in HTML and RTF format. Access is by month of decision, first party, second party, or keyword search.

This site provides easy-to-use and straightforward access to these cases. While the time period is limited, this is an excellent resource for recent cases.

Subject Heading: Cases—Full Text

[631] U.S. Court of Appeals, Fourth Circuit

Sponsoring Agencies: Court of Appeals. Fourth Circuit; Emory University. School of Law

Primary Access: http://www.law.emory.edu/4circuit/

Resource Summary: Electronic versions of the opinions from the Fourth Circuit of the Federal Court of Appeals are available from January 1995 to the present. The electronic versions are available in HTML and RTF format. Access is by month of decision, first party, second party, or keyword search.

Emory provides an easy-to-use and straightforward access mechanism to these cases. While the time period is limited, for recent cases this is an excellent resource.

Subject Heading: Cases—Full Text

[632] U.S. Court of Appeals, Sixth Circuit

Sponsoring Agencies: Court of Appeals. Sixth Circuit; Emory University. School of Law

Primary Access: http://www.law.emory.edu/6circuit/

Resource Summary: Electronic versions of the opinions from the Sixth Circuit of the Federal Court of Appeals are available from January 1995 to the present. The electronic versions are available in HTML and RTF format. Access is by month of decision, first party, second party, or keyword search.

Emory provides an easy-to-use and straightforward access mechanism to these cases. While the time period is limited, for recent cases this is an excellent resource.

Subject Heading: Cases—Full Text

[633] U.S. Court of Appeals, Tenth Circuit

Sponsoring Agencies: Court of Appeals. Tenth Circuit; Emory University. School of Law

Primary Access: http://www.law.emory.edu/10circuit/

Resource Summary: Electronic versions of the opinions from the Tenth Circuit of the Federal Court of Appeals are available from August 1995 to the present. The electronic versions are available in HTML and RTF format. Access is by month of decision, first party, second party, or keyword search.

Emory provides an easy-to-use and straightforward access mechanism to these cases. While the time period is limited, for recent cases this is an excellent resource.

Subject Heading: Cases—Full Text

[634] U.S. Court of Appeals for the D.C. Circuit

Sponsoring Agencies: Court of Appeals. District of Columbia Circuit; Georgetown University Law Center Library

Primary Access: http://www.ll.georgetown.edu/Fed-Ct/cadc.html

Resource Summary: Electronic versions of the opinions from the D.C. Circuit of the Federal Court of Appeals are available from March 1995 to the present. The electronic versions are available in HTML and RTF format. Access is by month of decision, first party, second party, or keyword search.

This site provides easy-to-use and straightforward access to these cases. While the time period is limited, for recent cases this is an excellent resource.

Subject Heading: Cases—Full Text

[635] U.S. Court of Appeals for the Second Circuit Decisions

Sponsoring Agencies: Court of Appeals. Second Circuit; Pace University School of Law

Primary Access: http://www.law.pace.edu/legal/us-legal/judiciary/second-circuit.html

Resource Summary: Electronic versions of the opinions from the Second Circuit of the Federal Court of Appeals are available from September 1995 to the present. The electronic versions are available in HTML format. Access is by month of decision and then alphabetically by case name.

This site provides relatively easy access to these cases. Access by first party, second party, and keyword would be a useful addition. The time period covered is limited, but for recent cases this is an excellent resource.

Subject Heading: Cases—Full Text

[636] U.S. Federal Courts Finder

Sponsoring Agency: Emory University. School of Law

Primary Access: http://www.law.emory.edu/FEDCTS/

Resource Summary: This is a simple image map, and it provides text-based links to the Web sites that provide access to cases from the Federal Circuit Courts of Appeals and the Supreme Court.

While not as broad a finding aid as the Federal Court Locator, this is an effective way to connect to the various sources for recent federal case law.

Subject Heading: Finding Aid—Laws

[637] United States Court of Appeals, Eleventh Circuit

Sponsoring Agencies: Court of Appeals. Eleventh Circuit; Emory University. School of Law

Primary Access: http://www.law.emory.edu/11circuit/

Alternative Access Method: http://www.mindspring.com/~wmundy/opinions.html

Resource Summary: Electronic versions of the opinions from the Eleventh Circuit of the Federal Court of Appeals are available from November 1994 to the present. The electronic versions are available in HTML and RTF format. Access is by month of decision, first party, second party, or keyword search. The alternate site includes versions from the past few months only, and all are originally WordPerfect 5.1 files compressed in .zip format.

Emory provides an easy-to-use and straightforward access mechanism to these cases. While the time period is limited, for recent cases this is an excellent resource.

Subject Heading: Cases—Full Text

[638] United States Court of Appeals, First Circuit

Sponsoring Agencies: Court of Appeals. First Circuit; Emory University. School of Law

Primary Access: http://www.law.emory.edu/1circuit/

Resource Summary: Electronic versions of the opinions from the First Circuit of the Federal Court of Appeals are available from 1995 to the present. The electronic versions are available in HTML and RTF format. Access is by month of decision, first party, second party, or keyword search.

Emory provides an easy-to-use and straightforward access mechanism to these cases. While the time period is limited, for recent cases this is an excellent resource.

Subject Heading: Cases—Full Text

[639] United States Court of Appeals for the Third Circuit

Sponsoring Agencies: Court of Appeals. Third Circuit; Villanova Center for Information Law and Policy

Primary Access: http://www.law.vill.edu/Fed-Ct/ca03.html

Alternative Access Method: telnet://dial3rd@anthrax.law.vill.edu for the Third Circuit Court of Appeals Bulletin Board System

Resource Summary: Electronic versions of the decisions from the Third Circuit of the Federal Court of Appeals are available from May 1994 to the present. The electronic versions are available in multiple formats: HTML, ASCII, MS Word, WordPerfect 5.1, and by fax to selected regions. Access to the decisions is by month, by first or second party name (not yet functional), and via a keyword search.

The online availability of this information on the Internet is commendable. The HTML and common word processor formats make the decisions easy to read online or offline.

Subject Heading: Cases—Full Text

Legal Information: Law Enforcement

[640] Attorney General

Sponsoring Agency: Department of Justice (DOJ). Office of the Attorney General

Primary Access: http://www.usdoj.gov/offices/oag.html

Resource Summary: This site describes the Office and has some biographical information on the current Attorney General, Janet Reno. It also provides links to speeches, annual reports, and information on the anti-gang and youth violence initiative.

Subject Heading: Law Enforcement

[641] Bureau of Justice Assistance

Sponsoring Agencies: Bureau of Justice Assistance; Department of Justice (DOJ); National Criminal Justice Reference Service (NCJRS)

Primary Access: http://www.ojp.usdoj.gov/BJA/

Resource Summary: As part of the NCJRS' site, this page gives a basic description of the Bureau and its mission. The site includes informatin on a number of grant programs under the heading Funding Assistance. Under the Technical Assistance heading is a link to the Justice Information Center's search screen and to a section entitled Evaluation/Technical Assistance and Training.

The site itself has few documents, but there are many Bureau publications available through the Justice Information Center.

Subject Headings: Grants; Criminal Justice

[642] Counter-Terrorism Rewards Program (HEROES)

Sponsoring Agencies: Bureau of Diplomatic Security; Diplomatic Security Service; Department of State

Primary Access: http://www.heroes.net/

Alternative Access Methods: http://www.heroes.net/spanish/servicio.html [Spanish version] http://www.heroes.net/french/service.html [French version]

Resource Summary: Featuring information on security for Americans at home and abroad, this site features sections including Counter-Terrorism Rewards Program; Counter-Narcotics Rewards Program; and Passport and Visa Fraud Investigations Programs. These along with the News and Information section include wanted posters, descriptions of well-known terrorism incidents, and information on the rewards programs.

While this site does not cover all aspects of terrorism in the U.S. and abroad, it does provide an interesting discussion of one of the federal agencies involved in the fight against terrorism.

Subject Headings: Terrorism; Wanted People

[643] Deputy Attorney General

Sponsoring Agency: Department of Justice (DOJ). Office of the Deputy Attorney General

Primary Access: http://www.usdoj.gov/offices/dag.html

Resource Summary: This page provides information on the office and the current Deputy Attorney General, Jamie S. Gorelick. It also provides access to recent speeches.

Subject Heading: Law Enforcement

[644] Drug Enforcement Administration

Sponsoring Agency: Drug Enforcement Administration (DEA)

Primary Access: http://www.usdoj.gov/dea/

Resource Summary: The Drug Enforcement Administration site offers basic information about the agency and includes the following categories: Mission, Administrator, Congressional Testimony, Press Releases, Employment Opportunities, Publications, and Items of Interest. Under the Publications heading, several documents published since 1995 are available including *Speaking Out Against Drug Legalization*. A few topical categories are also available including Diversion Control, Demand Reduction, Trends and Statistics, and DEA Fugitives.

Subject Headings: Law Enforcement; Drug Abuse

SuDoc Number: J 24.2: D 84/20 *Speaking Out Against Drug Legalization*

[645] Federal Bureau of Investigation

Sponsoring Agency: Federal Bureau of Investigation (FBI)

Primary Access: http://www.fbi.gov/

Resource Summary: The FBI features a broad collection of information resources on its Web site. It has a section on individuals wanted by the FBI which includes pictures. The FBI Overview, History, and Employment Opportunities area includes the location of FBI field offices and a section on Famous Cases. The Major Investigations section features information on well-known recent investigations such as the Unabomber, TWA flight 800, and the Arizona Train Wreck. Other primary sections include FBI Congressional Affairs, FBI Public Affairs, and FBI Law Enforcement Support.

The site includes access to full-text ASCII articles from the *FBI Law Enforcement Bulletin* from November 1994. It also includes highlights and extracts from the *Uniform Crime Reports for the United States*.

The wide variety of information on popular law enforcement topics and the full-text availability of popular FBI publications make this a frequently visited site.

Subject Headings: Electronic Periodicals; Kidnapping; Law Enforcement; Wanted People

SuDoc Numbers: J 1.14/7: *Uniform Crime Reports for the United States*
J 1.14/8: *FBI Law Enforcement Bulletin*

[646] Federal Law Enforcement Training Center

Sponsoring Agency: Federal Law Enforcement Training Center (FLETC)

Primary Access: http://www.ustreas.gov/bureaus/fletc/homepage.html

Alternative Access Method: http://www.ustreas.gov/bureaus/fletc/contents.html

Resource Summary: The main FLETC page consists primarily of a welcome message from the director. At the bottom is a link to the contents,where the full contents of the FLETC site are much more easily accessible. Most of the informational links are listed under General Information and consist of items such as History of the FLETC Campuses, Key Addresses and Phone Numbers, On-Site Participating Organizations, and FLETC Operations—What We Do For You.

These pages will be of interest primarily to those considering attending FLETC training or to those trying to contact FLETC.

Subject Heading: Law Enforcement—Training

[647] Financial Crimes Enforcement Network

Sponsoring Agencies: Department of the Treasury; Financial Crimes Enforcement Network (FinCEN)

Primary Access: http://www.ustreas.gov/treasury/bureaus/fincen/

Resource Summary: FinCEN oversees and implements the Department of the Treasury's policies to prevent and detect money laundering. The Network is becoming a leader in international efforts to build effective counter-money laundering policies and cooperation throughout the world. Their Web site supports this mission with sections such as Press Releases, Advisories (in PDF format), and Bank Secrecy Act Forms. It also has sections entitled: Cyberpayments, the Borderless World, and Publications. The Cyberpayments category discusses law enforcement concerns about electronic money transfers and Internet-based payment systems.

This should be a useful site for those researching money laundering or interested in electronic payments.

Subject Headings: Criminals; Money Laundering

[648] Fugitives - Wanted

Sponsoring Agencies: Department of Justice (DOJ); Drug Enforcement Administration (DEA); Federal Bureau of Investigation (FBI); Marshals Service

Primary Access: http://www.usdoj.gov/bureaus/fugitives.html

Resource Summary: This site includes links to lists of wanted fugitives from the FBI, the DEA, and the U.S. Marshals Service. For the FBI, they include their list of the Ten Most Wanted Fugitives as well as a Fugitive Publicity page with information on other wanted criminals. The DEA fugitives are listed by DEA region. The Marshals Service lists its 15 most wanted fugitives. These pages include pictures, descriptions of the crimes, and information on contacting the appropriate law enforcement agency.

Subject Headings: Criminals; Wanted People

[649] IGnet—Internet for the Federal Inspectors General

Sponsoring Agencies: Offices of Inspectors General (IG); President's Council on Integrity and Efficiency (PCIE)

Primary Access: http://www.sbaonline.sba.gov/ignet/

Alternative Access Methods: gopher://www.sbaonline.sba.gov/11/ignet
mailto:majordomo@www2.sbaonline.sba.gov with "lists" in body

Resource Summary: IGnet serves the IG community which consists of the Offices of Inspector General who conduct audits, investigations, and inspections in more than 60 federal agencies. The IGnet Web site features two main sections: The IG Community and IGnet Tools.

The IG Community category includes the headings IG Information, which includes IG reports and component IG home pages; the IG Directory, which includes hotline numbers and information on reporting fraud, waste, and abuse; the IG Community Manual with laws, regulations, and standards; President's Council on Integrity and Efficiency Reports and Publications; and News of the IG Community including press releases and testimony.

The heading IGnet Tools features sections including Virtual Library with materials for A-128 and A-133 audits; Job Opportunities; Training Information; and Search IGnet—a keyword search engine for the entire site. The IGnet site also includes an HTML version of the *Yellow Book*, known officially as *Government Auditing Standards*.

The alternate mailto: URL provides access to IGnet e-mail discussion lists. These include numerous lists such as ig-audit, ig-aiga, ig-insp, and ig-inv. Send the command "lists" for a complete list of available discussion groups, and send the command "info listname" for more information on each of the lists.

IGnet provides a broad range of materials for both IG employees and whistleblowers interested in contacting one of the IG offices.

Subject Heading: Fraud

SuDoc Number: GA 1.2:AU 2/14/ *Government Auditing Standards*

[650] MPP Presents the U.S. Sentencing Commission

Sponsoring Agencies: Marijuana Policy Project (MPP); Sentencing Commission

Primary Access: http://www.mpp.org/~mpp/theussc.html

Resource Summary: This is simply an HTML document describing the United States Sentencing Commission, federal sentencing guidelines, and members of the Commission. It appears that this may be an electronic reproduction of a print document, but the source is not cited. This document is not hosted on an official government site, but rather on the Marijuana Policy Project server.

Although this descriptive page is hosted on an unofficial site, it seems to provide a non-biased description of the Commission. See also the official United States Sentencing Commission site at http://www.ussc.gov/.

Subject Headings: Sentencing; Criminal Justice

[651] National Institute of Justice

Sponsoring Agency: National Institute of Justice (NIJ)

Primary Access: http://ncjrs.aspensys.com/nijhome.htm

Resource Summary: This site describes the mission of the National Institute of Justice and includes information on applying for National Institute of Justice grants. A more detailed description of its research agenda can be found under these categories: Reduce Violent Crime; Reduce Drug- and Alcohol-Related Crime; Reduce the Consequences of Crime; Improve the Effectiveness of Crime Prevention Programs; Improve Law Enforcement and the Criminal Justice System; and Develop New Technology for Law Enforcement and the Criminal Justice System.

While there is not a great deal of information at this site, the NIJ does have numerous publications available through the Justice Information Center.

Subject Heading: Criminal Justice

[652] NCJRS Mailing Lists

Sponsoring Agencies: Department of Justice (DOJ); National Criminal Justice Reference Service (NCJRS); Office of Juvenile Justice and Delinquency Prevention (OJJDP); Office of Justice Programs

Primary Access: mailto:listproc@ncjrs.aspensys.com with "sub listname" in body

Resource Summary: There are two e-mail lists sponsored by NCJRS that provide announcements—JUVJUST is a listserv for those in the juvenile justice system or related professions. The listserv contains announcements from the Office of Juvenile Justice and Delinquency Prevention. JUST INFO, an electronic newsletter, is designed to provide criminal justice professionals with accurate, current, and useful criminal and juvenile justice-related information. Published on the 1st and 15th of every month, JUST INFO reports on a wide variety of topics including updates and information from the Office of Justice Programs agencies, new products and services from NCJRS, updates on federal legislation, important criminal justice resources on the Internet, and international services from NCJRS.

Subject Headings: Criminal Justice; E-mail Lists; Juvenile Offenders

[653] Office of Juvenile Justice and Delinquency Prevention

Sponsoring Agencies: Department of Justice (DOJ); Office of Juvenile Justice and Delinquency Prevention (OJJDP)

Primary Access: http://www.ncjrs.org/ojjhome.htm

Resource Summary: As part of the NCJRS' site, this page gives a basic description of the Office and its mission. Most of the substantive links connect to the sections of the Justice Information Center that contain the most relevant documents. The Highlights page gives information on and links to sections entitled National Juvenile Justice Action Plan; Creating Safe and Drug-Free Schools; Funding Opportunities; and Newly Released Publications.

While most of the Office's materials are available on the Justice Information Center site, this page does provide a starting point for finding some of their major publications.

Subject Headings: Criminal Justice; Juvenile Offenders

SuDoc Number: J 32.21: *OJJDP Fact Sheet*

[654] Office of National Drug Control Policy

Sponsoring Agencies: National Criminal Justice Reference Service (NCJRS); Office of National Drug Control Policy

Primary Access: http://www.whitehouse.gov/WH/EOP/ondcp/html/ondcp.html

Alternative Access Methods: http://www.whitehouse.gov/WH/EOP/ondcp/html/ondcp-plain.html [text version]
gopher://ncjrs.aspensys.com:71/11/drugs

Resource Summary: Although this Office is organized within the executive office of the president, many publications are available from NCJRS on its Justice Information Center site. On this server, there is information about the Office, its mission, and drug control priorities in the areas of treatment, prevention, domestic law enforcement, interdiction, and international drug policies.

Subject Heading: Drug Abuse

[655] Office of the Associate Attorney General

Sponsoring Agency: Department of Justice (DOJ). Office of the Associate Attorney General

Primary Access: http://www.usdoj.gov/offices/aag.html

Resource Summary: This site simply offers a brief description of the Office and a link to information on the current Associate Attorney General, John Schmidt.

Subject Heading: Law Enforcement

[656] Official Office of Justice Programs

Sponsoring Agency: Office of Justice Programs (OJP)

Primary Access: http://www.ojp.usdoj.gov/

Alternative Access Method: http://www.ojp.usdoj.gov/text.htm [text version]

Resource Summary: The Office of Justice Programs provides federal leadership, coordination, and assistance to the nation's justice system. OJP and its five program bureaus are responsible for collecting statistical data and conducting analyses; identifying emerging criminal justice issues; developing and testing promising approaches to address these issues; evaluating program results; and disseminating these findings and other information to state and local governments. The Web site consists primarily of descriptive information on the agency. The major content is available via links to the component agencies and to the Justice Information Center.

Subject Headings: Criminal Justice; Judicial System

[657] U.S. Immigration and Naturalization Service

Sponsoring Agency: Immigration and Naturalization Service (INS)

Primary Access: http://www.usdoj.gov/ins/

Alternative Access Method: http://www.usdoj.gov/ins/textonly/ [text version]

Resource Summary: The INS Web site features these sections: The Agency; Frequently Asked Questions; Public Information; and Employer Information. The Frequently Asked Questions section is fairly extensive, offering information on asylum, green cards, citizenship, employers and employees, naturalization, residency, and visas. Under the Public Information section, numerous online publications are available including press releases, *Immigration to the United States*, and other INS statistical publications. The Employer Information section has information on Employment Verification Pilot Programs.

While this site is by no means a comprehensive source, it is an excellent starting point for anyone with questions about immigration. All of the information is in English, so the site will not be useful to those who do not speak English.

Subject Headings: Law Enforcement; Immigration

SuDoc Numbers: J 21.2:W 89 *Worksite Enforcement: Reducing the Job Market*

[658] United States Marshals Service

Sponsoring Agency: Marshals Service

Primary Access: http://www.usdoj.gov/marshals/

Resource Summary: The Marshals site contains information on the Service, employment opportunities, and lists of auctions and wanted fugitives. The main sections are: Overview of the U.S. Marshals Service; Directory of U.S. Marshals Service District Offices; U.S. Marshals 15 Most Wanted Fugitives; How the Public Can Purchase Forfeited Assets; Listing of U.S. Marshals Service Auctions; Recruitment Information for Deputy U.S. Marshals; Current Status of Deputy U.S. Marshal Recruiting; and Directors' Speeches.

Subject Headings: Auctions; Employment; Law Enforcement; Wanted People

[659] Welcome to the Border Patrol

Sponsoring Agency: Border Patrol

Primary Access: http://members.aol.com/usbp1/

Resource Summary: This is an unofficial site for information on the U.S. Border Patrol and is designed to give an overview of the Border Patrol, its mission, organization, and history. The site also features the following categories: The Album, a collection of Border Patrol photographs; Air Operations; and Hiring and Training. Other sections include Life on the Line; Agent Down, a list of Border Patrol agents killed in the line of duty; and News and Current Events.

Although this is an unofficial site, it does provide a great deal of information on the agency, its activities, and topics of interest to the public.

Subject Heading: Immigration

CHAPTER 10: LIBRARIES

Numerous federal libraries provide information resources on the Internet ranging from their online public access catalogs to specialized databases and unique archival resources. Many of these federal libraries offer little more than basic information for their users and a link to their catalog. Others make some specialized services or databases available that will be of broad interest to those beyond their immediate users. This chapter includes resources of special interest to librarians in the Federal Depository Library Program.

The featured sites for this chapter are LC Web and NOAA Central Library sites. Of all the federal library sites, the Library of Congress' site is not only the best known, but the most frequently used. It offers a significant number of resources of broad general interest alongside specific resources for librarians. While there is not a single site that lists all of the federal library sites, the NOAA Central Library site comes the closest by listing links to other NOAA libraries.

Featured Sites

[660] Library of Congress World Wide Web (LC Web)

Sponsoring Agency: Library of Congress (LC)

Primary Access: http://www.loc.gov/

Alternative Access Methods: http://lcweb.loc.gov/
http://marvel.loc.gov/

Resource Summary: As the largest library in the world, it is only fitting that the Library of Congress Web site, known as LC Web, should be one of the most extensive and useful governmental library Web sites. Its American Memory Project, with its scanned images, movies, audio files, and other reproductions of historic documents, is an example of the great potential that the Internet has for making rare collections available to the public. Through its Services area, LC Web offers sections including Preservation, Cataloging, Acquisitions, and Reference. Other areas of the site offer an information for publishers section and a section on standards. The site features a rotating series of online exhibitions. Like the LC collection, the LC Web includes resources in many diverse subject areas. While the Web offers only a very small fraction of the material available in the Library itself, it does provide an important collection of material to the Internet community.

Many sections of LC Web are described elsewhere in this directory, but there are many other areas worth exploring as well. This is a large site and it is continually growing, offering substantial resources of interest to librarians, historical researchers, publishers, lawyers, Congress, and the general public.

Subject Headings: Exhibitions; Geography; History; Humanities; Libraries; Library Science

SuDoc Numbers: D 101.22:550- *Area Handbook Series*
LC 1.32/5: *FEDLINK Technical Notes Newsletter*

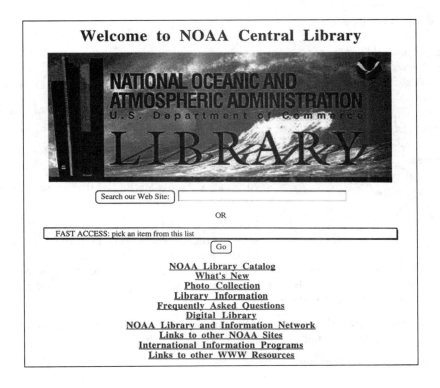

Welcome to NOAA Central Library

NATIONAL OCEANIC AND ATMOSPHERIC ADMINISTRATION
U.S. Department of Commerce
LIBRARY

Search our Web Site: [   ]

OR

FAST ACCESS: pick an item from this list

[Go]

NOAA Library Catalog
What's New
Photo Collection
Library Information
Frequently Asked Questions
Digital Library
NOAA Library and Information Network
Links to other NOAA Sites
International Information Programs
Links to other WWW Resources

[661] NOAA Central Library

Sponsoring Agencies: National Oceanic and Atmospheric Administration (NOAA); National Oceanographic Data Center (NODC)

Primary Access: http://www.lib.noaa.gov/

Resource Summary: The central NOAA library (managed under the direction of the NODC) describes its services, hours and policies, and lists links to other NOAA libraries. It also includes the ability to submit electronic reference questions. Their journal list and new items list is available on the page, but their online catalog is not. Under the NOAA Library and Information Network heading, there is an image map of the U.S. and a list of other NOAA library sites. Some of the links merely connect to NOAA laboratories and not specifically to NOAA libraries. Even so, it is one of the few government sites that lists more than a dozen other federal libraries.

The list of journals can be useful to interlibrary loan departments, but access to the full catalog would be even more useful. While the full catalog is available for dial-up, it is not accessible on the Internet.

Subject Headings: Finding Aid—Libraries; Libraries—Environment

The Libraries resources in this chapter are subdivided into three sections. The first section covers resources that are general library-related sites or federal library sites thar do not fit into the other two categories. This section runs from entry numbers 662 to 701. The second subchapter, Depository, features resources of interest to the depository library community and includes entries 702-717. The third section, National, contains resources from the national libraries such as the Library of Congress and runs from entries 718-724.

Libraries: General

[662] AFIT Academic Library

Sponsoring Agency: Air Force Institute of Technology (AFIT). Library

Primary Access: http://www.afit.af.mil/Schools/LD/afitld.htm

Alternative Access Methods: http://sabre.afit.af.mil/ telnet://sabre.afit.af.mil

Resource Summary: This fairly extensive Web site presents the categories AFIT Library Information, Library News, and Research Tools and Connections. Like many library sites, it provides basic information about the AFIT Academic Library and its services. It features an online new book list, library journal holdings, a Web interface to its online catalog, and some AFIT library bibliographies.

This is an informative and well-organized page. It is useful for patrons of the AFIT Library and those wanting to search its holdings.

Subject Headings: Library Catalogs; Libraries—Education

[663] Air University Library

Sponsoring Agency: Air University. Library

Primary Access: http://www.au.af.mil/au/aul/aul.htm

Resource Summary: The Air University Library Web site provides information on the Library and its services. Though the Web version of their catalog is only available to Air University personnel, there are other portions of the Web site that are not so restricted. These include their list of periodicals, bibliographic databases, descriptions of services, and bibliographies. The Library compiles many bibliographies on topics ranging from air base defense to the Yom Kippur War. Some of the recent bibliographies are available under the Bibliographies section.

Overall, this site provides a substantial amount of information about the library. It would be nice to have open access to the Library catalog. Although there is a brief description of the Air University Library *Index to Military Periodicals* CD-ROM, this is not accessible from the Web site. It would be a significant service if they offered an Internet version of the database.

Subject Heading: Libraries—Education

[664] Aiso Library

Sponsoring Agency: Defense Language Institute (DLI). Library

Primary Access: http://www.dli.army.mil/support/daa/library/default.htm

Alternative Access Method: http://206.102.94.201/ [catalog]

Resource Summary: This basic page contains Library hours, a description of the Library mission, the collections, borrowing policies, and a link to a Web interface to the library catalog. The library catalog interface uses the Library Corporation software.

Subject Heading: Library Catalogs

[665] Center for Electronic Records

Sponsoring Agencies: Center for Electronic Records; National Archives and Records Administration (NARA)

Primary Access: http://www.nara.gov/nara/electronic/

Resource Summary: This page provides sections including: Introduction to the Center; Information for Researchers; Information for Federal Records Managers; and Information Resources Personnel. The subsequent pages describe the holdings of data files, services available to federal agencies, how to request files, and technical specifications of the data files. The site also includes a brief bibliography of staff publications relating to electronic records.

The information on this site is descriptive, but otherwise the resources are relatively scarce.

Subject Headings: Archives; Electronic Publications

[666] Daedalus: The Aeromedical Library Online

Sponsoring Agency: Brooks Air Force Base. Library

Primary Access: http://www.brooks.af.mil/AL/SD/DAEDALUS/

Alternative Access Method: telnet://daedalus.brooks.af.mil

Resource Summary: The Aeromedical Library site features telnet access to the library catalog. It also offers online submission of interlibrary loan requests by patrons, customer comments, and finding aids for journals on the Web, libraries on the Web, and organizations on the Web.

This site aims to serve the Library's users, but other government librarians may find it useful for comparing service offerings.

Subject Headings: Aeronautics—Medical Aspects; Libraries—Health Sciences; Libraries—Military; Library Catalogs

[667] Dudley Knox Library

Sponsoring Agency: Naval Postgraduate School. Dudley Knox Library

Primary Access: http://vislab-www.nps.navy.mil/~library/

Alternative Access Methods: http://web.nps.navy.mil/uhtbin/cgisirsi/0/1/0 [catalog]
gopher://peacock.nps.navy.mil/11/Library

Resource Summary: This library site features the categories: News from the Library, Services, Resources, Library Hours, Communicating with the Library, and BOSUN—the Online Catalog. The catalog uses Sirsi software with a Web interface. The other sections provide basic information about the Library and its services.

The site uses a simple presentation style and delivers its information and access to the catalog effectively.

Subject Headings: Libraries—Education; Libraries—Military

[668] EPA National Online Library System

Sponsoring Agency: Environmental Protection Agency (EPA)

Primary Access: telnet://epaibm.rtpnc.epa.gov/

Alternative Access Method: http://www.epa.gov/natlibra/

Resource Summary: The Web page gives a little information about the EPA National Library Network Program along with a telnet link to the Online Library System (OLS). The OLS is the main source for information about the EPA libraries and their holdings. After connecting, choose the Public Access option, and then choose OLS. Once connected to the OLS, the primary EPA union catalog is listed as the National Catalog. The Catalog provides access to the holdings of all EPA libraries.

The OLS includes more than just the National Catalog. The menu also includes databases on Subsurface Remediation, Hazardous Waste, Environmental Financing Information Network, and National Center for Environmental Publications and Information (NCEPI). NCEPI offers a listing of EPA publications with publication titles, EPA publication numbers, and National Technical Information Service and/or Government Printing Office numbers. The full text of *Access EPA* is also available on the OLS.

The OLS also contains a substantial body of full-text and bibliographic information sources from the EPA. The telnet interface is difficult for many people to use, and conversion to the Web would greatly broaden its appeal.

Subject Headings: Bibliographic Databases; Libraries—Environment; Library Catalogs

SuDoc Number: EP 1.8/13: Ac 2/ *Access EPA*

[669] Federal Bureau of Prisons Library

Sponsoring Agency: Federal Bureau of Prisons. Library

Primary Access: http://206.102.94.227/

Resource Summary: This library Web site is primarily a Web interface to their Federal Bureau of Prisons library catalog. The site also includes a brief description of the Library, information on the archives, and a list of periodicals.

Subject Heading: Library Catalogs

[670] Fermilab Information Resources Library

Sponsoring Agency: Fermi National Accelerator Laboratory. Library

Primary Access: http://www-lib.fnal.gov/library/welcome.html

Alternative Access Method: http://fnlib.fnal.gov/MARION/ [catalog]

Resource Summary: The Fermilab Library Web site features access to a Web interface to its catalog, a list of journal holdings, and a bibliography of Fermilab preprints. The preprints are available via a New Preprints on Display section, which has weekly updates, and via the link, Monthly Lists of Fermilab Preprints. While not all of the preprints are available in full text, those that are available online have direct links to their location in a preprint archive. This Web site also lists numerous external resources such as various preprint archives.

Subject Headings: Libraries—Research Laboratories; Library Catalogs; Preprints

[671] General Services Administration Library Catalog

Sponsoring Agency: General Services Administration (GSA). Library

Primary Access: http://206.102.94.228/

Resource Summary: This page provides some basic information on the GSA library collection, and also includes information not available in the collection, borrowing information, and contact information. However, the primary function of the page is to offer a Web interface to their library catalog using the Library Corporation software.

Subject Heading: Library Catalogs

[672] GOVDOC-L [e-mail list]

Primary Access: mailto:listserv@lists.psu.edu with "sub govdoc-l name" in body

Alternative Access Methods: news:bit.listserv.govdoc-l
gopher://burrow.cl.msu.edu/11/news/archives/bit.listserv.govdoc-l

Resource Summary: This is the oldest, and primary e-mail list for documents librarians. While it is neither hosted by nor sponsored by the federal government, the discussions, questions, and announcements relate directly to the practice of government documents librarianship. The list includes needs and offers notices, announcements and answers direct from GPO personnel, job announcements, and discussions of government Internet sites. The GPO's *Administrative Notes* are also sent to this list.

The newsgroup is supposed to echo all postings to the listserv, but the gateway sometimes fails to send all postings. Thus, the archives at the Gopher site may not include all postings. Search functions are also available directly from the listserv.

Subject Headings: E-mail Lists; Documents Librarians; Government Publications—Discussion

SuDoc Number: GP 3.16/3-2: *Administrative Notes*

[673] Homer E. Newell Memorial Library

Sponsoring Agency: Goddard Space Flight Center (GSFC). Library

Primary Access: http://www-library.gsfc.nasa.gov/

Resource Summary: The GSFC Library Web site features a Goddard Technical Report Server, a Balloon Library database, and a NASA acronym database. The Technical Report Server provides bibliographic information and abstracts for technical reports coming from Goddard. Their Special Collection's Balloon Library database has bibliographic references to literature on balloons.

Another interesting link is the Goddard Library Online Bibliographic Access/Locator which is designed as an expert system to assist library patrons in selecting library resources. Other links provide information on the Library and its services. While the library catalog is accessible via a telnet link from the Web site, it requires a username and password that must be requested from the library.

While many sections of this site are restricted to local users only, it does provide an excellent example of how a library Web site can provide access to a broad range of library services. It would be helpful, however, if they provided the username and password for their catalog on the Web site.

Subject Headings: Balloons; Bibliographic Databases; Libraries—Science

[674] INTL-DOC [e-mail list]

Sponsoring Agency: Government Documents Round Table (GODORT). International Documents Task Force (IDTF)

Primary Access: mailto:listserv@listserv.acns.nwu.edu with "sub intl-doc name" in body

Alternative Access Method: http://www.library.nwu.edu/govpub/idtf/intl-doc.html

Resource Summary: INTL-DOC features discussions by international documents librarians and users of International Governmental Organization (IGO) materials. The United Nations Library posts notices regarding the UN depository program and other matters on this list. The list is intended primarily for those working with IGO documentation. However, it also welcomes items related to the literature of foreign national governments and of international affairs in general.

This is an essential list for government documents librarians that work with IGO publications.

Subject Headings: E-mail Lists; Government Publications—Discussion; Government Publications—International

[675] LLNL Library Services

Sponsoring Agency: Lawrence Livermore National Laboratory (LLNL). Library

Primary Access: http://www.llnl.gov/tid/Library.html

Alternative Access Method: telnet://patron@library.llnl.gov

Resource Summary: The Lawrence Livermore National Library site features a telnet link to its online catalog and descriptions of its services and collections. Full-text, LLNL-authored unclassified technical reports are available in PDF format.

While this page includes a decent amount of information about the Library and its services, the presentation could be better organized.

Subject Headings: Libraries—Research Laboratories; Library Catalogs; Reports—Full Text

[676] Los Alamos Library

Sponsoring Agency: Los Alamos National Laboratory (LANL). Library

Primary Access: http://lib-www.lanl.gov/

Alternative Access Methods: telnet://library.lanl.gov:9001 [catalog]
http://lib-www.lanl.gov/edata/catalog.htm [catalog]

Resource Summary: The LANL Library Web site features information about the Library, its services, and its move toward becoming a digital library. Some portions of the site are restricted to LANL personnel only, including the experimental Los Alamos Unclassified Publications database. However, under the Los Alamos Publications section, some reports and publications are available in full-text format. The Web interface to their library catalog is an experimental project using Z39.50. The other http URL opens a telnet window to the telnet catalog address.

This site offers a good overview of the Library and many of its projects. Even with some sections restricted in access, the other portions make this site well worth a visit.

Subject Headings: Libraries—Research Laboratories; Library Catalogs

[677] Lunar and Planetary Institute Library

Sponsoring Agency: Lunar and Planetary Institute (LPI). Library

Primary Access: http://cass.jsc.nasa.gov/library/library.html

Resource Summary: This library site features two Web interfaces to its online catalog—easy and expert. Beyond this library catalog interface, the site has some information on LPI slide sets and Regional Planetary Image Facilities.

Subject Headings: Libraries—Science; Library Catalogs

[678] The Marine Corps University Libraries

Sponsoring Agency: Marine Corps University Library

Primary Access: http://www-mcu.mqg.usmc.mil/www/MCRC/library/library.htm

Resource Summary: After a link to the Libraries' mission statement, the site divides resources into two sections: The Collections and Collections Guides. The only link currently functioning under either category is one to The New Science Collection page. Other sections which may be enabled soon include: Journals, Microforms, Collection Development Plan, Bibliographies, and Research Guides. There are also links to two remote sites—University Library and the Quantico Family Library.

This site will be of most interest to the Libraries' patrons. While resources on the site look like they will soon be expanded, there is not much information available.

Subject Headings: Libraries—Education; Libraries—Military

[679] NASA Langley Research Center Technical Library

Sponsoring Agency: Langley Research Center (LaRC). Library

Primary Access: http://library-www.larc.nasa.gov/

Resource Summary: This site offers information for users of the LaRC Technical Library. Under the Information, Resources, and Services heading, this page offers information on the Library including reference services, circulation, a library overview, and information for visitors. The Electronic Desktop Access page provides connections to the Web version of the library catalog and bibliographic databases, electronic journals, and RECONSelect. The Library News and Events section offers information on library workshops and how to "borrow" an information specialist.

Subject Headings: Libraries—Science; Library Catalogs

[680] National Defense University Library

Sponsoring Agency: National Defense University Library

Primary Access: http://www.ndu.edu/ndu/library/home01.html

Resource Summary: This site includes descriptive information about the Library, its services, and its special collections and archives. It appears that further developments are planned such as an Information Quest section and issues of their in-house current awareness system, named Current Journal Articles. No link to a catalog is available. Part of the Library's Internet Resource Guide, its Defense Nexus section, provides an excellent finding aid for other military sites.

While the site is rather limited in terms of library information, future expansion appears to be in the works.

Subject Headings: Libraries—Education; Finding Aid—Military

[681] National Institute for Literacy

Sponsoring Agency: National Institute for Literacy (NIFL)

Primary Access: http://novel.nifl.gov/

Resource Summary: The main categories on this server include Current Events and Information; Literacy Forums and Listservs; NIFL Regional Hubs and States Literacy Resources; National Adult Literacy and Learning Disabilities Center; and Literacy Americorps. There are relatively few publications available from any of these links, but they do provide contact information and some toll-free phone numbers.

The primary information on this site is within the directory information sections. It could use some basic full-text documents on literacy and literacy programs.

Subject Heading: Literacy

[682] National Institutes of Health Library

Sponsoring Agency: National Institutes of Health (NIH). Library

Primary Access: http://libwww.ncrr.nih.gov/

Alternative Access Methods: telnet://nih-library.nih.gov:23/
gopher://gopher.nih.gov/11/lit/nih_library

Resource Summary: The NIH Library site features information about the Library, its services, and a connection to its catalog. Main categories include: Services, Electronic Resources, Requests (which can only be submitted by NIH users), News; Calendar; and Hours. The library catalog is accessible by telnet. The link to the library catalog on the Web page did not work, but the one on the Gopher server did.

The site will primarily be of interest to NIH researchers and other Library users.

Subject Headings: Libraries—Health Sciences; Library Catalogs

[683] National Radio Astronomy Observatory Library

Sponsoring Agency: National Radio Astronomy Observatory (NRAO). Library

Primary Access: http://info.cv.nrao.edu/html/library/library.html

Alternative Access Method: http://www.aoc.nrao.edu/NRAOLIB.html [catalog]

Resource Summary: This site features the Library's catalog and many external resources, particulary preprint sites. The NRAO RAPSheet is a bibliographic listing of astronomy and astrophysics preprints received in the Charlottesville Library of the National Radio Astronomy Observatory from 1986 forward. Another section features NRAO staff and visitor preprints, and published papers including both full-text preprints and bibliographic listings. That section also includes instructions to authors for submitting their papers for the full-text page.

Not much information on the Library or its services is available on this site. A brief description would be helpful.

Subject Headings: Libraries—Science; Library Catalogs; Preprints

[684] Navy Department Library

Sponsoring Agency: Department of the Navy. Library

Primary Access: http://navy.library.net/

Alternative Access Method: http://206.102.94.230/

Resource Summary: This Web interface to the navy's library uses software from the Library Corporation. Search options include browse and keyword searches by author, title, and subject. In addition, this site includes some basic information about the Library including sections entitled Subjects Emphasized; Special and Rare Collections; and Location.

This catalog is useful for finding books in the areas of maritime history, naval customs and traditions, shipbuilding, naval stations, canals, and navigation.

Subject Headings: Military History; Library Catalogs

[685] NCAR Library

Sponsoring Agency: National Center for Atmospheric Research (NCAR)

Primary Access: http://www.dir.ucar.edu/iss/lib/

Alternative Access Methods: telnet://library.ucar.edu/ [catalog]
http://www.ucar.edu/LIBRARY/libhome.html

Resource Summary: This site includes information on the National Center for Atmospheric Research Library and its services including a list of CD-ROM titles and document delivery information. Other featured sections include the Archives Home Page; Zap Interlibrary Loan Requests; and The Collection. A telnet link connects to the online catalog which includes an archives and manuscripts database in addition to the library catalog database.

This site provides a fair amount of information on the Library and its services. The pages are of interest to NCAR library patrons and to other librarians who may want to compare service offerings.

Subject Headings: Libraries—Environment; Library Catalogs; Scientific and Technical Information

[686] NIEHS Library

Sponsoring Agency: National Institute of Environmental Health Sciences (NIEHS). Library

Primary Access: http://library.niehs.nih.gov/home.htm

Resource Summary: The National Institute of Environmental Health Sciences Library serves primarily the scientific and administrative staff of NIEHS, but it also provides limited services to the public. The NIEHS Web site offers information on new books, copy services, interlibrary loans, book ordering, journal subscriptions, reference services, and CD-ROM and LAN support. The catalog is supposed to be available via the Web soon.

Subject Heading: Libraries—Health Sciences

[687] Nimitz Library

Sponsoring Agency: Naval Academy. Library

Primary Access: http://www.nadn.navy.mil/Library/

Alternative Access Method: telnet://131.121.188.001 [for catalog]

Resource Summary: The Nimitz Library Web site features information about the Library and its services including interlibrary loan request forms, reserves forms, online searching requests, library hours, and a newsletter. A Research Guides section is being designed to offer guidance for research in the Nimitz Library. Most of the other links point to external resources.

This site is well designed, but some of the sections are empty at this point.

Subject Headings: Libraries—Education; Library Catalogs

[688] NIST Virtual Library

Sponsoring Agency: National Institute of Standards and Technology (NIST). Library

Primary Access: http://nvl.nist.gov/

Alternative Access Method: telnet://ricmenu.nist.gov:7172/

Resource Summary: While providing basic information about the Library and its services, this site goes far beyond those basics. It features pages for electronic journals, a telnet Interface to its Sirsi online catalog, subject guides, databases, and NIST publications. The site uses frames, but it also has a very well designed customization capability. Users can customize the appearance of the page and what links should be included in a favorite pop-up menu. The NIST Publications section includes access to an online version of the *Journal of Research*, in PDF format. It also features a list of other NIST sites with online publications which can be a useful finding aid when searching for a specific NIST document. The Databases page includes access to NIST's Fire Research Information Service (FRIS)—an online bibliographic database on fire research-related topics.

Subject Headings: Libraries; Library Catalogs

SuDoc Number: C 13.22: *Journal of Research of the National Institute of Standards and Technology*

[689] NOAA Seattle Regional Library

Sponsoring Agencies: National Oceanic and Atmospheric Administration (NOAA). Library and Information Services Division; National Oceanic and Atmospheric Administration (NOAA). Western Region. Library

Primary Access: http://www.wrclib.noaa.gov/lib/

Resource Summary: This regional NOAA library serves NOAA agencies in the Western region. Basic Library information such as hours, policies, and services are provided along with a journals list, a new books list, and an electronic reference questions submission. The Sirsi library catalog is available via the Web.

This page is aimed at the Library's clientele.

Subject Headings: Libraries—Science; Library Catalogs

[690] Northwest and Alaska Fisheries Science Centers Library

Sponsoring Agency: Northwest Fisheries Science Center. Library

Primary Access: http://listeria.nwfsc.noaa.gov/library/library.htm

Resource Summary: This site provides a basic description of Library services including a new books list, their serials list, and a list of electronic products available in the Library. It also includes information on its archival collections. Another section, the Endangered Species Salmon Files, will be made available only on CD-ROM and in the Library itself.

This site is primarily of interest to users of the Library.

Subject Headings: Fish and Fishing; Libraries—Science

[691] NRL Library InfoWeb

Sponsoring Agencies: Naval Research Laboratory (NRL); Ruth H. Hooker Research Library and Technical Information Center

Primary Access: http://infonext.nrl.navy.mil/

Alternative Access Method: http://libsun.nrl.navy.mil/uhtbin/cgisirsi/26/1/1 [catalog]

Resource Summary: The NRL Library Web site features information on the Library and its services under the following sections: Catalogs and Databases, Computer Support, Government Information, Internet Directory, Science Resources, and Torpedo. Torpedo is a full-text journal service that is only available to authorized users. The catalog uses Stilas software from Sirsi Corporation, and its search options include browse and keyword searching by author, title, and subject. The Science Resources category consists of pointers to external resources.

In general the site is well organized, but it would be helpful if the catalog were directly accessible from the top level menu.

Subject Headings: Libraries—Research Laboratories; Library Catalogs; Navy

[692] Phillips Laboratory Technical Library

Sponsoring Agency: Kirtland Air Force Base. Phillips Laboratory. Library

Primary Access: http://library.plk.af.mil/

Alternative Access Method: http://library.plk.af.mil/uhtbin/cgisirsi/9/1/1 [catalog]

Resource Summary: By providing access to information on the Library and a connection to its catalog, this site is typical of many of the other government library sites. The catalog uses Stilas software from Sirsi Corporation. A main link, Excalibur's WebFile (EFS) is an interactive image retrieval system that provides a full-text search capability on all currently-archived unlimited distribution materials in the Library's collection. However, it is only available to government agencies.

This site provides basic information about the catalog. Like other Stilas sites, access to the catalog could be more direct.

Subject Headings: Libraries—Research Laboratories; Library Catalogs

[693] Research Library at Brookhaven National Laboratory

Sponsoring Agency: Brookhaven National Laboratory (BNL). Library

Primary Access: http://www.bnl.gov/RESLIB/reslib.html

Alternative Access Method: telnet://brookhaven@inform.bnl.gov

Resource Summary: The BNL Research Library features the categories: General Information; Online Catalogs; Electronic Subscriptions; and the BNL Digital Archive. While the site is designed for the BNL staff, some sections are freely available to outsiders. The library catalog is available through the telnet connection and through a Web interface.

Subject Headings: Libraries—Research Laboratories; Library Catalogs

[694]   Sandia National Laboratories Technical Library

Sponsoring Agency: Sandia National Laboratories. Library

Primary Access: http://www.sandia.gov/library/

Resource Summary: This site provides basic information about the Library and its services. However, its library catalog is only available in-house and through the Sandia Internal Restricted Network. Under the heading Electronic Resources, the Library makes a few *SAND Reports* available in PDF format. It appears that the Library will be expanding this section by providing access to many of the unclassified *SAND Reports*.

The site is useful for finding standard information about the Library. The *SAND Reports* section will make the site of broader interest when more of the *SAND Reports* become available there.

Subject Headings: Libraries—Research Laboratories; Reports—Full Text

SuDoc Number: E 1.28:SAND *SAND Reports*

[695]   SILIBS-L [e-mail list]

Sponsoring Agency: Smithsonian Institution

Primary Access: mailto:listserv@sivm.si.edu with "sub silibs-l name" in body

Resource Summary: This e-mail list, sponsored and hosted by the Smithsonian, is maintained for the purpose of disseminating announcements and information from Smithsonian Institution libraries.

Subject Headings: E-mail Lists; Libraries

[696] Smithsonian Institution Libraries

Sponsoring Agency: Smithsonian Institution

Primary Access: http://www.sil.si.edu/

Alternative Access Methods: telnet://siris.si.edu [catalog]
tn3270://siris.si.edu [catalog]

Resource Summary: This principal starting point for information about the various Smithsonian Institution Libraries begins with links to branch Libraries' home pages. This section provides links to the branch Libraries that have Web sites. Project Access gives information on the Libraries' various CD-ROMs and online services. The Electronic Publications section provides access to a few Bureau of American Ethnology *Bulletins* and a newsletter from the Smithsonian Libraries. Another section lists current exhibitions, including an online version of the Science and the Artist's Book exhibition.

The library catalog includes different catalogs. The main catalog is listed as Smithsonian Libraries while the other catalogs include sections titled Art Inventories, Archives and Manuscripts, Research/ Bibliographies, and Smithsonian Chronology.

This Smithsonian Libraries' Internet site provides both an excellent overview of the libraries and some unique resources as well. Watch the Electronic Publications section for an expanded number of online documents and the Exhibitions section for more online exhibits.

Subject Headings: Libraries—Science; Library Catalogs

SuDoc Number: SI 2.3: *Bulletin* / Smithsonian Institution. Bureau of American Ethnology

[697] U.S. Department of State Library

Sponsoring Agency: Department of State. Library

Primary Access: http://usds.library.net/

Resource Summary: Boldly proclaiming itself as the "oldest federal library," the State Department Library site features its online catalog. Using software from the Library Corporation, it has the usual search features. Other information about the Library on this page includes location, description, mission statement, and borrowing policies.

Given the establishment date of 1789, we can only hope that this library will soon make some of its historic collections available online.

Subject Heading: Library Catalogs

[698] U.S. Naval Observatory Library

Sponsoring Agency: Naval Observatory (USNO). Library

Primary Access: http://www.usno.navy.mil/library/lib.html

Alternative Access Method: telnet://urania@urania.usno.navy.mil [catalog]

Resource Summary: In addition to a telnet connection to its catalog, this site features sections including Recently Cataloged Books, Journal Holdings, and Recent Papers by USNO Staff Members. The last of these is a bibliography, but it does not provide access to full-text versions of the papers. Almost all of the other links are to external resources. The catalog requires decent vt100 emulation to function properly.

A functional Web interface to their catalog would greatly improve its Internet accessibility.

Subject Headings: Libraries—Science; Library Catalogs

[699] U.S. Waterways Experiment Station Research Library

Sponsoring Agency: Waterways Experiment Station (WES). Library

Primary Access: http://libweb.wes.army.mil/

Alternative Access Method: telnet://134.164.84.4 [catalog]

Resource Summary: The WES Research Library site features information about the Library's services and a number of search options. The Search section provides links to the online library catalog, Internet searches, and an internal WES Web search. The library catalog is available via a Web Z39.50 interface as well as through the telnet connection.

Subject Headings: Libraries—Research Laboratories; Library Catalogs

[700] Wallops Technical Library

Sponsoring Agencies: Goddard Space Flight Center (GSFC). Library; Wallops Technical Library

Primary Access: http://www-library.gsfc.nasa.gov/wff/

Resource Summary: This library is a component library of the Goddard Space Flight Center Library (the Homer E. Newell Memorial Library). This Web page is almost a duplicate of the Homer E. Newell Memorial Library Web site.

Subject Heading: Libraries—Science

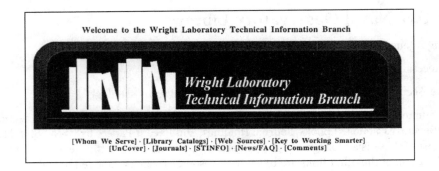

Welcome to the Wright Laboratory Technical Information Branch

Wright Laboratory
Technical Information Branch

[Whom We Serve] · [Library Catalogs] · [Web Sources] · [Key to Working Smarter]
[UnCover] · [Journals] · [STINFO] · [News/FAQ] · [Comments]

[701] Wright Laboratory Technical Information Branch

Sponsoring Agency: Wright-Patterson Air Force Base. Library

Primary Access: http://www.wl.wpafb.af.mil/library/

Alternative Access Method: telnet://chui@techlib.wpafb.af.mil [catalog]

Resource Summary: In addition to the telnet connection to their library catalog, this Web site features a journals holdings list, service request forms, and more. The Scientific and Technical Information Office of the library provides information on submitting camera-ready reports for publication. Another section, Keys to Working Smarter, provides suggestions and advice on using specific library services.

This site is primarily of interest to Wright-Patterson personnel.

Subject Headings: Libraries—Military; Library Catalogs

[702] Basic Depository Library Documents - The Unauthorized HTML Editions

Sponsoring Agencies: University of Denver Library; Government Printing Office (GPO)

Primary Access: http://www.du.edu/~ttyler/bdldhome.htm

Resource Summary: This is a collection of documents for the depository library community. Thomas Tyler began this effort at the University of Denver Library as an experiment to see if the *List of Classes* available from ftp://fedbbs.access.gpo.gov/ could be automatically converted into HTML format. After the success of that project, he began converting other management documents of the Depository Library Program that were available in machine-readable form.

By making these documents available on the Web in a usable form, this page provides great service for government documents librarians.

Subject Headings: Depository Libraries; Electronic Publications

SuDoc Numbers: GP 3.24: *List of Classes*
GP 3.29:D 44/ *Collection Development Guidelines for Selective Depository Libraries*
GP 3.2:C 56/8/ *Explanation of the Superintendent of Documents Classification System*
GP 3.26:D 44/992 *Instructions to Depository Libraries*
GP 3.29:D 44/993 *Federal Depository Library Manual*
GP 3.29:D 44/993/supp.2 *Guidelines for the Federal Depository Library Program*
GP 3.29:P 88/993 *GPO Classification Manual*
GP 3.2:Su 7 *Superseded List*
GP 3.3.32/2: *Union List of Item Selections*

[703] Claitor's GPO Publication Reference File Master Index

Sponsoring Agencies: Government Printing Office (GPO); Claitor's Law Books

Primary Access: http://www.claitors.com/prf/prfindex.htm

Resource Summary: The *Publications Reference File* (PRF), an essential tool for documents librarians, is a catalog of in-print and out-of-print titles available from the GPO. Claitor's version of the PRF is a direct hypertext version of the information available from the GPO and contains all information from the GPO PRF. Although there is no keyword search option, Claitor's provides browse access by stock number, agency source, SuDoc number, and title. There is also a section called PRF Latest Releases. Some of the out-of-print items are available direct from Claitor's, as are most of the in-print items. Claitor's also provides ordering information and an online order form.

This is a very useful resource to have online. While keyword search capabilities would be nice, the browse access points are sufficient for most needs.

Subject Headings: Bibliographic Databases; Documents Librarians; Government Publications—Bibliographies

SuDoc Number: GP 3.22/3: *GPO Sales Publications Reference File*

[704] Depository Library Council

Sponsoring Agency: Depository Library Council (DLC)

Primary Access: http://www.library.okstate.edu/govdocs/dlc/toppages/dlcindex.htm

Resource Summary: While this is not an official Web site for the Depository Library Council, its goal is to provide a historical compilation of information dealing with the Depository Library Council to the Public Printer. Sections include DLC Chairs and Members from 1973-1995; DLC Locations; and DLC Recommendations and Responses. In addition, it has some basic information on the DLC.

While this is a useful historical collection of sources for documents librarians, it has not been updated for awhile. It may take some time before the most recent DLC information is added, so check the "last updated" date on the bottom of the page and compare that with the date of the latest meeting.

Subject Heading: Depository Libraries

[705] Federal Depository Library Program Administration

Sponsoring Agencies: Government Printing Office (GPO); Superintendent of Documents

Primary Access: http://www.access.gpo.gov/su_docs/dpos/fdlppro.html

Resource Summary: This site was established by the GPO to provide news, information, and communication for and about the Federal Depository Library Program (FDLP). It includes online full-text versions of *Administrative Notes*, *Administrative Notes Technical Supplement*, LPS contacts, and various FDLP instructions, manuals, and guides. *Administrative Notes* is available from August 1996, and *Administrative Notes Technical Supplement* is available from July 1996. The FDLP site also features an option titled Locate Regional Depository Libraries by State. As the program moves toward providing more documents online, a new addition to this site is the Internet Information Product Notification Form. This is the form which GPO requests when government agencies initiate, substantially modify, or terminate a government information product.

This site is useful primarily for documents librarians and those interested in the FDLP. Some of the documents make good training material as well.

Subject Headings: Depository Libraries; Federal Depository Library Program

SuDoc Numbers: GP 3.16/3-2: *Administrative Notes*
GP 3.16/3-3: *Administrative Notes Technical Supplement*

[706] GODORT Handout Exchange

Sponsoring Agencies: Government Documents Round Table (GODORT); University of Michigan. Documents Center

Primary Access: http://www.lib.umich.edu/libhome/Documents.center/godort.html

Resource Summary: The GODORT Handout Exchange is a collection of guides to government information sources written by library staff across the United States and distributed by GODORT. These guides are arranged by broad subject classification. Each is identified with a brief title, author, library affiliation, and date of GODORT distribution—which is not necessarily the date of publication. The guides can be searched with jughead or WAIS from the Gopher version. While many of the handouts are in ASCII, others are only available as Microsoft Word or WordPerfect formats.

The Exchange can be useful for librarians and others that work with government documents and need to produce handouts to help their users.

Subject Heading: Government Publications—Guides

[707] Government Publications Network

Sponsoring Agency: Bernan Associates

Primary Access: http://www.bernan.com/

Alternative Access Methods: gopher://gopher.bernan.com/
telnet://gpn@bernan.com
ftp://ftp.bernan.com/

Resource Summary: In addition to an online version of the *GPO Sales Publications Reference File* (PRF), Bernan offers news and catalogs for documents from the United Nations, the European Communities, the British government, UNESCO, the Food and Agriculture Organization, and other international governmental organizations. Along with the bibliographic catalogs, documents within the catalogs can be ordered directly from Bernan. The PRF and the other searchable databases use a WAIS search engine that supports nested Boolean searching and truncation, but note that the Boolean operators must be in all uppercase characters.

The full-text indexing and the variety of government publication catalogs make this site an excellent way to browse for and order print government publications.

Subject Headings: Bibliographic Databases; Documents Librarians; Government Publications—Bibliographies; Government Publications—International—Bibliographies

SuDoc Number: GP 3.22/3: *GPO Sales Publications Reference File*

[708] GPO Shipping Lists

Sponsoring Agencies: Government Printing Office (GPO); Superintendent of Documents

Primary Access: http://www1.uta.edu/isc658

Alternative Access Method: gopher://gopher1.uta.edu:70/1/ISC658

Resource Summary: Paper, separate, and electronic GPO shipping lists are available on this site in ASCII text format. (The paper lists go back to shipping list 96-0136-P.) This site offers more than just the shipping lists. It offers a Shipping List Exclusion/Label Program that is designed to help check the shipping lists against a library's selection profile and get the SuDoc numbers on the documents. Using scanned shipping lists that are available on this site soon after their release, the program matches a specific library's profile and prints the labels needed.

Be aware that these are scanned versions of the shipping lists, so errors could occur. It also excludes microfiche shipping lists. This site can be of signifant assistance to those who process federal documents.

Subject Heading: Depository Libraries

[709] Impact/Online WebPAC™

Sponsoring Agencies: Auto-Graphics, Inc.; Government Printing Office (GPO); Superintendent of Documents

Primary Access: http://www.auto-graphics.com/cgipac/mmx/gdcs

Resource Summary: As a demonstration for its software products, Auto-Graphics has made the full *Monthly Catalog of Government Publications* freely available. Unlike the GPO version at http://www.access.gpo.gov/su_docs/dpos/ adpos400.html, which only goes back to 1994, the Auto-Graphics version goes back to 1976. It also has more search options. Users can search by title, author, subject, or note field and can set options for limiting by date, media, or language. Boolean searching is available with a forms interface. The Options link is available for number searching. When records are displayed, a follow-up search can be run from certain fields in the record. Records are displayed in a labeled format by default, but MARC format and Card format are only a click away. There is even a download option. The location feature of Holdings does not work in the demonstration version.

This is an excellent demonstration product, and in most cases it is more useful than the GPO version. One drawback of the Auto-Graphics version is that it does not list the day that the database was last updated, so the GPO version may be more current. However, the Auto-Graphics version is much easier to use than the GPO version for most users and librarians. Unfortunately, the demonstration project ceased to be available for free in April 1997. A very small demonstration database is still available, but the full version is now available only to subscribers.

Subject Headings: Bibliographic Databases; Government Publications

SuDoc Number: GP 3.8: *Monthly Catalog of Government Publications*

[710] List of United States Depository Libraries

Sponsoring Agency: Joint Committee on Printing

Primary Access: gopher://gopher.umsl.edu/11/library/govdocs/gdep

Alternative Access Method: ftp://ftp.fedworld.gov/pub/misc/dlprof.zip

Resource Summary: These listings provide basic directory information for federal depository libraries including address, phone, fax, and the name of the government documents librarian. The data originated as a dBase file on the Fedworld ftp site. On the Gopher site, the entire converted dBase file is available in ASCII text as one large file or in portions by state.

This is a useful resource for anyone looking for depository library locations or personnel. It does not include e-mail addresses, library catalog telnet addresses, or home page URLs. While it is not exactly the same as *A Directory of U.S. Government Depository Libraries*, it contains similar information.

Subject Heading: Depository Libraries

SuDoc Number: Y 4.P93/1-10: *A Directory of U.S. Government Depository Libraries*

[711] Monthly Catalog of Publications (MOCAT)

Sponsoring Agencies: Government Printing Office (GPO); Superintendent of Documents

Primary Access: http://www.access.gpo.gov/su_docs/dpos/adpos400.html

Resource Summary: This is GPO's version of their *Monthly Catalog of United States Government Publications* which they have made Web-accessible. The search interface is available as a single line entry form or via a "fielded search" that allows field searching by title, year, SuDoc number, item number, and stock number. In either option, the search software requires using quotation marks to identify phrases and numbers. Boolean operators (AND, OR, NOT, ADJ) can be used but must be in uppercase. From the citation display, a link is available that identifies which depository libraries receive that publication. The database contains cataloging records published in the *Monthly Catalog* since January 1994, and it is updated daily.

This is a commendable service to offer, especially the link to specific depository library holdings. However, the search structure is not intuitive and is more difficult to use than Auto-Graphics' demonstration version of the *Monthly Catalog* at http://www.auto-graphics.com/cgipac/mmx/gdcs. It did help when GPO added some help statements on the top level screen, but it would be even more effective if they offered more intuitive search software.

Subject Headings: Bibliographic Databases; Government Publications

SuDoc Number: GP 3.8: *Monthly Catalog of Government Publications*

[712] Needs and Offers List

Sponsoring Agency: University of the South. Library

Primary Access: http://docs.sewanee.edu/nando/nando.html

Resource Summary: This electronic edition enables government documents librarians to trade government publications. Some depository libraries receive duplicate copies while others fail to receive specific publications. The Needs and Offers List facilitates communication between libraries to fill those needs. This online version includes the sections: Guidelines; Needs; Offers; and Search.

While not all depository libraries participate in the list, those that do may find it very useful.

Subject Headings: Depository Libraries; Government Publications—Trade

[713] Pathway Services Browse Titles

Sponsoring Agencies: Government Printing Office (GPO); Superintendent of Documents

Primary Access: http://www.access.gpo.gov/su_docs/dpos/btitles.html

Resource Summary: This Browse Electronic Titles page from GPO's Superintendent of Documents site offers a very lengthy listing of published government information products available via the Internet. The list includes both monographic and serial titles available on official federal agency Internet sites. Arrangement of the list of titles is first alphabetically by major agency, then alphabetically by title within agency or subagency groupings. The page provides links to lower sections of the page by major agency and links back to the top. Each entry includes title, item number, SuDoc number, and a link to the resources. The page states that titles may remain on this page for only 90 days.

By putting all of the file onto one very long page, the resulting file is quite large and takes some time to load and navigate, even on a fast Internet connection. The 90-day roll-over policy also limits the usefulness of this site. Significant resources may fail to appear on this list after they have been on it for over 90 days. For comprehensive coverage, be sure to check the *Monthly Catalog* and other similar lists such as the Uncle Sam Migrating Government Publications page.

Subject Headings: Electronic Publications; Government Publications—Bibliographies

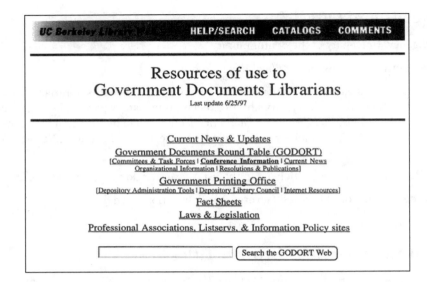

[714] Resources of use to Government Documents Librarians

Sponsoring Agencies: Depository Library Council; Government Documents Round Table (GODORT)

Primary Access: http://www.lib.berkeley.edu/GODORT/

Alternative Access Method: gopher://infolib.lib.berkeley.edu/11/resdbs/gove/godort/

Resource Summary: This site has gathered many documents and links of interest to documents librarians. The Government Documents Round Table section includes a GODORT directory, bylaws, policies, and much more. The GPO section nicely organizes links to adminstrative tools used by depositories and has a section for the Depository Library Council. Other sections include several fact sheets from *Administrative Notes* and a list of professional associations.

This is an excellent starting point for government documents librarians that work at depository libraries. Documents that are not available elsewhere are housed on this server. The organization is clear, and it is updated frequently.

Subject Headings: Depository Libraries; Government Publications

[715] Superintendent of Documents

Sponsoring Agencies: Superintendent of Documents; Government Printing Office (GPO)

Primary Access: http://www.access.gpo.gov/su_docs/

Alternative Access Method: http://www.gpo.gov/su_docs/

Resource Summary: Proclaiming itself a pathway to federal government information, the Superintendent of Documents Web site is an entry point for a significant number of resources. Many of these are described elsewhere in this directory, including the *Monthly Catalog*, GPO Access, and the Federal Bulletin Board. Principal categories on this site include Electronic Information, Information for Sale, Information for Free Use, and Services to the Public.

Within the Electronic Information category is the link Online, On-Demand, and Locator Services, which provides the significant full-text resources of GPO Access and the Federal Bulletin Board. (See under their own entries elsewhere in this directory.) This is also the access point for the GPO version of the *Monthly Catalog*. Other links in this category include the GPO GILS (Government Information Locator Service) database and information about U.S. Fax Watch. GPO has its own version of GPO Access, and many depository libraries have established GPO Access gateways as well. All are accessible from this section, but it may take some work to identify which link goes where.

The category Information Available for Free Public Use in Federal Depository Libraries includes a variety of links to information on the Federal Depository Libraries Program and to lists of Regional Depository Libraries and Depository Libraries. Links to both the *Monthly Catalog* and the *DOE Reports Bibliographic Database* can show which depository libraries should have certain documents.

Information for Sale by the Superintendent of Documents provides a variety of sources to help in identifying specific documents available for purchase. Under the Publications heading, GPO *Subject Bibliographies* are available in full text with links to online ordering of items. Also under this section are lists of subscriptions, CD-ROMs, and U.S. Government Bookstores. However, the *GPO Sales Publications Reference File* is not available here. The Superintendent of Documents' Services to the Public section points back to the GPO Access databases, to information on depository libraries, to the sales section, and to the Consumer Information Center.

Until the organization is improved, it may be most efficient to bookmark the appropriate subsections, and hope that the subsidiary URLs do not change.

Subject Headings: Depository Libraries; Finding Aid; Government Information Locator Service (GILS); Government Publications

SuDoc Number: GP 3.22/2: *Subject Bibliographies*

[716] U.S. Government Printing Office

Sponsoring Agency: Government Printing Office (GPO)

Primary Access: http://www.access.gpo.gov/

Alternative Access Method: http://www.gpo.gov/

Resource Summary: The GPO home page is a primary source for information on government documents and Congress. The top level begins with information about the GPO including the GPO mission, the organizational structure, and a multimedia sample of the office. The other parts of this page link to major resources such as the Superintendent of Documents pages, GPO Access, the U.S. Congress page with many congressional documents, and the General Accounting Office. Most of these links are described separately in this directory. See GPO Access, U.S. Congress, and GAO Web Services for these major GPO sites.

The GPO site also includes information on GPO services available to federal agencies, such as their customer service and information on electronic prepress and document creation. Another section, Business and Contracting Opportunities, includes links to the section, Printing Procurement and Materials Management Service.

This site is a major starting point for finding some of the most significant collections of government documents on the Internet. Unfortunately, the arrangement of resources can be best understood only by those familiar with the depository library system, the GPO, and government organization in general. It can be difficult to navigate because there is so much available on the site.

Subject Heading: Congress

[717] Uncle Sam Migrating Government Publications

Sponsoring Agency: University of Memphis. Library

Primary Access: http://www.lib.memphis.edu/gpo/mig.htm

Resource Summary: This is one of a number of lists of federal depository library program government publications which are available on the Internet. It offers both Migrating Government Publications by Title and Migrating Government Publications by SuDoc categories. Each category gives alphabetical access to the list, and each record contains the title, SuDoc number, URL, and a direct link to the source. Some records also have brief informative notes. The scope of this list is limited to serials and periodicals.

While the list is not comprehensive and there are a few inaccuracies, it is an excellent supplement to the other lists. The most prominent of which is the GPO's own Pathway Services Browse Titles which includes both monographs and serials.

Subject Headings: Government Publications—Bibliographies; Electronic Publications

[718] Library of Congress E-mail Lists

Sponsoring Agency: Library of Congress (LC)

Primary Access: mailto:listserv@loc.gov with "lists" in body

Alternative Access Methods: http://lcweb.loc.gov/acq/conser/consrlin.html
http://lcweb.loc.gov/catdir/lccn/

Resource Summary: The Library of Congress hosts a number of e-mail lists on their listserver. Some of these lists are only for LC employees or are otherwise limited to specific groups. The other e-mail lists are distribution lists and not discussion lists. For example, CONSRLIN sends out the CONSER (Conversion of Serials) Program Newsletter—*CONSERline* which is available on the Web at the first alternate URL. LCCN distributes the *Library of Congress Cataloging Newsline* (which is also available at the second alternate URL), and PRESS is used for sending out announcements from the Office of the Librarian.

Most of the other lists are discussion lists focusing on a specific area within library science. The following is a partial listing:
CONSRLST - CONSER cataloging discussion list
CONSRPOL - CONSER Policy Committee discussion list
FEDLIB - Federal librarians discussion list
FEDLIBIT - Federal librarians information technology discussion
FEDPOL - FLICC Policy Working Group
FEDREF-L - Federal reference librarians discussion list
USMARC - USMARC discussion list
ZCLIENT - Public domain Z39.50-1995 client discussion list

Subject Headings: E-mail Lists; Electronic Periodicals; Library Science

[719] Library of Congress Information System

Sponsoring Agency: Library of Congress (LC)

Primary Access: telnet://locis.loc.gov

Alternative Access Methods: http://lcweb.loc.gov/catalog/
tn3270://locis.loc.gov
http://lcweb.loc.gov/z3950/gateway.html

Resource Summary: The Library of Congress Information System (LOCIS) is the original LC
Internet resource. The telnet and tn3270 are the original versions of LOCIS. LOCIS includes the
following sections: LC Catalog, Federal Legislation, Copyright Information, Braille and Audio,
Organizations, and Foreign Law. The LC Catalog section is the main category and it provides
access to separate catalogs titled LC Books; Serials; Maps; Subject Terms and Cross References;
and Older, Incomplete Books and Serial Records. The main LC Book catalog is divided by date
into three sections. The Older, Incomplete Books and Serials Records section covers items
cataloged from 1898 to 1980.

The Federal Legislation databases track and describe bills and resolutions introduced in the U.S.
Congress from 1973 (93rd Congress) to the present. There is a separate file for each congressional
session along with the capability to search all of them. Searches can be done by member name,
bill number, and subject words. This database tracks the status of legislation, but it rarely has any
full-text versions of bills or resolutions.

The Copyright Information section includes references to works registered for copyright since
1978. It also includes serials and selected other documents related to copyright. The Braille and
Audio database includes publications intended for those who are unable to read print. The
Organizations database features the National Referral Center Master File of organizations and
associations. Unfortunately, this database has not been updated since 1992. Foreign Law includes
abstracts of legislation from other countries (primarily Hispanic countries) and article citations
related to the Hispanic legal system.

The Z39.50 Web interface only searches some of the databases available on the full telnet version
of LOCIS. The Web has two search options: Word Search and Browse Search. The Web searches
do not yet include all of the catalog files or the extra databases available on LOCIS.
The telnet versions of LOCIS are neither easy to use nor easy to learn. Successful searching in any
of the databases requires some significant time spent learning the peculiarities of both the search
system and the particular database. For those willing to take the time, LOCIS is a significant
information source in that it provides access to material not elsewhere available. The Web version
is much easier to use, but it does not offer as many resources as LOCIS. All versions of LOCIS list
its hours of availability. Note that unlike most other Internet resources, it is not available at all
times.

Subject Headings: Copyright; Legislation; Library Catalogs; Z39.50 Databases

[720] Library of Congress MARVEL

Sponsoring Agency: Library of Congress (LC)

Primary Access: gopher://marvel.loc.gov/

Alternative Access Method: gopher://gopher.loc.gov/

Resource Summary: The Library of Congress Machine-Assisted Realization of the Virtual Electronic Library (MARVEL) Gopher server was one of the first substantial information sources from the federal government using Gopher technology. It rapidly grew in its goal of combining information about the LC with access to electronic resources on the Internet. Some of the many major categories include Events, Facilities, Publications, and Services; Research and Reference (Public Services); Libraries and Publishers (Technical Services); Copyright; Library of Congress Online Systems; Employee Information; Government Information; and Global Electronic Library (by Subject).

The original goal of MARVEL was to serve LC staff, the U.S. Congress, and constituents throughout the world. The MARVEL team did such an excellent job of both gathering and arranging resources, that MARVEL had become one of the most useful Gopher-based finding aids, especially for government information. However, when the Web began to eclipse Gopher, MARVEL became less used. And, as a result of the increased effort that has been put into the LC's Web servers, MARVEL is beginning to languish. While it still remains an excellent finding aid for government Gopher servers, some sections are getting dated. The sections that are still useful on MARVEL include those that provide information about the LC, and the Government Information section for links to Gopher servers.

Subject Headings: Copyright; Finding Aid

SuDoc Numbers: LC 1.18: *Library of Congress Information Bulletin*
LC 33.10: *LC Science Tracer Bulletin*
LC 39.10: *Folklife Center News*

[721] National Agricultural Library

Sponsoring Agency: National Agricultural Library (NAL)

Primary Access: http://www.nal.usda.gov/

Alternative Access Methods: http://www.nalusda.gov/
telnet://isis@opac.nal.usda.gov [catalog]
gopher://gopher.nal.usda.gov/
ftp://ftp.nalusda.gov/
http://www.agnic.org/

Resource Summary: As a major international source for agricultural information, NAL provides access to many resources and acts as a gateway to its associated institutions through this Web site. Primary categories include General Information; Answers to Your Questions; How to Access the Collection; ISIS (Integrated System for Information Services); and AgNIC (the Agriculture Network Information Center).

General Information describes NAL's collections, products, and services. It also includes a mission statement, visitor information, and a staff locator. The Answers to Your Questions section tells how to obtain answers to general reference questions and how to get help from NAL's 10 specialized information centers. The section titled How to Access the Collection provides instructions for connecting to NAL's online collection of agricultural images and other information products. A number of NAL publications can be found in the Other NAL Information Products subsection.

The online system, ISIS, includes both the library catalog and a Journal Article Citation database. The latter contains records from Agricola for 1989 to the present and is updated daily. The search software is not overly intuitive, but there is a menu interface that can make it easier.

The Agriculture Network Information Center provides access to agriculture-related information, subject area experts, and other resources. Many of the links connect to resources beyond NAL. AgNIC includes sections such as Agricola Subject Category Codes; a Calendar for Agricultural Conferences, Meetings, and Seminars; and a directory of Experts in Agriculture.

This site can be used as an excellent starting point for finding agricultural information. With the availability of Agricola on ISIS and NAL's own catalog, it is also useful for finding print resources.

Subject Headings: Agricola; Bibliographic Databases; Libraries—Agriculture; Library Catalogs

SuDoc Numbers: A 1.2/13: *Priorities for Research, Education and Economics*
A 17.1: *Annual Report. National Agricultural Library*
A 17.18/4: *Quick Bibliography Series*
A 17.18/5: *List of Journals Indexed in Agricola*
A 17.23: *Agricultural Libraries Information Notes*
A 1.77:232 *Nutrition and Your Health: Dietary Guidelines for Americans*

[722] National Archives and Records Administration

Sponsoring Agency: National Archives and Records Administration (NARA)

Primary Access: http://www.nara.gov/

Alternative Access Method: gopher://gopher.nara.gov/

Resource Summary: The National Archives and Records Administration offers materials about the National Archives along with other materials that might not be expected to originate from NARA. For example, NARA oversees the Presidential Libraries, and the Web site has links to descriptive information on each of these libraries. NARA also oversees the Electoral College and thus their Web site includes statistics and summaries of the votes in the Electoral College for every presidential election since George Washington.

However, the main focus of the site is on the National Archives and their services. The Looking for Information at the National Archives section discusses genealogical research (although NARA does not yet have any genealogical records online) and historical records of government agencies. Under the latter category is the online version of the *Guide to Federal Records in the National Archives of the United States*.

The Visitor's Gallery features pages such as the Online Exhibit Hall, Gift Shop, Book Store, Digital Classroom, and Public Programs. The Digital Classroom provides initial ideas and methods for teaching with primary sources and sample lesson plans. The Online Exhibit Hall features selected exhibits from the National Archives and reproductions of documents like the Magna Carta. For the archivist, the NARA site also has sections titled Records Management, Preservation, and Archival Management. The Records Management section includes access to *NARA Bulletins* pertaining to federal records management.

This site is unusual in the scope of materials available. While very little actual archival material is available online, NARA has put selected high-interest items online. The electoral voting information, the Digital Classroom, and the *Guide to Federal Records in the National Archives of the United States* provide substantial information content, even if it is only a small fraction of NARA's actual holdings.

Subject Headings: Archives; Exhibitions; Genealogy; Libraries—Presidential; Voting

SuDoc Numbers: AE 1.103: *NARA Bulletin*
AE 1.108:G 94/ *Guide to Federal Records in the National Archives of the United States*
AE 1.126: *Quarterly Compilation of Periodical Literature Reflecting the Use of Records in the National Archives*

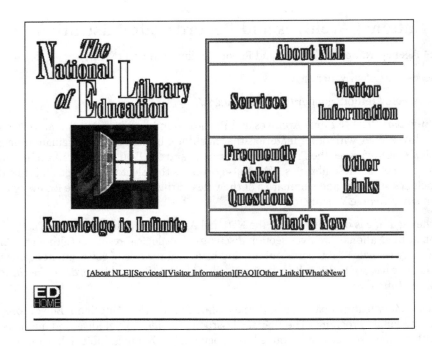

[723] National Library of Education

Sponsoring Agency: National Library of Education (NLE)

Primary Access: http://www.ed.gov/NLE/

Resource Summary: The newly designated National Library of Education (formerly the Education Research Library of the Department of Education) offers some descriptive information about itself, its services, visitor information, and links to external resources. Within the NLE Services section, the library offers some topic-oriented bibliographies on education.

While the site provides some interesting reading about the Library, there is no link to its catalog nor is there a mention of it. The bibliographies can be useful, although they are relatively short.

Subject Heading: Libraries—Education

[724] U.S. National Library of Medicine

Sponsoring Agency: National Library of Medicine (NLM)

Primary Access: http://www.nlm.nih.gov/

Alternative Access Methods: gopher://gopher.nlm.nih.gov/
ftp://ftp.nlm.nih.gov/

Resource Summary: As a major resource for information on health sciences literature, the National Library of Medicine offers many resources through these pages. The General Information section provides the usual descriptions of hours, services, job openings, and location, but it also has a special section of services for libraries and researchers at a distance. Press releases and announcements can be found under the New/Noteworthy heading. The Databases category describes the NLM databases such as Medline, and different methods for connecting to them. The NLM Publications section includes the full text of *NLM Fact Sheets*, the *NLM Technical Bulletin*, and other NLM publications. The Grants, Acquisitions section includes a variety of descriptions and announcements of extramural funding opportunities.

The NLM Web site also features the Visible Human Project. This project is involved in creating complete, anatomically detailed, three-dimensional representations of a male and female human body. The current phase of the project is collecting transverse computerized tomography, magnetic resonance imaging, and cryosection images of representative male and female cadavers at one millimeter intervals. The long-term goal of the Visible Human Project is to produce a system of knowledge structures that will transparently link visual knowledge forms to symbolic knowledge formats such as the names of body parts.

The NLM site is an excellent example of a Web site that provides information about the Library and its services, but the site also provides information products of use to professionals and the general public.

Subject Headings: Anatomy; Bibliographic Databases; Grants—Health Sciences; Libraries—Health Sciences; Health Sciences

SuDoc Numbers: HE 20.3603/2: *NLM Technical Bulletin*
HE 20.3612/4: *List of Journals Indexed in Index Medicus*
HE 20.3618/2: *List of Serials Indexed for Online Users*
HE 20.3615/2: *Current Bibliographies in Medicine*
HE 20.3619: *National Library of Medicine News*
HE 20.3621: *NLM Fact Sheets*
HE 20.3625: *Gratefully Yours*

CHAPTER 11: MILITARY

The U.S. military has been an active participant in the Internet since the inception of Internet networking technology. They have a number of their own networks and continue to maintain an internetwork that, for security reasons, is completely separated from the Internet. On the public Internet itself, the military claims the top level domain of .mil and has over 250,000 Web pages available. These range from basic descriptions of specific Department of Defense agencies to technical standards and specifications.

The two featured sites for this chapter are all finding aids for military sources on the Internet: AJAX, DefenseLINK, and Mil-Cat. AJAX presents easy access to top level military sites. DefenseLINK covers far more sites and is probably the best single starting point for a military search.

[725] AJAX: U.S. and International Government Military, Intelligence, and Law Enforcement Agency Access

Sponsoring Agency: Sagal Computer Systems

Primary Access: http://www.sagal.com/ajax/

Alternative Access Method: http://www.sagal.com/ajax/ajax.htm [non frames version]

Resource Summary: The AJAX site supplies entries for other sites by the following categories and then alphabetically by acronym: Government Intelligence and Law Enforcement Servers; Military Branch Servers; Military and Defense Agency Servers; Military and Defense Laboratory Servers; International Intelligence and Law Enforcement Servers; NATO and International Military Servers; United States Regulatory Agency Servers; United States Government Agency Servers; and Private Intelligence, Law Enforcement, and Task Force Servers. The single line entries include acronyms and full names of the linked agencies.

This is a very basic finding aid and it is easy to use. While the total number of sites included is not large, AJAX does link to the important top level agency servers from military, intelligence, law enforcement, and other government agencies.

Subject Headings: Finding Aid—Military; Intelligence Service; Law Enforcement

[726] DefenseLINK

Sponsoring Agencies: Defense Technical Information Center (DTIC); Department of Defense (DoD). Office of the Assistant Secretary of Defense

Primary Access: http://www.dtic.mil/defenselink/

Resource Summary: DefenseLINK provides access to the other top level defense sites both from an image map at the top of the page and through a hierarchical listing. In addition to links to the main military sites, the top DefenseLINK page includes links to two sections, Other Organizations (related to defense) and Other Information. The latter of these includes the headings Biographies, Career Opportunities, Doing Business with the Department of Defense, Deployments and Exercises, Education, and History.

Under the Publications heading, the site features the full text of *Defense Issues* in HTML, starting with 1995; the index and full text of selected *DoD Directives*, the *Annual Reports* since 1995, and *Weapon Systems*. The *DoD Directives* are in a searchable WAIS database. Press releases, DefenseLINK photos, and speeches are available under the News section. All releases are archived and available for searching—the archive began October 15, 1994.

With its clear organization, frequent updates, and search features, DefenseLINK is an excellent starting point when looking for U.S. military Web sites or U.S. military information. The *Directives* are a good supplement to depository library collections since only selected *Directives* come through the depository program.

Subject Heading: Finding Aid—Military

SuDoc Numbers: D 1.1: *Annual Report to the President and Congress (Annual Defense Report)*
D 1.6/8-2: *DoD Directives*
D 2.15/4: *Defense Issues*
D 101.95: *Weapon Systems*

The Military resources are divided into four sections. The first section covers general military information resources as well as sites that are not directly connected to one of the three major branches of the military. This section runs from entry numbers 727 to 764. The second section features resources from or about the air force and includes entries 765-786. Sources from or about the army are available in the third section, which ranges from entries 787 to 797. The last subchapter is for navy sites and includes entries 798-804.

Military: General

[727] ACQWeb

Sponsoring Agency: Department of Defense. Office of the Under Secretary of Defense for Acquisition and Technology USD(A&T)

Primary Access: http://www.acq.osd.mil/

Resource Summary: ACQWeb offers a variety of resources including documents published by Under Secretary of Defense for Acquisition and Technology, projects executed and under development by its many offices, and personnel data. Under the heading USD(A&T) Documents, the full texts of press releases, speeches, and testimony before Congress are available. The Office Navigator page presents a large image map complete with a graphic presentation of the component offices and agencies arranged by subject, including logistics, environmental security, and acquisition reform. Those agencies without a Web presence are in darkened type. The Office Index link provides an alphabetical list. Search Bot uses an artificial intelligence search engine to search the entire ACQWeb.

Primarily of interest to military and acquisition professionals, these pages are well designed and may be of interest to those curious about a wide variety of military topics.

Subject Headings: Acquisitions; Military Logistics

[728] Arms Control and Disarmament Agency

Sponsoring Agency: Arms Control and Disarmament Agency (ACDA)

Primary Access: http://www.acda.gov/

Resource Summary: This site contains general information on disarmament as well as specific documents and statements from ACDA. The site is arranged in the following categories: About ACDA, Fact Sheets, Speeches, Treaties, Reports, and Historical Documents. Through these sections, ACDA makes numerous press releases, issues, briefs, fact sheets, occasional papers, and official texts available in ASCII format.

While it would be more visually appealing to have the documents available in PDF or HTML, this site offers a great deal of official information on arms control.

Subject Headings: Arms Control; Disarmament

SuDoc Numbers: AC 1.1: *ACDA Annual Report*
AC 1.16: *World Military Expenditures and Arms Transfers*

[729] BosniaLINK

Sponsoring Agency: Department of Defense (DoD). Office of the Assistant Secretary of Defense for Public Affairs

Primary Access: http://www.dtic.mil/bosnia/

Resource Summary: BosniaLINK contains a variety of resources about U.S. military activities in Operation Joint Endeavor—the NATO peacekeeping mission in Bosnia. The site includes operations maps; fact sheets; press releases; biographies of key commanders and leaders; and transcripts of briefings, speeches, and testimony. There is a keyword searching capability, and the full text of *The Talon*, a newsletter for the troops in Bosnia, is available since 1995 in large PDF files.

This is an especially rich resource for those with friends or family serving in Bosnia and for anyone else interested in researching the Bosnian peacekeeping mission.

Subject Heading: Bosnian Conflict

[730] The Central Imagery Office

Sponsoring Agency: Central Imagery Office (CIO)

Primary Access: http://www.odci.gov/ic/usic/cio.html

Resource Summary: This single-page site consists of a brief description of the Central Imagery Office.

This site should at least include an address and phone number for the office.

Subject Heading: Intelligence Service

[731] Chemical Warfare/Chemical-Biological Defense Information Analysis Center

Sponsoring Agencies: Chemical Warfare/Chemical-Biological Defense Information Analysis Center (CBIAC); Defense Technical Information Center (DTIC)

Primary Access: http://www.cbiac.apgea.army.mil/

Resource Summary: CBIAC is another Defense Information Analysis Center that provides information about combat readiness, biological warfare, chemical identification, and medical effect and treatment on its Products and Services page. While the Basic Products page provides a bibliographic listing of available publications, not online versions of the publications themselves. The lists include price, distribution restrictions, date, and availability. The site also boasts a Current Awareness service, an Inquiry and Referral Service, and a CBIAC newsletter.

While this site gives pointers to useful information on these topics, few publications are available online.

Subject Headings: Chemical Warfare; Biological Warfare; Information Analysis Center

[732] Cooperative Programs for Reinvestment Web

Sponsoring Agency: Defense Technical Information Center (DTIC)

Primary Access: http://www.dtic.mil/cpr/

Alternative Access Method: gopher://gopher.dtic.mil/11/CPR%20-%20Cooperative%20Programs%20for%20Reinvestment

Resource Summary: The Cooperative Programs for Reinvestment (CPR) service contains descriptions and points of contact for government assistance programs and technology transfer opportunities. The Department of Defense developed CPR to assist defense industry firms impacted by the drawdown in defense spending. This assistance focuses on supporting defense industry efforts toward reinvestment and conversion.

Subject Headings: Defense Contractors; Downsizing

[733] Crew Systems Ergonomics Information Analysis Center

Sponsoring Agencies: Crew Systems Ergonomics Information Analysis Center (CSERIAC); Defense Technical Information Center (DTIC)

Primary Access: http://www.dtic.mil/iac/cseriac/cseriac.html

Resource Summary: CSERIAC provides access to resources for ergonomics and human factors information. This includes a variety of products and services to government, industry, and academia to promote the use of ergonomics in the design of human-operated equipment. Available sections include: Crew System Ergonomics Defined, Products Catalog, Points of Contact, Services Catalog, Government Points of Contact, and the Human Factors and Ergonomics Internet Index.

The site is aimed at designers, engineers, researchers, and human factors specialists. Few online publications are available.

Subject Headings: Ergonomics; Human Factors; Information Analysis Center

[734] Defense Automated Printing Service

Sponsoring Agencies: Defense Automated Printing Service (DAPS); Defense Printing Service

Primary Access: http://www.ddas.mil/

Resource Summary: Formerly known as the Defense Printing Service, DAPS offers information about its headquarters, area offices, major field offices, and local offices. The Our Business and Yours section provides information on DAPS' automated PDF conversion services. The site also features a fairly detailed DAPS Strategic Plan.

This site is of most use to the defense community for locating nearby DAPS offices. This site will also be of interest to organizations investigating automated printing and document conversion options.

Subject Heading: Printing

[735] Defense Fuel Supply Center Entry Point

Sponsoring Agency: Defense Fuel Supply Center (DFSC)

Primary Access: http://www.dfsc.dla.mil/

Resource Summary: The Defense Fuel Supply Center Entry Point includes staff phone and fax directories, standard fuel prices from the previous year, organizational information, and a biography of the commander. An online version of the *DFSC Fact Book* is available in HTML and in a self-extracting version.

The site is useful for information about the organization itself, on fuel pricing, and on gasoline and alternative fuels in general.

Subject Headings: Energy; Petroleum Products

SuDoc Number: D 7.1/6-2: *DFSC Fact Book*

[736] Defense Information Systems Agency

Sponsoring Agency: Defense Information Systems Agency (DISA)

Primary Access: http://www.disa.mil/

Resource Summary: The DISA Web site includes directories of key personnel, descriptions of programs and field commands, and DISA field and line organizations. The DISA's Core Mission Areas section features information on the Global Command and Control System, the Defense Information Systems Network, the Defense Message System, and the Global Combat Support System.

The site provides basic information about the agency, its major mission areas, and its programs and field commands.

Subject Headings: Computer Networking; Military Computing

[737] Defense Intelligence Agency

Sponsoring Agency: Defense Intelligence Agency (DIA)

Primary Access: http://www.dia.mil/

Resource Summary: The Defense Intelligence Agency aims to provide military intelligence to warfighters, decisionmakers, and policymakers in the Department of Defense and the federal government. Their Web site includes a bit of information about the Agency under the heading About the DIA and has employment ads under Employment at the DIA. The Doing Business with the DIA section features information on procurement opportunities at the DIA.

While none of the sections contain detailed information, the site does give a basic agency overview, information for job seekers, and helpful procurement information for businesses.

Subject Headings: Intelligence Service; Military Intelligence; Procurement

[738] Defense Modeling, Simulation, and Tactical Technology Information Analysis Center

Sponsoring Agencies: Defense Technical Information Center (DTIC); Defense Modeling, Simulation, and Tactical Technology Information Analysis Center (DMSTTIAC)

Primary Access: http://dmsttiac.hq.iitri.com/

Resource Summary: Featuring information on DMSTTIAC's services and products, this site offers sections such as Information Services, Calendar of Events, Electronic Conferences, and Modeling Products.

The site is primarily for authorized users of DMSTTIAC.

Subject Headings: Information Analysis Center; Military Modeling

[739] Defense Programs Internal Home Page

Sponsoring Agency: Department of Energy (DOE). Defense Programs Organization

Primary Access: http://www.dp.doe.gov/

Alternative Access Method: http://www.dp.doe.gov/TPhome.html [text version]

Resource Summary: The Defense Programs Organization helps manage the military's nuclear weapons. The page includes categories such as Defense Program's Organizational Chart, Photo Album, Stockpile Stewardship and Management Workshop Program Plan, News and Highlights, and Tritium Project Office. The Stockpile Stewardship and Tritium Project Office links provide some information on the agency's management of nuclear weapons and materials.

The site does not provide detailed information, but it does present a starting point for research on the government's management of nuclear weapons.

Subject Heading: Nuclear Weapons

[740] Defense Sciences Engineering Division

Sponsoring Agency: Lawrence Livermore National Laboratory (LLNL). Defense Sciences Engineering Division

Primary Access: http://www-dsed.llnl.gov/

Resource Summary: The Defense Sciences Engineering Division designs and tests systems in support of both defense and non-defense activities. Their Web site includes information on the Division's core areas of specialization which include chemistry and material science, instrumentation and data acquisition, visualization, power conversion technologies, and electromagnetics. The site also features information on special areas of research such as pulsed plasma processing of effluent gases and toxic chemicals, plasma heated waste remediation methods, and ground-penetrating imaging radar systems.

The page provides a good overview of the Division's research areas and current projects.

Subject Heading: Electrical Engineering

[741] DefenseLINK Guide to DoD Organization and Functions

Sponsoring Agency: Department of Defense (DoD). Office of the Secretary of Defense

Primary Access: http://www.dtic.mil/defenselink/pubs/ofg.html

Resource Summary: This online hypertext guide describes the functions of the Office of the Secretary of Defense, other Defense agencies, and DoD field activities. Where appropriate, the description cites the pertinent *DoD Directive,* which charters the organization and provides more detailed information on the authorities, responsibilities, and functions of the organization.

This can be a useful source to find the official functions of different parts of the DoD. While the site links to an online version of the *DoD Directives*, it does not include links within the descriptions when a specific *Directive* is cited. It also does not link to any of the component DoD agency Web sites.

Subject Heading: Military—Directories

[742] Department of Defense Single Stock Point for Specifications and Standards

Sponsoring Agency: Defense Automated Printing Service Detachment Office Philadelphia

Primary Access: http://www.dtic.mil/dps-phila/

Alternative Access Method: telnet://163.12.140.70

Resource Summary: This site provides access to information about military specifications and standards. It includes access to a searchable WAIS version of the DoD *Index of Specifications and Standards* (DODISS). Authorized users can link to the Acquisition Streamlining and Standardization Information System (ASSIST) database, a management and research tool that includes DODISS and other military specifications and standards documents.

This site is very useful for looking up bibliographic information on specific military standards and for finding ordering information for the standards.

Subject Heading: Standards

SuDoc Number: D 1.76: *Index of Specifications and Standards*

[743] DFAS Lane

Sponsoring Agency: Defense Finance and Accounting Service (DFAS)

Primary Access: http://www.dfas.mil/

Resource Summary: The Defense Finance and Accounting Service Lane features information on accounting and related areas within the DoD. Under the heading Money Matters, DFAS Lane provides information about military pay, civilian pay, retired and annuitant pay, vendor pay, travel pay, transportation pay, garnishment and involuntary allotments, and government credit card programs. The What's New section features press releases, new additions to the Web site, and full-text PDF versions of its magazine, *DFAS*, since December 1995. The site also includes a directory of DFAS personnel and a reference library, which contains a DFAS acronyms list, archival information, and Government Information Locator Service records.

The pay scales section will be of most interest to non-Defense users. For Defense users, the Customer Service area, with its contact information for questions about pay would be beneficial. The availability of *DFAS* on this site is a nice addition since this title is not distributed to depository libraries.

Subject Headings: Accounting; Government Information Locator Service (GILS); Pay Scales

SuDoc Number: D 1.104: *DFAS*

[744] DISA Center for INFOSEC

Sponsoring Agencies: Center for Information System Security (CISS); Defense Information Systems Agency (DISA)

Primary Access: http://www.disa.mil/ciss/

Resource Summary: The DISA Center for Information Security (INFOSEC) Web site describes the Center and its mission. It also features the categories: Security and Certification Department; the Training Department; the Assessments Department; and a Security Products Database.

Subject Headings: Computer Networking; Security

[745] Electronic Data Interchange Standards

Sponsoring Agency: Defense Information Systems Agency (DISA)

Primary Access: http://www.itsi.disa.mil/edi/edi-main.html

Resource Summary: This DoD (EDI) site contains a variety of background and current information related to the use of Electronic Data Interchange (EDI) within the Department of Defense. It features information on EDI standards and their implementation within the DoD.

This site is useful to those in the DoD EDI community and for others interested in EDI.

Subject Headings: Electronic Data Interchange (EDI); Standards

[746] GuardLINK

Sponsoring Agency: National Guard

Primary Access: http://www.dtic.dla.mil/defenselink/guardlink/

Resource Summary: This site provides information about the National Guard Bureau, the Army National Guard, the Air National Guard, and National Guard sponsored organizations and events. It features sections with information on the Guard by State, Around the World, and In the Communities. Other sections link to pages on the National Guard Bureau and Research Materials.

Subject Headings: National Guard; Military Reserves

[747] Guidance and Control Information Analysis Center

Sponsoring Agencies: Defense Technical Information Center (DTIC); Guidance and Control Information Analysis Center (GACIAC)

Primary Access: http://gaciac.iitri.com/

Resource Summary: The GACIAC site features sections titled Directory, Points of Contact, User Guide, Bulletins, Calendars, Documents, and Databases. The Bulletins section contains an online current awareness publication. The User Guide and Databases areas describe GACIAC bibliographic and other databases that are available to subscribers, although not through this Web site. The Documents section includes an acronym handbook and the *Polarimetric Technology Handbook*.

This site is useful for describing the research areas of the Center.

Subject Headings: Guidance Systems; Information Analysis Center; Military Research

[748] Information Assurance Technology Analysis Center

Sponsoring Agencies: Defense Technical Information Center (DTIC); Information Assurance Technology Analysis Center (IATAC)

Primary Access: http://surviac.flight.wpafb.af.mil/IATAC/home.htm

Alternative Access Methods: http://surviac.flight.wpafb.af.mil/IATAC/2home.htm [HTML 2.0 version]
http://surviac.flight.wpafb.af.mil/IATAC/1home.htm [text version]

Resource Summary: This new Information Analysis Center has been charged with gathering information on information assurance technologies, system vulnerabilities, research and development, and models and analyses to support the development and implementation of effective defenses against information warfare attacks. The Web site features sections titled Frequently Asked Questions, News and Publications, Products and Services, Calendar of Events, and Query IATAC. As a new center, there is little information within any of these categories now, but expect them all to grow.

The site will be more useful once more content is added.

Subject Headings: Information Analysis Center; Information Assurance; Information Warfare

[749] Joint Chiefs of Staff

Sponsoring Agency: Joint Chiefs of Staff

Primary Access: http://www.dtic.dla.mil/jcs/

Resource Summary: This page provides basic information on the Joint Chiefs of Staff, the organization of the office, member biographies, and some press releases, speeches, and other documents.

Subject Heading: Military Command

[750] Joint Strike Fighter Information System

Sponsoring Agency: Department of Defense (DoD)

Primary Access: http://www.jast.mil/

Resource Summary: The Joint Strike Fighter (JSF) is a joint services program that is designing the basics for the next generation of strike weapon systems for the navy, marine corps, air force, and allied forces. JSF is sponsored by the navy, marines, and air force, and this Web site features descriptions of the project, an FAQ file, and the JSF Master Plan.

This site should be of interest to those investigating future military technology.

Subject Headings: Air Force; Aircraft; Marines; Navy

[751] Marine Corps Intelligence

Sponsoring Agency: Marine Corps

Primary Access: http://www.odci.gov/ic/usic/mci.html

Resource Summary: This single-page site features a brief description of the office.

The information on a minimal page like this would be enhanced by including an address and phone number for the agency.

Subject Headings: Marines; Military Intelligence

[752] MarineLINK

Sponsoring Agency: Marine Corps

Primary Access: http://www.usmc.mil/

Resource Summary: MarineLINK features unclassified information from and about the Marine Corps. The major categories cover the following information, News includes press releases; Opportunities includes recruiting information; Public Events lists events open to the public, including Marine Band performances; and Fact File contains fact sheets on Marine Corps weapons and equipment systems. Other sections include: History, Good Scoop, Publications, Answers, Marine Corps Mission, and Marine Sites. *Marines* and *Warfighting* can be found under the Publications category.

This site has a substantial amount of information on the marines and it appears to be updated frequently.

Subject Heading: Marines

SuDoc Numbers: D 214.9/4:1 *Warfighting*
D 214.24: *Marines*
D 214.27: *Concepts and Issues*

[753] Military City Databases Page

Primary Access: http://www.militarycity.com/member/locate.html

Resource Summary: The databases at this site use a WAIS search engine for finding people in the military. The five databases include: Active Duty Personnel Database, Overseas Personnel Database, Duty Losses Database, Reserves Database I, and Reserves Database II. The only difference described between the last two databases is that the Reserves II database often contains less information, since in many instances there is no unit affiliation.

Subject Headings: Military Personnel

[754] National Reconnaissance Office

Sponsoring Agency: National Reconnaissance Office

Primary Access: http://www.odci.gov/ic/usic/nro.html

Resource Summary: This single-page site has a brief description of the Office and its mission in spaceborne reconnaissance.

A single-page site such as this should include an address and phone number for the Office.

Subject Headings: Military Intelligence; Space

[755] National Security Agency

Sponsoring Agencies: National Security Agency (NSA); National Cryptologic Museum

Primary Access: http://www.nsa.gov/

Resource Summary: The NSA Web site includes non-sensitive information about this sometimes secretive agency. The site includes the Agency's mission statement, a director's page, and information about NSA. Another section is devoted to employment opportunities at the NSA. Other sections include information on the National Cryptologic Museum with some sample exhibits, the Mathematics Education Partnership Program, and the VENONA Project. Documents from the VENONA project—a 1940's era decryption of Soviet messages project—are being declassified and made available here.

This is a very basic site and it is easy to navigate. It gives only a small amount of information, but the addition of the VENONA Project documents make this an interesting site for research into the history of cryptography.

Subject Headings: Cryptography; Employment; Military Intelligence

[756] Nonproliferation and International Security Division

Sponsoring Agency: Los Alamos National Laboratory (LANL). Nonproliferation and International Security Division

Primary Access: http://www.lanl.gov/Internal/divisions/nis/

Alternative Access Method: http://sst.lanl.gov/

Resource Summary: The aim of this Division is to develop and apply preeminent science and technology to deter, detect, and respond to proliferation and to ensure U.S. and global security. Their Web site features a research section with information on their research projects and a publications section that gives access to their annual report. The rest of the publications area is limited to internal use only.

This site is useful primarily for information about the Division's activities.

Subject Headings: National Security; Nonproliferation; Nuclear Weapons

[757] Nonproliferation and National Security

Sponsoring Agency: Department of Energy (DOE). Office of Nonproliferation and National Security

Primary Access: http://www2.nn.doe.gov/nn/

Alternative Access Method: http://www.nn.doe.gov/nn/

Resource Summary: This site includes information from the DOE on nonproliferation topics. It includes organizational information relating to the Office, mission and function statements, budget information, organizational charts, testimony to Congress, and unclassified publications. It also provides topical information about the Office's activities, links to related government sites, and contact names, numbers, and e-mail addresses. The publications are in PDF format. Information on the agency's involvement in energy intelligence is also available.

This is a solid, basic site with some of the standard information about the Office and a few recent publications. The site should be of interest to people concerned with nonproliferation and nuclear weapons.

Subject Headings: Intelligence Service; Nonproliferation; Nuclear Weapons; National Security

[758] Selective Service System

Sponsoring Agency: Selective Service System (SSS)

Primary Access: http://www.sss.gov/

Resource Summary: The Selective Service site features topics such as What Happens If There's a Draft and What Does the SSS Provide for America? Other areas include: Induction Numbers; Publications; Registration Information; and Frequently Asked Questions. The Publications section contains no online documents but offers online ordering of free SSS publications.

The site provides a good, basic overview of Selective Service.

Subject Heading: Draft

[759] Survivability/Vulnerability Information Analysis Center

Sponsoring Agencies: Defense Technical Information Center (DTIC); Survivability/Vulnerability Information Analysis Center (SURVIAC)

Primary Access: http://surviac.flight.wpafb.af.mil/

Resource Summary: SURVIAC is a DoD information analysis center covering nonnuclear survivability/vulnerability data, information, methodologies, models, and analysis relating to U.S. and foreign aeronautical and surface systems. Their Web site features sections entitled What is SURVIAC? Calendar of Events; Current Awareness Information; and Products and Services. The latter includes information on a variety of databases, models, and products.

The site has a fairly narrow focus, but it should be of great interest to researchers in the area of military survivability.

Subject Headings: Information Analysis Center; Military Research; Survival

[760] United States Coast Guard

Sponsoring Agency: Coast Guard

Primary Access: http://www.dot.gov/dotinfo/uscg/

Resource Summary: The principal areas of interest on the Coast Guard Web site include: News and Current Events; Commandant's Corner; Recruiting and Academy; Roles and Missions; Areas, Districts and Units; and Facts, Images, and History. The News and Current Events category includes press releases and operations highlights. The Commandant's Corner page includes a biography, speeches, and interviews.

Only basic information about the Coast Guard and its divisions can be found on this site. Some of the divisional sites have more detailed information resources.

Subject Headings: Coast Guard; Coastlines

SuDoc Numbers: TD 5.3/9: *Coast Guard*
TD 5.8:SA 1/2/ *Marine Safety Manual*
TD 5.4/2: *Navigation and Vessel Inspection Circulars*
TD 5.6:IN 8/ *Navigation Rules: International-Inland*
TD 5.13: *Proceedings of the Marine Safety Council*
TD 5.14: *The Reservist Magazine*

[761] United States Institute of Peace Highlights

Sponsoring Agency: Institute of Peace (USIP)

Primary Access: http://www.usip.org/

Alternative Access Method: gopher://gopher.igc.apc.org:7001/1

Resource Summary: The United States Institute of Peace is an independent, nonpartisan federal institution created and funded by Congress. Its mission is to strengthen the nation's capacity to promote the peaceful resolution of international conflict. Their Internet sites feature sections such as About the Institute; Highlights; Publications; Research Areas; Library and Links; Education and Training; and Grants and Fellowships. The Publications section includes a list of books available from USIP and an online full- text version of *Peace Watch*, the Institute's magazine. While this section also lists regional and topical reports, they are not yet linked anywhere. Presumably, these will be new online publications available from the USIP Web site

For research into peace and the U.S. involvement in peace processes, this can be a very useful site. It does not offer much historical information, but for recent years, it has fair coverage.

Subject Headings: Grants; Peace

SuDoc Number: Y 3.P 31:15-2/ *Peace Watch*

[762] United States Marine Corps

Sponsoring Agency: Marine Corps

Primary Access: http://www.hqmc.usmc.mil/hqmcmain/hqmc.htm

Alternative Access Method: http://www.hqmc.usmc.mil/

Resource Summary: Organized by the component divisions of the Marine Corps headquarters, this site offers information and links to divisions including the Office of the Commandant; the Public Affairs Division; the Manpower and Reserve Affairs Division; the Installations and Logistics Division; Command, Control, Communication, Computer, and Intelligence; and the Safety Division.

This site is mainly of interest to marines on active duty.

Subject Heading: Marines

[763] USGS: Release of Declassified Inventory

Sponsoring Agency: Geological Survey (USGS)

Primary Access: http://sun1.cr.usgs.gov/dclass/dclass.html

Alternative Access Method: http://edcwww.cr.usgs.gov/dclass/dclass.html

Resource Summary: This site describes how satellite photographs from the 1960s have been declassified and made available to the public. Samples are available on this page.

Subject Headings: Military Intelligence; Satellite Imagery

[764] The Wall on the Web

Primary Access: http://grunt.space.swri.edu/thewall/thewallm.html

Resource Summary: This site provides a listing of names on the Vietnam Veterans Memorial. This huge list—totalling 58,000 names—is divided into files, one for each letter of the alphabet. While there is not yet a searchable interface, the straight alphabetical breakdown does make the list accessible, if somewhat slow to load.

Subject Headings: Veterans; Vietnam War

Military: Air Force ──────────────────────────

[765] AIAlink

Sponsoring Agency: Air Intelligence Agency (AIA)

Primary Access: http://tecnet2.jcte.jcs.mil:8000/cybrspke/aialink.html

Resource Summary: The AIAlink home page provides information on the air force's Air Intelligence Agency, a Field Operating Agency headquartered at Kelly Air Force Base in San Antonio, Texas. It includes descriptive information about the Agency, press releases under the heading Cutting Edge, biographies of AIA leaders, and an online version of the AIA magazine, *Spokesman*, called the *cyberSpokesman*.

While not as well organized in presentation as it could be, this site does provide basic information about the Agency. The press releases and *cyberSpokesman* help to present an even broader picture of the agency and its activities.

Subject Headings: Military Intelligence; Intelligence Service

[766] Air Chronicles

Sponsoring Agency: Air University

Primary Access: http://www.cdsar.af.mil/air-chronicles.html

Resource Summary: This online publication gateway from Air University includes the full text of articles from *Airpower Journal* from the spring 1994 issue. The articles are available in HTML and in WordPerfect 5.2 format. Future issues plan to have articles available in Acrobat PDF format. Other plans include loading the Spanish and Portuguese versions of the articles, loading all the past articles from the journal, and also providing the *Airpower Journal Index*.

The electronic presentation of this print journal demonstrates how well print publications can be disseminated on the Web. There are plans to develop an even more extensive and effective site.

Subject Heading: Electronic Periodicals

SuDoc Number: D 301.26/24: *Airpower Journal*

[767] Air Combat Command (ACC)

Sponsoring Agency: Air Combat Command (ACC)

Primary Access: http://www.acc.af.mil/

Resource Summary: With some links restricted to access by af.mil or .mil sites only, the site still offers some sections open to the full Internet. These sections include Air Combat Command Bases, History of ACC, Biographies of ACC Staff, and Other Air Combat Command Pages. Unfortunately, the Publications link is one that has restricted access.

Due to access restrictions, this site is most useful to air force personnel, but it does provide basic agency information for the general public.

Subject Heading: Combat Readiness

[768] Air Force Command Section

Sponsoring Agency: Department of the Air Force. Command Section

Primary Access: http://www.hq.af.mil/

Resource Summary: This site consists of information about the Command Section and its supporting offices.

This page is primarily useful for finding brief, descriptive information on the Air Force Command Section and its subsidiary offices.

Subject Heading: Air Force

[769] Air Force Communications Agency

Sponsoring Agency: Air Force Communications Agency (AFCA)

Primary Access: http://infosphere.safb.af.mil/

Resource Summary: This site offers the categories: AFCA Fact Sheet, Key Leader Biographies, Year 2000; *Intercom*; and Visitor's Center Photo Tour. The *Intercom* online section features selected articles from the current issue of this publication. For authorized domains, a different page will show up.

This site is useful for basic information on the Agency. The Year 2000 page may also be of broader interest.

Subject Headings: Communications; Year 2000

SuDoc Number: D 301.101: *Intercom*

[770] Air Force Development Test Center

Sponsoring Agencies: Air Force Development Test Center (AFDTC); Eglin Air Force Base

Primary Access: http://www.eglin.af.mil/afdtc/

Resource Summary: The AFDTC is responsible for nonnuclear testing of munitions. The site is organized around the sections AFDTC Wings, Support Groups, and Squadrons.

The site is primarily of interest to AFDTC personnel.

Subject Headings: Munitions; Testing

[771] Air Force Link - Official Web Site of the United States Air Force

Sponsoring Agency: Department of the Air Force

Primary Access: http://www.dtic.mil/airforcelink/

Alternative Access Method: http://www.af.mil/

Resource Summary: This central air force top level page divides its wealth of information into categories such as News, Careers, Library, Sites, Images, and Navigate. The News section features well-organized and searchable press releases from the Air Force News Service. Job opportunities, pay charts, recruiting information, and more can be found under the Careers category. The Library section does not link to an air force library site, but to a collection of FAQs, publications (including *Airman* magazine), biographies, fact sheets, and speeches.

This site offers an alphabetical listing of air force sites that are accessible to the public without restrictions. It also provides a listing by major command. A list of internal air force sites is available only to .mil users. Both photographs and art from the Air Force Institute of Technology Art Gallery can be found under Images. The Navigate section gives a basic graphical representation of the site in both images and in text.

For air force information, this is the first place to look. The site is well organized, offers substantial information, and is easy to navigate.

Subject Heading: Air Force

SuDoc Numbers: D 301.60: *Airman*
D 301.120:INTERNET *U.S. Air Force Policy Letter Digest*

[772] Air Force Logistics Management Agency

Sponsoring Agency: Air Force Logistics Management Agency (AFLMA)

Primary Access: http://www.hq.af.mil/AFLG/AFLMA/AFLMA1/lma_home.html

Alternative Access Method: http://www.hq.af.mil/AFLG/AFLMA/AFLMA1/afjlhome. html

Resource Summary: The main URL points to a page that has a description of the Agency. Use the alternate URL to get access to the AFLMA publications.

Subject Headings: Electronic Periodicals; Military Logistics

SuDoc Number: D 301.91: *Air Force Journal of Logistics*

[773] Air Force Office of Scientific Research

Sponsoring Agencies: Department of the Air Force. Office of Scientific Research (AFOSR); Federal Information Exchange, Inc. (FIE)

Primary Access: http://web.fie.com/web/fed/afr/

Resource Summary: AFOSR directs the air force's entire basic research program. This is a Fedix site which provides access to information on AFOSR funding opportunities, job openings, descriptions of ongoing programs, and minority information.

The site features the usual Fedix information and a brief description of the agency, but it gives a different appearance than an agency-maintained Web site.

Subject Headings: Grants; Military Research

[774] Air Force Reserve

Sponsoring Agency: Air Force Reserve (AFRES)

Primary Access: http://www.afres.af.mil/

Resource Summary: With its publicly-accessible pages and limited access pages, this Air Force Reserve site makes the limited access pages available to anyone in the .mil or .gov domains and to Air Force Reserve members by username and password. The sites features categories such as News and Information, Online Training, AFRES Units, and Want to Join? In addition, it has an AFRES FAQ, information on obtaining passwords, and keyword searching of the entire site.

Of most interest to members of the Air Force Reserve, the site also provides basic information about the organization and information for prospective members.

Subject Headings: Air Force; Military Reserves

[775] Eglin

Sponsoring Agency: Eglin Air Force Base

Primary Access: http://www.eglin.af.mil/

Resource Summary: The Eglin site offers information about the Eglin Air Force Base and its programs. Main areas on the Web site include Public Affairs, Business Opportunities, Organizations, Announcements, and Eglin Facilities. The site also has a link to Eglin Information that is available only to .mil domains.

The site offers basic information about the Eglin Air Force Base.

Subject Headings: Air Force Bases; Munitions

[776] Eielson Air Force Base

Sponsoring Agency: Eielson Air Force Base

Primary Access: http://www.eielson.af.mil/

Resource Summary: The main section on this site is the 354th Fighter Wing link. It also includes sections for Tenant Units and General Aviation Information.

Subject Heading: Air Force Bases

[777] Headquarters Air Education and Training Command

Sponsoring Agency: Air Education and Training Command (AETC)

Primary Access: http://www.aetc.af.mil/AETC-Bases/aetcinfo.html

Resource Summary: The AETC site features a list of directorates, including those without Web sites, and links to a few Numbered Air Forces. The category Other Areas of Interest Within AETC includes the links AETC Leadership and Development Catalog/Schedule; Air Force Occupational Measurement Squadron; Communications and Information Integration Updates; AETC Virtual Training Technology Forum; and Mentoring Programs. There is also an imagemap which is a map of AETC sites.

Although of interest to the air force community, others in military education may find useful sections as well.

Subject Headings: Higher Education—Military; Military Training

[778] Headquarters Materiel Command

Sponsoring Agencies: Wright-Patterson Air Force Base; Materiel Command (AFMC)

Primary Access: http://www.afmc.wpafb.af.mil/

Resource Summary: The section Programs, Projects, and Bulletin Board lists many AFMC projects and provides information about them, although some of the listings have restricted access. The Publications and Forms category includes AFMC electronic forms and links to other air force or DoD forms as well as to a few online publications. The Organizations section is a hypertext-linked directory to AFMC departments, field operating agencies, air logistics centers, product centers, test centers, laboratories, and more.

Subject Heading: Air Force

[779] Headquarters Pacific Air Forces

Sponsoring Agencies: Department of the Air Force; Pacific Air Forces

Primary Access: http://www.hqpacaf.af.mil/

Resource Summary: This site primarily links to subsidiary Web sites. It does provide basic information on the Pacific Air Forces and offers a staff directory. Within the section titled Pacific Air Force Bases, the site links to the Web sites of other bases including Andersen, Eielson, Elmendorf, Hickam, Kadena, Kunsan, Misawa, Osan, and Yokota.

Subject Heading: Air Force Bases

[780] Kunsan Air Base

Sponsoring Agency: Kunsan Air Force Base

Primary Access: http://www.kunsan.af.mil/

Resource Summary: The Kunsan Air Force Base in Korea has a Web site with a variety of descriptive information. Featured categories on the top level page include News, Base Fact Sheet, Wing History, Photo Gallery, Mission Statements, About Kunsan, Sponsor Information, Cultural Tips, and Organizations.

The site is quite useful in providing information about Kunsan, but has little beyond that.

Subject Headings: Air Force Bases; South Korea

[781] Rome Laboratory

Sponsoring Agencies: Department of the Air Force; Rome Laboratory

Primary Access: http://www.rl.af.mil/

Resource Summary: Some of the few featured sections on the top level page include Current News and Events; Business Opportunities, Inside Rome Laboratory, and Technology Transfer. For a more extensive list, look under the heading, Information Directory. This site also features information on research projects at the lab and technology transfer opportunities.

The Rome Laboratory site has more to offer businesses interested in technology transfer than it has to offer researchers, but it should still be useful to both.

Subject Headings: Military Research; Research Laboratories; Technology Transfer

[782] United States Air Force Auxiliary - Civil Air Patrol National Headquarters

Sponsoring Agencies: Civil Air Patrol (CAP); Maxwell Air Force Base

Primary Access: http://www.cap.af.mil/

Alternative Access Methods: ftp://ca0408.cap.gov/pub/
mailto:cap-info-request@cap.af.mil with "subscribe" in body

Resource Summary: The Civil Air Patrol site features sections such as What is Civil Air Patrol? How Do I Find or Join CAP? Civil Air Patrol News, National Headquarters, CAP Mission Activity, Unit and Wing Web Pages, and CAP Publications Online. The Publications section features a few forms, memoranda of understanding, and monthly mission reports. The mission reports are also available under the CAP Mission Activity section.

Useful for CAP members and those interested in joining, this site also provides useful background information on the CAP.

Subject Headings: Air Patrol; Aeronautics—Education

[783] United States Air Forces in Europe

Sponsoring Agency: Air Forces in Europe (USAFE)

Primary Access: http://www.usafe.af.mil/

Resource Summary: The USAFE Web site features some basic information on the air forces in Europe. The Sites section links to Web sites for the individual air force bases by name and on an imagemap. Press releases are available under the category News. The Events page offers a brief list of conferences and other events while the Library category includes fact sheets, publications, and forms.

Except for the Sites section, none of the other main categories have much in them. The site is most useful for finding information about specific bases in Europe.

Subject Headings: Europe; Air Force Bases

[784] Welcome to Brooks Air Force Base

Sponsoring Agency: Brooks Air Force Base

Primary Access: http://www.brooks.af.mil/

Alternative Access Method: http://www.brooks.af.mil/homeframes.html [frames version]

Resource Summary: This central page for the Brooks Air Force Base (AFB) primarily serves to link to subsidiary Web sites including Armstrong Laboratory, Human Systems Center, 70th Air Base Group, Air Force Center for Environmental Excellence, Air Force Medical Support Agency, and the Air Force School of Aerospace Medicine. It also features a Business Opportunities page and a full list of Brooks organizations with Web sites.

For basic information on Brooks AFB and its divisions, especially with regard to aerospace medicine, the site is well worth visiting.

Subject Headings: Acquisitions; Air Force Bases; Aeronautics—Medical Aspects

[785] Wright Laboratory Armament Directorate

Sponsoring Agencies: Eglin Air Force Base; Wright Laboratory Armament Directorate

Primary Access: http://www.wlmn.eglin.af.mil/

Resource Summary: This Directorate develops conventional armament technologies for the air force. The Web page features information on its divisions along with sections titled: Ordnance, Advanced Guidance, Weapon Flight Mechanics, and Assessment and Instrumentation. It also has the text of the nondepository *Conventional Armament Technology Area Plan*.

Subject Heading: Armaments

[786] Wright-Patterson Air Force Base Bulletin Board

Sponsoring Agencies: Aeronautical Systems Center; Wright-Patterson Air Force Base (WPAFB)

Primary Access: http://www.wpafb.af.mil/

Alternative Access Method: http://www.wpafb.af.mil/oldindex.html [former version]

Resource Summary: This is the main Web site for the Wright-Patterson Air Force Base. The site features information about the Base under the heading, About WPAFB. About WPAFB contains the links: History, the Air Force Museum, and Base Services. Under the Business and News heading, there is information on procurement and on doing business with Wright- Patterson and the Aeronautical Systems Center. The site also features a keyword search option of the entire Web site, a What's New section, and the WPAFB Bulletin Board (which is restricted to .mil access only).

Due to the many restricted access sections, this site is most useful for military personnel. However, the general public can find basic information about the Base, its services, and business opportunities.

Subject Headings: Air Force Bases; Aeronautics

Military: Army ───────────────────────────────

[787] Army Intelligence Center and Fort Huachuca

Sponsoring Agencies: Army Intelligence Center; Fort Huachuca Garrison

Primary Access: http://huachuca-usaic.army.mil/

Alternative Access Method: http://huachuca-usaic.army.mil/homepage-basic.html [non-Netscape version]

Resource Summary: While this site serves as the home page for both the Army Intelligence Center and for Fort Huachuca Garrison. All of the Fort Huachuca links are only available to authorized users. Under the Army Intelligence Center site, the sections are openly available. These feature the headings, Doctrines and Publications, Training, Center Units and Organizations, and Other Sites of Interest. Of these, the Doctrines and Publications area presents the most interest, with online official doctrinal publications, an online version of *Military Intelligence Professional Bulletin*, and conference proceedings.

Designed primarily to serve the Army Intelligence Center and Fort Huachuca personnel, this site may also be of interest to other military intelligence professionals.

Subject Heading: Military Intelligence

[788] Army Research Laboratory

Sponsoring Agency: Army Research Laboratory (ARL)

Primary Access: http://info.arl.army.mil/

Resource Summary: The primary sections on the ARL site are: Organization Information, Public Affairs, Technical Program, Visitor Information, and Business Opportunities. Organization Information includes a mission statement, initiatives, and an organizational chart. Press releases and a calendar of events are listed under the heading, Public Affairs. The Technical Program section lists technical directorates, facilities, and major shared resources. The Business Opportunities area features some technology transfer programs.

Subject Headings: Military Research; Research Laboratories; Technology Transfer

[789] ArmyLink: U.S. Army Public Affairs

Sponsoring Agencies: Department of the Army. Office of the Secretary of the Army (Public Affairs); Army Broadcasting Services (ABS)

Primary Access: http://www.dtic.mil/armylink/

Resource Summary: ArmyLink is designed to provide a link between the army and the public. While its major sections point only to other army sites, ArmyLink does offer its own sections including: Army Broadcasting Services (ABS), News (with a variety of press releases), Photos, and Questions.

This site is most useful for finding army press releases and broadcast information.

Subject Headings: Army; News

[790] Branch Marketing

Sponsoring Agency: Army Signal Center. Branch Marketing

Primary Access: http://147.51.101.5:80/OCOS/BM/DOC1.HTM

Resource Summary: Branch Marketing seeks to educate soldiers about the army's Regimental System and to keep soldiers and civilians abreast of Signal Corps activities. This page describes the Branch and has links to information on the staff and to the online *Army Communicator*.

Subject Headings: Ceremonies; Electronic Periodicals

SuDoc Number: D 111.14: *Army Communicator*

[791] Fort Knox Television

Sponsoring Agencies: Fort Knox Television (FKTV); Armor Center

Primary Access: http://knox-tv.army.mil/

Resource Summary: Fort Knox Television is an army video production facility located at the Armor Center in Fort Knox, Tennessee. The FKTV provides broadcast-quality video production and duplication services. The Web site provides a description of its video production, electronic graphics, library/duplication, engineering, and telemedia services. Under the Telemedia section, there are a few clips, mostly stills with a few sound files and video included.

This site could use more online samples of its work.

Subject Heading: Television

[792] Picatinny Arsenal

Sponsoring Agency: Picatinny Arsenal

Primary Access: http://www.pica.army.mil/

Alternative Access Method: http://www.pica.army.mil/index.html [no frames version]

Resource Summary: The Picatinny Arsenal in northern New Jersey is a principal army research center in armaments and munitions. This framed Web site presents a navigation frame with links that include Visitor's Guide, What's New, Reference, 411, and Library Search. Press releases and a few issues of the Arsenal's online newsletter can be found within What's New. The Library Search section connects to a local Excite search engine for keyword and concept searching of the entire Web site. Reference links to external sources, internal pages such as Technical Information Resources and Picatinny Production Pages, and internal documents such as *Combat Connection*. Local directory information is available in the 411 section.

The site has substantial information about the Arsenal, but not a great deal about its research efforts.

Subject Headings: Armaments; Arsenals; Military Research; Munitions

[793] Soldiers Online

Sponsoring Agency: Department of the Army

Primary Access: http://www.redstone.army.mil/soldiers/home.html

Alternative Access Method: http://www.redstone.army.mil/soldiers/texthome.html [text version]

Resource Summary: This is the online version of the well-known print publication *Soldiers*, the official magazine of the army. It is not intended to be a simple reproduction of the paper version, but rather an "electronic sister" to the print version. The site features the most recent version, but it also maintains archives back to July 1994, with a keyword search capability. It also has another section for online feedback and a section with information for ordering a print subscription.

Well designed and arranged, this site offers a substantial amount of information. It gives a comprehensive view of what is available in *Soldiers* along with an archive of older issues of the publication. This should be of interest to subscribers and nonsubscribers.

Subject Heading: Electronic Periodicals

SuDoc Number: D 101.12: *Soldiers*

[794] Team Redstone Online

Sponsoring Agencies: Army Missile Command; Redstone Arsenal

Primary Access: http://www.redstone.army.mil/

Resource Summary: Under the heading Public Information, the Team Redstone site features sections titled History, Acquisition, Command Group, Army Community Service, Integrated Materiel Management Center, Corporate Information Center, and Safety Information. The Government Information section has some of the same links, along with sections such as Army Regulations and Government Travel. Some sections of the site are restricted.

This site is most useful for finding basic information about Redstone Arsenal and military organizations housed there.

Subject Heading: Armaments

[795] The United States Army Corps of Engineers Information Network

Sponsoring Agency: Army Corps of Engineers

Primary Access: http://www.usace.army.mil/

Resource Summary: The Corps of Engineers site offers sections including: What We Do, Information, News, Organization, and Search. The Organization category features a long list of subsidiary Corps Web sites arranged geographically and alphabetically. What We Do is an HTML version of a pamphlet that explains the Corps' functions. The Information area consists of a long alphabetical list of sub-pages. The News section includes the publication, *Engineer Update* (available in HTML back to April 1996) and press releases.

This site offers a substantial number of links and information about the Corps of Engineers' activities. However, beyond the press releases and publications, most of the information is actually on the Web sites of the districts, divisions, and directorates.

Subject Heading: Engineering

SuDoc Numbers: D 103.116: *Monthly Bulletin of Lake Levels for the Great Lakes*
D 103.69: *Engineer Update*

[796] Welcome to the Center of Military History

Sponsoring Agency: Center of Military History (CMH)

Primary Access: http://www.army.mil/cmh-pg

Resource Summary: The CMH site offers a large collection of military history information including dozens of full-text books and documents, and a museum display of army art. The majority of the collection can be found under the Books and Documents section, where the CMH is now putting all new publications online in full-text format. This section is arranged by subject and then by title. The full text of the publications is also keyword searchable, but from the top page, not from the Books and Documents section. Under the heading Army Museum System, this is a selection of army photographs and art reproduced online. The Finding Aids section provides a number of online finding aids to print holdings of the CMH and other agencies.

This site is a must see for any military historian.

Subject Headings: History; Military History

[797] Welcome to the U.S. Army

Sponsoring Agency: Department of the Army

Primary Access: http://www.army.mil/

Resource Summary: This is the central Web site for the army. The main section of the page offers search options for finding army Web sites by organization name, keyword, or alphabetically (with over 500 listings). Below the search options, this page features current stories from the Army News Service. The main outline of the site is available in the margin, which divides the content of the army Web into main categories such as Leadership Organization, Finding Information, Warfighter Online, and Management and Administration.

The Leadership Organization section includes links to the mission statement, performance review, posture statement, and the Public Affairs Office. The Finding Information section includes an FAQ, retirement services, and indexes to Army organizations, subjects, and alumni. Warfighter Online includes an alphabetical listing of army installations around the world, recruiting online, a photo library, and more. The Management and Administration section provides Web management links such as E-mail to the Web Master, Registering an Army Web Site, and Security and Privacy.

Well designed and well organized, the army's site should be one of the first stopping points for anyone seeking information about the army. This site could serve as a model on how to design a Web site for all other major government agencies.

Subject Headings: Army; Finding Aid—Military

Military: Navy

[798] Fleet Hospital Support Office

Sponsoring Agency: Fleet Hospital Support Office

Primary Access: http://www.fhso.navy.mil/

Resource Summary: This site describes the Office's function and has a searchable e-mail directory. The page also provides a contact for reservists and a training schedule.

Subject Heading: Medicine—Military Support

[799] Naval Intelligence

Sponsoring Agency: Department of the Navy. Office of Naval Intelligence

Primary Access: http://www.odci.gov/ic/usic/ni.html

Resource Summary: This single-page site has a brief description of the Office. It would be helpful if an address and phone number for the office were included.

Subject Headings: Military Intelligence; Navy

Welcome to World Wide Web Home of
The Naval Undersea Warfare Center (NUWC)
Newport, Rhode Island

[800] Naval Undersea Warfare Center

Sponsoring Agency: Naval Undersea Warfare Center (NUWC)

Primary Access: http://www.nuwc.navy.mil/

Resource Summary: NUWC is the navy's research, development, test, evaluation, engineering, and fleet support center for submarines, autonomous underwater systems, and offensive and defensive weapons systems associated with undersea warfare. The Web site features information on its divisions in Keyport, Washington, and Newport, Rhode Island. Other sections include/NUWC History, Publications, and Library. The Publications section is slim, with a strategic plan and a standard. The Library page points to other external Web resources.

With a focus on its two divisions, the site will be of most interest to NUWC personnel. However, it also provides basic information about NUWC and underwater warfare in general.

Subject Headings: Military Research; Submarines; Underwater Warfare

[801] Navy Online

Sponsoring Agency: Department of the Navy

Primary Access: http://www.navy.mil/

Resource Summary: Navy Online is the official Web site of the navy. It features the sections Navy Public Affairs Library, Naval Web Sites, Naval-Related Web Sites, Navy Internet Dialup Service, and News and Information Services. The Dialup Service was terminated at the end of 1996, so the category will likely disappear in time. The Public Affairs Library consists of a large collection of online documents, images, calendars, and announcements, including an online version of *All Hands* and many other online publications. The Navy Web Sites section covers well over 100 other Navy sites from the Hampton Roads Navy Housing site to specific vessels' Web sites. By default, this is presented as an alphabetical listing, but other options include Category Listing and a Title Keyword Search.

For any information about the navy, this site should be the first stop. While the design is not as elegant as many other sites, it is quite functional.

Subject Headings: Finding Aid—Military; Navy

SuDoc Number: D 207.17: *All Hands*

[802] Navy Opportunities

Sponsoring Agency: Department of the Navy

Primary Access: http://www.navy.com/

Resource Summary: This is the primary navy recruiting site, which lists all sorts of navy jobs. The site features headings such as Jobs in the Fleet, Health Care Professions, Money for College, Worldwide Travel, Naval Reserve, and Naval Benefits.

This is an excellent resource for anyone interested in a navy job or in researching employment in the navy.

Subject Heading: Employment

[803]   Space and Naval Warfare Systems Command

Sponsoring Agency: Naval Command, Control, and Ocean Surveillance Center (NCCOSC)

Primary Access: http://www.nosc.mil/spawar/welcome.page

Resource Summary: This site offers information on Space and Naval Warfare (known on this site as SPAWAR). It features sections including: Organization; Command Briefings; Visiting; Weather; Programs, Products, and Services; Publications; Newsletter; Phone Book; and Employment Information. Another section offers the links: Advanced Technology; Space Systems; Information Support Systems; Information and Electronic Warfare; Command, Control, and Communications; and Intelligence, Surveillance, and Reconnaissance.

Users interested in advanced military technology, space warfare, and information warfare should find this site interesting.

Subject Headings: Information Warfare; Military Technology; Space Warfare

[804]   U.S. Naval History

Sponsoring Agency: Naval Historical Center

Primary Access: http://www.history.navy.mil/

Resource Summary: With a broad collection of online historical information, the Naval Historical Center's site divides its numerous links into two sections, Naval Historical Center Overview and Branches. Under the latter, featured sections include Contemporary History; Photographic Section; Early History; Naval Aviation History; Naval Aviation News; Navy Art Gallery; the Navy Museum; Ships History; and Underwater Archaeology. The Overview page offers the sections: Introduction to the Naval Historical Center; Frequently Asked Questions; History of the U.S. Navy; Naval History Bibliography Series; Publications; Fellowships and Grants; Internships; Events at the Naval Historical Center; and Visiting the Naval Historical Center. The Naval History Bibliography Series is available in full text, online and offers a broad collection of references for further research.

While there is not much in-depth online historical material here, the broad scope of the collection and the reference to print resources make this an excellent starting point for historical information about the navy.

Subject Headings: Bibliographic Databases; History; Military History

SuDoc Numbers: D 202.9: *Naval Aviation News*
D 221.17:1 *United States Naval History: A Bibliography*

CHAPTER 12: POPULAR GOVERNMENT REFERENCE SOURCES

This chapter includes popular ready reference resources. These government resources can be used to provide answers to frequently asked questions, do quick fact checks, and look up basic information. Inclusion of sources in this chapter is a subjective decision, and many of the resources found elsewhere in this directory can also provide quick answers. For statistical questions, see also the resources in Chapter 3—Census and Other Statistics, which includes the Bureau of Labor Statistics and the Government Information Sharing Project. For legal reference sources, the Supreme Court Decisions and GPO Gate give access to other standard reference sources. Some of the sources in this chapter are available on larger sites listed elsewhere in this directory, but they are present here to provide easier access.

One site that proves an excellent finding aid for many other government reference sources is the U.S. Government Information Reference Shelf from the University of Virginia Library. It is the featured resource for this chapter.

Government Information Resources

UNIVERSITY OF VIRGINIA LIBRARY

WALTER'S

U.S. GOVERNMENT INFORMATION REFERENCE SHELF

This selected list of Internet sites is based loosely on titles in the print reference collection in the Government Information Section of the University of Virginia Library. It is a mixture of both government and nongovernment sites. *User's should note that this is a highly selective list; a much more comprehensive list of titles of government electronic information products on the Internet is available via* GPO's Pathway Services.

Search for Titles Beginning With

A|B|C|D|E|F|G|H|I|K|M|N|O|P|R|S|T|U|W|Y

[805] U.S. Government Information Reference Shelf

Sponsoring Agency: University of Virginia. Library

Primary Access: http://www.lib.virginia.edu/govdocs/refshelf/walt_ref.html

Resource Summary: This selected list of Internet sites is based loosely on titles in the print reference collection in the Government Information Section of the University of Virginia Library. Arranged alphabetically by title, it provides the title, item number, and SuDoc number for each entry. Unlike some of the larger lists of government documents available on the Internet, this is a highly selective list specializing in reference resources.

While it is a mixture of both government and nongovernment sites, it is one of the best starting points for finding ready reference government document titles that may be available on the Internet. The occasional brief notes, such as a statement that the Web version is not as current as the print version, can also be very helpful.

Subject Headings: Depository Libraries; Finding Aid

The remainder of the resources are listed alphabetically in one general section and range from entry numbers 806 to 835.

Popular Government Reference Sources: General

[806] 1996 *Digest of Education Statistics*

Sponsoring Agency: National Center for Education Statistics (NCES)

Primary Access: http://www.ed.gov/NCES/pubs/D96/

Alternative Access Method: ftp://ftp.ed.gov/ncesgopher/publications/majorpub/digest/

Resource Summary: One of the best known sources for summary educational statistics, the *Digest of Education Statistics* provides a broad selection of statistics for both K-12 and postsecondary education. Other sections include Outcomes of Education; International Comparisons of Education; and Learning Resources and Technology. The document is available in a series of well-organized HTML documents. The separate chapters are also available in zipped files for quicker downloading. After unzipping these files, the component parts are in straight ASCII format.

This is an excellent resource for educational statistics.

Subject Heading: Educational Statistics

SuDoc Number: ED 1.326: *Digest of Education Statistics*

[807] Alpha Command and Control Information System Table of Contents

Sponsoring Agencies: Central Intelligence Agency (CIA); North Atlantic Treaty Organization (NATO)

Primary Access: http://cliffie.nosc.mil/toc.cgi

Resource Summary: This NATO site, housed on a U.S. military Web server, features some very useful resources. Under the heading Geographic Reference Information, resources provide quick country information, maps, and flags from around the world. There is a full copy of the text from the CIA's *World Factbook*, which can be useful if the CIA's site is unavailable. There is also a fairly complete section on Flags of the World, with large GIF format images for flags from almost all countries. The *World Factbook* does not include the maps like the one on the CIA's pages, but it does pull flag images from the Flags of the World section and makes them available at the beginning of each country's listing. There is also an Atlas of the World, which includes scanned maps for the world, continents, countries, and selected cities. Most of the maps are scanned versions of CIA maps, and thus they do not have very detailed information. Basically they cover major political boundaries, roads, and geographical features.

Despite the beauracratic-sounding title of this page, it provides an excellent ready reference resource for country information, maps, and flags. While a standard world atlas will give much more detail than this online Atlas of the World, it is well worth using for quick checks on boundaries or major features. If using the *World Factbook*, check to be sure it is the latest edition. The 1995 edition was still available here even after the 1996 edition became available on the CIA's site.

Subject Headings: Flags; Geography; Maps and Mapping

SuDoc Number: PrEx 3.15: *World Factbook*

U.S. Department of State

Background Notes

Background Notes provide information on geographic entities and international organizations and are updated periodically.

Geographic Regions

Africa (Directory)
Middle East and North Africa (Directory)
East Asia and the Pacific (Directory)
South Asia (Directory)
Europe and Canada (Directory)
Latin America and the Caribbean (Directory)

International Organizations

Association of Southeast Asian Nations (3/92)
European Community (1/93)
Organization of American States (5/97)
United Nations (10/95)

To **automatically receive via email** all newly released Background Notes, subscribe to the Department of State Background Notes listserv.

Selected Background Notes also are available **for sale in print by annual subscription** or individually from the Superintendent of Documents, U.S. Government Printing Office.

[808] *Background Notes*

Sponsoring Agency: Department of State

Primary Access: http://www.state.gov/www/background_notes/

Alternative Access Methods: http://www.access.gpo.gov/su_docs/aces/aces820.html
gopher://dosfan.lib.uic.edu:70/1D-1%3A22525%3ABackground%20Notes%20Series
gopher://gopher.umsl.edu/11/library/govdocs/bnotes
mailto:listserv@listserv.uic.edu with "sub dosback" in body

Resource Summary: This popular publication series of brief country overviews comes from the Department of State and is available in multiple forms on the Internet. The main site primarily points to ASCII text versions that are actually located on the first Gopher server. Some of the most recent versions are also available in HTML format. The version of the *Background Notes* from GPO are all taken from the *U.S. Foreign Affairs* on CD-ROM and are in PDF format. However, they can be more dated than the versions available on the other sites. Subscribe to the e-mail list to receive the latest *Background Notes* in text format by e-mail.

The *Background Notes* are useful for providing basic political, economic, and geographic information for each country.

Subject Headings: Foreign Countries; E-mail Lists; Geography; Travel

SuDoc Number: S 1.123: *Background Notes*

[809] *Catalog of Federal Domestic Assistance*

Sponsoring Agency: General Services Administration (GSA)

Primary Access: http://www.gsa.gov/fdac

Alternative Access Method: telnet://database.carl.org [under Open Access Information Databases]

Resource Summary: The General Services Administration regularly updates this Web-searchable version of the *Catalog of Federal Domestic Assistance* (CFDA). Searching is by way of a form that then runs a WAIS against the full text of the databases. Unfortunately, subject searching of the records using the official subject headings for each record is not directly available using WAIS. While keyword searching can pull up relevant records, it may not be as effective as using the index to the print version. Boolean searching is available, but the operators must be in upper case. The Web version also can sort output by date, alphabetically, and by size. The telnet version, available from the Colorado Association of Research Libraries is also keyword searchable, but without the capability to browse subject headings. The Gopher version does not even have keyword search capabilities.

Unlike earlier editions of the CFDA, the GSA Web version gives the date of the last database update. It also gives the date of the specific edition of the CFDA that serves as the basis for the database. Search capabilities are limited by the limitations to WAIS searching. The most notable absence is the ability to browse subject headings. Regardless, this is a very useful reference tool even if the search options need significant improvements.

Subject Heading: Grants

SuDoc Number: PrEx 2.20: *Catalog of Federal Domestic Assistance*

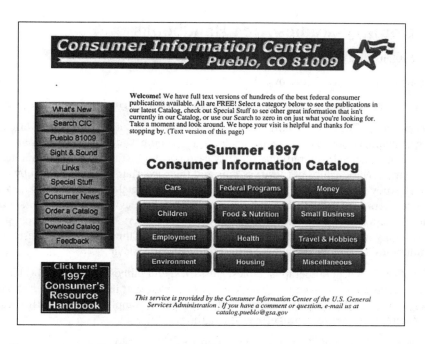

[810] Consumer Information Center

Sponsoring Agency: Consumer Information Center

Primary Access: http://www.pueblo.gsa.gov/

Alternative Access Methods: http://www.pueblo.gsa.gov/textver/t_main.htm [text version]
gopher://gopher.gsa.gov/11/staff/pa/cic
ftp://ftp.gsa.gov/pub/cic
mailto:cic.info@pueblo.gsa.gov with "SEND INFO" in body
mailto:catalog.pueblo@gsa.gov

Resource Summary: This page and the Gopher site give access to the well-known *Consumer Information Catalog*. Unlike the print *Catalog* which simply lists the various free federally-produced consumer publications, this online version of the catalog actually includes online versions of the publications as well. The publication order form can be downloaded and print copies of publications can be ordered. In addition, the ads (print, radio, and at least one TV ad) that have been used to advertise the *Consumer Information Catalog* are also available at the Sight and Sound link.

This is a treasure trove for consumer information. Having the full text of the publications available makes it easier to simply browse the publication as opposed to ordering it from the catalog.

Subject Heading: Consumer Information—Full Text

SuDoc Number: GS 11.9: *Consumer Information Catalog*

[811] Country Studies/Area Handbooks

Sponsoring Agencies: Department of the Army; Library of Congress (LC)

Primary Access: http://lcweb2.loc.gov/frd/cs/cshome.html

Alternative Access Method: gopher://gopher.umsl.edu/11/library/govdocs/armyahbs

Resource Summary: The *Area Handbooks* are excellent sources of information on other countries. Each work in the series covers a particular foreign country, describing and analyzing its political, economic, social, and national security systems and institutions. These publications examine the interrelationships of those systems and the ways that they are shaped by cultural factors. Each study is written by a multidisciplinary team of social scientists. The Library of Congress site offers full-text search capabilities across all of the available *Handbooks*, but the alphabetical access by country name and then by table of contents is the main access point. The alternate site only includes a few of the *Handbooks* including China, Egypt, Indonesia, Israel, Japan, Philippines, Singapore, Somalia, South Korea, and Yugoslavia.

This initial offering lacks photographs, tables, glossaries, and bibliographies, but LC plans on adding these items in the near future. The LC states up front that information on some countries may not be up to date. However, they do provide a "research completed" date at the beginning of each study so that the user can properly evaluate the reliability of the content.

Subject Headings: Electronic Books; Foreign Countries; Geography; Travel

SuDoc Number: D 101.22:550- *Area Handbook Series*

[812] Department of State Consular Affairs

Sponsoring Agencies: Bureau of Consular Affairs; Department of State

Primary Access: http://travel.state.gov/

Resource Summary: This State Department site links to a variety of other reference sites including the Travel Warnings pages, the Postal Service site, and travel health information from the Centers for Disease Control. It also provides other useful travel information such as links to embassy and consulate Web pages, passport information, visa information, and travel publications. The Publications section includes a variety of full-text pamphlets including several *Tips for Travelers*.

This is an excellent site for finding basic information about traveling abroad.

Subject Headings: Consulates; Embassies; Travel

SuDoc Numbers: S 1.2: *Tips for Travelers. . .*
S 1.2:F 76 E/ *Foreign Entry Requirements*
S 1.3/4: *Visa Bulletin*

[813] *Dictionary of Occupational Titles* Index

Sponsoring Agency: Employment Service

Primary Access: http://www.wave.net/upg/immigration/dot_index.html

Resource Summary: Only the index of the *Dictionary of Occupational Titles* (DOT) is available on this site. It is accessible via a hypertext alphabet and then by subdivisions such as "roadability through row." The entries are listed exactly as they appear in the printed volume.

Having the index available online is useful up to a point, especially for those that just need the DOT number. However, it is a far cry from the complete version with the descriptions of each of the job categories.

Subject Heading: Job Titles

SuDoc Number: L 37.2:Oc 1/2/991 *Dictionary of Occupational Titles*

[814] FedWorld Federal Job Search

Sponsoring Agency: Office of Personnel Management (OPM)

Primary Access: http://www.fedworld.gov/jobs/jobsearch.html

Alternative Access Methods: ftp://ftp.fedworld.gov/pub/jobs/jobs.htm
telnet://fjob.mail.opm.gov/
ftp://fjob.mail.opm.gov/APPS/FJOB_ftp/PUB/

Resource Summary: This interface to federal job opening files uses a WAIS search engine and a forms input. The input form includes scripted Boolean search capabilities, different sort orders, geographic limits, and a limit for the number of hits retrieved. The peculiarities of the database, of WAIS searching, and of the update frequency are all well documented on this page. There are even links to software packages which can be used for applying for federal jobs.

The telnet-accessible electronic bulletin board system (BBS) can only run eight sessions at a time, so it may be easier to reach the ftp site. On the BBS, search options include searches by job series, job title, agency, and state. Keyword searches, browse searches, and forms are available. The ftp sites includes the job vacancy listings in the jobs/directory where files are broken down by state. Other job-related files, including some application forms, are available in other directories. The filelist.txt file gives an explanation of the different directories and contents.

This is a well-designed site with excellent information value. It should be the first stop for anyone seeking a federal job.

Subject Heading: Employment

[815] FTC ConsumerLine

Sponsoring Agency: Federal Trade Commission (FTC)

Primary Access: http://www.ftc.gov/bcp/conline/conline.htm

Alternative Access Methods: gopher://consumer.ftc.gov:2416/11/ConsumerLine
http://www.webcom.com/lewrose/brochures.html
http://www.ftc.gov/bcp/coned.htm

Resource Summary: These sites feature well over 100 full-text pamphlets with advice for consumers and businesses from the Federal Trade Commission. These online versions of *Facts for Consumers* are available in HTML format in the following categories: General Information, Automobiles, Buying and Working at Home, Consumer Credit, Investments, Health and Fitness, Telemarketing, Homes and Real Estate, Products, Services, Young Consumers, and Business Publications. The alternate site, Advertising Law on the webcom server, lists available brochures alphabetically by title. On the FTC Web site, the pamphlets are found under the Publications heading, and there are also links to information on reporting complaints about fraud and a full-text version of the FTC Telemarketing Sales Rule.

Although brief, these consumer and business information brochures can be excellent sources of information. It would be helpful to have a keyword search option on the full text of all the publications. The alternate site, Advertising Law, has a search capability that covers the entire site, not just the FTC brochures.

Subject Heading: Consumer Information—Full Text

SuDoc Number: FT 1.32: *Facts for Consumers*

[816] General Schedule Pay Tables by Locality

Sponsoring Agency: Office of Personnel Management (OPM)

Primary Access: http://www.federaltimes.com/pay.html

Resource Summary: This is a Web form rather than a straight listing. Enter the General Schedule (GS) rating and choose a geographic area from the list provided. The database will respond with the GS pay scale and available steps for the specified geographic area and rank. The database is hosted by a commercial company, the *Federal Times*, but the data comes from the Office of Personnel Management.

This is an easy-to-use interface to sometimes hard-to-find data. The *Federal Times* is to be commended for making this site available. The information is more up-to-date than the information on the Library of Congress Gopher and more detailed than the information on the OPM Web site. It is especially valuable for finding information based on geographic area. Other sites include some of this information, but it is often just for a single local area.

Subject Heading: Pay Scales

[817] GS Pay Schedules

Sponsoring Agency: Office of Personnel Management (OPM)

Primary Access: gopher://marvel.loc.gov/11/employee/employ/pay

Alternative Access Method: http://www.usajobs.opm.gov/b5a.htm

Resource Summary: The Gopher site contains the pay schedules for government employees on the General Schedule (GS) scale, with steps. Files are available for the 1993, 1994, and 1995 Schedules. The alternate site, direct from OPM, has the current Schedule, but it does not include steps.

It is convenient to have all the levels listed in one document, but the Gopher site does not include variations based on geographic region, and the OPM Web site does not include steps. The site sponsored by the *Federal Times* (entry number 816) includes both steps and regional variations.

Subject Heading: Pay Scales

[818] *How Our Laws Are Made*

Sponsoring Agency: Congress

Primary Access: http://thomas.loc.gov/home/lawsmade.toc.html

Alternative Access Method: http://thomas.loc.gov/home/lawsmade.html [full version]

Resource Summary: This is the 1989 edition of this classic guide to the legislation process, revised and updated by Edward F. Willett. It is available both as one entire HTML file and by section in separate files. The handbook is intended to provide a readable and nontechnical outline of the background and the numerous steps of the federal lawmaking process. It starts with the origin of an idea for a legislative proposal and follows it through its publication as a statute.

The hypertext markup of the text is organized so that it is easy to read the entire text or just browse relevant sections.

Subject Heading: Legislation—Handbooks—Full Text

SuDoc Number: Y 1.1/7:101-139 *How Our Laws Are Made*

[819] Make a Tide Prediction: USA Coast

Sponsoring Agencies: Coastal and Estuarine Oceanography Branch; National Ocean Service

Primary Access: http://www-ceob.nos.noaa.gov/makepred.html

Alternative Access Method: http://www-ceob.nos.noaa.gov/tidetext.html [text version]

Resource Summary: This service can be used for predicting tide levels at specific coastal points in the United States, including Alaska and Hawaii. Choose a region and then a more specific area. Tide predications are available for the current day and for the next three days. Times are given with daylight savings times factored in, and measurements are given in feet.

While this site is useful for getting estimates for the current day or next few days, it only gives access to tide predictions for a very limited time period. For more options, see the WWW Tide/ Current Predictor from the University of South Carolina.

Subject Heading: Tides

[820] National Address and ZIP+4 Browser

Sponsoring Agencies: Postal Service (USPS); Semaphore Corporation

Primary Access: http://www.semaphorecorp.com/cgi/form.html

Alternative Access Method: http://www.semaphorecorp.com/cgi/navy.html

Resource Summary: The Semaphore Corporation provides a searchable version of the ZIP+4 database to advertise their CD-ROM product. This search form asks for address, city, state, and/or ZIP code. It uses automatic address correction software and guessing of incomplete street or city names. In the search results screen, any search warnings, changes, or errors are listed, along with an option for browsing addresses near the entered one. The alternate URL lists ZIP+4 codes for U.S. naval vessels.

Like the official USPS site, the availability of the ZIP+4 database is a useful source for addressing. Unlike the ZIP+4 search on the USPS site, the search does not present the results in all uppercase characters, which the Postal Service prefers. This can be a useful adjunct reference resource to the USPS offering.

Subject Heading: ZIP Codes

SuDoc Number: P 1.10/9: *ZIP + 4 State Directories*

[821] *Occupational Outlook Handbook*

Sponsoring Agency: Bureau of Labor Statistics (BLS)

Primary Access: http://stats.bls.gov/ocohome.htm

Alternative Access Methods: gopher://gopher.umsl.edu/11/library/govdocs/ooha
http://www.claitors.com/ooh/ooh.htm

Resource Summary: The most recent version of the *Handbook* is available on this site direct from the Bureau of Labor Statistics. It is available in full HTML format with links to definitions of terms and to other occupations. Entries for each occupation are found using the keyword search feature, which supports Boolean operators. Entries can also be found by browsing through the table of contents under the Outlook for Specific Occupations heading.

The alternate sites include the full text of older versions of the *Handbook* but not the most recent version. The text is in ASCII on the Gopher and in HTML on the alternate site.

This is an excellent implementation of an online version of a standard reference source. The hypertext links to definitions and cross references to other occupations make this source easy to browse. It is missing the pictures found in the print version, but that is no great loss to the information value. The initial page could be designed to make it more obvious that the main body of the *Handbook* is best browsed under the Outlook for Specific Occupations category.

Subject Heading: Employment

SuDoc Number: L 2.3/4: *Occupational Outlook Handbook*

[822] Per Diem Rates

Sponsoring Agencies: General Services Administration (GSA); UUcom, Inc.

Primary Access: http://www.uucom.com/perdiem/perdiem.html

Alternative Access Method: ftp://ftp.hq.nasa.gov/pub/travel.rates/

Resource Summary: This unofficial site includes federal per diem rates for travel. The rates are divided into three sections: Foreign Countries, U.S., and Non-Foreign Countries. The U.S. section includes only the continental U.S. while the Non-Foreign section includes American commonwealths, possessions, Alaska, and Hawaii. They also provide the date the files were last updated. The source for the data on this page comes from the alternate ftp site where it is available in ASCII, Microsoft Word, and spreadsheet formats.

UUcom, Inc., has provided a welcome service by publishing this data on the net in an easy-to-browse fashion. The data can be found on the alternate site, but it is more difficult to use. While the GSA also makes this information on their Policy Works Travel and Transportation Services site (entry number 824), it may be more easily browsed on the UUcom site.

Subject Heading: Travel—Per Diem Rates

[823] *The Plum Book*

Sponsoring Agencies: Government Printing Office (GPO); House of Representatives. Committee on Government Reform and Oversight

Primary Access: http://www.access.gpo.gov/plumbook/toc.html

Resource Summary: This publication, commonly known as the *Plum Book*, contains data on over 8,000 federal civil service leadership and support positions in the legislative and executive branches of the federal government that may be subject to noncompetitive appointment. It includes positions such as agency heads and their immediate subordinates, policy executives and advisors, and aides who report to these officials. This online version is primarily in HTML with a few sections in PDF format.

Although there will be plenty of changes to appointments after this is published, it can still be a useful source for finding basic directory information about salaries for appointed government officials.

Subject Headings: Government Employees—Directories; Pay Scales

SuDoc Number: Y 4.P 84/10:P 75/ *United States Government Policy and Supporting Positions*

[824] Policy Works Travel and Transportation Services

Sponsoring Agency: General Services Administration (GSA)

Primary Access: http://www.policyworks.gov/org/main/mt/homepage/mtt/perdiem/travel.shtml

Alternative Access Methods: ftp://policyworks.gov/pub/policyworks/mt/mtt/
gopher://dosfan.lib.uic.edu:70/1D-1%3A7898%3A03Foreign%20Per%20Diem%20Rates
http://www.dtic.mil/perdiem/opdrform.html

Resource Summary: This General Services Administration site lists the prescribed federal maximum per diem rates for the continental United States. A hypertext listing of the 48 contiguous states provides access to specific localities within the state. The alternate ftp site has spreadsheet and ASCII format versions of the full file. This site also has the previous year's per diem rates. Links are available to external sites that offer foreign per diem rates and rates for Alaska, Hawaii, and U.S. possessions.

The Web page is a very easy-to-use interface to this frequently requested information. This information is being provided by the GSA—the official government agency responsible for reporting the per diem rates. The unofficial per diem rates site (entry number 822) may be easier to use.

Subject Heading: Travel—Per Diem Rates

[825] *Sourcebook of Criminal Justice Statistics*

Sponsoring Agencies: Bureau of Justice Statistics (BJS); Hindelang Criminal Justice Research Center, University at Albany

Primary Access: http://www.albany.edu/sourcebook/

Resource Summary: This site has made the *Sourcebook of Criminal Justice Statistics* available on the Web. This online version of the *Sourcebook* has tables and entire sections available in Adobe PDF format. Access is by keyword search or by browsing by section. Although its print counterpart is only issued annually, this Web site is regularly updated to reflect new data that will appear in the next print edition.

The is an important reference source for criminal justice statistics and can include more recent data than the printed source.

Subject Heading: Criminal Justice—Statistics

SuDoc Number: J 29.9/6: *Sourcebook of Criminal Justice Statistics*

[826] Standard Industrial Classification Search

Sponsoring Agency: Office of Management and Budget (OMB)

Primary Access: http://www.osha.gov/oshstats/sicser.html

Alternative Access Methods: http://www.gsionline.com/guide/APP_E.htm
http://weber.u.washington.edu/~dev/sic.html
gopher://gopher.lib.virginia.edu:70/00/socsci/other/codes/sic_cbp.asc

Resource Summary: This page provides a searchable version of the 1987 *SIC Manual* by keyword and by four digit Standard Industrial Classification (SIC) code. It also has a hyperlinked table of contents for browsing the SIC structure. Search options include truncation and the Boolean AND and OR operators. The other URLs listed are connected to some of the other online versions of the *SIC Manual* that are Internet accessible.

The server is not very fast at returning results of a search, especially a complex one with a large retrieval set. However, it is quite easy to use and the descriptive information of each SIC code is as complete as that in the printed manual. Browsing nearby sections is also easy as there are links up to the major group (two digit level) and the descriptions of the even broader divisions.

Subject Heading: SIC Codes

SuDoc Number: PrEx 2.6/2:In 27/987 *Standard Industrial Classification Manual*

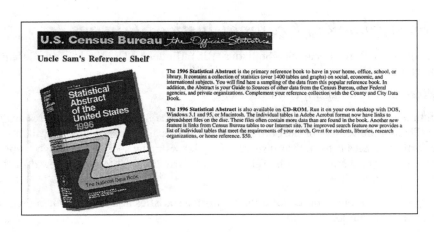

[827] *Statistical Abstract*

Sponsoring Agency: Economics and Statistics Administration

Primary Access: http://www.census.gov/stat_abstract/

Alternative Access Method: ftp://ftp.census.gov/pub/statab/

Resource Summary: This site provides the full text of both the *Statistical Abstract of the United States* and the *USA Statistics in Brief*. While only selected information is available in HTML, the full text of *Statistical Abstract* is available in PDF format. Unfortunately, each chapter is one large PDF file. This site also features access to other statistics which are included under the headings, State Rankings and State and County Profiles. These three categories provide statistics in HTML or ASCII format.

The print version is still far easier to use, but for those without ready access to a print copy, the PDF version can be quite useful. Some of the other tables available on this site are also useful for providing quick statistical information.

Subject Heading: Statistics

SuDoc Numbers: C 3.134: *Statistical Abstract of the United States*
C 3.134/2-2: *USA Statistics in Brief*

[828] Time Service Department

Sponsoring Agency: Naval Observatory (USNO). Time Service Department

Primary Access: http://tycho.usno.navy.mil/

Resource Summary: The Time Service Department site provides a wide variety of well-documented and authoritative ready reference information. A variety of links use the Naval Observatory Master Clock to provide an accurate, up-to-the-second time reading. Under the What Time Is It? heading, there is a Java applet that compares the Master Clock reading to the user's own computer clock, options for the correct time in all the major U.S. time zones, and instructions for adding a clock to your own home page that uses the Master Clock for authoritative time readings. Under the heading World Time Zones, there is non authoritative worldwide information on the time.

This site is not only useful for checking time. The section Times of Sun/Moon Rise/Set/Phases is a sophisticated interface for finding local times for sunrise, sunset, moonrise, moonset, and moon phases. Using a form entry, users can designate specific dates and locations within the U.S. and retrieve daily or yearly reports. The daily results also include times for the beginning and end of civil twilight, a term that is defined under the heading Rise, Set, and Twilight Definitions. This section also offers an option for entering longitude and latitude, which can be used for non-U.S. locations.

This is an excellent ready-reference resource for checking the time and for looking up specific sunrise, sunset, and moon phase times for specific locations. The information on this site is well documented, stating clearly which information is authoritative and which is not.

Subject Headings: Moon Phase; Sunrise and Sunset; Time

[829] Title IV School Code Database

Sponsoring Agency: Department of Education (ED). Office of Postsecondary Education

Primary Access: http://oeri.ed.gov:8888/TITLE4/search/SF

Resource Summary: This site provides searchable access to the Title IV School Codes required on many financial aid forms. Access is by way of a form that offers keyword and state searches. Search results provide the Title IV School Code and offer access to a school address.

This is a handy source for Title IV School Codes, especially when a print source is not readily available.

Subject Heading: Financial Aid

[830] Trakrouter - Amtrak's Online Scheduler

Sponsoring Agency: National Railroad Passenger Corporation

Primary Access: http://www.amtrak.com/cgi-bin/amtrains/scheduler/all_intr.pl

Resource Summary: Formerly hosted on an unofficial site, the Amtrak schedules now appear on Amtrak's own Web site. With Trakrouter, users can get a schedule by choosing two points along the routes, by train number, and by train name.

Some of the pages are fairly graphics-intensive which can make for slow response time, especially over a modem connection.

Subject Headings: Amtrak; Railroads—Schedules

[831] Travel Warnings and Consular Information Sheets

Sponsoring Agency: Department of State

Primary Access: http://travel.state.gov/travel_warnings.html

Alternative Access Method: mailto:travel-advisories-request@stolaf.edu with "subscribe" in body

Resource Summary: Travel Warnings are issued for selected countries when the State Department recommends that Americans avoid travel to particular countries. Consular Information Sheets are available for every country of the world and include such information as location of the U.S. embassy or consulate in the subject country, unusual immigration practices, health conditions, minor political disturbances, unusual currency and entry regulations, crime and security information, and drug penalties. They may also mention unstable conditions. These useful online pamphlets are arranged alphabetically by country.

The site also includes a section titled Public Announcements, which includes information about terrorist threats and other relatively short-term and/or transnational conditions posing significant risks to the security of American travelers. These announcements are made any time there is a perceived threat that includes Americans as a target group.

From 1991 to 1995, St. Olaf College distributed the State Department Travel Warnings and Consular Information Sheets. They still maintain the e-mail service which together with the Information Sheets are very useful services for the traveler. While they do not mention all possible risks, they do provide a good overview of the situation in a specific country.

Subject Headings: Foreign Countries; Travel

[832] *U.S. Industrial Outlook*

Sponsoring Agency: International Trade Administration (ITA)

Primary Access: http://www.ita.doc.gov/industry/otea/usio/usio95.html

Alternative Access Method: gopher://gopher.umsl.edu/11/library/govdocs/usio94

Resource Summary: In March 1995, the International Trade Administration published *The U.S. Global Trade Outlook, 1995-2000*. This report highlights export growth and trade trends in key countries and sectors. This publication is the successor to the *U.S. Industrial Outlook*, a standard reference for industry forecasts. The last edition, from 1994, is also available online at the alternate URL and selected tables are available at the primary URL.

Subject Headings: Importing and Exporting; Industry Statistics; International Trade

SuDoc Numbers: C 61.34: *U.S. Industrial Outlook*
C 61.34/2: *U.S. Global Trade Outlook*

[833] *United States Government Manual*

Sponsoring Agency: National Archives and Records Administration (NARA)

Primary Access: http://www.access.gpo.gov/nara/nara001.html

Alternative Access Method: gopher://una.hh.lib.umich.edu/11/socsci/poliscilaw/govman/

Resource Summary: This link into GPO Acess offers the most current version of the *Government Manual*, unlike the alternate URL which provides an older copy. One problem with this version is that the print manual is not divided into small units. For example, a search on the National Park Service does not simply retrieve that portion of the *Government Manual*. It retrieves the entire Department of the Interior section, along with several other links that are not in the National Park Service section. In many ways, the print version is easier to use.

Subject Headings: Government Employees—Directories; Agency Information—Directories

SuDoc Number: AE 2.108/2: *United States Government Manual*

[834] United States Postal Service

Sponsoring Agency: Postal Service (USPS)

Primary Access: http://www.usps.gov/

Resource Summary: The Postal Service Web site features a variety of useful reference resources for the general public and for businesses. Stamp collectors will appreciate the Today's Features section with its subcategory of What's New in Stamps and the Stamps section under Your Post Office. Other sections of the Your Post Office area include the headings Postal Rates, Postal Calculator, Addressing, and ZIP Codes. The ZIP Codes section includes a ZIP+4 Code Lookup form, City and State to ZIP Code Associations, and a page with official addressing abbreviations.

The Business Section features a wide variety of business reference sections including Express Mail Tracking, Information on Selling to the U.S. Postal Service, Printable Business Forms, a Locate Local Postal Business Centers service, and Business Publications (including the *Postal Bulletin* and *Memo to Mailers*). Under the For Your Information section is a post office locator, press releases, and information about the USPS, including *Postal Life* magazine and their *Annual Reports*.

With a collection of useful reference sources for addressing and stamp collecting, this site is well worth visiting. It does not have the Browse Nearby Addresses feature that the National Address and ZIP+4 browser has, but it handles most other ZIP code questions. The Information on Stamps section could be greatly expanded, but it does have information on new stamps.

Subject Headings: Addresses; Missing Children; Stamps; ZIP Codes

SuDoc Numbers: P 1.1: *Annual Report of the Postmaster General*
P 1.3: *Postal Bulletin*
P 1.10/9: *ZIP + 4 State Directories*
P 1.43: *Postal Life*
P 1.47: *Memo to Mailers*
P 1.47/2:INTERNET *The Mailroon Companion*

[835] WWW Tide/Current Predictor - Site Selection

Sponsoring Agency: University of South Carolina

Primary Access: http://tbone.biol.sc.edu/tide/

Resource Summary: This services gives both tide and current speed predictions for the United States. Access to the predictions is available via a clickable image map, a geographic region, or an alphabetical list. The default display provides predictions for just a few days, but there are many options available for changing the start date, displaying the data in different formats, and modifying the number of days to display. The predictions can also be displayed as a graphic plot for those that prefer to visualize such information.

This prediction service offers more choices than the Make a Tide Prediction service from the Coastal and Estuarine Oceanography Branch. The addition of current speed information is also helpful for boaters. However, note that the site itself still recommends that users check the predictions against officially sanctioned tables.

Subject Heading: Tides

CHAPTER 13: SCIENCE

This chapter covers scientific resources that are not listed in the other, more specialized chapters on science topics. For any of the medical or health sciences, see Chapter 7, Health Sciences. The broad environmental sciences including biology, climatology, oceanography, and weather, can be found in Chapter 6, Environment. Chapter 1, Agriculture, covers the agricultural sciences, and Chapter 16, Technology and Engineering encompasses the applied sciences. So what is left for this chapter? The resources here focus on physics and the spaces sciences, geology, earth sciences, and resources that have a broad interdisciplinary focus within the sciences. Be sure to also use the index for more specific scientific subjects.

The featured sites, NASA Organization and Science on the Internet, are general finding aids for science-related government resources. Both provide access to government science resources by topic. The NASA Organization site features access to the hundreds of NASA sites by agency and by subject. Science on the Internet also takes a topical approach, but it features United States Geological Survey sites. Try both for a more comprehensive search.

[836] NASA Organization

Sponsoring Agency: National Aeronautics and Space Administration (NASA)

Primary Access: http://www.nasa.gov/hqpao/nasa_subjectpage.html

Resource Summary: Few government sites take a broad approach to providing links to other scientific government sites. This NASA page is one of the few that does, even though it is limited primarily to other NASA sites. The top part of the site links to NASA Headquarters Offices' sites. This is followed by an image map and list of NASA Centers. While these links provide basic access to NASA sites, it is the next section, Information by Subject, that is the most useful. Information by Subject uses broad subject categories that follow those used by NASA's Science and Technical Information Program in its RECONSelect bibliographic database. Under these topics, programs and divisions of NASA are listed throughout. The topics are not just related to space or aeronautics but also to chemistry, engineering, life sciences, geosciences, mathematics, and even social sciences.

While this site is far from comprehensive, it makes an excellent starting point for finding scientific information from NASA by broad topics.

Subject Heading: Finding Aid—NASA

[837] Science on the Internet

Sponsoring Agency: Geological Survey (USGS)

Primary Access: http://www.usgs.gov/network/science/

Resource Summary: Maintained by the United States Geological Survey, this site still offers a broad range of science-oriented sites. Featuring USGS sites, this page starts with an Index of U.S. Geological Survey Servers and another link to the USGS by Theme. Under the heading of Non-USGS Resources by Topic, other scientific disciplines are available which include Astronomy and Space Science; Atmospheric Science; Biology; Computer Science; Earth and Environmental Science; Physics; and Other Science Resources. While not all of the resources under this heading are government sites, this listing is limited to those that are educational and not for-profit. The USGS sections, however, include all government sites.

While the coverage of non-USGS governmental science sites could be much larger, this is one of the few sites that provides some level of subject access to government science sites. Combine this with the central NASA site for more complete coverage.

Subject Heading: Finding Aid—Science

Science: General

[838] BIOCIS-L Biology Curriculum Innovation Study [e-mail list]

Sponsoring Agency: Smithsonian Institution

Primary Access: mailto:listserv@sivm.si.edu with "sub biocis-l name" in body

Resource Summary: This is an e-mail discussion list sponsored and hosted by the Smithsonian. Topics of discussion are focused on innovative curriculum design in biology.

Subject Headings: E-mail Lists; Biology—Study and Teaching

The scientific resources in this chapter are divided into four sections. The first section covers general scientific information resources as well as sites that do not fit under the other categories or other science chapters. This section runs from entry numbers 838 to 855. Earth Sciences, the second section, features resources on geology and the other earth sciences and covers entries 856-884. The third section, Physics, contains resources related to physics that are not related directly to space exploration and includes entries 885-898. The related category of Space Exploration covers space sciences information for the general public and for research scientists. This section includes entries 899-930.

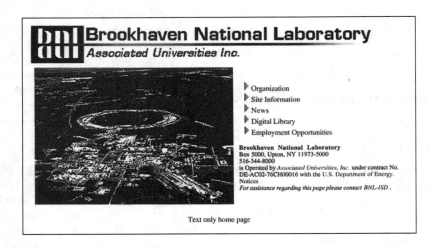

Brookhaven National Laboratory
Box 5000, Upton, NY 11973-5000
516-344-8000
is Operated by *Associated Universities, Inc.* under contract No.
DE-AC02-76CH00016 with the U.S. Department of Energy.
Notices
For assistance regarding this page please contact BNL-ISD .

Text only home page

[839] Brookhaven National Laboratory

Sponsoring Agency: Brookhaven National Laboratory (BNL)

Primary Access: http://www.bnl.gov/

Alternative Access Method: http://www.bnl.gov/bnl_textonly.html [text version]

Resource Summary: Brookhaven National Laboratory is a nondefense research institution that conducts basic and applied investigations in a multitude of scientific disciplines including experimental and theoretical physics, medicine, chemistry, biology, environmental research, engineering, and more. Their Web site serves as an entryway to its many research projects and divisional sites. The Organization section features the links Departments; User Facilities; Databases; Administration; and Telephone Book. The Departments link provides easy access to the many subsidiary BNL sites including the Alternating Gradient Synchrotron, the National Nuclear Data Center, and the Relativistic Heavy Ion Collider. Under Site Information, the page includes the headings About BNL, Calendar of Events, BNL News, and Jobs. The Digital Library link headings Scientific and Technical Reports and full text Research Publications. The BNL Reports are available from the BNL Scientific and Technical Reports Bibliographic Database which offers bibliographic information but not the full text of the reports. Under Research, some full text publications are available including the *Protein Data Bank Quarterly Newsletter*, the *National Synchrotron Light Source Newsletter*, and *Cleanupdate*.

Offering a variety of research information in many scientific disciplines, this site should be a definite stopping point for researchers in any of the areas covered by BNL.

Subject Headings: Bibliographic Databases; Biology—Research; Chemistry Research; Engineering Research; Medical Research; Physics; Research Laboratories

[840] Cold Regions Research and Engineering Laboratory

Sponsoring Agency: Cold Regions Research and Engineering Laboratory (CRREL)

Primary Access: http://www.crrel.usace.army.mil/

Alternative Access Method: http://www.usace.army.mil/crrel/

Resource Summary: With main headings such as Organization; News; and Information, the top level CRREL page offers more descriptive divisions such as Military and Civil Research and Engineering; Technical Information Resources; and Business Information. These sections provide access to lists of CRREL publications, some full-text technical reports (from1996 on, in PDF format), an Ice Jam Database, and the CRREL consulting services. CRREL has been involved with supporting Operation Joint Endeavor in Bosnia, and it offers links to some of its support operations there.

The CRREL site should be of interest to researchers in cold regions studies. The availability of technical reports and Bosnia information may be of interest to a broader audience.

Subject Headings: Arctic Regions Research; Bosnian Conflict; Reports—Bibliography; Reports—Full Text

[841] Explore Art, Science, and History with *Smithsonian Magazine*

Sponsoring Agency: Smithsonian Institution

Primary Access: http://www.smithsonianmag.si.edu/

Resource Summary: This electronic version of the *Smithsonian Magazine* provides the table of contents, selected articles, and images from the print version. Access is by date, topic, or keyword, with access back to the February 1995 issue. Most of the articles are available as abstracts of the originals and do not include the full text. The site also includes the instructions to authors information, membership information, and an image gallery.

The site presents a nice overview of what is in the print publication. However, it gives the impression that it contains the full text of its print counterpart, even though most of the articles are only abstracts or extracts of the original.

Subject Headings: Electronic Periodicals; *Smithsonian Magazine*

[842] Institute for Computer Applications in Science and Engineering

Sponsoring Agency: Institute for Computer Applications in Science and Engineering (ICASE)

Primary Access: http://www.icase.edu/

Alternative Access Method: mailto:majordomo@icase.edu

Resource Summary: The ICASE is a center of research in applied mathematics, numerical analysis, computer science, and physical sciences, with emphases on aeronautics, materials, and structures. The Research section is a compendium of research topics under investigation at ICASE. The Publications link features the full text of the *Research Quarterly* and some ICASE technical reports in Postscript and/or PDF format back to 1991. The site also features links to Colloquia, Meetings, and Mail Lists. The Mail Lists section provides the names of mailing lists that distribute new technical reports and notification of colloquia.

Subject Headings: Computer Science—Research; Mechanics; Mathematics—Research

[843] Lawrence Berkeley National Laboratory

Sponsoring Agency: Lawrence Berkeley National Laboratory (LBL)

Primary Access: http://www.lbl.gov/

Alternative Access Method: telnet://cat@csa1.lbl.gov/

Resource Summary: LBL conducts basic research in a wide range of fields including biological, physical, materials, chemical, energy, and environmental sciences. Their Web site features many categories including Welcome to Berkeley Lab; Scientific Programs; Research News; Publications; Educational Programs; and Computing Sciences. For an overview of the many programs and projects at LBL, see the Scientific Programs page. It lists the numerous divisions, groups, and projects at LBL by subject. However, it is not comprehensive. The LBL Search option is available for searching either the main LBL Web server or all of the Lab Web servers. There is also an index and directory for access to LBL pages and personnel. Both the Research News and the Publications pages provide access to publications from Berkeley Lab. These include the *LBL Research Review*, press releases, annual reports, and a Catalog of Laboratory Reports accessible via the alternate telnet URL.

The LBL site is well-organized and provides a substantial set of scientific information. The large number of subsidiary sites accessible from the top level LBL page make this an important searching site for scientists from many fields.

Subject Headings: Biology—Research; Chemistry Research; Energy—Research; High Energy Physics; Materials Science; Particle Accelerators; Research Laboratories

SuDoc Number: E 1.53/2: *LBL Research Review*

Text version

[844] Lawrence Livermore National Laboratory

Sponsoring Agency: Lawrence Livermore National Laboratory (LLNL)

Primary Access: http://www.llnl.gov/

Alternative Access Method: http://www.llnl.gov/llnl/home-text.html [text version]

Resource Summary: The broad range of research areas of Lawrence Livermore National Laboratory include nuclear weapons, renewable energy, and bioscience research. Within the About the Lab section, the site provides an LLNL phone directory, job opportunities, and educational programs. The Laboratory Research section provides access to Lab programs and projects by topic. For online versions of the Lab's published research papers, reports, and periodicals, look under the Publications heading. This heading includes full-text HTML and PDF format issues of *Science and Technology Review* as far back as 1994 (where it appears under its previous title of *Energy and Technology Review*). Another category, More Resources, links to press releases and visitor information.

The LLNL provides a substantial number of online full-text documents of interest to researchers. The site should be the starting point for anyone seeking more information on the Lab's programs or on some of its areas of expertise.

Subject Headings: Biology—Research; Renewable Energy—Research; Nuclear Weapons; Research Laboratories

SuDoc Number: E 1.53: *Science and Technology Review*

[845] NASA Dryden

Sponsoring Agencies: Dryden Flight Research Center; National Aeronautics and Space Administration (NASA)

Primary Access: http://www.dfrf.nasa.gov/

Alternative Access Methods: ftp://ftp.dfrc.nasa.gov/
gopher://gopher.dfrc.nasa.gov/

Resource Summary: Dryden is responsible for flight research and flight testing. Their Web site features the categories Dryden Flight Research Center Information; Dryden Organizations; and Dryden Information Services. The latter category includes workshops, an employee phone directory, and access to some of Dryden's technical reports, which are also available through the central NASA technical reports server. The Dryden Organizations category links to the sections, Flight Research Projects, Dryden History, and Education Programs. Many of the remaining links links are aimed at Dryden staff.

Much of the material here is primarily of interest to Dryden staff, but the Flight Research Projects, Images, Technical Reports, and History page should have broader appeal.

Subject Heading: Aeronautics—Research

[846] NASA/JPL Imaging Radar

Sponsoring Agency: Jet Propulsion Laboratory (JPL)

Primary Access: http://southport.jpl.nasa.gov/

Resource Summary: This site aims to inform the public about the work NASA and the Jet Propulsion Laboratory are conducting in radar remote sensing of the Earth's surface. It describes how to obtain, use, and analyze radar data and images; and it provides educational outreach. Featured categories includes Images and Video; How to Get Data; Education; Science and Applications; Projects; Products; and Software. The Images and Videos section provides access to the remote sensing images available on this site via a clickable world map and other access points.

Only a very few areas have pictures or videos available. This site would be more useful if it had a larger collection of imaging radar pictures.

Subject Headings: Imaging; Radar; Remote Sensing

[847] NASA Wallops Island Flight Facility

Sponsoring Agency: Wallops Island Flight Facility

Primary Access: http://www.wff.nasa.gov/

Resource Summary: Wallops is responsible for the management and implementation of suborbital research programs including sounding rockets, scientific balloons, and scientific aircraft. Available categories include Welcome, Mission, Organizations, Projects, Visitor Center, Local Interest, and Related Links. The Mission page provides access to videos, images, and project descriptions. The Projects page includes schedules for projects at Wallops, and the Organization page provides a hierarchical listing of Wallops directorates and divisions.

Subject Headings: Aeronautics—Research; Balloons; Rockets

[848] National Research Council

Sponsoring Agencies: Congress; Institute of Medicine (IOM); National Academy of Engineering (NAE); National Academy of Sciences (NAS); National Research Council (NRC)

Primary Access: http://www.nas.edu/

Resource Summary: Chartered by Congress to advise the federal government on scientific and technical matters, the National Academy of Sciences is a private, non-profit, self-perpetuating society of distinguished scholars. The NAS, along with the National Academy of Engineering and the Institute of Medicine, are supervised by the National Research Council. All four provide scientific advice to Congress on a variety of topics. The Web site features sections on all four organizations and a topical list of "focus areas." These include Education; Agriculture; Behavioral and Social Sciences; Computer Sciences and Technologies; Engineering; Environment and Earth Sciences; Life Sciences; Medicine and Health; Physical Sciences and Mathematics; and Transportation. Another section offers advice for beginning scientists and engineers. The publications and reports section includes bibliographic lists of publications along with full-text access to the *Proceedings of the National Academy of Sciences* (free through 1997, but a commercial service after that).

This site should be of interest to the scientific and science policy community. The topical lists provide summaries and, in some cases, full-text reports from these distinguished bodies. It is also useful for the availability of the prestigious *Proceedings of the National Academy of Sciences*. Enjoy the free access while it lasts.

Subject Headings: Engineering Research; Medical Research; Science and Technology Policy

[849] National Science Foundation

Sponsoring Agency: National Science Foundation (NSF)

Primary Access: http://www.nsf.gov/

Alternative Access Methods: http://stis.nsf.gov/
gopher://stis.nsf.gov/

Resource Summary: As one of the government's major scientific agencies, the National Science Foundation promotes science and engineering research and education. Their Internet sites feature a topical breakdown of NSF program areas into broad subjects. Within the category, More Information the Web site includes the links, Grants and Awards; National Science Board; Office of the Director; Public Information; Students and Educators; U.S. Science Statistics; Directory and Staff; and Visitor Information.

The NSF sites are a major source for information on NSF grants. The Grants and Awards section features the sections, Grants and Awards Opportunities; Program Deadlines; Policies, Guidelines, and Procedures; and Search Awards. This last section offers information about research projects that NSF has funded since 1989 including abstracts and the names of principal investigators. A Documents Online button provides keyword search and browse access to the many NSF publications that are available online. Many of these are in multiple formats, including ASCII, HTML, PDF, and Lotus 1-2-3.

For those involved with NSF grants or interested in applying for one, this is an essential site to visit. It provides very useful information on grants in the sciences. The NSF also provides useful statistics and publications on science and engineering education. The NSF offers a substantial number of documents online, but access to those documents could be improved by adding a basic alphabetical title listing.

Subject Heading: Grants—Science

SuDoc Numbers: NS 1.3: *NSF Bulletin*
NS 1.11/3: *SRS Data Brief*
NS 1.20: G76/2/ *Grant Policy Manual*
NS 1.28/2: *Science and Engineering Indicators*
NS 1.44: *Science and Engineering Doctorate Awards*
NS 1.49: *Women, Minorities, Persons with Disabilities in Science and Engineering*
NS 1.53: *Science Engineering Research Facilities at Universities and Colleges*

[850] Naval Observatory

Sponsoring Agency: Naval Observatory (USNO)

Primary Access: http://www.usno.navy.mil/

Resource Summary: The Naval Observatory is responsible for determining the positions and motions of the Earth, Sun, Moon, planets, stars, and other celestial objects. The Observatory also provides astronomical data; determines precise time; measures the Earth's rotation; and maintains the Master Clock for the United States. The Web site provides access to divisions of the USNO, including the Directorate of Astrometry; the Astronomical Applications Department; the Time Service Department; the Earth Orientation Department; and the Public Affairs Office. It also offers sections titled About the Observatory; The Precision Measuring Machine Project; USNO Colloquia; USNO Telephone Numbers; and Jobs at the USNO.

This site is useful for information on the official current time and general information on the Naval Observatory and its programs.

Subject Headings: Astronomy; Observatories; Time

[851] The Naval Research Laboratory

Sponsoring Agency: Naval Research Laboratory (NRL)

Primary Access: http://www.nrl.navy.mil/

Alternative Access Method: http://www.cmf.nrl.navy.mil/home.html

Resource Summary: This is the top level site for the many directorates and divisions of the Naval Research Laboratory. The research focus is broad and covers a variety of scientific areas within the Navy's concern with the sea, sky, and space. Major research areas include oceanography and atmospheric science, materials science, and space science. The site offers some overall mission statements and breakdowns by directorates. The directory listings point to subsidiary Web sites of directorates and divisions. There are also links titled Employee Activities, Publications and Announcements, Public Affairs Office, and Resources. A featured resource is Clementine, which provides access to over 170,000 lunar images, including pictures of all named lunar features.

This site can serve as a starting point to a very rich collection of scientific research. While much may be buried in the divisional Web pages, take some time to learn the organization of the site and then determine which direction to go.

Subject Headings: Atmospheric Studies; Materials Science; Military Research; Moon—Images; Oceanography; Research Laboratories; Space—Research

[852] The NSF Grants Database

Sponsoring Agencies: Community of Science; National Science Foundation (NSF)

Primary Access: http://cos.gdb.org/best/fedfund/nsf-intro.html

Resource Summary: This NSF Grants Database contains information about all NSF grants given since 1989, and it is updated at least every month. It includes a complete listing, for each institution, of dollar amounts for grants awarded. Like other Community of Science databases received from the federal government, the Community of Science does an excellent job of providing a powerful search interface to the Database. Searches can be run against the entire database, just the new records, or institution-specific subfiles. There is also broad science discipline subject access.

Subject Heading: Grants—Science

[853] Pacific Northwest National Laboratory

Sponsoring Agency: Pacific Northwest National Laboratory (PNNL)

Primary Access: http://www.pnl.gov/

Resource Summary: The Pacific Northwest National Laboratory conducts research in nearly every field of basic science with the goal of solving problems in the environment, energy, health, and national security. Their Web site features information on the Lab and its research projects. The At-A-Glance section provides basic information, the history, and the mission of the Lab. The Partnering section offers information on technology transfer, education programs, and its economic development office. Science and Technology is one of the major sections and presents the research areas of PNNL by topic, with specific programs underneath. These topics include Atmospheric Sciences; Biology; Chemistry; Energy Research; Environmental Science and Technology; Health; Information Technology; National Security; Nuclear Research; and Sensors and Instrumentation. The News link includes press releases, job opportunities, and some newsletters including *ER News*—Energy Research News.

With such a variety of basic research projects, it can be difficult to predict which researchers may be most interested in the PNNL site beyond those working closely with it. However, at least scientists working in the area of environmental science and technology should look at the offerings here.

Subject Headings: Atmospheric Studies; Biology—Research; Chemistry Research; Energy—Research; Environmental Science and Technology; Medical Research; National Security; Research Laboratories

SuDoc Number: E 1.19/4: *ER News*

[854] Sandia National Laboratories

Sponsoring Agency: Sandia National Laboratories

Primary Access: http://www.sandia.gov/

Resource Summary: Primarily involved in the design of nonnuclear components of the nation's nuclear weapons, Sandia is also involved in long-term energy issues research. Their Web site features contact information, job opportunities, and contracting opportunities. The National Security section features research projects related to national security and a summary of Sandia's involvement in national security issues. Under the Energy and Environment section, Sandia's programs include energy research, applied energy, nuclear energy, nuclear waste management, and environment. Another section, Research and Technology, provides a lengthy list of research programs arranged by topic.

Subject Headings: National Security; Nuclear Weapons; Research Laboratories

[855] Welcome to Armstrong Laboratory

Sponsoring Agencies: Brooks Air Force Base; Armstrong Laboratory

Primary Access: http://www.brooks.af.mil/HSC/AL/al-home.html

Resource Summary: The Armstrong Laboratory focuses on human-centered science and technology. Some topics the lab researches include human resources, crew systems, aerospace medicine, environmental quality, and occupational and environmental health. The Web site features the headings Lab Announcements; Publications; Information by Organization; and Projects, Products, and Services. The Publications section features some brochures, an index to the Lab's reports and papers, and a PDF version of their newsletter. The Information by Organization section provides access to the Lab's component organizations and sections.

This site is most useful for locating information about the Lab. However, there is information about the Lab's research contained within the Lab's subsidiary organization Web sites.

Subject Headings: Air Force; Environmental and Occupational Health; Military Research

Science: Earth Sciences

[856] Aeronomy Laboratory

Sponsoring Agency: Aeronomy Laboratory

Primary Access: http://www.al.noaa.gov/

Resource Summary: The Aeronomy Laboratory conducts basic research on the chemical and physical processes of the Earth's atmosphere. This research concentrates on the lower two layers of the atmosphere—the troposphere and stratosphere. The Web site offers information on the Lab's research projects in both technical and nontechnical descriptions.

Subject Headings: Atmospheric Studies; Global Change; Research Laboratories

[857] Alaska Volcano Observatory

Sponsoring Agency: Geological Survey (USGS). Alaska Volcano Observatory (AVO)

Primary Access: http://www.avo.alaska.edu/

Resource Summary: The Alaska Volcano Observatory site has sections titled Updates; General Information; Monitored Volcanoes; Other Volcanoes; Inside AVO; and Resources. It provides weekly updates and periodic information releases that describe the current state of volcanic activity along the Aleutian arc. The Updates section provides updates of the last two months while the Update Archive contains those older than two months. This site also offers weekly Kamchatkan volcanic activity reports. The General Information section includes collections of photographs and satellite imagery as well as a database of tremor and earthquake swarms.

The AVO site is of interest to scientists and also to people who are in the vicinity of these volcanoes.

Subject Headings: Alaska; Observatories; Volcanoes

[858] BIA Division of Energy and Mineral Resources

Sponsoring Agency: Bureau of Indian Affairs (BIA). Division of Energy and Mineral Resources

Primary Access: http://snake2.cr.usgs.gov/

Resource Summary: The primary goal of the Division is to provide professional geotechnical, engineering, and economic advice to Indian landowners seeking to manage and develop their mineral resources. Their Web site offers a variety of databases including the National Indian Oil and Gas Evaluation and Management System; Oil and Gas Exploration Opportunities; and the National Indian Seismic Evaluation System. The site also features a Native American Children's Art Gallery.

This site should be of interest to anyone following mining or other mineral extraction activities on Indian lands.

Subject Headings: American Indians; Art—American—Exhibitions; Energy; Mining

[859] Bureau of Reclamation

Sponsoring Agency: Bureau of Reclamation (USBR)

Primary Access: http://www.usbr.gov/

Resource Summary: Agency information at this site includes press releases, organizational charts, and job opportunities. Under the heading Reclamation Activities, descriptions and links to many USBR programs are listed under these categories: Cultural Resources; Disaster Response; Environmental Activities; Facility Operations and Maintenance; Geographic Information System; International Activities; Native American Issues; Policy Issues; Recreation; and Research. Most of the pages accessible from these links contain only descriptions of the programs and links to other sites. A few, such as Environmental Activities, contain links to full-text publications.

Well designed and well organized, this site contains substantial descriptive information and links to other sites. It could be enriched by adding more full-text publications from the USBR itself.

Subject Headings: Environmental Issues; Geographic Information Systems

[860] Cascades Volcano Observatory

Sponsoring Agency: Geological Survey (USGS). Cascades Volcano Observatory (CVO)

Primary Access: http://vulcan.wr.usgs.gov/

Resource Summary: The Cascades Volcano Observatory observes volcanoes and other natural hazards including earthquakes, landslides, and debris flows in the western United States. Their goal is to provide accurate and timely information that is pertinent to the assessment, warning, and mitigation of natural hazards. Their Web site offers a Volcano Information section, with information on hazards, monitoring, features, and individual volcanoes. Other sections include CVO Information, Hydrologic Information, and Educational Outreach. The site includes a collection of pictures, a glossary of volcano terms, information on the USGS Volcano Hazards Program, and basic information about volcanoes in general.

This site is of interest to volcanologists and to members of the general public living near or visiting the areas of volcanic activity in the Cascades. In addition, the basic information available makes the site useful to anyone searching for background information on volcanoes.

Subject Headings: Observatories; Volcanoes

[861] Earth Observing System Project Science Office

Sponsoring Agencies: National Aeronautics and Space Administration (NASA);
Earth Observing System (EOS) Project Science Office

Primary Access: http://eospso.gsfc.nasa.gov/

Resource Summary: This office serves as the primary interface between the earth science community and NASA's Mission to Planet Earth program. The Web site features the categories: Publications; Directory; Validation; Calibration; and Earth Observing System Data Services Information (EOSDSI). The EOSDIS page provides access to hundreds of earth sciences data, product, and services. The Publications link offers access to some newsletters, handbooks, and reports from EOS.

Subject Heading: Remote Sensing

[862] Earth Resources Observation Systems Data Center

Sponsoring Agency: Geological Survey (USGS). Earth Resources Observation Systems (EROS)

Primary Access: http://edcwww.cr.usgs.gov/eros-home.html

Alternative Access Method: ftp://edcftp.cr.usgs.gov/

Resource Summary: The EROS Data Center (EDC) handles data collection and distribution of satellite and aerial data and photos. The Web site does not offer access to their entire digital collection, but there is a lot of information available. Featured categories include About EROS Data Center; Products and Services; Programs; Partners; and Publications. The Publications section contains a bibliographic list of recent scientific and technical publications from the EDC staff, but the vast majority of these are not available online in full-text format. The Programs section links to Earthshots, a collection of images from the EDC's National Satellite Remote Sensing Data Archive. The Products section offers access to some of their products, including ftp access to some Digital Line Graphs.

For researchers seeking remote sensing data sets, the site is definitely worth a visit.

Subject Headings: Maps and Mapping; Remote Sensing

[863] Earthquake Info from the USGS

Sponsoring Agency: Geological Survey (USGS). Earthquake Data Center

Primary Access: http://quake.wr.usgs.gov/

Resource Summary: This USGS site features a broad range of earthquake information. Major sections include: Latest Quake Information; Hazards and Preparedness; More About Earthquakes; and Studying Earthquakes. The Latest Quake Information page provides geographic summaries for regions all over the globe. The Studying Earthquakes link highlights USGS efforts to understand earthquakes and to reduce earthquake hazards. For USGS hazard reduction fact sheets and seismic hazard maps, the Hazards and Preparedness link provides a large collection.

For anyone interested in earthquakes, this site offers a rich collection of information about the movements of the Earth's crust.

Subject Heading: Earthquakes

[864] Federal Geographic Data Committee

Sponsoring Agency: Federal Geographic Data Committee (FGDC)

Primary Access: http://fgdc.er.usgs.gov/

Resource Summary: The Federal Geographic Data Committee coordinates the National Spatial Data Infrastructure (NSDI), which encompasses policies, standards, and procedures for organizations to cooperatively produce and share geospatial data. Their Web site offers information on the FGDC and the NSDI along with a calendar of events. Another section connects to the National Geospatial Data Clearinghouse via a geospatial data form. The FGDC Development Areas section features some of the NSDI standards, including those out for review, along with cooperative agreements, partnerships, and metadata information.

Subject Headings: Data Products; Geography

[865] Global Change Master Directory

Sponsoring Agency: National Aeronautics and Space Administration (NASA)

Primary Access: http://gcmd.gsfc.nasa.gov/

Alternative Access Method: ftp://gcmd.gsfc.nasa.gov/pub/

Resource Summary: NASA's Global Change Master Directory (GCMD) aims to be a comprehensive source of information about satellite and in-site earth science data, with broad coverage of the atmosphere, hydrosphere, oceans, solid earth, and biosphere. The GCMD is accessible via both a Controlled Search and a Free-Text Search option. The GCMD records contain information on the data sets including personnel, data center, attributes, and a summary. In addition, the GCMD site has categories such as Register Your Data Set; Software and Documentation; Earth Science Links; and Projects and Outreach.

The availability of this directory can assist researchers in finding data sets that will be relevant and useful in their research.

Subject Headings: Data Products—Directory; Global Change

[866] Global Land Information System

Sponsoring Agency: Geological Survey (USGS)

Primary Access: http://sun1.cr.usgs.gov/glis/glis.html

Alternative Access Methods: http://edcwww.cr.usgs.gov/webglis/
telnet://xglis.cr.usgs.gov [for X terminals]

Resource Summary: The Global Land Information System (GLIS) provides a directory of data sets for scientists seeking sources of information about the Earth's land surfaces. GLIS contains metadata—descriptive information about available data sets. With GLIS, scientists can evaluate data sets, determine their availability, and place online requests for products. The site also offers online samples of earth science data that may be ordered through the system. While this main page consists primarily of descriptive information, it provides links to the alternate URLs, which offer a Web version of GLIS and an X version, accessible via an X Window telnet client.

Subject Headings: Data Products—Directory; Geographic Information Systems

[867] Goddard Distributed Active Archive Center

Sponsoring Agency: Goddard Space Flight Center (GSFC)

Primary Access: http://xtreme.gsfc.nasa.gov/

Alternative Access Method: ftp://daac.gsfc.nasa.gov/data/

Resource Summary: The Goddard Distributed Active Archive Center (DAAC) provides data and related services for global change research and education, especially for the upper atmosphere, atmospheric dynamics, and the global biosphere. This site provide access to information on the various data sets available from DAAC.

Subject Headings: Atmospheric Studies; Data Products; Global Change

[868] Minerals Management Service

Sponsoring Agency: Minerals Management Service (MMS)

Primary Access: http://www.mms.gov/

Resource Summary: The Minerals Management Service is charged with managing the mineral resources of the outer continental shelf. It also collects, verifies, and distributes mineral revenues from federal and Indian lands. Some of the links available include About MMS, Environment and Science, Collecting and Distributing Revenues, Managing Offshore Resources, and Reading Room. A variety of publications are available in the Reading Room including press releases, a publications catalog, statistics, and some PDF issues of their newsletter, *MMS Today*.

Subject Headings: Mining; Oceanography

SuDoc Number: I 72.17: *MMS Today*
I 72.18: *Offshore Stats*
I 72.13: *Royalty Management Program Mineral Yearbook*

[869] NASA Goddard Institute for Space Studies

Sponsoring Agencies: Goddard Institute for Space Studies (GISS); Goddard Space Flight Center (GSFC)

Primary Access: http://www.giss.nasa.gov/

Resource Summary: Goddard Institute for Space Studies is a Goddard Space Flight Center research institute that does basic research in space and earth sciences in support of Goddard programs. It emphasizes a broad study of global change and the prediction of atmospheric and climate changes for the next couple of decades. Their Web site includes pages on education, publications, data sets and images, and research. The publications section is primarily a bibliographic listing of publications from GISS staff, although a few are available in compressed PostScript format.

While most of the site is geared toward the research scientist or graduate/postdoc students, the Popular Science page offers nontechnical summaries of many of their research projects.

Subject Headings: Climatology; Global Change; Space—Research

[870] National Earth Orientation Service

Sponsoring Agencies: National Earth Orientation Service (NEOS); Naval Observatory (USNO)

Primary Access: http://maia.usno.navy.mil/

Resource Summary: The National Earth Orientation Service was organized to coordinate, collect, analyze, and distribute data from the various operational U.S. programs that monitor variations in the orientation of the Earth. Their Web site features answers to questions including What is Earth orientation? and What is a leap second? The NEOS Products and Publications section provides access to various announcements, bulletins, and current notices regarding shifts in Earth orientation.

Due to the very technical nature of most of this information, the site is primarily of interest to navigators, geodesists, and those involved in timekeeping.

Subject Headings: Geodesy; Time

[871] National Geodetic Survey

Sponsoring Agency: National Geodetic Survey (NGS)

Primary Access: http://www.ngs.noaa.gov/

Alternative Access Method: ftp://ftp.ngs.noaa.gov/pub/

Resource Summary: The National Geodetic Survey develops and maintains the National Spatial Reference System (NSRS) using geodetic, photogrammetric, and remote sensing techniques. The NSRS is a national coordinate system that defines latitude, longitude, height, scale, gravity, and orientation throughout the U.S., including how these values change with time. The NGS Web site's featured categories include What's New; Federal Geodetic Control Subcommittee; Search; Who We Are; Products and Services; and Geodetic Resources. Their substantial Products and Services page includes access to Aerial Photos, Aeronautical Data, Calibration Base Lines, Global Positioning System Orbital Data, and Geodetic Software Programs.

The technical nature of the material available on this site means that it will be of interest primarily to researchers in geodesy and remote sensing.

Subject Headings: Geodesy; Maps and Mapping; Remote Sensing

[872] National Geophysical Data Center

Sponsoring Agency: National Geophysical Data Center (NGDC)

Primary Access: http://www.ngdc.noaa.gov/

Alternative Access Methods: gopher://gopher.ngdc.noaa.gov/
ftp://ftp.ngdc.noaa.gov/

Resource Summary: The National Geophysical Data Center provides data in the fields of solar-terrestrial physics, solid earth geophysics, marine geology and geophysics, paleoclimatology, and glaciology (snow and ice). Subject categories that have their own links to data sets and software access tools include Solid Earth Geophysics, Solar-Terrestrial Physics, Marine Geology and Geophysics, Paleoclimate Program, and the Defense Meteorological Satellite Program (DMSP) Satellite Data Archive. An NGDC personnel directory is also available.

The site contains numerous data products of use to research professionals in the relevant disciplines.

Subject Headings: Marine Geology; Glaciology; Geophysics; Solar-Terrestrial Physics

[873] National Imagery and Mapping Agency

Sponsoring Agencies: Defense Mapping Agency; National Imagery and Mapping Agency (NIMA)

Primary Access: http://www.nima.mil/

Resource Summary: Formerly known as the Defense Mapping Agency, the NIMA Web site provides access to imagery, imagery intelligence, and geospatial information. Their site features sections titled Organization, Commercial Advocate, Geospatial Information, Imagery Information, General Information, and Publications. The Commercial Advocate link includes procurement and customer service information. The remaining sections feature technical resources related to imagery, geodesy, and mapping. The Publications page includes an HTML edition of *Geodesy for the Layman*. The Geospatial Information page provides access to the GEOnet Names Server—a database of foreign geographical feature names.

Subject Headings: Geodesy; Imaging; Maps and Mapping; Place Names

SuDoc Number: D 5.302:G 29 *Geodesy for the Layman*

[874] Office of Surface Mining

Sponsoring Agency: Office of Surface Mining (OSM)

Primary Access: http://www.osmre.gov/

Alternative Access Methods: http://www.osmre.gov/osmx.htm [non-frames version]
ftp://ftp.osmre.gov/pub/

Resource Summary: This site primarily features information about the office, such as a biography of the director, the mission statement, the OSM budget, and a contact directory. Other content links include the text of the 1977 Surface Mining Control and Reclamation Act and a year-in-review report for mining in 1995.

Subject Heading: Mining

[875] PALCLINE - Paleoclimate, Paleoecology [e-mail list]

Sponsoring Agency: Smithsonian Institution

Primary Access: mailto:listserv@sivm.si.edu with "sub palcline name" in body

Resource Summary: This e-mail discussion list, sponsored and hosted by the Smithsonian, covers paleoclimate and paleoecology for the late Mesozoic and early Cenozoic periods.

Subject Headings: E-mail Lists; Paleoclimatology; Paleoecology

[876] Topex/Poseidon Mission

Sponsoring Agencies: Centre National d'Etudes Spatiales; Jet Propulsion Laboratory (JPL)

Primary Access: http://topex-www.jpl.nasa.gov/

Resource Summary: The Topex/Poseidon Mission is a partnership between the U.S. and France established to monitor global ocean circulation, discover the tie between the oceans and atmosphere, and improve global climate predictions. The Web site offers basic information about the mission, near real-time data, images from the satellite, and educational resources. The satellite measures global sea level every 10 days.

Subject Heading: Global Change

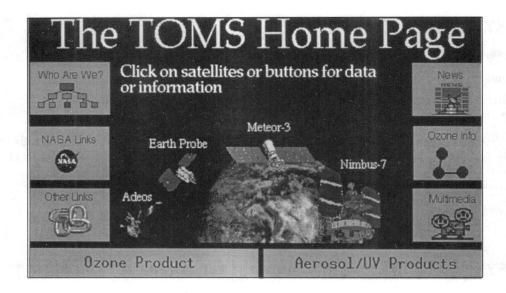

[877] Total Ozone Mapping Spectrometer

Sponsoring Agency: Goddard Space Flight Center (GSFC)

Primary Access: http://jwocky.gsfc.nasa.gov/

Resource Summary: This site features information, data, and images for the Total Ozone Mapping Spectrometer (TOMS) instruments. NASA's TOMS instruments provide global measurements of total column ozone on a daily basis. Nimbus-7 TOMS and Meteor-3 TOMS together provided daily ozone data from November 1978 to December 1994. After a gap of one and a half years, two new TOMS instruments were launched and are now providing near real-time data. The Multimedia section includes animated images video files that show ozone depletion and the ozone hole, and other related multimedia files. Choose the specific TOMS instrument for access to the most current images and data available along with access to archives of images and data. The site also states that aerosol and ultraviolet data will be available in the future.

While this site is geared toward researchers, the Multimedia section and some of the images present the data in a manner that is easily grasped by the layman as well.

Subject Headings: Global Change; Ozone

[878] U.S. Geological Survey

Sponsoring Agency: Geological Survey (USGS)

Primary Access: http://www.usgs.gov/

Resource Summary: As one of the government primary scientific agencies, the U.S. Geological Survey offers a broad range of scientific material on their Web site. The site includes functional categories such as Ordering Products; Publications and Data; Fact Sheets; and The Learning Web along with primary subject categories of Biology, Geology, Mapping, and Water. These four primary subject categories point to separate USGS sites which are described separately in this directory. However, the main page also has additional thematic subdivisions which include: Hazards, Natural Resources, Environment, and Information Management. The thematic pages gather links to USGS resources from many different USGS Web sites and provide broad subject access to the resources.

The Publications and Data page provides links to many USGS monographic publications and series. While there are links to major USGS series such as the *Bulletin*, *Open-File Reports*, and *Circulars*, only a few are available for each series including the current one. The *New Publications of the U.S. Geological Survey Catalog* provides a far more complete list of USGS publications, and the online version does have links to any publications that are available online.

With links to its major subsidiary sites by subject, theme, and keyword search, the USGS site provides multiple access points to its rich collection of scientific resources. While only a small percentage of the agency's vast output of reports and publications is available online, these include some significant resources, fact sheets, and series.

Subject Headings: Geology; Maps and Mapping

SuDoc Numbers: I 1.94/2: *Selected Water Resources Abstracts*
I 19.1: *USGS Yearbooks*
I 19.3: *USGS Bulletins*
I 19.4/2: *USGS Circulars*
I 19.14/4: *New Publications of the USGS*
I 19.42/4: *Water-Resources Investigations Reports*
I 19.76: *Open-File Reports*
PrEx 2.6/2: G 29 *Manual of Federal Geographic Data Products*

[879] U.S. Geological Survey Geologic Information

Sponsoring Agency: Geological Survey (USGS). Geologic Division

Primary Access: http://geology.usgs.gov/

Resource Summary: The graphic banner at the top of the page highlights one of the research programs or themes conducted by the USGS Geologic Division. However, the banner and its caption change on each reload. For a more static look at what is available from this site, see the categories which include: Geologic Research Activities; Research Results and Products; What's New; and Customer Support. The Geologic Research Activities section provides information on major research programs with access by theme, geographic location, and scientific discipline. The site also features an Ask-A-Geologist page, which provides a form to ask scientific questions about geology, geophysics, or geochemistry. A USGS geologist should respond within a few days, although they do not guarantee a response.

This site is a useful starting point for finding geology information from the USGS. However, many other geology sources are available on the main USGS server, so it may require looking on both.

Subject Heading: Geology

[880] USGS Coastal and Marine Geology Program

Sponsoring Agency: Geological Survey (USGS)

Primary Access: http://marine.usgs.gov/

Resource Summary: This site features the USGS investigations of geologic issues of coastal and marine areas. The main topics include: Environmental Quality and Preservation; Natural Hazards and Public Safety; Natural Resources; and Earth Sciences Information and Technology. The Features section includes the links: the National Plan; Current Research; Research Fact Sheets; and Web Highlights. Within these sections, this site offers a substantial quantity of information on research in marine geology, including many images of the areas being studied.

This should prove a useful site for questions relating to marine geology.

Subject Heading: Marine Geology

[881] USGS Hawaiian Volcano Observatory Volcano Watch

Sponsoring Agency: Geological Survey (USGS). Hawaiian Volcano Observatory

Primary Access: http://www.soest.hawaii.edu/hvo/

Resource Summary: This site provides online access to *Volcano Watch*, a weekly newsletter for the general public written by scientists at the USGS Hawaiian Volcano Observatory. The newsletter is in HTML, and the site offers archives back to 1994.

This site will be of interest to anyone living in Hawaii. For the general public, the newsletter presents a good picture of what it is like to live near a volcano.

Subject Heading: Volcanoes

[882] USGS Mapping Information

Sponsoring Agency: Geological Survey (USGS)

Primary Access: http://mapping.usgs.gov/

Alternative Access Method: http://mapping.usgs.gov/index1.html [text version]

Resource Summary: As the central site for USGS map-related information, this site offers a substantial amount of information on maps, geographic features, and data products. It includes access to the *Geographic Names Information System* (*GNIS*) and a large database of official USGS place and geologic feature names. The records include longitude and latitude, elevation, topographic map name, and feature type. The site also includes the categories: Geospatial Data Standards; National Mapping Programs and Activities; Educational Resources; Data and Information Products and Services; Biological Resources; Water Resources; and Geology. For those looking for specific print maps, the site offers the links Map and Product Ordering; Map Prices; and Map Dealers.

While this site does not yet have online versions of all USGS topographical maps, it does have much to offer anyone interested in map or mapping information. The availability of *GNIS* makes this an excellent source for basic information on place names.

Subject Headings: Biology; Maps and Mapping; Place Names

SuDoc Number: I 19.120:G 25/ *GNIS: Geographic Names Information System: Digital Gazeteer*

[883] USGS Mineral Information

Sponsoring Agencies: Geological Survey (USGS); Bureau of Mines

Primary Access: http://minerals.er.usgs.gov/minerals/

Resource Summary: This USGS site offers access to minerals information formerly supplied by the now-defunct Bureau of Mines. The site features statistics and information on the worldwide supply, demand, and flow of minerals and materials and offers online access to publications such as the *Mineral Industry Surveys* and the *Minerals Yearbook*. Access to this information is by publication, commodity, country, or state. The site also features a Contacts section which lists mineral specialists by commodity, country, and resource. Note that the SuDoc numbers given for the publications are Bureau of Mines SuDoc numbers. As more recent editions are published, the SuDoc numbers will change and begin with I 19.

This is a very useful site for finding statistical information on minerals as commodities.

Subject Headings: Geology; Minerals

SuDoc Numbers: I 19.129: *Metal Industry Indicators*
I 28.37: *Minerals Yearbook*
I 28.37/6: *Statistical Compendium*
I 28.54/2: *Manganese in . . . (Mineral Industry Surveys)*
I 28.55/2: *Mercury in . . . (Mineral Industry Surveys)*
I 28.84/2: *Chromium in . . . (Mineral Industry Surveys)*
I 28.95/2: *Antimony in . . . (Mineral Industry Surveys)*
I 28.107/2: *Peat (Mineral Industry Surveys)*
I 28.122: *Pumice and Pumicite in . . . (Mineral Industry Surveys)*
I 28.123: *Asbestos in . . . (Mineral Industry Surveys)*
I 28.127: *Diatomite in . . . (Mineral Industry Surveys)*
I 28.130: *Mica in . . . (Mineral Industry Surveys)*
I 28.133: *Perlite in . . . (Mineral Industry Surveys)*
I 28.135: *Sodium Compounds in . . . (Mineral Industry Surveys)*
I 28.136: *Talc (Mineral Industry Surveys)*
I 28.145: *Rhenium in . . . (Mineral Industry Surveys)*
I 28.148: *Mineral Commodity Summaries*
I 28.151:ST *Statistical Compendium*
I 28.161: *Garnet in . . . (Mineral Industry Surveys)*
I 28.163: *Iron Oxide Pigments in . . . (Mineral Industry Surveys)*
I 28.173: *Metal Industry Indicators*

[884] Western Region Marine and Coastal Surveys

Sponsoring Agency: Geological Survey (USGS). Western Region Marine and Coastal Surveys

Primary Access: http://walrus.wr.usgs.gov/

Resource Summary: This site offers a list of research activities, a staff list, and a public information page. The main focus of their mapping and research activities is to provide access to information on the site. Categories on the site include: Environmental Quality and Preservation; Natural Hazards and Public Safety; Natural Resources; and Information and Technology. Under each category, descriptive information on the Surveys' studies is available. Their Public Information page features some information designed for children, teachers, and the general public.

Subject Headings: Maps and Mapping; Marine Geology

Science: Physics

[885] Advanced Spaceborne Thermal Emission Reflectance Radiometer

Sponsoring Agency: Jet Propulsion Laboratory (JPL)

Primary Access: http://asterweb.jpl.nasa.gov

Resource Summary: ASTER (Advanced Spaceborne Thermal Emission and Reflection Radiometer) is an imaging instrument that will fly a NASA satellite planned for launch in 1998. ASTER will be used to produce detailed maps of surface temperature, emissivity, and reflectance elevation. The Web site consists of a collection of pages that relate to ASTER activities, data product architecture, the spectral library, and simulated data sets.

Subject Heading: Imaging

[886] Fermi National Accelerator Laboratory

Sponsoring Agencies: Department of Energy (DOE); Fermi National Accelerator Laboratory

Primary Access: http://www.fnal.gov/

Resource Summary: Fermilab is a research lab that focuses on the fundamental nature of matter and energy. The lab provides the resources so that basic research can be conducted in high energy physics and related disciplines. The research focuses on the world's highest-energy particle accelerator—the Tevatron. Available sections include Laboratory Index, What's New, The Laboratory, The Directorate, Particle Physics, Education, Clickable Tour, Visitors Information, Cultural Events, Directories, and Fermilab at Work.

This site is useful for both researchers and the general public. The Education, Particle Physics, Cultural Events, and Clickable Tour sections all provide information for the general public, while other sections can provide contact and technical information for researchers.

Subject Headings: Particle Accelerators; High Energy Physics; Research Laboratories

[887] Harvard-Smithsonian Center for Astrophysics

Sponsoring Agencies: Smithsonian Institution; Smithsonian Astrophysical Observatory; Harvard University

Primary Access: http://cfa-www.harvard.edu/

Resource Summary: The Center for Astrophysics combines the resources and research facilities of the Smithsonian Astrophysical Observatory and the Harvard College Observatory. The purpose of this collaboration is to study the basic physical processes that determine the nature and evolution of the universe. The Web site features Archives and Services and Educational Opportunities. The Archives and Services section provides access to preprints, images, and press releases from the Center for Astrophysics.

Subject Headings: Astrophysics; Observatories

[888] High Energy Astrophysics Science Archive Research Center (HEASARC)

Sponsoring Agency: Goddard Space Flight Center (GSFC)

Primary Access: http://heasarc.gsfc.nasa.gov/

Resource Summary: The purpose of the HEASARC is to support a multimission archive facility in high energy astrophysics for scientists all over the world. Data from space-borne instruments on spacecraft are provided, along with a knowledgeable science-user support staff and tools to analyze multiple data sets. The Archives section provides access to the catalogs and astronomical archives using a W3Browser interface. Also within the Archives section is SkyView, a virtual observatory that generates images of any part of the sky at wavelengths in all regimes from radio to gamma-ray.

Primarily useful for the professional astronomer and astrophysicist, this site does offer some information for the general public. The Public Outreach and Education section links to their Learning Center, which provides some educational material on high energy astrophysics for various age levels.

Subject Headings: Astrophysics; High Energy Physics

[889] NASA Astrophysics Data System

Sponsoring Agencies: Harvard University; National Aeronautics and Space Administration (NASA)

Primary Access: http://adswww.harvard.edu/

Alternative Access Method: http://cdsads.u-strasbg.fr/ [mirror]

Resource Summary: The Astrophysics Data System (ADS) is a NASA-funded project whose main resource is an Abstract Service. The Service includes three sets of abstracts: astronomy and astrophysics—containing approximately 255,000 abstracts; instrumentation—containing approximately 460,000 abstracts; and physics and geophysics—containing approximately 220,000 abstracts. Each data set can be searched by author, object name (astronomy only), title, or abstract text words. In addition to the ADS Abstracts Database, the site also provides an ADS Article Service with access to scanned images of over 40,000 journal articles in HTML and/or PDF format and an ADS Digital Library with access to scanned astrophysics books.

This is an important site for anyone searching for information in the astrophysics field.

Subject Headings: Astrophysics—Abstracts; Bibliographic Databases

[890] National Radio Astronomy Observatory

Sponsoring Agency: National Radio Astronomy Observatory (NRAO)

Primary Access: http://www.nrao.edu/

Alternative Access Method: http://info.aoc.nrao.edu/

Resource Summary: The National Radio Astronomy Observatory site groups its links under headings such as Telescopes, Major Initiatives, Astronomical Tools, Employment Opportunities, and Public Information. Most of the information is very technical in nature. The NRAO Preprints and Published Papers page provides citations to NRAO visitor and staff preprints and published articles, but not to the full text of the papers.

The site is well organized and will be of interest to researchers. It could be improved with the addition of a general description, mission statement, and goals summary.

Subject Headings: Astrophysics; Observatories; Radio Waves

[891] National Space Science Data Center

Sponsoring Agencies: Goddard Space Flight Center (GSFC); National Space Science Data Center (NSSDC)

Primary Access: http://nssdc.gsfc.nasa.gov/nssdc/

Alternative Access Method: http://nssdc.gsfc.nasa.gov/nssdc/gen_public.html

Resource Summary: The NSSDC site provides access to a wide variety of astrophysics, space physics, solar physics, lunar, and planetary data from NASA space flight missions. It also provides access to other data and some models and software. The NSSDC provides access to online information bases about NASA and non-NASA data at the National Space Science Data Center and elsewhere. There is also information about the spacecraft and experiments that have or will provide public access data. Featured categories include Disciplinary Services and Multidisciplinary Services. The Disciplinary Services page provides subject access. The alternate URL points to an NSSDC page designed to guide the public to NSSDC data and services that would be of interest to the nonscientist.

While this site contains data of interest primarily to scientists, the addition of the general public page provides easy access to some of its less technical information resources.

Subject Headings: Astrophysics; Planets; Solar Physics

[892] Princeton Plasma Physics Laboratory

Sponsoring Agencies: Department of Energy (DOE); Princeton Plasma Physics Laboratory (PPPL)

Primary Access: http://www.pppl.gov/

Resource Summary: Princeton Plasma Physics Laboratory is dedicated to the development of fusion energy science. The Laboratory is engaged in a broad spectrum of plasma physics research. The site features information about the Lab, its research, and its equipment. Categories include Overview of the Laboratory; Tokamak Fusion Test Reactor; National Spherical Torus Experiment; PPPL Colloquia; PPPL Visitor's Handbook; PPPL Reports; Subject Locator; and Employee Locator. The PPPL Reports page provides access to abstracts and preprints of technical reports from the Lab. These are available in HTML and PostScript format as they are approved and finalized. Access is by date (back to 1994) and via a searchable form.

Subject Headings: Fusion; Plasma Physics; Research Laboratories

[893] Space Environment Center Home

Sponsoring Agency: Space Environment Laboratory

Primary Access: http://www.sel.noaa.gov/

Alternative Access Methods: gopher://gopher.sel.noaa.gov/
http://www.sel.bldrdoc.gov/

Resource Summary: The site includes various solar images and descriptions of space between the Sun and the Earth. The Center provides real-time monitoring and forecasting of solar and geophysical events, conducts research in solar-terrestrial physics, and develops techniques for forecasting solar and geophysical disturbances. Under the heading, Today's Space Weather is a quick overview of the space environment between the Sun and Earth. Included are the most recent full-disk images of the Sun; x-ray plots from the satellites; plots of the satellite environment; estimated auroral ovals; and partial text from the solar-terrestrial forecast. Additional images are available under the Solar Images heading.

Available data sets, primarily housed on the Gopher server, are available in the following categories: Latest Solar-Geophysical Data; Solar Products by Vocational Interest; Solar Alerts, Forecasts, and Summaries; Weekly Report of Solar and Geophysical Data; Indices; Events; Region Data; Lists of Solar-Geophysical Data; and Plots of Solar-Geophysical Data.

These sites present a wealth of data for researchers in solar-terrestrial physics.

Subject Headings: Research Laboratories; Solar-Terrestrial Physics

[894] Stanford Linear Accelerator Center

Sponsoring Agencies: Department of Energy (DOE); Stanford Linear Accelerator Center (SLAC)

Primary Access: http://www.slac.stanford.edu/

Resource Summary: This page provides a public-oriented introduction to the Stanford Linear Accelerator Center. The site also provides links to Highlighted Home and Detailed Home, which offer a version for SLAC researchers, collaborators, and staff. The public-oriented section titled, What We Do gives a basic overview of the Center. The Learn About Science at SLAC page offers information for visitors and the education community. The site also provides access to *Beam Line*, a quarterly journal of particle physics and databases of scientific preprints by SLAC authors and others in the high-energy physics community.

Subject Headings: High Energy Physics; Particle Accelerators; Preprints; Research Laboratories

[895] The Superconducting Super Collider Project

Sponsoring Agencies: Department of Energy (DOE). Office of Superconducting Super Collider; High Energy Physics Information Center

Primary Access: http://www.hep.net/ssc/

Alternative Access Method: http://www.ssc.gov/ [defunct]

Resource Summary: The Superconducting Super Collider (SSC) Laboratory was a DOE supported facility until Congress halted funding in 1993. The laboratory is in the final shutdown phase, but this Web site provides some information on the Project including a History of the Project page. The Scientific and Technical Electronic Repository page features access to some SSC documents, and the Utilization of the SSC Assets section suggests potential projects for using the site, although none are funded as yet.

This is now a non-governmental site hosted by the High Energy Physics Information Center. While they are to be commended for continuing to provide access to information from and about the SSC, some of it is a bit biased in favor of keeping the SSC functioning.

Subject Headings: High Energy Physics; Particle Accelerators; Superconductivity

[896] T-2 Nuclear Information Service

Sponsoring Agency: Los Alamos National Laboratory (LANL). Theoretical Division

Primary Access: http://t2.lanl.gov/

Alternative Access Methods: gopher://t2.lanl.gov/
ftp://t2.lanl.gov/

Resource Summary: Run by Group T-2 (Nuclear Theory and Applications) of the Theoretical Division of LANL, this site covers nuclear modeling; nuclear data; cross sections; nuclear masses; nuclear astrophysics; radioactivity; radiation shielding; data for medical radiotherapy; data for high-energy accelerator applications; and data and codes for fission and fusion systems. Available categories include Data (sets of nuclear data); Codes (computer coding developed by T-2); Publications; and News.

The technical nature of this data means that the site will be of interest primarily to nuclear physicists.

Subject Heading: Nuclear Physics

[897] The Unitary Plan Wind Tunnels

Sponsoring Agency: Ames Research Center (ARC). Aerodynamics Division

Primary Access: http://ccf.arc.nasa.gov/ao/

Resource Summary: The Unitary Plan Facility is the most heavily used wind tunnel in all of NASA. In addition to a brief description of the facility, the Web site features sections titled Heavily Used Wind Tunnels, Wind Tunnel Measurements, Examples of Aircraft and Spacecraft Tested, and Diversity of the Test Programs. The Wind Tunnel Measurements page includes a brief description of the measurements taken in the wind tunnel.

All the descriptions on this site are fairly brief. The site gives the basic idea behind wind tunnel testing and measurements. For more technical details, it would be wise to look elsewhere.

Subject Headings: Aeronautics—Research; Wind Tunnels

[898] xxx e-Print Archive

Sponsoring Agency: Los Alamos National Laboratory (LANL)

Primary Access: http://mentor.lanl.gov/

Alternative Access Methods: http://xxx.lanl.gov/
ftp://xxx.mentor.gov/
http://xxx.lpthe.jussieu.fr/
http://xxx.uni-augsburg.de/
http://xxx.tau.ac.il/
http://xxx.sissa.it/
http://www.yukawa.kyoto-u.ac.jp/
http://xxx.snu.ac.kr/
http://xxx.sf.nchc.gov.tw/
http://xxx.soton.ac.uk/
http://xxx.if.usp.br/

Resource Summary: This is one of the primary sites for finding preprints of journal articles in physics, mathematics, the nonlinear sciences, and computation and language. Started in August 1991, the LANL site and its many mirrors provide an archive for the distribution of electronic preprints. Each of the topical subdivisions is available as an e-mail list where subscribers automatically receive a listing of title, author, and abstract information for newly submitted papers. The full text of preprints is available via the archive through ftp, the Web, or automated e-mail commands. The preprints are available in a variety of formats, including PostScript and PDF. Beyond the e-mail list alerting service, access to these preprints is by keyword search, author list, date, and number.

The formats of these preprints work best for technically savvy users on an X window platform. Some of the fonts required to display the PDF version must be downloaded for Windows and Mac users. Other technical modifications to Windows and Mac browser or viewer applications may be necessary to view these files, but the target audience of research physicists is often using X window.

Subject Headings: Mathematics; Physics; Preprints

Science: Space Exploration

[899] AEROSP-L Aeronautics and Aerospace History [e-mail list]

Sponsoring Agency: Smithsonian Institution

Primary Access: mailto:listserv@sivm.si.edu with "sub aerosp-l name" in body

Resource Summary: This is an e-mail list for discussion of the history of aeronautics and space.

Subject Headings: E-mail Lists; Aeronautics—History; Space—History

[900] Ames Imaging Library System

Sponsoring Agency: Ames Research Center (ARC)

Primary Access: http://ails.arc.nasa.gov/

Resource Summary: The Ames Imaging Library System is an online library of still images that chronicle the projects and activities of the ARC. Access is by the category index listing or by keyword. A larger, more easily viewed image is also available by clicking on the thumbnail image. The reproductions of photographs are in JPEG format, and each image carries a unique number.

Subject Headings: Aeronautics—Images; Space Flight—Images

[901] Asteroid and Comet Impact Hazard

Sponsoring Agency: National Aeronautics and Space Administration (NASA). Space Science Division

Primary Access: http://ccf.arc.nasa.gov/sst/

Resource Summary: The site provides access to congressional documents and NASA studies related to asteroid and comet impact hazards. The site also provides a complete listing of all known Earth-crossing asteroids and of predicted close approaches to the Earth in the near future. It also offers a bibliography of key scientific papers on the impact hazard.

With recent popular movies exploring the concept of a major impact hazard, this site should prove popular with the general public as well as with scientists taking a more scholarly interest in the phenomena.

Subject Headings: Asteroids; Comets

[902] Center for Mars Exploration

Sponsoring Agency: Ames Research Center (ARC). Space Science Division

Primary Access: http://cmex-www.arc.nasa.gov/

Resource Summary: The Center for Mars Exploration (CMEX) site features a wide range of materials on Mars. These include historical references to Mars, previous Mars mission information, tools to analyze Mars, current Mars news, and papers related to the possibility of life on Mars. This lengthy page includes sections such as Educational Resources, CD-ROM Image Archives, CMEX Software, Mars News and Information, Mars Images, and Mars Tools.

This large collection of Mars-related information is an excellent resource for anyone, from students to professionals, who is interested in researching Mars.

Subject Headings: Mars; Planets

[903] Crustal Dynamics Data Information System (CDDIS)

Sponsoring Agency: Goddard Space Flight Center (GSFC)

Primary Access: http://cddis.gsfc.nasa.gov/cddis.html

Alternative Access Method: ftp://cddis.gsfc.nasa.gov/

Resource Summary: The Crustal Dynamics Data Information System (CDDIS) supports data archiving and distribution activities for the space geodesy and geodynamics community. The main objectives of the system are to store space geodesy- and geodynamics-related data products in a central data bank; to maintain information about the archiving of these data; and to disseminate this data and information. These sites offers access to CDDIS data sets, documents, programs, and reports.

This site is primarily of interest to researchers in this field.

Subject Headings: Data Products—Research; Geophysics

[904] EnviroNET: The Space Environment Information Service

Sponsoring Agency: Goddard Space Flight Center (GSFC)

Primary Access: http://envnet.gsfc.nasa.gov/

Resource Summary: EnviroNET provides models and information on the space environment for the entire space environment community. It is dedicated to supporting NASA's engineering and scientific goals and is aimed at the space scientist and engineer. The site offers information on EnviroNET projects, services, Web computational models, and publications. For contact information, it also features a staff directory.

Although it sports the slogan "Space Environment Information at Your Fingertips," a heavy reliance on large, multimedia files and graphics can make for slow loading. It is also difficult to navigate and would benefit from a simpler design.

Subject Heading: Space

[905] Goddard Space Flight Center

Sponsoring Agency: Goddard Space Flight Center (GSFC)

Primary Access: http://pao.gsfc.nasa.gov/

Alternative Access Method: http://www.gsfc.nasa.gov/

Resource Summary: The mission of Goddard Space Flight Center is to expand knowledge of the Earth and its environment, the solar system, and the universe through observations from space. Goddard is the lead Center in the Mission to Planet Earth program, NASA's long term, coordinated research effort to study the Earth as a global environmental system. The Welcome page has information about Goddard, its goals, and its facilities. The Goddard Missions section offers information about observatories in orbit, upcoming flight missions, sounding rockets, and balloons that carry payloads into the atmosphere. The Space Sciences page focuses on orbiting spacecraft and their observations, while the Earth Sciences page covers the Earth as a global environmental system. For access to the many offices and subsidiary programs at GSFC, the Goddard Organizations page and the Goddard Organizations and Projects page provide a hierarchical listing of the many Goddard links. The site also features sections such as the Newsroom, Education Programs, and Public Services and Information.

With a great deal of descriptive information on Goddard and its research areas, this site is useful for people who are interested in the space and earth sciences.

Subject Headings: Atmospheric Studies; Global Change; Space—Research

[906] International Space Station

Sponsoring Agency: National Aeronautics and Space Administration (NASA). International Space Station Office

Primary Access: http://issa-www.jsc.nasa.gov/

Resource Summary: The International Space Station Office is using the Web site as a gateway to information on establishing a permanent human presence in space. The site provides up-to-date information on the space station's progress. In addition, it offers pages on building of the station, technical details, and education tools. For publications, see the Library section, which has some fact sheets and a fact book. The Onboard page gives information on some of the research projects that are being planned for the space station.

Subject Heading: Space Station

[907] John C. Stennis Space Center

Sponsoring Agency: Stennis Space Center (SSC)

Primary Access: http://www.ssc.nasa.gov/

Resource Summary: SSC is NASA's primary Center for testing large rocket propulsion systems for the space shuttle and for future generation space vehicles. The Web site offers a list of links about the SSC, organizations within the SSC, and SSC services.

Most of the material on this site is descriptive of the Center or is research-level information.

Subject Headings: Propulsion; Space Shuttle

[908] Johnson Space Center

Sponsoring Agency: Johnson Space Center (JSC)

Primary Access: http://www.jsc.nasa.gov/

Resource Summary: With a primary focus on manned space flights and the selection and training of astronauts, the Johnson Space Center organized its Web site by kind of visitor rather than by topic. The kinds of visitors include the Public; Kids; Educators; News Media; Business; and Employees. The Employees page points to an intranet available only to JSC employees and contractors; however, the link does offer access to information on how to become an employee or contractor. The Public page provides access to a staff directory, press releases, a virtual tour, and detailed information on the space shuttle and international space station programs.

Most of the material on this site is geared toward the public, the press, and business users. Researchers not affiliated with JSC will have a difficult time finding much research-level information. It is an excellent site for students and teachers to find material for education related to humans in space, manned space flights, and basic astronomy.

Subject Headings: Astronauts; Astronomy—Study and Teaching; Space—Effects on Humans—Research; Space Flight; Space Shuttle; Space Station

[909] Lewis Research Center

Sponsoring Agency: Lewis Research Center (LeRC)

Primary Access: http://www.lerc.nasa.gov/

Resource Summary: Researching aeronautics and propulsion technologies is LeRC's main focus, but its research areas also include space applications involving power and on-board propulsion; commercial communications and launch vehicles; and microgravity research. Their Web site presents basic information about LeRC, and then makes the bulk of their site available by Subject Area, Organization, Project, Information Resource, or Search Query. Under the Subject Area section, the Online Publications category provides access to LeRC technical reports, LeRC images, and a guide to technical report writings.

Subject Headings: Aeronautics—Research; Power; Propulsion; Research Laboratories

[910] Liftoff to Space Exploration

Sponsoring Agency: National Aeronautics and Space Administration (NASA)

Primary Access: http://liftoff.msfc.nasa.gov/

Alternative Access Methods: http://liftoff.msfc.nasa.gov/home/liftoffnpi.html [non-plug-in version]
http://astro-2.msfc.nasa.gov/

Resource Summary: With daily updates, NASA news and headlines, and astronaut information, the Liftoff site provides an excellent overview of U.S. space program news and current missions. On the main pages, news and current events information includes top headlines from NASA news, the day's events at NASA, the day's events in space, and a historical look at the current day in space history. Liftoff also has pages entitled Visitor's Port; Mission Operations; Station; Astronauts; Space Academy; and Kid's Space. It includes a Java implementation of a spacecraft tracking program, J-Track. This can be used to track current positions of the Hubble Telescope, the space station Mir, and the space shuttles.

Geared toward the public and children, this site offers a substantial amount of news and information for anyone interested in the space program. The Kid's Space section makes this an excellent site to show to children interested in the space program.

Subject Headings: Astronauts; Hubble Telescope; Space—Education; Space Station; Space Shuttle

[911] Lunar and Planetary Institute

Sponsoring Agency: Lunar and Planetary Institute (LPI)

Primary Access: http://cass.jsc.nasa.gov/

Resource Summary: The Lunar and Planetary Institute is a research institute that focuses on research into the current state, evolution, and formation of the solar system. The Web site features links to Research Resources, Meetings and Conferences, Education Resources, Publications, and Exploring the Moon. The Research Resources page includes access to some information-rich sources such as the Stereo Atlas of the Solar System, Clementine Images of the Moon, and Crater Databases for Ganymede and Venus. The Publications page features an online version of the *Lunar and Planetary Information Bulletin*, some conference publications, and the *Solar System Express*, a monthly abstract journal from LPI.

Subject Headings: Moon; Planets; Solar System

[912] Mars Exploration Program

Sponsoring Agency: Jet Propulsion Laboratory (JPL)

Primary Access: http://www.jpl.nasa.gov/mars/

Resource Summary: With detailed information on the various exploratory missions on Mars, this site features the sections: Mars Pathfinder; Mars Global Surveyor; Sojourner Rover; and *The Martian Chronicle*, the electronic newsletter. A more recent addition is the Mars Exploration Education page which provides resources specially tailored for the education community. The subsidiary pages provide detailed information on the missions, on Mars as a planet, and on current events in the program.

Despite the initial appearance, this site offers substantial information resources for the study of Mars.

Subject Headings: Mars; Planets

[913] Marshall Space Flight Center

Sponsoring Agency: Marshall Space Flight Center

Primary Access: http://www.msfc.nasa.gov/

Resource Summary: Marshall's primary mission is to develop and maintain space transportation and propulsion systems and to conduct microgravity research. Their Web site provides a broad range of technical and background information on the many projects, scientific disciplines, and specific space flight missions with which the Center is involved. The General Information page gives basic information on the Center. The Space Science Missions and Space Flight Projects pages give information on specific flights and ongoing research and the Technical Home Page link gives access to a directory of Marshall Web sites.

Subject Headings: Propulsion; Space Flight

[914] NASA Ames Research Center

Sponsoring Agencies: Ames Research Center (ARC); National Aeronautics and Space Administration (NASA)

Primary Access: http://www.arc.nasa.gov/

Resource Summary: The top level page for the Ames site offers three different sets of pages for text browsers; for enhanced browsers that support frames and Java; and for basic graphical browsers that do not support frames or Java. After choosing a browser, the site features sections related to its research mission in the aeronautics, space, and intelligent systems areas. These sections include News; About Ames; Organization; Doing Business; Kids and Teachers; Resources Support; and the Hi-Bandwidth Zone. The Organization section offers links to the many subsidiary ARC Web sites organized by directorate. The Hi-Bandwith Zone features large video and virtual reality files demonstrating some ARC equipment and facilities.

The site offers a substantial amount of research and popular information, but much is buried within the directorates and offices sites. While some information is readily available from the main pages for students and teachers, for businesses and for researchers it may take some time to locate more substantial resources. The site map and the keyword search options can be helpful in the search process.

Subject Headings: Aeronautics; Research Laboratories; Space—Research

[915] NASA Jet Propulsion Laboratory

Sponsoring Agency: Jet Propulsion Laboratory (JPL)

Primary Access: http://www.jpl.nasa.gov/

Resource Summary: The Jet Propulsion Laboratory is the lead U.S. center for robotic exploration of the solar system. JPL spacecraft have visited all known planets except Pluto. Their Web site features information on Earth, the other planets, the universe and space technology. The JPL Missions page gives information on specific robotic spacecraft and the accomplishments of their missions.

For multimedia information on the planets or the universe, see the Pictures and Videos page. The Information section includes press releases, fact sheets, status reports, an educator archive, and historical records. The Web Directory provides an alphabetical list of all the JPL Web pages.

Subject Headings: Planets; Space Flight

[916] NASA Kennedy Space Center

Sponsoring Agency: Kennedy Space Center (KSC)

Primary Access: http://www.ksc.nasa.gov/

Alternative Access Methods: http://www.spaceportusa.com/main.html
ftp://ftp.ksc.nasa.gov/

Resource Summary: The Kennedy Space Center has the primary responsibility for ground turnaround and support operations, prelaunch checkout, and launch of the space shuttle and its payloads, including NASA's eventual Space Station. The site features information on recent NASA missions; an unorganized list of other KSC Web sites under the heading Additional KSC Servers; and general information pages on KSC. These latter pages include a shuttle reference manual, frequently asked questions, a staff directory, and information on KSC facilities.

While the primary KSC page consists of a long page of links with little visual organization, the KSC Visitor Center page (at the first alternate URL) functions much better as an entry point for the general public and for prospective visitors to KSC. Another alternative is the Public Affairs site.

Subject Headings: Space Flight; Space Shuttle; Space Station

[917] NASA Langley Research Center

Sponsoring Agency: Langley Research Center (LaRC)

Primary Access: http://www.larc.nasa.gov/

Resource Summary: As a major center for aeronautics, atmospheric sciences, and space technology, The Langley Research Center offers a Web site featuring information about itself and its research areas. The General Information category includes procurement information, announcements, directories, and an overview of the LaRC. The Langley Projects, Teams, and Initiatives Online section provides an alphabetical listing of projects with Web sites. Langley Organizations Online provides access to the major administrative components of LaRC along with an organizational browser for lesser divisions. Much of the primary content on the site is available under the Langley Technology Access Services, which presents some targeted customer interfaces, software, images, technical reports, and special highlights and showcases.

With a wide collection of aeronautical information, this site is an important resource for researchers in aeronautics.

Subject Headings: Aeronautics—Research; Research Laboratories; Space Flight

[918] NASA Observatorium

Sponsoring Agency: National Aeronautics and Space Administration (NASA)

Primary Access: http://observe.ivv.nasa.gov/

Resource Summary: NASA's Observatorium is designed for the general public and provides access to images of and information about the Earth, the planets, and stars. Access to this information is through categories such as Image Gallery, Space Science, Spaceflight, Fun and Games, Education, Aeronautics, and Planet Earth. The level of material is demonstrated by titles such as See How It Flies and Earth —The Everchanging Planet.

This is an excellent site for students, teachers, and the public who they are searching for basic information on aeronautics and the space sciences.

Subject Headings: Planets; Space—Education; Space—Images

[919] NASA Online Information

Sponsoring Agency: National Aeronautics and Space Administration (NASA)

Primary Access: http://www.larc.nasa.gov/nasaonline/

Resource Summary: This site provides a list of links to other NASA sites. Beginning with links to the main NASA site and NASA Information by Subject Area, the site then provides a hierarchical listing of some of the many NASA Internet sites.

While this page does not come close to covering all of the NASA Web sites, it has good coverage of NASA Gopher servers, ftp archives, telnet resources, and even a WAIS directory.

Subject Heading: Finding Aid—NASA

[920] NASA Shuttle Web

Sponsoring Agency: National Aeronautics and Space Administration (NASA)

Primary Access: http://shuttle.nasa.gov/

Resource Summary: The official space shuttle site provides up-to-the-minute information on the latest space shuttle mission. Preflight, launch, orbit, and landing information are readily accessible along with an overview and a crew listing. A photo gallery and video gallery feature multimedia clips from recent events. There is a visitor's guest book to sign, functional help screens, and an archive of past space shuttle information. Available real-time data on the shuttle includes telemetry data, tracking displays, and sightings.

Not only is the layout of this site beautifully arranged, but the information content is current and available in various multimedia formats. It is an excellent example of what the Web can offer and features information of broad popular appeal.

Subject Heading: Space Shuttle

[921] NASA Space Calender

Sponsoring Agency: National Aeronautics and Space Administration (NASA)

Primary Access: http://newproducts.jpl.nasa.gov/calendar/

Resource Summary: NASA's Space Calendar covers space-related activities and anniversaries for the coming year. Included are over 700 links to related Web pages. The Calendar includes historical events such as the launching of various spacecraft, conferences, current launch dates, and celestial events such as an eclipse or perihelion.

This is an excellent resource for amateur astronomers and those interested in the history of space exploration.

Subject Headings: Daily Events; Space—History

[922] National Aeronautics and Space Administration

Sponsoring Agencies: National Aeronautics and Space Administration (NASA); National Aeronautics and Space Administration. Information Services

Primary Access: http://www.nasa.gov/

Alternative Access Method: http://www.gsfc.nasa.gov/NASA_homepage.html

Resource Summary: The central NASA Web server provides access to the hundreds of NASA Web sites and to basic information on the agency itself. A Welcome page includes a welcome message, user tips on helper applications, and a search engine for top level NASA pages. The Today@NASA link features breaking news such as recent Hubble Space Telescope Images, links to the shuttle Web site, and the latest news releases. For organizational access to other NASA pages, the NASA Organization, Go To, and NASA Centers links can be used. Subject approach to NASA information is available through pages titled Aeronautics, Space Science, Mission to Planet Earth, Human Space Flight, and Technology Development. The Questions and Answers page lists answers to frequently asked questions.

While other NASA sites can provide more direct access to specific sections of NASA projects, they can also all be found from this page.

Subject Headings: Aeronautics; Space

[923] The Planetary Rings Node

Sponsoring Agency: Ames Research Center (ARC)

Primary Access: http://ringside.arc.nasa.gov/

Resource Summary: The Rings Node of the Planetary Data System is devoted to archiving, cataloging, and distributing scientific data sets relevant to planetary ring systems. For the general public, the page features a Fun Stuff section which includes images, animations, and artwork for Jupiter, Saturn, Uranus, and Neptune. For the scientist, the site features Tools—which provides online tools and calculation routines; Data Sets—which includes the Rings Node Data Set Catalog; history, background, instrument descriptions, and data from the Voyager Mission; and the 1995-1996 Saturn Ring Plane Crossings.

Subject Heading: Planets—Ring Systems

[924] Planetary Sciences at the NSSDC

Sponsoring Agency: National Space Science Data Center (NSSDC)

Primary Access: http://nssdc.gsfc.nasa.gov/planetary/

Resource Summary: The National Space Science Data Center is responsible for the distribution of planetary images and other data to scientists, educators, and the general public. This site offers a separate page for each planet as well as for asteroids and comets. Each of these sections features fact sheets, images, and Frequently Asked Questions files. In addition, information about space-craft missions to the various planetary bodies is provided.

This site offers a substantial body of textual and pictorial information for all the planets in our solar system. Information is available at many levels, from children to research scientists. It is definitely worth a visit for anyone needing basic information of images of the planets, asteroids, or comets.

Subject Headings: Asteroids; Comets; Planets

[925] Project Galileo: Bringing Jupiter to Earth

Sponsoring Agency: Jet Propulsion Laboratory (JPL)

Primary Access: http://www.jpl.nasa.gov/galileo/

Alternative Access Methods: http://galileo.ivv.nasa.gov/ [mirror]
mailto:majordomo@sender.jpl.nasa.gov with "subscribe galileo" in body

Resource Summary: The Galileo site provides an extensive collection of information on the Galileo spacecraft and on the planet Jupiter. The site includes just-released images and data from Jupiter, a brief introduction to the mission, and an online guide to Galileo's exploration of Jupiter. Available sections of the page include Latest News, Countdown, Spacecraft, Jupiter, Images, Mission, K-12, and Online. The Galileo status reports and press releases are available via e-mail at the alternate mailto URL listed.

Much of the material is obviously aimed at students and teachers, although the site is equally useful for the general public. Researchers would probably prefer more ready access to some of the data from Galileo.

Subject Headings: Jupiter; Planets; Space—Education

[926] Shuttle Solar Backscatter Ultraviolet Project

Sponsoring Agency: Goddard Space Flight Center (GSFC)

Primary Access: http://ssbuv.gsfc.nasa.gov/

Resource Summary: Offering general information and measurement of atmospheric ozone, this site uses ozone measurements made during space shuttle flights. Each specific shuttle mission that has had an ozone measurement component has a link to that mission. The site also offers the sections, Ozone Maps and Solar Spectral Irradiance Plots. The flight results appear in their Publications section. For the general public, the site has an online factsheet titled, Ozone: What Is It, and Why Do We Care About It?

Subject Headings: Ozone; Space Shuttle

[927] SOHO - The Solar and Heliospheric Observatory

Sponsoring Agencies: European Space Agency; National Aeronautics and Space Administration (NASA)

Primary Access: http://sohowww.nascom.nasa.gov/

Alternative Access Methods: http://sohowww.nascom.nasa.gov/index-text.html [text version] mailto:majordomo@sohomail.nascom.nasa.gov with "subscribe sohonews" in body ftp://sohoftp.nascom.nasa.gov/

Resource Summary: The SOHO Internet sites provide information, status, and goals of the SOHO mission. The information is aimed at the public as well as to the international solar physics and solar-terrestrial physics communities. The Web site offers a broad range of information on the mission in categories such as What's New; Contents; The Mission; Instruments; Institutions; Publications; Gallery; SOHO Archive; Operations; Latest Images; and Space, Solar Physics, and Astrophysics. Both the What's New page and the mailing list provide updates of changes to the site along with new features. The Contents page provides a hierarchical display of the Web site while the Publications page features press releases, a SOHO bibliography (in Postscript format), SOHO documentation, and a few SOHO scientific reports and publications.

Subject Headings: Observatories; Solar Physics; Solar-Terrestrial Physics

[928] Space Station Biological Research Project

Sponsoring Agency: Ames Research Center (ARC)

Primary Access: http://pyroeis.arc.nasa.gov/

Resource Summary: The Space Station Biological Research Project is responsible for the facilities that will be used to conduct life sciences research on board the International Space Station. Their Web site describes the gravitational biology laboratory that is being planned for the Space Station and it provides links to more information on some of the instrumentation. Additional links are available including Science and Research Information, Space Life Sciences, and Frequently Asked Questions.

Subject Headings: Biology—Research; Space Station

[929] Spacelink

Sponsoring Agency: National Aeronautics and Space Administration (NASA)

Primary Access: http://spacelink.msfc.nasa.gov/

Resource Summary: Spacelink is a NASA resource developed specifically as an aeronautics and space resource for educators. It is designed to provide current and historical educational information on space, NASA, and aeronautics to teachers and students. Offerings include teacher guides; pictures; computer software; and science, mathematics, engineering and technology education lesson plans. Further offerings include: information on NASA educational programs and services; current status reports on agency projects and events; news releases; and television broadcasts schedules for NASA Television.

By creating this site specifically for the education community and by building a large collection of relevant files, NASA has created becomes an essential stop for anyone in the education community interested in space and aeronautical sciences.

Subject Headings: Aeronautics—Education; Lesson Plans; Space—Education

SuDoc Numbers: NAS 1.49/2: *Educational Horizons*

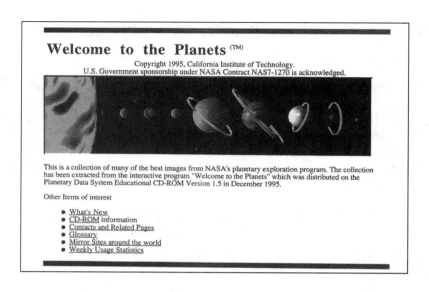

Welcome to the Planets (TM)

Copyright 1995, California Institute of Technology.
U.S. Government sponsorship under NASA Contract NAS7-1270 is acknowledged.

This is a collection of many of the best images from NASA's planetary exploration program. The collection has been extracted from the interactive program "Welcome to the Planets" which was distributed on the Planetary Data System Educational CD-ROM Version 1.5 in December 1995.

Other Items of interest

- What's New
- CD-ROM information
- Contacts and Related Pages
- Glossary
- Mirror Sites around the world
- Weekly Usage Statistics

[930] Welcome to the Planets

Sponsoring Agency: Jet Propulsion Laboratory (JPL)

Primary Access: http://pds.jpl.nasa.gov/planets/

Alternative Access Methods: http://scruffy.phast.umass.edu/welcome.html [mirror]
http://www.phys.ttu.edu/www_root/planets/welcome.htm [mirror]
http://www-hpcc.astro.washington.edu/mirrors/planets/ [mirror]
http://www.eps.mcgill.ca/wtp/planets/ [mirror]
http://www.ast.cam.ac.uk/Pictures/planets/ [mirror]
http://www.univ-rennes1.fr/ASTRO/planets/welcome.html [mirror]
http://www.curtin.edu.au/mirror/planets/ [mirror]
http://titan.ica.luz.ve/planets/ [mirror]

Resource Summary: This is a collection of many of the best images from NASA's planetary exploration program. The collection has been extracted from the interactive CD-ROM *Welcome to the Planets*. The basic organization of the site provides links to pictures of each of the planets in our solar system. It then links to the category, The Explorers which include information about the spacecraft and other instruments that took the pictures. Each link provides basic information on the planet or explorer, along with a list and explanation of the available images.

This is an excellent site for anyone seeking background information and images of the planets.

Subject Heading: Planets

SuDoc Number: NAS 1.86:P 69/CD *Welcome to the Planets*

CHAPTER 14: SOCIAL SERVICES

The government has been active in social services for decades, but this area of government information has lagged far behind most others in disseminating its information on the Internet. However, the Social Services category includes some sites with significant resources for consumers, veterans, Native Americans, welfare recipients, and workers.

The featured site for this chapter is from a link off of the White House's Web site—Commonly Requested Federal Services. This is one of the very few finding aids for information on government services.

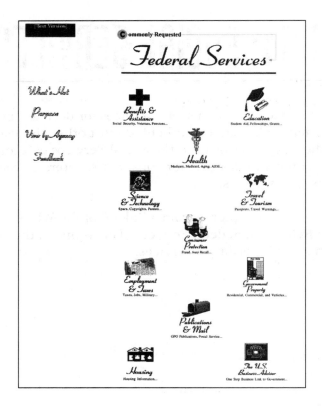

[931] Commonly Requested Federal Services

Sponsoring Agency: White House

Primary Access: http://www.whitehouse.gov/WH/Services/

Alternative Access Method: http://www.whitehouse.gov/WH/Services/index-plain. html [text version]

Resource Summary: While there is no single government site which points to all of the government social services sites, sections of this page can at least point to some of the sites. As part of the White House Web page, check under the headings Benefits and Assistance; Housing; and Consumer Protection for social services information. Under each of these headings are descriptions of frequently requested services, links to the Web site of the agency providing the services, and links to specific subsections of those Web sites that answer particular questions.

While this site is broader than just social services, it can be a helpful finding aid for many commonly asked questions regarding social services.

Subject Heading: Finding Aid—Social Services

Social Services: General

[932] Ancestry's Social Security Death Index Online Search

Sponsoring Agencies: Ancestry, Inc.; Social Security Administration (SSA)

Primary Access: http://www.ancestry.com/SSDI/Main.htm

Resource Summary: Made available by a commercial genealogical publishing company, the Social Security Death Index is searchable by name, Social Security number, location issued, birth information, death information, and last residence or lump sum payment information. Records include the individual's birth date, death date, Social Security number, and last residence.

The Social Services resources are divided into four sections. The first section covers general resources as well as sites that do not fit under the other categories. This section runs from entry numbers 932 to 945. Housing and Community Development, the second section, features resources related to social services for homes and communities and covers entries 946-952. The third section, Welfare and Benefits, contains sites with information on public welfare and benefits programs and includes entries 953-961. The last category, Workers, has sites that deal with issues related to labor and displaced workers. This section runs from entry 962 to 970.

Ancestry, Inc., should be commended for making this database available on the Internet and for clearly giving the date of the database near the title. Searching is easy and the database should prove useful to genealogists and anyone interested in tracking family ancestry.

Subject Heading: Genealogy

[933] Bureau of Indian Affairs

Sponsoring Agency: Bureau of Indian Affairs (BIA)

Primary Access: http://www.doi.gov/bureau-indian-affairs.html

Resource Summary: The BIA site features a variety of descriptive information on the agency, its functions, and services. Major categories include Native American Ancestry, BIA Press Releases, Area Offices, Tribal Leaders List, Tribal Courts List, Freedom of Information Act and Privacy Act Officers and Coordinators, BIA's Division of Energy and Mineral Resources, Water Resources Technician Training Program, Office of Indian Education Programs, and Indian Health Services.

Providing a good descriptive overview of the BIA, the site is useful for basic information. It will not be useful for searching for more in-depth information such as details on individual tribes or reservations.

Subject Heading: American Indians

[934] Child, Youth, and Family Network

Sponsoring Agency: Cooperative State, Research, Education and Extension Service

Primary Access: http://www.cyfernet.mes.umn.edu/

Alternative Access Method: gopher://cyfer.esusda.gov/11/CYFER-net

Resource Summary: The Child, Youth, and Family Network (CYFERNet) provides practical, research-based, children, youth, and family information within these categories: Health, Child Care, Building Organizational Collaborations, Promoting Family Strength, Science and Technology Programs, and Strengthening Community-Based Programs. In addition to these links, the site offers sections divided by kind of user: Resources for Children, Youth, and Family Professionals; Especially for Parents; and Kidspace Especially for Children and Youth.

Originally a Gopher resource, both the Web and Gopher versions continue to provide a large collection of material for children, parents, and family professionals on a wide variety of subjects relevant to children and families.

Subject Headings: Children; Families

[935] CodeTalk

Sponsoring Agencies: Department of Agriculture (USDA); Department of Commerce (DOC); Department of Housing and Urban Development (HUD)

Primary Access: http://www.codetalk.fed.us/

Resource Summary: CodeTalk is an information-sharing network for and about Native Americans. It is sponsored by federal agencies that operate Native American programs. The name is based on the Native American CodeTalkers, heroes of two World Wars. Included in the site is government program information, an electronic consultations feature, and links to other interesting Native American Internet information. The site includes the headings: News Clips; Topics of Interest; Consultation; About CodeTalk; Document Library; Planet Youth; Calendar of Events; Scenes from Indian Country; and Resources and Contacts. Press releases related to Indians from the different agencies are available under the heading News Clips. A special area for youth is entitled Planet Youth section. The Document Library section includes relevant online publications from various federal agencies, although very few have online links at this point.

This is an excellent site for a broad overview of federal activities of interest to the American Indian community.

Subject Heading: American Indians

[936] Consumer Product Safety Commission

Sponsoring Agency: Consumer Product Safety Commission (CPSC)

Primary Access: http://cpsc.gov/

Alternative Access Methods: http://www.cpsc.gov/
gopher://cpsc.gov/

Resource Summary: The Consumer Product Safety Commission site aims to further the organizations mission of reducing the risk of injury or death from consumer products. It includes sections entitled: About Us/Vacancies; Business/Contracts; Consumer; News Desk; Library; Public Calendar; Talk to Us; and Search. The Talk to Us area is used for reporting unsafe products. Product recalls can be found within the Press Releases section under the Consumer and News Desk area. The Search feature, which uses a WAIS search, also can retrieve product recalls. The Publications section includes access to the full text of the *Consumer Product Safety Review*. The *Annual Report* is available on the Gopher.

Both for reporting defective consumer products and for seeing what products have been recalled, this is a useful site. The Search option and titling of documents could be improved since search results may just show up with a numeric title. An alphabetical product title list would be helpful as well.

Subject Headings: Consumer Information; Safety

SuDoc Numbers: Y 3.C 76/3:28 *Consumer Product Safety Review*
Y 3.C 76/3:1 *Annual Report*

[937] Corporation for National Service

Sponsoring Agency: Corporation for National and Community Service

Primary Access: http://www.cns.gov/

Resource Summary: This Web site features information on the volunteer and service organization which the Corporation for National and Community Service oversees. These include Americorps, Senior Corps, Learn and Serve America (for students), and National Service Scholars. The site also features a section on Resources for service volunteers.

Subject Headings: Americorps; Volunteerism

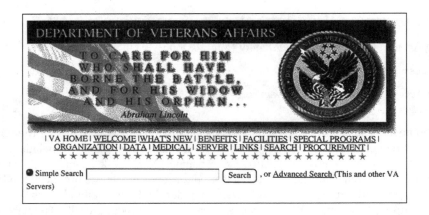

[938] Department of Veterans Affairs

Sponsoring Agency: Department of Veterans Affairs (VA)

Primary Access: http://www.va.gov/

Resource Summary: The VA Web site features a variety of sections useful to veterans and those helping veterans claim benefits. The principal categories include: What's New; Benefits; Facilities; Special Programs; Medical; Data; and Organization. Under the Benefits heading, the site provides English and Spanish versions of *Federal Benefits for Veterans and Dependents* along with a list of VA cemeteries and various VA forms. The Facilities section includes lists of contact numbers and locations of VA facilities. The Special Programs area includes a section for Bosnia veterans and a Persian Gulf Veteran's Illness page.

This well-designed site provides useful information in many of the VA service areas. It should prove useful to veterans and anyone involved in assisting veterans.

Subject Headings: Gulf War Veterans' Disease; Veterans

SuDoc Numbers: VA 1.10/3: *Persian Gulf Review*
VA 1.19:80 *Federal Benefits for Veterans and Dependents*
VA 1.43/5: *Summary of Medical Programs*
VA 1.95/2: *Board of Veterans' Appeals Decisions*

[939] Food and Consumer Service

Sponsoring Agency: Food and Consumer Service (FCS)

Primary Access: http://www.usda.gov/fcs/

Alternative Access Methods: ftp://fwux.fedworld.gov/pub/fcs/fcs.htm
ftp://fwux.fedworld.gov/pub/fcs/

Resource Summary: This Food and Consumer Service site features information on its services such as the Women, Infants, and Children (WIC) and food stamps programs. The site includes a brief collection of documents on Welfare Reform. Its main sections include FCS Library of Files, FCS Research and Evaluation, Food Stamp Program, Food Distribution Programs, Child Nutrition Programs, WIC Program, Gleaning and Food Recovery, Team Nutrition, and Center for Nutrition Policy and Promotion. Each section provides basic information on the programs including information on applying, hotline numbers, and basic fact sheets.

This site provides an excellent overview of FCS programs and should prove useful to anyone needing information on them.

Subject Headings: Consumer Information; Food Stamps; Nutrition; Welfare

SuDoc Numbers: A 1.38:1528 *Expenditures on Children by Families*
A 98.17: *WIC Program and Participants Characteristics*
A 98.19/2: *Cost of Food at Home Estimated for Food Plans at Four Cost Levels*

[940] Inter-American Foundation

Sponsoring Agency: Inter-American Foundation (IAF)

Primary Access: http://www.iaf.gov/

Resource Summary: The Inter-American Foundation is a foreign assistance program. The IAF has worked in Latin America and the Caribbean to promote equitable, responsive, and participatory self-help development by awarding grants directly to local organizations throughout the region. Their Web site features a descriptive brochure along with sections titled Fellowship Programs, Program Guidelines, Resource Mobilization, and Local Development. It also offers links to information in Spanish and Portuguese.

Subject Headings: Central America; Foreign Assistance; South America

[941] Library of Congress Prisoner of War Database

Sponsoring Agencies: Library of Congress (LC); Task Force Russia

Primary Access: http://lcweb2.loc.gov/pow/powhome.html

Resource Summary: This database has been established to assist researchers interested in investigating U.S. government documents pertaining to U.S. military personnel killed, missing, or imprisoned in Southeast Asia during or after the conclusion of American involvement in the Vietnam War. The title of this collection is Correlated and Uncorrelated Information Relating to Missing Americans in Southeast Asia. The database does not contain full-text documents, but the site explains how the actual documents can be obtained. The site also provides access to documents from Task Force Russia—an attempt to locate Americans thought to have been held in the former Soviet Union.

Subject Headings: Bibliographic Databases; Prisoners of War; Veterans; Vietnam War

[942] PAVNET Online: Partnerships Against Violence

Sponsoring Agencies: Department of Agriculture (USDA); Department of Defense (DoD); Department of Education (ED); Department of Health and Human Services (HHS); Department of Housing and Urban Development (HUD); Department of Justice (DOJ); Department of Labor (DOL)

Primary Access: http://www.pavnet.org/

Alternative Access Methods: gopher://cyfer.esusda.gov/11/PAVnet
mailto:majordomo@nal.usda.gov with "subscribe pavnet" in body

Resource Summary: PAVNET Online seeks to provide information about effective violence prevention initiatives. The sites include information about violence and youth-at-risk, representing data from seven different federal agencies. The Web site is primarily a front-end to the Gopher, which contains most of the information content. The main Gopher sections include the headings, About PAVNET Online; Promising Programs; Funding Sources for Violence Prevention; and Information Sources and Technical Assistance. The Web site also features forms for individuals to add their anti-violence program or for researching the PAVNET database.

PAVNET is a useful resource for finding basic and advanced information on violence prevention.

Subject Headings: Families; Violence

[943] Public Health Service

Sponsoring Agencies: Department of Health and Human Services (HHS); Public Health Service (PHS)

Primary Access: http://phs.os.dhhs.gov/phs/phs.html

Resource Summary: The Public Health Service Web site is shutting down due to the reorganization of the Department of Health and Human Services. However, for now at least, the page still points to the Web sites for the components formerly overseen by the PHS. These links consist of Public Health Service Agencies; Public Health Service Program Offices; Public Health Service Support Activities; and PHS Vacancy Announcements.

This site is still useful for finding information formerly available from the PHS, however, it does not say how long the site will be operating. Once it is finally down, look for the relevant agencies from the main HHS Web site.

Subject Heading: Public Health

[944] U.S. Access Board

Sponsoring Agencies: Access Board; Architectural and Transportation Barriers Compliance Board

Primary Access: http://www.access-board.gov/

Resource Summary: The U.S. Access Board, also known as the Architectural and Transportation Barriers Compliance Board serves as the only independent federal agency whose primary mission is to create accessibility for people with disabilities. Their Web site features links entitled: About the Access Board, Building and Facility Design Guidelines, Transportation Vehicle Guidelines, Enforcement, Publications, Training, and Telecommunications. The Publications section includes access to an online version of their newsletter, *Access Currents*, and to bibliographic lists of publications. The online version of the Americans with Disabilities Act *Accessibility Guidelines for Buildings and Facilities* is available on the Building and Facility Design Guidelines page.

Subject Headings: Americans with Disabilities Act; Disabilities

SuDoc Numbers: Y 3.B 27: *Access Currents*
Y 3.B 27:8 AM 3/2/ *Accessibility Guidelines for Buildings and Facilities*

[945] United States Commission on Civil Rights

Sponsoring Agency: Commission on Civil Rights

Primary Access: http://www.usccr.gov/

Resource Summary: After a brief description of the Commission, this site features categories such as Commission Information; Publications; Commission Meeting Calendar; State Advisory Committee Meeting Schedule; Regional Offices; Information on Filing a Complaint; and News Releases.

The site provides basic information on the Commission and its regional office. It has relatively little content beyond that.

Subject Heading: Civil Rights

Social Services: Housing and Community Development

[946] Community Connections: Putting People First

Sponsoring Agency: Department of Housing and Urban Development (HUD). Office of Community Planning and Development (CPD)

Primary Access: http://www.comcon.org/

Resource Summary: This site serves state and local agencies, nonprofit organizations, public interest groups, and others interested in housing and community development. The site features sections including: About Community Connections; What's New; Newsletter; Consolidated Plan Summaries; CPD Program Information; Funding Information; and Databases. The Databases section promises that a Training and Technical Assistance Database will be available in that category. The Newsletter section includes a few PDF versions of the newsletter, *Community Connections*.

This site still needs to grow in the depth of its content and assuming it does, it will be a very useful site for those researching community development.

Subject Headings: Community Development; Housing

SuDoc Number: HH 1.108/2: *Community Connections*

[947] Federal Housing Finance Board

Sponsoring Agency: Federal Housing Finance Board

Primary Access: http://www.nal.usda.gov/ric/fhfb/

Resource Summary: This site features background information on the Federal Housing Finance Board, some of its programs, and other information on federal government home finance programs. It includes descriptions of the Affordable Housing Program and the Community Investment Program along with case studies from each.

Subject Headings: Housing; Mortgages

[948] Homes and Communities

Sponsoring Agency: Department of Housing and Urban Development (HUD)

Primary Access: http://www.hud.gov/

Alternative Access Method: gopher://gopher.hud.gov/

Resource Summary: The HUD Web site features a For Citizens section and a For Community and Business Partners area. Under the heading For Citizens there are tips on home buying, mortgage shopping, finding affordable rental housing, and getting involved in the local community. In the For Community and Business Partners area there is information about funding, technical assistance, best practices, contracting opportunities, and major HUD initiatives. Other links off the top level page include: Site Map; Local Offices; Search; and Comments.

Beautifully designed, this site offers a great deal of information useful for consumers and for businesses. Multiple access points are provided making it an easy site to navigate. The Gopher does not provide as much information or such easy access, but it does contain updated information.

Subject Headings: Community Development; Housing

[949] HUD's Client Information and Policy System

Sponsoring Agency: Department of Housing and Urban Development (HUD)

Primary Access: http://www.aspensys.com/hudclips/

Alternative Access Methods: http://www.hud.gov/hudclip.html
gopher://srv1.aspensys.com/11/hudclips
telnet://bbs@198.77.70.82:23/

Resource Summary: HUDCLIPS (HUD Client Information and Policy System) is a searchable online database containing the entire inventory of official HUD policies. HUDCLIPS is only available to registered users, but registration is free. It offers full-text search and retrieval capabilities.

While this site is useful only to subscribers, it does offer access to an important collection of HUD-related documents. There is also a HUDCLIPS-Plus server available from the Gopher URL for which a fee is required.

Subject Headings: Housing; Electronic Publications

[950] HUD User

Sponsoring Agency: Department of Housing and Urban Development (HUD). Office of Policy Development and Research

Primary Access: http://www.huduser.org/

Alternative Access Methods: http://huduser.aspensys.com/
gopher://huduser.org:73/11/
gopher://huduser.aspensys.com:73/

Resource Summary: HUD User is the primary source for federal government reports and information on housing policy and programs, building technology, economic development, urban planning, and other housing-related topics. HUD User also creates and distributes a variety of other information products and services. The main sections of the site include: About HUD User; What's New; Publications; HUD User Database; Data Available From HUD User; and Search HUD User. While there are a few online full-text publications available under the Publications heading, the HUD User Database offers access to bibliographic information on thousands of reports, articles, case studies, and other research literature on topics related to housing and community development. The Data section includes a significant number of statistical data sets.

HUD User offers a great deal of useful information for the researcher. Perhaps someday, the database will include links to full-text reports, but even without that it can be extremely useful.

Subject Headings: Bibliographic Databases; Community Development; Economic Development; Housing

SuDoc Numbers: HH 1.75/2: *Cityscape*
HH 1.84: *Recent Research Results*
HH 1.120/2: *U.S. Housing Market Conditions*

[951] Neighborhood Networks

Sponsoring Agency: Department of Housing and Urban Development (HUD)

Primary Access: http://www.hud.gov/nnw/nnwindex.html

Resource Summary: Neighborhood Networks aims to enhance the self-sufficiency, employability, and economic self-reliance of low-income families and the elderly living in HUD properties. It accomplished this by providing these residents with on-site access to computer and training resources. Major sections of the site include: About Neighborhood Networks; What's New; Publications; and Locations and Information. The Publications area includes a few PDF pamphlets and newsletters.

The site is useful primarily for providing a description of the program.

Subject Headings: Community Development; Computers; Economic Development; Housing

[952] Office of University Partnerships

Sponsoring Agency: Department of Housing and Urban Development (HUD). Office of University Partnerships (OUP)

Primary Access: http://oup.aspensys.com/

Resource Summary: This Office of University Partnerships functions as a national clearinghouse for disseminating information about HUD's Community Outreach Partnership Centers Program. Their Web site features the categories: About OUP; What's New; OUP Programs; Publications; and OUP Forums. The Forums section offers some Web-based electronic communication forums on the OUP programs. The Publications area points to some OUP publications available from HUD User. The rest of the site contains descriptive information about OUP and its programs.

This site will be of most interest to those involved in OUP programs.

Subject Headings: Community Development; Higher Education

Social Services: Welfare and Benefits

[953] Administration for Children and Families

Sponsoring Agency: Administration for Children and Families (ACF)

Primary Access: http://www.acf.dhhs.gov/

Alternative Access Methods: telnet://158.71.4.8
ftp://158.71.4.8/

Resource Summary: Focusing on child support and programs that strengthen families and help children to succeed, this site offers information on a wide range of federal programs aimed at helping children and families. Main categories featured on this site include: ACF Programs and Administrative Services; Organizational Structure and Staff Information; and ACF in the News. The ACF bulletin board system, available from the alternate URLs, includes additional files of policy documents.

Although it can take awhile to find all the relevant information, this site does offer a substantial number of resources related to children and families and benefits available to them from the government.

Subject Headings: Child Support; Children; Families; Welfare

SuDoc Numbers: HE 24.1: *Office of Child Support Enforcement Annual Report*
HE 24.9: *Child Support Report*
HE 24.15: *Information Memorandum*

[954] Federal Poverty Guidelines

Sponsoring Agency: Department of Health and Human Services (HHS)

Primary Access: http://aspe.os.dhhs.gov/poverty/poverty.htm

Resource Summary: This site includes both a reprint of the Federal Poverty Guidelines as published annually in the *Federal Register* and information about the Guidelines. A brief definition differentiates the Federal Poverty Guidelines from the poverty threshold while the section, For Further Information provides contact numbers and citations.

This is a useful site for checking the current poverty guidelines, especially since it includes additional explanatory information.

Subject Heading: Poverty Level

[955] Green Book

Sponsoring Agencies: Department of Health and Human Services (HHS); House of Representatives. Committee on Ways and Means

Primary Access: http://www.access.gpo.gov/congress/wm001.html

Alternative Access Methods: http://aspe.os.dhhs.gov/GB/gbpage.htm
ftp://ftp.os.dhhs.gov/pub/Greenbook/

Resource Summary: The *Green Book* is a unique collection of program descriptions and historical data on a wide variety of social and economic topics. These topics include Social Security, employment, earnings, welfare, child support, health insurance, the elderly, families with children, poverty, and taxation. The files available from the alternate site are for the 1994 edition and were derived from the CD-ROM version of the book. The most recent edition is at the main URL, available from the House Ways and Means Committee Prints site. For that version, be sure to include the phrase "green book" (including the quotation marks) in the search box to limit the search to just sections from the *Green Book*.

The *Green Book* offers a wealth of information about entitlement programs, and it includes detailed historical statistics. The Web interface presents the table of contents in HTML, and the sections themselves are displayed in an ASCII fixed font so that the tables line up properly.

Subject Headings: Entitlements; Welfare; Social Security

SuDoc Number: Y 4.W 36: 10-7 *Green Book*

[956] Head Start Bureau

Sponsoring Agencies: Administration for Children and Families; Head Start Bureau

Primary Access: http://www.acf.dhhs.gov/programs/hsb

Alternative Access Method: telnet://hsbbs.org

Resource Summary: This site seeks to improve access to resources and communications within the Head Start community. It features the headings: Programs; Current Initiatives and Events; Training and Technical Assistance Regional Network; National Head Start Bulletin Board System; Resource Library; and Frequently Asked Questions.

These sites provide basic information on Head Start programs for the general public and offer some services specific to those involved with Head Start programs.

Subject Headings: Children; Head Start

[957] Health Care Financing Administration - The Medicare and Medicaid Agency

Sponsoring Agency: Health Care Financing Administration

Primary Access: http://www.hcfa.gov/

Resource Summary: This site features detailed information about the Health Care Financing Administration and its Medicare and Medicaid programs, including statistics and publications related to those two programs. Featured categories include: Customer Service; Medicare; Medicaid; Statistics and Data; Laws and Regulations; Publications and Forms; Research and Demonstrations; Public Affairs; and Local Information.

The Publications section includes forms, technical publications, online pamphlets, the *Medicare Handbook*, the *Guide to Health Insurance for People with Medicare*, *Directory of State and Federal Medicaid Officials*, and a wide selection of other manuals and miscellaneous publications.

Fortunately, much of the site clearly differentiates consumer resources from researcher resources. This is an excellent starting point for the general public as well as for those seeking more in-depth information on Medicare and Medicaid.

Subject Headings: Health Insurance; Medicare and Medicaid

SuDoc Numbers: HE 22.8/16: *Medicare Handbook*
HE 22.8/17: *Guide to Health Insurance for People with Medicare*
HE 22.114:St 2/ *Directory of State and Federal Medicaid Officials*

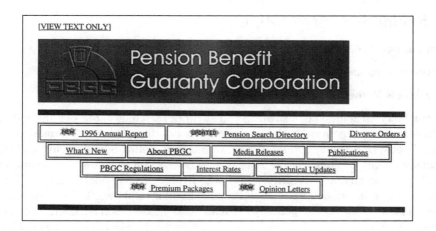

[VIEW TEXT ONLY]

[958] Pension Benefit Guaranty Corporation

Sponsoring Agency: Pension Benefit Guaranty Corporation (PBGC)

Primary Access: http://www.pbgc.gov/

Alternative Access Method: http://www.pbgc.gov/pbgch_ng.htp [text version]

Resource Summary: PBGC is a federal agency that insures and protects pension benefits in certain pension plans. Their Web site features a variety of sections related to pensions insured through PBGC including Pension Search Directory; Premium Packages; Divorce Orders and PBGC What's New; About PBGC; Media Releases; Publications; PBGC Regulations; Interest Rates; and Technical Updates. The Publications area includes a full-text version of the PBGC *Annual Report*.

The site offers a fair amount of information content and should prove useful to anyone seeking information on one of the PBGC-insured pension plans.

Subject Headings: Pensions; Retirement

SuDoc Number: Y 3.P 43:1/ *Annual Report*

[959] Social Security Online

Sponsoring Agency: Social Security Administration (SSA)

Primary Access: http://www.ssa.gov/

Alternative Access Method: http://www.ssa.gov/SSA_Home.html

Resource Summary: In addition to a site map and keyword searching of the site, the SSA site features the following categories: About Social Security's Benefits; Medicare Information; Facts and Figures; Forms; Our Agency and Its History; Online Transaction Services; Financial Status of our Programs; Services for Employers and Businesses; Laws and Regulations; Public Information Resources; How to Reach Social Security; and How to Report Fraud to Social Security. A newly introduced feature is the online request for a Personal Earnings and Benefit Estimate Statement which shows a person's own Social Security earnings history, how much Social Security taxes that person paid into the program, and estimates of future benefits. Publications such as the *Social Security Handbook* are available from the About Social Security's Benefits section. Statistical publications are under Facts and Figures at the Research and Statistical Data and Publications links.

For anyone interested in the Social Security program, this site is a rich source of information.

Subject Headings: Medicare and Medicaid; Social Security

SuDoc Numbers: SSA 1.8/3: *Social Security Handbook*
SSA 1.17: *Recipients by State and County*
SSA 1.17/3: *Earnings and Employment Data for Wage and Salary Workers Covered Under Social Security by State and County*
SSA 1.17/4: *OASDI Beneficiaries by State and County*
SSA 1.24: *Social Security Programs Throughout the World*
SSA 1.26: *Fast Facts and Figures About Social Security*

[960] Thrift Savings Plan

Sponsoring Agency: Federal Retirement Thrift Investment Board

Primary Access: http://www.tsp.gov/

Resource Summary: The Thrift Savings Plan (TSP) is a retirement savings plan for federal employees. This site offers basic information on the TSP. Major sections of the site include TSP Features, Rates of Return, Current Information, Forms and Publications, Calculators, and a Site Map.

Subject Headings: Banking; Government Employees

[961] U.S. Railroad Retirement Board

Sponsoring Agency: Railroad Retirement Board

Primary Access: http://www.rrb.gov/

Resource Summary: Featuring a broad range of information and publications, the site includes categories including News, Publications, Contact Information, Programs Index, and Organization Index. Under the News and Publications heading, there is statistical information, press releases, tax information, and a list of publications, including some online general publications. The Programs Index category includes the links Retirement and Survivor Benefits, Unemployment and Sickness Benefits, Social Security Benefits, Medicare, and Taxation of Benefits. The Organization Index describes the Board, its activities, and its programs.

This site will be of most interest to those involved in the Railroad Retirement program, for whom it offers a considerable amount of useful information on their benefits.

Subject Headings: Railroads; Retirement

Social Services: Workers

[962] Electronic Archive

Sponsoring Agencies: Cornell University. Martin P. Catherwood Library; Commission on Family and Medical Leave; Commission on the Future of Worker-Management Relations; Federal Glass Ceiling Commission; Task Force on Excellence in State and Local Government Through Labor-Management Cooperation

Primary Access: http://www.ilr.cornell.edu/library/e_archive/

Alternative Access Method: ftp://ftp.ilr.cornell.edu/pub/

Resource Summary: The Catherwood Library offers this online archive of government reports from various commissions and task forces that focus on the employer-employee relationship. The documents are in various formats including ASCII, HTML, PostScript, PDF, Microsoft Word, and WordPerfect. All of the newest documents are being converted to PDF or HTML.

This is an excellent archive of reports from commissions that might not otherwise be available on the Web.

Subject Headings: Child Labor; Equal Opportunity; Labor; Minorities; Reports—Full Text

SuDoc Numbers: L 1.2:B 96 *Good for Business: Making Full Use of the Nation's Human Capital*
L 1.2:F 11/4 *Commission on the Future of Worker-Management Relations. Final Report*
L 1.2:W 89/36 *Working Together for Public Service*
L 29.2:C 43 *Forced labor: The Prostitution of Children*
Y 3.2:F 21/W 89 *A Workable Balance*
Y 3.2:G 46/B96 *Good for Business: Making Full Use of the Nation's Human Capital*
Y 3.2:G 46/IN 8 *A Solid Investment: Making Full Use of the Nation's Human Capital*

[963] Empowerment Zone and Enterprise Communities

Sponsoring Agencies: Department of Agriculture (USDA); Department of Housing and Urban Development (HUD)

Primary Access: http://www.ezec.gov/

Alternative Access Method: http://www.ezec.gov/tindex.cgi [text version]

Resource Summary: The Empowerment Zone/Enterprise Communities site is designed to promote the exchange of information about the Presidential Empowerment Initiative. It includes information about the purposes and organization of the Initiative and the Empowerment Zones, Enterprise Communities, and Champion Communities participating in the Initiative. In addition, it provides a toolbox of information to help communities develop and implement effective strategic plans for community and economic development.

This will be of most interest to community leaders who would like to get their communities involved in these initiatives.

Subject Headings: Economic Development; Rural Development

[964] Federal Labor Relations Authority

Sponsoring Agency: Federal Labor Relations Authority (FLRA)

Primary Access: http://www.access.gpo.gov/flra/

Resource Summary: The Federal Labor Relations Authority is an independent agency responsible for administering the labor-management relations program for federal employees. Their Web site includes information on the FLRA, decisions, policies, guidelines, and announcements. The two publications, *FLRA Bulletin* and *FLRA News* are located under the Announcements heading.

Subject Headings: Collective Bargaining; Labor—Government Employees

SuDoc Numbers: Y 3.F 31/21-3:15/ *FLRA Bulletin*
Y 3.F 31/21-3: *FLRA News*

[965] Federal Mediation and Conciliation Service

Sponsoring Agency: Federal Mediation and Conciliation Service (FMCS)

Primary Access: http://www.fmcs.gov/

Alternative Access Method: http://www.fmcs.gov/alt-site/a-welcome.htm [non-frames version]

Resource Summary: FMCS is an independent agency set up to promote sound and stable labor-management relations. Their Web site describes the Service, its programs, and its services. It also offers a phone directory for FMCS and a Public Information page.

Subject Headings: Labor-Management Relations; Mediation

[966] Merit Systems Protection Board

Sponsoring Agency: Merit Systems Protection Board

Primary Access: http://www.access.gpo.gov/mspb/

Resource Summary: The Board serves as guardian of the federal government's merit-based system of employment, principally by hearing and deciding appeals from federal employees of removals and other major personnel actions. The Board also hears and decides other types of civil service cases, reviews significant actions and regulations of the Office of Personnel Management, and conducts studies of the merit systems. Their Web site includes additional descriptive information on the Board along with links to Board Decisions on FedWorld; Forms and Publications;Regional and Field Offices and Geographical Areas Served; the Office of Policy and Evaluation Reports and Publications; and Customer Service Standards. The Office of Policy and Evaluation Reports and Publications includes access to their newsletter, *Issues of Merit*.

Subject Headings: Government Employees; Labor—Government Employees

SuDoc Number: MS 1.17: *Issues of Merit*

[967] *National Longitudinal Surveys of Labor Market Experience Annotated Bibliography*

Sponsoring Agency: Bureau of Labor Statistics (BLS)

Primary Access: http://www.chrr.ohio-state.edu/nls-bib/

Resource Summary: The *National Longitudinal Surveys (NLS) of Labor Market Experience Annotated Bibliography* is an online version of the *NLS Annotated Bibliography* that combines newly-found, current research with retrospective entries from all previously published editions and supplements. The last printed version of the bibliography was published in 1995, and this is a continuation of that effort to provide a bibliography of research based on NLS data of Labor Market Experience.

Subject Headings: Bibliographic Databases; Labor—Bibliography

[968] Office of Compliance

Sponsoring Agency: Office of Compliance

Primary Access: http://www.compliance.gov/

Resource Summary: The Office of Compliance is responsible for implementing a law that extends the rights and protections of 11 employment and labor laws to employees in the legislative branch of the federal government. Their Web site offers the categories General Information on the Office, Organization, and Agency Publications. The Publications section includes links to relevant laws and regulations as well as to a manual and a poster from the Office.

Of most interest to federal employees in the legislative branch, this site can also prove useful to the general public interested in employee rights.

Subject Headings: Civil Rights; Labor—Government Employees

[969] Office of Economic Conversion Information

Sponsoring Agencies: Department of Commerce (DOC); Department of Defense (DoD)

Primary Access: http://netsite.esa.doc.gov/oeci/

Resource Summary: The OECI Web site is a clearinghouse for information related to defense downsizing. It provides information about defense adjustment, defense conversion, economic development, and technology transfer. Their database contains a compendium of government programs and other materials designed to assist businesses, communities, and workers affected by defense budget cutbacks and other economic development challenges. The sections on the Web site include: About OECI; Search the OECI System; View the OECI System; and the Parcels Information System. The Parcels Information System is an interactive database for developers and companies interested in investing in or locating on closed military bases or in the neighboring communities.

While this service is targeted very specifically at those directly affected by defense downsizing, the economic and supplemental data in their database can be of use to others as well.

Subject Headings: Downsizing; Economic Development; Military

[970] Office of Worker and Community Transition

Sponsoring Agency: Department of Energy (DOE). Office of Worker and Community Transition (OWCT)

Primary Access: http://www.stat-usa.gov/owct/owct.html

Resource Summary: The goal of the OWCT is to minimize social and economic impacts on workers and communities affected by the downsizing of the defense-related facilities. This Web site includes a variety of documentation including press releases, workshop summaries, secretarial memorandums, contact lists, and general information related to OWCT. Major categories include Program Documentation; Comment Board; Documents for Review and Comment; For More Information; and Job Opportunity Bulletin Board.

The site includes potentially useful information for its target audience of downsized workers from the defense industry.

Subject Headings: Economic Development; Downsizing; Military

CHAPTER 15: STATE GOVERNMENTS

There are many resources available from and about state governments. In this chapter, only selected resources are listed for each state. The primary focus is on the major executive, legislative, and judicial sites for each state. There is at least one site included for each state. Many official state home pages are not specifically designed just for government information. Especially in the administrative branch, some of the sites are more focused to providing tourist information. In such cases, the primary URL will point to a government section, if one is available.

The two featured sites for this chapter are useful finding aids for state government information. State and Local Government on the Net features an excellent hierarchical classification of state and local government sites. State Law focuses more on legislative and judicial sites, and its classification by function makes it quite useful.

Featured Sites

[971] State and Local Government on the Net

Sponsoring Agency: Piper Resources

Primary Access: http://www.piperinfo.com/state/states.html

Resource Summary: The initial listing on this site is divided alphabetically by state. Each state listing is categorized under the following headings: State Home Page; Statewide Offices; Legislative Branch; Judicial Branch; Executive Branch; Boards and Commissions; and Counties; and Cities. In addition to the state listings, the site features additional state-oriented categories such as Multi-State Sites; Federal Resources; National Organizations; and Other Links.

This is an excellent finding aid for state and local government resources. The categorizations with each state's listings make it especially useful.

Subject Heading: Finding Aid—States

[972] State Law: State and Local Government - Executive, Legislative, and Judicial Information

Sponsoring Agency: Washburn University School of Law

Primary Access: http://lawlib.wuacc.edu/washlaw/uslaw/statelaw.html

Resource Summary: Organized by state, this site lists Internet resources that are geared toward state governments, legislative information, and legal information. Within each state site, the categories include: Home Page, Legislative Information, Court Opinions, Statutes, Bills, State Agencies, Local Government, and Miscellaneous. Another section provides links to sites of interest that are related to all states.

The clear classification of different state sites makes this one of the easiest finding aids for state Internet resources. Since the developers take a broad view of legal resources, it is useful both for those interested in legislative information and general state and local governmental information.

Subject Headings: Finding Aid—Laws; Finding Aid—States

State Governments: General

[973] Government of Guam Information on Kuentos

Sponsoring Agencies: Guam. Government; Kuentos Communications, Inc.

Primary Access: http://www.guam.net/gov/

Resource Summary: With a few government links for this U.S. territory, this site includes the headings Guam Telephone Authority, Guam Laws Online, Guam Legislature, and Guam Department of Education Federal Programs Division.

Subject Heading: Guam

The remaining state government resources are divided into two sections. The first section covers other general finding aids for state government sites and the governmental sites for U.S. possessions and territories. This section runs from entry number 973 to 982. The second subchapter, entries 983-1129, features resources for the individual states, arranged alphabetically by state.

[974] Government of Puerto Rico - Office of the Governor

Sponsoring Agency: Puerto Rico. Governor

Primary Access: http://fortaleza.govpr.org/

Resource Summary: This site offers both an English and Spanish version of its pages. After the governor's welcome message page, the site offers information on the government of Puerto Rico. Major categories include: Services; Activities; Government; and Official Information.

Subject Heading: Puerto Rico

[975] National Conference of State Legislatures

Sponsoring Agency: National Conference of State Legislatures (NCSL)

Primary Access: http://www.ncsl.org/

Resource Summary: Also known as NCSLnet—the Electronic Information Network for State Legislatures—this site features a broad range of materials for state legislatures and officials that work in state legislative bodies. One part of the site has recent announcements from NCSL. Other principal sections include: About State Legislatures; Guide to NCSL and Its Services; Foundation for State Legislatures; and Links to the Internet. Under the latter section is a finding aid for direct links to state legislatures' Web sites.

This site should be of broad interest to state legislators and to officials, managers, and administrators of state legislative bodies.

Subject Headings: Finding Aid—States; Finding Aid—Laws; Legislation

[976] The State Court Locator

Sponsoring Agency: Villanova Center for Information Law and Policy

Primary Access: http://www.law.vill.edu/State-Ct/

Resource Summary: The State Court Locator provides links to the sites of state and local courts. It includes sites with state court opinions that can be viewed and downloaded. The page is arranged alphabetically by state.

Subject Headings: Cases; Finding Aid—Laws—States; Finding Aid—States

[977] The State Web Locator

Sponsoring Agency: Villanova Center for Information Law and Policy

Primary Access: http://www.law.vill.edu/State-Agency/

Resource Summary: Broader in scope than The State Court Locator, The State Web Locator is another finding aid for state government sites on the Internet. It includes links for all 50 states and for a few U.S. territories and possessions. Under each state, the sites are categorized under headings such as State Home Page; Executive Branch; Legislative Branch; Departments and Agencies; and Judicial Branch.

This site is not as detailed or as up-to-date as the State Law or State and Local Government on the Net sites. It can, however, be a useful adjunct to those two sites as well as to other state finding aids.

Subject Heading: Finding Aid—States

[978] StateSearch - Sponsored by NASIRE

Sponsoring Agency: National Association of State Information Resource Executives (NASIRE)

Primary Access: http://www.nasire.org/ss/

Resource Summary: NASIRE represents information resource executives and managers from the 50 states, 6 U.S. territories, and the District of Columbia. StateSearch, introduced by NASIRE in 1995, provides a directory of state government information by subject areas such as Education, Revenue, Treasurers, and State Legislatures.

This can be used to find state agencies and administrative departments grouped by function, rather than by state. While it is not completely comprehensive, it is updated frequently and appears fairly accurate.

Subject Heading: Finding Aid—States

[979] U.S. House of Representatives - Internet Law Library - U.S. State and Territorial Laws

Sponsoring Agency: House of Representatives

Primary Access: http://law.house.gov/17.htm

Resource Summary: This site presents an alphabetical list of states with separate pages for any state-related legal material. On the top level page, it also has a section for model acts and inter-state compacts. Under each state the categories include: state constitutions; codes; cases; legislative information; individual acts; and local regulations. The lists are presented alphabetically, although links to major sites for the constitution, code, and cases are listed first.

At first look, this site appears to be disorganized, however, it can be helpful for finding state legal information that may not be easily found elsewhere. Conversely, some of the links lead to dead ends. It could use more frequent updating and verification.

Subject Headings: Finding Aid—Laws—States; Finding Aid—States

[980] U.S. State Fact Sheets

Sponsoring Agency: Economic Research Service

Primary Access: http://www.econ.ag.gov/epubs/other/usfact/

Alternative Access Method: mailto:listserv@ers.bitnet with "get <state code> data f=mail" in body

Resource Summary: The fact sheets contain basic demographic and farm statistics for each state. The Web version makes the fact sheets accessible by state name and through an image map of the U.S. The same statistics are also available for the U.S. as a whole.

This is a useful service for finding basic demographic and agricultural information.

Subject Headings: Agriculture—Statistics; States—Statistics

[981] World Wide Web Virtual Library: Law: State Government

Sponsoring Agency: Indiana University School of Law

Primary Access: http://www.law.indiana.edu/law/v-lib/states.html

Resource Summary: This listing, part of the World Wide Web Consortium's Virtual Library, is a list of links to state government sites arranged alphabetically by state. Within each state section, there is no obvious order to the listed links.

Because this site does not categorize the links under each state heading by function, it is not as useful as the State Law or the State and Local Government on the Net sites. However, it can be a useful supplement to those other two sites.

Subject Heading: Finding Aid—States

[982] Yahoo! Government: U.S. States

Sponsoring Agency: Yahoo! Inc.

Primary Access: http://www.yahoo.com/Government/States/

Resource Summary: This section of the well-known Yahoo! directory includes links to governmental sites in all 50 states. It also features some multi-state categories such as Organizations; State Government Jobs; and Indices. Within each state's section, the main government page is listed first, followed by subcategories that might be available, and then an alphabetical list of other government sites.

This site has much broader coverage of state governments than some of the other finding aids, but it is not categorized as neatly as the State Law site. It is useful for expanding a list of state government sites available from the other finding aids.

Subject Heading: Finding Aid—States

State Governments: Individual States ———————————

Alabama

[983] Alabama's Legal Information Center

Sponsoring Agency: Alabama. Supreme Court

Primary Access: http://alalinc.net/

Alternative Access Method: telnet://204.29.92.2/

Resource Summary: The site serves a variety of purposes. It provides access to Alabama's Appellate Court opinions, and it will soon feature some information on the Alabama Supreme Court. Some of the Web sections are still under development, and the use of the system requires either a telnet connection or the use of a Netscape plug in.

There is little information available directly on the Web site, but it does provide some basic access.

Subject Heading: Cases—Alabama

[984] Alabama State Legislature

Sponsoring Agency: Alabama. Legislature

Primary Access: http://www.asc.edu/archives/legislat/legislat.html

Resource Summary: This site provides descriptive information about the legislature, but it does not yet have any online bills.

Subject Heading: Legislation—Alabama

[985] AlaWeb Government

Sponsoring Agency: Alabama State Government

Primary Access: http://alaweb.asc.edu/govern.html

Resource Summary: The site features links to categories such as the Governor's Office; State Agencies; Legislature; Economic Development; and the Lieutenant Governor. It is a useful starting point for state government information for Alabama.

Subject Heading: Alabama

Alaska

[986] Alaska Court System

Sponsoring Agency: Alaska. Court System

Primary Access: http://www.alaska.net/~akctlib/homepage.htm

Alternative Access Method: http://www.touchngo.com/sp/sp.htm

Resource Summary: This site includes Alaska Supreme Court and Court of Appeals slip opinions from 1991. Access is by date or keyword search. Unfortunately, opinions are removed from this site once they are printed. The alternate URL, however, includes the full text of the Supreme Court cases from 1991 through the present.

Subject Headings: Alaska; Cases—Alaska—Full Text

[987] Alaska State Legislature Textual Infobases

Sponsoring Agency: Alaska. Legislature

Primary Access: http://www.legis.state.ak.us/

Alternative Access Method: http://www.legis.state.ak.us/default2.htm [text version]

Resource Summary: This site provides the Alaska Statutes from 1993; a current bill tracking system; and older legislative material back to 1983. The statutes are searchable using the Folio Infobase software.

Subject Heading: Legislation—Alaska—Full Text

[988] State of Alaska

Sponsoring Agency: Alaska State Government

Primary Access: http://www.state.ak.us/

Resource Summary: The Alaska site includes the categories: Top 10 List; Agency Directory; Visitor Information; State Employee Directory; and News. The Subject Search uses AltaVista to limit the search just to the main server. The primary access to state government sites is under the Agency Directory section which is available in a hierarchical or straight alphabetical list.

Alaska has pages for most of its agencies, and this site makes it relatively easy to find them.

Subject Heading: Alaska

Arizona

[989] Arizona Judicial Department

Sponsoring Agency: Arizona. Supreme Court

Primary Access: http://www.state.az.us/sp/

Resource Summary: Despite its title, this is also the central page for the Arizona Supreme Court. No cases are yet available on the site, but it does give basic information and current news about the Court.

Subject Heading: Arizona

[990] Arizona Legislative Information System

Sponsoring Agency: Arizona. Legislature

Primary Access: http://www.azleg.state.az.us/

Resource Summary: This site features an online version of the *Arizona Revised Statutes*; current legislation status; committee agendas; and a members directory. The full text of bills is available along with the current status and subsequent versions of the bills. Archival coverage dates back to the 1995 legislative session.

This is a well-designed site with a great deal of full-text legislative material available.

Subject Heading: Legislation—Arizona

[991] State of Arizona

Sponsoring Agency: Arizona State Government

Primary Access: http://www.state.az.us/

Alternative Access Method: gopher://gopher.state.az.us/

Resource Summary: This central governmental page includes prominent links to all three branches of the Arizona state government. Major administrative departments and their logos are featured with direct links to their respective sites. The State Services section provides access to agencies by function. A keyword search option is also available.

This site provides easy access to Arizona government sites and to government information.

Subject Heading: Arizona

Arkansas

[992] Arkansas General Assembly

Sponsoring Agency: Arkansas. Legislature

Primary Access: http://www.arkleg.state.ar.us/

Resource Summary: This site features sections entitled: Legislators and Committees; Meetings and Events; Committee Agendas; Access Current Session Bills and Resolutions; and Access Current Session Acts. The session bills and session acts are accessible by number or via the keyword search option. They are available in both Microsoft Word and WordPerfect formats. A separate option provides current bill status information.

Subject Heading: Legislation—Arkansas

[993] Arkansas Judiciary

Sponsoring Agency: Arkansas. Supreme Court

Primary Access: http://www.state.ar.us/supremecourt/

Resource Summary: This site provides access to opinions of the Arkansas Supreme Court and the Arkansas Court of Appeals from 1996. Access is by date and the opinions are available in ASCII and WordPerfect 5.1 formats. The site also features information on the Arkansas court system.

Subject Heading: Cases—Arkansas

[994] State of Arkansas

Sponsoring Agency: Arkansas State Government

Primary Access: http://www.state.ar.us/

Resource Summary: The Arkansas site provides access to the various branches of government along with the headings: Educational Resources in Arkansas; Visitor's Center; Arkansas Economic Development; and Parks and Tourism Travel Information Request. The government section includes a listing of administrative agencies, some of which have Web sites available.

While not the most elegant of designs, the site supports a basic funcationality and easy access to Arkansas government agencies that are Internet accessible.

Subject Heading: Arkansas

California

[995] California Courts and Judicial System

Sponsoring Agency: California. Judicial System

Primary Access: http://www.courtinfo.ca.gov/

Resource Summary: Linking to many of the different California court and judiciary sites, this page is a central starting point for judicial information from California. The site has links entitled: Supreme Court; Court of Appeals; Trial Courts; Court Opinions; and Judicial Council Rules. The Court Opinions area contains the slip opinions of the Supreme Court and Court of Appeal issued in the last 60 days in Microsoft Word 6.0 and PDF formats.

This site offers a great deal of information on the California courts. However, only the most recent 60 days worth of cases are available in full text.

Subject Headings: California; Cases—California—Full Text

[996] California State Home Page

Sponsoring Agency: California State Government

Primary Access: http://www.ca.gov/

Resource Summary: The focus of this site is the governor, but it also provides links to other California government sites. Look under the headings, Your Government or Hello May We Help You? to get a list of state agencies with links to their sites.

The site design is aimed at the general public and is quite popular in tone. Unfortunately, that can actually make it more difficult to find relevant California government sites, especially for those looking by agency name.

Subject Heading: California

[997] Official California Legislative Information

Sponsoring Agency: California. Legislature

Primary Access: http://www.leginfo.ca.gov/

Resource Summary: This central site for the California Legislature features the headings: Bill Information; California Law; Legislative Publications; Today's Events; and Your Legislature. It includes daily updates of both Assembly and Senate bills, and the full text of the California Codes. The bills are available back to the 1993-94 session and are searchable by keyword or author.

While response time can be slow, this site contains a wealth of California legislative information that is available in an accessible manner.

Subject Headings: California; Legislation—California—Full Text

Colorado

[998] Colorado Courts

Sponsoring Agency: Colorado. Supreme Court

Primary Access: http://www.rmii.com/slv/courts/colcts.htm

Alternative Access Method: http://www.cobar.org/coappcts/scndx.htm

Resource Summary: The Colorado Courts Web site provides a wide variety of information on the courts and the judicial system. However, it takes some searching to find the full text of recent Colorado Supreme Court opinions. These opinions are available at the alternate URL—cases are arranged chronologically and are available in HTML format.

The site would benefit from some reorganization. The link to the slip opinions should be elevated to a higher level.

Subject Headings: Cases—Colorado—Full Text; Colorado

[999] Colorado General Assembly

Sponsoring Agency: Colorado. Legislature

Primary Access: http://www.state.co.us/gov_dir/stateleg.html

Alternative Access Method: http://crs.aescon.com/

Resource Summary: The Colorado Legislative site offers directories of the House and Senate along with current bill information. The Bill Information section features the 1996 Digest of Bills and the full text of current bills, arranged by bill number and available in HTML. The alternate URL provides access to the Colorado Revised Statutes, however, it is a commercial service and requires a fee.

Subject Headings: Colorado; Legislation—Colorado—Full Text

[1000] Colorado Government

Sponsoring Agency: Colorado State Government

Primary Access: http://www.state.co.us/gov_dir/govmenu.html

Resource Summary: Near the top of this page, the Colorado Government site connects to the headings Legislature and Colorado Tax Forms. The rest of this online directory features the sections: Elected Officials; State Agencies; Boards, Committees and Commissions; Judicial Branch; and Legislative Branch.

With a standard organization, this site provides easy access to Colorado government sites on the Web.

Subject Heading: Colorado

Connecticut

[1001] State of Connecticut

Sponsoring Agency: Connecticut State Government

Primary Access: http://www.state.ct.us/

Alternative Access Method: http://www.state.ct.us/homenf.htm [no frames version]

Resource Summary: The official Connecticut home page features divisions for the executive, judicial, and legislative branches as well as directories and a subject index. The section titled Directories includes links to various government staff directories, while the Subject Index section offers access to government agencies by topic.

Subject Heading: Connecticut

[1002] State of Connecticut Judiciary

Sponsoring Agency: Connecticut. Courts

Primary Access: http://www.state.ct.us/judic.htm

Alternative Access Method: http://www.cslnet.ctstateu.edu/judicial/

Resource Summary: Although this site does not yet have any online opinions, the site does include the sections Judicial Directory "Blue Book," Overview of Connecticut Courts, List of Supreme Court Justices, and List of Appellate Court Judges. It also has sections entitled Court Information and Judicial Departments Alphabetically.

Subject Heading: Connecticut

[1003] State of Connecticut Legislative Branch of Government

Sponsoring Agency: Connecticut. Legislature

Primary Access: http://www.state.ct.us/legis.htm

Resource Summary: While not yet fully functional, this site allows browsing and direct retrieval of bill status; the bills themselves; and fiscal impact statements. Daily journals will provide details on each house's session and activities. The site already includes the sections Connecticut Legislators' E-mail Directory, Connecticut 1995 Public and Special Acts, the General Statutes of Connecticut, and Election and Voting Information.

Subject Headings: Connecticut; Legislation—Connecticut—Full Text

Delaware

[1004] Delaware Court System

Sponsoring Agency: Delaware. Courts

Primary Access: http://www.ncsc.dni.us/court/delaware/homepage.htm

Resource Summary: While no information is yet available on this page, there is a placeholder page.

Subject Heading: Delaware

[1005] State Legislature

Sponsoring Agency: Delaware. Legislature

Primary Access: http://www.state.de.us/govern/statlegi.htm

Resource Summary: This page includes the headings: State Senators; State Representatives; Controller General; and the Legislative Information System. The Legislative Information System includes two links, Bill Tracking System and Daily Agendas. Access to the full text of bills and their status is by bill number, bill title, and sponser.

Subject Headings: Delaware; Legislation—Delaware—Full Text

[1006] State of Delaware

Sponsoring Agency: Delaware State Government

Primary Access: http://www.state.de.us/

Alternative Access Method: http://www.state.de.us/weltext.htm

Resource Summary: The categories on this central site for the state of Delaware include: Government, Education, Economic Development, Tourism, Delaware Facts, and What's New. Sections under the Government heading include: State Agencies; Statewide Elected Officials; State Legislature; State Court System; and State Government Phone Directory.

Subject Heading: Delaware

District of Columbia

[1007] Washington D.C.

Sponsoring Agency: District of Columbia Government

Primary Access: http://www.dchomepage.net/dcmain/index.html

Resource Summary: Opening with a banner proclaiming this site the Official DC Home Page, the site features the categories: Mayor's Office; the Office of International Business; the Office of Tourism and Promotions; and the Minority Business Opportunity Commission.

The site contains little substantive information. One major improvement would be the addition of some information on the city council.

Subject Heading: District of Columbia

Florida

[1008] Florida Communities Network

Sponsoring Agency: Florida State Government

Primary Access: http://www.state.fl.us/

Resource Summary: This page provides a list of general interest topics in one frame, but the bulk of the site consists of sections entitled: Access to Government Area for a State Agency Listing; Florida Government Job Vacancy System; Florida Statewide Telephone Directory; and the One-Stop Service Centers. The primary government area is within the Access to Government section and features a list of state agencies and services available on the Web.

Although the design and organization of the site are unusual, it is still effective for delivering Florida government information.

Subject Heading: Florida

[1009] Judicial Online Superhighway User Access System

Sponsoring Agency: Florida. Courts

Primary Access: http://justice.courts.state.fl.us/

Alternative Access Method: http://justice.courts.state.fl.us/non_gui.html [text version]

Resource Summary: The Judicial Online Superhighway User Access System (JOSHUA) offers the sections: Florida Court System; Judicial Administration; Legal Research; and Court Opinions and Rules. The opinions of the Supreme Court of Florida since September 1995 are available in HTML and Rich Text Format. Access to the opinions is by keyword searching or indexes of first party, second party, and date.

Subject Headings: Florida; Cases—Florida—Full Text

[1010] Online Sunshine - The Florida Legislature

Sponsoring Agency: Florida. Legislature

Primary Access: http://www.leg.state.fl.us/

Resource Summary: The legislature's site features statutes, bills, calendars, and lobbyist information. The site offers the status and full text of bills from 1995. The *Florida Statutes* are online from 1993 to the present. Both the bills and the statutes can be searched by keyword.

Florida offers a significant set of legislative information on this site.

Subject Headings: Florida; Legislation—Florida—Full Text

Georgia

[1011] GeorgiaNet Legislative Services

Sponsoring Agency: Georgia. Legislature

Primary Access: http://www.ganet.org/services/

Resource Summary: Current bills are available in full text with access by keyword, bill number, code section, date, author, committee, and sponsor. The bills are in ASCII, and older bills are available back to the 1995 session. The *Georgia Code* (unannotated) is also available with access by keyword or code number.

Subject Headings: Georgia; Legislation—Georgia—Full Text

[1012] State of Georgia

Sponsoring Agency: Georgia State Government

Primary Access: http://www.ganet.org/

Alternative Access Method: http://www.state.ga.us/

Resource Summary: The two main sections of this site link to the Governor's page and to a Services section. The Services section includes the links: Legislative Session; Purchasing; Corporate Search; Banking and Finance; Georgia Code; and State Agencies. The latter section provides easy access to many of the other Georgia state agencies on the Web. The alternate URL points to Georgia Online which also features a variety of state government resources including information about state agencies, the Governor, and the legislative and judicial branches. However, it is far more difficult to navigate due to the background image and poor organization of the site into one long page.

Subject Heading: Georgia

[1013] Supreme Court of Georgia

Sponsoring Agency: Georgia. Supreme Court

Primary Access: http://www.state.ga.us/Courts/Supreme/

Resource Summary: Although the opinions are not yet available on this site in full text, it does offer the sections: The Court Calendar; Opinion Summaries; Recent Certioraris; Rules and Procedures; and a History of the Supreme Court.

Subject Headings: Georgia; Cases—Georgia

Hawaii

[1014] ACCESS Legislative Information Service

Sponsoring Agency: Hawaii. Legislature

Primary Access: telnet://fyi@fyi.icsd.hawaii.gov

Resource Summary: After connecting to the URL and logging in as fyi, choose the first option, ACCESS Legislative Information Service. This service offers timetables, directories, and drafts of bills. Access to the bills is by bill number or keyword—only bills from the current session are available.

While a Web version of this information would make it more accessible to the public, this system is quite functional for those that understand how to make a telnet connection.

Subject Headings: Hawaii; Legislation—Hawaii

[1015] Hawaii State Judiciary

Sponsoring Agencies: Hawaii. Courts; Hawaii State Bar Association

Primary Access: http://www.hawaii.gov/jud/

Alternative Access Method: http://www.hsba.org/Hawaii/Court/cour.htm

Resource Summary: The main URL links to a site with the categories: Hawaii Supreme Court, Intermediate Court of Appeals, Circuit Courts, District Courts, and Family Courts. This site includes information on judges and caseload activity. For online access to some of the courts' opinions, use the alternate URL to connect to the Hawaii State Bar Association's AccessLine. The most recent month's worth of Supreme Court and Intermediate Court of Appeals cases are available from this site. Access to earlier cases requires a subscription fee.

Subject Headings: Hawaii; Cases—Hawaii—Full Text

[1016] Hawaii State Government

Sponsoring Agency: Hawaii State Government

Primary Access: http://www.hawaii.gov/

Resource Summary: This site offers a basic directory of state government Web sites organized under the topics: Business; Human Resources; Permits and Licenses; Taxes; and Social Services.

The subject approach can be very useful, but it would also be helpful to have a hierarchical listing.

Subject Heading: Hawaii

Idaho

[1017] Idaho Judicial Branch

Sponsoring Agency: Idaho. Courts

Primary Access: http://www.state.id.us/judicial/judicial.html

Resource Summary: In addition to the *Idaho Courts Annual Report*, this site provides access to all Idaho Supreme Court and Court of Appeals appellate opinions. Opinions are posted the day of their release but are removed after 60 days. They are available in ASCII format and are accessible by broad topic and then in reverse chronological order.

Subject Headings: Cases—Idaho—Full Text; Idaho

[1018] Idaho Legislature

Sponsoring Agency: Idaho. Legislature

Primary Access: http://www.state.id.us/legislat/legislat.html

Resource Summary: Idaho's legislative site includes documents and reports regarding the activities of the Idaho Legislature, information that describes the Legislature, and a section describing how the legislative process works. Bills are available in full text by bill number or keyword from the 1996 session. This site also provides access to the Idaho Constitution and the *Idaho Statutes*.

Subject Headings: Idaho; Legislation—Idaho—Full Text

[1019] State of Idaho

Sponsoring Agency: Idaho State Government

Primary Access: http://www.state.id.us/

Alternative Access Method: http://www.state.id.us/home.html [text version]

Resource Summary: The main Idaho site presents a hierarchical table of contents. The Government section includes links to the executive, judicial, and legislative branches along with an Agency Directory Search and a hierarchical State Government Agencies section.

Subject Heading: Idaho

Illinois

[1020] Illinois Supreme and Appellate Courts Opinions

Sponsoring Agency: Illinois. Courts

Primary Access: http://www.state.il.us/court/

Resource Summary: This site features the full text of opinions from both the Illinois Supreme Court and Appellate Courts since 1996. The slip opinions are available in both WordPerfect and ASCII formats—access is by date. An index of Supreme Court opinions provides access by date and by case name or docket number.

A search option takes the user to an alphabetical listing of the file names (the docket number of the case doubles as the file name).

Subject Headings: Cases—Illinois—Full Text; Illinois

[1021] Legislative Information

Sponsoring Agency: Illinois. Legislature

Primary Access: http://www.state.il.us/cms/hp0040.htm

Alternative Access Method: http://www.state.in.us/acin/iga/

Resource Summary: This site provides directories of state representatives and senators by district and by name. No bills or other full-text legislative information is available on the site.

Subject Heading: Illinois

[1022] State of Illinois

Sponsoring Agency: Illinois State Government

Primary Access: http://www.state.il.us/

Alternative Access Method: http://www.state.il.us/CMS/HP00T.HTM [text version]

Resource Summary: This central state page serves as a link to state government information. The sections entitled: Governor and Lieutenant Governor; State Agencies; Legislative Information; and the Capitol Complex point directly to Illinois government sources. The State Agencies page provides an alphabetical list of state agencies, many of which have an Internet presence.

Subject Heading: Illinois

Indiana

[1023] Indiana General Assembly

Sponsoring Agency: Indiana. Legislature

Primary Access: http://www.state.in.us/legislative/

Resource Summary: Featuring the categories: Calendars, Committees, Legislators, and Bill Information, this is a substantial site. The Bill Information section includes introduced and approved bills, committee reports, amendments, fiscal impact statements, and an actions list. The bills are available in HTML, and they can be searched by bill number, keyword, or phrase. This page also links to online versions of the *Indiana Code* and the *Indiana Administrative Code*

Subject Headings: Indiana; Legislation—Indiana—Full Text

[1024] Indiana Judicial System

Sponsoring Agency: Indiana. Courts

Primary Access: http://www.ai.org/judiciary/welcome.html

Alternative Access Method: http://www.law.indiana.edu/law/incourts/incourts. html

Resource Summary: The main URL points to a brief welcoming page while the bulk of the content is actually at the alternate URL for Indiana Judicial Decisions. The Indiana Judicial Decisions site contains the full text of Indiana Supreme Court, Court of Appeals, and Tax Court cases since 1995. The cases are available in HTML, WordPerfect, and ASCII formats. Browse access is by first party, second party, date, or month, while keyword searching access is available for keywords and subjects.

While this site provides a substantial number of cases, it does not appear to be updated regularly. Some information is up to nine months behind. With this in mind, it may not be a useful resource for recent opinions.

Subject Headings: Cases—Indiana—Full Text; Indiana

[1025] Indiana State Government

Sponsoring Agency: Indiana State Government

Primary Access: http://www.state.in.us/state.html

Resource Summary: This Indiana Government site links to categories including: Government Offices; Governor and Lieutenant Governor; Judiciary; State Forms; General Assembly; and Meetings and Agenda. The Government Offices section is an alphabetical list of state agencies on the Web. State Forms provides a variety of applications, registration forms, and even state tax forms.

Subject Heading: Indiana

Iowa

[1026] Functional Iowa List: Branches and Departments

Sponsoring Agency: Iowa State Government

Primary Access: http://www.state.ia.us/government/

Alternative Access Method: http://www.state.ia.us/government/indextxt.html [text version]

Resource Summary: Featuring the standard breakdowns by executive, judicial, and legislative Branches, this page offers access to state government sites via an alphabetical list and a function listing.

Subject Heading: Iowa

[1027] Iowa General Assembly

Sponsoring Agency: Iowa. Legislature

Primary Access: http://www.legis.state.ia.us/

Alternative Access Method: gopher://gopher.netins.net:70/11/showcase/IPTN/

Resource Summary: This site features the categories: Legislation; the Code of Iowa; Members and Committees; Interim Study Committees and Information; and Calendars. Under the Legislation heading, the full text of bills (in HTML), bill history, and House and Senate journal pages are available. Access is by bill number and bills are available from the main URL back to 1996. The alternate site contains older information, apparently from 1994 and 1995.

Subject Headings: Iowa; Legislation—Iowa—Full Text

[1028] The Judicial Branch

Sponsoring Agency: Iowa. Courts

Primary Access: http://www.sos.state.ia.us/register/r3/judpage.htm

Alternative Access Methods: http://www.netins.net/showcase/IPTN/legal.html
http://ialaw.giant.net/

Resource Summary: This site only provides brief descriptions and short biographies for the judges on the Iowa Supreme Court; Iowa Court of Appeals; Iowa District Court; and judicial boards and commissions. The two alternate URLs are supposed to provide some level of access to court opinions, but the first is still under construction and the second is a commercial service.

Subject Heading: Iowa

Kansas

[1029] Kansas Judicial Branch

Sponsoring Agencies: Kansas. Courts; University of Kansas School of Law. Library

Primary Access: http://www.law.ukans.edu/kscourts/kscourts.html

Resource Summary: In addition to providing information about the Kansas courts, the jury system, and judicial rules, this site features slip opinions from the Kansas Supreme Court and Court of Appeals in HTML format. Access to the cases is by docket number, date, case name, and keyword searching. Cases are available back to October 1996. The site also offers information on Kansas District and Municipal Courts.

Subject Headings: Cases—Kansas—Full Text; Kansas

[1030] Kansas Legislative Services

Sponsoring Agency: Kansas. Legislature

Primary Access: http://www.ink.org/public/legislative/

Resource Summary: This site offers bill tracking and the full text of bills for the current legislative session. Access to the bills is by bill number or keyword, and the full-text versions are in HTML. Other information is available under the headings: Bill Packets; Calendars; Journals; Enrolled Bills; and a Bill Subject Index. The site also offers information about legislative committees, legislators, the *Kansas Statutes*, the *Kansas Register*, and campaign finance data.

Subject Headings: Kansas; Legislation—Kansas—Full Text

[1031] State of Kansas

Sponsoring Agency: Kansas State Government

Primary Access: http://www.state.ks.us/

Resource Summary: While the offical Kansas Web site includes more than just government resources, it does link to categories which include: Governor; Elected Officials; State Agencies; Legislative; and Local Governments. The State Agencies section is an alphabetical list of the state agencies with Web sites.

Subject Heading: Kansas

Kentucky

[1032] Commonwealth of Kentucky

Sponsoring Agency: Kentucky State Government

Primary Access: http://www.state.ky.us/govtinfo.htm

Resource Summary: This page features a nonhierarchical alphabetical list of state agencies. It includes state agencies that do not have an Internet presence.

The lack of a hierarchical display or even a top level breakdown for the executive, legislative, and judicial branches makes this site difficult to navigate and to find appropriate state agencies.

Subject Heading: Kentucky

[1033] Kentucky Legislature

Sponsoring Agency: Kentucky. Legislature

Primary Access: http://www.lrc.state.ky.us/home.htm

Alternative Access Methods: http://www.lrc.state.ky.us/lrcindex.htm [text version] gopher://gopher.state.ky.us/

Resource Summary: This is an extensive site, with a large collection of descriptive information about the legislature along with access to legislation. Bills are accessible by bill number and are in Word 2.0c format. The full text of recent bills is available as are summaries of older bills back to 1994.

Subject Headings: Kentucky; Legislation—Kentucky—Full Text

Louisiana

[1034] Louisiana Legislature

Sponsoring Agency: Louisiana. Legislature

Primary Access: http://www.state.la.us/state/legis.htm

Alternative Access Methods: http://www.senate.state.la.us/
http://www.house.state.la.us/

Resource Summary: This page links to the categories: Louisiana House of Representatives; the Louisiana Senate; and the Legislative Auditor. The Senate and House pages also aim to be central Louisiana Legislature sites, and they link to each other. Most of the sites consist of information about the legislative process, current legislators, committee information, and bill information. Most of the bill information available from both the House and Senate pages offers only summaries of legislation but not full text. The bill summaries are accessible by author and bill number. On the Senate page, the Senate bills are available in full text, PDF format by bill number only

Subject Headings: Legislation—Louisiana; Louisiana

[1035] Supreme Court of Louisiana

Sponsoring Agency: Louisiana. Supreme Court

Primary Access: http://www.gnofn.org/~lasc/

Resource Summary: Beginning with a History of the Supreme Court section, this site also features information on the sitting justices, court rules, press releases, and full-text slip opinions. The opinions are available by linking from the press releases for opinion decrees and are available since February 1996. The cases are in self-extracting, compressed, WordPerfect 5.1 format.

Subject Headings: Cases—Louisiana—Full Text; Louisiana

[1036] Welcome to Info Louisiana

Sponsoring Agency: Louisiana State Government

Primary Access: http://www.state.la.us/

Resource Summary: Info Louisiana is designed to be the entry point to state government information on Louisiana. The primary links include Governor; Lieutenant Governor; Legislature; Judiciary; State Departments; Local Government; and Contact People in State Government. The latter provides access to state agency telephone directories. The State Departments page provides a basic list of the primary state agencies along with the headings Governmental Subdivisions and Frequently Requested Information Phone Numbers.

Subject Heading: Louisiana

Maine

[1037] Maine State Government

Sponsoring Agency: Maine State Government

Primary Access: http://www.state.me.us/

Resource Summary: With more than a dozen main categories, Maine's official Web site links to the categories: Agencies; Cities and Towns; Government Directories; Governor; Judicial Branch; Legislature; and Quasi-State Agencies among others. The Agencies section is the primary source for state executive branch agencies—it is a straight alphabetic arrangement. A hierarchical option could make it easier to find specific state agencies.

Subject Heading: Maine

[1038] State of Maine Judicial Branch

Sponsoring Agency: Maine. Courts

Primary Access: http://www.courts.state.me.us/

Resource Summary: The Judicial Branch site for Maine includes the categories: The Chief Justice's Page; Directory of Maine Courts; About the Court System; Court Publications; Schedule of Court Fees; and Supreme Court Opinions. The Opinions are available in full-text HTML, WordPerfect 3, or PDF format. Accessible by date, the cases go back to the beginning of 1997.

Subject Headings: Cases—Maine—Full Text; Maine

[1039] State of Maine Legislative Home Page

Sponsoring Agency: Maine. Legislature

Primary Access: http://www.state.me.us/legis/

Resource Summary: This site features links to the categories: Calendar of Events; House; Senate; Offices; Bill Information; and Maine Constitution and Laws. The Bill Information page only includes some summaries of bills and a discussion of the bill making process, no full-text versions are online yet. The Maine Constitution and Laws page only includes the full text of the constitution. The Maine Statutes page may eventually appear here since there is a heading for them, but there is no link available yet.

Subject Headings: Legislation—Maine; Maine

Maryland

[1040] Maryland Electronic Capital

Sponsoring Agency: Maryland State Government

Primary Access: http://www.mec.state.md.us/

Resource Summary: The official Maryland Web site includes more than just government links. The primary sections are: State Government; State Agencies; Governor's Office; Counties; and Cities. The State Government page points to the executive, judicial, and legislative branches. The State Agencies page links to the cabinet agencies and an alphabetical list of independent agencies, boards, and commissions.

Subject Heading: Maryland

[1041] Maryland General Assembly

Sponsoring Agency: Maryland. Legislature

Primary Access: http://mlis.state.md.us/

Resource Summary: This site includes information on the legislature and includes the categories: About the General Assembly; Contact or Find a Legislator; Bill Information and Status; House and Senate Proceedings; Bill Indexes and Profiles; and Hearing Schedules. The Bill Information section provides summaries of the bills, legislative history, sponsors, statute affected, and the full text. Bills are available in full text in RTF format while fiscal notes and amendments are in WordPerfect 6.1 format. Bills are available back to the 1996 session.

Subject Headings: Legislation—Maryland—Full Text; Maryland

[1042] The State of Maryland Court System

Sponsoring Agency: Maryland. Courts

Primary Access: http://www.courts.state.md.us/

Alternative Access Method: http://www.mec.state.md.us/mec/mecjudic.htm

Resource Summary: Providing a fair amount of descriptive information about the Maryland court system, this site provides lists of judges and their phone numbers. Additionally, the Court Opinions section provides some WordPerfect, full-text opinions from the Court of Special Appeals Opinions and Court of Appeals Opinions since 1992. Access to these cases is only by the very cryptic file names which appear to be based on the year and number of the opinion.

Subject Headings: Cases—Maryland—Full Text; Maryland

Massachusetts

[1043] Commonwealth of Massachusetts

Sponsoring Agency: Massachusetts State Government

Primary Access: http://www.magnet.state.ma.us/

Alternative Access Method: http://www.magnet.state.ma.us/index2.htm [no frames version]

Resource Summary: This official Massachusetts site features sections entitled: Agencies; Services; Reference Shelf; Transactions; and Commonwealth Communities. The first two provide two different approaches to finding state government sites. The Reference Shelf page is a list of online press releases and other publications from state agencies. The Transactions page lists informational and financial transactions that can be conducted online. The category, Commonwealth Communities offers information on the cities and towns in Massachusetts.

Subject Heading: Massachusetts

[1044] The General Court

Sponsoring Agency: Massachusetts. Legislature

Primary Access: http://www.magnet.state.ma.us/legis/

Resource Summary: The General Court of the Commonwealth of Massachusetts, despite its name, is the legislature for the state. Their Web site features the categories: Member Directory; Committee Directory; Committee Hearings; Constitution; and Current Legislation. This last section includes bill status but not the full text of the bills.

Subject Headings: Legislation—Massachusetts—Full Text; Massachusetts

[1045] Massachusetts Court System

Sponsoring Agencies: Lawyers Weekly Publications; Massachusetts. Courts; Social Law Library

Primary Access: http://www.state.ma.us/courts/courts.htm

Alternative Access Methods: http://www.lweekly.com/masslaw.htm
http://www.socialaw.com/

Resource Summary: The primary URL offers a selection of descriptive information on the Massachusetts court system and a Frequently Asked Questions area. However, at this time, no opinions are available on that site. For Supreme Judicial Court and Court of Appeals decisions, see the alternate URLs. The first alternate URL, from Lawyers Weekly Publications provides free access to cases from the last three months. The second alternate URL points to a commercial, fee-based source for opinions that go back to 1937.

Subject Headings: Cases—Massachusetts—Full Text; Massachusetts

Michigan

[1046] Michigan Cases, Statutes, and Guides

Sponsoring Agencies: Institute of Continuing Legal Education; Michigan. Courts

Primary Access: http://www.icle.org/michlaw/index.htm

Resource Summary: The Institute of Continuing Legal Education provides access to the full text of Michigan Supreme Court opinions issued since October 1995; Michigan Court Rules; Administrative Orders; and Michigan Court of Appeals opinions since August 1996. The cases are available in HTML or WordPerfect formats. Access is available by date or by keyword searching.

Subject Headings: Cases—Michigan—Full Text; Michigan

[1047] Michigan State Government

Sponsoring Agency: Michigan State Government

Primary Access: http://www.migov.state.mi.us/

Resource Summary: This primary site for Michigan government information offers the basic three branches of government as starting points. In addition, it has links to the categories, Areas Updated Regularly and Important Issues. The listing of state agencies is found under the Departments and Agencies heading.

Subject Heading: Michigan

[1048] The Michigan State Legislature

Sponsoring Agency: Michigan. Legislature

Primary Access: http://www.migov.state.mi.us/legislature.html

Alternative Access Method: http://www.icle.org/leg-sums/leglist.htm

Resource Summary: This very simple page consists of links to the Michigan House and Senate Web sites. Both of these sites provide member directories and descriptive information, but neither yet offers much information on legislation. A summary of important recent legislation can be found at the alternate URL.

Subject Heading: Michigan

Minnesota

[1049] Minnesota State Court System

Sponsoring Agency: Minnesota. Courts

Primary Access: http://www.courts.state.mn.us/

Resource Summary: Featuring a substantial amount of court-related information, this site provides recent news from the courts and links to the categories: Court Information Office; the Minnesota State Law Library; the Lawyer's Professional Responsibility Board; and the Client Security Board. Supreme Court opinions and Court of Appeals opinions are available in WordPerfect, RTF, and HTML formats and are available back to 1996. For the older cases, try the Minnesota State Law Library link.

Subject Headings: Cases—Minnesota—Full Text; Minnesota

[1050] Minnesota State Legislature

Sponsoring Agency: Minnesota. Legislature

Primary Access: http://www.leg.state.mn.us/

Resource Summary: The primary links on this site are entitled: Minnesota House of Representatives; Minnesota Senate; Legislation and Bill Tracking; Schedules; Minnesota Statutes and Minnesota Session Laws; and Joint Legislative Departments and Commissions. The Bill Tracking section includes both the bill status and the full text of bills in HTML format back to the 1993 session. The Minnesota Statutes and Minnesota Session Laws section includes a browsable verions of the *Minnesota Statutes* in HTML. A keyword search option is made available by using Infoseek. The page also includes an online copy of the Minnesota constitution and the *Minnesota Session Laws* back to 1993.

Subject Headings: Legislation—Minnesota; Minnesota

[1051] North Star: Minnesota Government Information and Services

Sponsoring Agency: Minnesota State Government

Primary Access: http://www.state.mn.us/mainmenu.html

Alternative Access Methods: http://www.state.mn.us/text/index.html [text version]
http://www.state.mn.us [for other options]
gopher://x500.state.mn.us/

Resource Summary: Designed to be "one-start government," North Star offers information on the state as well as links to government servers. Primary government sections include: Government Offices; Northern Highlights; Tools of Democracy; and Search North Star. The Government Offices section is the best starting point for finding specific agencies. This page is organized under sections such entitled: Legislative Branch; Executive Branch; Judicial Branch; Local Government; and State Boards, Commissions, Councils, Ombudsmen Offices, and Task Forces.

Subject Heading: Minnesota

Mississippi

[1052] Mississippi State Legislature

Sponsoring Agency: Mississippi. Legislature

Primary Access: http://www.ls.state.ms.us/

Alternative Access Method: ftp://billstatus.ls.state.ms.us/

Resource Summary: Links to the House and Senate provide member biographies, committee information, and mailing addresses for each chamber. Use of the Bill Status section requires downloading and installing software to view the bill status, but even with the extra software, it does not offer access to the full text of the bills. However, the ftp site gives access to the full text of bills for the current session in WordPerfect 5.2 format.

Subject Headings: Legislation—Mississippi—Full Text; Mississippi

[1053] Mississippi Supreme Court

Sponsoring Agency: Mississippi. Supreme Court

Primary Access: http://www.mslawyer.com/mssc/

Resource Summary: This site includes all of the Mississippi Rules of Practice along with opinions of the Mississippi Supreme Court and Court of Appeals. The Cases section provides access to the opinions from both courts back to 1996. Available in HTML or compressed WordPerfect 6.1 formats, the cases are accessible by date, name, or keyword. The site also has directories of court judges and staff at the circuit, county, and state levels.

Subject Headings: Cases—Mississippi—Full Text; Mississippi

[1054] State of Mississippi

Sponsoring Agency: Mississippi State Government

Primary Access: http://www.state.ms.us/

Resource Summary: This site consists primarily of an alphabetical list of state agencies and other state government Web sites. As such, it is useful as a starting point but it would be improved with more descriptive state information.

Subject Heading: Mississippi

Missouri

[1055] Missouri General Assembly

Sponsoring Agency: Missouri. Legislature

Primary Access: http://www.moga.state.mo.us/

Resource Summary: The General Assembly site features the categories: Bill Tracking Information; Missouri Revised Statutes; Missouri Constitution; Missouri House of Representatives; Missouri Senate; and Legislative Joint Committees. The Bill Tracking Information section provides the status and full text of bills in HTML. The bills are accessible by bill number, keyword, and sponsor. This HTML version of the *Missouri Revised Statutes* is accessible by keyword and is browsable by title.

Subject Headings: Legislation—Missouri—Full Text; Missouri

[1056] Missouri State Government

Sponsoring Agency: Missouri State Government

Primary Access: http://www.state.mo.us/

Resource Summary: Featuring a different government site each week, Missouri's official Web site organizes the rest of its links under the headings: Executive Branch; Executive Departments; Judicial Branch; and Legislative Branch. In addition, it offers the categories: State Government Open Meeting Notices; State Government E-mail Directory; State Government; State Government Telephone Directory; State Job Opportunities; and State Bid Opportunities.

Although it packs a lot of information onto one page, this site is well designed and very easy to navigate.

Subject Heading: Missouri

[1057] Supreme Court of Missouri

Sponsoring Agency: Missouri. Supreme Court

Primary Access: http://www.state.mo.us/sca/mosupct.htm

Resource Summary: This site provides the categories: Dockets and Meet the Judges for the Supreme Court and the Eastern District Court of Appeals. Cases are available for the heading Court of Appeals from December of 1996 in HTML format. The Supreme Court cases are found under the Monthly Dispositions section, also in HTML but only for the past month.

Subject Headings: Cases—Missouri—Full Text; Missouri

Montana

[1058] Montana Legislative Branch

Sponsoring Agency: Montana. Legislature

Primary Access: http://www.mt.gov/leg/branch/branch.htm

Resource Summary: Montana's legislative site features access to the full text of bills and also to the state code. Under the heading Legislature, the bills are available in WordPerfect and HTML formats back to 1995. Access is by bill number, keyword search, or via a subject index. This area also includes the headings: Hearing Schedules; Agenda; Cumulative Bill Status; Budget Analysis; and Calendar. The *Montana Code Annotated* can be searched by keyword or browsed by title as a Folio Infobase.

Subject Headings: Legislation—Montana—Full Text; Montana

[1059] Montana Supreme Court Opinions

Sponsoring Agency: Montana. Supreme Court

Primary Access: http://www.lawlibrary.mt.gov/OPININS.HTM

Resource Summary: Beginning with 1997, the Montana Supreme Court slip opinions are available by date at this site. The cases are in ASCII text and no keyword searching is available. Check at the root URL for the Montana State Law Library in case this URL changes.

Subject Headings: Cases—Montana—Full Text; Montana

[1060] State of Montana: State and Local Government

Sponsoring Agency: Montana State Government

Primary Access: http://www.mt.gov/gov/gov.htm

Resource Summary: This page provides an alphabetical list of state agencies and other state government Web sites. Despite the title, it includes no local government links.

Subject Heading: Montana

Nebraska

[1061] Nebraska Legislature

Sponsoring Agency: Nebraska. Legislature

Primary Access: http://unicam1.lcs.state.ne.us/

Resource Summary: Nebraska's single-chamber legislature provides this site with the full text of bills and the state statutes. The site also features descriptive and historical information on the Legislature. Under the heading, Nebraska Statutes, the full text of statutes is available in a Folio Infobase and is searchable by keyword or chapter. The Bills and Other Current Legislative Documents section features daily agendas, worksheets, and summaries; hearing schedules; past summaries; and the current session's bills. Available in both HTML and RTF formats, the bills can be searched by number or keyword.

Subject Headings: Legislation—Nebraska—Full Text; Nebraska

[1062] Nebraska State Government

Sponsoring Agency: Nebraska State Government

Primary Access: http://www.state.ne.us/

Alternative Access Method: http://www.state.ne.us/text/index.html [text version]

Resource Summary: Nebraska's Web site provides basic information about Nebraska's government along with links to agency information and a state government phone directory. Primary categories include: Elected Officials; State Agencies with Internet Sites; Subject Guide; State Phone Directory; and Unicameral Legislature. The State Agencies link is an alphabetical list with some hierarchical breakdowns while the Subject Guide section offers topical access to state agencies. Choose the option, Search this Site for keyword searching.

Subject Heading: Nebraska

Nevada

[1063] Nevada State Legislature

Sponsoring Agency: Nevada. Legislature

Primary Access: http://www.leg.state.nv.us/

Alternative Access Method: ftp://ftp.leg.state.nv.us

Resource Summary: Nevada's legislative site features the sections: Session Information; Daily Agendas; Legislators and Committees; Legislative Counsel Bureau; General Information; and Search Nevada Law. Current bills are found under the heading, Session Information. They are available in HTML format, accessible by bill number and keyword. Session Information also includes the links Assembly and Senate Journals and Announcements. The Search Nevada Law section provides keyword access to the *Nevada Revised Statutes and Administrative Code*.

While this site offers a commendable quantity of state legislative information, the access could be improved. It would be helpful to have browse access by title for the *Nevada Revised Statutes and Administrative Code*.

Subject Headings: Legislation—Nevada—Full Text; Nevada

[1064] State of Nevada

Sponsoring Agency: Nevada State Government

Primary Access: http://www.state.nv.us/

Resource Summary: Nevada's official site organizes most of its links under the heading General Categories of Information and Interest. The section lists state government sites by general topics. The Index of Agencies and Departments link provides a straight alphabetical list of agencies. Other featured categories include Press Releases and New Additions.

Subject Heading: Nevada

New Hampshire

[1065] New Hampshire General Court

Sponsoring Agency: New Hampshire. Legislature

Primary Access: http://www.state.nh.us/gencourt/gencourt.htm

Resource Summary: Despite its name, this is the site of New Hampshire's legislature. The site features rosters, calendars, and journals for both the House and Senate. It provides lists of introduced bills with brief summaries back to 1996. The only bills available in full text are the final versions of those that passed. These bills are under the Session Laws section in HTML format, accessible by chapter.

Subject Headings: Legislation—New Hampshire—Full Text; New Hampshire

[1066] New Hampshire Judicial Branch

Sponsoring Agency: New Hampshire. Courts

Primary Access: http://www.state.nh.us/courts/home.htm

Resource Summary: This simple page links to the pages for New Hampshire's Supreme Court; Probate Court; Administrative Office of the Courts; and Law Library. The Supreme Court page includes the full text of slip opinions in HTML and zipped ASCII formats since 1995. Access is by date in reverse chronological order. The Probate Court link offers only probate court forms and a few administrative orders.

Subject Headings: Cases—New Hampshire—Full Text; New Hampshire

[1067] The New Hampshire State Government Online Information Center

Sponsoring Agency: New Hampshire State Government

Primary Access: http://www.state.nh.us/

Resource Summary: Also known as Webster, the New Hampshire State Government Online Information Center offers sections including: State Government; State Information by Subject; Local Government; New Hampshire Almanac; and Employment. The State Government section uses a hierarchical breakdown of sites under the headings: Governor's Office; State Agencies; Legislative Branch; Judicial Branch; and Directory of State Agencies. The State Information by Subject divides agency links by general topics.

Subject Heading: New Hampshire

New Jersey

[1068] New Jersey Judiciary

Sponsoring Agency: New Jersey. Courts

Primary Access: http://www.state.nj.us/judiciary/

Resource Summary: While this site does not yet offer any slip opinions online, it does provide basic information about New Jersey courts down to the county and vicinage level. The site also has information about the Administrative Office of the Courts. Many of the other links point to federal or additional state court information.

Subject Heading: New Jersey

[1069] New Jersey State Legislature

Sponsoring Agency: New Jersey. Legislature

Primary Access: http://www.njleg.state.nj.us

Resource Summary: This site features the sections: Information on Members of the New Jersey Legislature; An Interactive Map of New Jersey Legislative Districts; The Text, Indexes, and History of Bills; The New Jersey Statutes; The New Jersey Constitution; The Latest Legislative Calendar; and The Latest and Previous Issues of the Legislative Digest. The full-text bills, the Legislative Calendar, and the Legislative Digest are only available in Envoy format, although brief summaries are available in HTML. The bills are accessible by bill number, sponsor, subject, and keyword in a Folio Infobase. The full-text search of the *New Jersey Statutes* is also in a Folio Infobase, accessible by keyword and is browsable by title.

Subject Headings: Legislation—New Jersey—Full Text; New Jersey

[1070] The State of New Jersey

Sponsoring Agency: New Jersey State Government

Primary Access: http://www.state.nj.us/

Resource Summary: Also called the New Jersey In Touch Home Page, this site aims to help the public keep in touch with what's happening throughout the state and find information on government services. Featured sections include: Office of the Governor; Of Special Interest; and Government in Action. The Of Special Interest section covers general interest topics while the Government in Action section points to the primary branches of state government.

Subject Heading: New Jersey

New Mexico

[1071] New Mexico Legislature

Sponsoring Agency: New Mexico. Legislature

Primary Access: http://www.technet.nm.org/legislature/

Alternative Access Methods: http://www.nm.org/legislature
http://www.michie.com/Code/NM/NM.html

Resource Summary: The legislative pages for New Mexico feature the links: Bill Finder; House; Senate; Current Issues; and Archives. The Bill Finder section provides access to the bills by chamber, type of bill, keyword, sponsor, category, and bill number. The bills are available in ASCII format with a link to bill status information. Older bills are available back to 1996. The Archives section has a link to the *New Mexico Statutes* and *Administrative Code*, but it points to a dead end. Check the second alternate URL for access to these publications at The Michie Company. Free registration is required to view the publications.

Subject Headings: Legislation—New Mexico—Full Text; New Mexico

[1072] State of New Mexico Government Information

Sponsoring Agency: New Mexico State Government

Primary Access: http://www.state.nm.us/

Resource Summary: The official New Mexico site organizes its links under the headings: Information Resources; Contact Us; Elected Officials; and In General. The main state government agency links are under the heading Information Resources by both agency name and by subject.

Well designed, with the appropriate use of Southwestern colors and design schemes, this site is quite effective in providing easy access to New Mexico government information on the Web.

Subject Heading: New Mexico

[1073] The Virtual Court House / The Second District Court of New Mexico

Sponsoring Agency: New Mexico. Second District Court

Primary Access: http://www.cabq.gov/cjnet/dst2alb/

Resource Summary: At this point, this is apparently the only state court in New Mexico with an Internet presence. It does not include online cases, but it does have descriptive information on the Second District Court.

Subject Heading: New Mexico

New York

[1074] New York Court of Appeals Decisions

Sponsoring Agencies: Legal Information Institute (LII); New York. Court of Appeals

Primary Access: http://www.law.cornell.edu/ny/ctap/overview.html

Alternative Access Method: mailto:listserv@lii.law.cornell.edu with "subscribe liibulletin-ny" in body

Resource Summary: Note that while in most states the highest court is called the Supreme Court, New York's highest court is the Court of Appeals. This site offers access to decisions since 1992 by date, name, topic, and keyword. The opinions are in HTML format. The mailing list is a current awareness mailing list that analyzes the more significant decisions of the New York Court of Appeals. These commentaries are also available on the Web site.

Subject Headings: Cases—New York—Full Text; New York

[1075] New York State Assembly

Sponsoring Agency: New York. Legislature

Primary Access: http://assembly.state.ny.us/

Alternative Access Methods: telnet://assembly.state.ny.us/
gopher://assembly.state.ny.us/

Resource Summary: New York's legislative sites features: Assembly Legislative Information System; an Assembly member directory; press releases; and information on the legislative process. The Assembly Legislative Information System provides access to the sections: Bill Information; Assembly Calendar; Public Hearing Schedule; Committee Agendas; New York State Laws; and Legislative Reports. The Bill Information section offers access by bill number or keyword. The results show a bill summary, actions, votes, and a memo record. The full text is in ASCII format, and only the current session is available. Under the heading New York State Laws, both the *New York State Consolidated Laws* and the *New York State Unconsolidated Laws* are available, with access only by subject.

Subject Headings: Legislation—New York—Full Text; New York

[1076] Welcome to New York

Sponsoring Agency: New York State Government

Primary Access: http://www.state.ny.us/

Resource Summary: The official New York state page points to more than just government information. Try the top level links to the Governor and Citizen's Access to Government section for state government information. Within the Citizen's Access to Government page, choose either the State or Local sections. The State section is arranged alphabetically, while the Local is divided by type and location.

The organization of this site can make it difficult to find specific state agencies. The state agency listing should be higher in the site's hierarchy and a topical index to state services would be helpful.

Subject Heading: New York

North Carolina

[1077] North Carolina General Assembly

Sponsoring Agency: North Carolina. Legislature

Primary Access: http://www.ncga.state.nc.us/

Alternative Access Methods: ftp://www.ncga.state.nc.us/
ftp://ftp.legislature.state.nc.us/

Resource Summary: This site offers the sections: House; Senate; Bills; Search; Calendars; County Representation; Committees; and Legislative Services. Both the Bills and Search sections provide access to the full text of recent bills in HTML and ASCII formats. The Bills section also includes the headings Bill History; Bill Status; History of Votes; Fiscal Information; and other sections relevant to the legislative process. Access to bills via the Search section is by bill number, key-word, or sponsor.

Subject Headings: Legislation—North Carolina—Full Text; North Carolina

[1078] North Carolina Information Server

Sponsoring Agency: North Carolina State Government

Primary Access: http://www.state.nc.us/

Resource Summary: This official North Carolina site offers government information from categories including Public Info; Business Info; Employee Info; Education; and State Agencies. Except for the last, these all provide topic access to various state agency sites. The Employee Info page is designed specifically for current and prospective state employees. The State Agencies section lists links to state agencies in a hierarchical display.

Subject Heading: North Carolina

[1079] North Carolina Judicial Branch

Sponsoring Agency: North Carolina. Courts

Primary Access: http://www.aoc.state.nc.us/

Alternative Access Method: http://www.nando.net/insider/supreme/supco.html

Resource Summary: The site features a broad range of information on the North Carolina Courts, including opinions, press releases, speeches, and information from the Administrative Office of the Courts. The Supreme Court and Court of Appeals links provides access to those courts' opinions, calendars, and biographies. The slip opinions are available in HTML and WordPerfect formats and are accessible by date and case name back to December 1995. The alternate URL also has HTML copies of slip opinions acessible by date, but that site goes back to November 1994.

Subject Headings: Cases—North Carolina—Full Text; North Carolina

North Dakota

[1080] North Dakota Legislative Branch

Sponsoring Agency: North Dakota. Legislature

Primary Access: http://www.state.nd.us/lr/

Resource Summary: Offering information on past, present, and future legislative sessions, this site provides basic information about the Legislative Assembly including the sections: Legislative Council Interim Studies; How to Contact a Legislator; How a Bill Becomes a Law; How to Testify Before a Legislative Committee; and Legislative Deadlines. The Bill Status System which provides the status and full text of bills in PDF format is a subscription service.

Subject Headings: Legislation—North Dakota—Full Text; North Dakota

[1081] North Dakota Supreme Court

Sponsoring Agency: North Dakota. Supreme Court

Primary Access: http://www.court.state.nd.us/

Resource Summary: The Supreme Court site offers information on the whole state court system with sections including: Opinions; Rules; Calendar; Notices; The Court; District Courts; Lawyers; Resources; Committees; and Filing. Slip opinions are available by date for the past two years and by name, topic, citation, and keyword for older opinions back to 1993. The decisions are in HTML. The full text of various North Dakota court rules are available in HTML under the Rules heading.

Subject Headings: Cases—North Dakota—Full Text; North Dakota

[1082] The State of North Dakota

Sponsoring Agency: North Dakota State Government

Primary Access: http://www.state.nd.us/

Resource Summary: North Dakota's site provides a basic breakdown of government servers by the three branches of government. It also provides the links: Eduction; Road Reports; and General Information and Services. Look under the Executive Branch heading for a basic breakdown of state agency Web sites. The General Information and Services section includes the links, Electronic Mail Addresses and Employment Opportunities.

Subject Heading: North Dakota

Ohio

[1083] Legislative Branch

Sponsoring Agency: Ohio. Legislature

Primary Access: http://www.ohio.gov/ohio/legislat.htm

Alternative Access Methods: http://www.avv.com/orc/
http://www.gongwer-oh.com/general.html

Resource Summary: This main URL only provides access to a directory of the House and Senate. No current bill information is available yet, but the first alternate URL provides access to the *Ohio Revised Code* and *Ohio Session Law*. The *Code* can be browsed by title or searched by keyword. *Ohio Session Law* includes the full text of all bills passed by the legislature since 1995. Access to these is by bill number.

State legislative leaders have indicated that the Ohio General Assembly will make the full text of House and Senate bills; amendments to bills; analysis of bills prepared by the Ohio Legislative Service Commission; and fiscal impact statements of bills prepared by the Ohio Legislative Budget Office available. While this information is not yet there, check the three URLs to see if it becomes available soon.

Subject Headings: Legislation—Ohio—Full Text; Ohio

[1084] Ohio Government Pages

Sponsoring Agency: Ohio State Government

Primary Access: http://www.ohio.gov/

Alternative Access Method: http://www.state.oh.us/

Resource Summary: Also listed as Ohio Government Information and Services, this site features information divided into the standard three branches of government. In addition, the Information by Topic section features the headings: Online Transactions; Job Opportunities; Popular Resources; and Telephone and E-mail Directories. Under the Executive Branch heading, the Agencies by Name section provides an alphabetical list of state agencies on the Web.

Subject Heading: Ohio

[1085] Supreme Court of Ohio

Sponsoring Agency: Ohio. Supreme Court

Primary Access: http://www.sconet.ohio.gov/

Alternative Access Method: ftp://ftp.sconet.ohio.gov/

Resource Summary: In addition to a few links to information on recent events or expected descisions, the primary link on this page is Announcements and Opinions, which points to the FTP site. Slip opinions are accessible by date and then docket number (which is embedded in the file name) back to 1992. All are in ASCII text format with more recent cases also available in Microsoft Word format.

Subject Headings: Cases—Ohio—Full Text; Ohio

Oklahoma

[1086] Oklahoma

Sponsoring Agency: Oklahoma State Government

Primary Access: http://www.oklaosf.state.ok.us/

Resource Summary: With an opening banner reading "Oklahoma Native America," this site is Oklahoma's State Government Information Server. There is a link to a listing of state agency home pages which provides both an online phone directory and a list of state agencies with Web sites arranged alphabetically by keyword. (Often the chosen keyword is in the middle of the agency name.) The primary organization of the top level page is by broad topics such as Budget, Revenue, and Pension; Commerce; Education, Science, and Technology; or Arts, Tourism, and Recreation. Under these topical headings are links to state agencies that deal with that subject area.

The organization could be improved with providing a straight alphabetical listing of agencies and by offering clear and direct access to the main three branches of the state government.

Subject Heading: Oklahoma

[1087] Oklahoma Legislative Information System

Sponsoring Agency: Oklahoma. Legislature

Primary Access: http://www.lsb.state.ok.us/

Resource Summary: This simply-designed page points directly to the House and Senate sites. While no full-text bill information is available, these sites offer member directories, committee information, and brief legislation summaries. The Text of Bills section provides information on how to obtain copies of the bills. While some electronic services are listed, no Internet connection information is provided for any of those services.

Subject Headings: Legislation—Oklahoma; Oklahoma

[1088] Oklahoma Public Legal Research System

Sponsoring Agencies: Oklahoma. Courts; Oklahoma Bar Association

Primary Access: http://www.onenet.net/oklegal/

Resource Summary: The Oklahoma Public Legal Research System provides access to Oklahoma statutes, cases, and other law-related information. The site is sponsored by the Oklahoma Bar Association and maintained through the efforts of volunteers. Its principal sections are: Oklahoma Constitution; *Oklahoma Statutes*; Oklahoma Decisions; and State Department of Labor Administrative Decisions. The *Oklahoma Statutes* are keyword searchable. The Oklahoma Decisions section offers access to the links: Oklahoma Supreme Court Opinions; Court of Appeals Opinions; Court of Criminal Appeals Opinions; Attorney Generals Opinions; Attorney Generals Unpublished Opinions; and Merit Protection Opinions. They vary in date coverage with the Supreme Court opinions going back to 1994 and the Attorney Generals opinions going back to 1948. Keyword searching can be on the full text, date, appellant, appellee, or jurisdiction.

This is a commendable volunteer effort that makes a large collection of Oklahoma legal material available on the Web.

Subject Headings: Cases—Oklahoma—Full Text; Legislation—Oklahoma—Full Text; Oklahoma

Oregon

[1089] Oregon Law Online

Sponsoring Agency: Oregon. Courts

Primary Access: http://www.or-law.com/~ccrowell

Alternative Access Method: http://www.willamette.edu/~ccrowell/law/osct/osct. htm

Resource Summary: This site offers ASCII versions of recent Oregon Supreme Court and Oregon Court of Appeals decisions. The Oregon Court of Appeals section includes lists of cases and summaries only. Additional descriptive information about these courts is supposed to be added soon. The alternate site has some of the older opinions, arranged by date.

The site could be improved with better organization and clearer descriptions of what is available.

Subject Headings: Cases—Oregon—Full Text; Oregon

[1090] Oregon Online Government

Sponsoring Agency: Oregon State Government

Primary Access: http://www.state.or.us/governme.htm

Resource Summary: This page consists of a long list of state departments, boards, commissions, and divisions that have Web sites. The list is alphabetical by keyword. It also links to statewide e-mail and telephone directories of government workers.

The organization of this page could be much improved to provide easier access to many state agencies with Web sites. A hierarchical or topical list would help greatly.

Subject Heading: Oregon

[1091] Oregon State Legislature

Sponsoring Agency: Oregon. Legislature

Primary Access: http://www.leg.state.or.us/

Alternative Access Methods: gopher://gopher.leg.state.or.us/
ftp://landru.leg.state.or.us/

Resource Summary: This collection of sites provides a significant amount of legislative information. The Web site includes the sections Senate, House, Bills and Laws, Capitol Information, Committees, and Legislative Gopher. The links to the chambers provides information on members, committee assignments, and leadership. The Bills and Laws section provides access to the *Oregon Revised Statutes*, housed on the Gopher server. It supports keyword searching or browsing by chapter. The Legislative Measures and Related Publications section provides access to bills from 1995. Once again, the information is housed on the Gopher server and is accessible by bill number or keyword searching.

Since most of the information content is on a Gopher server, it is mostly in ASCII format. Moving these resources to the Web would allow for additional formatting options.

Subject Headings: Legislation—Oregon—Full Text; Oregon

Pennsylvania

[1092] Pennsylvania Senate

Sponsoring Agency: Pennsylvania. Senate

Primary Access: http://www.pasen.gov/

Alternative Access Method: http://moose.erie.net/~italo/bills.html

Resource Summary: This site offers relatively little information on the Senate or the legislature in general, but it does include a directory of officers and members. Some bills that were enacted are available from 1995-1996 on the alternate URL.

While no bills are yet available, the site does offer a note saying that the technical changes necessary to provide bill history and text are being reviewed with the intent of providing that information in the future.

Subject Headings: Legislation—Pennsylvania; Pennsylvania

[1093] Pennsylvania State Government

Sponsoring Agency: Pennsylvania State Government

Primary Access: http://www.state.pa.us/govstate.html

Resource Summary: This page features a hierarchical listing of state agencies that have information on the Web. The first level of the hierarchy divides links into the executive, legislative, and judicial branches.

Subject Heading: Pennsylvania

[1094] The Supreme Court of Pennsylvania

Sponsoring Agency: Pennsylvania. Courts

Primary Access: http://www.cerf.net/penna-courts/

Resource Summary: This site offers press releases, session calendars, court rules, and opinions from the Pennsylvania Supreme Court and Commonwealth Court. The slip opinions are available in WordPerfect 5.0 format and are accessible by month back to November 1996. Within each month, the cases are listed roughly by date. The site displays case name, docket number, and date posted.

It is not easy to find specific cases on this site and as more cases are added, the confusion will get worse. More access points should be developed, and HTML or ASCII formats for the decisions would be helpful as well.

Subject Headings: Cases—Pennsylvania—Full Text; Pennsylvania

Rhode Island

[1095] Rhode Island Courts Information

Sponsoring Agencies: Rhode Island. Courts; Rhode Island Bar Association

Primary Access: http://www.ribar.com/courts.html

Resource Summary: Sponsored by the Rhode Island Bar Association and hosted on their Web server, a few recent Rhode Island Supreme Court opinions are available in HTML, accessible by an unordered list by name only. It appears as though the Bar Association plans on adding more content to this site.

Subject Headings: Cases—Rhode Island—Full Text; Rhode Island

[1096] Rhode Island General Assembly

Sponsoring Agency: Rhode Island. Legislature

Primary Access: http://www.rilin.state.ri.us/

Alternative Access Method: http://www.sec.state.ri.us/submenus/leglink.htm

Resource Summary: Beyond a few audio welcome files, the main content on the site is found within the categories: House; Senate; General Assembly; Press Releases; Ocean State; and Student/Teacher Guide. Under the General Assembly heading, the full text of bills from the current session, committee calendars, committee agendas, public laws back to 1994, and the *Rhode Island General Laws* are available. The HTML versions of the bills may be searched by the bill number, sponsor, citation, or keyword. The *Rhode Island General Laws* are accessible by title or keyword and are in HTML format. The alternate site also provides some access to the full text of current bills.

While this site provides a substantial quantity of Rhode Island legislative information, a few small improvements would help. The *Rhode Island General Laws* sections should at least provide a date for the source files that is more obvious.

Subject Headings: Legislation—Rhode Island—Full Text; Rhode Island

[1097] Rhode Island State Government

Sponsoring Agency: Rhode Island State Government

Primary Access: http://www.info.state.ri.us/

Alternative Access Method: http://www.state.ri.us/

Resource Summary: The State Government Information Service section features some budget documents followed by sections for the executive and legislative branches. Another link points to the heading, Rhode Island Cities and Towns. Under the heading Executive Branch, the State Government Agencies section offers a topical listing of state agencies that have Web sites. The alternate URL points to the Secretary of State's Public Information Kiosk which has direct access to the full text of bills and also to the links: State Officials; Elections; Legislative Information; and State Departments and Quasi Public Agencies.

Subject Heading: Rhode Island

South Carolina

[1098] Opinions of the Supreme Court of South Carolina

Sponsoring Agencies: South Carolina. Supreme Court; University of South Carolina Law Center. Library

Primary Access: http://www.law.sc.edu/opinions/opinions.htm

Alternative Access Method: http://www.state.sc.us/judicial/

Resource Summary: The University of South Carolina Law Center's Library has made these cases available in HTML format. Accessible by date, first party, second party, and by keyword search, these slip opinions are available back to March of 1996. The alternate URL provides access to the Judicial Branch of South Carolina State Government, but it only consists of some addresses and a link to the central URL.

Subject Headings: Cases—South Carolina—Full Text; South Carolina

[1099] State of South Carolina Public Information

Sponsoring Agency: South Carolina State Government

Primary Access: http://www.state.sc.us/

Resource Summary: This central site for the state links to the sections: Education; Commerce and Tourism; Government in the Palmetto State; State Agencies; and South Carolina State Jobs. The Government in the Palmetto State section points to a variety of state government information areas including: Governor's Office; Lt. Governor's Office; Comptroller General's Office; State Treasurer's Office; Legislature; State Agencies; The Judicial Branch; and State Employee Office Phone Numbers. The State Agencies page offers an alphabetical list of the major state agencies that have an Internet presence.

Subject Heading: South Carolina

[1100] Welcome to the South Carolina General Assembly

Sponsoring Agency: South Carolina. Legislature

Primary Access: http://www.leginfo.state.sc.us/

Alternative Access Method: http://www.lpitr.state.sc.us/

Resource Summary: Both sites provide basic information on the legislature along with access to bill status and to the full text of bills. The main URL is better organized with the links Chambers; Bills; Sponsors; Committees; Actions; Subjects; Status; and Past Legislation. The actual HTML full-text copies of the bills are located on the server for the alternate URL, but both starting points provide easy access to the legislation. The Past Legislation link provides access to information on bills from 1975.

Subject Heading: Legislation—South Carolina—Full Text

South Dakota

[1101] Legislative Branch

Sponsoring Agency: South Dakota. Legislature

Primary Access: http://www.state.sd.us/state/legis/legis.htm

Alternative Access Method: gopher://gopher.state.sd.us/1%201%5Cfiles%5Clegis

Resource Summary: This page links to the headings Legislative Research Council and Legislative Audit. Choose the Legislative Research Council for address information on the Council and a link to current legislative information. The Legislative Information page provides access to the full text of current bills in HTML format and to bill status information. Access is by bill number, bill tracking list name, sponsor, and keyword. The Gopher server listed under the alternate URL hosts an online version of the *Administrative Rules of South Dakota*, the 1994 session laws, and the 1994 special session laws, all in WordPerfect 5.1 format.

Subject Headings: Legislation—South Dakota—Full Text; South Dakota

[1102] South Dakota Supreme Court Opinions

Sponsoring Agencies: South Dakota. Supreme Court; State Bar of South Dakota

Primary Access: http://www.sdbar.org/opinions/index.htm

Alternative Access Method: http://www.state.sd.us/state/judicial/ujs.htm

Resource Summary: This site offers HTML versions of the opinions from the South Dakota Supreme Court since 1996. Access to the cases is by date, in reverse chronological order. The alternate URL points to a page that contains address information on the State Court Administrator of the Unified Judicial System for South Dakota. There are no links at the alternate URL, not even to the Supreme Court opinions.

Subject Headings: Cases—South Dakota—Full Text; South Dakota

[1103] State of South Dakota

Sponsoring Agency: South Dakota State Government

Primary Access: http://www.state.sd.us/

Alternative Access Methods: http://www.state.sd.us/texthome.htm [text version]
gopher://gopher.state.sd.us/

Resource Summary: With hot topics and current events links on one side of the page, the main categories run down the other side. These include Government (with Executive, Legislative, Judicial, and Services as subcategories); Tourism; Game, Fish, and Parks; Education and Cultural Affairs; Labor; and Business. These categories provide topical access to South Dakota government sites. The Government section presents a more detailed topical breakdown of government agencies, including those without Web sites. The site also offers a keyword search option.

Subject Heading: South Dakota

Tennessee

[1104] Administrative Office of the Courts

Sponsoring Agency: Tennessee. Courts

Primary Access: http://www.tsc.state.tn.us/

Alternative Access Method: http://www.tsc.state.tn.us/texthome.htm [text version]

Resource Summary: This site features the sections: Supreme Court; Court of Appeals; Criminal Appeals; Workers' Compensation; Court Rules; and Press Releases. Full-text opinions are available from the Supreme Court, Court of Criminal Appeals, and Court of Appeals back to 1995 in WordPerfect 6 format. Access is by date only—the date of posting on the Web, not necessarily the date the opinion was filed.

The availability of the cases is commendable, but it would be very helpful to have more access points or other formats. The use of dates posted to the Web rather than filing date can be confusing.

Subject Headings: Cases—Tennessee—Full Text; Tennessee

[1105] Tennessee Sounds Good To Me

Sponsoring Agency: Tennessee State Government

Primary Access: http://www.state.tn.us/

Resource Summary: This page offers a single link to the main body of the site that begins with a welcome message from the governor. After the welcome, the site offers the categories: Executive Branch; Legislative Branch; Judicial Branch; The Governor's Web Links; News Releases; Weekly Schedule; and Search. The press releases and the weekly schedule pertain to the governor. Under the Executive Branch heading, the site offers links to all the state departmental sites. The Search option uses the Excite search engine to search by keyword or concept.

Subject Heading: Tennessee

[1106] Welcome to the Tennessee General Assembly

Sponsoring Agency: Tennessee. Legislature

Primary Access: http://www.legislature.state.tn.us/

Resource Summary: This site briefly describes the General Assembly and offers the links Senate; House of Representatives; Legislative Information; and Legislative Staff Offices. Under the heading Legislative Information, the site offers the sections: Filed Legislation; Calendars; Committees; Daily Service; and the Legislative Record. The Filed Legislation section includes the full text of bills, amendments, fiscal notes, and history. Access is by bill number, but a keyword search is being constructed. The bills are in HTML format.

Subject Headings: Legislation—Tennessee—Full Text; Tennessee

Texas

[1107] State of Texas Government

Sponsoring Agency: Texas State Government

Primary Access: http://www.state.tx.us/

Alternative Access Method: http://www.texas.gov/

Resource Summary: Texas' site offers a substantial collection of information from its main page with the categories Traveling in Texas; Working in Texas; Doing Business in and with Texas; Texas Government; Texas Electronic Library; Texas Agencies; Counties; Cities; and Councils of Government. While not all of these point directly to government information, many do. For state government links, the Texas Government section offers the links Texas Law; State Agencies, Commissions, Universities, and Boards; Office of the Governor; Legislative Information; Councils of Government; Capitol Complex Maps; and Lotto Texas Results. An alphabetical list of state agencies on the Web is under the State Agencies, Commissions, Universities, and Boards section.

With the numerous links and the substantial content on this site, it might be easier to navigate with links to the main three branches of government or with a hierarchical list.

Subject Heading: Texas

[1108] Texas Judicial Web Server

Sponsoring Agency: Texas. Courts

Primary Access: http://sll.courts.state.tx.us/

Resource Summary: This beautifully designed site offers the sections Texas Judicial System Overview; Courts of the State; and Support Organizations. Under the Courts of the State section, basic descriptive information is available for the Supreme Court, the Court of Criminal Appeals, and the 14 Courts of Appeals. The past three months' worth of opinions from the Court of Criminal Appeals are available in a compressed, self-extracting WordPerfect format. They are accessible by date in reverse chronological order.

Subject Headings: Cases—Texas—Full Text; Texas

[1109] Texas Legislature Online

Sponsoring Agency: Texas. Legislature

Primary Access: http://www.capitol.state.tx.us/

Resource Summary: The Texas Legislature Online offers the full text of bills; state codes; the Texas constitution; legislative calendars; committee membership and schedules; and a calendar of events. The full text of the bills can be found under the sections Search Bill Text; Search for Bills By; or View Individual Bill Information. These three sections provide access to text; fiscal notes; bill analyses; author; caption; and legislative actions. Multiple access points are available to the bills which are available in WordPerfect 6, RTF, and ASCII formats. The online bill system offers access to bills back to 1993. The *Texas Statutes* provide the table of contents for each code in HTML format, but the text itself is basically in ASCII. ASCII versions of entire codes are also available as zipped ASCII files.

Subject Headings: Legislation—Texas—Full Text; Texas

Utah

[1110] Official Web Site for the State of Utah

Sponsoring Agency: Utah State Government

Primary Access: http://www.state.ut.us/

Resource Summary: With a prominent position for state government news and an events calendar, this site offers a broad range of information. Primary categories include: Services; Agencies; Legislature; Legal System; and State Directory. The Agencies page presents a hierarchical list of state agencies on the Web while the Services page presents a topical directory. The State Directory is a phone directory of state government employees.

Subject Heading: Utah

[1111] Utah State Court System

Sponsoring Agency: Utah. Courts

Primary Access: http://courtlink.utcourts.gov/

Resource Summary: This site is being completely revised, but it still offers a link to the Utah Digital Signature Law page. After the reconstruction, it should offer basic information on the Utah courts. Check back to this site later to see if it also provides the full text of recent cases.

Subject Heading: Utah

[1112] Utah State Legislature

Sponsoring Agency: Utah. Legislature

Primary Access: http://www.le.state.ut.us/

Resource Summary: This site offers access to full-text bills and to the state code. Major categories include About the Legislature; Legislation; Committees; Utah Code; Legislators; and Staff Office. The Legislation section features calendars, schedules, agendas, journals, and the fulltext bills, back to 1996. Access is by bill number and keyword search. The bills are available in HTML and zipped WordPerfect 6.1 format. The *Utah Code* can be browsed by title or searched using the keyword engine. The text is available in HTML with links to zipped WordPerfect 6.1 formats for downloading.

It would be helpful if users could provide an e-mail address so that they could be notified when specific bills are changed.

Subject Headings: Legislation—Utah—Full Text; Utah

Vermont

[1113] State of Vermont

Sponsoring Agency: Vermont State Government

Primary Access: http://www.cit.state.vt.us/

Resource Summary: Offering an alphabetical list of state agencies with an Internet presence, this site is the official Vermont home page. Below the list of state agencies, the site provides links to the judicial and legislative branches. The Government link near the top points to other governmental links, including federal and other states.

Subject Heading: Vermont

[1114] Vermont Judiciary

Sponsoring Agency: Vermont. Courts

Primary Access: http://www.state.vt.us/courts/

Alternative Access Method: gopher://dol.state.vt.us/11GOPHER_ROOT3%3A%5BSUPCT%5D

Resource Summary: This site provides links to just a few subsidiary pages including Vermont Courts; Court Administration; Court Calendars; and Rule Amendments. Under the Vermont Courts heading, each of the courts has brief descriptive information and a court calendar. Unfortunately, the Judiciary site does not link to the alternate URL. That Gopher server offers slip opinions in ASCII format back to 1993. Access is by date or keyword search.

Subject Headings: Cases—Vermont—Full Text; Vermont

[1115] Vermont Legislative Home Page

Sponsoring Agency: Vermont. Legislatures

Primary Access: http://www.leg.state.vt.us/

Resource Summary: The full text of both bills and the state statutes are available on this site. Featured sections include Today's Legislative Service; Legislative Bill Tracking System; Legislative Documents; Legislative Reports; Legislative Directory; and the Vermont Statutes Online. The Legislative Bill Tracking System provides access by sponsor, bill number, or keyword to bill information from 1987. The bills are in HTML with an option to download a WordPerfect 6.1 version. The Vermont Statutes Online section provides access by title or keyword to the full text of the *Vermont Statutes* in HTML format.

Subject Headings: Legislation—Vermont—Full Text; Vermont

Virginia

[1116] Virginia Government

Sponsoring Agency: Virginia State Government

Primary Access: http://www.state.va.us/home/governmt.html

Resource Summary: This site offers a list of links including The Governor; The Virginia General Assembly; and Virginia State Agencies, Boards, Commissions, and Councils. This last category provides an alphabetical list of state agencies.

Subject Heading: Virginia

[1117] Virginia's Judicial System

Sponsoring Agency: Virginia. Courts

Primary Access: http://www.courts.state.va.us/

Resource Summary: The Virginia Courts Web site features full-text opinions and information on the court system, individual courts, and judges. The Opinions section provides access to a synopsis of opinions from the Supreme Court of Virginia as well as to the full text of opinions from both the Supreme Court and the Court of Appeals. The opinions are available in WordPerfect 5.1 and ASCII formats, with the ASCII versions searchable by keyword. The only other access is by date, in reverse chronological order, for cases back to June 1995.

Subject Headings: Cases—Virginia—Full Text; Virginia

[1118] Welcome to the Virginia General Assembly

Sponsoring Agency: Virginia. Legislature

Primary Access: http://legis.state.va.us/

Resource Summary: The Virginia General Assembly's Web site features the headings Legislative Agencies, the State Legislature, and the Legislative Information System. The State Legislature page offers information on the Legislature with links to the House and Senate and to the page How a Bill Becomes a Law. The Legislative Agencies page links to the sites of several agencies including the Virginia Code Commission. Their page offers access to full-text versions of the *Code of Virginia*, the *Virginia Administrative Code*, and the *Virginia Register of Regulations*. Access to the first two is by keyword, and access to the *Virginia Register of Regulations* is by date. The Legislative Information System section also offers links to the *Code of Virginia* and the *Virginia Administrative Code,* as well as to the full text of bills. These bills are in HTML format and can be searched by bill number, date, subject, or keyword.

Subject Headings: Legislation—Virginia—Full Text; Virginia

Washington

[1119] Home Page Washington

Sponsoring Agency: Washington State Government

Primary Access: http://www.wa.gov/

Resource Summary: Home Page Washington features information from all three branches of government along with a Washington State Government Index and a Local and Regional Government Index, which present a list of state and local agencies with Web sites. Further down on the top level page, a list of topics provides subject access to state agencies. Below that, the site even offers a special section titled Just for Kids, which has resources for researching school reports and making Web pages.

Subject Heading: Washington

[1120] Washington State Courts

Sponsoring Agencies: CD Law, Inc.; Washington. Courts

Primary Access: http://www.wa.gov/courts/

Alternative Access Method: http://www.cdlaw.com/cases.htm

Resource Summary: This site offers its information under the two headings of Court Information and Assistance. The Court Information page includes press releases, a directory of Washington courts, and basic descriptions of the courts. The Assistance section provides links to the following sections: Supreme Court and Court of Appeals Opinions; Court Rules; Employment Opportunities; Reporter of Decisions; Court Forms and Instructions; among others. The Supreme Court and Court of Appeals opinions are available only from the past 90 days. These slip opinions are accessible by date and keyword and are in ASCII format.

The alternate URL from CD Law, Inc., also offers three months, worth of opinions for free. CD Law also has a commercial service that provides access to Washington Supreme Court and Court of Appeals decisions back to 1948 along with access to many other legal databases.

Subject Headings: Cases—Washington—Full Text; Washington

[1121] Washington State Legislature

Sponsoring Agency: Washington. Legislature

Primary Access: http://www.leg.wa.gov/

Alternative Access Methods: gopher://leginfo.leg.wa.gov/
ftp://leginfo.leg.wa.gov/

Resource Summary: The Washington State Legislature's Internet sites offers the links House and Senate; Legislative Agencies; Legislative Info; Bill Info; District Lookup; and a Kid's Page. The Bill Info section provides access to the full text of current bills. The bills are in ASCII format and are not connected directly to any bill status information. The only status information available in this section is in the Daily Status Report. The Report is composed of one long list that uses codes to provide status information. Access to the bills is by number or keyword. Although a Topical Index is available, it is not hyperlinked to the bills, so the user must take the bill number and go back to the listing by number. The full text of the *Revised Code of Washington* is available in ASCII format under the heading Legislative Info and is accessible by title and keyword search.

Subject Headings: Legislation—Washington—Full Text; Washington

West Virginia

[1122] West Virginia: A Welcome Change

Sponsoring Agency: West Virginia State Government

Primary Access: http://www.state.wv.us/

Resource Summary: The official West Virginia Web site features the sections News and Event; Government Highlights; and Departments. The News and Events section provides reports on recent government events primarily from the governor's office. The Government Highlights area provides links to the sections Governor's Office; State Legislature and Elected Officials; Employment Programs; and State Employee Phone Directory. The Departments section provides an unorganized short list of state agencies with an Internet presence.

While this page provides basic connections to the state's government resources, it could be much better organized, especially in the Departments section.

Subject Heading: West Virginia

[1123] West Virginia Legislature

Sponsoring Agency: West Virginia. Legislature

Primary Access: http://www.wvlc.wvnet.edu/legisinfo/legishp.html

Resource Summary: This site does not yet include the full text of any legislation, but it does provide the sections Legislative Session Daily Summary and Committee Meetings and Hearings and a listing of senators and delegates.

Subject Headings: Legislation—West Virginia; West Virginia

Wisconsin

[1124] Badger: State of Wisconsin Information Server

Sponsoring Agency: Wisconsin State Government

Primary Access: http://www.state.wi.us/

Alternative Access Method: gopher://badger.state.wi.us/

Resource Summary: Badger is Wisconsin's official site, and it provides information on Wisconsin state agencies, departments, and other governmental branches. It also links to information resources at the University of Wisconsin campuses. Primary sections of the site include Wisconsin State Agencies; The Wisconsin Legislature; University of Wisconsin; Local Government and Community Sites; General Statewide Information; and Directory Information. The Wisconsin State Agencies page offers an alphabetical list of agencies, departments, and governmental branches that have information available in either Web or Gopher format. It also links to the Online Departmental Directory, which provides addresses and main phone and fax numbers.

Subject Heading: Wisconsin

[1125] WisBar Legal Resources

Sponsoring Agencies: State Bar of Wisconsin; Wisconsin. Courts

Primary Access: http://www.wisbar.org/legalres/

Alternative Access Method: http://www1.binc.net/legalres/

Resource Summary: WisBar users can search Wisconsin Supreme Court and Court of Appeals cases by using the Supreme Court and Court of Appeals search engines. Access to the cases is also available by docket number, petitioner's name, respondent's name, and date. The archive goes back to 1995. The older opinions are available in HTML, RTF, and compressed, self-extracting WordPerfect formats. Since January 1997, the Supreme Court cases are available in HTML and compressed, self-extracting Microsoft Word 7 formats, but only while the Court of Appeals opinions are in HTML and compressed, self-extracting WordPerfect format. In addition to the court opinions, this site offers court rules from the Circuit Courts and the Supreme Court.

Subject Headings: Cases—Wisconsin—Full Text; Wisconsin

[1126] The Wisconsin Legislature

Sponsoring Agency: Wisconsin. Legislature

Primary Access: http://www.legis.state.wi.us/

Resource Summary: The Wisconsin Legislature provides information on the Web from the Legislature and its support offices. The Bill Tracking section provides the full text of bills in PDF format and the histories and status of bills in HTML format. Access is by bill number or subject index. The Legislative Information area offers legislative publications and e-mail addresses of legislators. The *Wisconsin Statutes* are available in PDF format under the Statutes heading and are accessible by chapter.

Subject Headings: Legislation—Wisconsin—Full Text; Wisconsin

Wyoming

[1127] Welcome to the State of Wyoming

Sponsoring Agency: Wyoming State Government

Primary Access: http://www.state.wy.us/

Alternative Access Method: gopher://ferret.state.wy.us/ [defunct]

Resource Summary: The top level page offers the choice between a graphical page or a textual page. It also provides links to the sections Legislative Web Site; Judicial Web Site; and State Library Information. On the Web pages, top level sections include: Governor's Welcome; Governor's Office; Government; Tourism; Business and Industry; and Education. The Government link points to federal, state, and local government pages. For access to Wyoming agencies, try the Governor's Office section and then the State Agencies or Boards and Commissions links.

Subject Heading: Wyoming

[1128] Wyoming State Legislature

Sponsoring Agency: Wyoming. Legislature

Primary Access: http://legisweb.state.wy.us/

Resource Summary: Wyoming's site offers access to bills from legislative sessions back to 1995, and also to the sections State Statutes; Legislative Schedule; and Interim Activities. Under the session links, the full text of bills and the status of bills is available. The bills are in ASCII format, with access by bill numbers only. The State Statutes page provides access to the full text of the *Wyoming Statutes*. Access is by title or keyword search to this ASCII version of the state code.

Subject Headings: Legislation—Wyoming—Full Text; Wyoming

[1129] Wyoming State Supreme Court

Sponsoring Agency: Wyoming. Supreme Court

Primary Access: http://courts.state.wy.us/

Resource Summary: With full-text opinions and court rules, this site offers a basic collection of legal materials, including the sections Supreme Court Opinions; Law Library; Wyoming Court System; Supreme Court Justices; Clerk of Court; Court Administrator; Judicial Directory; and Rules of Procedure. The Supreme Court Opinions section offers slip opinions in HTML format back to 1996. Access is by date or keyword search. The Rules of Procedure page provides HTML versions of *Rules of Civil Procedure*, *Rules of Criminal Procedure*, and *Rules of Appelate Procedure*.

Subject Headings: Cases—Wyoming—Full Text; Wyoming

CHAPTER 16: TECHNOLOGY AND ENGINEERING

Since the Internet grew out of government engineering experiments, the Internet is a natural source for government technology and engineering resources. These resources cover a broad range of disciplines, from computer networking to telecommunications, to railroads. See also related information in the other science chapters.

While they are not general finding aids for government technology and engineering sites, the two featured sites for this chapter offer significant information. The Department of Energy Energy Information, Products, and Programs site is a significant resource for energy data and technology information. The NASA Scientific and Technical Information Server demonstrates the amount of technical information that the government produces and provides bibliographic access to a significant portion of that information.

Web Site of the Energy Resources Board

Energy Information, Products, and Programs

Member Offices
Energy Efficiency and Renewable Energy
Energy Information Administration (EIA)
Fossil Energy
Energy Research
The Office of Policy
Nuclear Energy -- Not active

[1130] Energy Information, Products, and Programs

Sponsoring Agency: Department of Energy. Energy Resources Board

Primary Access: http://www.eia.doe.gov/energy/

Resource Summary: The Energy Information, Products, and Programs Web site is the home page of the Energy Resources Board of the Department of Energy. It offers access to energy data, analysis products, information on energy technology, and energy efficiency. It also includes information on outreach programs, links to the individual offices and national labs, and a suggestion form. Under a Points of Interest heading, the page links to weekly production, stocks, and prices data for petroleum, crude oil, and distillate.

The broad range of energy information available from this site and its numerous links makes this an excellent starting point for anyone seeking energy-related information.

Subject Headings: Coal; Energy—Research; Energy Efficiency; Finding Aid—Energy; Nuclear Energy; Petroleum Products; Renewable Energy

[1131] NASA Scientific and Technical Information Server

Sponsoring Agencies: Center for Aerospace Information (CASI); National Aeronautics and Space Administration (NASA); National Advisory Committee for Aeronautics (NACA)

Primary Access: http://www.sti.nasa.gov/

Alternative Access Methods: ftp://ftp.sti.nasa.gov/
gopher://gopher.sti.nasa.gov/

Resource Summary: The NASA Scientific and Technical Information Program Web site provides access to over three million citations in aerospace, aeronautics, and related topics. The main body of its citation database is the CASI Technical Report Server (also known as RECONselect). The CASI Technical Report Server contains bibliographic citations for *Scientific and Technical Aerospace Reports* (STAR file series), journal articles, conference proceedings (Open Literature file series), and citations from the National Advisory Committee for Aeronautics (NACA) collection—NASA's predecessor organization. This bibliographic database uses WAIS indexing, but easy field searching is available through the search form. There are detailed explanations to assist in searching, and document delivery is available for a fee from CASI (although online ordering is not yet available). While the All Files Search option lists the dates of 1962 to the present, citations to older literature are included at least as far back as 1948.

The *STI Bulletin, STAR*, and most of the other publications are available under the STI Program Bibliographic Announcements section, although the Technical Report Server also includes the bibliographic content of these publications in its database. Most of the the publications are in PDF format, which can make browsing and using the indexes to locate bibliographic citations difficult. The Technical Report Server may provide more effective access. The *Thesaurus* has a separate link and is in HTML format, although the supplement is a PDF file.

This site provides a major bibliographic database of broad interest to the engineering and scientific communities. The Technical Report Server, with its field search options, is fairly easy to use for a beginning searcher, and the availability of the *Thesaurus* and more detailed help information make it a functional tool for the information professional as well. Anyone searching for citations to technical reports should try this site.

Subject Headings: Bibliographic Databases; Reports—Bibliography; Scientific and Technical Information

SuDoc Numbers: NAS 1.1/4: *Spinoff*
NAS 1.9/4: *Scientific and Technical Aerospace Reports* (*STAR*)
NAS 1.21: *NASA Thesaurus*
NAS 1.21:7037 *Aeronautical Engineering*
NAS 1.21:7011 *Aerospace Medicine and Biology*
NAS 1.21:7039 *NASA Patent Abstracts Bibliography*
NAS 1.76: *STI Bulletin*

The technology and engineering resources are divided into five sections. The first section covers general technology or engineering information resources as well as technological sites that do not fit under the other categories. This section runs from entry number 1132 to 1156. Communications, the second subchapter, features tele-communications and broadcasting resources and covers entries 1157-1169. The third section, Computer Science, contains resources specific to computer science and includes entries 1170-1198. The Engergy subchapter, entries 1199-1216, includes a number of Department of Energy resources. And the last section, Transportation, entries 1217-1232, cover travel by air, land, and sea.

Technology and Engineering: General

[1132] Advanced Materials and Processes Technology Information Analysis Center

Sponsoring Agencies: Advanced Materials and Processes Technology Information Analysis Center (AMPTIAC); Defense Technical Information Center (DTIC)

Primary Access: http://rome.iitri.com/amptiac/

Alternative Access Method: http://cindas.www.ecn.purdue.edu/ciac/ [former location]

Resource Summary: The Advanced Materials and Processes Technology Information Analysis Center is an Information Analysis Center sponsored by the DTIC. The site offers resources under the sections: User Guide; Products and Services; Data/Information; Calendar of Events; Newsletters; Bulletin Board; and Site Search.

While little information content is available under many of the categories, the site states that the Center is busy working to provide more substantial resources on the site.

Subject Headings: Information Analysis Center; Materials Science

[1133] The Advanced Technology Program

Sponsoring Agencies: Community of Science; National Institute of Standards and Technology (NIST)

Primary Access: http://cos.gdb.org/best/stc/atp.html

Resource Summary: This site promotes the economic growth and competitiveness of U.S. business and industry by accelerating the development and commercialization of promising, high-risk technologies with substantial potential for enhancing U.S. economic growth. It contains information on ATP projects including title, abstract, keywords, proposer, total project cost, and more.

With only a single search line available, the advanced search options in other Community of Science databases are not available here. The site could also better document the content of the database and the frequency of updates.

Subject Headings: Grants; Research and Development

[1134] Cold Regions Science and Technology Information Analysis Center

Sponsoring Agencies: Cold Regions Research and Engineering Laboratory (CRREL); Cold Regions Science and Technology Information Analysis Center

Primary Access: http://www.usace.army.mil/crrel/crstiac/crstiac.html

Resource Summary: The Cold Regions Science and Technology Information Analysis Center serves as the nation's corporate repository for data generated by CRREL. This unique area of science and engineering covers knowledge of the winter battlefield, the environment, basic physical processes, and engineering technology that works in the cold. The Cold Regions Science and Technology Information Analysis Center gathers, processes, analyzes, and disseminates this collection of cold regions knowledge. However, their Web site consists primarily of information about the Information Analysis Center, its activities, and its information services.

Subject Headings: Arctic Regions Research; Engineering Research; Information Analysis Center; Military Research

[1135] Construction Engineering Research Laboratories

Sponsoring Agencies: Army Corps of Engineers; Construction Engineering Research Laboratories (CERL)

Primary Access: http://www.cecer.army.mil/

Alternative Access Method: http://www.cecer.army.mil/hometext.html [text version]

Resource Summary: CERL is involved in research to support sustainable military installations and to increase the Army's ability to more efficiently construct, operate, and maintain its installations while ensuring environmental quality and safety. The Web site includes pages titled Business Areas; Research and Support Services; Points of Contact; Contracting Opportunities; Employment; News; Fact Sheets; and The Cutting Edge—the CERL quarterly publication. Most of these pages give information on the Lab, its personnel, and its divisions. For more detailed information on its projects, the Fact Sheets and the The Cutting Edge sections are the places to look.

Subject Headings: Army; Construction; Research Laboratories

[1136] Defense Nuclear Facilities Safety Board

Sponsoring Agencies: Defense Nuclear Facilities Safety Board (DNFSB); Department of Energy (DOE)

Primary Access: http://www.dnfsb.gov/

Resource Summary: The Board is responsible for independent, external oversight of all activities in the DOE's nuclear weapons complex that affect nuclear health and safety. The Board reviews operations, practices, and occurrences at DOE's defense nuclear facilities. Their site offers information on the Board members along with general information on the Board. Press releases are also available from the General Information page. The Reports and Documents page features the sections DNFSB Recommendations; the Technical Document Log; DNFSB Technical Reports; Travel Reports; and Weekly Reports.

Subject Headings: Nuclear Weapons; Safety

[1137] Defense Research and Engineering

Sponsoring Agencies: Department of Defense (DoD). Office of the Under Secretary of Defense for Acquisition and Technology; Defense Research and Engineering

Primary Access: http://www.dtic.mil/ddre/

Resource Summary: This site includes a number of publications and information on activities of the Director of Defense Research and Engineering. The main categories include Articles and Papers; Plans and Documents; Briefings and Speeches; Testimony; News and Announcements; Calendar of Events; Organization Chart; and Science and Technology Programs. The site also links to component Defense Research and Engineering Web sites.

This site is primarily useful for providing agency information.

Subject Headings: Engineering; Military Research

[1138] Defense Technical Information Center

Sponsoring Agency: Defense Technical Information Center (DTIC)

Primary Access: http://www.dtic.mil/

Alternative Access Methods: http://www.dtic.dla.mil/
ftp://ftp.dtic.dla.mil/pub/

Resource Summary: The Defense Technical Information Center is the Department of Defense's central distribution point for technical defense-related information. The DTIC offers the defense community, including contractors, a broad range of services for locating and delivering technical reports and other relevant publications. While some services available on this site are restricted to registered users only, other portions are available to the entire Internet community.

The primary area for locating DTIC-accessible information is the Products and Services page. It features links to the sections Customized Searches; Referral Services; Document Identification and Ordering; Document Status/Inquiries; DTIC Business Process Reengineering; Defense Online System; Current Awareness Services; Training; Focus Programs; and much more. The Defense Locator page provides access to a DTIC GILS directory.

For defense contractors and defense personnel, this should be the first site to visit when searching for defense technical material. Even for the general public, the site offers some sections that may be useful for verifying citations to defense technical reports. Registered users can search the site for specific information, but the site also explains how to have DTIC personnel conduct the search.

Subject Headings: Government Information Locator Service (GILS); Reports; Scientific and Technical Information

SuDoc Numbers: D 10.11: *DTIC Digest*
D 10.12:P 94/ *DTIC's Nonprint Products Catalog*
D 301.1/3: *Nation's Air Force Issues Book*

[1139] Flexible Computer Integrated Manufacturing Information Server

Sponsoring Agencies: Computer Systems Development Corporation; Department of Defense (DoD)

Primary Access: http://fcim.csdc.com/

Alternative Access Method: ftp://ftp.csdc.com/pub

Resource Summary: The DoD Flexible Computer Integrated Manufacturing (FCIM) program integrates equipment, software, communications, human resources, and business practices within an enterprise to rapidly manufacture, repair, and deliver items on demand with continuous improvements in the process. The vision for the FCIM program is to reduce the lead time for in-house production of parts. This Web site features descriptive information on the program, an FCIM Information Repository, FCIM reverse and re-engineering process assistant, and a What's New page.

Subject Heading: Manufacturing

[1140] HTECH-L [e-mail list]

Sponsoring Agency: Smithsonian Institution

Primary Access: mailto:listserv@sivm.si.edu with "sub htech-l name" in body

Resource Summary: This is an e-mail discussion list—sponsored and hosted by the Smithsonian—on the history of technology.

Subject Headings: E-mail Lists; Technology—History

[1141] Idaho National Engineering and Environmental Laboratory

Sponsoring Agencies: Department of Energy (DOE); Idaho National Engineering and Environmental Laboratory (INEEL)

Primary Access: http://www.inel.gov/

Resource Summary: The INEEL site is updated frequently and hosts information about INEEL research breakthroughs; data on the national programs they manage; and history and background on the Lab and its staff. The site also features a searchable INEEL phone book, employment opportunities, and information about INEEL cleanup and waste management programs. INEEL's research strengths include systems integration and applied engineering, environmental technology and waste management, and nuclear power generation and infrastructure capabilities. The site provides basic descriptive information on the programs and research areas, primarily in the Lab Capabilities and Technologies, and Cleanup and the Environment sections.

Subject Headings: Environmental Engineering; Nuclear Energy; Research Laboratories; Waste Management

[1142] Information Analysis Center Hub

Sponsoring Agencies: Department of Defense (DoD); Defense Technical Information Center (DTIC)

Primary Access: http://www.dtic.mil/iac

Resource Summary: This page is a directory to the home pages of the DoD Information Analysis Centers (IACs). The IACs establish databases of historical, technical, scientific, and other data and information on a variety of technical topics. The databases are worldwide in scope. Information collections include unclassified, limited distribution, and classified information. The IACs also collect, maintain, and develop analytical tools and techniques including databases, models, and simulations. Most of the home pages of the IACs describe the databases that they maintain, although they rarely provide access.

The IACs include the Advanced Materials and Processes Technology Information Analysis Center; the Chemical Warfare/Chemical and Biological Defense IAC; the Ceramics Information Analysis Center; the Chemical Propulsion Information Agency; the Cold Regions Science and Technology Information Analysis Center; and the Crew System Ergonomics Information Analysis Center. Other IACs include the Data and Analysis Center for Software; the Defense Modeling, Simulation, and Tactical Technology Information Analysis Center; the Guidance and Control Information Analysis Center; High Temperature Materials Information Analysis Center; the Information Assurance Technology Analysis Center; Infrared Information Analysis Center; the Metals Information Analysis Center; the Metal Matrix Composites Information Analysis Center; the Manufacturing Technology Information Analysis Center; the Nondestructive Testing Information Analysis Center; the Reliability Analysis Center; and the Survivability/Vulnerability Information Analysis Center. Some of the IAC's Web sites have separate entries in this directory.

Due to access restrictions, most of the resources from the IACs will only be of interest to the defense community. However, there are a few databases of unclassified material available.

Subject Headings: Bibliographic Databases; Engineering Research; Information Analysis Center; Military Research

[1143] Infrared Information Analysis Center

Sponsoring Agencies: Defense Technical Information Center (DTIC); Infrared Information Analysis Center (IRIA)

Primary Access: http://www.erim.org/IRIA/iria.html

Alternative Access Methods: gopher://gopher.erim.org/11/IRIA
ftp://ftp.erim.org/IRIA

Resource Summary: The IRIA Web site offers information about this Information Analysis Center, the symposiums it sponsors, and its area of research. It includes a searchable bibliographic database of unclassified IRIA reports.

The site is useful for finding information about IRIA, but there does not seem to be much research data available on the site. Unfortunately, the bibliographic database is not always dependable and may result in errors or empty sets.

Subject Headings: Bibliographic Databases; Information Analysis Center; Infrared Radiation; Military Research

[1144] Manufacturing Engineering Laboratory

Sponsoring Agencies: National Institute of Standards and Technology (NIST); Manufacturing Engineering Laboratory (MEL)

Primary Access: http://www.mel.nist.gov/

Alternative Access Methods: ftp://ftp.cme.nist.gov/
http://www.cme.nist.gov/ [defunct]

Resource Summary: With a research focus in manufacturing infrastructure technology, measurements, and standards, MEL provides manufacturing engineering tools, interface standards, manufacturing systems architectures, and traceability. The MEL Overview and Context page describes the Lab, its mission, and its research areas. It also has links to more detailed descriptions under the headings Basic Resources for Manufacturers, Information-Driven Manufacturing, Pushing the Limits, and Tapping the Resources. The Organization page provides links to the major divisions of the Lab including Precision Engineering; Automated Production Technology; Intelligent Systems; Manufacturing Systems Integration; and Fabrication Technology. These subsidiary pages contain the main substantive collection of research and project information from the Lab, including research summaries, project reports, and division publications.

Subject Headings: Manufacturing; Research Laboratories

[1145] Manufacturing Technology (ManTech) Program

Sponsoring Agency: Department of Defense (DoD)

Primary Access: http://mantech.iitri.com/

Resource Summary: The ManTech Web site offers information on the DoD ManTech Program and its activities. It includes information on what the program is, how it works, some of its successes, links to other sites, and points of contact for further information.

This site should be useful to anyone searching for information about this program.

Subject Heading: Manufacturing

[1146] Manufacturing Technology Information Analysis Center

Sponsoring Agencies: Defense Technical Information Center (DTIC); Manufacturing Technology Information Analysis Center (MTIAC)

Primary Access: http://mtiac.hq.iitri.com/

Resource Summary: MTIAC aims to promote the exchange of manufacturing technology information. The Center will serve any U.S. manufacturing interest, although some of its services are limited to unclassified information. The Web site offers the headings Customized Research; Current Awareness Bulletin; Calendar of Events and Publications as well as descriptions of its other Information Resources.

While the site offers little in the way of online publications or data sets, it does offer a good description of its services.

Subject Headings: Information Analysis Center; Manufacturing

[1147] NACA Report Server

Sponsoring Agencies: National Advisory Committee for Aeronautics (NACA); National Aeronautics and Space Administration (NASA)

Primary Access: http://www.larc.nasa.gov/naca/

Resource Summary: This site, for the defunct National Advisory Committee for Aeronautics, provides information on NACA publications. NACA is NASA's predecessor and was operational from 1917-1958. This page provides keyword searching of the technical reports published by NACA as well as access to the full text of some reports. The full-text reports are available in PDF format.

Subject Headings: Aeronautics—Research; Reports—Bibliography; Reports—Full Text

[1148] National Institute of Standards and Technology

Sponsoring Agency: National Institute of Standards and Technology (NIST)

Primary Access: http://www.nist.gov/

Alternative Access Methods: http://www.nist.gov/homepgtx.htm [text version]
gopher://gopher.nist.gov/ [now defunct]

Resource Summary: With a mission of promoting economic growth by working with industry to develop and apply technology, measurements, and standards, the NIST Web site provides information on NIST programs and a directory of NIST contacts. General interest sections include: NIST Image Gallery; News; Frequently Asked Questions; and NIST At-a-Glance (providing basic statistics). The Products and Services page includes topical access to NIST information including the Metric Program; Small Business Innovation Research Program; Standards in Trade; Standards Information and Services; Standard Reference Data; and Standard Reference Materials (which includes the *SRM Quarterly Updates*). The News page provides access to press releases, the *NIST Conference Calendar*, *NIST Update*, speeches, congressional testimony, and *Technology At-a-Glance*.

This is a very useful site for anyone involved with NIST standards. For the general public, the metric system information may be of interest.

Subject Headings: Standards; Manufacturing; Metric System

SuDoc Numbers: C 13.10/3-2: *NIST Conference Calendar*
C 13.36/7: *NIST Update*
C 13.48/4-3: *SRM Quarterly Updates*
C 13.75: *Technology at a Glance*

[1149] National Technology Transfer Center

Sponsoring Agencies: National Aeronautics and Space Administration (NASA); National Technology Transfer Center (NTTC)

Primary Access: http://www.nttc.edu/

Resource Summary: The National Technology Transfer Center is the hub of a national network linking U.S. companies to federal laboratories with the goal of turning government research into commercially relevant technology. The Web site features announcements of new federal technologies available for licensing; technology transfer opportunities; Small Business Innovative Research (SBIR) grant solicitations; a directory of contacts, resources, and current research activities; and access to NTTC's collection of databases. The NTTC databases include a directory of federal lab resources, SBIR grant databases, Department of Agriculture and Department of Justice databases, the *Catalog of Federal Domestic Assistance*, and licensable technologies. The search interface uses BRS/Search software.

This site collects numerous resources for technology transfer and makes them easily accessible. However, the site also notes that the information available from their Web site is only a portion of what is available from NTTC, so they also list contact information and their toll-free number.

Subject Headings: Grants—Business; Small Businesses; Technology Transfer

SuDoc Number: PrEx 2.20: *Catalog of Federal Domestic Assistance*

[1150] Naval Facilities Engineering Command

Sponsoring Agency: Naval Facilities Engineering Command

Primary Access: http://www.navy.mil/homepages/navfac/

Resource Summary: Focusing on the engineering needs of Navy facilities, this site features the links Information Technology Strategic Plan; Civil Engineer Corps Graduate Education; Public Works Field Support; Planning and Engineering Support; Environmental Services Information; and Navy Housing Program Information. In addition, another section provides information on Field Activities; Engineering Field Divisions; Construction Battalion Centers; Officers in Charge of Construction; and Public Works Centers.

The information available on this site is useful to those working with Navy engineers or involved with some of these facilities.

Subject Headings: Engineering—Military; Navy

[1151] Nondestructive Testing Information Analysis Center

Sponsoring Agencies: Defense Technical Information Center (DTIC); Nondestructive Testing Information Analysis Center (NTIAC)

Primary Access: http://www.dtic.mil/iac/ntiac/

Resource Summary: This DoD Information Analysis Center's Web site features the sections NTIAC Research Areas; Publications; Current Awareness; and Products and Services.

This Web site may be difficult to read due to the choice in background images and text colors. Its arrangement is also confusing. However, there is some useful information available for those interested in nondestructive testing.

Subject Headings: Information Analysis Center; Military Research; Nondestructive Testing

[1152] Oak Ridge Centers for Manufacturing Technology

Sponsoring Agency: Oak Ridge National Laboratory (ORNL). Centers for Manufacturing Technology (ORCMT)

Primary Access: http://www.ornl.gov/orcmt/

Resource Summary: The Oak Ridge Centers for Manufacturing Technology feature a broad collection of manufacturing expertise and information. The site is very simply arranged, with sections titled ORCMT Overview; How To Work With Us; Best Manufacturing Practices; Scientific and Technical Capabilities; Success Stories; and Conferences and Workshops. The site is useful for finding the areas of expertise that are available. For actual technical assistance, the site describes how to contact ORCMT.

Subject Heading: Manufacturing

[1153] Reliability Analysis Center

Sponsoring Agencies: Defense Technical Information Center (DTIC); Reliability Analysis Center (RAC)

Primary Access: http://rome.iitri.com/rac/

Resource Summary: The Reliability Analysis Center's mission is to collect, analyze, and disseminate data and information in the fields of reliability, maintainability, and quality. Their Web site's primary section is titled Data and Information. This page includes access to a fairly small bibliographic database on reliability and specialized databases that contain quantitative or qualitative reliability data on components.

The bibliographic database would be much more useful if it included subject indexing.

Subject Headings: Bibliographic Databases; Information Analysis Center; Reliability (Engineering)

[1154] STINET

Sponsoring Agency: Defense Technical Information Center (DTIC)

Primary Access: http://www.dtic.mil/stinet/public-stinet/

Alternative Access Method: http://www-sec.dtic.mil/S-STINET [authorized subscribers]

Resource Summary: The Scientific and Technical Information Network (STINET) is available in a restricted public version. The primary URL points to the version accessible to the general public, which allows searching of the unclassified, unlimited bibliographic citations of over 10 years of DTIC's Technical Report Database. This is a WAIS search system, and the query screen lists numerous databases that can be searched singly or together. These include both defense databases and NASA databases.

This is an important bibliographic resource. Public users should be aware that some of the defense publications may have access restrictions on them and might be difficult to obtain.

Subject Headings: Bibliographic Databases; Reports—Bibliography; Scientific and Technical Information

[1155] Technology Transfer Information Center

Sponsoring Agencies: Agricultural Research Service (ARS); National Agricultural Library (NAL); Technology Transfer Information Center (TTIC)

Primary Access: http://www.nal.usda.gov/ttic/

Resource Summary: The Technology Transfer Information Center aims to assist in the transfer of research results to commercial products. The Web site includes access to the Tektran database, which consists of prepublication notices of Agricultural Research Service research. The TTIC Publications section offers reports, technology transfer opportunities, and educational programs. Other sections provide access to ARS patents and new technologies.

Subject Headings: Agriculture—Research; Technology Transfer

[1156] Waterways Experiment Station

Sponsoring Agencies: Army Corps of Engineers; Waterways Experiment Station (WES)

Primary Access: http://www.wes.army.mil/

Alternative Access Method: http://www.wes.army.mil/Old_Welcome.html [text version]

Resource Summary: The Waterways Experiment Station is charged with conceiving, planning, studying, and executing engineering investigations and research and development studies in support of the civil and military missions of the Corps of Engineers and other federal agencies. The opening screen of the WES Web site has a single link that connects to the main Waterways Experiment Station welcome page. This page features a General Information section and a Major Mission Area section. The General Information section provides activity summaries, a welcome, online documentation, and management teams. The Major Mission Areas section includes the pages Coastal Engineering; Environmental; Geotechnical; Hydraulics; Information Technology; and Structures.

Subject Headings: Military Research; Research Laboratories; Rivers

Technology and Engineering: Communications

[1157] Cable Services Bureau

Sponsoring Agency: Federal Communications Commission (FCC). Cable Services Bureau

Primary Access: http://www.fcc.gov/Bureaus/Cable/WWW/csb.html

Alternative Access Methods: ftp://ftp.fcc.gov/pub/Bureaus/Cable/
http://www.fcc.gov/csb.html

Resource Summary: This site features recent press releases, orders, proposed rules, public notices, and a couple of informal reports, available in ASCII text and WordPerfect formats.

While the site includes useful documents, they could be better organized. For example, the press releases are not accessible by date, only by title, but they are not listed alphabetically. In addition, little information about the Bureau is included, not even an address or phone number.

Subject Heading: Television, Cable

[1158] Common Carrier Bureau

Sponsoring Agency: Federal Communications Commission (FCC). Common Carrier Bureau

Primary Access: http://www.fcc.gov/ccb/

Alternative Access Method: ftp://ftp.fcc.gov/pub/Bureaus/Common_Carrier/

Resource Summary: The Common Carrier Bureau is responsible for administering the FCC's policies concerning telephone companies that provide long-distance and local service to consumers. In addition to basic agency information, this site features a number of documents, including fact sheets and a FAQ on the bureau. Recent press releases, orders, proposed rules, public notices, and reports are available in ASCII text and WordPerfect formats. The Consumer Resources section provides access to fact sheets and a common carrier score card. Under the Exploring the Issues heading, the site links to information on universal service, access charge reform, and local competition.

Subject Headings: Consumer Information; Telecommunications

[1159] Compliance and Information Bureau

Sponsoring Agency: Federal Communications Commission (FCC). Compliance and Information Bureau

Primary Access: http://www.fcc.gov/cib/

Alternative Access Method: ftp://ftp.fcc.gov/pub/Bureaus/Compliance/

Resource Summary: The site contains agency information, press releases, public notices, and a variety of information about broadcasting regulation enforcement. There are self-inspection checklists for television and radio stations, information on the emergency alert system, and a list of top consumer issues.

Subject Headings: Broadcasting; Law Enforcement; Communications

[1160] Federal Communications Commission

Sponsoring Agency: Federal Communications Commission (FCC) `

Primary Access: http://www.fcc.gov/

Alternative Access Methods: http://www.fcc.gov/Welcometextonly.html [text version] ftp://ftp.fcc.gov/pub/

Resource Summary: The Federal Communications Commission site provides a wide variety of information. The top level Web page includes a section with recent FCC news. The FCC Headlines Archives page provides access to older press releases. The Daily Digest heading provides access to the full text of the FCC's *Daily Digest* in ASCII and HTML format. This publication, available online since February 1994, includes actions and announcements of the FCC. A Hot Topics section offers subject access to FCC documents on various topics of current interest including the Internet, the V-Chip, and Universal Service. LearnNet, the FCC's education page, is also listed under Hot Topics. The Bureaus/Offices section provides quick access to subsidiary FCC organizations. Employment opportunities, a phone directory, and forms can be found in the Information section.

For anyone following the telecommunications industry, the FCC site can function as a primary information and current awareness source. The availability of the *Daily Digest* is especially useful for librarians as this item is not distributed to depository libraries.

Subject Headings: Broadcasting; Communications; Telecommunications

SuDoc Numbers: CC 1.55/2: *FCC Forms*
CC 1.53: *Telephone Directory*
CC 1.54: *Daily Digest*

[1161] Institute for Telecommunications Sciences

Sponsoring Agencies: Institute for Telecommunications Sciences; National Telecommunications and Information Administration (NTIA)

Primary Access: http://www.its.bldrdoc.gov/

Alternative Access Method: ftp://ftp.its.bldrdoc.gov/

Resource Summary: The Institute for Telecommunications Sciences (ITS) is the research and engineering branch of the National Telecommunications and Information Administration. This site includes the sections ITS Research, Engineering and Standards Development; ITS Organization; National Information Infrastructure; the Global Information Infrastructure; ITS Online Documents; and ITS Telecommunications Analysis Services. It also features a glossary of telecommunications terms.

Subject Headings: National Information Infrastructure; Telecommunications—Research

[1162] International Bureau

Sponsoring Agency: Federal Communications Commission (FCC). International Bureau

Primary Access: http://www.fcc.gov/ib/

Alternative Access Method: ftp://ftp.fcc.gov/pub/Bureaus/International/

Resource Summary: In addition to basic agency information, this site features a number of documents, including recent press releases, public notices, orders, proposed rules, and some informal documents. Most are available in both ASCII and WordPerfect formats. A Hot Topics section provides ready subject access to some of these documents.

Subject Heading: Telecommunications—International

[1163] Mass Media Bureau

Sponsoring Agency: Federal Communications Commission (FCC). Mass Media Bureau

Primary Access: http://www.fcc.gov/mmb/

Alternative Access Method: ftp://ftp.fcc.gov/pub/Bureaus/Mass_Media/

Resource Summary: This Mass Media Bureau regulates the television and radio stations in the United States. Their site provides access to press releases, orders, and notices. Most are available in ASCII text and WordPerfect formats. The site also provides access to information on radio and television stations, children's television, and digital television.

Subject Headings: Broadcasting; Radio; Television

[1164] Mass Media Databases

Sponsoring Agency: Federal Communications Commission (FCC). Mass Media Bureau

Primary Access: http://www.fcc.gov/Bureaus/Mass_Media/Databases/

Resource Summary: This site features engineering databases for radio and television. The databases are available without any search interface and must be downloaded, decompressed, and loaded into a compatabile database program for use. The following databases are available: AM Engineering Database, TV Directional Antenna Database, FM Engineering Directional Antenna Database, FM Engineering Database, FM Engineering Comments Database, and TV Engineering Database.

While most users would prefer some kind of a searchable front end to these databases, at least they are made available here. It does take a bit of computer expertise to be able to retrieve and process the files for use on a desktop machine.

Subject Headings: Broadcasting; Radio; Television

[1165] National Telecommunications and Information Administration

Sponsoring Agency: National Telecommunications and Information Administration (NTIA)

Primary Access: http://www.ntia.doc.gov/

Resource Summary: The main body of information from this site is organized into sections titled NTIA Activities; NTIA Organizations; Minority Telecommunications Development Resource Center; NTIA Reports, Filings, and Related Material; Spectrum Management; and Grants and Assistance. It also features a Frequency Allocation Chart.

This Web site uses a clever combination of background images and inline images to build upon the information superhighway concept. For anyone interested in Internet or networking grants, this is an essential site to visit.

Subject Headings: Grants; National Information Infrastructure; Telecommunications

[1166] Office of Engineering and Technology

Sponsoring Agency: Federal Communications Commission (FCC). Office of Engineering and Technology

Primary Access: http://www.fcc.gov/oet/

Alternative Access Method: ftp://ftp.fcc.gov/pub/Bureaus/ Engineering_Technology/

Resource Summary: This site provides information on the Office's function and organization. Under the Information Online heading, various documents are available, including recent press releases, public notices, orders, proposed rules, software, databases, and informal documents. These are available in ASCII and WordPerfect formats. This site also includes information on radio frequency safety and a frequently asked questions area.

Subject Headings: Radio Waves; Telecommunications

[1167] PBS Online

Sponsoring Agency: Public Broadcasting Service (PBS)

Primary Access: http://www.pbs.org/

Resource Summary: While not directly a government site, it does receive federal funding. The PBS Web site provides a wide range of information on its television programming and on popular PBS programs as well as a listing of PBS stations.

This is an excellent site for information on PBS programs and on the organization of PBS itself.

Subject Headings: Broadcasting; Educational Resources; Television

[1168] Welcome to NPR

Sponsoring Agency: National Public Radio (NPR)

Primary Access: http://www.npr.org/

Resource Summary: While not directly a government site, National Public Radio does receive federal funding. NPR offers a site with information on NPR member stations, programs, and NPR news. The NPR News section features access to RealAudio files of NPR hourly news as well as archives of All Things Considered and other programs. Look on the Programs page for a list of popular NPR programs along with schedule information and RealAudio archives for selected programs.

With the RealAudio files of news and other programs, this is an important resource for news. Note that the current programs that can be heard on the radio will not be available in RealAudio format on the site until after they have broadcast on the air.

Subject Headings: Broadcasting; News; Radio

[1169] Wireless Telecommunications Bureau

Sponsoring Agency: Federal Communications Commission (FCC). Wireless Telecommunications Bureau

Primary Access: http://www.fcc.gov/wtb/wirehome.html

Alternative Access Method: ftp://ftp.fcc.gov/pub/Bureaus/Wireless/

Resource Summary: In addition to basic agency information, this site features a number of documents such as recent press releases, public notices, commission decisions, open proceedings, and auctions. Documents are available in either ASCII, PDF, or HTML formats. Other available sections of the site include the Auctions Page; Wireless Facilities Siting Issues; Public Safety; and Headlines.

Subject Headings: Auctions; Wireless Communications

Technology and Engineering: Computer Science ─────────

[1170] Advanced Computing Laboratory

Sponsoring Agency: Los Alamos National Laboratory (LANL). Advanced Computing Laboratory

Primary Access: http://www.acl.lanl.gov/

Resource Summary: The Advanced Computing Laboratory is involved in high-performance computing research that can involve projects from many other disciplines. Their Web site features links entitled: Who We Are; What We Do; Resources; User Information; Highlights; Bulletin Board; and Internal. The Highlights page provides some idea of recent research that the Lab has been doing, including Global Climate Modeling and Quantum Chromodynamics. That page also outlines the major software and hardware platforms available at the Lab.

Subject Headings: Research Laboratories; Computers—Research

[1171] Advanced Laboratory Workstation Project

Sponsoring Agency: National Institutes of Health (NIH). Advanced Laboratory Workstation Project

Primary Access: http://www.alw.nih.gov/

Resource Summary: The NIH Advanced Laboratory Workstation (ALW) System is a general-purpose, open, distributed computing system. This site describes the ALW program, and its uses for NIH researchers. To an NIH researcher without access to local computer expertise and support, an ALW provides a high level of computing power and storage capacity on the desktop.

Of interest to open systems fans, the site is primarily intended for the NIH researchers it serves.

Subject Headings: Computers—Research; Computer Networking—Research; Medical Research

[1172] Advanced Technology Demonstration Network

Sponsoring Agencies: Advanced Research Projects Agency (ARPA); Defense Information Systems Agency (DISA)

Primary Access: http://www.atd.net/atdnet.html

Resource Summary: The Advanced Technology Demonstration Network (ATDnet) is a high-performance networking testbed located in the Washington, D.C., area. It is intended to be representative of possible future Metropolitan Area networks. Established to enable collaboration among defense and other federal agencies, ATDnet has a primary goal of serving as an experimental platform for diverse network research and demonstration initiatives. Emphasis is on early deployment of emerging Asynchronous Transfer Mode and Synchronous Optical Network technologies. The Web site provides an overview and status of ATDnet.

Subject Heading: Computer Networking—Research

[1173] Army High Performance Computing Research Center

Sponsoring Agencies: Department of the Army; Army High Performance Computing Research Center (AHPCRC)

Primary Access: http://www.arc.umn.edu/

Resource Summary: This High Performance Computing (HPC) Center works to establish joint programs between academia and the army for collaborative research into the use of HPC for solving army and defense grand challenges. It also aims to develop educational programs and curricula in HPC and its application. The Web site offers the sections AHPCRC Support; Information on High Performance Computing at the AHPCRC; Education; and Technology Transfer. The Technology Transfer area provides information on job openings, research projects, and publications. The available publications include the nondepository *AHPCRC Bulletin*, *AHPCRC Briefs*, and *AHPCRC Preprints*.

This should be a useful site for anyone interested in HPC training or in some of the AHPCRC publications.

Subject Headings: Army; Computer Science—Education; High Performance Computing; Technology Transfer

[1174] Comprehensive Approach to Reusable Defense Software

Sponsoring Agency: Department of the Air Force

Primary Access: http://www.cards.com/

Resource Summary: The Comprehensive Approach to Reusable Defense Software (CARDS) site supports the missions of the CARDS program. The program aims to enable new and innovative approaches to system development by advocating a product line approach supported by a systematic reuse-based systems engineering discipline. The site includes the sections Reuse Technology, Products and Services; Practical Applications of Reuse Technology Transfer; CARDS History; Product Line Asset Support; and CARDS News.

Mostly of interest to those involved in the CARDS program, the site may also interest those in information techology in the commercial sector.

Subject Headings: Air Force; Military Computing; Software

[1175] Data and Analysis Center for Software

Sponsoring Agencies: Data and Analysis Center for Software (DACS); Defense Technical Information Center (DTIC)

Primary Access: http://www.utica.kaman.com:8001/

Resource Summary: A Department of Defense (DoD) Information Analysis Center, DACS serves as a source for software information and provides technical support to the DoD software community. The Web site is a guide to discovering Web and non-Web literature and information, in particular, software topic areas that are of interest to DACS users.

Subject Headings: Computer Science; Information Analysis Center; Military Computing; Software

[1176] Defense Advanced Research Projects Agency

Sponsoring Agency: Defense Advanced Research Projects Agency (DARPA)

Primary Access: http://www.arpa.mil/

Alternative Access Method: ftp://ftp.arpa.mil/

Resource Summary: As a primary military research agency, the DARPA Web site offers information on the Agency and its projects. The Organization section includes links to DARPA's component offices and their Web sites in a descriptive list or an abbreviated list. The Info section features information available to the public and information for small businesses. For press releases, see the News area. DARPA's budget can be found under the Budget heading. The Solicitations section lists current solicitations for the technical offices of DARPA.

As one of the federal agencies most responsible for the development of the Internet, this site is worth a visit. But it has much more than just computer networking technology information.

Subject Headings: Computer Networking—Research; Military Research; Small Businesses

[1177] Digital Library Technology Project

Sponsoring Agency: National Aeronautics and Space Administration (NASA)

Primary Access: http://dlt.gsfc.nasa.gov/

Resource Summary: The Digital Library Technology (DLT) project supports the development of new technologies to facilitate public access to NASA data via computer networks. The top level screen provides a Shockwave multimedia opening and a link to the main content page. The main page includes sections titled DLT Projects; Project Sites; Program Reports; and Digital Studio. The Project Sites page includes access to some of the current programs, including Retrieval of Digital Images by Means of Content Search; Project Horizon—a Public Scientific Data Server; and Compression and Progressive Transmission of Digital Images.

The DLT site and its projects will be of greatest interest to other researchers in imaging and in network research.

Subject Headings: Computer Networking—Research; High Performance Computing; Imaging

[1178] Division of Computer Research and Technology

Sponsoring Agency: National Institutes of Health (NIH). Division of Computer Research and Technology

Primary Access: http://www.dcrt.nih.gov/

Resource Summary: This site contains information about the Division's activities and programs. The publications that are available include computer manuals, technical documentation, and a newsletter. Other sections link to computer training in NIH, visitor information, and job opportunities.

This site will primarily be of interest to employees of the NIH that need computer support.

Subject Headings: Medical Research; Computer Support

[1179] DoD Information Systems Technology Insertion

Sponsoring Agencies: Defense Information Systems Agency (DISA); Advanced Communications Technology Department

Primary Access: http://disa11.disa.atd.net/

Resource Summary: This Web site is designed to provide information about technology insertion activities for information systems in the Department of Defense. It features information on ATM and Synchronous Optical Network technologies for computer networking.

Mostly of interest to those involved with the Defense Information Systems Agency, some of the background information on the ATM may be of interest to others in the computer networking community.

Subject Headings: Asynchronous Transfer Mode (ATM); Computer Networking; Military Computing

[1180] Energy Sciences Network

Sponsoring Agency: Department of Energy (DOE). Office of Energy Research

Primary Access: http://www.es.net/

Resource Summary: Energy Sciences Network (ESnet) is a nationwide data communications network managed and funded by the Office of Energy Research for the purpose of supporting multiple-program, open scientific research. ESnet facilitates online remote access to major DOE scientific facilities. Online services available through their Web site include ESnet Network Information Centers; Network Security; White Pages; and Network Statistics. The Partners in Research section provides information on ESnet pilot projects, research partners, and telecommuting.

This Web site is aimed at existing and potential ESnet customers. It is useful for finding descriptive information on the network and its services.

Subject Headings: Computer Networking; Internet

[1181] The Federal Networking Council

Sponsoring Agencies: Federal Networking Council (FNC); National Science Foundation (NSF)

Primary Access: http://www.fnc.gov/

Resource Summary: The FNC's mission is to act as a forum for networking collaborations among federal agencies to meet their research, education, and operational mission goals. The site includes a calendar of events, information from working groups and the advisory committee, background material, and initiatives and reports.

There is not much depth to the Initiatives and Reports page, which makes this site only of interest to those involved with the FNC or curious about its role.

Subject Heading: Computer Networking

[1182] High Data Rate Mobile Internet

Sponsoring Agency: Naval Command, Control, and Ocean Surveillance Center (NCCOSC)

Primary Access: http://fury.nosc.mil/

Resource Summary: This High Data Rate Mobile Internet site aims to demonstrate the technologies required to develop a Department of Defense network that is interoperable with the future carrier networks. The network will also need to provide reliable high-data-rate connectivity using mobile communication links supporting all types of media including data, voice, imagery, fax, and video teleconferencing. Some links on this site are marked "limited access."

Subject Headings: Navy; Military Computing; Computer Networking—Research

[1183] High Performance Computing Modernization Program

Sponsoring Agencies: High Performance Computing Modernization Program (HPCMP); Department of Defense (DoD). Office of the Secretary of Defense

Primary Access: http://www.hpcmo.hpc.mil/

Resource Summary: This program aims to provide advanced hardware, computing tools, and training to DoD researchers, utilizing the latest high-performance computing (HPC) technology in support of the warfighter. These pages provide information on the program, its goals, and its activities. The three initiatives of the HPCMP are the HPC centers, networking, and software.

While this site focuses on the military HPC, this site will be of interest to others in the HPC community.

Subject Headings: Computer Networking; High Performance Computing; Military Computing

[1184] Imaging and Distributed Computing Group

Sponsoring Agency: Lawrence Berkeley National Laboratory (LBL). Imaging and Distributed Computing Group

Primary Access: http://george.lbl.gov/ITG.html

Resource Summary: Featuring a diverse group of links under the Imaging and Distributed Computing Projects heading, this site provides access to the well-known Interactive Frog Dissection Kit and to the Whole Frog Project. These projects provide an interactive educational experience through the experience of dissecting a frog. However, the site also features other projects such as Electronic Notebooks; High Speed Networking; Imaging Processing and Manipulation Systems; and Computer Vision and Robotics Applications. Other sections of this site include a program overview, a group bibliography, and links to staff home pages.

Subject Headings: Biology—Study and Teaching; Computer Networking—Research; Imaging; Robotics

[1185] Information Infrastructure Task Force

Sponsoring Agencies: Department of Commerce (DOC); Information Infrastructure Task Force; White House

Primary Access: http://iitf.doc.gov/

Alternative Access Methods: http://iitf.doc.gov/index-t.html [text version]
gopher://iitf.doc.gov/

Resource Summary: Formed by the White House, the Information Infrastructure Task Force is coordinating the implementation of the National Information Infrastructure. The site features categories including About Us; What's New; Calendar of Events; Committees and Working Groups; Press Releases; Activity Reports; Documents; and Speeches and Testimony. These pages outline the activities of the Task Force and future directions.

This site should be of interest to anyone following the government's involvement and sponsorship of parts of the Internet.

Subject Headings: Computer Networking; National Information Infrastructure

[1186] IT Policy OnRamp

Sponsoring Agency: General Services Administration (GSA). Office of Information Technology Policy and Leadership

Primary Access: http://www.itpolicy.gsa.gov/

Resource Summary: The Information Technology (IT) OnRamp is provided by the General Services Administration as a central government location for IT-related topics, pages, and sites. Of the many available sections on this page, it includes Strategic IT Analysis; IT Management Practices; Emerging IT Applications; Software; Process Improvement; and Effective Practices.

This site is aimed at the government IT professional.

Subject Heading: Information Technology

SuDoc Number: GS 1.37/2:INTERNET *Information Technology Newsletter*

[1187] Major Shared Resource Center

Sponsoring Agencies: Department of Defense (DoD); Wright-Patterson Air Force Base

Primary Access: http://msrc.wpafb.af.mil/

Resource Summary: This DoD high-performance computing site provides information on the Center, its services, and its available hardware and software resources. There is also a Customer Support section that includes Online Documentation.

Primarily of interest to users of the Center, this site may also be of interest to others active in high-performance computing.

Subject Headings: Computer Science; High Performance Computing; Software

[1188] NASA Internet

Sponsoring Agency: Ames Research Center (ARC)

Primary Access: http://nic.nasa.gov/ni/

Resource Summary: The NASA Internet delivers a high-performance network to NASA's science and research communities. This network integrates internetworking technology into NASA aeronautics and space missions and provides wide area computer networking services to NASA researchers. This Web site consists of a brief description of the NASA Internet and links to an online version of their annual project report and to the NASA Network Information Center.

Subject Headings: Computer Networking; Internet

[1189] National Consortium for High Performance Computing

Sponsoring Agencies: Advanced Research Projects Agency (ARPA); National Science Foundation (NSF)

Primary Access: http://www.nchpc.lcs.mit.edu/

Resource Summary: In early 1992, a multiagency effort led by ARPA and the NSF resulted in the formation of the National Consortium for High Performance Computing (NCHPC). The Consortium's goal is to accelerate the nation's transition to a scalable computing base by stimulating relevant collaborations among Defense Department, industrial, and academic scientists and engineers, and to provide broad access to large-scale parallel systems. Their Web site consists of descriptive documents that explain the function of the Consortium, along with information on meetings, some published articles and notes about NCHPC, and a user's guide.

Much of this site does not appear to have been updated in years. For example, the list of upcoming conferences only includes one held in 1993. Use information on this with caution.

Subject Headings: Computers—Research; High Performance Computing

[1190] National Coordination Office

Sponsoring Agency: National Coordination Office for Computing, Information, and Communications

Primary Access: http://www.hpcc.gov/

Alternative Access Method: gopher://gopher.hpcc.gov/

Resource Summary: The National Coordination Office (NCO) is responsible for coordinating federal activities in computing, information, and communications, including the Federal High Performance Computing and Communications (HPCC) Program. The site includes sections titled About the NCO; HPCC Publications; Applications Council; Grants and Awards; Legislation and Testimony; and Agency and Activity Servers. HPCC Blue Books are available on the HPCC Publications page, along with implementation plans, program fliers, and agency reports.

Subject Headings: Computers—Research; Grants—Science; High Performance Computing

[1191] National Energy Research Scientific Computing

Sponsoring Agencies: Department of Energy (DOE). Office of Energy Research; Lawrence Livermore National Laboratory (LLNL); National Energy Research Scientific Computing Center (NERSC)

Primary Access: http://www.nersc.gov/

Resource Summary: The National Energy Research Scientific Computing Center provides high-performance computing services to researchers supported by the DOE Office of Energy Research. Major features of the site are the supercomputers, which include a Cray T3E, a cluster of Cray J90s, and a Cray C90. The links offer information about access and programming environments.

This site provides information for researchers that use the resources of NERSC. Therefore, it is primarily of interest to those users and prospective users.

Subject Headings: Computers—Research; Energy—Research; Supercomputers

[1192] National Information Infrastructure Virtual Library

Sponsoring Agency: National Institute of Standards and Technology (NIST)

Primary Access: http://nii.nist.gov/

Alternative Access Method: http://nii.nist.gov/nii_txt.html [text only]

Resource Summary: This site offers access to NIST's collection of information on the National Information Infrastructure (NII) and the related Global Information Infrastructure (GII). Some of the available links on this site include Publications, GII, Government, Industry, and Standards. The Publications page provides access to a list of online publications by title or by title with brief abstracts. This publications list points to many external documents on the topic of the NII and the GII, and not just to NIST publications.

Subject Headings: Computer Networking; National Information Infrastructure

[1193] Network Information Center

Sponsoring Agencies: Department of Defense (DoD). Network Information Center (NIC); Defense Information Systems Agency (DISA)

Primary Access: http://nic.ddn.mil/

Alternative Access Methods: mailto:nic@nic.ddn.mil
ftp://nic.ddn.mil/

Resource Summary: The DoD NIC is responsible for assigning DoD Internet hosts and domains, assigning Internet Protocol network numbers and Autonomous System Numbers for DoD entities, and providing domain name system server files to DoD agencies. The NIC handles the whois database for U.S. military sites, and the Web site can be used for whois queries. Another section can be used for reporting security incidents.

The DoD NIC is an essential point of contact for any U.S. military organization that desires to establish or expand its Internet presence. It is also a useful site for finding information on registered domains and users in the military.

Subject Headings: Domain Names; Internet; Military; Security

[1194] NIST Computer Security Resource Clearinghouse

Sponsoring Agency: National Institute of Standards and Technology (NIST)

Primary Access: http://csrc.ncsl.nist.gov/

Alternative Access Methods: gopher://csrc.ncsl.nist.gov/
ftp://csrc.ncsl.nist.gov/pub/

Resource Summary: Offering a collection of links and pages related to computer security, this page divides its offerings under the headings Announcements; Programs; Topics; and Forums. The Programs section features links to the pages Advanced Authentication; Cryptographic Standards Validation Programs; Encryption, Public Key Infrastructure; Role-Based Access Control; and Trust Technology Assessment. The Topics heading includes the links Alerts; Organizations; Other Computer Security Servers; Patches; Publications; Tools; and Viruses. The Forums section points to external discussions and discussion archives on computer security topics.

For systems adminstrators and others concerned with computer security, this site is worth a visit. However, the Alerts page includes some very outdated links. For example, the most recent NIST security bulletins were a couple of years old.

Subject Headings: Security; Computer Viruses

[1195] Numerical Aerospace Simulation Systems

Sponsoring Agency: Ames Research Center (ARC)

Primary Access: http://www.nas.nasa.gov/

Resource Summary: The Numerical Aerospace Simulation Facility provides research in large-scale computing solutions, supercomputing software tools, and high-performance hardware platforms, and consulting support in the area of aerospace design. The site offers information about the Facility, its technology, and its services. The Publications and Media section provides access to some technical reports and documentation from the researchers and writers at the Facility.

Subject Headings: Aeronautics—Research; Supercomputers

[1196] SHOTHC-L [e-mail list]

Sponsoring Agency: Smithsonian Institution

Primary Access: mailto:listserv@sivm.si.edu with "sub shothc-l name" in body

Resource Summary: This e-mail discussion list, sponsored and hosted by the Smithsonian, features discussion on issues related to the history of computing.

Subject Headings: E-mail Lists; Computers—History

[1197] Virtual Environment Generator (VEG)

Sponsoring Agency: Johnson Space Center (JSC)

Primary Access: http://lslife.jsc.nasa.gov/ipdl/VEGhome.html

Resource Summary: The Virtual Environment Generator (VEG) is designed as a possible experiment to be used in support of a Spacelab mission called Neurolab, a research mission dedicated to the neurosciences.

This page is descriptive in nature, providing basic information on VEG but little in the way of an actual virtual reality environment.

Subject Headings: Neurology; Virtual Reality

[1198] Welcome to NRaD

Sponsoring Agency: Naval Command, Control, and Ocean Surveillance Center (NCCOSC) Research, Development, Test, and Evaluation Division (NRaD)

Primary Access: http://www.nosc.mil/nrad

Resource Summary: The NRaD (an older acronym for Naval Research and Development, which is still used despite the new name) Web site features the sections: About NRaD; Visitor Information; Employment; and Phone Book. Other available sections providing more detailed information include Doing Business with NRaD; Programs; Publications; and Patents and Licensing. The Publications page contains a collection of online brochures and technical documents.

Despite the descriptive information available on this site, it will be of most use to those working for or already familiar with NRaD and its research areas.

Subject Headings: High Performance Computing; Navy

Technology and Engineering: Energy

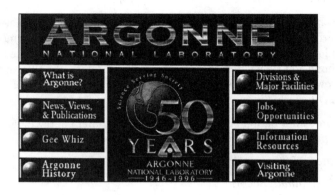

[1199] Argonne National Laboratory

Sponsoring Agency: Argonne National Laboratory (ANL)

Primary Access: http://www.anl.gov/

Alternative Access Methods: http://www.anl.gov/OPA/hometext.html [text version]
gopher://gopher.ctd.anl.gov/

Resource Summary: As one of the largest energy research centers within the Department of Energy, the ANL Web site is the central starting point for access to research-level information from ANL. The site features the categories What is Argonne? News, Views, and Publications; Divisions and Major Facilities; Jobs and Opportunities; Information Resources; and Gee Whiz. Access to information related to ANL's major research areas, which include the Advanced Photon Source; Energy and Environmental Science and Technology; Engineering Research; and Physical Research, can be found under both the Divisions and Major Facilities and the Information Resources sections. Gee Whiz features sections on Argonne's site that are of more general interest, such as the Rube Goldberg Contest, the Telepresence Microscopy Project, and Virtual Reality.

This site contains a substantial amount of information that will be of interest to research scientists. For the general public, the Gee Whiz section includes a number of intriguing links.

Subject Headings: Chemistry Research; Energy—Research; Engineering Research; Physics—Research; Research Laboratories

SuDoc Number: E 1.86/3: *logos*

[1200] Bonneville Power Administration

Sponsoring Agency: Bonneville Power Administration (BPA)

Primary Access: http://www.bpa.gov/

Resource Summary: The Bonneville Power Administration is a Department of Energy agency that administers dams in the Columbia-Snake River Basin. Their Web site features information on energy efficiency and power transmission. For information on the BPA itself, see the About BPA; Corporate; or Telephone and E-mail Search pages. For subject access, the BPA site offers the pages Energy Efficiency; Power; and Transmission. The Publications page provides access to recent BPA *Annual Reports* and *Quarterly Financial Reports*.

While this site has some information on energy efficiency and other energy topics, it will be of interest primarily to people seeking information on the BPA itself.

Subject Headings: Energy Efficiency; Power

SuDoc Numbers: E 5.1: *Annual Report*
E 5.1/2: *Quarterly Financial Reports*

[1201] Center of Excellence for Sustainable Development

Sponsoring Agencies: Center of Excellence for Sustainable Development; Department of Energy (DOE). Office of Energy Efficiency and Renewable Energy

Primary Access: http://www.sustainable.doe.gov/

Resource Summary: The Center of Excellence for Sustainable Development has been established by the DOE to help communities design and implement innovative and sustainable development strategies. Their Web site is designed to offer a tool kit of sustainable information including manuals, workbooks, databases, case studies, and model codes and ordinances. While the Welcome; Who We Are; What's New; and Website Road Map sections of this site describe the Center and its services, the resources will be found primarily on the Sustainable Development Toolkit page.

For urban and rural planners, the resources on this site should prove useful in learning how other communities solve similar problems.

Subject Headings: Community Development; Renewable Energy

[1202] DOE Explorer

Sponsoring Agency: Department of Energy (DOE)

Primary Access: http://www.explorer.doe.gov/

Resource Summary: The DOE Explorer page is set up to serve as a central Internet point for access to several DOE programs. The page features the links DOE Technology Information Network (DTIN); DOE Directives; Success Through Sharing Program; and DOE Quality Management. The DOE Directives are available in PDF format and include access to old series, new series, draft, and archived directives. The DTIN page is available for locating technical capabilities and resources in any of the DOE labs and can be used for technology transfer research and for establishing partnerships with the DOE.

Subject Headings: Directives; Finding Aid—Energy; Technology Transfer

[1203] Department of Energy

Sponsoring Agency: Department of Energy (DOE)

Primary Access: http://www.doe.gov/

Alternative Access Method: http://apollo.osti.gov/

Resource Summary: The central Department of Energy Web site provides a great deal of information on energy topics along with links to the many DOE laboratories, offices, and programs. Sections providing descriptive information include About The Department of Energy; People, Places, and Organizations; and Departmental Resources. The Department of Energy News and Hot Topics page provides press releases, notices of upcoming public meetings, speeches, DOE Directives, and DOE Acquistion Regulations. The OpenNet link provides access to a database of documents declassified and made publicly available after October 1, 1994, along with some other declassified older document collections. The Electronic Exchange Initiative section provides information on how to submit scientific and technical documents to the DOE's Office of Scientific and Technical Information.

This is a well-organized site and is easy to navigate. It is makes an excellent starting point for anyone searching for any level of energy-related information.

Subject Headings: Bibliographic Databases; Energy; Finding Aid—Energy

[1204] DOE Reports Bibliographic Database

Sponsoring Agencies: Department of Energy (DOE). Office of Scientific and Technical Information; National Technical Information Service (NTIS)

Primary Access: http://www.doe.gov/html/dra/dra.html

Alternative Access Method: http://www.osti.gov/html/dra/dra.html

Resource Summary: This bibliographic resource contains citations to DOE-sponsored scientific and technical reports in depository libraries, from January 1, 1994, to the present. The DOE database can also point to depository libraries in a specific state that should have the reports. The search form permits straight keyword searching or fielded searching by title, author, subject, and date. The only sorting of results is by WAIS-determined relevance score. The records include full bibliographic information along with an abstract, NTIS number, and SuDoc number.

The Web search engine is a front-end to a WAIS database. Therefore, despite the well-constructed search form, access is subject to all the problems with WAIS databases. It is also important to note that it includes no records prior to 1994. That being said, this is an important service. The inclusion of both the SuDoc and NTIS numbers for the reports is to be commended, as is the easy method for finding nearby depository libraries that have received the document.

Subject Headings: Bibliographic Databases; Depository Libraries; Reports— Bibliography

[1205] Energy Efficiency and Renewable Energy Network

Sponsoring Agency: Department of Energy (DOE)

Primary Access: http://www.eren.doe.gov/

Resource Summary: The Energy Efficiency and Renewable Energy Network (EREN) is the primary page for obtaining information from the DOE's Energy Efficiency and Renewable Energy programs and offices. The Search Option link provides access to an alphabetical list of sites and to a keyword search box. For information on EREN, see the What's New section or the News, Events, and Hot Topics page. For student science projects, there is a special Kids' Stuff page, with information on solar, wind, and other clean energy technologies. There is even an Ask an Energy Expert page, which can be used to submit questions to EREN specialists about energy efficiency and renewable energy technologies.

Subject Heading: Renewable Energy

SuDoc Number: E 1.128: *OTT Times*

[1206] Energy Information Administration

Sponsoring Agency: Energy Information Administration (EIA)

Primary Access: http://www.eia.doe.gov/

Alternative Access Methods: http://www.eia.doe.gov/indexframes.html [frames version] ftp://ftp.eia.doe.gov/pub/

Resource Summary: The EIA provides a site rich in energy-related information topics. The site organizes most of its information under the headings Fuel Groups; Other Energy Groups; Special Features; and Customer Services. Other categories include: EIA Publications; Search; and Applications. The EIA Publications section includes *U.S. Energy Industry Financial Developments*, which has been discontinued in paper. The Data Queries page (under the Special Features heading) provides an interactive query system for searching for selected EIA data series. The Fuel Groups heading includes links to the Petroleum; Natural Gas; Coal; Nuclear; Alternative/ Renewables; and Electricity pages.

With its broad range of energy resources available , this site makes an excellent starting point for anyone searching for information on energy, power, or fuel. For a more comprehensive search, this site should be used in conjunction with another EIA site—the Energy Information, Products, and Programs page featured at the beginning of this chapter.

Subject Headings: Coal; Energy; Finding Aid—Energy; Nuclear Energy; Petroleum Products; Power; Renewable Energy

SuDoc Numbers: E 3.1/2: *Annual Energy Review*
E 3.1/4: *Annual Energy Outlook*
E 3.9: *Monthly Energy Review*
E 3.11: *Natural Gas Monthly*
E 3.11/2-2: *Natural Gas Annual*
E 3.11/2-11: *Natural Gas Issues and Trends*
E 3.11/5: *Petroleum Supply Monthly*
E 3.11/5-6: *International Petroleum Statistics Report*
E 3.11/9: *Quarterly Coal Report*
E 3.11/17-8: *Electric Power Monthly*
E 3.11/17-10: *Electric Power Annual*
E 3.11/20 *International Energy Outlook*
E 3.13/4: *Petroleum Marketing Monthly*
E 3.13/4-2: *Petroleum Marketing Annual*
E 3.13/6:INTERNET *Motor Gasoline Watch*
E 3.31: *Short-Term Energy Outlook*
E 3.32: *Weekly Petroleum Status Report*
E 3.34: *U.S. Crude Oil, Natural Gas, and Natural Gas Liquids Reserves*
E 3.42: *State Energy Data Reports*
E 3.42/3: *State Energy Price and Expenditure Reports*
E 3.46/5: *Uranium Industry Annual*
E 3.56: *U.S. Energy Industry Financial Developments*
E 3.59: *Emissions of Greenhouse Gases in the United States*

[1207] Fossil Energy Gateway

Sponsoring Agency: Department of Energy (DOE). Office of Fossil Energy

Primary Access: http://www.fe.doe.gov/

Alternative Access Method: http://www.fe.doe.gov/fehome_t.html [text version]

Resource Summary: Functioning as a gateway to information on the Department of Energy's coal, oil, natural gas, and petroleum reserves programs, this site features a broad range of resources. For information about the Office, the site features the sections News Releases; Speeches and Events; Budget; Organization; and Procurements. Information on the fuel reserves managed by the Office is available on pages titled Strategic Petroleum Reserve, and Naval Petroleum and Oil Shale Reserves. The Technology Research and Development Programs page provide access to more details on current research programs. The Scientific and Technical Reports page provides keyword search access to abstracts of *Fossil Energy Technical Reports* in PDF format .

Access to full-text technical reports and to the *Strategic Petroleum Reserve Annual Report* makes this an important site for anyone interested in the strategic reserves or in the fossil fuels in general.

Subject Headings: Coal; Fuel Reserves; Petroleum Products

SuDoc Number: E 1.30: *Strategic Petroleum Reserve Annual Report*

[1208] Los Alamos National Laboratory

Sponsoring Agency: Los Alamos National Laboratory (LANL)

Primary Access: http://www.lanl.gov/

Resource Summary: Created to help in the development of nuclear weapons, the Los Alamos National Laboratory's major areas of research now include nuclear and advanced materials; nuclear weapons science and technology; nuclear science, beams and plasmas; analysis and assessment; theory, modeling, and high-performance computing; bioscience and biotechnology; and earth and environmental sciences. Their Web site is undergoing a redesign, but it currently offers information in these subject areas under Science and Technologies Subject Areas in the Science and Technology section. The Management page provides a hierarchical list of LANL organizations and offices. The Education page lists LANL programs that support education from K-12 through graduate level. For information on LANL itself, see the Welcome; Museum; News; Community; or Jobs sections.

While the site offers a broad range of materials, it does need some redesign to provide quicker subject access to the available online resources.

Subject Headings: Biotechnology; High Performance Computing; Nuclear Energy; Research Laboratories

[1209] National Renewable Energy Laboratory

Sponsoring Agency: National Renewable Energy Laboratory (NREL)

Primary Access: http://www.nrel.gov/

Resource Summary: The National Renewable Energy Laboratory was originally established as a national center for federally sponsored solar energy research and development. It has since expanded into the areas of energy efficiency, photovoltaics, wind energy, advanced vehicle technologies, biofuels, biomass electric, fuels utilization, and other renewable energy fields. The NREL Web site features the sections About NREL; Science and Technology; News and Events; Global and Local Partnerships; Data and Documents; and Clean Energy Basics. The Science and Technology page provides subject access to the NREL areas of research, with descriptive information on the topics and more detailed information on related NREL programs. The Data and Documents section features a bibliographic listing of all recent NREL publications, with many available in full text.

The availability of many full-text documents and detailed project descriptions makes this an excellent site for finding information on solar, wind, and other renewable energy topics.

Subject Headings: Energy Efficiency; Renewable Energy; Research Laboratories; Solar Energy

SuDoc Number: E 1.114/3: *Alternative Fuels in Trucking*

[1210] Nuclear Regulatory Commission

Sponsoring Agency: Nuclear Regulatory Commission (NRC)

Primary Access: http://www.nrc.gov/

Alternative Access Method: http://www.nrc.gov/NRC/textmenu.html [text version]

Resource Summary: The Nuclear Regulatory Commission site features information on nuclear reactors, nuclear materials, and radioactive wastes. Information on the NRC is available on the following pages: What Is NRC; Welcome; News and Information; Public Involvement with NRC; Contracting with NRC; Rulemaking; and Strategic Assessment Initiative. The News and Information page includes press releases and publications such as the *Weekly Information Report* and the *NMSS Newsletter* from the Office of Nuclear Material Safety and Safeguards (NMSS).

The NRC site does an excellent job of arranging its information sources and providing subject access to it reports, standards, and notices.

Subject Headings: Nuclear Energy; Nuclear Waste

SuDoc Numbers: Y 3.N 88:57 *NMSS Licensee Newsletter*
Y 3.N 88:57-2 *Sealed Source and Device Newsletter*
Y 3.N 88:14/ *Telephone Directory*
Y 3.N 88:50/ *Weekly Information Report*

[1211] Oak Ridge National Laboratory

Sponsoring Agency: Oak Ridge National Laboratory (ORNL)

Primary Access: http://www.ornl.gov/

Resource Summary: ORNL's Web site offers information on its research areas and on some electronic publications. The Headline News section includes press releases, the director's column, and conference information. The Research link provides information on Core Competencies Research Organizations at the Laboratory and, Research News and Highlights. For finding ORNL Directorates, Divisions, Centers, Offices, and Programs, look under the Organizations link or the Other ORNL Web Servers link. The Site Business Information section provides phone numbers, a mailing list, employment, and education information. The Publications section features a bibliographic database of ORNL publications, online full-text versions of ORNL's *Review*, some ORNL technical reports in PDF format, newsletters (including *Human Genome News*), and brochures.

While this site is large, it is well organized and provides a great deal of information for researchers in energy and related fields.

Subject Headings: Energy—Research; Materials Science; Research Laboratories

SuDoc Numbers: E 1.28/17: *Review (Oak Ridge National Laboratory)*
E 1.99/3: *Human Genome News*

[1212] Office of Civilian Radioactive Waste Management

Sponsoring Agency: Department of Energy (DOE). Office of Civilian Radioactive Waste Management (OCRWM)

Primary Access: http://www.rw.doe.gov/

Resource Summary: Charged with building a system for disposal of spent nuclear fuel and high-level radioactive waste, the Office of Civilian Radioactive Waste Management offers its Web site to provide   current information on its activites. Primary headings include Introduction to OCRWM; Congressional Testimony and Speeches; Current Events; Resource Information; and Waste Acceptance, Storage, and Transportation, which features information about OCRWM activities related to the storage and transportation of spent nuclear fuel. The Resource Information page features publications, reports, educational materials, and fact sheets. Of special note is the Technical Publications Database, which searches for recent information on the management of spent nuclear fuel and high-level radioactive waste. The database contains abstracts of OCRWM's scientific and technical reports published since July 1995.

With resources for an audience ranging from students to professionals, the OCRWM site should prove useful to anyone seeking information on the problems with and possible solutions for long-term storage of nuclear waste.

Subject Headings: Bibliographic Databases; Hazardous Waste; Nuclear Waste

[1213] Savannah River Site

Sponsoring Agencies: Savannah River Site (SRS); Department of Energy (DOE)

Primary Access: http://www.srs.gov/

Resource Summary: A former production site for weapons-grade nuclear materials, the Savannah River Site is now more focused on national security work; economic development and technology transfer initiatives; and environmental and waste management activities. Press releases are available on the News and Notes page. A Get to Know Us page features site maps, historical highlights, and River Site plans. The People, Partners, and Programs page includes sections for educational outreach and technology transfer. Information on SRS environmental programs, conferences, and waste management is on the Science and Technology page.

Subject Headings: Economic Development; National Security; Nuclear Weapons; Nuclear Waste; Technology Transfer

[1214] Technical Information Services

Sponsoring Agency: Office of Environment, Safety, and Health

Primary Access: http://www.eh.doe.gov/

Alternative Access Methods: http://nattie.eh.doe.gov/tis_text.html [text version] http://nattie.eh.doe.gov/tis_graphics.html [high graphics version]

Resource Summary: The top level page links to the graphics-intensive and text versions of the main page, but it also has links to the mission statement, a list of relevant Department of Energy organizations, and a welcome page. On the main pages, there are numerous links to a substantial body of environmental, safety, and health sites, documents, publications, and databases. Among other reports, this site includes an HTML version of the *Advisory Committee on Human Radiation Experiments, Final Report*.

Some links, such as ones to the Counterpoint version of the *CFR* and the *Federal Register*, are only available for DOE users.

Subject Headings: Environmental and Occupational Health; Radiation

SuDoc Number: Pr 42.8:R 11/H 88/ *Advisory Committee on Human Radiation Experiments, Final Report*

[1215] Tennessee Valley Authority

Sponsoring Agency: Tennessee Valley Authority (TVA)

Primary Access: http://www.tva.gov/

Resource Summary: The Tennessee Valley Authority site features the sections Investor Information; About Us; What's News; Contacts; and Our Product. Information about the TVA is available within the sections Investor Information (including the *Annual Report*); About Us; and Contacts. The What's News section includes the full text of *Today Online*, as well as an employee newsletter; press releases, and speeches by the TVA chairman. The Our Product page features information on power generation, TVA environmental and energy services, power transmission, and economic development. A Kid Page icon leads to a few children's resources.

Subject Headings: Electricity; Power

SuDoc Number: Y 3.T 25:1 *Annual Report of the Tennessee Valley Authority*

[1216] Yucca Mountain Project

Sponsoring Agencies: Department of Energy (DOE). Office of Civilian Radioactive Waste Management; Yucca Mountain Project

Primary Access: http://www.ymp.gov/

Resource Summary: Yucca Mountain has been proposed as an underground storage facility for nuclear wastes. The Yucca Mountain Project is a research project that aims to understand the suitability of this area as an underground storage facility. This site offers information about the research being conducted, answers to frequently asked questions, some educational material, press releases, and other relevant publications.

This site provides basic information on the project, the risks of an underground storage facility at Yucca Mountain, and the suitability of its location.

Subject Headings: Nuclear Energy; Nuclear Waste; Waste Management

Technology and Engineering: Transportation

[1217] Chemical Propulsion Information Agency

Sponsoring Agencies: Chemical Propulsion Information Agency (CPIA); Defense Technical Information Center (DTIC)

Primary Access: http://www.jhu.edu/~cpia/

Alternative Access Method: http://www.jhu.edu/~cpia/text.html [text version]

Resource Summary: This Information Analysis Center covers chemical propulsion technologies. The site features the headings Products and Services; Calendar of Events; Propulsion News; CPIA Publications; People in Propulsion; Meeting Reviews; and Technology Reviews. It also provides access to the Propulsion Database, which contains over 16,000 citations to nonclassified technical reports and conference papers covering 25 years of propulsion technology.

This is an excellent site for research into propulsion technology and for keeping current with such research. It has fewer restricted sections than many other military sites.

Subject Headings: Bibliographic Databases; Chemical Propulsion; Information Analysis Center; Space Flight

[1218] Commission on Aviation Safety and Security

Sponsoring Agencies: Office of the Vice President; White House Commission On Aviation Safety and Security Commission

Primary Access: http://www.aviationcommission.dot.gov/

Alternative Access Method: http://www.aviationcommission.dot.gov/texthome.html [text version]

Resource Summary: Although this White House Commission completed its work in February 1997, the Web site still provides access to the Commission's charter, initial report, final report, and a few other historical documents related to the Commission's activities. The site also features sections titled Safety; Security; and Air Traffic Control. The pages provide a message area for public comments and summaries of input received in each of the subject areas.

Subject Headings: Aeronautics; Aircraft; Safety

[1219] Department of Transportation

Sponsoring Agency: Department of Transportation (DOT)

Primary Access: http://www.dot.gov/

Alternative Access Methods: gopher://gopher.dot.gov/
ftp://ftp.dot.gov/pub/

Resource Summary: The central Department of Transportation Web site offers an excellent starting point for tracking down a wide variety of transportation resources. The Browse the DOT Administrations category provides easy access to component DOT offices, bureaus, and administrations. For additional information on the DOT, see the DOT News and Press Releases page or the What's New section for recent additions to their Web site. The Quick Locator displays a hierarchical site map of the DOT Web—up to three levels deep. This can be quite useful in locating specific resources when the orginating DOT agency is not known.

For subject access, the General Information page offers broad topical headings including Business Information; Safety; Research Projects; and Documents and Publications. Unfortunately, not all publications are easily accessible under the Documents and Publications section. For example, to find the *Dotted Line*, a user has to go under the Office of the Secretary link and then under the Grant Information link. The *ITS Update* is under the General Information heading, then Intelligent Transportation Systems (ITS), then ITS Reading Room, and then ITS Publications and Reports.

Finding publcations on the DOT site would be much easier if the site had a single page that provided access to all DOT publications. Otherwise, the site is very useful for finding specific federal transportation information.

Subject Heading: Transportation

SuDoc Numbers: TD 1.6/2: *Aviation Economic Orders*
TD 1.9: *DOT Telephone Directory*
TD 1.59:INTERNET *The Dotted Line*
TD 1.60:INTERNET *ITS Update*
TD 2.19: *Public Roads*
TD 2.30/13-2: *Focus: News from SHRP, The Strategic Highway Research Program*
TD 2.70: *Research and Technology Transporter*
TD 2.74: *The Red Light Reporter*

[1220] FAA Information Services via World Wide Web

Sponsoring Agencies: Federal Aviation Administration (FAA); National Transportation Safety Board (NTSB)

Primary Access: http://www.faa.gov/

Alternative Access Method: gopher://gopher.faa.gov/

Resource Summary: Other than links to information about the agency and aviation safety, most of this site is organized around divisions of the FAA. These links include: Centers and Regions; FAA-Supported Sites; Headquarters Office; Airports; Air Traffic Systems; Regulation and Certification; and Research and Acquisitions. The Aviation Safety Information link, made available in February 1997, provides detailed information on airline and aircraft safety along with aviation safety press releases and public information. The Aviation Safety Data page features access to databases, including the Aviation Accident/Incident Database, Incident Data System, and the NTSB Safety Recommendations to the FAA with FAA Responses database.

The News and Information page includes press releases, speeches, and a link to the section FAA Publications, Guides, and Reports. This Publications page provides access to online versions of *TD Intercom*, *FAA Aviation News*, and *Aviation System Indicators*. A How Do I? page provides directions for navigating the site and answers to frequently asked questions.

While the Aviation Safety Information section has attracted the most public interest, this site offers many other resources that can be useful to aviation professionals as well as to the general public.

Subject Headings: Aeronautics; Safety

SuDoc Numbers: TD 4.5/2: *Intercom*
TD 4.9: *FAA Aviation News*
TD 4.75: *Aviation System Indicators*

[1221] Federal Highway Administration

Sponsoring Agency: Federal Highway Administration (FHWA)

Primary Access: http://www.fhwa.dot.gov/

Alternative Access Method: telnet://febbs.dot.gov

Resource Summary: The Federal Highway Administration offers access to a wide range of textual and statistical information related to the nation's highways and roads. The Program Areas page provides information and links to the FHWA's major programs and activities. The Publications and Statistics page provides access to the FHWA publications catalogs back to 1991, to several reports, and to some serials such as *Highway Information Quarterly*, *Monthly Motor Fuel*, and *Traffic Volume Trends*. For more information on the FHWA including job openings, divisions, offices, and procurement information, look under the What's New; Field Offices; Organization; and Procurements pages.

Subject Heading: Roads

SuDoc Numbers: TD 2.23/4: *Highway Information Quarterly*
TD 2.23/5:INTERNET *Highway Information Update*
TD 2.46/2: *Monthly Motor Fuel*
TD 2.50: *Traffic Volume Trends*

[1222] Federal Maritime Commission

Sponsoring Agency: Federal Maritime Commission (FMC)

Primary Access: http://www.fmc.gov/

Resource Summary: The Federal Maritime Commission is responsible for the regulation of shipping in the foreign trades of the United States. Their Web site is designed for consumers and providers of international shipping services who want to know how to contact the FMC. It does not provide detailed instructions on how to file a tariff or agreement or how to apply for a freight forwarder license, but it does direct users to the appropriate section of the Commission's Rules in the *Code of Federal Regulations* and advises customers of which office to contact for further information.

Subject Headings: International Trade; Shipping—Regulations

[1223] Federal Railroad Administration

Sponsoring Agency: Federal Railroad Administration (FRA)

Primary Access: http://www.fra.dot.gov/

Resource Summary: This site describes the agency and includes the headings FRA's Mission and Vision, and Customer Service Plan. It also has separate pages for its component offices. On the information content side, it links to information on High Speed Ground Transportation from the Bureau of Transportation Statistics and features information on the Gage Restraint Measurement System.

The FRA's site is primarily of interest to those in the railroad business.

Subject Heading: Railroads

[1224] Federal Transit Administration

Sponsoring Agency: Federal Transit Administration (FTA)

Primary Access: http://www.fta.dot.gov/

Resource Summary: The FTA site features access to its pages by subject and by organization. In addition, it offers a keyword search feature. Major subject areas include Access to Transit; Bicycles and Transit; Facilities Design; Facilities Maintenance, History, Intermodalism, Land Use, the National Transit Database; Planning and Sample Plans; Public Participation and Outreach; Safety and Security; and Transit Technology. The level of information varies among the categories but can include a variety of publications on the topic, mostly in ASCII text versions.

This is a useful site for anyone interested in public transportion.

Subject Headings: Mass Transit; Public Transportation

[1225] National Highway Traffic Safety Administration

Sponsoring Agency: National Highway Traffic Safety Administration (NHTSA)

Primary Access: http://www.nhtsa.dot.gov/

Resource Summary: The National Highway Traffic Safety Administration Web site features a wide range of resources on motor vehicle and driving safety. The NHTSA General Information section includes announcements, a hotline, and a welcome message. The bulk of the material on the site is arranged under one of two headings: Cars or People. The Cars section includes vehicle and equipment information including test results; problems and issues; regulations and standards; and research and development. The test results are searchable by make, model, and year of car. The People section includes the subsections Injury Prevention; Communications and Outreach; Driver Performance; and Crash Information.

This site offers a substantial collection of information on the government's testing of vehicles and their safety ratings. Any consumer interested in safety ratings for their car should check this site.

Subject Headings: Automobiles; Consumer Information; Roads; Safety

[1226] National Railroad Passenger Corporation (Amtrak)

Sponsoring Agency: National Railroad Passenger Corporation

Primary Access: http://www.amtrak.com/

Resource Summary: With train schedules and reservations available from the Amtrak site, passengers can use this site to plan rail trips. Main sections include: Amtrak News; Travel Planner; Schedules; Reservations; and Promotions. The Travel Planner includes the National Route Map, and the Schedules section can be used to find the schedule between two selected points. The Reservations page currently only provides the toll-free reservation phone number, but Amtrak plans on having an interactive ticketing and reservation system up on the Web soon.

For anyone planning travel on Amtrak, this site provides useful information. The addition of online reservations would make pricing information available, which is not currently on the site.

Subject Headings: Amtrak; Railroads; Railroads—Schedules

[1227] National Transportation Safety Board

Sponsoring Agency: National Transportation Safety Board (NTSB)

Primary Access: http://www.ntsb.gov/

Resource Summary: On its Web site, the National Transportation Safety Board provides information on its progams and on the Board's activities. Information about NTSB includes press releases, job openings, speeches, upcoming events, office locations, and an organization chart. The Recommendations link points to a page of Most Wanted Safety Improvements. The NTSB page also has links to pages on each of its major areas of accident investigation: aviation, highway, marine, pipeline/hazardous material, and railroad. Each of these pages includes a listing of recent accidents and a publications list of accident reports and studies.

Subject Headings: Automobiles; Aircraft; Safety

[1228] Navigation Information Connection

Sponsoring Agency: Army Corps of Engineers

Primary Access: http://www.ncr.usace.army.mil/nic.htm

Alternative Access Method: http://www.ncr.usace.army.mil/navdata/nic.htm

Resource Summary: Covering inland waterways in the U.S. and navigation concerns on all of those waterways, this site is a significant resource. It offers lock and river conditions, public notices, and rules. Its numerous links feature the categories Basic Navigation Information; Transportation Mode Comparison; Environmental Advantages of Barge Transportation; and Map of Inland Rivers. The site has both current and historical information. Under the heading Half Hour Updates, there is current information on vessel locations in lock pools and vessels queued at locks.

This site is an important resource for anyone in the navigation industry. It is also worth a visit for anyone interested in water transportation within the 48 contiguous states, the workings of locks, or ships in general.

Subject Headings: Inland Waterways; Navigation

[1229] The Office of Aeronautical Charting and Cartography

Sponsoring Agency: Office of Aeronautical Charting and Cartography

Primary Access: http://www.nos.noaa.gov/acc/welcome.html

Resource Summary: This site describes the Office and how to order its products. No publications or data products are available at this site.

Subject Heading: Maps and Mapping

[1230] Saint Lawrence Seaway Development Corporation

Sponsoring Agency: Saint Lawrence Seaway Development Corporation (SLSDC)

Primary Access: http://www.dot.gov/slsdc/

Resource Summary: This site offers information on the SLSDC and its history under the heading About the Seaway. The site also provides pilotage and port contact information under the Contacts heading. The Briefing Room section includes press releases and articles, while annual reports are available under a separate heading. It also provides a current toll schedule.

This can be useful for research on the St. Lawrence Seaway and for current users of the Seaway.

Subject Headings: Canada; Shipping

[1231] U.S. Maritime Administration

Sponsoring Agency: Maritime Administration

Primary Access: http://marad.dot.gov/

Resource Summary: The Maritime Administration promotes the United States merchant marine for both waterborne commerce and as a naval and military auxiliary in time of war or national emergency. The Web site offers information on the Maritime Administration in the Virtual Tour; Administrator; Key Personnel; and Telephone Book sections. Publications of the agency are available under the Press Releases; Publications; and Annual Reports headings. The Publications page features access to some full-text brochures and pamphlets.

Subject Headings: Merchant Marine; Shipping

SuDoc Number: TD 11.9:97004760 *Maritime Publications Index*

[1232] William J. Hughes Technical Center

Sponsoring Agency: Federal Aviation Administration (FAA). Technical Center

Primary Access: http://www.tc.faa.gov/

Resource Summary: The William J. Hughes Technical Center is an aviation research, development, engineering, test, and evaluation facility. Their Web site provides information on their research and development programs and general information on the Center. Under the Research and Development Programs heading, the site features information on aviation simulation and human factors, air traffic control, and airport and aircraft safety.

This site will be of most interest to aeronautics researchers.

Subject Headings: Aeronautics—Research; Human Factors; Research Laboratories; Safety

CHAPTER 17: WHITE HOUSE

The White House has made excellent use of the Internet for distributing government information and for receiving input. This chapter does not include many sites, but the sites that are listed provide access to a significant portion of presidential documents and information on the chief executive.

The featured resources for this chapter could be nothing other than pages from the main White House Web site. For information on the president and the executive branch, this well-designed and highly used Web site is an excellent starting point. It functions as a finding aid for White House information and for government information in general.

[1233] Welcome to the White House

Sponsoring Agency: White House

Primary Access: http://www.whitehouse.gov/

Alternative Access Method: http://www.whitehouse.gov/White_House/html/White_House_Home-plain.html [text version]

Resource Summary: The White House's Web site is one of the principal government finding aids and the most obvious place to start when looking for information about the president, vice president, their families, and their current activities. The President and Vice President section provides contact information, an interactive form for sending e-mail, and additional information. The Interactive Citizens' Handbook section offers advice and links on how to find online government information with search tools or by subject categories. The Virtual Library section features access to White House press releases, audio files of speeches, and other presidential documents. For the most current documents, look in the Briefing Room section, which contains the most current press releases as well as recent federal statistics. For visitors and historical questions, the White House History and Tours area features the link Information on Past Presidents and First Families; Art in the President's House; and White House Tour Information. The Commonly Requested Federal Services category provides links to various administrative agencies that provide social and public services. The site also includes an HTML version of *Inside the White House*, a quarterly newsletter for young people.

The White House site is quite rich in its coverage of the president and of White House activities. It should be the first stop for anyone seeking online versions of official presidential documents. In addition, it serves as a top level finding aid for much frequently requested federal government information.

Subject Headings: Finding Aid; President; Vice President

SuDoc Number: PrEx 1.12/2: *Inside the White House*

White House: General

The remainder of the White House resources are listed alphabetically in one section and range from entry numbers 1234 to 1249.

[1234] Council of Economic Advisers

Sponsoring Agency: Council of Economic Advisers (CEA)

Primary Access: http://www.whitehouse.gov/WH/EOP/CEA/html/CEA.html

Alternative Access Method: http://www.whitehouse.gov/WH/EOP/CEA/html/CEA-plain.html [text version]

Resource Summary: The CEA's site is relatively small, with a brief biography of the chairwoman and several working papers available. It also links to copies of the CEA's *Economic Report of the President* and to *Economic Indicators*, but these are housed at GPO Access and not on the CEA's site.

The site would benefit from a brief description of the Council's mission and activities and a list of members.

Subject Heading: Economics

SuDoc Numbers: Pr 42.9: *Economic Report of the President*
Y 4.Ec 7: *Economic Indicators*

[1235] Department of State

Sponsoring Agency: Department of State

Primary Access: http://www.state.gov/

Alternative Access Methods: http://www.state.gov/text.html [text version]
gopher://gopher.state.gov/
gopher://dosfan.lib.uic.edu/

Resource Summary: The State Department sites, run with the help of the University of Illinois Chicago Library, provide a wealth of information on the president's foreign policy actions and initiatives. The main sections of the site include About State; International Policy; Travel; Business Services; Careers; and Hot Topics. While many of the publications are directly accessible from the top level page, the names of the links may vary from the actual titles of the publications. The *Foreign Relations of the United States* is only partially available, and that is on the Gopher server under the heading, Historic Declassified Documents. The *Diplomatic List* is also difficult to find, hiding on the Gopher under the heading Contacts and Phone Numbers. Like the National Trade Databank, this site also has online copies of the *Country Commercial Guides*.

This is an especially rich source of country information and diplomacy. Note that some of the publications available online are not as up-to-date as their print counterparts, so be sure to check the dates listed.

Subject Headings: Geography; Foreign Policy

SuDoc Numbers: S 1.1: *Foreign Relations of the United States*
S 1.1/7: *World Refugee Report*
S 1.1/8: *Voting Practices in the United Nations*
S 1.3/5: *Dispatch*
S 1.8: *Diplomatic List*
S 1.21: *Telephone Directory*
S 1.40/5: *Key Officers of Foreign Service Posts*
S 1.69/2: *Foreign Consular Offices in the U.S.*
S 1.76/3-2: *Maximum Travel per Diem Allowances for Foreign Areas*
S 1.123: *Background Notes*
S 1.138: *Patterns of Global Terrorism*
S 1.146: *International Narcotics Control Strategy Report*

[1236] Hillary Rodham Clinton, First Lady of the United States

Sponsoring Agencies: Office of the First Lady; White House

Primary Access: http://www.whitehouse.gov/WH/EOP/First_Lady/html/HILLARY_Home.html

Alternative Access Method: http://www.whitehouse.gov/WH/EOP/First_Lady/html/HILLARY_Home-plain.html [text version]

Resource Summary: The First Lady's Web site includes some biographical information, audio files of greetings to the site, and links to speeches of the First Lady.

The availability of the speeches provides a link to material that might not otherwise be readily accessible.

Subject Headings: First Lady; President—Family

[1237] National Performance Review

Sponsoring Agencies: National Performance Review (NPR); Office of the Vice President

Primary Access: http://www.npr.gov/

Alternative Access Method: mailto:almanac@ace.esusda.gov with text "send npr catalog"

Resource Summary: As the central effort for reinventing government, Vice President Al Gore's National Performance Review makes extensive use of its Web site. The principal sections on the site include Who We Are; Latest Additions; Initiatives; Customer Service; News Room; Accomplishments; Awards; How To Tools; Library; and Web Links. The NPR Library link features over 400 reinventivon documents and publications. Some of the many reports of the National Performance Review include the first executive document from the president, in multimedia format.

While the NPR goal of creating a government that works better and costs less is a worthy one, the Web site itself will be of interest primarily to those seeking in-depth information on the NPR process and accomplishments.

Subject Headings: Government Reform; National Performance Review

SuDoc Number: PrVp 42.15: *Reinvention Roundtable*

[1238] National Security Council

Sponsoring Agency: National Security Council (NSC)

Primary Access: http://www.whitehouse.gov/WH/EOP/NSC/html/nschome.html

Resource Summary: The primary sections of the NSC site include NSC Function; Membership; Staff; Documents; Speeches; and National Security Strategy. The most substantial sections of the site are the Documents and Speeches areas. The Documents section contains numerous fact sheets, for both transnational and area-specific issues. The Speeches section has links to full-text versions of some of the main speeches made by NSC staff.

While the site does not come close to providing comprehensive foreign policy coverage, the fact sheets and speeches make it an excellent starting point in researching current foreign policy.

Subject Headings: Foreign Policy; Security

[1239] Office of Management and Budget

Sponsoring Agency: Office of Management and Budget (OMB)

Primary Access: http://www.whitehouse.gov/WH/EOP/omb

Alternative Access Methods: http://www.whitehouse.gov/WH/EOP/OMB/html/ombhome-plain.html [text version]
http://pula.financenet.gov/omb.htm
gopher://gopher.financenet.gov/11/docs/central/omb

Resource Summary: As the primary federal budget agency in the executive branch, the OMB Internet sites feature information on its activities, the president's budget, and the administration of the budget. Primary categories include OMB's Role; Organization of OMB; Federal Budget; OMB Documents; Employment Information; Index; and OMB Locator. The budget documents are linked from the OMB site, although they actually reside on GPO Access. This is the primary source for *OMB Circulars* and other miscellaneous OMB documents, which can be easily found under the OMB Documents section.

Most useful for the availability of the *OMB Circulars*, the OMB site also has an area for reporting regulations and paperwork currently under review by OMB. This should be of interest to any group that could be affected by changes in OMB regulations.

Subject Heading: Budget

SuDoc Number: PrEx 2.4: *OMB Circulars*

[1240] President's Committee on Employment of People with Disabilities

Sponsoring Agency: President's Committee on Employment of People with Disabilities

Primary Access: http://www.pcepd.gov/

Alternative Access Method: http://janweb.icdi.wvu.edu/pcepd/pcpubs.htm

Resource Summary: The first page on this site includes an initial image and then a few links to the contents page, which has the detailed organizational breakdown of the site. The featured categories include About the President's Committee; President's Committee Projects; Job Accommodation Network; Business Focus; State Liaisons; Publications; Washington Fax; Speeches; and Press Releases. These categories include a broad collection of informative documents relating to disabilities, jobs for the disabled, and the Americans with Disabilities Act. See also the alternate URL for additional publications.

Although the lack of information on the initial page may discourage some users, the site offers an excellent overview on many issues related to employment for the disabled.

Subject Headings: Americans with Disabilities Act; Disabilities

[1241] President's Park: Pennsylvania Avenue at the White House

Sponsoring Agency: National Park Service (NPS)

Primary Access: http://www.nps.gov/dsc/dsgncnstr/pennave/

Resource Summary: In 1995, out of safety concerns for the president, Pennsylvania Avenue was closed to vehicle traffic. Since then, the National Park Service began coordinating a plan for the long-term design of the area. This site primarily consists of an Environmental Assessment (EA) for the long-term design of Pennsylvania Avenue. The EA document, newsletters, and a list of open houses are all available on this site.

While there is not a great deal of content on this site, it should be watched by anyone interested in this planning process or by those concerned with the fate of this section of Pennsylvania Avenue.

Subject Headings: National Parks; Pennsylvania Avenue; Presidential Safety

[1242] Secret Service

Sponsoring Agency: Secret Service

Primary Access: http://www.ustreas.gov/treasury/bureaus/usss/usss.html

Resource Summary: This single page site has a brief description of the Secret Service and its director, along with a couple links to the Department of the Treasury home page and to the U.S. Customs site.

A brief document such as this one should include the address and phone number for the agency.

Subject Heading: President—Protection

[1243] Spotlight—Bill Clinton

Sponsoring Agency: Counsel Connect

Primary Access: http://www.counsel.com/spotlight/archive/clinton.html

Resource Summary: This page consists of an HTML transcript of the videotaped testimony at the fraud and conspiracy trial of James and Susan McDougal and Jim Guy Tucker in Little Rock, Arkansas. This trail was relevant to the Whitewater investigation.

Subject Headings: President; Whitewater Investigation

[1244] Spotlight—The Special Committee's Whitewater Report

Sponsoring Agencies: Counsel Connect; Special Committee to Investigate Whitewater Development Corporation and Related Matters

Primary Access: http://www.counsel.com/spotlight/white/

Alternative Access Method: http://www.counsel.com/spotlight/archive/white/

Resource Summary: This site contains the full text of the special committee's report on the Whitewater affair including both the 759 pages from the Republicans and almost 400 pages from the Democrats. The HTML files are accessible via a table of contents, but they are not keyword searchable. The alternate URL is the more permanent location.

Subject Headings: President; Whitewater Investigation

[1245] Texas A&M's White House Archives

Sponsoring Agencies: Texas A&M University; White House

Primary Access: http://www.tamu.edu/whitehouse/

Alternative Access Method: gopher://gopher.tamu.edu/11/.dir/president.dir

Resource Summary: One of the earliest Internet sites to archive and arrange presidential material, the site includes White House press releases, speeches, memoranda, executive orders, proclamations, and other public documents from the president. The site begins with materials from 1992, but it stopped adding to the archives in September 1995. The material is accessible by year and then type of document, or it can be searched by keyword.

Although the site has not been updated since September 1995, it is still useful as an archive of press releases and other presidential documents from 1992-1995.

Subject Heading: President

[1246] Vice President Al Gore

Sponsoring Agency: Office of the Vice President

Primary Access: http://www.whitehouse.gov/WH/EOP/OVP/html/GORE_Home.html

Alternative Access Method: http://www.whitehouse.gov/WH/EOP/OVP/html/GORE_Home-plain.html [text version]

Resource Summary: The vice president's Web site includes a brief biography, an e-mail link, and brief descriptions of his activities. These activities are within the categories Environmental Issues; National Performance Review; Empowerment Zone and Enterprise Community Program; Science, Space, and Technology Policy; National Information Infrastructure; and Foreign Policy. Each of these areas links to a longer description of his involvement and/or links to his speeches in that area.

While this site has a decidedly political tone, it does give access to online copies of some of the vice president's speeches, which could otherwise be difficult to locate.

Subject Heading: Vice President

[1247] White House

Sponsoring Agencies: White House; Carnegie Mellon University

Primary Access: http://english-www.hss.cmu.edu/govt/whitehouse.html

Resource Summary: This site presents a well-organized front-end to White House information sources available from the Texas A&M Gopher. It only covers information from 1992-1994, although the Texas A&M Web site contains some of the 1995 documents.

This is primarily useful for finding some of the older information, primarily from 1992, that is not readily available from the official White House site.

Subject Headings: President; President—Press Releases

[1248] White House Information

Sponsoring Agencies: University of North Carolina; White House

Primary Access: http://sunsite.unc.edu/white-house/

Resource Summary: This is a quintessential example of a site that has not been maintained. At one time it was an excellent front-end to current White House press releases and a few other documents such as the Budget and the State of the Union addresses. The maintenance appears to have lapsed in early 1995, and now most of the links point to dead ends.

Unless the site is resurrected, it is only useful for finding older information. Most of the material formerly available here can be found on the central White House Web site.

Subject Headings: Budget; President—Press Releases

[Text version]

Welcome to the White House for Kids

Hi. My name is Socks. I am a member of the Clinton family. I will be your guide to the White House web site. If this is your first time here, begin your adventure by clicking on my picture below.

The White House

Location

White House Kids

History

White House Pets

3 Our President

For Kids

6 Write the President

[1249] Whitehouse for Kids

Sponsoring Agency: White House

Primary Access: http://www.whitehouse.gov/WH/kids/html/home.html

Alternative Access Method: http://www.whitehouse.gov/WH/kids/html/home-plain.html [text version]

Resource Summary: This section of the main White House site is specially designed for children. The graphics are illustrations rather than pictures, and Socks the Clinton's pet cat is the virtual tour guide. The child-oriented sections on this site include: Location; History; Our President; White House Kids; White House Pets; and Write the President.

While these pages contain much less information than the main site, it succeeds at delivering information at a child's level and could be quite useful for school reports. It is written at a level more appropriate for grade school and middle school students rather than high school students.

Subject Headings: Children; President—Material for Children

CHAPTER 18: MISCELLANEOUS

Miscellaneous resources in this chapter do not fall neatly into any of the categories of the other chapters. This collection of miscellaneous sites includes sites from agencies such as the Peace Corps, the Voice of America, the Office of Government Ethics, and the General Services Administration.

While there is no general finding aid for miscellaneous government resources because of the nature of a miscellaneous collection, two of these miscellaneous resources are presented as featured sites. The Central Intelligence Agency has offered its World Factbook in electronic format for years. This handbook of background information on countries and other offerings make this one of the featured sites. The second, the Federal Bulletin Board, is featured for the broad range of miscellaneous materials available on that site.

[1250] Central Intelligence Agency

Sponsoring Agency: Central Intelligence Agency (CIA)

Primary Access: http://www.odci.gov/cia/ciahome.html

Alternative Access Method: http://www.odci.gov/cia/

Resource Summary: The CIA Web site features sections titled About the CIA; CIA Publications; CIA Public Affairs; What's New; and Other Intelligence Community Links. Press releases, statements, speeches, and testimony can be found under the Public Affairs section. All of this aside, the CIA Web is best known on the Internet for its *World Factbook*. The CIA Web site features this well-known compendium of country information in full HTML text complete with maps. The latest version of the *Factbook* should always be available here, even though many older versions of the *Factbook* are circulating elsewhere on the Web. Also within the Publications category is an online version of the nondepository *Central Intelligence Agency Factbook on Intelligence* and *Handbook of International Economic Statistics*, along with other publications and publications lists.

The CIA Web site provides a variety of useful geographical and intelligence publications, not all of which are typically available in depository libraries. After suffering a break-in, the CIA's Web site was unavailable for over a week in the fall of 1996. Assuming this does not happen again, the site should be available to the public.

Subject Headings: Geography; Intelligence Service

SuDoc Numbers: PrEx 3.11/2: *Chiefs of State and Cabinet Members of Foreign Government*
PrEx 3.15: *World Factbook*
PrEx 3.16: *Handbook of International Economic Statistics*

[1251] Federal Bulletin Board

Sponsoring Agencies: Government Printing Office (GPO); Superintendent of Documents; Federal Labor Relations Authority; Food and Drug Administration (FDA); Department of State; Department of the Treasury; Environmental Protection Agency (EPA); Merit Systems Protection Board; Office of Government Ethics; Senate. Republican Policy Committee; Supreme Court

Primary Access: http://fedbbs.access.gpo.gov/

Alternative Access Methods: ftp://fedbbs.access.gpo.gov/gpo_bbs/ telnet://fedbbs.access.gpo.gov/

Resource Summary: The Federal Bulletin Board (FBB) is an electronic bulletin board service (BBS) offered by the Superintendent of Documents. It is designed to enable federal agencies to provide access to their information in electronic form. Many of the files available from the FBB are also available from other Internet sources. There are over 100 different file libraries available through the FBB. Not all government agencies contribute files, but those that do include: the Food and Drug Administration; the Department of State; the Department of the Treasury; the Environmental Protection Agency; the Merit Systems Protection Board the Federal Labor Relations Authority; the Office of Government Ethics; the Supreme Court; the Senate Republican Policy Committee; and the Federal Depository Library Program. Documents available include Supreme Court opinions, Senate voting analyses, *Background Notes*, *Access EPA*, *Dispatch*, and many other publications.

Although the interface, even via the Web, is not always easy to navigate, this site offers a substantial number of government publications. The organization of documents needs work because there is no easy way to tell which documents might be available on the FBB versus being available on an agency's site. Also, it is not always clear what kind of format the files are in. For example, the Senate Voting Analyses appear to be in WordPerfect format, but they are not labeled as such, so most browsers will attempt to display them in ASCII. This source will most likely be used by those already familiar with the specific files that are available here.

Subject Headings: Depository Libraries; Electronic Publications; Finding Aid

SuDoc Numbers: JU 6.8/B: *Slip Oinions of the United States Supreme Court*
S 1.123: *Background Notes*
S 1.3/5: *Dispatch*

The resources in this chapter do not divide easily into subcategories. Thus, the first section consists of general miscellaneous sites and runs from entry number 1252 to 1272. However, there were enough entries related to Museums and the Arts to make that a separate subcategory. It includes entries 1273-1282.

Miscellaneous: General

[1252] Americans Communicating Electronically

Sponsoring Agency: Americans Communicating Electronically (ACE)

Primary Access: http://www.sbaonline.sba.gov/ace/

Alternative Access Methods: http://www.sba.gov/ace/
mailto:majordomo@donq.sbaonline.sba.gov with "lists" in body

Resource Summary: ACE is a team of volunteers, both private and public citizens, dedicated to providing open access to information and learning from every home and community across the nation. ACE is committed to the provision of internetworked access to U.S. government information and services at centers open to all Americans. For example, ACE supports access in public libraries, neighborhood electronic kiosks, shopping centers, and rural cooperatives. Links on the ACE page include ACE Vision Statement, ACE Progress Report, Calendar of Events, Local Community Networks, and Connect Your School to the Internet. ACE runs a number of e-mail lists, which can be subscribed to through the mailto: URL or by using the form on the Registration For ACE Mailing List page.

Subject Headings: Government Publications; Public Advocacy

[1253] Federal Emergency Management Agency

Sponsoring Agency: Federal Emergency Management Agency (FEMA)

Primary Access: http://www.fema.gov/

Alternative Access Method: http://www.fema.gov/index_t.htm [text version]

Resource Summary: As the primary federal emergency response and preparedness unit, FEMA offers Web site information in a variety of categories including FEMA News Desk; Reducing Risk Through Mitigation; Emergency Preparedness and Training; Tropical Storm Watch; Reference Library; Global Emergency Management System; Working For a Fire Safe America; and Help After a Disaster. The Reference Library area includes publications, archives, press releases, and pages for specific disasters. The Tropical Storm Watch section features a national flood summary, press releases related to tropical storms, situation reports, and key telephone numbers.

The various documents and reports available from the FEMA site will be of interest to those preparing for emergencies, those recovering from them, or those tracking the current status of disasters such as tropical storms.

Subject Headings: Emergencies; Hurricanes

[1254] Federal Employees News Digest

Sponsoring Agency: Federal Employees News Digest, Inc.

Primary Access: http://www.clubfed.com/

Resource Summary: This commercial site includes a variety of resources from the government and from their own sources related to federal jobs. Categories include Civil Service Reform Plan, Report on the Administration's Job Cutting Efforts; Survivor Benefits; Per Diem Rates; and the 1996 General Schedule Pay Tables.

This site will be of interest to federal employees and those interested in working for the federal government.

Subject Headings: Employment; Pay Scales; Travel—Per Diem Rates

[1255] Federal Information Center—United States Government

Sponsoring Agencies: General Services Administration (GSA); Federal Information Center (FIC)

Primary Access: http://www.gsa.gov/et/fic-firs/fichome.htm

Resource Summary: The Federal Information Center has been established to direct enquiries to the appropriate federal offices. Their Web site features FIC phone numbers, which are available by state with toll-free service, by metropolitan area with toll-free service, and by nationwide TDD/TTY toll-free service. The site also features quick answers for frequently requested U.S. federal information.

For contacting a Federal Information Center, this site has all the necessary information. The FAQ could be longer, but the FIC is set up to answer questions and to direct users to the correct information. The FIC should be used by those who cannot find answers on one of the many Internet sites.

Subject Heading: Referrals

[1256] Federal Information Exchange (FEDIX)

Sponsoring Agency: Federal Information Exchange, Inc. (FIE)

Primary Access: http://web.fie.com/

Alternative Access Methods: http://web.fie.com/htdoc/fie/any/any/any/menu/ any/index_.htm [text version]
gopher://fedix.fie.com/
telnet://fedix.fie.com

Resource Summary: The Federal Information Exchange is a commercial service that aims to provide federal information to the higher education and research communities. Major FIE categories include: Fedix; Molis; Alert; Used Equipment; and Scholarship Resource Network. Fedix provides access to federal agency information on research programs, contact information, educational programs and services, equipment grants, and procurement notices. The Alert feature sends Fedix opportunity announcements out via e-mail. The Molis category provides information on minority colleges and universities, such as institutional capabilities, student and faculty profiles, educational programs, and research centers.

While this site includes a wide variety of government information, it is aimed specifically at the education and research audiences—specifically at administrators within those audiences. Others may find the system difficult to navigate.

Subject Headings: Higher Education; Minorities; Procurement; Research and Development

[1257] General Services Administration

Sponsoring Agency: General Services Administration (GSA)

Primary Access: http://www.gsa.gov/

Alternative Access Method: http://www.gsa.gov/textonly.htm [text version]

Resource Summary: Featuring a variety of procurement resources, the GSA site divides its resources into the following categories: GSA Advantage; Fleet Management and Federal Travel; Federal Information; Real and Miscellaneous Property; Government-Wide Policy; Business and Finance; GSA Publications; Publications; About GSA; and Education and Training. The GSA Advantage is a secure-transaction, online shopping system for federal government agencies. The Education and Training area provides the following GSA training programs: Federal Acquisition Institute Training; GSA Interagency Training Center; and Information Systems Security Training.

This site will be of most interest to those in federal government procurement and to people interested in learning more about the GSA's activities.

Subject Heading: Procurement

SuDoc Numbers: GS 1.6/10: *Federal Acquisition Regulations*
GS 1.17:P 96/ *Publications of the General Services Administration*
GS 1.26: *GSA Training Center Interagency Catalog and Schedule*
GS 1.34:G 29 *Geographic Locator Codes*
GS 1.37/2:INTERNET *Information Technology Newsletter*

[1258] Government Information Locator Service

Sponsoring Agency: Geological Survey (USGS)

Primary Access: http://info.er.usgs.gov/gils/

Resource Summary: This site, hosted by one of the primary Government Information Locator Service (GILS), proponents, gives an overview of GILS. The Demonstration Sampler section gives actual examples of the use of GILS, and for the technical audience, the site has sections on software and technical topics. This GILS information is part of the Global Information Locator Service (which shares the GILS acronym) pages.

While the aim of both the Government Information Locator Service and the Global Information Locator Service is to enable the free flow of information, the actual use of GILS has not lived up to its promise, at least at this point. However, this is a useful site for anyone interested in learning more about GILS.

Subject Heading: Government Information Locator Service (GILS)

[1259] Government Information Locator Service Initiative Documents

Sponsoring Agencies: Coalition for Networked Information (CNI); Office of Management and Budget (OMB)

Primary Access: gopher://gopher.cni.org/11/cniftp/pub/gils/

Alternative Access Method: ftp://ftp.cni.org/pub/gils/

Resource Summary: This site contains documents related to the GILS initiative. GILS attempts to identify information resources, to describe the information available in those resources, and to provide assistance in how to obtain the information. Documents on this site are available in various directories. The Global directory contains documents related to the Global GILS initiative while the Policy directory contains policy documents related to the GILS initiative. The Profile directory provides documents related to the application profile for the GILS initiative. The site also includes the archives of the GILS electronic form.

Much of the material on this site is dated. Except for the GILS discussion group archives, all the materials date from 1994. See other GILS sites for more current documents.

Subject Heading: Government Information Locator Service (GILS)

[1260] Governmentwide Electronic Messaging Program Management Office

Sponsoring Agency: Center for Electronic Messaging Technologies (CEMT)

Primary Access: http://www.fed.gov/

Alternative Access Method: http://www.fed.gov/hptext/hptext.html [text version]

Resource Summary: This CEMT site is designed for federal, state, and local employees to gain knowledge in the messaging, electronic directory, and applied technologies field. It offers information on electronic messaging; assistance and guidelines for getting started in electronic messaging; direct access to the Directory Registration Service; and an e-mail encyclopedia. In addition to CEMT reports and strategic plans, the site also offers access to Government Blue Pages Telephone Listings. The e-mail and telephone directories should be of use to both government employees and the general public.

Subject Headings: E-mail; Government Employees—Directories; Telephone Numbers

[1261] The International GovNews Project

Sponsoring Agencies: Office of the Vice President; National Science Foundation (NSF)

Primary Access: news:gov.*

Alternative Access Method: http://www.govnews.org/

Resource Summary: The International GovNews Project seeks to stimulate electronic access to public government information by establishing a dedicated government hierarchy for Usenet news. That goal was accomplished in March 1997 with the release of over 200 newsgroups. These newsgroups are not directly accessible on all news servers, but they should be available on most in the near future. A list of initial gov.news groups and brief descriptions follows:

gov.org.admin.financenet - FinanceNet - information on public financial management. (Moderated)

gov.org.g7.announce - Announcements on G7 activities. (Moderated)

gov.org.g7.environment - G7 Environment and Natural Resources Project. (Moderated)

gov.org.g7.misc - General G7 related discussions. (Moderated)

gov.topic.admin.finance.accounting - Public accounting. (Moderated)

gov.topic.admin.finance.asset-liab-mgt - Asset-liability management. (Moderated)

gov.topic.admin.finance.audits - Financial audits of government agencies. (Moderated)

gov.topic.admin.finance.budgeting - Appropriations and budgeting management. (Moderated)

gov.topic.admin.finance.calendar - Calendar of public finance events. (Moderated)

gov.topic.admin.finance.int-controls - Internal financial controls. (Moderated)

gov.topic.admin.finance.misc - General public finance topics. (Moderated)

gov.topic.admin.finance.municipalities - Municipal financial issues. (Moderated)

gov.topic.admin.finance.news - General government finance news. (Moderated)

gov.topic.admin.finance.payroll - Government payroll issues. (Moderated)

gov.topic.admin.finance.perf-measures - Financial performance measures. (Moderated)

gov.topic.admin.finance.policy - Government financial policy. (Moderated)

gov.topic.admin.finance.procurement - Procurement management. (Moderated)

gov.topic.admin.finance.reporting - Financial statements and reporting. (Moderated)

gov.topic.admin.finance.state-county - State and county financial issues. (Moderated)

gov.topic.admin.finance.systems - Financial software and hardware systems. (Moderated)

gov.topic.admin.finance.training - Financial personnel and training. (Moderated)

gov.topic.admin.finance.travel-admin - Travel administration. (Moderated)

gov.topic.admin.privatization - Privatization of government, Public/Private partnerships. (Moderated)

gov.topic.finance.banks - Banking, monetary supply, currency exchange. (Moderated)

gov.topic.finance.securities - Securities, commodity futures, etc. (Moderated)

gov.topic.forsale.misc - Miscellaneous government asset sales. (Moderated)

gov.topic.info.systems.epub - Government use of electronic publishing. (Moderated)

gov.topic.info.systems.year2000 - Accommodating dates after the year 2000.

gov.topic.telecom.announce - Telecommunications related announcements. (Moderated)

gov.topic.telecom.misc - Telecommunications- telephone, radio, TV, Internet. (Moderated)

gov.topic.transport.air - Aviation, aircraft, travel by air. (Moderated) gov.topic.transport.misc - General international transportation. (Moderated)

gov.topic.transport.navigation - Navigation systems. (Moderated)

gov.topic.transport.rail - Railroad transportation. (Moderated)

gov.topic.transport.road - Transportation over roads, auto safety, mass transit. (Moderated)

gov.topic.transport.shipping - International shipping and package delivery. (Moderated)

gov.topic.transport.water - Maritime related issues, transportation over water. (Moderated)

gov.us.fed.cia.announce - Central Intelligence Agency announcements. (Moderated)

gov.us.fed.congress.announce - Announcements about Congress. (Moderated)

gov.us.fed.congress.bills.house - Bill text from the House. (Moderated)

gov.us.fed.congress.bills.senate - Bill text from the Senate. (Moderated)

gov.us.fed.congress.calendar.house - House calendar of activities. (Moderated)

gov.us.fed.congress.calendar.senate - Senate calendar of activities. (Moderated)

gov.us.fed.congress.discuss - Followup discussions on Congress. (Moderated)

gov.us.fed.congress.documents - Congressional documents. (Moderated)

gov.us.fed.congress.gao.announce - Announcements about the Government Accounting Office. (Moderated)

gov.us.fed.congress.gao.decisions - Decisions from the Comptroller General. (Moderated)

gov.us.fed.congress.gao.discuss - Discussion on the Government Accounting Office. (Moderated)

gov.us.fed.congress.gao.reports - Reports from the Government Accounting Office. (Moderated)

gov.us.fed.congress.record.digest - Digest from the Congressional Record. (Moderated)

gov.us.fed.congress.record.extensions - Extension of remarks in the Congressional Record. (Moderated)

gov.us.fed.congress.record.house - House pages from the Congressional Record. (Moderated)

gov.us.fed.congress.record.index - Index to the Congressional Record. (Moderated)

gov.us.fed.congress.record.senate - Senate pages from the Congressional Record. (Moderated)

gov.us.fed.congress.reports - Congressional reports. (Moderated)

gov.us.fed.courts.announce - U.S. Courts announcements. (Moderated)

gov.us.fed.dhhs.announce - Department of Health and Human Services announcements. (Moderated)

gov.us.fed.dhhs.fda.announce - Food and Drug Administration announcements. (Moderated)

gov.us.fed.dhhs.ssa.announce - Social Security Administration announcements. (Moderated)

gov.us.fed.doc.announce - Department of Commerce announcements. (Moderated)

gov.us.fed.doc.cbd.awards - Contract awards in Commerce Business Daily. (Moderated)

gov.us.fed.doc.cbd.forsale - Surplus Property Sales in Commerce Business Daily. (Moderated)

gov.us.fed.doc.cbd.notices - General notices in Commerce Business Daily. (Moderated)

gov.us.fed.doc.cbd.solicitations - Procurement solicitation in Commerce Business Daily. (Moderated)

gov.us.fed.doc.cbd.standards - Foreign standards notices in Commerce Business Daily. (Moderated)

gov.us.fed.doc.census.announce - Census Bureau announcements. (Moderated)

gov.us.fed.doc.noaa.announce - National Oceanic and Atmospheric Administration announcments. (Moderated)

gov.us.fed.dod.announce - Department of Defense announcements. (Moderated)

gov.us.fed.dod.army.announce - Department of the Army announcements. (Moderated)
gov.us.fed.dod.navy.announce - Department of the Navy announcements. (Moderated)
gov.us.fed.dod.usaf.announce - Department of the Air Force announcements. (Moderated)
gov.us.fed.doe.announce - Department of Energy announcements. (Moderated)
gov.us.fed.doi.announce - Department of the Interior announcements. (Moderated)
gov.us.fed.doj.announce - Department of Justice announcements. (Moderated)
gov.us.fed.dol.announce - Department of Labor announcements. (Moderated)
gov.us.fed.dot.announce - Department of Transportation announcements. (Moderated)
gov.us.fed.dot.faa.announce - Federal Aviation Administration announcements. (Moderated)
gov.us.fed.dot.nhtsa.announce - National Highway Traffic Safety Administration announcements.
  (Moderated)
gov.us.fed.dot.uscg.announce - United States Coast Guard announcements. (Moderated)
gov.us.fed.ed.announce - Department of Education announcements. (Moderated)
gov.us.fed.eop.announce - Executive Office of the President announcements. (Moderated)
gov.us.fed.eop.white-house.announce - The President and White House Staff announcements.
  (Moderated)
gov.us.fed.epa.announce - Environmental Protection Agency announcements. (Moderated)
gov.us.fed.fcc.announce - Federal Communications Commission announcements. (Moderated)
gov.us.fed.fdic.announce - Federal Deposit Insurance Corporation announcements. (Moderated)
gov.us.fed.fema.announce - Federal Emergency Management Agency announcements. (Moderated)
gov.us.fed.ferc.announce - Federal Energy Regulatory Commission announcements. (Moderated)
gov.us.fed.fmc.announce - Federal Maritime Commission announcements. (Moderated)
gov.us.fed.frs.announce - Federal Reserve System announcements. (Moderated)
gov.us.fed.gsa.announce - General Services Administration announcements. (Moderated)
gov.us.fed.hud.announce - Department of Housing and Urban Development announcements.
  (Moderated)
gov.us.fed.nara.announce - National Archives and Records Administration announcements.
  (Moderated)
gov.us.fed.nara.fed-register.announce - Announcements about the Federal Register. (Moderated)
gov.us.fed.nara.fed-register.authoring - Discussion for Federal Register authors. (Moderated)
gov.us.fed.nara.fed-register.contents - Contents and Indexes of the Federal Register. (Moderated)
gov.us.fed.nara.fed-register.corrections - Corrections in the Federal Register. (Moderated)
gov.us.fed.nara.fed-register.notices - Notices in the Federal Register. (Moderated)
gov.us.fed.nara.fed-register.presidential - Presidential Documents in the Federal Register.
  (Moderated)
gov.us.fed.nara.fed-register.proposed-rules - Proposed Regulations in the Federal Register.
  (Moderated)
gov.us.fed.nara.fed-register.rules - Rules and Regulations in the Federal Register. (Moderated)
gov.us.fed.nasa.announce - National Aeronautics and Space Administration announcements.
  (Moderated)
gov.us.fed.nasa.ksc.announce - NASA Kennedy Space Center specific announcements.
  (Moderated)
gov.us.fed.nrc.announce - Nuclear Regulatory Commission announcements. (Moderated)

gov.us.fed.nsf.announce - National Science Foundation announcements. (Moderated)

gov.us.fed.nsf.documents - National Science Foundation documents. (Moderated)

gov.us.fed.nsf.grants - National Science Foundation grant information. (Moderated)

gov.us.fed.opm.announce - Office of Personnel Management announcements. (Moderated)

gov.us.fed.sba.announce - Small Business Administration announcements. (Moderated)

gov.us.fed.sec.announce - Securities and Exchange Commission announcements. (Moderated)

gov.us.fed.state.announce - Department of State announcements. (Moderated)

gov.us.fed.treasury.announce - Department of the Treasury announcements. (Moderated)

gov.us.fed.treasury.irs.announce - Internal Revenue Service announcements. (Moderated)

gov.us.fed.usaid.announce - US Agency for International Development, IDCA, OPIC. (Moderated)

gov.us.fed.usaid.pib - USAID Procurement Information Bulletin. (Moderated)

gov.us.fed.usda.announce - Department of Agriculture announcements. (Moderated)

gov.us.fed.va.announce - Department of Veterans Affairs announcements. (Moderated)

gov.us.org.admin.aga - Association of Government Accountants. (Moderated)

gov.us.org.admin.fasab - Federal Accounting Standards Advisory Board. (Moderated)

gov.us.org.admin.gfoa - Government Finance Officers Association. (Moderated)

gov.us.org.info.ace - Americans Communicating Electronically. (Moderated)

gov.us.org.info.ala - American Library Association. (Moderated)

gov.us.topic.agri.farms - Farming- growing crops, raising livestock. (Moderated)

gov.us.topic.agri.food - Food production and distribution, nutrition of food. (Moderated)

gov.us.topic.agri.misc - General agricultural issues. (Moderated)

gov.us.topic.agri.statistics - Detailed statistics on crop, livestock, and food production. (Moderated)

gov.us.topic.ecommerce.announce - Government electronic commerce infrastructure announcements. (Moderated)

gov.us.topic.ecommerce.misc - Discussions concerning government electronic commerce.
(Moderated)

gov.us.topic.ecommerce.standards - Standards for government electronic commerce. (Moderated)

gov.us.topic.emergency.alerts - Important bulletins for immediate broadcasting. (Moderated)

gov.us.topic.emergency.misc - Natural disasters, recovery, prevention. (Moderated)

gov.us.topic.energy.misc - Generation and delivery of energy. (Moderated)

gov.us.topic.energy.nuclear - Nuclear power and radioactive materials. (Moderated)

gov.us.topic.energy.utilities - Regulated utilities providing gas and electricity. (Moderated)

gov.us.topic.environment.air - Air quality, ozone, greenhouse gases, noise. (Moderated)

gov.us.topic.environment.announce - Announcements on environmental protection. (Moderated)

gov.us.topic.environment.misc - General environmental protection. (Moderated)

gov.us.topic.environment.toxics - Hazardous material use, disposal, cleanup. (Moderated)

gov.us.topic.environment.waste - Waste disposal, recycling. (Moderated)

gov.us.topic.environment.water - Water issues: drinking, irrigation, sewage. (Moderated)

gov.us.topic.finance.banks - Banking, monetary supply, currency exchange. (Moderated)

gov.us.topic.finance.securities - Securities, commodity futures, etc. (Moderated)

gov.us.topic.foreign.news - Selected news media reports from outside the U.S. (Moderated)

gov.us.topic.foreign.trade.leads - Information on trade opportunities collected by U.S.
governments.(Moderated)

gov.us.topic.foreign.trade.misc - Issues involving foreign trade, importation, customs. (Moderated)
gov.us.topic.foreign.trade.statistics - Detailed statistical reports on imports/exports. (Moderated)
gov.us.topic.gov-jobs.employee.issues - Discussions on government employee issues. (Moderated)
gov.us.topic.gov-jobs.employee.news - News of interest to government employees. (Moderated)
gov.us.topic.gov-jobs.hr-admin - Human Resources administration. (Moderated)
gov.us.topic.gov-jobs.offered.admin - Administrative job opportunities in government. (Moderated)
gov.us.topic.gov-jobs.offered.admin.finance - Jobs in public financial management. (Moderated)
gov.us.topic.gov-jobs.offered.admin.ses - Senior Executive Service job opportunities. (Moderated)
gov.us.topic.gov-jobs.offered.announce - Announcements on job hunting in government. (Moderated)
gov.us.topic.gov-jobs.offered.clerical - Clerical job opportunities in government. (Moderated)
gov.us.topic.gov-jobs.offered.engineering - Engineering related job opportunities in government. (Moderated)
gov.us.topic.gov-jobs.offered.foreign - Federal job opportunities located outside the U.S. (Moderated)
gov.us.topic.gov-jobs.offered.health - Medical and health-related job opportunities in government. (Moderated)
gov.us.topic.gov-jobs.offered.law-enforce - Law enforcement job opportunities in government. (Moderated)
gov.us.topic.gov-jobs.offered.math-comp - Math and computer related job opportunities in government. (Moderated)
gov.us.topic.gov-jobs.offered.misc - Unclassified public sector job opportunities. (Moderated)
gov.us.topic.gov-jobs.offered.questions - Questions and answers on job hunting in government. (Moderated)
gov.us.topic.gov-jobs.offered.science - Physical sciences job opportunities in government. (Moderated)
gov.us.topic.gov-jobs.offered.technical - Technical job opportunities in government. (Moderated)
gov.us.topic.grants.research - Grant opportunities for research. (Moderated)
gov.us.topic.info.abstracts.cdrom - Abstracts of new CD-ROM releases. (Moderated)
gov.us.topic.info.abstracts.epub - Abstracts of new publications available electronically. (Moderated)
gov.us.topic.info.abstracts.infosystems - Abstracts of new online systems and services. (Moderated)
gov.us.topic.info.abstracts.print - Abstracts of new publications available in hard copy. (Moderated)
gov.us.topic.info.libraries.govdocs - Government documents libraries. (Moderated)
gov.us.topic.info.libraries.technology - Library information technology discussion. (Moderated)
gov.us.topic.info.policy.announce - Announcements on government information policy. (Moderated)
gov.us.topic.info.policy.misc - Discussions on government information policy. (Moderated)
gov.us.topic.law.pub-contract - Lawyers discuss Federal public contract law. (Moderated)
gov.us.topic.nat-resources.forests - Forestry, logging, and wood production. (Moderated)

gov.us.topic.nat-resources.land - Other uses of public land, e.g., grazing, wetlands, watershed. (Moderated)

gov.us.topic.nat-resources.marine - Fishing, aquaculture, marine sanctuaries. (Moderated)

gov.us.topic.nat-resources.minerals - Extraction and transportation of minerals. (Moderated)

gov.us.topic.nat-resources.oil-gas - Extraction and transportation of oil and gas. (Moderated)

gov.us.topic.nat-resources.parks - Public land for recreation and tourism, and museums. (Moderated)

gov.us.topic.nat-resources.wildlife - Wildlife management, hunting. (Moderated)

gov.us.topic.statistics.announce - Brief announcements on economic and demographic statistics. (Moderated)

gov.us.topic.statistics.reports - Detailed reports on economic and demographic statistics. (Moderated)

gov.us.topic.telecom.announce - Announcements on general telecom policy issues. (Moderated)

gov.us.topic.telecom.misc - Discussion on general telecom policy issues. (Moderated)

gov.us.topic.transport.air - Aviation, aircraft, travel by air. (Moderated)

gov.us.topic.transport.misc - General transportation in the U.S. (Moderated)

gov.us.topic.transport.rail - Railroad transportation. (Moderated)

gov.us.topic.transport.road - Transportation over roads, auto safety, mass transit. (Moderated)

gov.us.topic.transport.shipping - International shipping and package delivery. (Moderated)

gov.us.topic.transport.water - Maritime related issues, transportation over water. (Moderated)

gov.us.usenet.admin - Discussion of gov.us news admin.

gov.us.usenet.announce - Admin announcements. (Moderated)

gov.us.usenet.answers - FAQs and periodic articles. (Moderated)

gov.us.usenet.control - Control messages for U.S. gov newsgroup changes. (Moderated)

gov.us.usenet.groups - Discussion of gov.us management.

gov.us.usenet.lists - News related statistics and lists. (Moderated)

gov.us.usenet.questions - Q & A for users new to gov.us newsgroups.

gov.us.usenet.software - Discuss gov.us specific software.

gov.us.usenet.test - Use in testing news software setups.

gov.usenet.admin - Discussion of gov news admininstration.

gov.usenet.announce - Admin announcements. (Moderated)

gov.usenet.answers - FAQs and periodic articles. (Moderated)

gov.usenet.control - Control messages for top gov newsgroup changes. (Moderated)

gov.usenet.groups - Discussion of gov hierarchy management.

gov.usenet.lists - News related statistics and lists. (Moderated)

gov.usenet.questions - Q & A for users new to gov newsgroups.

gov.usenet.software - Discuss gov news specific software.

gov.usenet.test - Use in testing news software setups.

Subject Heading: Newsgroups

[1262] National Capital Planning Commission

Sponsoring Agency: National Capital Planning Commission

Primary Access: http://www.ncpc.gov/

Resource Summary: The National Capital Planning Commission coordinates all federal planning activities in the National Capital Region that includes Washington, D.C., and the surrounding communities in Maryland and Virginia. The Web site features sections on the Commission; the Location; its Vision; Guidelines and Submission Requirements for Antenna; and a Public Information.

Subject Heading: District of Columbia

[1263] National Endowment for the Humanities

Sponsoring Agency: National Endowment for the Humanities (NEH)

Primary Access: http://www.neh.fed.us/

Alternative Access Method: http://www.neh.fed.us/textonly.html [text version]

Resource Summary: The National Endowment for the Humanities site provides information on applying for NEH grants, listings of NEH-sponsored programs, and the usual agency information. The Applying for a Grant page provides application forms, deadlines, and guidelines. The Around the Country category includes a sampling of NEH-sponsored programs on a state-by-state basis. The Inside the Endowment section gives information about the NEH, a staff directory, and publications information.

This site provides an easy-to-use overview of the NEH and its sponsored programs. It will be a very useful site for those interested in applying for NEH grants.

Subject Headings: Grants; Humanities

[1264] National Technical Information Service

Sponsoring Agency: National Technical Information Service (NTIS)

Primary Access: http://www.ntis.gov/

Alternative Access Method: http://www.ntis.gov/text/ntishome.html [text version]

Resource Summary: NTIS is one of the government's major publishing arms, featuring thousands of technical reports. However, since it is run on a cost recovery basis, many of its services require payment. Information about NTIS is available in the sections Our Organization; About This Site; News; Ordering; and Services for Federal Agencies. The Products and Information Tools sections describe some of NTIS's data products, publications, and services, most of which come at a price. The NTIS OrderNow, available under the Ordering and Information Tools categories, does offer free access to the last 30 day's worth of the NTIS bibliographic database of technical reports.

With limited free resources, the NTIS site is most useful for providing information on its various commercial products. However, NTIS also runs FedWorld, which provides access to a great deal of free government information.

Subject Headings: Bibliographic Databases; Reports

[1265] National Zoological Park

Sponsoring Agencies: National Zoological Park; Smithsonian Institution

Primary Access: http://www.si.edu/organiza/museums/zoo/homepage/nzphome.htm

Alternative Access Method: ftp://photo1.si.edu/images/gif89a/science-nature/

Resource Summary: The National Zoo's Web site presents a beautifully designed, if somewhat slow-loading, virtual visit to the Zoo. Pictures of the animals on location, news, and information about the Zoo combine to make this site an excellent introduction to the Zoo. The animal pictures are located on the ftp server. The site also features reports on Zoo research projects and electronic newsletters such as *Dragon Doings*, which covers news on the Zoo's Komodo dragons.

Subject Headings: Animals; Biology—Research; Zoos

[1266] Office of Government Ethics

Sponsoring Agency: Office of Government Ethics (OGE)

Primary Access: http://www.access.gpo.gov/usoge/

Resource Summary: The Office of Government Ethics coordinates activities in the executive branch that relate to the prevention of conflicts of interest on the part of government employees. The Office also resolves conflicts of interest that do occur. Their Web site, hosted by GPO Access, features the topics Introduction to OGE; Matters Outside of OGE's Jurisdiction; Ethics Program Topics; Ethics Community Services; Informational Resources and Reference/Educational Materials; Ethics Resource Library; and What's New In Ethics. The top level page also has a hierarchical table of contents for the Web site which aids in navigation. The Ethics Resource Library includes a variety of OGE forms, relevant legislation, and some publications in PDF format.

This site will be useful to government employees concerned with possible conflict of interest situations. It is also an excellent starting point for members of the general public interested in exploring topics in government ethics.

Subject Heading: Ethics in Government

SuDoc Number: Y 3.ET 3:15/ *Government Ethics Newgram*

[1267] Office of Personnel Management

Sponsoring Agency: Office of Personnel Management (OPM)

Primary Access: http://www.opm.gov/

Alternative Access Method: http://www.usajobs.opm.gov/

Resource Summary: As the federal government personnel office, the OPM is a primary source for information on federal jobs. The USA Jobs link includes an online application and listings for current job openings. The section titled Current Job Openings is browsable by category or by alphabetically ordered job titles. Under the headingVeterans and Uniformed Services, the OPM provides information on veterans' preferences in hiring for federal jobs.

For finding information on federal jobs, this site is an excellent starting point. It should provide additional information about working for the federal government,particularly for current employees, but it does at least provide a database of job openings.

Subject Heading: Employment

[1268] Peace Corps

Sponsoring Agency: Peace Corps

Primary Access: http://www.peacecorps.gov/

Alternative Access Method: ftp://ftp.peacecorps.gov/

Resource Summary: Formed to promote world peace and mutual understanding, the Peace Corps uses its Web site to feature information on its programs and current projects. The Volunteer category provides information on becoming a Peace Corps volunteer. The Countries section offers regional and country-specific overviews of basic geographical information as well as information on the activities of the Corps in a specific area. The World Wise Schools page includes information on the Corps' global education program. Other sections include Returned Peace Corps Volunteers; Contribute; Press; Technical Information; and Agency Information. The Essay section highlights a monthly essay on service in the Corps.

With a wide variety of information on the Peace Corps, this site will be useful to anyone interested in information about the Corps, describing possibilities for volunteering, and providing some basic country information from the Peace Corps' perspective.

Subject Headings: Peace; Service; Volunteerism

[1269] U.S. Agency for International Development

Sponsoring Agencies: Information Agency (USIA); Agency for International Development (USAID)

Primary Access: http://www.info.usaid.gov/

Alternative Access Methods: http://www.info.usaid.gov/welcome/usaid_txt.html [text version]
gopher://gopher.info.usaid.gov/
ftp://ftp.info.usaid.gov/pub/
mailto:listproc@info.usaid.gov with "subscribe usaid_press_release" in body
mailto:listproc@info.usaid.gov with "subscribe ofda-l" in body

Resource Summary: To see the range of humanitarian programs with which the Agency for International Development is involved, browse some of the headings on their Web site. The Democracy; Population and Health; Economic Growth; and Environment sections each give brief descriptions of USAID projects in these areas by country. The Humanitarian Response section describes the way USAID responds to crises. Regions and Countries provides a clickable image map or text access to USAID projects by region or country.

The Regions and Countries sections includes information on areas all over the world, including pertinent sections from the Congressional Presentation. The Presentation is the Agency's annual submission to Congress in support of the president's budget request for USAID's economic and humanitarian assistance activities. Additional agency information can be found under the sections About USAID; Publications; In the News; Development Links; and Business and Procurement.

There is a substantial amount of Agency information available on these Gopher and Web sites. The user must often look deeper than two levels to find the information, but after finding it the user will see why this site is a valuable resource.

Subject Headings: Developing Countries; Emergencies; Foreign Assistance; Foreign Countries

SuDoc Numbers: S 18.1/3: *USAID Congressional Presentation*
S 18.2:P 41/ *Agency Performance Report*
S 18.45: *SD Abstracts*
S 18.62: *SD Developments*
S 18.62:AF 8/ *African Voices: A Newsletter on Democracy and Governance in Africa*

[1270] United States Information Agency

Sponsoring Agency: Information Agency (USIA)

Primary Access: http://www.usia.gov/

Alternative Access Method: gopher://gopher.usia.gov/

Resource Summary: The activities of the United States Information Agency encompass a broad range of programs. Their Web site features detailed information on their exchange programs under the heading International Exchanges/Training. This section includes the links Fulbright Scholarships, Arts America, Citizen Exchanges, Foreign Student Advising, and International Visitors. Under the Products/Services heading, are descriptions of other USIA programs such as their International Broadcasting (including Voice of America) and Foreign Commentary on the United States which includes recent digests of foreign media reactions to various foreign policy issues. The full text of various laws and regulations relevant to the USIA can be found under the Regulations/Laws/General Counsel heading.

The site contains little information on the USIA broadcasting endeavors, and it does not link to the Internet versions of such programs as the Voice of America. However, the site will definitely be useful to those interested in international exchange programs. The Foreign Commentary on the U.S. section contains some hard-to-find information, but the site only keeps recent issues of the digests.

Subject Headings: Foreign Exchange Programs; Fulbright Program; Grants—Education

[1271] Voice of America

Sponsoring Agencies: Voice of America (VOA); Information Agency (USIA)

Primary Access: http://www.voa.gov/

Alternative Access Methods: http://www.voa.gov/text-only.html [text version]
gopher://gopher.voa.gov/
ftp://ftp.voa.gov/

Resource Summary: The Web, Gopher, and ftp servers all provide access to publicly available VOA radio scripts, audio files, program schedules, frequency information, and free software. Selected original VOA radio scripts are available in the Chinese national character-encoding standard (Guo Biao).

This site provides a variety of VOA resources. U.S. users should bear in mind that in accordance with federal law, the program materials are intended exclusively for recipients outside of the United States.

Subject Heading: Radio

[1272] World News Connection

Sponsoring Agencies: National Technical Information Service (NTIS); Foreign Broadcast Information Service (FBIS)

Primary Access: http://wnc.fedworld.gov/ntis/

Resource Summary: This is a subscription-based service that features news and information from thousands of non-U.S. media sources gathered by FBIS. All articles in this service are translated into English. Content includes the latest two year's worth of full text and summaries of newspaper articles, speeches, television and radio broadcasts, books, and reports. Under the Latest Headlines section, nonsubscribers are able to browse the titles of recent headlines, but only subscribers have access to the full text of articles.

This could be a very useful service, but the cost of subscriptions keeps most of the general Internet public out. Time will tell if NTIS can make enough money off this service to support the subscriber system or if it will eventually offer some of its content for free.

Subject Headings: News—Foreign; Translations

Miscellaneous: Museums and the Arts ─────────────

[1273] Archeology: National Archaeological Database

Sponsoring Agencies: National Park Service (NPS). Archeological Assistance Program; University of Arkansas. Center For Advanced Spatial Technologies

Primary Access: http://www.cast.uark.edu/other/nps/nadb/

Alternative Access Method: telnet://nadb@cast.uark.edu

Resource Summary: The National Archaeological Database (NADB) includes inventories of over 120,000 archeological investigations; guidance on compliance with the Native American Grave Protection and Repatriation Act (NAGPRA); and maps displaying archeological and environmental data at the state/country level. The NADB-Reports database is updated yearly and consists of about 120,000 reports of archeological investigations, primarily as limited distribution reports. Access to this database is by search form. The NADB-NAGPRA database contains publications in ASCII and PDF formats related to NAGPRA including congressional reports; statutes; proposed regulations; guidance; review committees; *Federal Register* Notices of Completion of Inventory; and intents to repatriate. The Map database includes Geographic Information Systems (GIS) layers. The GIS layers available include site counts and densities, citation counts and densities, and property densities.

Subject Headings: Archeology; American Indians; Geographic Information Systems

[1274] Institute of Museum Services Overview

Sponsoring Agency: Institute of Museum and Library Services

Primary Access: http://www.ims.fed.us/

Resource Summary: Set up to increase and improve museum services throughout the United States, the Institute's Web site is designed to ensure effective communication with its public. It offers information on the Institute's grants in the following sections: Programs; Deadlines; Eligibility; and Awards. The site also includes a PDF version of its General Operating Support Application Guidelines. Also, note that on October 1, 1996, the Institute of Museum Services became the Institute of Museum and Library Services, so users should begin to see more public library information on it in the near future.

Those seeking funding for public museums, and now libraries, should be sure to browse this site. The availability of past awards can help inform future applicants.

Subject Headings: Grants; Libraries; Museums

[1275] NASNEWS National Air and Space Museum Events [e-mail list]

Sponsoring Agencies: National Air and Space Museum; Smithsonian Institution

Primary Access: mailto:listserv@sivm.si.edu with "sub nasnews name" in body

Resource Summary: This e-mail list, sponsored and hosted by the Smithsonian, is used to disseminate announcements from the National Air and Space Museum about upcoming events.

Subject Headings: E-mail Lists; Aeronautics; Space

[1276] National Center for Preservation Technology and Training Gopher

Sponsoring Agency: National Center for Preservation Technology and Training (NCPTT)

Primary Access: gopher://gopher.ncptt.nps.gov/

Alternative Access Method: http://www.cr.nps.gov/ncptt/

Resource Summary: With its major content still on the Gopher, the NCPTT provides access to libraries, archives, museums, preservation organizations, and National Park Service resources. Other resources include the NCPTT's newsletter; text of preservation laws; preservation briefs; job announcements; conferences; grants; and workshops.

This is one of the few government servers that still contains most of its content on a Gopher server, though much may be moved to the Web pages in the future. The site will be of interest to those involved in historic preservation.

Subject Headings: Archeology; Grants; Historic Preservation

[1277] National Endowment for the Arts

Sponsoring Agency: National Endowment for the Arts (NEA)

Primary Access: http://arts.endow.gov/

Alternative Access Method: http://arts.endow.gov/NEAText/Homepage/Homepage.html [text version]

Resource Summary: This well-designed site shows the artistic touch of the National Endowment for the Arts while providing a substantial body of information about the NEA and its sponsored programs. The major components of the site include *arts.community*, a hyperlinked periodical with features and news about the arts; *Guide to the National Endowment for the Arts*, an overview of the grantmaking programs of the NEA; and the Arts Resource Center, which includes a catalog of NEA publications.

Subject Headings: Art; Grants; Music

SuDoc Numbers: NF 2.1: *NEA Annual Report*
NF 2.8:N 21/ *Guide to the National Endowment for the Arts*

[1278] National Museum of American Art

Sponsoring Agencies: National Museum of American Art; Smithsonian Institution

Primary Access: http://www.nmaa.si.edu/

Alternative Access Method: http://www.nmaa.si.edu/hometextmostly.html [text version]

Resource Summary: This site includes an electronic version of a number of exhibits, images of hundreds of works of art, and reports of upcoming and recent events. It also presents an option for interacting with staff and some of the artists in the collection.

With solid design, this is an informative and well-organized site.

Subject Heading: Art—American

[1279] Ocean Planet

Sponsoring Agencies: National Museum of Natural History; Smithsonian Institution

Primary Access: http://seawifs.gsfc.nasa.gov/ocean-planet.html

Resource Summary: The Web pages give access to this specific exhibit by inviting users to wander through the exhibit halls by subject or to take a special tour designed by the curator. Keyword searching is available for images, objects, and exhibit sections. The site also has links to educational materials associated with the exhibition.

Subject Headings: Museums; Exhibitions; Oceanography; Biology—Study and Teaching

[1280] The Smithsonian Institution

Sponsoring Agency: Smithsonian Institution

Primary Access: http://www.si.edu/

Alternative Access Methods: http://www.si.edu/strttxt.htm [text version]
http://www.si.sgi.com/sgi.htm [mirror site]

Resource Summary: The Smithsonian's Web site includes press releases; speeches of the Secretary of the Smithsonian (including a new message each month); information on current exhibits; hours and locations of the Smithsonian Museums; and a staff directory. Some of the links include Museums and Organizations; Activities; You and the Smithsonian; and Resources. The Resources section includes extracts of articles from the *Smithsonian Magazine* and *Encyclopedia Smithsonian*, an online source that provides answers to frequently asked questions.

The Web site provides an excellent overview of the Smithsonian's component institutes and programs. The breadth of the resources provides something for everyone, including visitors, scientists, and other museum personnel.

Subject Heading: Museums

[1281] Smithsonian Natural History Web

Sponsoring Agencies: National Museum of Natural History; Smithsonian Institution

Primary Access: http://www.nmnh.si.edu/

Alternative Access Methods: http://nmnhwww.si.edu/
gopher://nmnhgoph.si.edu/

Resource Summary: This Web site contains documents and data about the Museum of Natural History research and its national collections. These collections comprise more than 120 million scientific specimens and cultural artifacts from around the world. The site also includes information about programs and projects at the Museum or about projects produced in cooperation with other organizations that support the Museum's mission. The Bulletin of the Global Volcanism Network is available from the Global Volcanism Program page under the Research and Collections section.

Subject Headings: Museums; Natural History; Volcanoes

SuDoc Number: SI 3.13: *Bulletin of the Global Volcanism Network*

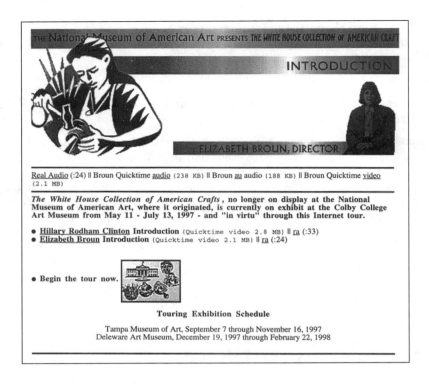

The National Museum of American Art PRESENTS THE WHITE HOUSE COLLECTION OF AMERICAN CRAFT

INTRODUCTION

ELIZABETH BROUN, DIRECTOR

Real Audio (:24) ‖ Broun Quicktime audio (238 KB) ‖ Broun au audio (188 KB) ‖ Broun Quicktime video (2.1 MB)

The White House Collection of American Crafts , no longer on display at the National Museum of American Art, where it originated, is currently on exhibit at the Colby College Art Museum from May 11 - July 13, 1997 - and "in virtu" through this Internet tour.

- Hillary Rodham Clinton Introduction (Quicktime video 2.8 MB) ‖ ra (:33)
- Elizabeth Broun Introduction (Quicktime video 2.1 MB) ‖ ra (:24)

- Begin the tour now.

Touring Exhibition Schedule

Tampa Museum of Art, September 7 through November 16, 1997
Deleware Art Museum, December 19, 1997 through February 22, 1998

[1282] The White House Collection of American Crafts

Sponsoring Agencies: National Museum of American Art; Smithsonian Institution

Primary Access: http://www.nmaa.si.edu/WHC/AmericanCrafts/

Alternative Access Method: http://www.nmaa.si.edu/WHC/americancrafts/

Resource Summary: The virtual exhibit includes graphics of the pieces, artist's statements, and videos of some artists at work. Finding aids include indexes by artist, White House room, object title, and object medium. Other features include a glossary, links to the artists' own Web site (when applicable), and selected audio files.

The site is well organized and uses the online medium well in its presentation of a museum exhibit. The pages present a number of options to tour the exhibits, including graphic reproductions, videos, and audio files. Despite the emphasis on high-end multimedia, the user can select the text-heavy pages for easy access to the textual portions of the exhibition, such as artist statements and biographies.

Subject Headings: Museums; Art—American—Exhibitions

INDEXES

Index of Primary and Alternative Access URLs

NOTE: The numbers in these indexes refer to the entry number, not the page number.

SuDoc Number Index

NOTE: The numbers in these indexes refer to the entry number, not the page number.

Publication Title Index

NOTE: The numbers in these indexes refer to the entry number, not the page number.

NOTES: The numbers in these indexes refer to the entry number, not the page number.
Boldface entry numbers indicate a primary site for that organization.

GOVERNMENT INFORMATION ON THE INTERNET

National Institutes of Health (NIH).
Library: 682
National Institutes of Health (NIH). Office
of Policy for Extramural Research
Administration: 436
National Institutes of Health (NIH). Section
of Developmental Biology: 435
National Institutes of Health Library: 682
National Integrated Pest Management
Network: 26
National Labor Relations Board (NLRB): 93
National Library for the Environment: 195
National Library of Education (NLE): 231, **723**
National Library of Medicine (NLM): . 391, 396,
417, 441, 445, 446, **724**
National Longitudinal Surveys of Labor
Market Experience Annotated
Bibliography: 967
National Marine Fisheries Service
(NMFS): **313**, 314
National Marine Fisheries Service (NMFS).
Office of Protected Resources: 316
National Museum of American
Art: **1278**, 1282
National Museum of Natural History: 1279,
1281
National Ocean Service: **349**, 819
National Ocean Service. Coastal Programs
Division: 338
National Ocean Service. Sanctuaries and
Reserves Division: 354
National Oceanic and Atmospheric
Administration (NOAA): ... 25, 274, **290**, 298,
348, 661
National Oceanic and Atmospheric
Administration (NOAA). Library and
Information Services Division: 689
National Oceanic and Atmospheric
Administration (NOAA). Western Region.
Library: 689
National Oceanographic Data Center
(NODC): **344**, 661
National Parent Information Network: 283
National Park Service (NPS): **300**, 1241
National Park Service (NPS). Archeological
Assistance Program: 1273
National Performance Review
(NPR): 3, 59, 112, 121, 440, **1237**

National Plant Data Center (NPDC): 28, 30
National Public Radio (NPR): 1168
National Radio Astronomy Observatory
(NRAO): 890
National Radio Astronomy Observatory
(NRAO). Library: 683
National Railroad Passenger Corporation
(Amtrak): 830, **1226**
National Reconnaissance Office: 754
National Renewable Energy Laboratory
(NREL): 292, **1209**
National Research Council (NRC): 848
National Rural Development Council
(NRDC): 34
National Rural Development Partnership
(NRDP): 35, 39
National Science Foundation (NSF): . 124, 274,
849, 852, 1181, 1189, 1261
see also Chapter 13 in general
National Science Foundation (NSF). Director-
ate for Education and Human Resources
(EHR): 223
National Science Foundation (NSF). Division of
Elementary, Secondary, and Informal
Education: 265
National Science Foundation (NSF). Division of
Graduate Education: 243
National Science Foundation (NSF). Division of
Undergraduate Education (DUE): 244
National Security Agency (NSA): 755
National Security Council (NSC): 1238
National Severe Storms Laboratory: 331
National Space Science Data Center
(NSSDC): **891**, 924
National Spatial Data Infrastructure (NSDI): 27
National Technical Information Service
(NTIS): 2, 72, 1204, **1264**, 1272
National Technology Transfer Center
(NTTC): 15, **1149**
National Telecommunications and Information
Administration (NTIA): 309, 1161, **1165**
National Toxicology Program (NTP): 455
National Transportation Safety Board
(NTSB): 1220, **1227**
National Weather Service (NWS): 319, **332**
National Weather Service-Tallahassee: 341
National Zoological Park: 1265
NATO Official Home Page: 468
Natural Resources Conservation Service

GOVERNMENT INFORMATION ON THE INTERNE

Subject Index

NOTE: The numbers in these indexes refer to the entry number, not the page number.

Reports—Bibliography: 198, 840, 1131, 1147, 1154, 1204
Reports—Full Text: 135, 195, 199, 203, 209, 391, 584, 602-605, 675, 694, 840, 962, 1147
Research and Development: 1133, 1256
Research Laboratories: 50, 298, 438, 443, 781, 788, 839, 843, 844, 851, 853, 854, 856, 886, 892-894, 909, 914, 917, 1135, 1141, 1144, 1156, 1170, 1199, 1208, 1209, 1211, 1232
Retirement: 958, 960, 961
Rhode Island: 1095-1097
Rivers: 306, 319, 1156
Roads: 1221, 1225
Robotics: 1184
Rockets: 847
Romania: 556, 557
Rural Development: 21, 34-39, 41, 467, 963
Rural Education: 29, 272
Russia: 142, 153, 558
Safety: 380, 936, 1136, 1218, 1220, 1225, 1227, 1232
Sanctuaries: 354
Satellite Imagery: 348, 763
Satellites: 290
Saudi Arabia: 559
Savings Bonds: 63
School Meals: 387
Science and Technology Policy: 848
Science Education: 223, 232-244, 261, 265, 268, 269, 274, 278
Scientific and Technical Information: 140, 685, 1131, 1138, 1154
Security: 744, 1193, 1194, 1238
Sentencing: 616, 650
Service: 1268
Sexually Transmitted Diseases: 423
Shipping: 136, 1230, 1231
Shipping—Regulations: 1222
SIC Codes: 188, 826
Singapore: 560, 561
Slovakia: 562
Slovenia: 563, 564
Small Businesses: 80, 82-84, 94, 138, 145, 1149, 1176
Smithsonian Magazine: 841
Smoking: 425
Social Science Research: 169

Social Security: 955, 959
Social Services *see* Chapter 14 in general
Social Studies Education: 273
Software: 1174, 1175, 1187
Soils: 27
Solar Energy: 1209
Solar Physics: 891, 927
Solar System: 911
Solar-Terrestrial Physics: 872, 893, 927
Solvents: 359
South Africa: 566
South Africa—Finding Aid: 565
South America: 470, 940
South Carolina: 1098, 1099
South Dakota: 1101-103
South Korea: 567, 780
Space: 279, 754, 904, 922, 1275
see also Chapter 13, Space Exploration section
Space—Education: 910, 918, 925, 929
Space—Effects on Humans—
Research: 457, 908
Space—History: 899, 921
Space—Images: 918
Space—Legislation: 607
Space—Research: 255, 851, 869, 905, 914
Space Flight: 908, 913, 915-17, 1217
Space Flight—Images: 900
Space Shuttle: 907, 908, 910, 916, 920, 926
Space Station: 906, 908, 910, 916, 928
Space Warfare: 803
Spain: 568
Sri Lanka: 569
Stamps: 834
Standards: 27, 742, 745, 1148
States: 39
see also Chapter 15 in general
States—Statistics: 165, 980
Statistics: 66, 157, 159, 163, 169, 234, 313, 412, 463, 827
see also chapter 3 in general
Stock Exchanges: 110
Storms: 329, 331
Streamflow Data: 302
Strokes: 430
Student Services: 225, 254
Submarines: 800
Sunrise and Sunset: 828

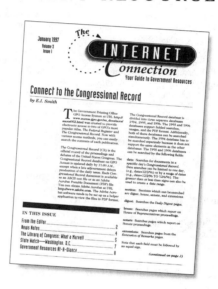

BERNAN ASSOCIATES   4611-F ASSEMBLY DRIVE   LANHAM, MD 20706

Call Toll-Free (800)274-4447   *Fax Toll-Free (800)865-3450*   **E-mail: order@bernan.com**

ORDER FORM

QUANTITY	ISBN	TITLE	BEGIN STANDING ORDER?	PRICE
	—	The Internet Connection Newsletter (sample)	—	FREE
	ISSN 1080-8493	The Internet Connection Newsletter (10 issues)	—	$69.00
	—	Bernan Associates Standing Order Catalog	—	FREE
	0-89059-071-0	1997 County and City Extra ❖	☐ yes ☐ no	$109.00
			Subtotal	
			*Postage & Handling	
			**Tax	
			TOTAL	

METHODS OF PAYMENT

Deposit Account
Requires a minimum initial deposit of $100.00 and an ongoing balance of $50.00. Upon receipt of the check or money order, an account will be established and a special account number will be assigned. The cost of ordered publications will be deducted from the funds on deposit.

Invoice Statement Account
Send in the order on an authorized purchase order. An invoice will be included with the shipment of publications. An account number will be assigned after the first purchase. All future orders can be charged against this account number with an authorized purchase order.

Prepayment
Prepay all orders with a check or money order in U.S. dollars, drawn from a U.S. bank, payable to *Bernan Associates*.

RETURN POLICIES
❖Titles published by Bernan Press may be purchased on a 30-day trial basis. Review any title published by Bernan Press for 30 days. If not completely satisfied, simply return for a full refund or credit to your account.

For titles *not* published by Bernan Press, returns are allowed only if publications received are damaged/defective or titles are incorrect.

*Add Postage and Handling as follows:
as follows:
U.S.: 6%, minimum $5.00
Canada and Mexico: 10%, minimum $6.00
Outside North America: 30%, minimum $15.00

****MD, D.C., and NY add tax; Canada add GST**

Rush Service
Rush Service is available for an additional fee of $15.00.

Prices are subject to change

Terms: Net 30 days

IF USING A PURCHASE ORDER, PLEASE ATTACH THIS FORM

☐ Bill Me (attach purchase order) P.O. No._____   Date _____

☐ Check or Money Order Enclosed (payable to *Bernan Associates*)

☐ VISA   ☐ MasterCard   Card No. _____   Exp. Date_____

Signature_____   Bernan Associates Acct. No. _____

BILL TO

Name _____

Organization _____

Address _____

_____

Phone_____ Fax_____

SHIP TO

Name _____

Organization _____

Address _____

_____

Phone_____ Fax_____